Theremin

Music in American Life

A list of books in the series appears at the end of this book.

THEREMIN

Ether Music

and Espionage

Albert Glinsky

Foreword by Robert Moog

UNIVERSITY OF ILLINOIS PRESS

URBANA AND CHICAGO

Library of Congress Cataloging-in-Publication Data
Glinsky, Albert.
Theremin : ether music and espionage / Albert Glinsky ;
foreword by Robert Moog.
p.   cm. — (Music in American life)
Includes bibliographical references and index.
ISBN 0-252-02582-2
1. Theremin, Leon, 1896–1993.
2. Musicians—Biography.
3. Spies—Biography.
4. Theremin.
5. Electronic music—History and criticism.
6. United States—Foreign relations—Soviet Union.
7. Soviet Union—Foreign relations—United States.
I. Title. II. Series.
ML429.T43G6   2000
786.7'3—dc21   00-008024

C 5 4 3 2 1

To my parents,
Cleo Hartwig and Vincent Glinsky,

to
Linda, Luka, and Allegra,

and to
Lev Sergeyevich Theremin,
Electronic Art Pioneer
and
Citizen of the Twentieth Century

CONTENTS

ILLUSTRATIONS FOLLOW PAGES 128, 202, AND 274

Robert Moog

After years of meticulous research, Albert Glinsky has written this wondrous story of Lev Sergeyevich Termen (Leon Theremin), the inventor of the space-control electronic musical instrument that bears his name. Leon Theremin has touched the lives of countless musicians and scientists, and his work is a vital cornerstone of our contemporary music technology. In this short foreword, I would like to tell some ways in which Leon Theremin and his work have influenced my career.

Leon Theremin has been my hero and virtual mentor for most of my life. I became a designer of electronic musical instruments because of my fascination with the theremin. I first learned about the theremin over a half century ago, from a do-it-yourself construction article in an electronics hobbyist magazine. Back then, it was easy to be an electronics hobbyist. A circuit for a typical project contained maybe a few dozen simple parts, which you could purchase at a radio parts store for a few cents to a few dollars each. Using an electric drill, a soldering iron, and a few hand tools, you could put your project together on the kitchen table. Printed circuit boards were exotic, high-tech objects that were not available to mere hobbyists, so your wiring was "point-to-point." If you did the wiring carefully, your completed project would be an object of elegance and beauty, which you would then show off with pride to all your fellow nerds. And if your project actually *worked,* your sense of accomplishment and prestige did wonders for your self-esteem.

Building a theremin has always been a popular hobby project. I've seen well over a dozen do-it-yourself theremin articles, the oldest of which was published in a 1932 German electronics hobbyist magazine. Then as now, a theremin is about as easy as a radio to build and, when completed, can be used to amaze and amuse everybody who sees it or tries to play it. After building my first theremin in 1949, I was hooked. By my senior year in high school, I had "designed" my own theremin and demonstrated it at a school assembly. ("Moog," my physics teacher told me afterward, "that was *damn* good.")

Looking back on those times, I now realize that, compared to most do-it-yourself theremins, the instruments that Leon Theremin built in the late 1920s and early 1930s embodied a unique elegance of design. Theremin's instruments sounded wonderful and could be played expressively by accomplished thereminists. Do-it-yourself instruments, on the other hand, were not at all as carefully designed as Theremin's original instruments.

During the late forties and early fifties, few thereminists were performing in public, and very little was known about the technical aspects of Leon Theremin's instruments. Even less was known about Theremin himself. He attracted a lot of attention when he arrived in New York in 1927, then mysteriously disappeared a few years later. Since he was a citizen of the Soviet Union, and since the cold war was in full swing when I was a young student, all I knew about Theremin was the incomplete and often inaccurate information that appeared in the popular press from time to time.

My first direct contact with Theremin's work came when I ordered a service manual for the RCA Theremin from the Radio Corporation of America. That particular service manual was then out of print, but somebody in the RCA service department kindly sent me a faded copy on blueprint paper. I spent many hours studying the schematic diagrams of the RCA Theremin (which, I learned later, Theremin himself had designed). Little by little, I came to understand the subtle technical principles underlying Theremin's designs. Throughout the late 1950s I continued to design my own versions of the theremin, but now I had the benefit of knowing what Leon Theremin had actually done. I also benefited from having studied electrical engineering, so I could approach my design work as a professional engineer, rather than as a young amateur experimenter. As a graduate student in the engineering physics department of Cornell University, I used my landlord's furnace room to design and build theremins. Many of my customers at that time were itinerant musicians who performed religious music at churches throughout the country. They found that the theremin, with its ethereal sound and visually dramatic playing technique, provided an effective medium for religious music performance.

From time to time, I learned bits and pieces of theremin lore. I heard about the great theremin virtuosa Clara Rockmore. I discovered that Mrs. Rockmore had concertized widely since the 1930s, and that her home was in New York City. At one point I arranged to show her one of my instruments, a feat of incredible bravery for a young, shy engineering student. She graciously welcomed me into her apartment and tried out the instrument that I had brought. My instrument had a tiny built-in radio loudspeaker, so the sound was weak, to say the least. Mrs. Rockmore complimented me for taking an interest in the theremin but told me that she wasn't personally interested in my instrument. She pointed out that she played a theremin that Leon Theremin himself had built especially for her. In addition to the tone-generating circuit itself, Mrs. Rockmore's instrument had a large amplifier and speaker, which enabled her to play at full volume with symphony orchestras. This was an important lesson for me: no matter how well its tone circuit is designed, an electronic instrument can sound only as good as its amplifier and speaker.

In 1960 I used my knowledge of theremin technology to design a simple instrument for the do-it-yourselfer. My design used just four transistors, which were then becoming available to hobbyists. I wrote an article describing the circuit and then published it in the hobbyist magazine *Electronics World*. At the same time I offered a kit of parts for the construction of the *Electronics World* theremin. The article was a big success, and I found it necessary to take six months off from my graduate school studies to deal with the kit orders that I received.

I completed my graduate studies in 1965, and then, using the experience and insights I gained by designing theremins, I started designing and building synthesizers. Theremin orders all but disappeared as the general public's attention turned to the new music technology. Two decades later, synthesizer technology had gone through several stages of evolution. Moog Music Inc., the company I founded in 1954, became a division of Norlin Music in 1973. By 1985, Norlin ceased operating as a musical instrument company and I went to work for Kurzweil Music Systems, a maker of sophisticated digital synthesizers. I remained with Kurzweil until 1989.

The year 1989 also marked the resurgence of a worldwide interest in Leon Theremin's work. In that year, I, along with many other musicians and scientists, was able to meet Theremin for the first time at a new-music festival in Bourges, France. Theremin had not left his native Russia for fifty-one years before coming to Bourges. For me it was the realization of a lifelong dream—to stand in the same room with the person who, virtually single-handedly, launched the field of electronic music technology.

Around this time, the documentary filmmaker Steven Martin contacted me. He told me that he planned to produce a feature-length documentary film on Theremin's life and work, and he asked for my assistance. He wanted to film Clara Rockmore as she played her theremin in public, but her instrument was not working at the time, and in fact had not been working for several years. Martin asked me to come to Mrs. Rockmore's apartment to help restore her instrument. The opportunity to work on an instrument that Leon Theremin himself had built was too attractive to resist, so I agreed to do it. I arrived at Mrs. Rockmore's apartment with my tool kit and test equipment on a Friday. Michael Jasen (Mrs. Rockmore's regular technician) and I completely dismantled her instrument. We found many components that were faulty and had to be replaced. By Sunday afternoon we had reassembled the instrument. Mrs. Rockmore then tried it by playing a few notes. "No," she said impatiently, "it doesn't play right." Michael and I reset some of the internal adjustments, and Mrs. Rockmore tried the instrument again. "No, it's still not right," she said. Once again, we reset the adjustments. Mrs. Rockmore tried a few notes, then proceeded to play George Gershwin's "Summertime" from beginning to end. At the end, tears were in her eyes. She turned to us and said, "I was afraid I would never be able to play my instrument again." At that moment I sensed a strong spiritual connection with Leon Theremin, a feeling that remains with me even now. I would say that that moment was the high point of my professional career.

Fast-forward to the present: I published another do-it-yourself theremin article in 1996, this time in *Electronic Musician* magazine. Big Briar Inc., my current company, is selling theremins worldwide. The CD *The Art of the Theremin — Clara Rockmore* is enjoying wide acceptance, as is the video *Clara Rockmore, the World's Greatest Theremin Virtuosa*. I helped produce both of these. These accomplishments are milestones in my life. But they are mere footnotes to the story of Leon Theremin. The complete story is in this book, carefully researched and artfully written by Albert Glinsky. Leon Theremin was a creative genius and a prolific inventor. His lifetime spanned the entire existence of the Soviet Union, and then some. At various times in his life, Theremin was a technological sensation, a political prisoner, a major contributor to the war effort of the Soviet Union, a beloved teacher, a forgotten hero, and an object of adulation by thousands of modern-day music technologists. This story of Theremin and his time will amaze you and probably, from time to time, overwhelm you. I'm sure you will enjoy reading it.

ACKNOWLEDGMENTS

The thirteen years of research for this book involved the compilation of an enormous personal archive of materials in order to chronicle Theremin's vast story. My gathering, shaping, and interpreting of these materials in the context of contemporary history was shepherded along by individuals who were very generous with their time and knowledge.

I would like to thank my editor, Judith McCulloh, for her vision and faith—not to mention her patience—as this project ambled to completion, held up by late-breaking details and endless tidbits of research that filtered into the final manuscript. The musicologist Olivia Mattis deserves special mention for her initial endorsement of this work, and for her unflagging encouragement and assistance as each chapter fell into place. Particular thanks also go to Norm Cohen, who offered cogent technical advice and supported the publication of this chronicle as a book. Nick Holonyak Jr. was most gracious in reviewing a late copy of the manuscript, helping me to fine-tune significant engineering details, and adding his vote for publication.

Among those who shared vital information with me, Leon Theremin himself must go at the top of the list, not only for his valuable comments but for the sheer inspiration of his presence. Anne Stern, daughter of Lucie Bigelow Rosen, unlocked a treasure house of Theremin documentation by making her mother's rich archive available to me, in addition to granting me a number of interviews over many years. Lydia Kavina, granddaughter of Leon Theremin's first cousin—and a leading composer and thereminist—gave richly of her time and energy with several extensive interviews and a regular correspondence in which she sent me piles of valuable Russian archival and press information, family documents, photographs, and contacts for further research. Bulat Galeyev, Theremin's friend, colleague, and Russian biographer, was more than gracious in helping me track down elusive information, supplying me with rare journal and manuscript articles, and offering a gallery of photographs. Robert Moog was most obliging in telling me his life story—much of which he was surely rehashing for the umpteenth time. Tanya Seroka, my invaluable Russian translator, spent countless hours helping me navigate through hundreds of pages of Russian text, interpreting not only words, but shades of historical meaning and political innuendos. Hilton M. Bailey, director of business administration at the Caramoor Center for Music and the Arts in Katonah, New York, untiringly assisted me in my frequent research visits to the center.

Various people, either directly or indirectly connected with Leon Theremin, his associates, or his instruments, generously granted me interviews. They include: Burnett Cross, Herbert Deutsch, Gary Hoffman, Yolanda Bolotine Kulik, Otto Luening, Clare Morgenstern, Pamela Mia Paul, Clara Rockmore, Eric Ross, Frances Schillinger, John Scholz, Walter Sear, Nicolas Slonimsky, Paul O. W. Tanner, and Rosalyn Tureck.

I am indebted to those individuals in Russia who provided me with valuable articles, documents, and personal reminiscences: Natalia Constantinova, Anton Diachenko, Alexander Kalmykov, Anatoly Kisselev, Vladimir Kossarev, Ludmila Mikheyeva, Natalia Skatova, Helena Theremin, and Sergei Zorin.

Particular thanks are extended to those whose custodial skills aided my archival research: Norman Brouwer at the South Street Seaport Library in New York; Lynn Falk, my steadfast facilitator of interlibrary loans; Don Manildi at the International Piano Archives, University of Maryland at College Park; Ned Quist, head librarian, and Elizabeth Schaaf, archivist, at the Arthur Friedheim Library, Peabody Institute; Elliot Sivowitch of the Division of Electricity and Modern Physics, National Museum of American History, Smithsonian Institution; Marian L. Smith, historian, U.S. Immigration and Naturalization Service; Phyllis Smith, David Sarnoff Research Center; and Natalia Zitzelsberger, Slavic and Baltic Division, New York Public Library. I am grateful to the archivists of the U.S. National Archives and Records Administration who repeatedly assisted me in locating important government files and documents—at Archives I, Washington, D.C.: William R. Ellis, Claire Prechtel-Kluskens, and Mitchell Yockelson; at Archives II, Textual Reference Branch, College Park, Maryland: Marjorie Ciarlante, Wayne de Caesar, Greg M. Gluba, Milton Gustafon, Tab Lewis, Martin F. McGann, and Frederick Romanski; at the Northeast Region, New York: Richard Gelbke. My thanks also to the librarians and staff members at the Library of Congress who offered their expertise: Elizabeth Aumen, Bryan Cornell, Jan McKee, Jon Newsom, and Wayne Shirley.

Several people provided me with specialized information from their personal collections: Kit Basquin offered me valuable items on Mary Ellen Bute; Diana Dunbar made available interview materials, photographs, and personal recollections of her dance mentor, close friend, and research subject, Lavinia Williams; Gary Hoffman provided me with extensive archival material on his father, Samuel Hoffman; Karen Shaw and Sandra Shaw Murphy furnished me with considerable materials from the collection of their mother, the American pianist and thereminist Juliet Shaw; Michael Zinman provided me with significant papers from the archive of his father, M. Boyd Zinman.

The following museums and organizations graciously aided me in probing their archives: Alcatraz Island National Park; American Bureau of Shipping; Central Park Archives, New York City; Circuit Court House, New York City; Civil Court, New York City; Department of State, State of New York, Bureau of Corporations; Free Library of Philadelphia; Hagley Museum and Library, Wilmington, Delaware; Hoover Institution, Stanford University; Lloyd Seely Library, John Jay College of Criminal Justice, New York City; Mannes College of Music; Mariner's Museum, Newport News, Virginia; Metropolitan Museum of Art; Municipal Archives of the New York City Parks Administration; Ossining Historical Society, Ossining, New York; Peabody Essex Museum, Salem, Massachusetts; the Philadelphia Orchestra; Schenectady Museum, Schenectady, New York; Sing Sing Correctional Facility, Ossining, New York; Southern District Court, New York City; U.S. Bureau of Prisons; U.S. Department of Justice; and the U.S. Federal Bureau of Investigation. On my many visits to the branches and divisions of the New York Public Library I was provided generous assistance at the Dance, Drama, and Music Research Collections, the American Music Collection, and the Rogers and Hammerstein Archive of Recorded Sound at the New York Public Library for the Performing Arts, Astor, Lenox, and Tilden Foundations, as well as the New York Public Library Annex, the Central Research Library at Fifth Avenue and Forty-second Street, and the Science, Industry, and Business Library.

My gratitude also goes to the many people who assisted in various high-level translations and specific research tasks, or who facilitated personal contacts, corresponded over historical minutiae, advised me on technical matters, granted permission to use materials, performed long-distance research, and offered choice bits of information I would never have come upon in any other way: Bruce Abrams, Roberta Arminio, Margaret E. Barclay, Jason Barile, Joanne Barry, George Boziwick, Frank Braynard, Alison Campbell, Eric Canel, Celeste Clark, Linda Closs, William Corson, Hugh Davies, Anne Diestel, Luann Dragone, Floyd Engels, Elisa Fahnert, Fritz Fahnert, Marge Fessler, Earleen Glaser, Diane Golding, Charles Greiner, Sara Hassan, Robert Heibel, L. Douglas Henderson, Anthony J. Henk, David Icove, Dennis James, Darci Jones, Kyrill Kalmykov, David Kean, William King, Amy Knight, Edith and Richard Kobler, John Kobler, Peter Laki, Charlie Lester, Wayne Lovercheck, Harvey Maisel, David McCornack, Michael McQuillen, Eleanor Meier, Howard Mossman, David Miller, Jim Nemeth, Hayden Peake, Irina Pekelnaya,

Joan Peyser, Lou Pine, Jack Platt, Thomas Rhea, Gino Robair, Jason Rosenberger, Paul Rosenblum, Jacques Rossi, Jane Rubinsky, William A. Schell, John B. Scholz, Alex Sherman, John Snyder, Andrew Sokoloff, Michael Spudic, Jane Thiele, Jerry Trambly, Chris Troutman, John Vanco, Vera Volchansky, Vitaly Volchansky, Reid Welch, Vernon Wherry, Channan Willner, Roger Wright, and Youseff Yancy.

I would also like to extend my appreciation to H. Keith Melton for allowing me to reproduce his images of the Great Seal bug, and to R. Saifullin, R. Mukhametzyanov, and F. Gubaev, for the use of their photos of Leon Theremin, Lydia Kavina, and the "Prometheus" Institute, Kazan, Russia.

For encouragement and feedback during the early stages of research I would like to acknowledge Dr. John V. Gilbert, Dr. Kenneth Peacock, and Dr. David W. Ecker, of the New York University faculty.

Among my friends and colleagues who stood by with encouragement and psychological sustenance during my pit stops, I am grateful to Raymond Erickson, Richard Goode, Barbara Heyman, Robert Hoff, Lewis Kocher, Edith Leon, Stephen Marvin, and Mark Wait.

Finally, my deepest gratitude goes to my mother, Cleo Hartwig; to my wonderfully devoted and enduring wife, Linda Kobler—whose powerfully discerning musician's and writer's eyes, depth of understanding, love, synergistic discussions, and quality control kept my manuscript in check and on track always—and to my son, Luka, and my daughter, Allegra, for their patience and understanding during my frequent absences, literal and figurative, as this volume painstakingly came together.

Theremin

My father, the late American sculptor Vincent Glinsky, was born just outside
St. Petersburg, Russia, in 1895. Leon Theremin, the subject of this book, was
born in St. Petersburg the following year. Both spent their youth in the dusk
of imperial Russia. My father recalled wearing his military-style uniform to
school, standing each day with his classmates to salute the tsar's portrait. But
in the events of these formative years, the commonality of the two men's lives
ended.

With fateful timing, my father and his family boarded a ship in Bremen
and sailed to America only days before the outbreak of World War I. As a U.S.
citizen, he saw his dreams to fulfillment, living a peaceful life of creative accomplishment until his death in 1975. His brothers, embracing the capitalist
dream, all became successful businessmen.

In 1914, Theremin, a student of physics and astronomy at St. Petersburg
University, saw his life eclipsed by the shadow of the First World War. After
he was handed a Red Army uniform several years later, he found he couldn't
get it off—it was his new skin. Patriotism meant Bolshevism, Bolshevism meant
blind service to Lenin, and Lenin meant business. Once the leader had found
useful applications for Theremin's genius, the young inventor was ipso facto a
Soviet scientist. Like my father, Theremin managed to live a life of creative accomplishment, but his was not a peaceful one. He had ransomed his freedom
for the simple chance to invent—and he would never again be his own person.

For those of us who already know the highlights of Theremin's story—his
bewitching gallery of musical inventions and electronic legerdemain, and the
choice morsels of his improbable life—it might seem more than adequate to
shape this litany of gadgets and events into a delightful biography. Western
journalism, in fact, most often paints Theremin as the happy-go-lucky inventor of wild-and-wacky musical instruments, the icon of Hollywood's horror and
sci-fi film industry, and the avuncular hero of modern musical electronics.
These, of course, he is. But this view alone is one-dimensional at best. When
he lived in America, Theremin charmed thousands with his magical musical

instruments; at the same time he was feeding intelligence to the Soviet apparat. He was the toast of New York's glittering high society, yet his closest associates were Socialists and Communists. Where did his personal allegiance lie?

Many Western sketches of Theremin make passing reference to his dis-
appearance from the Western Hemisphere for decades, his Russian imprisonment, and his forced service to the Soviet military machine during World
War II. But precisely in these biographical details lies the true substance of
Theremin's character and life. Granted, his American years were the highlight
of his professional career, but they account for a mere 10 percent of his long
lifetime.

Russian scholarship on Theremin, which has focused on the remaining 90
percent, has brought hundreds of little-known facts to light. Scientists and
colleagues have written with personal empathy about the inventor's fate under the Soviets; journalists have drawn stupefying revelations out of him in the
free speech of post-Communism; authors have penned tributes to the near
science fiction achievements of his later years.

It was Theremin's Russian biographer, Bulat Galeyev, who was the first to
address the central conflicts and motivations in the inventor's life. Galeyev was
a close friend and admirer, and someone who understood the pain of twentieth-century Soviet politics. His 1995 book *Soviet Faust* lays out the premise
that the inventor, in order to pursue an abiding passion for scientific creation,
was essentially forced to sell his soul to the devil—meaning the KGB and its
insidious secret police predecessors. In his interviews with Theremin, Galeyev
even confronted his subject point blank about the dark side of his past—issues
that were answered by averting eyes. Although Western accounts parenthet-
ically cast Theremin as a victim of Soviet repression, the Faust analogy is the
truest. Ultimately, Galeyev's portrayal is a forgiving one, as any study of Theremin must be, lest we cast the first stone. He understands only too well how
many millions of ordinary people were forced into extraordinary compromises
to preserve their lives, save their families, or protect their work.

Interestingly, the interpretation of Theremin's motives has been the source
of a split in the theremin community, most of it along cultural lines. Non-
Russians seem to stand in denial of what Russians see as axiomatic: that under threat of death, every citizen had to soldier the cause, and that there was
precious little any one person could do to resist. The violinist Nathan Milstein
illustrated this quite plainly in his memoirs when he came to the defense of
his brilliant colleague, the violinist Leonid Kogan:

> I was aware that many people did not like him. Once there was even a protest
> demonstration against him, because of rumors that he was involved with the

KGB. I don't quite understand why Kogan was singled out. I've read the memoirs of Soviet intelligence officer Colonel Oleg Penkovsky, who wrote that all members of Soviet delegations to the West, whether scientists, musicians, or ballerinas, are obligated to report to the government on everything they see and hear. For instance, they're asked, "Well, you met with Rothschild, what did he say, what does he think?" And so on. Leonid Kogan was not an exception in that regard. I always wondered why the Soviets make their artists report on their contacts with the West. I mean, what useful information could a Kogan bring back? I once asked that marvelous violinist and dear man Isaac Stern whether the CIA or FBI invited him in for a chat after his trip to the Soviet Union. He said no. And it would never occur to Stern to go to a government agency with any information, even though he is a patriot. There are professionals for spying. But under the Soviet system, every citizen is made to engage in espionage, to humiliating and inefficient effect.[1]

The composer Dmitri Shostakovich was stunned and disgusted by Westerners who refused to see the Russian situation for what it was—who, for instance, bought every line Stalin fed them:

They all ate out of his hand. As I understand it, they don't like to remember this in the West. For they're always right, the great Western humanists, lovers of truthful literature and art. It's we who are always at fault. I'm the one who gets asked, "Why did you sign this and that?" But has anyone ever asked André Malraux why he glorified the construction of the White Sea Canal, where thousands upon thousands of people perished? No, no one has. Too bad. They should ask more often. After all, no one can keep these gentlemen from answering, nothing threatened their lives then and nothing threatens them now.[2]

To his credit, Theremin never evinced impatience with his Western interviewers when he was repeatedly asked the same uncomprehending questions: "Why were you arrested?" "What exactly did you do to deserve such a fate?" Hopefully, this book will do more than answer these questions; it will demonstrate how painfully self-evident those answers were to begin with.

If Theremin's role as an artist did not exempt him from espionage duty, his status as a scientist drew him in even more deeply. Richard Deacon, writing in *A History of the Russian Secret Service*, mentions that a prime aim of Meyer Trilisser, the head of the Russian Foreign Department of the United State Political Administration (OGPU) under Lenin,

was to develop industrial and scientific espionage in the Western world. He had direct encouragement from Lenin to achieve this. . . . Trilisser had the utmost contempt for the "worker-spy" in industry, maintaining that he was unprofessional . . . with insufficient technical knowledge to know what to look for. So he decided that if Russia were to obtain the West's scientific and technological secrets she must employ dedicated scientists who could be trusted to serve the cause. Or, alternatively, scientists must be used in this cause without their realising what was happening until, of course, it was too late and they were already compromised. . . .

Historians of the Russian Intelligence Services have almost completely neglected this vital role played by prominent young Russian scientists in enabling the Soviet Government to catch up on the lead which the Western powers had in the field of science in the 'twenties and 'thirties.[3]

While Russian literature on Theremin, with all its richness, has added immeasurably to an understanding of his life, it is spotty and inaccurate when it comes to his American years and tends to rehash the same spurious rumors that leaked into the story over the decades. One aim of my study has been to fuse concrete bodies of information from both East and West, stitching together the whimsical and the covert, the triumphant and the treacherous, into a single, multidimensional picture of the man.

But Theremin's life presents the historian with innumerable hurdles. To begin with, his paper trail is paltry and full of gaps. For over a quarter century the Soviet government prohibited him from carrying on correspondence; during the last third of his life, he himself was denied access to his own diplomas and any documentation of his earlier scientific achievements. And his long years of incarceration and forced service to the state are simply lost. The work he carried on then as a faceless drone was not documented, and the sensitivity of much of it kept him closemouthed in later years. In the letters and diaries that we do have, Theremin is rarely a confessional personality. He is formal and to the point. As someone who learned quickly that any spoken or written words were testimony in Soviet eyes, he measured out his sentences with icy precision. And of course anything he said to his American acquaintances in the United States was filtered through the constraints of his intelligence agenda and cannot be interpreted at face value.

Theremin routinely supplied different versions of the same incident to different interviewers at different times. And when he was finally politically free enough to tell his own story he could no longer be counted on to tell it reliably. Age had taken its toll on his memory. At the same time he was an enigmatic figure, one who vacillated between harmless storytelling and outright obfuscation. He routinely boasted to Russian journalists about the "700 registered theremin players" in 1930s New York, even though the figure was probably closer to fifteen. With a mischievous pride he told Galeyev he had been "something like a resident" in the United States (a "rezident" was a high-level Soviet agent planted for an extended time in a foreign country).[4] "I was carrying out the same mission in America as Richard Sorge did in Japan," he explained.[5] Any Russian historian, of course, would know in an instant that a bone fide agent like Richard Sorge could never have compromised his identity with lavish displays of musical instruments and great public fanfare. Obviously Theremin, in his late years, found a certain romance in grossly exaggerating his covert role. Again and again he confounded Galeyev, his close friend. In *Soviet Faust*, the author finds himself repeating the same refrain each time Theremin makes some fantastic claim: "And again, it is hard to understand. Is it a joke or not?"[6]

Repeatedly, the inventor crossed names and people, as when he claimed that it was Albert Einstein who collaborated in his studio with the filmmaker Mary Ellen Bute, whereas we know it was Joseph Schillinger. (The famous physicist was also crossed with his eponymous counterpart in the arts, the musicologist *Alfred* Einstein, and there are many cases of this sort of amplified mythology.) The list of stellar twentieth-century names who actually did cross the inventor's path is impressive enough—there is certainly no need to fatten up the résumé with apocryphal anecdotes.

Theremin sometimes had three different versions of the same incident, and not surprisingly, the same kind of inconsistencies in dates, sums, places, and faces dogged his many surviving friends and associates. Nicolas Slonimsky recalled that Theremin was "constantly in debt" in his New York years;[7] Galeyev and other Russians have often characterized the inventor as an "American millionaire."[8] The historian quickly learns the pitfalls of oral testimony: the subject doesn't remember what happened or doesn't *want* to remember, or perhaps remembers what he or she *wished* had happened.

Compounding the problem of personal amnesia is its sordid cultural twin: historical revisionism. That the Soviet government in the twentieth century made a specialty of rewriting history is well known. We have thousands of official photos that were literally airbrushed over to vaporize this or that political figure from history. Soviet libraries regularly received government packets with instructions to rip out a specific dictionary page and replace it with the new, enclosed page, omitting the original offending entry altogether. People and identities were summarily wiped out—only to be reinstated or "rehabilitated" later. A whole culture grew up regarding truth as an inconvenience (albeit one that could be conveniently enough overcome).

Unquestionably, the only hope of clearing a reliable path through this historical mine field is through slavish cross-checking of oral testimony with press accounts, archival documents, and impartial data from the historical record. Along with the many hours of interviews I conducted, my research led me through FBI and KGB files, New York County Court records, documents from the U.S. Departments of Labor and Justice, the Bureau of Prisons, and the National Archives, to cite just a few sources. I tracked down birth and death certificates, phone books from the '30s, old maritime records, and over one thousand newspaper and journal articles. Often, on a tip, I spent days sprinting down some circuitous path, only to turn up another tip that rendered the first one impossible, unlikely, or simply idle conjecture layered over existing folklore. I have run into dead-ends, tied up loose ends, and in general had no end of frustration in trying to separate the truth from legend in Theremin's life.

In the process, the good and the bad have emerged, and I have made a deliberate effort to refrain from smoothing out the painful, outrageous, and sometimes outright embarrassing moments in Theremin's roller coaster career. To fathom the complex personality that emerges, the reader sees the way the inventor was judged at each junction of his life, through the eyes of those who often relied on sketchy information or skewed encounters, as well as through the perspective of those who knew him well. In the end, I have aimed at a balanced picture, free from testimonial, but ultimately an admiring tribute to the man.

Wherever possible I have tried to let each era and personality speak directly to the reader in the savory quotations of the period—each with its own inimitable phrasing and cadence. We can eavesdrop, for instance, with a certain wistfulness, on an era when technology could still take one's breath away— an awe of a magnitude all but vanished in the blasé, daily one-upmanship of modern consumer electronics.

But here I have perhaps saved the best for last. In the personal history of Leon Theremin there lies a larger history—one that embraces the whole of the twentieth century. It is astounding to think that Theremin witnessed most of the major cataclysms of the century—World War I, the Russian Revolution and civil war, the Great Depression, Stalin's purge, World War II, the cold war, and perestroika—not as a passive observer, but as an active, if reluctant, participant. He knew capitalism because he had worked the system for all it was worth; he knew communism because he had donned the Red Army uniform and joined the cause; he saw the pitfalls of free enterprise because he lived through the Great Depression; he felt the full weight of Soviet repression because he suffered under the terror. Rarely do we have the opportunity to relive, up close, such an encyclopedia of world events and perspectives from the experience of one single human being.

A quick glance at the index of this book will reveal that Theremin's story takes in everyone from the Bolsheviks to the Beach Boys and runs from the gulags of Stalin to the inanities of a Jerry Lewis movie. Leon Theremin's story is nothing less than a metaphor for the divergence of communism and capitalism, totalitarianism and freedom, luxury and drudgery, hope and hopelessness. His life was a microcosm of these dueling scenarios and he spent most of his nearly one hundred years shuttling back and forth between them. A typical example illustrates this chasm between Soviet and American culture: when Theremin built one of the first televisions in the 1920s, the Soviet government seized it, made it top secret, and pressed it into service as a surveillance device for border guards and the Kremlin. At the other end of the world, David Sarnoff, RCA's guiding star at the birth of television in America—later to be Theremin's employer—worked to put a set in every home and spoke glowingly of television's possibilities: to introduce *Hamlet* to the people, and to offer night school courses. Surveillance versus *I Love Lucy*. The divergence of Soviet and American culture can be almost unfathomable. And it would be laughable, had it not been so tragic and so typical.

Leon Theremin will be remembered as the wizardly patriarch of electronic music. But as spectators on his amazing life, we may also learn from that part of his story for which he has not generally been remembered. We can relive the extraordinary century he inhabited, and the forces that shaped our protagonist and, in no small way, ourselves as well.

ONE

Soviet Power Plus Electrification

Electricity will take the place of God. Let the peasant pray to electricity; he's going to feel the power of the central authorities more than that of heaven.

—Vladimir Ilyich Lenin, 1918

Homes were searched, and thousands of citizens were seized and rounded up without warning by lieutenants, sergeants-at-arms, spies, and other informants. In jail, the will of the arrested was quickly worn down by hunger and lack of sleep. Legal counsel was denied them, and they would never learn the identity of their accusers. They were usually quick to admit to their alleged crimes at a tribunal. If not, any attempts at self-defense were met with Draconian measures, including torture, to exact a confession of guilt—the only admissible verdict in the end. Punishment was life imprisonment or execution. In either case, the goods and property of the convicted were confiscated, condemning their descendants to a life of penury.

Such was the fate of the Albigensian sect of the twelfth and thirteenth centuries, routed in southern France by a bloody Inquisition. The Albigenses were heretics who denied the veracity of Christ's redemptive power, the authority of the pope, and the teachings of the Roman church. They believed only in the constant struggle between good and evil. They preached that human souls, like Satan, had been cast out of heaven for rebelling against God and had been condemned to imprisonment on earth in physical bodies. Purification of the soul at death was their single goal. Any worldly perpetuation of the race—marriage, procreation—or any material want, was to be shunned. Suicide by starvation was encouraged in anyone who had reached a pure or "perfect" state, and those who were still "impure" at death were thought to transmigrate to a lower life form. The killing of animals was therefore forbidden, and meat and dairy products were thought to be contaminated.

The Inquisition left the Albigenses' homeland—the province of Languedoc, near Toulouse—virtually cleansed of their sect at the end of the fourteenth century. A scattered few managed to escape, and among them was a group bearing the name Théremin—a name that translated literally as "bath attendant," a Christian metaphor, ironically, for the "cleansing of the soul."

Reinventing themselves, the group adopted the metaphor literally and converted to Christianity as Huguenots, only to suffer persecution under the French monarchy in the sixteenth century. But their iron resolve sent them fleeing where they had to, repeatedly adapting for survival. They fanned out to Switzerland, Germany, Belgium, Prussia, and, in 1793, to St. Petersburg, where a Russian branch of the family was established.

The generations of Theremins that followed were a diverse lot. One offshoot flowered into a line of Protestant priests; some became rebels, storming the Bastille and fighting in the American Civil War; still others were artists, musicians, and professors, and a few distinguished themselves in law and medicine. One family member had been blessed by Calvin himself, while his brother was slaughtered in the St. Bartholomew's Day Massacre of 1572.

The Theremin family history was laden with leitmotifs: war, persecution, flight, emigration, spiritual fortitude, encounters with the nobility, disdain for material pursuits, artistic excellence, scientific and philosophical inquiry, and, above all, the perpetual interplay of good and evil. Tumbling down through the generations, these manifold fortunes, and the whole familial legacy of the sacred and the profane, the victorious and the tragic, would eventually be the single inheritance of one, extraordinary individual, set apart in every way, even by his earliest recollection:

> I remember myself before my official birthday. . . . there was complete darkness. Something was always turning, and it seemed to me I was falling into a neighboring place. I remember sounds gradually becoming louder, and at the end I saw a little red spot start to get bigger and bigger, brighter and brighter, and suddenly it was so big that my eyes were hurting. I was afraid. The spot changed color from red to white. Something began to push me from behind, and finally it pushed me out. The light was so bright that I tried to close my eyes. There were so many sounds around me. That was the day of my birth.[1]

That day was August 15, 1896, by the Old Style, Julian calendar. It was St. Petersburg. The boy's father, Sergei Emilievich Theremin, a graduate of St. Petersburg University and a respected lawyer, was the son of the tsar's court physician. Sergei's wife, Yevgenia Antonova Orzhinskaya, part Polish and part Russian, was of noble birth and liked to dabble in music and the arts.

The boy remembered: "I was held in someone's hands. Now I know it was my father. Everyone around me was talking loudly. Then I was put down. It was cold. Now I know it was cold water. It was my baptism."[2]

He was christened Lev Sergeyevich Termen (pronounced "Tair-MEN," with a flipped "r"—the Russian adaptation of the ancestral name, although the proper non-Cyrillic spelling remained "Theremin"). He was born into the responsibility of a heraldic tradition: atop the family emblem, lilies and a crown were meant to signify nobility. A shield with Christ's monogram and two olive branches denoted a high spirituality. Across a ribbon at the bottom, the rule of the "golden mean" echoed the motto of his medieval French forebears: *ne plous, ne moeins*—"no more, no less."

Life in the twilight years of the tsarist empire was cozy. Lev lived with his parents, grandmother, and younger sister, Helena Sergeyevna, in five comfortable rooms at 50 Nicolayevska Street, apartment 4. The family was close-knit. They were religious—Russian Orthodox—and read prayers together every morning and evening, but they rarely attended church. Lev shared a small room with his grandmother. On the surface, his childhood might have seemed as unspectacular as countless others playing out across the Russian capital at the turn of the century. But there was an odd intensity to Lev, a peculiar sense of drive and purpose for a child. When his father encouraged him to explore their big study, Lev quickly discovered a spinning bookshelf with the famous Brockhaus and Efron encyclopedia. "At three I tried to read this encyclopedia," he recalled, "and was fascinated by what I found. None of the other books were real to me." He puzzled over velocities and mechanical things. "I had blocks, and built walls and slides, and studied a pendulum on a rope."[3] His father often took him to rummage through the used-goods stands at the Nevsky Prospekt market for tools and small odds and ends, and by seven, Lev was dismantling and repairing his father's gold watches. Electricity fascinated him.

His parents played four-hand arrangements at the piano and Lev coaxed lessons out of them when he was five. At nine he took up the cello. He loved music, but he was impatient with the conditioned muscular training needed to extract even the simplest tunes from these instruments; it seemed to limit his inner expression. "I realized there was a gap between music itself and its mechanical production, and I wanted to unite both of them."[4]

When he entered St. Petersburg's First State Gymnasium, at the end of Nicolayevska Street, Lev stood out in a class of thirty boys. At the first physics lecture, he took issue with the instructor. "The teacher began to speak about the principle of pendulums. I felt he didn't explain things correctly, and it wasn't professional."[5] Lev was called to repeat the explanation in front of the class, but his perspective was so unlike the teacher's that he found himself mumbling. He received his first failing grade. Two days later he was asked to try again. This time, measuring his words, he made a case for his own viewpoint, disarming the instructor. "He was very interested and asked me where

I had learned all these things," Lev recalled.[6] The teacher sweetened the praise with an invitation to do independent electrical research in the gymnasium physics lab.

At home, Lev conducted experiments with high-frequency currents, optical devices, and magnetic fields, and he began studying astronomy by investigating all known stars. In the vegetable garden behind his parents' summer home, just outside the city, he constructed his own observatory where he discovered a new star. When he reported his find to the Astronomical Society, it must have turned a few heads, coming from a fifteen-year-old boy.

The next year he was invited by the principal of his school to stage a whimsical display for the gymnasium students and their parents—a foreshadowing of his future caprice and fancy in science. Ten feet over the heads of his audience he strung electrical wires receiving a high-frequency electrical current. Volunteers were each handed a Geissler tube—the earliest sealed glass vacuum tube containing two electrodes. When high voltage was applied, a wayward spray of electrons from current flowing between the electrodes would hit the inside wall of the tube and cause a green fluorescent glow. Participants were asked to rise individually and aim their Geissler tubes at the suspended wires. As the raised tubes came within eighteen inches of the wires, they entered the electromagnetic field and lit up. The participants were transformed into Statue of Liberty–like torchbearers.

When Lev was sixteen, his cousin, Kirill Fedorovich Nesturkh ("Kirusha"), invited him to witness the master's thesis defense of a rising star in Russian physics, Abram Fedorovich Ioffe. Lev never forgot that day in May 1913. He and Kirusha, a physicist at St. Petersburg University, jostled their way to front row seats as the hall filled up. Even the eminent physicist Vladimir Lebedinsky rushed to claim one of the remaining places at the back. It was a weighty event in the physics world—Ioffe's work was controversial. His thesis topic was "the photoelectric effect and magnetic fields of electrons," and Lev was struck by the unusual approach. It seemed to him "unlike others who operated more with mathematical indices, expressions, and formulas shaded with symbolism. It was about objects around us connected to our feelings . . . and perceived directly by our sensory organs." Ioffe's approach was an eye opener to Lev. "It was calling me to the real scientific—not the abstract—knowledge of the essence of matter, and probably life."[7] His pulse raced at the possibilities of empirical investigation—the thrill of experimental physics, of drawing back curtain after curtain from the mysteries of the physical world.

Kirusha tracked down Ioffe afterward and presented Lev to him as a young experimenter in physics and a future student at the university. Lev was young and impressionable, but he was sure he had met his role model. "Abram Fedorovich looked in my eyes with a friendly smile and gave me his hand, which I shook with great affection. I thought how wonderful it would be to work under his leadership as an adult."[8]

Lev graduated from the gymnasium in 1914 with a silver medal. In the fall he was to enter the School of Physics and Mathematics at St. Petersburg University. Astronomy and physics would be his concentration, but he hoped to keep a hand in music as well. Among his parents' coterie of friends, the cello soloist of the Imperial Ballet Orchestra, A. Garpf, agreed to audition him for the St. Petersburg Conservatory as his own pupil.

≪≫

On August 1, with little warning, the motherland was ignited by the spark of the First World War when Germany declared war on Russia. From the urbane, insular world of intellectual circles and scientific thought, Lev found himself at the epicenter of a cataclysm. Things began shifting and transforming themselves all around him—even his beloved St. Petersburg was rechristened with the more Russified name of "Petrograd." Fifteen million young men were suddenly mobilized and marched off by the tsar. At Tannenberg, the Germans crushed the first Russian offensive in a bloody, costly defeat.

Lev hoped the war would end swiftly, and he managed to begin his studies at Petrograd University. At the same time he was juggling classes at the conservatory in music theory and wound up in Professor Garpf's cello class. The physics circle he joined at the university was mostly made up of older students—the residue left behind when the draft swept away the majority of his peers.

In the spring of 1915 he heard that Ioffe was presenting his doctoral defense. It was a public lecture again, and afterward Lev nabbed the physicist in the corridor and let forth a storm of questions. "Ioffe listened attentively to me and commented on the importance of experiments with big electric and magnetic fields to determine the parameters of atomic and molecular structure."[9] Lev hung on every word. Seeing the student's earnestness, Ioffe took a chance and arranged for Lev to have his own room in the university's Physical Institute building to do independent research—an unheard-of honor for a second-year student, but obviously an endorsement of a new protégé.

Lev was in his element, but he kept a nervous eye over his shoulder, fearing the long arm of the draft would find him before long. The war was dragging on. By the autumn of 1915, the Austro-German army had driven the tsar's troops out of the Baltic provinces, pushing the Russian lines back hundreds of miles. In desperation, the tsar hurried to the front himself to supervise the army, leaving behind the Empress Alexandra and her erratic adviser—the mystic faith-healer Rasputin—to run domestic affairs. As the war escalated, the monarchy—haughty and unresponsive to rampant hunger among the masses—appeared to be crumbling.

Lev finally received the call early in 1916, but his prodigious electrical knowledge saved him from the front lines: the physics and astronomy deans maneuvered him into the Nicolayevska Military Engineering School in Petrograd, an avenue open only to fourth-year students. It was a blessing, yet it had taken him away from his ideal métier of practical research. He was unable to mask his disappointment. Ioffe took a philosophical outlook: "He comforted me that the war wouldn't last long, and my military engineering experience could be used successfully for the aims of science."[10]

Lev was tossed into the cogs of the raging war machine. He was pushed through a six-month shortened course at the Military Engineering School and relayed immediately to the doors of the Graduate Electrotechnical School for Officers to major in military radio engineering. When he graduated, late in 1916, he was fed back into the school's Radio Technical Department to instruct the next wave of recruits. His well-trained hands were also needed for transmitter work, and simultaneously he was cast in the role of lieutenant in the Reserve Electrotechnical Battalion. His first charge was to oversee the construction of a powerful radio station for the front at Saratov, on the Volga River, to open strategic communication with Moscow four hundred miles to the northwest.

Erecting radio towers was a far cry from Lev's dream of practical physics, but for the moment it offered sanctuary from the sorry lot of the tsar's troops. By late 1916, enemy blockades had stemmed the import of vital goods, and the railroad system was collapsing. Agricultural production was shrinking after hordes of peasant men were drafted into the war. Hunger was spreading among the population. Food riots, antigovernment strikes, and street demonstrations began to foment a climate of revolution.

Lev also perceived a seismic movement in the ideological ground beneath him. The lawyer's son would have to face up to the corrupt political and moral fabric of a society he had taken for granted: "It was the last year before the Revolution, and there was mental fermentation in the army. People had various personal opinions, often at odds with their officers. There were different political circles organized in the Battalion. I wasn't a Bolshevik yet, but we all expected changes in the life of our country. My strongest sympathies were with the Marxist circle."[11]

Discontent in the army set off mass desertions, and in February 1917, the tsar's soldiers began joining ranks with demonstrators. "Bread and freedom" became the cry. Police stations, courts, and jails were raided and burned. Cities all across Russia fell into the hands of insurgents. On March 2, Tsar Nicholas

II, recognizing that his authority was in eclipse, abdicated the imperial throne, ending the three-hundred-year reign of the Romanovs in Russia.

A Provisional Government was rushed into power, but its cabinet consisted mainly of intellectuals hoping to preserve private property and delay decisions affecting the working classes. The opposition, waiting in the wings, was the Petrograd Soviet and other soviets that sprouted around the country: governing councils of rank-and-file leaders elected by workers, peasants, and military personnel, with an ideology more in step with the needs of the masses.

In the midst of these upheavals, Lev managed to complete his degree from Petrograd University in 1917; at the same time he received a "freelance artist" diploma from the conservatory.

After another devastating rout of the Russian army by the Germans in July 1917, the Provisional Government suffered a loss of confidence, and the Bolsheviks gained a majority in the Petrograd and Moscow soviets. Of the leftist factions vying for power, the Bolsheviks were more radical than their Menshevik and Socialist Revolutionary counterparts. They advocated a true socialist state organized by and for the proletariat, against the bourgeois society. A showdown was imminent.

The Bolshevik party leader, Vladimir Ilyich Lenin, orchestrated a complete army insurrection, disarming the government and commandeering bridges, government buildings, communications, transport services, and munitions supplies in Petrograd. On the evening of October 25, revolutionary forces seized the Winter Palace—the former headquarters of the tsar—and arrested the cabinet of the Provisional Government holed up there. Later that night, a manifesto drafted by Lenin was read before delegates to the Congress of Soviets: a Revolutionary Soviet Socialist Government was to be formed immediately. It would secure prompt withdrawal from the war and seize private and church land for the soviets, to be parceled up and distributed among the peasants. The "October Revolution" was complete.

As the new head of the Soviet government, Lenin signed the Brest-Litovsk peace treaty with the Central Powers in March 1918. Russia's involvement in the First World War was over.

Lenin's deputy comrade in arms, Leon Trotsky—president of the Petrograd Soviet, and second in command during the staging of the October Revolution—was the new people's commissar for war. Trotsky was charged with rebuilding viable Russian armed forces for the Soviet state. In 1918, he formed the nonvolunteer Red Army, largely from peasants and workers—a force that burgeoned into the main defensive arm of the new regime.

To keep the seat of government farther from the border, Lenin moved the Soviet capital from Petrograd to Moscow. The gesture was also a symbolic one.

St. Petersburg had always been "Russia's window on the West," a European-style metropolis associated with the tsar and his aristocracy. Moscow, on the other hand, embodied Russia's Asiatic heritage, and a retreat from Western influences. The move resulted in Lev's reassignment to Moscow to serve as deputy chief of the new Red Army's Military Radiotechnical Laboratory—the Soviet reincarnation of the old Reserve Electrotechnical Battalion. As a job, it was a lateral shift, but there was one small change: he was wearing a Bolshevik uniform now. He had stepped into a realm with no exits.

When the Bolsheviks seized power, their victory left a large, disaffected faction of former upper and middle classes—Socialist Revolutionaries and Mensheviks—that rallied under its own military commanders to topple the Lenin-Trotsky leadership. These "White" forces were a serious threat, but Lenin felt if he could destroy them, he could destroy the bourgeoisie at the same time. In the spring of 1918 he precipitated a civil war that was, in reality, a class struggle against the "Whites." To accomplish his ends, Lenin met his adversaries with a monstrous barbarity that reduced his leadership to a nightmare of paranoia, repression, and terror.

Coupled with this, Lenin sanctioned one of the most notorious acts of regicide since the French Revolution: the assassination of the tsar and his family by a band of Bolsheviks in Ekaterinburg, where the former monarch was in custody. On July 17, 1918, the family, along with their physician, cook, and other attendants, were shot at point blank range in a relentless volley that wiped out the entire Romanov dynasty and any future threat it might pose, with a single, sudden act of terror.

For the Bolsheviks, terror was not merely a matter of combating resistance. It became a mandated state policy that transformed the Russian consciousness, turning the society virtually overnight into a frantic police state of arbitrary violence and mass repression. "The dictatorship," Lenin wrote in 1920, "means . . . unrestrained power based on force and not on law."[12] In December 1917, he founded the Cheka—the Extraordinary Commission to Combat Counterrevolution and Sabotage—an intelligence and secret police organization that carried out investigations, arrests, and executions. The Cheka was responsible for the extermination of tens of thousands, including many Bolsheviks, and became the model for later state terror organizations under Stalin. Working independently, the Cheka had its own internal system of justice and ultimately answered only to the head of the Party.

As part of Lenin's "cleansing" decrees, landowners and the middle class were singled out for special persecution. In 1918, he directed the people's commissar for food production to take twenty-five to thirty hostages from among the rich in every grain-producing district to be executed merely for belonging to the wrong class. In a cable to Trotsky he urged "remorseless destruction" in Kazan, and he directed the commissar for oil in a Caspian city to prepare to burn down the city completely in the event of resistance. He directed another commander to "carry out relentless terror against the kulaks [wealthy peasant farmers], the priests and the White Guards," and among his own military commanders he purposefully sowed the seeds of fear and paranoia to discourage any dissent. "From now on we're applying the model of the French Revolution," he cabled Trotsky, "and putting on trial and even executing the senior commanders if they hold back and fail in their actions."[13] In May 1919, nearly eighty thousand Red Army deserters were reportedly arrested.

After two separate attempts on Lenin's life, many former ministers of the Provisional Government were publicly executed. Former tsarist officers were arrested as a matter of course and imprisoned along with their entire families, including aunts and uncles. By 1918, Lenin began organizing concentration camps for those lucky enough to be spared the bullet. His new policy of forced labor became a potent weapon in the terror campaign that saw thousands of men, women, and children dying on their way to the camps, or as a result of conditions within them. By now, Lenin had extinguished any hopes of a democratic, decentralized Soviet state. He could cling to power only with a centralized dictatorship that held its own self-preservation over the interests of anyone, proletarian or otherwise.

In 1919, Lev was relocated to Petrograd. Like it or not, he was now at ground zero of an Armageddon, recruited to aid the Red Army's struggle for Bolshevik supremacy. The burden of trust he was shouldering was daunting: he was appointed broadcast supervisor (chief of the transmitter) at the most powerful radio station in the country. The installation was situated fifteen miles south of the city, in Tsarskoe Selo, a town where the tsar had lived with his family part of the year in the luxurious Alexander Palace.

The Petrograd Lev returned to bore little resemblance to the noble city of his youth—it was unrecognizable. Under siege from White forces led by General Yudenich, the city's Bolshevik defenders were forced to mobilize every available man, including seventy-year-old veterans. Plans were underway to close all factories so workers might be sent to the front. "Women will undergo military training," the *New York Times* reported, "and be formed into a medical corps, according to the same order."[14] Describing the city as a "hell" where "history's greatest tragedy was now being played," a recently escaped soldier recounted the situation in Petrograd in a cable to the paper on October 25, 1919—the second anniversary of the revolution:

For a long time most of the necessary victuals have been lacking, and if one did not possess at least 18,000 rubles a month it was impossible to get any but moldy bread and rotten herrings.

Many thousands are dying of famine and cold. The lack of coal and wood is now terrible. All wooden buildings are being torn down for fuel. Even the famous wooden pavement of Petrograd has been used and the streets are impossible for traffic. . . .

The nights are more than terrible. Every moment houses are searched by mariners or bands of factory girls, stealing everything eatable and dragging the inhabitants into the courts, accusing them of every crime.

All men have been forced into the Red Army, now a couple of hundred thousand in Petrograd alone. . . . Sickness of all kinds, especially cholera and typhoid fever, have had an immense number of victims, and it is now estimated that only a quarter of a million of civilians are alive in Petrograd. On account of the lack of wood there are no coffins, and corpses are heaped on big wagons and thrown into open graves.[15]

In a dispatch from London issued the day before, the *New York Times* reported that Trotsky's entire staff had been captured at Tsarskoe Selo, and that Trotsky himself had "escaped by clinging to a railway car and later fleeing from the scene in an automobile."[16] Pursued by White troops firing on his car, he managed to reach Petrograd safely.

Inside the radio facility, Lev obliged a tour to Alexander Chernishov, a professor he knew from university days. Chernishov hoped to pick Lev's brain and return to his colleagues at Petrograd Polytechnical Institute with a state-of-the-art knowledge of transmitters—a sign of the high respect Lev garnered from academics. On his way out, Chernishov mentioned that he worked with Ioffe now, who sent his regards and hoped that conditions would allow them all to collaborate in the future. Lev remembered that the words hit him like a thunderbolt: "This unexpected contact with my distant past brought up intense emotions in me. Until then, I considered that my past, which I held so deeply in my memory, had died in me forever. During this time, in my private life, there were many events which were very far from my university activity, far from my studies and my specific research desires. And suddenly it was back. Suddenly it became so real and very close."[17]

But at the moment, anti-Bolshevik forces led by General Yudenich were closing in on Tsarskoe Selo. Lev and others at the station were compelled to make quick decisions. "Yudenich was coming to capture the radio station," he remembered, "and announce through it to the whole world his victory over the Bolsheviks who 'illegally took power.' We immediately started preparation for transmitter evacuation to the East. For six days, with no sleep, we loaded everything on railway cars, and sent them toward the Ural Mountains. With the last train I left for Petrograd, and blew up all 120 meters of the radio mast."[18]

At Petrograd, Lev was put to work equipping an international-reception radio station under the transmitter tower of the Electrotechnical Institute. Simultaneously, he was pressed into service as an engineer-instructor for the radio department of Narkompochtel (the newly formed "People's Commissariat of Post and Telegraph"). "In addition to that," he despaired, "I read lectures to prepare radio specialists. It was a difficult time. It was difficult for food, and difficult to carry on technical work, especially the design of a radio station on a high technical level. Visiting specialists looked on everything with pessimistic eyes. It was not easy to work with them on the design of new machines needed for our country." Before long, he recalled, "on a day when my disappointment and hopelessness about overcoming philistine resistance were the strongest, I had a phone call. It was the voice of my beloved Abram Fedorovich [Ioffe]. He suggested I come to work under his leadership at the newly created Physico-Technical Institute, on the premises of the Polytechnical Institute."[19]

The next morning, Lev mounted his bicycle early for the long ride out to Sosnovka, at the outskirts of the city. Beyond the "Finland" stop on the tram—the last outpost of civilized travel—the institute was an additional five-mile hike, and students and workers routinely covered the distance on bikes until the fall muddy season claimed the road and the trek had to be made on foot. At number 2 Lesnoi Prospekt, Lev sprang up the steps of the "Polytechnic," two at a time, for his promised "negotiation." Ioffe was in his office. "He found me very grown up," Lev remembered,

> and was pleased to see I was still energetic and cheerful. He sat me on the couch and began to tell me about the newly organized Institute, and its technical and scientific challenges for the near future. He explained that we live at an important time for starting a new Soviet science to improve life.
>
> He suggested I take an active role in the work of the Physico-Technical Institute, and asked me to supervise a laboratory for high-frequency oscillations. It seemed I had again returned to that world I had felt the loss of for so long. I wanted to kiss him—but it wasn't acceptable—so we shook hands, and agreed that the next morning I would be given a room for my work.[20]

For Lev it was an innocent bargain. But under the banner of noble invention he had unwittingly been ushered to the inner sanctum of the Soviet machine, the nerve center of covert strategies and horrific mandates.

Ioffe knew that his own career, if he were to have one, would continue at the pleasure of the Bolshevik ideologues and their capricious schemes. He set about recruiting for the Physico-Technical Institute, attracting a host of the country's top scientists and engineers sympathetic to the revolution. A new Soviet science had to be raised up from the ashes if the fledgling Communist state were to become competitive in a world the Bolsheviks viewed as inherently hostile.

The institute, soon to be one of the largest research academies in Russia, was also a place of sanctuary. The revolution had sought an unprecedented leveling of the classes, and the Bolsheviks hoped to reconstitute the Russian people as a single class of manual laborers and peasants with no constitutional power or representation. The gentry, clergy, professionals, and the bourgeoisie ceased to be recognized as legitimate groups. Added to the confiscation of their private property, they received reduced food rations and were legally discriminated against. "Civilized" society as it had previously been known was disappearing. But among these newly persecuted intelligentsia, scientists could find a safe haven at the institute, as long as they were fulfilling a useful purpose in Lenin's plan.

Lev's first assignment was to observe the crystal structure of objects using X rays of various wavelengths. He supervised physics students and sometimes dabbled with hypnosis. Ioffe urged him to bring his findings on trance-induced subjects to the physiologist Ivan Pavlov, who invited Lev to perform joint experiments at the Military Medical Academy.

In a few months—by early 1920—space in the X-ray lab became tight as desks and tables began spilling over with circuits. Across the street, a former medical building recently occupied by the Roentgenology Institute of the Polytechnic's physics department (named for Wilhelm Roentgen, discoverer of X rays) had space available due to a shortage of students. Ioffe found Lev a large, unheated third-floor drafting hall with twenty desks, fourteen windows—patched together in spots with plywood—and two shielded X-ray chambers standing in the middle of the room. Lev was to clean up the space, arrange it to his liking, and assemble a research laboratory for radio oscillations under his direction.

Lev and his new assistants cobbled together two large brick stoves for heat, directing the smoke and soot out through openings in the windows with iron pipes. In the bone-chilling winter outside, Petrograd was withering under the ravages of famine and pestilence, but inside there was just enough warmth to take the nip off the drafts and put the mind to the revolutionary tasks at hand.

It was an irony that Lev's wartime broadcast work—which he so resented—had, in truth, prepared him for the path he would ultimately follow under Ioffe. Investigations of atomic and molecular structure would be put in abeyance, but perhaps his mentor sensed a more urgent need for utilitarian radio skills. It was a natural choice for him: the technology of radio itself had matured in tandem with his own childhood.

A mere nine years before Lev's birth, the very existence of electromagnetic waves, and their capacity to travel through the air, had been demonstrated for the first time by the German physicist Heinrich Hertz. In a simple lab experiment, Hertz had released a burst of energy by inducing a spark to jump across a gap between two electrically charged rods. The spark radiated electromagnetic waves into the atmosphere, which were received and registered as a second spark between two wires across the room. This was essentially the first transmitter and receiving antenna. For Hertz, the experiment also proved the existence of the "ether," the medium scientists had earlier postulated as filling all space, serving as a carrier of electromagnetic waves, since they could travel through a vacuum, without air. The term "ether waves" became associated henceforth with any form of radiated electrical energy.

In 1896, when Lev was born, the electrical beeps of telegraphic dots and dashes coursing through wires were the lone grammar of global communication. Three years later, those signals became airborne for the first time when the young Guglielmo Marconi sent a message across the English Channel in a landmark display of wireless telegraphy. Marconi's spark gap transmitter—a sophisticated version of Hertz's original experiment—produced weak, damped waves that were sufficient for Morse code signals but were incapable of transmitting voices or music through the atmosphere. A "continuous wave" transmitter generating high-frequency oscillations was needed to carry more sophisticated sounds.

By the time Lev was ten, shipboard operators off Brant Rock, Massachusetts, had picked up the first strains of speech and music riding the airwaves. Phonograph music, a Bible reading, singing, and violin playing—heard on Christmas Eve 1906, in what might be the first "broadcast"—were beamed out by Reginald Fessenden, a Canadian scientist testing his new alternator for General Electric. The device, essentially an ordinary electric generator stepped up to spin at twenty thousand revolutions per minute, made an effective high-frequency transmitter, but its technology left much to be desired. The centrifugal force of the mammoth rotating mechanism nearly tore apart the housing, and the horsepower required of its steam turbine engine was staggering. But "radiotelephony" was born, an infant science. By then, the term "radio" had superseded "wireless," suggesting the radiating of high-frequency signals.

The same year, the American inventor Lee De Forest was searching for a stronger detector of radio signals (on the receiving end) and came upon the pivotal invention in all of radio and electronics history: the three-element vacuum tube, or triode. De Forest began with the two-electrode detector tube commonly used to receive radio signals. Inside the glass bulb, in between the conventional electrodes, cathode and anode (each with its own power source), he added a third element—a platinum grid to which he applied the incoming antenna current. Now the weak incoming signal acted upon much larger currents flowing between the other two electrodes. The fluctuations in the signal, which carried the message pattern, became significantly amplified. The implications for radio were enormous. De Forest dubbed his new triode tube the "audion" (from *audio* and *ionize*). "I little realized that I held in my hand the long-sought Aladdin's lamp of our new world," he later wrote in his vainglorious autobiography, *Father of Radio,* "a lamp which when rubbed by gifted engineers would swiftly summon gigantic Genii to do our bidding, and all but remake our world."[21]

The lamp unquestionably had the power to remake the world, but not before it was rubbed by another "gifted engineer," Edwin Howard Armstrong. In 1912, as sixteen-year-old Lev was distributing Geissler tubes at the gymnasium, Armstrong, a Columbia University senior, summoned the genie from the audion at his home laboratory in Yonkers, New York. Armstrong, on a hunch, fed the current flowing from the output of the anode back to the input of the grid, to re-amplify it again—an action that then repeated itself many thousands of times a second, since electrons flow through a circuit at the speed of light. Feeding the signal back upon itself in this way greatly amplified the incoming message pattern. Now the audion was not simply a strong *detector* of signals, it could amplify them as well.

Armstrong pressed further with his feedback principle, observing that at maximum amplification, the tube itself oscillated and appeared to be generating high-frequency waves of its own. The discovery was earth-shattering: this small glass bulb was now a powerful transmitter of high-frequency radio waves, with a latent potential many times greater, and more efficient, than Fessenden's behemoth alternator.

The twin discoveries from Armstrong's "feedback" (or "regenerative") circuit—amplification and transmission—were the final bridge to large-scale commercial broadcasting. These principles also formed the bedrock for all modern electronics in everything from radar and television to early computers, and they remained central to later transistorized and integrated circuits that overturned vacuum tube technology.

Mass-production of radio receiving sets for the common household, however, did not become a reality until the early 1920s. The military demands of World War I intervened, and audion tube manufacturing soared to fill the needs of the U.S. Navy, as well as the waves of orders pouring in from foreign countries, including Russia.

In his work with the electrotechnical battalions, Lev had used De Forest's and Armstrong's cutting-edge technology. The huge transmitter towers at Tsarskoe Selo and the Electrotechnical Institute wouldn't have been possible without it. Now, early in 1920, in the big drawing hall of the Physico-Technical Institute, Lev pondered new roles for the little audion lamp. He could not have realized that this glass ovum stored the life material of nearly every future invention to spring from his mind, along with the vast empire of commercial radio and electronics yet to come.

Lev's first project for Ioffe used the human body as an electrical conductor—its ability to store up charges, or the property known as "capacitance." In an electrical circuit, the capacitance was regulated by a "capacitor"—known at that time as a "condenser"—made up of two conducting plates, separated by a nonconductor (a dielectric), which functioned to accumulate an electrical charge. Lev was intrigued by the notion that a person's natural body capacitance, when standing near an electrical circuit, could interfere with the capacity of the circuit, cause a change in its parameters, and set off a signaling device—a simple, invisible burglar alarm.

To build the apparatus, he used an oscillating audion as a radio transmitter to generate waves of a specific high frequency, directing them to an antenna. In this case the antenna functioned as what he called a "control conductor," radiating the waves (an electromagnetic field) only a short distance across the room—between thirteen and sixteen feet—not miles, as a radio transmitter would. He adjusted the circuits so the approach of a person within the radiating field of the antenna would affect the capacity of the circuit, alter its oscillating frequency, and cause a contact switch to close on an associated circuit, setting off an audible signal. He called it the "radio watchman."

Next, Ioffe asked him to devise an apparatus for measuring the density and dielectric constant of gases under varying conditions of pressure and temperature. Lev assembled a circuit and placed a gas between two plates of a capacitor. He found that a rise in temperature resulted in the expansion of the gas and a change in the circuit's capacity. The change was registered by fluctuations of a needle on a meter. The device was highly sensitive, interpreting the slightest motion of Lev's hand in the surrounding air as an increase in density, deflecting the needle.

To more accurately gauge the subtlety of the gas fluctuations, he adapted the system using an audion oscillator in a tuned circuit. This arrangement—employed in his radio watchman, and in radio transmitters in general—filtered out harmonics generated by the oscillator to capture a single frequency, which in this case he made audible through a pair of earphones. Lev added a condenser dial similar to those used by radios to tune in a given frequency. When he "tuned in" the density of a particular gas, the constant pitch of the oscillator's tone whistled in the earphones. The slightest drift in the properties of the gas altered the capacity of the circuit and changed the pitch of the whistling note.

Lev again noticed that movements of his hand near the circuitry were interpreted as fluctuations in density, this time registering as changes in pitch. As his hand moved closer to the capacitor, the whistle tone became higher; withdrawing the hand lowered the pitch. Shaking the hand in a gentle, tremulous motion created a subtle vibrato.

The dormant cellist was roused. There was some sort of music in this capacitometer, a new way of producing tones—maybe even an instrument. He summoned Ioffe and handed over the earphones. "That's an electronic Orpheus' lament!" Ioffe marveled.[22] Lev's imagination was seduced. This was electricity singing to him, pure and simple. No friction of physical soundmakers rubbing against each other. No mechanical energy. Just the free voice of electrons.

Lev began experimenting, stitching the air together with gentle back and forth motions of his hand, fishing for the notes of his favorite melodies. After a little practice he picked out approximations of Massenet's "Elegy" and the "Swan" of Saint-Saëns. Word quickly traveled among the students that "Theremin plays Gluck on a Voltmeter."[23] The following day, many flocked to the laboratory to see for themselves.

The principle was similar to that of the radio watchman. Again, natural body capacitance—this time from the hand, rather than the whole body—interfered with the electromagnetic field emanating from the device and induced a change in the capacity of the circuit, altering its oscillating frequency. In this case, the result was not the simple closing of a switch to sound an alarm, but the perception of the actual tuned circuit changing its frequency, made audible by the design itself. The phenomenon was related to the annoying "squeal" let off by early radio sets when the hand approached the tuning dial, momentarily altering the frequency of the oscillator. Ioffe encouraged Lev to refine the concept into a musical instrument.

To extend the range and offer more sensitive control for a player, Lev turned to the heterodyne principle, formulated by Reginald Fessenden in 1901. Heterodyning had just recently been explored for broadcasting technology in secret experiments by Edwin Armstrong in 1918, and it would not be ready for his RCA "superheterodyne" radio until 1923. This virgin concept was in Lev's hands just as the upstart American radio industry was mulling it over.

To "heterodyne" (from the Greek, *hetero* and *dyne,* or "different forces") meant to combine two frequencies to form a third, whose frequency resulted from the difference between the other two. The combination of a frequency of 3,000 cycles per second, it was known, with one of 2,000 per second, would acoustically coincide, or "beat together," producing an audible "beat frequency" of 1,000 cycles. Armstrong realized the importance of this as a means to detect the higher and higher frequencies radiated in broadcast transmission.

To tune in a frequency of 3,000,000 cycles on a 1918 receiver was straining the envelope. Armstrong reasoned, though, that by combining an incoming signal of that magnitude with a frequency of 2,900,000 generated by an oscillator inside the receiver itself, the two would be heterodyned and yield a more manageable 100,000-cycle frequency. This "intermediate" frequency could then be easily detected in the usual manner, "rectified," and converted to an acoustic signal that replicated the original speech or music broadcast. Armstrong had again found a simple and elegant idea that entered the lexicon of basic radio principles.

Independently, Lev devised his own application of Fessenden's concept. He began with two high-frequency oscillators that generated an identical note beyond the reach of human hearing (in the area of 300 kilohertz). One oscillator was fixed at its frequency, the other variable, meaning it could be made to slide out of sync with its partner. The variable oscillator circuit was connected to a vertical antenna that extended outside the housing, on the right-hand side of the box. This antenna radiated a weak electromagnetic field and served as one plate of the circuit's capacitor. The human hand, with its natural body capacitance, formed the complementary "plate." When the hand moved closer to the antenna (shortening the distance between the "plates"), the capacitance of the circuit increased, reducing the frequency of its oscillator to a pitch lower than that of the fixed oscillator. The two frequencies were then heterodyned by a detector (or mixer) circuit, resulting in a beat frequency (or "difference tone") that lay in the audible range. (The combination of 300,000 Hz in the fixed oscillator, for example, beating with 299,744 Hz in the variable oscillator, would yield a beat frequency of 256 Hz, or "middle" C, well within the limits of human hearing.) The closer the hand came to the antenna, the lower the variable oscillator would be pushed, creating a greater difference tone (of a higher frequency value), and thus a higher pitch. Moving the hand farther away from the antenna produced the opposite result, closing the frequency gap between the oscillators with a smaller difference tone, and a lower pitch. Withdrawing the hand completely to the shoulder brought the oscillators back to the unison, or "zero beat" state, with no heterodyning effect, and complete silence. To play a melody, Lev stopped his hand at various distances from the antenna, creating a series of beat frequencies.

It was a brilliant scheme: an electromagnetic field generated by high-frequency oscillators could detect extremely small capacitances in the human hand (less than one-trillionth of a farad) and made possible a very subtle control interface. The problem, Lev found, was to orient his right hand in free space. With no tactile point of reference, the basic gesture toward and away from the antenna made only a continuous rising and falling siren sound. To slice that sound into separate pitches required the stopping of the sound between notes.

At first, Lev fashioned a foot pedal to control volume and a control button operated by the left hand to cut off the sound during slides from note to note. But to provide a more balanced use of the upper body, and to create the illusion of a completely contact-free playing technique, he added new circuitry allowing the left hand to gesture in space as well. He designed a second antenna, in the shape of a loop, which sprouted from the left flank of the box in the horizontal plane. Setting it at a right angle to the vertical pitch antenna on the right allowed minimum interference between the two electromagnetic fields. The volume antenna circuit also resonated at a high frequency, but in a range well separated from the pitch oscillators, to avoid a conflict. A complementary oscillating circuit resonated at nearly the same frequency when the left hand was entirely removed from the antenna. In this state, maximum current flowed to the audio frequency amplifier tube, allowing maximum volume. As the left hand approached the antenna, the circuits were brought out of resonance relative to the distance of the hand, and the current flow to the amplifier was reduced by a corresponding degree, resulting in a reduction of volume. Loudspeakers were not yet available, so Lev concocted an enlarged earphone—the size of a plate—fitted with a paper horn, to project enough volume for demonstrations.

The new instrument boasted a range of three to four octaves—about the compass of the cello—and its tone suggested a likeness of that instrument in the lowest register. The higher octaves were an uncanny mimic of a violin, or a soprano intoning the syllable "oo." The instrument was monophonic (capable of producing only one note at a time).

Lev dubbed his invention the "etherphone," to "distinguish it from products of the contact or keyboard method." The reference also, of course, was to the "ether waves," an especially trendy notion in the delirious new era of broadcasting—one the layperson appropriated to explain, and sometimes mythologize, the magic of radio. In reality, the ether was a hotly contested issue among scientists by the 1920s. Many had long written it off as the vestige of nineteenth-century attempts to fathom electrical fields. Early twentieth-century physicists generally agreed that electromagnetic waves need no transporting medium other than the omnipresence of the electric force occupying all space. Still, the idea managed to linger in the public imagination.

Lev unveiled the etherphone to Professor Ioffe in October 1920. After a period of practice, he managed his first public "concert" the following month, performing and lecturing before students in the Mechanical Engineers' Group at the institute. It was easy to draw on his old cello repertoire. The program featured "Fiametta," from a ballet by Minkus, the Saint-Saëns "Swan," and Massenet's "Elegy." The sight of Lev, standing at attention, his arms outstretched, his two hands hovering, fluttering, and diving in air around two antennas, willing melodies into being, was spellbinding, even to the young physicists who took scientific wonders for granted. Ioffe addressed the gathering afterward, forecasting a big future for Lev, advising him to secure patents on the etherphone and radio watchman and to explore their possible use in foreign countries. Interestingly, the same month, another application of radio technology made its debut: station KDKA in Pittsburgh launched commercial radio broadcasting in the United States.

Periodically, Lev was drawn back to astronomy. At the famous Pulkovo Observatory he took part in research, and he was inducted as a charter member of the All-Union Association of Astronomy (VAGO) in 1920. Lev delivered a paper at the meeting on the "problems of radio physics and photometrical qualities of the planets' atmospheres." His growing professional status was apparent when he was appointed to the Commission for Connections with Foreign Scientists, after the ceremony.

Nineteen twenty-one was a banner year. In June, Lev filed for a Russian patent on the etherphone. In the fall, at the invitation of Professor Chernishov, he made his public debut with the instrument at the Eighth All-Union Electro-Technical Congress in Moscow. It was no small honor to be showcased at this national conference on the GOELRO Plan (GOELRO was the State Commission for the Electrification of Russia). The congress was a sort of Bolshevik exposition and symposium aimed at bringing the country up to speed on energy. It was a forum for new applications of electricity, and Lev proudly piped the voice of his instrument through the new technology of the loudspeaker, just then available in Russia. Gleb Anfilov described the October 5 demonstration at Moscow's Polytechnic Museum:

> The inventor came nervously onto the stage. In the auditorium he saw the famous scientists Krzhizhanovsky, Bonch-Bruevich and Chatelin, and a crowd of noisy, impatient and curious youths. He gave a brief description of his instrument and apologized that he would have to play unaccompanied. The grand which stood on stage was completely out of tune. Then a strange music, unlike anything yet heard, floated over the quiet audience. The vibrating electrical tone, now swelling and now falling, was singing familiar airs which sounded new and unusual. There were Russian folk songs, a selection from Tchaikovsky's *The Queen of Spades*, and "The Swan" from Saint-Saens's *Le carnaval des animaux*. When he had finished his modest repertoire, the physicist was given the kind of applause that is usually reserved for famous artists.[24]

Several days later Lev staged a repeat performance for the general public in the same auditorium. He was starting to feel his oats as a performer. The historical value of the invention and the novelty of his act did not escape him, and he saw a philosophical posture emerging that he could use to his advantage. When the State Institute of Musical Science convened on November 11, he mounted the speaker's podium to make a case for the instrument. Prior to high-frequency oscillators, he explained, early experiments with electrical music were restricted to audio frequency vibrators: "singing voltaic arcs, rotary dischargers, buzzers and alternating-current audiotone oscillators." These were unsatisfactory, "because controlling the sound has been difficult and the resulting sounds have been unsuitable for music." Radio frequency oscillators were the answer, he insisted, and he added, a bit boldly, that an instrument allowing "free movement of the hands in space . . . would have an advantage over traditional instruments."[25]

At the GOELRO demonstration, Lev had run into Akim Maximovich Nikolayev, an old colleague from Tsarskoe Selo who was now chairman of the Radiotechnical Council and Bolshevik commissar for radio. Several months later, Lev recognized his voice on the phone: "Vladimir Ilyich asked me to find you and see if you would demonstrate your radio musical device." It was a summons from the "Great Man"—*the* Vladimir Ilyich Lenin, father of the revolution. "Do you think it would interest him?" Lev pressed. Nikolayev reassured him. "Vladimir Ilyich places great value on radio engineering, and your device opens new, unpredictable possibilities."[26]

On an early spring morning in March 1922, Lev took off to rendezvous with Nikolayev in Moscow. They would meet at the Military Radiotechnical Lab— Lev's old Red Army post—where he had been commuting recently for odd assignments. The last leg from Kalanchovka Street to the lab was just under an hour by hansom cab, and that morning the old, half-dead horse clopped out to Molchanovka, urged on by the cabman. Nikolayev was waiting with a dilapidated Austin. Lev and his lab assistant, Grisha Fine, packed the etherphone, the radio watchman, and some batteries in the trunk. Even the commissar could not flaunt the comforts of government privilege. No bourgeois limousine for him. Just solid proletarian transportation. The car rattled into the city on a rough road, cackling like a machine gun, coughing, and trailing a stream of blue exhaust.

"At a specified time—10 o'clock in the morning—I arrived at the Kremlin with my assistant," Lev recalled.[27] The car pulled up to the gate and Nikolayev passed his documents to a guard. The trio carried their equipment through five or six cold rooms. "Vladimir Ilyich was at a meeting, and Nikolayev took us to a big office with a long table where we put down our large devices."[28] The radio watchman was set up at one end of the table and Lev connected it to a large metal vase rigged to emit an electromagnetic field. He placed the etherphone at the other end of the table. A piano stood in the corner.

"I forgot to warn you," he remembered suddenly, "I need a piano for the demonstration." Nikolayev was surprised. "Oh, I didn't think about that. You didn't have any accompaniment at the meeting."[29]

The commissar disappeared down the hall and came back with a young woman who extended her hand: "Fotieva. Vladimir Ilyich told me to accompany you. He's at a meeting and asked your forgiveness for his lateness. I will try to work with you, but I haven't played in a long time."[30] Lydia Alexandrovna Fotieva was Lenin's personal secretary—a graduate of St. Petersburg Conservatory who had abandoned a performing career in the climate of postrevolutionary Russia.

There was still a fluency in her fingers. After a few tries she easily read through the accompaniments to Lev's repertoire. The two rehearsed briefly and traded compliments. She told him about her background: "I studied at the Conservatory for some time. It was long ago, before the Revolution." "I was there too," Lev confided. Fotieva laughed. "So this is what we musicians do now!"[31]

"Everything was ready for the demonstration," Lev remembered.[32] "We spent nearly two hours preparing and testing everything. I was very worried. I was afraid the big boss would come and be displeased because we had arrived too early. Suddenly I was told, 'he's coming!' "[33] Then, "the door opened and Lenin entered the office along with a group of comrades. He greeted us, apologized for the unavoidable delay, and began to look at the equipment with great interest."[34] Lev's apprehension melted. "I had been afraid for no reason. He was a very nice, pleasant person—not very tall, and he treated me like a son."[35] There were about fifteen or twenty people gathered in the office. Among the faces, Lev recognized Mikhail Kalinin, future chief of the Soviet state.

Lenin shook hands with Lev and Grisha and sat down to watch the demonstration. When the group was seated and quiet, he turned to Lev. "What kind of magic have you prepared for us?"[36] Lev walked to the radio watchman at the end of the table and demonstrated how the alarm would sound when someone approached the "keep away" zone. "And here a funny incident occurred," Lenin later wrote in a letter. "One of the comrades didn't believe the inventor's warning. He put a scarf and a fur hat on his arm and started to tiptoe toward the charged vase, and it began to ring. Everyone was laughing hilariously."[37] It was just the sort of trap Lenin delighted in.

Lev signaled Fotieva to take her place at the piano. Then he raised his hands and began his now seasoned repertoire: a Scriabin etude and the Saint-Saëns "Swan." "As I played I watched the expression on Lenin's face. It changed with the character of the music."[38] Lenin's musical preferences were well known. He especially loved Tchaikovsky, Wagner, Chopin, and Schubert; Beethoven's "Appassionata" sonata was a particular favorite. Lev concluded with Glinka's "Skylark." "Vladimir Ilyich got up from the armchair quickly," Lev recalled. "He wanted to try it himself."[39] But "at first, I was afraid he wouldn't be able to extract clean notes."[40] When "he came up to the instrument . . . I stood behind him, taking his hands in mine so I could move them. Then with our four hands we started to play 'Skylark.' Fotieva accompanied, and I moved his hands. Soon I sensed Vladimir Ilyich could feel the music very well himself, and I slowly withdrew my hands. Vladimir Ilyich finished the second half of 'Skylark' practically by himself. Everyone applauded, and I thanked him very much. I was surprised that his musical ear was keen enough to grasp the technique of the instrument so quickly."[41]

When the room cleared out, Lev remained behind with Lenin: "Then we spoke alone. I told him about where I was working, my current projects, and my ideas. We talked at length about astronomy, microspace, and I explained my theories of human cells, and the brain. Vladimir Ilyich was very interested in all this. . . . He was very attentive and asked many questions. I was surprised how, without being a physicist, he grasped the essence of problems, and showed such an interest in them."[42] Lev was face to face with a man who also understood electricity and often bellowed his own pet aphorism: "Socialism equals Soviet Power plus Electrification!"

"Lenin spoke simply," Lev recalled, "almost all the time looking straight in the eyes of the interlocutor, with a barely noticeable smile. The hour and a half or two hours I happily spent with Vladimir Ilyich . . . revealed his great charm, his warmth, his benevolence."[43] Then Lenin "asked me about the needs of the laboratory, and suggested I ask for help without any shyness."[44]

The etherphone struck Lenin as an ideal propaganda tool for electricity. As they left, he told Lev he was pleased it was of Russian origin. "We must advertise this invention in every possible way," he urged.[45] "We have to show it to the whole country." "When we said goodbye," Lev recalled, "I wanted to kiss him for the strong and happy impression he made on me."[46]

Within weeks of the Kremlin audience, *Pravda* published Lenin's preface to E. Skvortsov-Stepanov's *Electrification of the Russian Socialist Federated Soviet Republic in Connection With the Transition Phase of World Economy*, a propaganda book touting Lenin's electrification plan. Lenin advocated "popular public readings" about electricity and technology and suggested Lev's inventions be included. On April 4, 1922, Lenin wrote to Trotsky asking if they should consider "whether the number of guard duties undertaken by the Kremlin cadets cannot be reduced by means of the introduction of electric signalling in the Kremlin. (One engineer, Termen, demonstrated his experiments to us in the Kremlin: the kind of signalling by which an alarm is set off simply by someone approaching the wire—before it is touched.)"[47]

Lev was welcomed back to the Physico-Technical Institute as a hero. "The fact that I was holding *both* Lenin's hands in mine," he beamed, "Ioffe thought that was an astounding thing, and none of us could ever have done that." Ioffe was especially impressed that Lev had permission to apply directly to Lenin if he needed help. Lev remembered how a rush of revolutionary fever came over Ioffe: "He said we must not let Lenin down, we must support his hopes for the possibilities of making wide propaganda among the people for the idea of electrification."[48]

Lev's triumph underscored Ioffe's confidence in him. His penchant for the daring, for thinking the unthinkable, went hand in hand with Ioffe's mandate to the whole institute: to invent new technologies, not modernize old ones. Lev personified that quest and even took it a step further, always attempting to wed fantasy and reality. But many of his colleagues considered him a dreamer— "light minded," they would say. Perhaps they felt he was fiddling with a musical instrument while Petrograd burned; playing Saint-Saëns while the country hungered for hard solutions from physics. Others might simply have been jealous of his European stage flair, or his burgeoning fame in a society where proletarian anonymity was the status quo.

There were occasional moments when he seemed to step over the line and prove them right. When a young student at the institute, one of Lev's former X-ray lab assistants, died of pneumonia, Lev refused to mourn.

> At that time I was studying how cells taken from the glacier could be restored to life. I was convinced that something of that nature was possible, and if so, I must try to save my assistant's life. I wanted to cool her body slowly, and for some time, not more than a year, bury her in the eternal frost. I believed I could do the job and return her to life. I explained this to Ioffe, and asked him to speak to her parents—he knew them very well. Ioffe was quite embarrassed. "You're probably right, perhaps it's possible," he said, "but such a suggestion could offend the girl's parents in their grief." He refused to speak with them about it. It was very unfortunate, because the girl was only 20 years old, and I was confident of my theory. But I didn't want to argue with Ioffe. I realized the time was not yet right for this work.[49]

In May 1922, Lenin suffered a stroke, and Lev would not see him or have contact with him again. But an important legacy of the Kremlin meeting had arrived in the mail several days afterward: a free pass for all railroads in the country. Lenin had been serious about "advertising" the etherphone everywhere. He had directed the secretary of the All-Union Central Executive

Committee, A. C. Yenukidze, to issue Lev a "Mandat," a train pass guaranteeing safe and unrestricted movement through all Soviet territories. The pass was a blatant directive: Lev was to embark on an agitprop tour. "Agitation and propaganda" often took the form of miniature road shows bringing musicians, actors, and other pariahs to the hinterlands to indoctrinate the unwashed. Since their class had never dirtied its hands, at least its eloquence could be put under the yoke to sing the Party's message. Lenin did not mean to promote electronic music per se, but to flaunt one achievement of "Soviet power"—to captivate the masses and galvanize popular sentiment for bending backs a little harder, in the name of modernization—in the name of a fortified Communist empire.

As a kickoff for his tour, Lev organized an ambitious program presented at the Grand Hall of the Petrograd Philharmonic Society on December 19, 1922. A poster promised feats to confound the skeptical:

ONE EVENING

L. S. THEREMIN

RADIO MUSIC

NEWLY INVENTED MUSICAL INSTRUMENTS

MAIN ACHIEVEMENTS: Sound operation with free spatial hand movements. . . . Wire and radio sound transmitting in any direction at any speed, without tone and timbre distortion. . . . Projection of different timbre curves on the screen. . . . Combination of light and sound. Possibilities for combining music with dance.

L. S. TERMEN DEMONSTRATES HIS DEVICE IN ACTION

It was a sound and light show auguring the multimedia events of future decades. Lev beguiled the crowd with his stock tricks, making the most of the "invisible" touch of the etherphone. There were the customary solo pieces with piano, songs performed by his aunt, Elena Emilievna Termen, and a lecture demonstration. He brought out a new electric fingerboard instrument—a stringless, bowless cello, a variation of his basic design—and his new "illumovox," a rotating color-wheel apparatus that, when connected to the etherphone, projected evolving hues of the spectrum in direct correspondence to pitch changes on the instrument. Then he coaxed the audience into his sphere of fantasy, asking them to imagine dancers moving their bodies in an electromagnetic field to materialize a new sort of spontaneous music. Among the dignitaries in the audience that night were Alexander Glazunov and the young Dmitri Shostakovich.

Within a month, Lev took to the road. In Moscow, posters advertised the performances, and sizable, curious throngs began collecting at demonstrations there in colleges, factories, recreational centers, and government offices. Lev drew huge crowds for recitals in the Timiryazev Academy and the Peter Arcades. His rail pass brought him to outlying cities: Minsk, Yaroslavl, Nizhny Novgorod, Pskov, and many others. The press began to notice, declaring that "Termen's invention is a musical tractor coming to replace the wooden plough," "Termen's invention has done almost what the automobile has done for transportation," and "The problem of producing the ideal instrument is solved."[50] Soon the man and his invention fused, and the papers began referring to the etherphone as "Termen's voice"—or the "Termenvox."

Lev donated proceeds from the concerts to the famine relief fund, set up to aid the nearly twenty-five million people starving in Russia—many clinging to life by scavenging among carrion and dead bodies. The help was especially needed to compensate for the government's deliberate dismantling of relief efforts by the bourgeoisie.

In 1923 Lev had staged enough propaganda concerts to inspire a follower, and a clone of the Termenvox that raised its status to that of a generic instrument. Konstantin Kovalsky, six years older than Lev, was a conservatory graduate who had injured his hand and found the contact-free Termenvox an ideal vehicle for rechanneling his musicianship. Kovalsky built and played a variant design of the ether instrument with a right-hand pitch antenna, similar to Lev's, but with a foot pedal to regulate volume. The left hand operated an assortment of buttons that controlled the attack and release of notes, making possible staccato effects, cleanly executed trills, and other subtle articulations that were either impossible or more taxing to produce on Lev's model. Kovalsky joined Lev in performance from time to time, and eventually he devoted his life to the instrument in more than three thousand solo and ensemble performances around Russia during a fifty-year period.

Between agitprop tours, Lev returned to work at the Physico-Technical Institute. In 1923 he arranged a job there for his closest friend, Alexander Pavlovich Constantinov. It would be a fateful reunion. The two had met as young recruits in the Reserve Electrotechnical Battalion in 1916 and later served side-by-side at the Tsarskoe Selo transmitter. When the station was detonated, Alexander transferred to the Baltic fleet ship *New Holland* for a tour of duty during the civil war, and in 1921 he made his way to the Pulkovo Observatory. The friends shared a passion for radio engineering and astronomy. Each had survived the monstrous devastation after the revolution, but their lives had become a study in contrasts. Lev's parents had lived well through the revolution and afterward were permitted to remain in their apartment on Nicolayevska Street—now called Marat Street. Alexander's family, like so many others, had been shattered by the Bolsheviks.

Before the revolution, Alexander's father was a successful building contractor, once awarded the title of "Hereditary Honorable Citizen" in St. Petersburg. Between 1915 and 1916 he built his family a house, but before they could move in, property started to be nationalized and former owners were often arrested. In 1918, he disappeared in Petrograd without a trace. Alexander, the oldest son, bore the responsibility of looking after his mother and eight younger brothers and sisters—four still under the age of ten. His mother moved to a village with the younger children, as people of "noble" birth were often forced to do in order to hide their identity and find food, sometimes even working for a peasant. But Alexander, his two oldest brothers, and his oldest sister, Ekaterina, remained in a big apartment in Petrograd where they endlessly battled cold and hunger.

Among the stream of young people who frequented the apartment, Lev was a constant presence. He was an uncle figure to Alexander's siblings, who adored and admired him for his small kindnesses. He often brought them food or helped them with their homework, and together with Alexander, he inspired several to take up careers in science. "Bobka"—little Boris—one of the youngest, later became director of the Physico-Technical Institute and vice president of the USSR Academy of Science.

Ekaterina—seven years Lev's junior—leaned toward the medical sciences. She was a "modest, melancholic woman—serious and plain," as her niece later described her, and "not very brave," but at the same time, "kind, naive, full of light," and sometimes given to enthusiasm.[51] Lev knew her as "Katia." She was petite—five feet four inches tall—with fair hair and brown eyes. Her admiration for Lev turned to devotion, and she soon fell in love.

In January 1924, Vladimir Ilyich Lenin finally succumbed to the toll taken by three strokes. Despite the efforts of twenty-six handsomely paid physicians summoned to his bedside from many countries, he died on the twenty-first from complications brought on by acute arteriosclerosis. Instantly, the deification of Lenin began. Leninism was elevated to a sweeping, totalitarian religion instituted in force by the state. Busts and statues were commissioned. The Politburo approved the renaming of Petrograd as "Leningrad." His name was given to streets, factories, palaces, and ships. New books canonized him as the immortal author of the revolution—the eternal secular god, the rock on which the Soviet state would forever rest. His spirit was enshrined in the socialist pantheon next to Marx and Engels.

Lev was "deeply struck with grief."

The most important person for me—Lenin—had died, and as soon as I heard about it I made a decision. He must be buried in the eternal frost, and then I could revive him. I said nothing to Ioffe about this anymore. I had a reliable assistant whom I sent to Gorky to find out how it could be done, and how to make it official. But he returned soon and told me it was too late for us to do anything. Lenin's brain and heart had already been removed. They had been put in a jar with alcohol poured all over them. The brain had been killed.[52]

Lev's desire to resurrect Lenin was actually right in step with the government's ideas, but the state was happy enough to settle for preserving the physical remains and allow the spirit to be incarnated in his followers to tyrannize the next generation. Elaborate procedures were carried out to embalm the body and install the mummy in a permanent mausoleum so an eternity of visitors could pass the catafalque and pay their respects. War veterans and the general populace would later languish at the edge of starvation while millions of rubles were lavished on preserving the body. In 1925, the Politburo even established a special laboratory to dissect and study Lenin's brain, hoping to find evidence of its superhuman constitution. Lev was disgusted. "I thought science had reached a level where we could determine the defects in human organs. For example, if the heart doesn't work, and you have to exchange it for another, you shouldn't have to take it from another person, but with the help of an engineer, you could construct one, like a part for a machine."[53]

But the pickling of Lenin's body was an insidious propaganda maneuver of the new regime. Josef Stalin had begun to man the controls of the Soviet vessel and, riding the crest of Lenin's posthumous consecration, he set himself up as chief interpreter of Vladimir Ilyich's ideas. By erecting a shrine to the perpetuity of Lenin, Stalin cleverly entrenched himself in the government hierarchy as the only "legitimate" heir to the country's highest office.

Lev was disheartened. "I no longer pinned my hopes on Ioffe's Institute. I dreamed of creating a laboratory, or a department, which would study these problems. Then, maybe in a few years we would be able to revive cells and build organisms. I wanted to make it the aim of our work."[54]

In the wake of Lenin's death, Lev returned to his concertizing on the Termenvox, hoping the new occupants of the Kremlin would still find a socialist agenda in it. On May 2, 1924, he appeared as soloist with the Leningrad Philharmonic conducted by V. Dranischnikov, in the premiere of the first original work written for the instrument, *A Symphonic Mystery* for Termenvox and orchestra, composed the previous year by Andrey Filippovich Pashchenko. With the evolution of the loudspeaker, Lev was able to unleash limitless dynamic range. Now the electronic howl could grow to stentorian levels and loom over a whole orchestra. Lev had also refined the instrument with the addition of twelve timbre-control "stops" to allow various changes in tone color.

One day, Katia Pavlovna Constantinova was returning some gardening equipment for her brother Alexander. "The bell rang in my apartment," Lev recalled, "and at the door there was a beautiful girl holding all those tools in her hands, whom I liked very much, and I decided I would be with her forever."[55] On May 24, 1924, at the age of twenty, Katia married Lev, within days of her brother Alexander's wedding. She and Lev moved into the Marat Street apartment with his parents. In the fall she resumed the five-year college program at the Medical Institute she had begun the year before.

In September, Lev was granted Russian patent number 780 for his Termenvox ("Musical Instrument with Cathode Tubes"). How the patent would serve him, he wasn't sure yet, but in the meantime his radio watchman had been dispatched to stand guard at major government strongboxes. Just as Lenin might have envisioned it, the impregnable ghost was now custodian of the GOHRAN (the state storehouse for expropriated church valuables from around the country). The GOHRAN held thousands of pounds of gold, silver, diamonds, gemstones, and sundry precious objects literally ransacked from houses of worship during Lenin's 1922 crusade to crush the church. Thousands of clergy were arrested and executed during the campaign, and large quantities of confiscated valuables were shipped to foreign Communist parties to bankroll propaganda and revolution abroad. The installation of Lev's system at the GOHRAN carried a chilling symbolism: in 1918 Lenin had warned, "electricity will take the place of God. Let the peasant pray to electricity; he's going to feel the power of the central authorities more than that of heaven."[56]

The radio watchman also stood sentinel at the Gosbank (the State Bank) and in the Scythian hall of gold at Leningrad's Hermitage. The Scythians were an ancient band of equestrian marauders who dominated a vast stretch of the European steppe (from the Danube, east through the Ukraine to the Caucasus Mountains). They were fierce nomads who fashioned drinking cups from their victims' skulls, and who grew so rich from their plunder they commissioned intricate gold ornaments from Greek craftsmen to deck their clothing, armor, and even their horses. Scythian tombs—huge mounds of earth called kurgans, some rising as high as sixty-five feet—yielded archaeologists abundant caches of the gold, much of it transferred to the Petrograd Hermitage. In the old hall, a patriarchal guard was steward of the Scythian treasure. Bearded and barrel-chested, his uniform emblazoned with gold, he was a lordly specter of the imperial age. No radio wires, he was convinced, could rival his seasoned vigilance. Only when he leaned through the window of the second-floor wing, hanging over Millionaya Street, did Lev's alarm ring in the new era for him.

The task of setting these electronic traps took Lev away from his research, but Ioffe cautioned him that security jobs were a priority. "Abram Fedorovich placed a great deal of significance on this work," Lev recalled, "because we had to show the fruits of technical achievement, and the ability of our Institute to produce something real. . . . He supported me and told me to cheer up when I was pulled away from the pure scientific research I liked so much."[57]

Ioffe could sense Lev's burnout over his work at the institute and began brainstorming for a new challenge to rekindle his imagination. "During one of our conversations," Lev recalled, "he mentioned that there was a very interesting problem, but we were probably not ready to solve it yet. This was long distance vision—the possibility of seeing at a great distance, not transmitting stationary pictures, but subjects and people in motion as though you were seeing them with your own eyes."[58]

Ioffe called the embryonic science of television "distance vision," after the phrase "distant electric vision," a term for television coined by A. A. Campbell Swinton in a 1908 article for *Nature* magazine. The idea reignited Lev. "These words were like a shot in the bullseye for me. I had long dreamed of devoting my time to solving this problem, but I was afraid to speak about it at the Institute because I was already occupied with electromusic, signalization, and measuring devices. I probably blushed, and Abram Fedorovich noticed it."[59]

Ioffe took the cue. Lev, who loved to face off with the impossible, was the man for the job. He would enroll at Ioffe's newly organized School of Physics and Engineering at the Leningrad Polytechnical Institute and tackle the question as a graduate thesis. The field was still wide open. No working television systems had been developed anywhere in the world yet, even though the integral concepts for transmission of visual images had been bandied about for some time. Lev jumped at the idea.

In reality, he had a head start. In 1921, on his own, he had researched over fifty articles and patents concerned with television, some going back as early as 1825. At the time, he shared his findings with a seminar at the institute and with the Russian Society of Radio Engineers. He found that the very term "television" had been coined in 1900 by Constantin Perskyi in the International Electricity Congress at the Paris Exhibition. The earliest practicable invention anticipating television, he discovered, was an 1884 patent by the German inventor Paul Nipkow.

The Nipkow disk was a large circular plate with twenty-four small holes arranged in a partial spiral near the outside edge. As the disk spun, these apertures scanned the light image of an illuminated object, directing the pattern onto a selenium cell that converted the information into a series of electrical impulses. At the receiving end, the impulses caused analogous light patterns to beam through a second disk that spun in synchronization with the first, resulting in a reassembling of the original image. This image was then projected on a screen or viewed through an eyepiece. Nipkow's concept was carried out by others and became the basis for mechanical television systems for the next fifty years—"mechanical," because of the unwieldy spinning disks.

Lev learned that one branch of research originated in his own city. In 1907, Boris Rosing, a lecturer at the St. Petersburg Technological Institute, filed for a patent that held the seminal clue for future television. In 1911, with the help of his student Vladimir Zworykin, Rosing successfully demonstrated a crude system based on the patent. A mechanical scanner was used to transmit the image, but the receiver consisted of a cold cathode ray tube—a sophisticated form of the Geissler tube Lev had used in 1912 at the gymnasium. Based on the same principle, air was evacuated from a glass tube, and two electrodes (anode and cathode) were inserted. When a high-voltage current was applied, some of the electrical "rays" moving inside the glass between the cathode and anode sprayed past the anode and hit the far inside surface of the tube, causing a fluorescent glow. By focusing these "cathode rays" (later discovered to be electrons) into a beam and controlling the deflection of the beam in both vertical and horizontal axes, received electrical impulses representing a scanned picture could be painted in flashing sets of lines continuously streamed on the interior wall of the tube. Chemical phosphors were added to the wall (the screen), which would prolong the fluorescent glow for several seconds after the electron beams had struck. This resulted in a perceived recreation of the original transmitted picture. Because this method attempted to do away with the precarious spinning disks (especially at the receiving end), it was considered "electronic" rather than "mechanical."

On May 9, 1911, Rosing and Zworykin successfully demonstrated the principle at the St. Petersburg Technological Institute, displaying a screen image of four luminous bands. While this was hardly a finished, functional system, it was considered important enough to win Rosing a gold medal from the Russian Technological Society. Vladimir Zworykin emigrated to the United States in 1919 and later pioneered the development of electronic television for the Radio Corporation of America.

When Lev presented his survey in 1921, little progress had been made since Rosing's demonstration, mostly due to the intervention of World War I. By 1924, research in the field was heating up again, but Lev was still at the starting gate with his foreign competitors, and the prize remained up for grabs. In November, under Ioffe's eye, he began testing his hypotheses in the lab.

Ioffe had spent significant periods away on "business trips" over the past few years, particularly in Berlin. In his letters from Germany, he routinely solicited requests for spare parts, equipment, or books from his institute workers. "I ask everyone who is working now to write me about what you need, what you are lacking," he wrote in one letter, "especially if it relates to Termen . . .

or Chernishov."[60] At first glance, these trips seemed innocent enough—an institute director shopping for raw materials and cementing relationships with foreign scientists. But as Lev would soon realize, Ioffe was trafficking in far more than trade journals and handfuls of audion tubes. And his well-worn path to Berlin was no coincidence.

The founders of the Soviet state, Trotsky in particular, envisioned a coming world socialist revolution—one that would set in motion the overthrow of the capitalist-imperialist presence worldwide. When Lenin and Trotsky occupied the tsar's former headquarters at the Kremlin in 1918, the musical clock tower that once chimed "God Save the Tsar" was reconstructed to peal the "Internationale," the Communist hymn of the revolution:

> *The earth shall rise on new foundations,*
> *We have been naught, we shall be all.*
>
> *'Tis the final conflict,*
> *Let each stand in his place,*
> *The International Soviet*
> *Shall be the human race!*

The "International Soviet" was not some idealist Nirvana. It was to be a pragmatic consummation of the revolution, put into place by the Communist International—the "Comintern." The Comintern called for an underground, illegal communist organization in every country and the unquestioned allegiance of each communist party to the Soviet Union. By kindling socialist brushfires throughout the world—civil wars and internal uprisings of the working masses—a brotherhood of the proletariat would eventually link arms around the globe. "Workers of the World, Unite!" was Trotsky's manifesto. "You have nothing to lose but your chains!"

Germany was a perfect test case. When the smoke cleared after the First World War, this defeated nation, with its shaky government and political rebellions and assassinations, was fertile ground for recruiting sympathizers to the German Communist Party. A new, fortified Soviet Germany could be Russia's first ally in the crusade. And the partnership would be politically expedient, given the strength of France in the postwar chemistry, and that country's potential as a future military power. Paris, in fact, was known to harbor the largest community of expatriate Russians hostile to the Kremlin. No sooner had Moscow reestablished diplomatic relations with Berlin in 1920 than it began furiously fanning the flames of revolution for a German Communist coup. Confidence ran high. Posters around Moscow promised, "The German October is at the gates."

Seeding a revolution from within involved elaborate intelligence opera-

tions. Beginning in the early '20s, Soviet espionage burgeoned. Two government organs controlled spying activities: the notorious Cheka—recast by 1924
as the United State Political Administration (the OGPU)—and the Fourth
Department of the Red Army (the GRU), founded by Trotsky. The main nerve
centers for intelligence were the official diplomatic legations in foreign cities.

The Russian embassy in Berlin was not what it seemed. Behind the facade
of ambassadorial protocol lay a diabolical nest of spies and provocateurs. High
"officials" coordinated clandestine tasks: the "military attaché" could be a GRU
representative; one of the "counselors" might be a member of the OGPU.
Agents and high-ranking Central Committee members masqueraded as door-
men, secretaries, or simple office personnel. Tangled in this network, rank-
and-file operatives recruited from the local populace worked through go-
betweens. Usually they were privy only to their small link in a much larger
chain. Moving unnoticed through the streets were "residents"—agents dispatched to live in the city to coordinate underground Comintern activities.

Beyond the agenda of a Communist transfusion in Germany, there was a
second covert strategy at work. Although the German armed forces were in
eclipse, and there were few secrets to be uncovered there, the country's future strength was in its industry, which offered a treasure chest of military
technology for the Soviets. In 1921, the GRU arrived in Berlin to set up a trade
mission. Together with the embassy, it was the second jab of a one-two punch
leveled at German vulnerability.

The Wostwag (Eastern Trading Company) was a commercial front—on the
surface it was established to export Soviet products to Germany, though few
such products existed. In reality it offered a "legitimate" cover for sweeping
industrial espionage. Besides camouflaging agents of the Comintern, the
OGPU, and the GRU, it offered access to manufacturing plants all over Germany. The chemical, steel, iron, aviation, and electrical industries were especially targeted. One method of building "trust" was to register Soviet inventions under German patents to cast the impression that these items might be
sold or manufactured there. Access to patent offices also provided an inex-
haustible reservoir of trade secrets to sluice. But agents of the apparat could
go only so far in assessing technical matters, and Soviet engineers and specialists needed to be imported to leech the significant flow of information.

Ioffe was recruited early on. He began moving between Moscow and
Berlin in 1921 and, at first, let slip only hints to his workers. "Ioffe told me of
his great wish," Lev remembered, "that right in our country we could find new
scientific and technical means, and use them to reach and exceed the level of
life in the capitalist countries. He felt that the close contact of our scientists
and our organization with foreign countries and colleges was very important

so our foreign colleagues would know that our possibilities were as great as theirs, and for their own success they would need contacts with us."[61]

In 1924, when Abram Fedorovich was on his way to Germany, Lev recalled, "he asked me for explanatory circuit diagrams, photos, and copies of patents in case it was necessary to make agreements with foreign companies."[62] On his trip, Ioffe wrote back that he had signed a contract, in the name of the institute, with M. J. Goldberg and Sons, a business that supplied medical equipment to the Soviet Union. The agreement covered the patent and commercial manufacture of the radio watchman and the Termenvox. When Ioffe returned, he was a bit more forthright. Lev recalled: "He told me in great detail about life in Germany, and about its relationship with the Soviet Union, and the future prospects for commerce. He also warned me that I must be prepared to go on a business trip to Germany to help prepare the patents, bring back much needed modern radio components for the Institute, and make a personal introduction to the owners and employees of the Goldberg company."[63] By December 8, 1924, Lev had two German Empire patent applications pending. It was his first professional step into the Western world. He couldn't have imagined where it would lead him.

As 1925 dawned, Lev pressed on with his distance vision work, testing separate system components based on known principles. From these he was hoping to assemble an original scheme for a working television. Several of his coworkers pitched in to help: his brother-in-law, Alexander Constantinov—later a television specialist—and A. N. Boiko, who designed an ultrasensitive selenium photo element accepting a pencil-ray of scanned light, to increase the quality of the image. Along the way, Lev and another colleague, V. E. Kovalenkov, acquired a Russian patent for a "spiral method of image focusing." Parts were hard to come by. Lev would scour Leningrad's Alexander market for cheap radio components or travel all the way to Moscow to the Suharevka Market—a sort of combination flea market and black market, where people sold and traded.

By late 1925, all the systems were linked for a test of the first complete prototype. The components were mechanical, but instead of a Nipkow disk, Lev used a mirror sweep (a rotating disk with mirrors that directed light from the original image onto the photocell). Rosing's 1907 patent and his 1911 demonstration, in fact, had used two mirror drums for scanning and dissecting the image at the transmitter. In Lev's experimental system, the received image—sent through wires and projected on a screen—had a resolution of sixteen lines. It was possible to perceive the semblance of an object, but not its details. A human face was recognizable, but the person's identity couldn't be discerned.

Neck and neck with Lev, a handful of foreign inventors labored to construct their own systems. In 1922, the American inventor Charles Francis Jenkins had filed for a patent on a wireless system of picture transmission. By December 1923, working with the General Electric and Westinghouse companies, he demonstrated a mechanical apparatus using rotating disks with prismatic mirrors. He was able to send simple images of still objects from a transmitter to a receiver across his laboratory—probably the earliest wireless picture transmission on record. Over a three-week period in April 1925, the Scottish inventor John Logie Baird displayed a mechanical television at Selfridge's Department Store in London. Curious shoppers took turns peering through a narrow tube to view Baird's tiny, shadowgraph-like images with a resolution of thirty vertical strips formed through the use of a Nipkow disk. Baird, who had applied for his first television patent in 1923, also managed to transmit the recognizable image of a boy's face by October of '25.

These systems began to prove that crude, still images could be sent through the air on radio waves, but the devices were essentially just wireless equivalents of facsimile machines. The task of transmitting actively moving objects remained.

On June 13, 1925, Jenkins broke new ground by televising the image of a revolving windmill over a five-mile distance from Maryland to Washington, D.C. At a resolution of forty-eight lines, the picture was fuzzy, but the event made the national headlines, for now a recognizable object could be seen in action.

Lev's work was interrupted again in the fall when he was summoned to Berlin. It was the "business trip" Ioffe had "warned" him about. At the firm of M. J. Goldberg and Sons, he met Yuri Mikhailovich Goldberg, a partner in the company. Yuri was a Russian citizen, born in 1888 in St. Petersburg, where he had attended the gymnasium. Later he moved to Germany to pursue training as a mechanical engineer at the Darmstadt Polytechnic Institute. In Berlin he assumed the name George Julius Goldberg.

On November 21, Lev—adopting a new German transliteration of his name—set his hand to a pivotal document in the presence of E. T. Smith, consul of the United States of America in Berlin:

> Whereas Leo Ssergejewitsch Thèremin of 50 Marat Street, Leningrad, Russia, has invented a Signalling Apparatus, for which he has filed application for letters patent of the United States
> And Whereas the firm of M. J. Goldberg und Söhne G. m. b. H. of Bleibtreustrasse 40, Berlin-Charlottenburg, is desirous of acquiring an interest in said invention, and in the letters patent to be obtained therefor:
> . . . in consideration of the sum of 5 Dollars to me in hand paid . . . I, the said Leo Ssergejewitsch Thèremin, have sold, assigned, and transferred . . .

unto the said firm of M. J. Goldberg und Söhne G. m. b. H. my entire rights in and to the said invention.[64]

It was a clever ruse. When the American consul set his "hand and official seal" to the papers, he might as well have signed a promissory note to the GRU or the Comintern. The German patent application Ioffe secured earlier had opened another Berlin doorway for Soviet intelligence, but this document went further. It was a decoy for capitalists. A United States patent would provide entrée to American industry, and beyond that, the assignment to Goldberg and Sons would give Western entrepreneurs interested in the invention the impression they were dealing with a German firm, and not directly with the Soviets—a prospect that gave many businessmen cold feet. Any shared technical data from the West, relating to the invention, would be relayed back to the GRU through the company, and profits from Western sales of the device would be passed via Goldberg and Sons to the Soviet apparat to fund intelligence operations against the capitalist countries.

Applications for United States patents on the watchman ("Signalling Apparatus") and the Termenvox ("Method of and Apparatus for the Generation of Sounds") were recorded on December 5. In Berlin, Lev also registered patent applications for France and Great Britain, countries the Soviets had staked out for massive surveillance. Along with his now standard duet of devices, he added applications covering recent condensers and airplane altimeters he had developed. In his luggage on the return trip he carried out radio parts, loudspeakers, and measuring equipment for Ioffe.

In January 1926, John Logie Baird welcomed the London press to a demonstration of his television system; the medium had emerged from the recesses of the laboratory. As the spring progressed in Leningrad, Lev, working on his own now, began fine-tuning his original apparatus. A second experimental version had a thirty-two-line resolution. In a third adaptation, he tried interlaced scanning and pushed the resolution up to sixty-four lines. This would be the basis for his diploma defense, which was approaching in a few months. Sleep was often put on the back burner, and many prearranged agitprop performances had to be canceled.

On June 5 he received a secret package from the department of invention of the REVVOENSOVET (The Revolutionary Military Council of the USSR). He was required to fill out papers and make preparations for an extended trip to Germany for more patent work. He complied with the directions, returned the forms, and would wait for a response.

On June 7 he defended his thesis. "The Mechanism of Electric Distance Vision" was shown in the Assembly Hall of the Physico-Technical Institute before a gathering of two hundred students and faculty from the Polytechnic physics department. On a five-foot-square screen, Lev projected images transmitted from a receiver in the adjoining room. A face could easily be recognized now if the person made no sharp movements, and motions of a waving hand were plainly visible on the receiving screen at virtually the same moment they happened. Compared with film technology the images appeared slightly out of focus, but the achievement of near-instantaneous transmission was groundbreaking.

The demonstration provoked a sensation at the Polytechnical Institute. "Termen's discovery is grand," Ioffe wrote in *Pravda*, "and on an all-European scale!"[65] Off the record, he spoke candidly. Lev remembered, "He recommended that I continue this work, not just for film applications, but for special tasks—for underwater research, or for conditions where a person's presence would be dangerous or unwanted."[66]

Another short Berlin excursion intervened in November. On the thirteenth, Lev sold, assigned, and transferred his entire rights for the Termenvox to Goldberg and Sons.

On December 16, Lev brought his distance vision apparatus before the Fifth All-Union Congress of Physicists in Moscow. The reactions of the distinguished gathering were summed up by Boris Rosing—known to be cautious with his appraisals. In a statement printed in *Izvestia* on December 29 he wrote: "Thanks to the experimental talent of the engineer Termen in the area of electrical telescopy based on the mechanical process, Russian electrical engineering had a partial victory almost simultaneously with the foreign experimenters Baird, Jenkins, and others."[67]

The sophistication of Lev's demonstration was underscored by events on the other side of the Atlantic one day before. At a meeting of the American Institute of Electrical Engineers on December 15 in St. Louis, Missouri, General Electric's resident television specialist, Ernst F. W. Alexanderson, revealed that the company was involved in television research. Alexanderson already had a well-established reputation as an engineer—he had worked on Reginald Fessenden's alternator in 1906, which made possible the landmark Christmas Eve "broadcast," and his work had advanced the status of wireless transmission. But his talk in St. Louis was curious for its cautious tone in light of advancements Lev had already made—advancements Alexanderson evidently knew nothing about. Speaking hypothetically, without demonstrating any equipment, Alexanderson confessed that GE could not hope to realize a viable television without reducing the transmission time of an event from the existing twenty minutes to about one-sixteenth of a second. Lev had already demonstrated a near synchronous reception in his display of hand movements, albeit within the confines of a lab, and not over large distances. Alexanderson bemoaned the almost "inconceivable" task of achieving a sufficiently large screen for viewing an image at the receiving end. Baird, Jenkins, and others were unable to expand their screen dimensions beyond several inches, and experimenters at the time were confined to postcard-sized viewing areas, at best. But in the system demonstrated in June and December, Lev had beamed the image onto a screen many times that size.

Lev's was the first functioning television apparatus in Russia. Predictably, the state wasted no time in finding a use for it. Early in 1927 Lev was summoned to the CTO (the Soviet of Labor and Defense). The directive was to design a special distance vision unit for the border patrol. The device was to conform to strict specifications: it had to operate in daylight, possess a sufficiently high resolution to identify the face of a subject, and be capable of following the progress of a moving object—rather tall orders given the state of television research.

While Lev tinkered furiously with these demands, his musical life crested one more time. Around the city, posters heralded the latest event at the Leningrad Philharmonic Society's Grand Hall:

LECTURE CONCERT

L. S. TERMEN

NEW DIRECTIONS IN MUSICAL ART

Technical Possibilities for Combining Music and Color,
Music and Movement, Music and Smells,
Music and Touch

The lecture is accompanied by a demonstration of the
electromusical instrument invented by L. S. TERMEN

CONCERT TO FOLLOW THE LECTURE.[68]

Lev's renown was at an apex. After the physicists' congress he was crowned with a new sobriquet, "the Russian Edison." In the public eye he had become the Merlin of electronic sensory perception. The demonstration on April 10, in the hall where Shostakovich and Glazunov had seen him in 1922, was a benefit for the physics circle of the Polytechnic. The recital portion included selections by Grieg, Scriabin, and others, with Lev's aunts assisting: Elena Emilievna Termen sang, and Olga Emilievna Termen—a Petersburg Conservatory graduate—accompanied at the piano. Lev again brought out his illumovox to demonstrate "music and color," and, anticipating the notion of "virtual reality" by a few generations, he mused over the thought of an enveloping amalgam of music, touch, movement, and fragrance.

By June, the secret, fourth version of distance vision was ready for a demonstration before Kremlin officials. The mirror sweep scanner used in the third version satisfied the requirement for telecasting in natural daylight. (Most other schemes at the time functioned only when the subject was indoors, flooded with deliberately bright, artificial light.) In the new system, Lev achieved a resolution of one hundred lines—a record for the time—permitting the clear recognition of a face, even when the person was moving.

Kliment Voroshilov, people's commissar for military and naval affairs—a member of Stalin's highest-ranking inner circle—headed the commission overseeing the project. The first test was arranged in his office in front of Stalin and a few of his top brass gathered to judge its potential as a surveillance device. It was an Olympian huddle: Mikhail Tukhachevsky, Red Army chief of staff; Semen Budenny, inspector of the cavalry—both future marshals of the Soviet Union—and Sergo Ordzhonikidze, a leading Bolshevik and future member of the Politburo.

The receiver for the portable system was installed in a secretary's study adjacent to Voroshilov's office so the commissar could monitor visitors below as they approached the Kremlin. The scanning-transmitting camera, set up outside on a tripod, was swiveled by an operator to follow people crossing the courtyard. Passers-by were tracked in the viewing field during their entire movement through the yard, at distances ranging from 100 to 160 feet from the camera. The picture signal was transmitted on a shortwave frequency, but a wired, closed circuit setup was also possible.

It was Lev's second triumph in the Kremlin in five years. "A few days later," he remembered, "Voroshilov told me Stalin had been impressed by the magic screen and sent his regards."[69] Voroshilov kept the device in his office for a short time and, convinced of its merits, he ordered Lev to arrange a similar setup as an electronic sentinel for troops patrolling the border. After the system was delivered, military officers of the border guard were trained in its use for several days. Lev was rewarded for his efforts with a coupon for "a big food parcel," courtesy of the government.

But the television was immediately made top secret. All writings and public statements about Lev's distance vision ceased, and no detailed technical data about the secret "fourth version" were ever disclosed.

For an instant, Lev had taken the lead among his competitors. By early 1927 he had achieved a screen resolution of 100 lines, while even the following year Alexanderson still claimed the known world's record of 48 lines, surpassed seven months later by Westinghouse with 60 lines, and eventually by RCA in 1931, with 120 lines. Lev also held the lead for image size at the receiver. The 5-by-5-foot screen dimensions he displayed in 1926 had no close contenders at the time. In 1927 and 1928, Alexanderson's mechanical systems used screens that varied from 3-inch squares to 8-by-10-inch surfaces. Lev's record would only be surpassed in 1930 with Alexanderson's public demonstration of a screen image measuring 6 by 8 feet. Lev also managed successful outdoor transmission before most of his colleagues, and in the technique of panning a moving subject his Kremlin courtyard system predated other similar attempts. (In September 1928, Alexanderson's broadcast of a play still required separate, immovable cameras to capture, alternately, the motions of the actors' faces and hands.)

Lev collected the accolades of colleagues and academicians, but he was powerless to develop his work any further. His distance vision scheme had been snatched and sealed in a vault. Apparently serving the state meant being cut out of the bargain eventually. Lenin's appropriation of the radio watchman was exceeded only by Stalin's delight in television as the perpetual hidden eye of the dictatorship.

As the curtain was drawn on television in Soviet Russia, RCA's commercial manager, the visionary David Sarnoff, began to muse, starry-eyed, about the future of television in America. "The greatest day of all will be reached," Sarnoff told the *Saturday Evening Post* in 1926,

> when not only the human voice, but the image of the speaker, can be flashed through space in every direction. On that day the whole country will join in every national procession. The backwoodsman will be able to follow the play of expression on the face of every leading artist. Mothers will attend child welfare clinics in their own homes. Workers may go to night school in the same way. A scientist can demonstrate his latest discoveries to those of his profession even though they be scattered all over the world.[70]

For Stalin, the notion of his own "backwoodsmen" getting their hands on a television receiver, or his scientists advertising their wares freely over the airwaves, would be out of the question.

"Voroshilov talked to me about my future activities in invention," Lev recalled,

> my work at the Physico-Technical Institute, and about creating devices for military purposes. In connection with the agreement Abram Fedorovich made with the Goldberg company about patent affairs, it was necessary for me to go to Germany to finally complete those documents. At the beginning of July 1927, Abram Fedorovich suggested I leave the Physico-Technical Institute for an extended business trip as a scientist-worker to learn about new foreign developments. It would be done on the basis of an international agreement for science and technical exchange.[71]

Every organization seemed to have its hand in the pie. Boris Krasin, head of the music department at the People's Commissariat of Education (Narkompros), and Professor Garbuzov, founder of the State Institute of the Science of Music, supported the notion of Lev as a cultural ambassador to demonstrate the Termenvox. The All-Union Society for Cultural Relations with Foreign Countries (VOKS) suggested he present the instrument at an international music exposition already in progress in Germany.

These ideas were feasible, but not exactly what Ioffe had in mind. Lev was a valuable commodity to the state, and his function abroad would have to include more than music. The trip to Germany was approved as a cultural exchange, but Lev was handed, as he put it, a "little extra assignment."[72] Before leaving for Germany, his marching orders would come from the GRU.

The Fourth Department of the Red Army (the GRU—official organ of military intelligence) was headed by Jan Karlovich Berzin. A Latvian, Berzin was an old Bolshevik veteran of the October Revolution, and a former member of the Cheka. When the Fourth Department was founded, he was appointed to direct its espionage activities—the most far reaching of any Soviet intelligence organization. Where observation of foreign industry and technology were concerned, Lev's experience as an engineer came under the purview of the Fourth Department. Henri Barbé, a French Communist, once described his own meeting with Berzin:

> We crossed Moscow in a car and arrived at a large building that did not have any special sign to indicate its identity; this was the headquarters of Soviet military intelligence.
>
> I was led into a large room with huge maps of Europe and Asia on the walls. ·At the desk stood a man of about fifty in military uniform, on his tunic two Red Banner decorations. The husky man was about five feet, eight inches tall; his skull was shaved. He looked at me with lively, piercing blue eyes. This was General Berzin, the head of the Intelligence Service of the Red Army. . . . He was animated, a bit nervous.
>
> Berzin greeted me cordially, shook my hand, and ordered tea and pastry. Then he started a long talk about the importance of information and intelligence work for the defense of the Soviet Fatherland.[73]

Berzin was to be Lev's principal contact, known to him henceforth only as "Peter Janovich," or, simply, "Peter."

On July 20, Lev set out for Germany with a company of musicians that included a quartet from the Moscow Philharmonic. Their first stop would be the Soviet embassy in Berlin, and from there they would disperse into German towns and cities. Lev's tour was to be a foreign extension of his agitprop barnstorming—by now he was a veteran of over 180 concerts in Russia. Katia was compelled to remain in Leningrad—insurance for the government that her husband wouldn't bolt in a moment of weakness.

To Lev it was a chance to stretch his wings and see if his ether music would fly in another culture. For the Fourth Department, in the end, it couldn't have been better. No GRU mastermind could have cooked up a subterfuge of such elegant simplicity: distract the population with a captivating new magician's music, and pick its pockets clean as they listen.

The Greatest Musical Wonder of Our Time

One way has ended.
Another way opens up and travels into the blueness.
White, over tracts and walls,
Flutter a scientist's sensitive hands
Like shrewd and knowing owls through the greyness.

One thousand human beings stare
Craning their necks
At the tiny foot of earthly iron
From which stretches out
The lonely guidepost of a space probe. . . .
One among them . . . they hear the music of his blood,
His blood, their blood.

    —from "Theremin," Gerhart Hermann Mostar, Berlin, 1927

Now he was Leon Theremin. It was a smooth transition to the Gallic origin of his name, and to the Western European culture that ran in his veins (reinforced by a noble upbringing in St. Petersburg). At the gymnasium he had studied French and German, and, though he was not fluent in either language, he moved easily within the refined society of his ancestors. Slender and dashing, with a gracious, cosmopolitan demeanor, he was anything but the dogmatic Bolshevik. As a Soviet ambassador with an auxiliary mission, he blended perfectly with his new surroundings.

Berlin, his first destination, had become the hub of Soviet intelligence in Western Europe. Because of its geographical proximity to Moscow, and the fact that many agents spoke German—along with the torpid state of the country in general—it made an ideal home base for receiving and dispatching espionage traffic. Theremin would establish a lab and residence in the city during the fall of 1927, always returning there between musical forays to other German cities. At the Russian embassy, before foreign diplomats, he gave his first performance and then took off to make his official Western debut.

The international exposition in Frankfurt, "Musik im Leben der Völker" (Music in the Life of the People), had opened on June 11. The Frankfurter Internationalen Ausstellung was a cornucopia of music from around the world, "almost worth a trip to Europe," according to one correspondent from the *Musical Observer.* Many countries were represented with individual exhibit halls. Theme rooms replicated historical epochs with furniture and antique instruments from each period; pianos from the collections of Beethoven, Liszt, and Clara Schumann mingled with instruments from China, Japan, and Java. There were hundreds of artifacts from famous composers: locks of hair, writing desks, paintings, and autograph scores. Viewers could stroll through whole evolutionary histories in the organ room and the piano department. There were exhibits on the casting of bells, violin manufacture, and the development of the phonograph (with a room for visitors to record their own voices); displays of mechanical instruments; examples of the latest technology of acoustic film, the radio, and movies; and recordings of exotic instruments. There was a quarter-tone piano and a jazz display. Three concert halls (the Bachsaal, Beethovensaal, and Haydnsaal) offered an assortment of chamber music recitals—"ultra-modern music," standard fare, and everything from Chinese music to a sound-and-movement demonstration by Jacques Dalcroze and his pupils.

On August 4, in the Bachsaal, Theremin presented "New Trails in Musical Creation," his prototype lecture-recital, which he would repeat many times over the following months. Near the edge of the stage, on the viewer's left, he stood in profile, arms outstretched before the latest version of his instrument: a steep, wedge-shaped mahogany box with vertical pitch and horizontal loop antennas, placed on a small table. Facing him on the right, also in profile, before a second table, was George Julius Goldberg, touring as Theremin's "pupil" and "assistant," after a hasty coaching from the inventor in "space-control" technique.

Goldberg's table held an adaptation of the earliest etherphone in the form of a tilted wooden music rack atop a small rectangular box. A single, vertical pitch antenna shot up from the right side. Goldberg controlled volume with a foot pedal and pressed a small button with his left hand to switch the tone on and off. This allowed a cleaner "attack" on each note, avoiding the swooping from note to note that was often unavoidable when the left hand, in space, attempted to jab downward over the loop antenna to cut off the volume between tones. Theremin offered the pedal and button schemes in his U.S. patent application, but in the end it seemed he was committed to perpetuating the visual illusion of two hands conducting in the air, whatever its musical debit might be.[1]

Behind the two men, a woman sat at a grand piano that supported a black, "swan's-neck" horn loudspeaker gaping at the audience like a shipboard air funnel. The instruments and speaker were connected to a dry cell battery on the floor in a tangle of wires draped from desk to desk that spilled down and snaked across the stage.

"Incredulous, we gaze upon the young engineer," an eyewitness reported.

> His looks grow tender. The inventor becomes the musician. The fingers of his right hand . . . vibrate in free air. . . . Invisibly a soul sings, and we listen, thrilled.
>
> Now it sounds deep as an organ note, and now like a perfect viola, or a violin from the hand of one of the old master craftsmen. Again it resembles a flute or a huntsman's horn. . . . The works of such composers as Grieg, Saint-Saëns, Scriabin, are played. . . .
>
> Now another young man takes his place in front of a second box, smaller than the first. These two technical musicians—tone engineers, let us call them—perform, merely by the raising and dropping and bending of their gently vibrating fingers, music which resounds through the great room in pure and perfect tones.[2]

The audience, another listener recalled,

> sat spell-bound. Finally our neighbor remarked: "We might as well throw our violins aside." . . . Prof. Theremin's assistant told a number of us after the performance that he played no musical instrument and had learned to play this instrument in two weeks. Imagine struggling some ten years with a violin and then suddenly learning to play in two weeks, equally beautifully, by mere movements of the hands in the air. . . . It will doubtless ere long be the greatest revolutionizer of music in the home since the advent of radio.[3]

Assessing the whole Frankfurt festival, one critic ranked Theremin's demonstration as "the most interesting thing we were permitted to hear and see,"[4] and another called it music "of a beauty hitherto undreamed of."[5]

A little piece of Europe had been won, and it was clear from the headlines ("The Latest Marvel in Music,"[6] "Electric Instrument Proves the Sensation of the Frankfort Festival"[7]) that Theremin would shortly have the whole continent at his feet. The exhibition's directors, sensing a hit, persuaded Goldberg and the inventor to remain on hand for an additional week—from the fifteenth to the twenty-third of August.

Publicity stunts were in order, and Theremin tried a new one: humoring local dignitaries with a go at the instrument. An artist's pen-and-ink rendering, syndicated in several German newspapers, shows Theremin standing before his instrument, directing the outstretched hand of a stout, mustachioed gentleman—a dead ringer for Teddy Roosevelt—who gestures before the pitch control antenna. A caption explained that Theremin, "the young, genial inventor of electrical music, guided the hand of the mayor of Frankfurt, Dr. Land-mann, in a rendition of the 'Pilgrim's Chorus' from *Tannhäuser.*"[8] The inventor was learning that his instrument could conveniently speak the musical tongue of any country.

The German press, sniffing something major cooking, came running from all corners of the country. Hyperbole, daring speculation, and heated debate rolled out in story after story about "Aetherwellen-Musik" (ether music) and "Theremins Sphärenmusik" (Theremin's music of the spheres). The inventor was now "Professor Theremin" or "Professor of Engineering Theremin" ("Prof. Dipl.-Ing. Theremin") and his instrument, the "Thereminvox."

The Frankfurt festival was important as an early international forum for electronic instruments. No one was quite sure what use they had, but there was a prevailing intuition that their technology might augment the future sound palette of composers. "One of the main demands of modern music is to produce new tone colors, new scales and systems," the musicologist Arno Huth wrote,

> the widening of the frequency range and the subdivision of the octave into small intervals. . . . All this has been impossible because traditional instruments are tied to a tempered system. As a result, modern music has been "cramped." Young composers complain, "we cannot go on, the instruments are not there." . . . It's not surprising, then, that in response to this crisis, new ways have been found. The most promising are shown in the exhibition "Music in the Life of the People" in Frankfurt—in that of electronic tone production.[9]

Huth was referring to Theremin, of course, but his praise also embraced another exhibitor at the Ausstellung.

Off in a corner, a plump, compact man with a large, bald head and a beaklike nose sat quietly waiting for occasional visitors to stroll past and inquire about his strange-looking contraptions. Jörg Mager was in every aspect the antithesis of Theremin. Born in 1880 in Eichstatt, Germany, he had devoted his life to the development and perfection of his instruments to the exclusion of his social and material well-being. He was an idealist—precise and systematic—but detached from the world. Mager was a communist, but also a pacifist, an ascetic opposed to the consumption of alcohol, and an Esperantist. He frequently suffered from hunger and financial straits that forced him to abandon his research and take up work as a schoolteacher and organist.

In the hot summer of 1911, an organ that had drifted out of tune prompted Mager's sudden fascination with quarter tones (the notes lying halfway between semitones, the smallest Western divisions of the octave). That year he constructed a quarter-tone harmonium that formed the basis for all his later instruments.

Mager came upon the idea of electronic music while doing temporary work in a radio technology factory. In a 1924 pamphlet, "A New Epoch in Music through Radio," he wrote, "With the technical means of radio, something much higher and powerful could be achieved, namely, to place at the disposal of music the totality of all additional tones on which the timbre depends. With this totality a new world of sounds can be created which can overshadow all that has been achieved until now."[10]

Mager's first instrument, the "Electrophon," was built around 1921 with the assistance of the Lorenz Company of Berlin. Like Theremin's instrument, it harnessed the heterodyne principle, using two radio frequency oscillators in the fifty-kilohertz range. But unlike the Thereminvox, it allowed pitch changes to be regulated manually, by turning a crank connected to the variable oscillator. Underneath the crank, notes of the chromatic scale were indicated on a semicircular plate. Tone color shifts were accomplished through filter chains. The microtonal composer Alois Hàba wrote with great excitement that the instrument represented "an epoch-making development, not only in the construction of instruments, but for music in general."[11]

Mager, however, was disturbed by the unavoidable glissando between notes—the characteristic impediment in Theremin's instrument—which in this case resulted when the crank moved over the chromatic increments. Mager corrected the problem by adding a second crank that allowed each note to be silently selected while another was being played. He renamed the instrument the "Sphärophon" and introduced it at the Donauschingen Music Festival in July 1926. Presentations of "mechanical music" at the event featured works of Paul Hindemith and Ernst Toch for electrical piano and Welte-Reproduktionsklavier, a mechanical organ. Oskar Schlemmer's robot figures danced to Hindemith's *Das Triadische Ballett*. Mager's instrument, presented at the Zeppelinsaal, fit in well. Hindemith called it "the most revolutionary invention in the field of musical instruments."[12] *Der Deutsche Rundfunk* ventured, "we can now say without exaggeration, that it is the instrument of the future."[13] Like Mager himself, though, the Sphärophon was easily overshadowed by the more flamboyant offerings at the festival and was hardly noticed, except by a few journalists.

Mager had little interest in showmanship and little cared how others saw him. Unlike Theremin, he was devoted to the pursuit of the hypothetical, perfect instrument. His equipment was regarded as advanced in design and workmanship, but it was unknown outside Germany. Mager was also suspicious and mistrustful, hoarding technical information that prevented the manufacture of his work. Theremin, on the other hand, was growing into a promoter, willing to stop short of perfection for the sake of disseminating his broader ideals.

The convergence of the two men in Frankfurt in 1927 touched off a debate in the music community. "In Mager's case," Arno Huth wrote, "the work is systematic, objective and scientific; in Theremin's case, it is genial and intuitive. . . . more directly dependent upon the performing artist."[14] "On the whole," the *Musical Courier* decided, "Theremin's instrument, as the simplest of all, seems to be regarded as being the farthest advanced."[15] But Max Eisler, reporting on the event in *Musique et instruments*, argued that Mager "remained almost completely overshadowed, although he had devised equipment both practically and scientifically superior to that of Theremin. . . . but whereas Theremin, by his publicity and gestures, attracted and enraptured the audience and captivated the press, the poor schoolteacher from Aschaffenburg, Jörg Mager, demonstrated his 'Sphaerophon' before a few rare wandering visitors in the obscure corner to which he had been relegated."[16]

Back in Berlin, Theremin filed two more German patent applications on August 27, and on the twenty-sixth of September, he strode onto the stage of the Bechsteinsaal for his formal Berlin debut. The invitation-only audience of several hundred musicians, scientists, and composers was scattered with a handful of luminaries who came out to assess the new Aetherwellen-Musik: Albert Einstein, the tenor Leo Slezak, the Nobel laureate playwright Gerhart Hauptmann, and the conductor Bruno Walter. Again, Theremin collected the press plaudits he was coming to expect. The instrument had "shortened the path from the brain of a human being to matter," allowing "a much more adaptable production of music," according to the *Hamburger Fremdenblatt*.[17] It was "undoubtedly a turning point in the theory of interpretive music," the *Düsseldorfer Nachrichten* reckoned.[18]

Five days later, the *Berliner Tageblatt* devoted a half-page spread to the new phenomenon. The first column was given over to an unabashed manifesto in the inventor's own words: "Mein Ziel": "The accelerating tempo of current life demands a similar change in the field of art. One continuously notices that the currently played musical instruments, which for tens or even hundreds of years have not changed, are incapable of meeting the demands of today's music and art. It therefore should be useful to work on new types of instruments which make use of the latest achievements of science and technology. My experiments have, in principle, solved many of the problems."[19] Across the next two columns, solicited testimonials two and three paragraphs long endowed the instrument and its inventor with the imprimatur of giants: "Professor Theremin's invention has made the deepest impression on me," Bruno Walter rhapsodized.

"Here indeed seems to be a new country. I cannot say which affected me most: the method of tone production which suggests the miraculous, or the completely novel character of the tone itself. . . . it was a moving experience." To Leo Slezak it was "overwhelming," an "invention of genius." "Without claiming to be a prophet," the composer Ottorino Respighi forecast, "I can already say that Theremin's instrument has great significance for the orchestra."[20]

Perhaps the brightest victory, though, was the first glimmer of fascination from the New World: the *New York Times* had come, seen, and been conquered. "Ether Wave Music Amazes Savants," Waldemar Kaempffert announced to his readers in boldface. It was "an astounding demonstration," he reported, and after a cursory technical explanation in the story, Kaempffert quoted one of the inventor's more grandiloquent statements: "With this instrument I have made it possible to produce tones of constancy of pitch not even remotely approached by the best piano or organ. My apparatus frees the composer from the despotism of the twelve-note tempered piano scale, to which even violinists must adapt themselves. The composer can now construct a scale of the intervals desired. He can have intervals of thirteenths, if he wants them. In fact any gradation detectable by the human ear can be produced."[21]

Theremin was aware, of course, that the general public, complacent as it was with the raptures of Brahms, Mahler, or Gershwin, didn't give two cents or a reichsmark about the so-called "problems" of modern composers. For them he needed another angle—one that appealed to the amateur musician: "ether wave music is created with a simplicity and a directness matched only by singing. There is no keyboard to obtrude itself, no catgut, no bow, no pedal, nothing but simple expressive gestures of the hands."[22] He had cast his bait into the capitalist sea. A header over his statement in the *Berliner Tageblatt*, in fact, was careful to reinforce the mass appeal, perhaps even the commercial utility, of the invention: "we can say that this instrument is not the art of the top ten thousand. In fact, one calculates that this easily played instrument, once it is mass-produced, will cost more or less what a radio costs—about 150 to 200 marks."[23]

Theremin was on a roll. On October 7, another demonstration followed in Berlin at the Beethovensaal, then an appearance in Hamburg on the twenty-fifth, back to Berlin on the thirty-first for a third presentation—this time at the Tonhalle—followed by a stop in Cologne on November 5. "I was just now in Dresden," he told a correspondent from the *Berliner Tageblatt*. "There they didn't even want to go home—even when the hall was darkened they were still standing and 'applauding with their feet.' And at the music exhibition in Frankfurt they were all so nice to me that as a thank you I gave gratuitous demonstrations for the Frankfurt youth. I like it very much in Germany."[24]

Gerhart Herrmann Mostar mythologized these moments in his poem "Theremin," published in Berlin's *Der Deutsche Rundfunk:*

One thousand human beings listen to the grand
"Come into being"
By which somebody out there will rouse the sounds of the future,
One among them . . . they hear the music of his blood,
His blood, their blood. . . .
They are seeking with souls outstretched
The singing of tomorrow . . .
And tremble to lose it.[25]

With Theremin's patents pending in the United States and the eager attentions of the *New York Times,* along with the gathering popular momentum in Germany, the Kremlin knew it was time to act. By mid-November the decision came down to send the inventor on a brief "business trip" to America for about "two to two-and-a-half months."[26] He would leave on December 5. In the meantime, a fourth Berlin concert took place at the Philharmonic on November 17.

Increasing numbers of tourists and foreign correspondents flooded into Berlin as word of the demonstrations spread across Europe. Charles B. Cochran, the recently appointed general manager of London's Royal Albert Hall, witnessed one of the concerts and told London's *Daily Telegraph,* "I found the experience . . . quite uncanny. The purity of the tone he extracts is remarkable."[27] On stage, afterward, Cochran took his turn at the instrument, poking out "The Keel Row." It was an impresario's dream. Theremin simply had to be lured to London. Arrangements were made to postpone the American departure, and a booking was confirmed for Albert Hall on December 12, with a small private demonstration to be held beforehand on the tenth.

In the meantime, Theremin had engagements to fulfill in Munich, Breslau, Stettin, Nuremburg, Leipzig, Mannheim, and once again in Hamburg. In between, he scrambled to finish several new projects. On a visit to the Berlin lab, Arno Huth saw two variations of the ether music design, one still in progress.

An electronic keyboard instrument, resembling a miniature upright piano, sat on a table. Forty-nine standard piano keys made up a 4-octave range (C to C). On the vertical surface rising up from the keyboard, 27 rotary condenser dials were arranged in 3 rows of 9 each. Pitch fluctuations of up to $\frac{1}{100}$ of a tone were adjustable on each note by twisting the dial assigned to that key. The calibration of 100 possible settings for each whole tone allowed for countless new tuning schemes. The instrument was polyphonic (capable of sounding multiple tones simultaneously). After Theremin designed it in Russia in 1926, he had apparently used it only for acoustic research, and never in performance. He called it the "electric harmonium," or "keyboard harmonium."

Huth found the inventor at work on a series of identical variants of the space-control model. "I am now building twelve instruments," Theremin had told the *New York Times*. "Good musicians will learn how to play them in a fortnight. With an orchestra thus constituted, with nothing but gestures these men will give us concerts that will reveal new beauties in tones and their combinations."[28]

In this fresh mutation of the instrument, Theremin played into the latest fantasy. Recent musings in the press had carried the ether wave myth to the extreme: now it was "music without instruments." Beginning with a collection of portable music stands constructed of thin metal, the inventor equipped each with a horizontal tube, disguised under the small shelf that supported the sheet music. Two antennas (vertical/pitch on the right, and horizontal/volume on the left) were easily camouflaged as extensions of the spindly stands. Electrical wires linked each stand to its own remote box that housed the main circuitry. A forest of these "stands" on a stage, with musicians gesturing only at the printed music before them, would be an invisible orchestra.

"When I return from America we will build more apparatuses," Theremin told the *Berliner Tageblatt*. "We already have so many orders that soon we won't be able to take care of them all. At first, we don't wish to make them on a production line but rather single models in the laboratory. Then we will give them to musicians and put an orchestra together. . . . The instruments will have the sound character of the various orchestral instruments."[29] To train performers he planned to open a school in Berlin. "At first, I myself will teach, and then I will train teachers. . . . I still have many other plans, and can't permit myself to travel and demonstrate for such a long time."[30]

At the American embassy in Berlin on November 25, as the Atlantic crossing drew closer, Theremin and Goldberg were granted temporary immigration visas to visit the United States. Under "Profession or Trade" on his permit, Theremin was listed as "Professor and Graduate engineer with the Physical Technical Institute, Leningrad." The "Purpose" was noted as "Temporary visit—to demonstrate inventions."[31]

Theremin started to wrap up his affairs and prepare for his quick side trip to London. French journalists in Berlin, however, were nearly as dogged as the Germans in covering ether wave activities, and when word got out about the upcoming Albert Hall event, Parisians decided they would have a last-minute slice of the cake as well.

A demonstration was scheduled at the modest-sized Salle des Concerts, in the Maison Gaveau, for December 6. With gales of publicity blowing in from

Germany, the event sold out virtually as notices were being released. Radio and wireless applications were all the rage in Paris—the letters "T.S.F." (*télégraphie sans fil*) were sprinkled into scores of newspaper and journal essays— and now the buzzword was "la musique des ondes éthérées." Only the likes of the Paris Opera could contain the expected throngs for an additional concert, and the sponsors cast a net to catch this spillover while they were still negotiating with the hall's management: "The MARCEL DE VALMALETE CONCERT BUREAU announces a second, unique hearing which will take place on Wednesday the 7th, or Thursday the 8th of December. Only one of these days is possible because M. Thérémin will present his apparatus at the Albert Hall in London on the 10th of December, and on the 14th, he will embark for America where he will negotiate the sale of his patent, for which he has been offered the sum of 500,000 dollars."[32]

Katia arrived in Paris for a quick reunion with her husband on the eve of his American sojourn. They stayed with his relatives on the rue Monsieur Le Prince, and the press descended on him. "We asked the magician himself . . . to speak to us about his discovery," the *Petit Journal* began.

—It's . . . very . . . simple, we gathered with much difficulty, because he can barely speak our language.

We were beginning to fear that a somewhat simple interview on this subject couldn't be very intricate under these circumstances, when an interpreter came to our aid, and the conversation commenced in an agreeable dialect mixing Russian, French, German, and English.[33]

Outside the Salle Gaveau, the crowd queuing up eyed a heavy truck parked by the entrance loaded with strange machines. A tangle of electrical cables spewing from the equipment was directed through the front door. Suspicion began to heat up about a fraud—perhaps this ethereal music was piped into the speakers from an external source. But before a melee erupted, patrons were reassured that it was only the Fox Film Company, recording the event on the new medium of sound film.

Inside the hall, "all scientific and medical Paris"[34] held its breath to see the man who had lately declared, "with my instrument I can play Berlioz's works with a clearer tone than any orchestra."[35] A reporter from the *Belfast Telegraph* took it all in:

The hall was full, and on the tiered stage, where orchestras of 60 are accommodated, one object riveted all attention—a dark wooden box, a little larger than a suitcase. . . .

The door opens at the back of the stage—the buzz of conversation dies down—a little youthful figure crosses the stage to the box. . . .

For a moment he manipulates the interior of his instrument, which emits not unfamiliar crackling and buzzings. Then he stands erect and his fingers grasp the music of the spheres. A note of the purest intensity floods the hall, falls and rises at the performer's will, expands or fades at his demand. . . .

One searches for an invisible violoncello. . . . All that has happened is that a pale, shy, young savant with deft, hovering hands sways the impalpable waves of harmony and one hears the sons of the morning sing together.[36]

Paris's *Petit Journal* swooned: "A revelation, better yet, a revolution."[37]

La Lanterne put the inventor on the spot: "Hasn't the Revolution hindered your work? Haven't political affairs overshadowed your art?" "I am not a musician," he was careful to emphasize. "I am an engineer. . . . The Revolution has not hindered my work, and I have always enjoyed great freedom. The laboratory at my disposal, and the stipends I have received, have successfully allowed me to conduct my research. Nowadays . . . savants can work in Russia under the same material and moral conditions as in Germany, France, or in England."[38]

L'Humanité, the French Communist newspaper, made the most of the event: "This magnificent invention comes to us from communist Russia! The inventor, assisted by the Soviet government, a soviet citizen, has been able to realize it in that worker and peasant Republic where the new world is found! Once again, the accusations of barbarity are reduced to nothing."[39] A second article in the same issue was dripping with sarcasm: "this marvel comes to us from barbarous communist Russia where 'robbery, pillage, arson and murder are legal tender' . . . where 'three hundred fifty thousand intellectuals have been massacred'!!?"

L'Humanité employed over one thousand "rabcors"—"worker-correspondents"—who constituted a new breed of petty operatives recruited by Moscow to keep an eye on local events through inquiring journalism. Many rabcor reports made their way from France to Jan Berzin's office, and Theremin's presence in Paris revved up the agitprop engines to high pitch. "Should we not report," the paper continued, "that this surprising invention which constitutes, without a doubt, the most powerful means of expression in the future life of the people, is the work of a young engineer . . . from the land of the Soviets? . . . The repercussions in the social realm of music are bound to be considerable. It has ended the whole aristocratic conception of music."[40]

Two nights later, a human wave rushed the entrance of the Paris Opera. Tickets totaling twenty-five thousand francs had sold in three days. "Police were called to keep order among the crowds," the *New York Times* reported. "Many hundreds were turned away. For the first time in the history of the Opera standing room was sold in boxes."[41] Among the elite procession of dignitaries and literati streaming into the hall were Paul Valéry, the Marquis and Marquise de Polignac, and the British ambassador.

At the first sound, "everyone shivered as if they had seen God inflate the dead instrument with life," *Le Courier Musical* observed.[42] But there were also skeptics present. "It would seem, according to some enthusiasts," one journalist quipped, "that the new instrument could replace an orchestra. What a joke! It can never play more than one note at a time."[43] "Some musicians were extremely pessimistic about the possibilities of the device," Henry Prunieres admitted in the *New York Times*, "because at times M. Theremin played lamentably out of tune. But the finest Stradivarius, in the hands of a tyro, can give forth frightful sounds. The fact that the inventor was able to perform certain pieces with absolute precision proves that there remain to be solved only questions of practice and technique."[44] The huge ovation at the end showed the French audience to be forgiving. The adoration of Parisians was summed up in one reviewer's panegyric: Theremin "beat time to the choirs of angels, to the celestial voices, to the fairy musicians, whom the intellect of this man has revealed, as if he had been given a wager to make us believe the beautiful fairy tales of our childhood."[45]

But even intoxicated columnists, awash in this lyricism, were clearheaded enough to recall another electronic music demonstration in Paris earlier that year. "Curiously enough," May Birkhead wrote in the *New York Times*, "the principle had already been demonstrated at the Trocadero last June by M. Givelet."[46] Armand Givelet was the vice president of the Radio Club of France. In 1918 he had accidentally discovered the effect of body capacitance when he simultaneously touched two different points of an audion amplifier and was surprised to hear a persistent whistling coming through the headset. Substituting a variable condenser for his fingers, he was able to adjust the pitch of the whistle. When he inscribed notes of the scale on the condenser dial, he found it was possible to play simple pieces of music by rotating the dial. Amplification was in its infancy, and Givelet realized that without loudspeakers, "the new music, admirable for its purity and its variety of timbres, could not be heard beyond a distance of several meters," and "this curious discovery found itself buried for a period of almost nine years."[47]

Givelet eventually refined his instrument with a keyboard and a system allowing fine gradations of tuning. He christened it the "Clavier à Lampe" and demonstrated it for the first time in public at the Trocadero on June 9, 1927. A week after Theremin's spectacle at the Opera, Givelet demonstrated a second instrument at the Grand-Palais of the Champs-Élysées during the Exposition des Sciences et Arts (December 15–29). The two loudspeakers used at that performance each contained 175 speaker cones and were fed by a 10,000-

volt amplifier installed in a car. Givelet later claimed he overheard people speculating about a colossal organ hidden in the high walls of the building.

Like Mager's instruments, Givelet's Clavier à Lampe invited comparison with Theremin's work. Although Givelet's device was well realized, it was not a finished concept but only a step toward more-sophisticated instruments he would build in the future. Luckily for Theremin, Givelet was not concerned with promoting or marketing his work, and he modestly saw himself as simply an engineer in the Eiffel Tower laboratory, engaged in musical research. In any event, Theremin seemed to be accorded the greater respect. "Professor Theremin has . . . made an instrument far more perfect and practical than that of M. Givelet," Henry Prunieres concluded in the *New York Times*.[48] "M. Theremin deserves to be called an artist," the *Paris Times* declared. "It is his artistic mastery of the instrument that constitutes the difference between his performance last night and that of M. Givelet. . . . For this is not a new invention."[49]

To some, this hairsplitting was academic. The whole issue of electronic music in the first place was just another nail in the coffin of nineteenth-century cultural heritage. After the Opera performance, *Le Figaro* published the reflections of one listener who wondered

> if the marvels of radioelectric science will encourage our youth to increase their diligence, and give them the desire to go out and make great discoveries, or, indeed, if students won't say that it's entirely pointless to expend even the slightest effort, because fortunes will fall into their laps. . . .
>
> The second hypothesis is more likely. After the astounding demonstrations of Professor Théremin at the Opera, we fear that mothers will have great difficulty persuading their daughters to take piano lessons, and their sons violin lessons. Many nice young ladies will lose out on the fees paid for the first prize at the Conservatory.
>
> After the typewriter, we have the calculator. . . . We anticipate soon having a machine to translate. . . .
>
> After that we will have a machine to think, which will furnish sensations of color, time, or adapt to the nervousness of each customer. . . . After we have other appliances to create solvency, or peace, or war, there will never be a way to invent a machine to create happiness. And it is then that we will discover that happiness is not automatic.[50]

≪≫

On the evening of December 9, 1927, Theremin and Goldberg arrived at London's Victoria Station with seventeen cases of equipment. The inventor was surrounded by a small army of reporters who pressed him with questions. "Through an interpreter," the *Daily Herald* reported, "Professor Theremin said he hoped and believed the day would come when his invention would be in every home, like the wireless."[51] "If a youth has the spirit of music in him," Theremin told the *Daily Chronicle,* "he can play with my instrument, in a fortnight, what a violinist can play only after two years' training. . . . There is no question yet of marketing it, but I think it could be produced and sold at the price of a three-valve radio set. People will learn to play it without much difficulty. . . . The volume can be varied from the softest to the loudest—loud enough for 150,000 people to hear."[52]

At the bottom of the column, the *Chronicle* matter-of-factly disclosed that Theremin had "received special leave from the Soviet Government to travel round the world demonstrating his invention to scientists and musicians and at the same time learning of other scientific developments." It was clearly a symptom of Western vulnerability and naiveté that the Soviets could so casually declare their purpose. The Kremlin, moreover, must have been delighted with Charles Cochran's invitation. Only six months earlier, the Soviets had been ceremoniously ejected from England following an espionage scandal.

Arcos (the All-Russian Cooperative Society)—the Soviet "trading mission" in London—was the counterpart of Wostwag in Berlin. Playing into Britain's designs on Russia as a limitless trade frontier (amid massive unemployment and a sagging English economy), Arcos induced British manufacturers, on the promise of high-volume purchases, to forward complete product samples and accompanying documentation to Moscow for consideration. When no sales materialized and the British firms sought the return of their materials, Arcos routinely had "no record" of the negotiations and referred all inquiries to the Soviet embassy. The embassy bounced questions back to Arcos, which referred matters to Moscow. Ultimately, the manufacturers were given the silent treatment.

Suspecting foul play, Scotland Yard officers, London police, and agents of MI5 (the British Military Intelligence section) orchestrated a raid on Arcos headquarters. When a search warrant was answered with a slammed door, a full-fledged assault ensued. Penetrating a steel door, agents torched locks as they heard breaking glass, shouting, and running on the upper floors. Arcos employees, overcome by smoke after kindling an inferno to destroy documents, were flushed out of smoldering offices by arresting officers. Diplomatic relations with Russia were severed, the Soviet embassy in London was closed, and the ambassador and his staff were expelled on June 3, 1927.

At Victoria Station in December, Theremin and Goldberg were met by the English music critic Edwin Evans, who would offer a spoken translation of the inventor's address at Albert Hall and provide the piano accompaniment. In Paris, Evans had recently witnessed one of the inventor's recitals.

At noon on Saturday, December 10, a private demonstration was held in the Abraham Lincoln Room of the Savoy Hotel. In honor of the occasion,

Charles Cochran had convened the senior academies of scientific, literary, and musical London into a sort of Victorian gentlemen's colloquium. Julian Huxley was present, as were the novelist Arnold Bennett, the conductor Henry Wood (founder of the British "Proms," perennially curious about new musical trends), and Sir Oliver Lodge, the English physicist famous for his ether research, his development of the "coherer" radio wave detector, and his pioneering laboratory demonstration of wireless telegraphy in 1894, even before Marconi. When Cochran extended an invitation to George Bernard Shaw, the crusty G.B.S. wrote back, "By all means, let us have a look in to hear Theremin. I am keen on all these new games."[53] Filling out the audience of two to three hundred were "a row of pretty debutantes," the hotel chef, and a cluster of music critics.

Charles Cochran introduced Theremin, who took his place on stage. To most observers, the instrument suggested "an ordinary wireless valve set" (a radio). Theremin was "a pale young Russian in a black suit"—a "slightly built" and "grave-looking academic young man." Edwin Evans took the floor to deliver the spoken part of the demonstration in English. He "conveyed to the audience the fact that the professor did not claim proficiency as an executant of *music,* and quoted a statement made by the demonstrator that 'A man will come who can play much greater music than I can.' "[54] The *Sunday Times* music critic, Ernest Newman, observed that "the inventor, a dark-haired handsome young man, more like a diffident film star than a scientist, stood bewildered (for he does not understand English) before the bearded experts, while Mr. Edwin Evans explained the manipulation of the instrument, and he looked half startled and nervous when the small distinguished audience laughed at occasional sallies."[55] The inventor walked over to his instrument and "tuned up by a process which to a layman could only be compared to that of a man testing the heat of a boiler with his naked hand."[56] Then, "when Mr. Evans sat down at the piano, and began a soft accompaniment for Schubert's 'Ave Maria,' the nervous, silent young man became more confident."[57] "Theremin, with the music in front of him, gazed at the metal rod and raised his hands."[58] "Then something as sweet as a well-played violin flowed delicately around the gilt and mirrors of the room."[59] "One had almost to rub one's eyes not to see the strings of the violin below the invisible bow which he seemed to be wielding. . . . His right hand was held up with the fingers drawn in to the palm. . . . His left hand meanwhile was occupied in pushing up and down an invisible pump or pedal. As his hand rose so did the volume of noise grow, as it fell so did it decrease."[60]

One journalist remembered, "There was a sort of muffled gasp from those of us who sat in the crowded hall. Sir Oliver Lodge, from whom modern scientific progress holds few secrets, sat up with a jerk. Bernard Shaw, in the front row, gripped more tightly the handle of a big umbrella. For the first time in my experience I saw Arnold Bennett looking surprised."[61] Another listener recalled, "Musicians sat, after the first miraculous opening, with eyes shut, rapt by the timbre of the music. Non-musicians leaned forward with staring eyes, hypnotised by the sight of the fragile, calm young man. . . . Spontaneous applause greeted his first experiment, followed by subdued murmurs of 'How does he do it?' 'Is it a fake?' and 'I hope he's going to play something gay.' He played nothing gay."[62]

Goldberg offered a solo on the earlier model, which was adjusted to the range of a contralto voice. "It was actually a song without words," Newman remarked, "and hinted at a possible thinning of the ranks of women singers."[63] "Professor Theremin then placed a black tube over the rod, and obtained 'cello effects with remarkable fidelity."[64] As a finale, Theremin and Goldberg played Glinka's "Elegy" in duet, accompanied by Evans.

Sir Oliver Lodge jumped to his feet at the end with a tribute to the inventor: "There is nothing miraculous about it. Here we have just the application of known principles applied with great skill. Indeed, I am so impressed by this skill that I am filled with admiration for the professor." Then he confessed, "How he manages to get the loudness I do not know."[65]

On the way out, according to the *Sunday Chronicle*, Bernard Shaw "declined an opinion." Another audience member remarked, "It is a wonderful invention. It has silenced Shaw." But a few days later the *Daily Express* reported: "When Mr. Bernard Shaw heard it at a private concert on Saturday he said that he had heard better noises on a comb covered with tissue paper!"[66]

Opinions at the newsstand ran the gamut. "The human voice, the violin, viola, cello, bass and double-bass, the cornet, horn, trombone, saxophone, organ, and almost every instrument you can think of, are all beaten at their own game by this one simple little apparatus," the correspondent for the *Musical Standard* was convinced.[67] For Ernest Newman, it was "the greatest musical wonder of our time."[68] Others were not so sure. "While Mr. Theremin is a great performer on the air," one critic wrote, "the air does not seem to be a very satisfactory instrument."[69]

The quibble was with the unavoidable "portamento" inherent in the instrument's design, and it came up again and again. It was ironic. The unbroken siren sound resulting from the to-and-fro motion of the right hand in the electrical field allowed the hand to describe any number of increments in the air, chopping an octave of sound into any number of parts, of any size, for the alleged "microtonal" capabilities. But this same "freedom" left the player groping in the air for the very major and minor scale increments already available, ironically, on standard instruments. Traditional music was harder to play than on other instruments. "The performer on the ether cannot, it is obvious, take a clean step from note to note," one critic complained. "No matter how quickly he moves his hand every intermediate sound is heard."[70] This left the instrument vulnerable to poor intonation. The sluggish response made slow music hard enough and fast passages virtually impossible. This also restricted concert selections to slow music—another debit in many critics' eyes. "Furthermore," the reviewer went on, "no note was steadily played—naturally, since it is almost impossible to keep one's hand absolutely still, holding it in the air without support, and the smallest oscillation of the hand causes the ethereal tone to wobble." It all boiled down to "melodious moans" as far as he was concerned.[71] Beyond the sliding between notes, some listeners were also annoyed by the persistent vibrato.

There was another issue as well. "If this new invention gave us the music of the spheres we might forgive the excessive tremolo and portamento, and go to great trouble to acquire the new art," one skeptic wrote. "Alas! It does not make new music but merely plays music that has already been composed."[72] This was a central dilemma for Theremin. Here was his instrument, an ambassador for the music of the future, condemned to repeat the music of the past in an unfair competition with established instruments. At this historical threshold, the guardians of musical tradition had to be convinced on their own terms, and the torchbearers of the avant-garde needed to be persuaded just how unconventional the new instrument was. It would be nearly impossible to please both.

On Monday evening, December 12, at 8:45 P.M. in the Albert Hall, "though that vast building was not nearly full, the audience was large enough to be counted in thousands."[73] Again, Edwin Evans took the speaker's podium and served as accompanist. Theremin, as he had in every demonstration, began with samples of the various timbral capabilities of his instrument. Morsels of "violin," "cello," and "human voice" colorings were demonstrated, and then came "some examples of mere noise . . . highly suggestive of the range of tones obtainable from the 'taming' of the wireless 'howl,'" the *Birmingham Post* reported. "M. Theremin gave us bellows, and moans, and child-like whimperings, and, last of all, a very realistic bleating of sheep."[74] The *Newcastle Journal* reported sounds "like those of a motor-horn and a factory syren. The audience could not refrain from laughing."[75] "Had he chosen to 'take us to the Zoo,'" another columnist suggested, "or to 'imitate a farmyard,' he could have perpetuated the funniest turn in London."[76]

While the audience tittered, few probably realized that in this bleating and whimpering lay the true crux of the issue. The real significance of the instrument was not in the drippy recital of romantic miniatures they were about to hear. The genuine revolution in this technology was that the raw materials of sound were now exposed and could be molded in every dimension. If electricity could beam voices and music through the air and transmit moving images, it could also become an architect with the bricks and mortar of sound itself.

It was this property, and this property alone, that fired up the critics of vision in the major cities. Even the most awestruck and deferential reviewers cautioned that the Thereminvox was not an end in itself, but a first step toward some future horizon. For those who heard only an inferior mockery of a soprano, or a sour cello, there was little point. The composer Ernst Toch, after hearing the instrument in Berlin, summed up the situation:

> The concrete material of music has consisted until now of a limited series of exactly fixed pitches and of a limited series of exactly fixed sound colors. The closer Theremin in his "concert" attempts to come to them . . . to produce them in a deceiving manner, the less interesting his demonstration becomes for the composer. . . . It is of no consequence for the composer whether the tone of the 'cello . . . comes from a real legitimately accepted 'cello or from an imitation of an instrument of any sort. . . . A true substitution cannot be seriously discussed, anyway, because . . . it lacks that variety . . . such as the almost infinite variety of bowings, double stops, pizzicati . . . which unquestionably is bound up in the substance of the instrument. . . . Had a 'cellist or violinist played a whole concert of "heavy" pieces in a cruelly uninterrupted vibrato, it would simply have had an unbearable effect and would in no event have been acceptable by the public with undivided enthusiasm. . . . Its expression remains . . . an insignificant plaything. . . .
>
> But things change if one considers material which, less amusing and interesting for a large audience, lies *between* the fixed pitches and *between* the fixed tone colors; rich, tempting, promising and . . . enchanting for the artist.[77]

Toch admitted that "the audience would have felt only modestly entertained by the sound phenomena, which, before the 'concert' and during the lecture as rough raw material, often similar to animal or climatological sounds of nature, appeared during the 'concert' as uncalled-for byproducts and waste products, hardly having been noticed. Just in those lies the fertile germ of a true new vista which Theremin lays open to the composer of music, still incalculable in its consequences."[78] What Toch found were the ingredients of the synthesizer.

At the same time, the inventor repeatedly undermined his credibility with critics by making exaggerated claims. "Hitherto the composer has had only about twenty tone colors," he had told Waldemar Kaempffert, "represented by as many different types of orchestral instruments. I give him literally thousands of tone colors."[79] It was no wonder some listeners puzzled over this boast when they heard only a handful of actual sounds. While many found the intrinsic tone quality of the instrument monotonous and annoying after a short period of time, the inventor was busy announcing to the *Chicago Tribune* reporter in Paris, "I can produce equally well the sounds of a violin, an alto, or a trumpet. The quality of the sound of my apparatus is even better than that produced by the instruments themselves."[80]

In his U.S. patent application, Theremin claimed that the invention could produce a "realistic imitation of the human voice and various known musical instruments," and he detailed several schemes for timbre control, but only a small sampler of variations was possible in practice.[81] "The inventor controls the tone-colour," an English reviewer noticed, "by a kind of little signal-box on the left of the instrument, making, for example, the sound of a drum a moment after he has been making fiddle sounds."[82] These effects were achieved by using the inherent irregularities in the response curve of the loudspeaker to accentuate different overtones. Filters for this purpose were turned on and off with five switches located on the side of the instrument. But even Givelet had discovered a method to vary tone color and was able to obtain timbres resembling cello, oboe, clarinet, and saxophone, all with a single tube. Mager, of course, had his own designs for timbre.

All of these experiments revealed, in embryo, the virtually infinite tone color resources that would awaken in future synthesizers. Theremin sensed this, but in the meantime he seemed intent on passing off figurative musings as literal capabilities.

For the moment, it was still the consumer, and not the composer, who interested Theremin. If his instrument couldn't literally retire cellos and violins, at least it offered a novel tool for personal expression, and he went to pains to show that the common person—Mager, Givelet, and timbre control aside—could use his "apparatus" as an emotional outlet for interpretive gestures, like conducting in the air, or dancing. Science was beside the point: "It is generally considered that electricity is a symbol of automatic technology and soullessness," Theremin admitted. "This is not surprising. We already have a number of electrically generated instruments to produce tones with various levers and switches. A musical instrument, however, can only be considered in relation to its interaction with the individuality of the artist in producing the work of art."[83]

For his parting European bow, Theremin charmed the Albert Hall crowd with two last displays of legerdemain. One of his pet stunts was to create the illusion that tones were projected from the roof, or the rear of the auditorium. After playing a few bars of music, he would "throw" the next phrase to the far reaches of the hall as an echo, by reversing the current. "It was as perfect an echo," the *Birmingham Post* fancied, "as is obtained in the Albert Hall when bugles are sounded near the organ and other bugles in a far gallery repeat their notes."[84] "It was ventriloquism with a vengeance," another paper jested.[85]

Then, as the first strains of Scriabin's "Etude" rose, hall lights were extinguished and against the black background a prismatic play of light evolved from "gold to green, from green to a misty violet, so that beyond the darkness one could see the colours of the setting sun melting as they might on a stormy sky."[86] The illumovox, thirty feet across the stage from the inventor, projected a beam of light through a rotating disk containing a strip of gelatin tinted with a color spectrum. Notes played in different registers of the Thereminvox triggered the projection of corresponding areas of the color range. Low pitches on the instrument yielded a deep red color; successively higher pitches produced yellows, greens, blues, and violets, shifting through the complete spectrum.

"There were extraordinary scenes at the finish," the *Daily Sketch* reported, "the audience rushing the platform, as at a Kreisler recital, and refusing to go until the professor had played four more pieces." Hangers-on trickled up onto the stage to dabble their hands in the ether wave field. "Edythe Baker played 'My Heart Stood Still,' and everybody recognised what she was playing, which I call very high praise," one observer remarked. "Mrs. Patrick Campbell also tried her hand, but perhaps the most successful of all was Lord Londonderry, who produced some very modern music, which was agreed to be Prokofiev."[87]

The next day, on cue, the press broke ranks along the usual lines. The *Daily Chronicle* was captivated: "M. Theremin caressed the air, patted it quickly, stroked it, worked his fingers through it as if he were crumbling pieces of bread, touched it as if he were plucking the strings of a violin." But ultimately, this reviewer saw alchemy: "If Leo Theremin had lived 500 years ago he would probably have been burnt as a sorcerer. Last night his magic again held enchanted the thousands of people who filled the Albert Hall. He . . . filled the great hall with wistful, ghostly music . . . extraordinary enough to suggest . . . that it might be a tune from another world."[88] Arthur Eaglefield Hull, in the *Monthly Musical Record,* represented the school of impatience: "The tone . . . is of the steam-syren order, and allied to the hooting of the wireless apparatus when 'tuning-in'. . . . The invention represents an interesting scientific advance; but at present it has no value for musicians. In fact, it is only by courteously straining the term that it can yet be described as *music* from the ether."[89] But the levelheaded Ernest Newman, in London's *Sunday Times,* concluded: "The Theremin invention may have results fifty years hence, of which we can at present form no conception. . . . The pity of it, for us of to-day, is that we shall not enter into the Promised Land."[90]

≪ ≫

"Ether Music Inventor Sails Today," the *New York Times* reported by wireless: "LONDON, Dec. 13.—Professor Leo Theremin, the Russian, who has given demonstrations in Berlin, Paris and London of his apparatus for producing music from the ether, sails tomorrow on the Majestic for New York. He expects to spend six weeks in the United States experimenting and making demonstrations."[91] On the pier, London's *Daily News* extracted one last statement:

> Bad News for Burglars.
> Professor Leon Theremin . . . said yesterday when he sailed for New York: "I have also an invention which will give immediate alarm should robbers approach any valuable within its sphere of influence."[92]

According to his plans, the inventor would come back to London in March for two more demonstrations on the invitation of Charles Cochran, and continue on for concerts in Manchester and Glasgow before returning to Berlin and Leningrad. Katia would remain in Paris with her in-laws until the inventor returned from the States. Strangely, her husband's marital status was listed as "single" on the ship's alien passenger manifest.

Goldberg and Theremin enjoyed luxurious, first-class cabin accommodations on the 915-foot White Star liner *Majestic*. Sharing passage with the inventor and his "assistant" were doyens of the world's musical elite: the violinist Joseph Szigeti, the cellist Pablo Casals and the pianist Ignacy Paderewski. Szigeti, who had met Theremin earlier that year in Russia, later recorded a memoir of their on-board encounter:

> Our loungings in the winter garden of the ship, during which the Soviet inventor indulged in the romantic pastime of composing little Russian poems in the form of anagrams, were every so often interrupted by wireless messages bearing some of the biggest industrial and commercial names in America, offering Theremin Caruso-like fees (I distinctly remember one offer of $5,000) for the privilege of a "preview" of the invention during a soiree in their homes or, in the case of a cable signed by the owner of a great department store, in the auditorium of that store. As Theremin and his secretary spoke no English, my wife and I had to convey to him the meaning of all this competition between Chicago's Mr. S., Detroit's Mr. F., and Philadelphia's Mr. W. But all we succeeded in conveying to him was names and figures, which did not seem to interest the young Soviet scientist. . . . However, Theremin, imbued with the socialist ideology, was calmly emphatic in his refusal to consider any of these offers and stuck to the original plan of giving the first demonstration free of charge in the presence of the Press, of noted musicians, scientists, radio engineers, and the like."[93]

By the time Theremin had finished his sweep through Europe, he had accomplished something no one else ever had: he managed to ignite large-scale curiosity and genuine interest in the idea of electrical music. His mounting critical acclaim fed back upon itself like the audion oscillator, continually amplifying his popularity and mystique. His "apparatus" and his public persona managed to inspire poetry, caricatures, political cartoons, newspaper "funnies," and even references in articles on other subjects. A cartoon in London's *Sunday Pictorial,* which hit the newsstands as the inventor strolled the decks of the *Majestic,* bore the heading, "When the Ether Becomes Our Fairy Godmother." "A Professor now produces music from the ether," the caption read. "When the idea is developed we may be able to extract all our wants from it." Cocktails, money, cigarettes, the sketches suggested, would be up for grabs in the ether.[94]

The avalanche of hyperbole from the other side of the Atlantic no doubt sent conflicting, if not intriguing, messages to Americans. "Europe is so baffled and bewildered by Theremin's demonstration that one hears speculation of recovering the sound waves of the eons of the past," one London reporter wrote. "It has even been suggested that the eloquence of Cicero and Demosthenes may be recaptured for all to hear."[95] Emile Vuillermoz, the French musicologist, spoke of the "great pathetic cry of the subjugated wave."[96]

Just what was "Professor Theremin's Music of the Spheres," this "Music Out of Space," "Music without Instruments"? And who was the "Magician of Music"? "Since this revelation," May Birkhead wrote in the *New York Times,* "Paris, artistic and intellectual, mundane and technical, has talked of little else. What can happen when the imagination of Paris is sympathetically aroused was shown in the case of Lindbergh."[97] The commentary ran from the sublime to the ridiculous. One piece of wry London invective compared Theremin's demonstration to Samuel Johnson's remark about the dog who walked on two legs: "he didn't do it very well but the wonder was that he could do it at all." For the same writer, the "moral of it all" was that "even if it became possible to turn the racket of the streets into music, a far more useful invention would be a silencer of sound."[98] To another critic, the instrument called to mind a "drunken violinist playing with a buttered bow."[99]

Reckoned with all this was the comment of the distinguished German musicologist Alfred Einstein, that "in the twentieth century we have, once again, an event similar to when prehistoric man coaxed a tone from a string with his bow. . . . the sound obtained freely out of space is a new phenomenon. It hardly permits comparison."[100]

Steam-syren, or music from another world, the free-enterprise system was next to decide. "An American piano corporation," the *New York Times* revealed, had "offered the youth a large fortune for the rights to his invention. . . . The power of producing beautiful harmony, until now denied all but a few, may soon be within the reach of thousands. . . . The American concern, having examined the instrument, said it is convinced that it can manufacture it in large numbers."[101] The "concern" obviously hadn't consulted with London's *Truth,* which, five days after this *New York Times* announcement, assured readers: "It is obvious that a great deal of further development is necessary, and in the meantime makers of violins, pianofortes, and other musical instruments may sleep undisturbed in their beds."[102]

Nevertheless, the *New York Times* also disclosed that Theremin had been offered a record sum for a single appearance in the United States: thirty-five thousand dollars.[103]

THREE

Capitaliʒm Pluʒ Electrificatiọn

*On the terrace of one of the sky-palace apartment houses with which
our Island of Manhattan will bristle, the New Yorker of the future sits in
the twilight and out of the blue ether plucks his own music—the song of
his day's work accomplished. . . .*

*The music thoughts that well up in every human soul at evening. The
musical impulse—mute through the centuries—articulate at last in
every human creature.*

*Stretch out the hand. Command the ether. . . . A high, thin note,
swelling to grandeur, pulsates from the imagination of the man of the
future. His strife, his sorrow, his overcoming, his longing and his love—
he paints them on the sky.*

—Don Ryan, *New York American,* 1927

Reporters from the major dailies clambered onto the *Majestic* when it docked
for quarantine at Ellis Island on December 20, 1927. Pressmen and sob sisters armed with notepads, slung with cameras, shouldered for the story before the professor hit dry land. New York's Russian community had already
learned from the *Russkaya Gazeta* that the ether instrument "allows you to
play without any training and eliminates the 'monopoly' of professional, well-
trained musicians in the savoring of music."[1] As the liner steamed up the
Hudson, an interpreter juggled a mix of Russian and German. The *New York
Times* observed the scene. "As Professor Theremin sat answering questions
on the Majestic yesterday, with his thin, sensitive face, a small blond mustache
and the intense eyes of a scientist, he was still a modest and almost diffident
physicist and not a world-famous inventor."[2] Every paper wanted a statement
out of him. "He expressed confidence that his technical apparatus will super-
sede all other instruments of music in the home," the *New York Sun* explained."[3] "Someday, he predicted . . . it would be more popular in homes than
the piano is today."[4] "He claims that all persons will soon learn to 'wave their
hands and express their own musical personality, providing they possess a
musical feeling.'"[5] American radio firms, the inventor announced, had already
bid on production of the device. "Of course I hope the apparatus will be man-

ufactured in quantities in the United States, but I am not old enough to worry about the money I may obtain. I am more interested at present in demonstrating my musical discovery, and I hope to test the musical preferences of the American people."[6]

Right off the gangplank on the West Seventeenth Street pier, Theremin was swept up in the rhythm and bustle of the Jazz Age. New York was racing in overdrive near the end of a decade-long party of prosperity. The American dream was rocketing forward, unstoppable—washing machines, automobiles, and the latest fashions were seducing buyers into woozy debt. Consumers were drunk on technology. It was the age of flight. Lindbergh had just landed American pride in Paris. Radio was the focal entertainment in millions of homes, and 1927 had seen the first nationwide broadcasts. RCA Radiola sets were the furniture of choice. *The Jazz Singer* had just inaugurated movie "talkies" with the new Vitaphone bellowing sound into theaters. Babe Ruth and Jack Dempsey carried the nation's athletic torch.

It was the "Era of Wonderful Nonsense," of fads and trivial contests—dance marathons of somnambulant couples staggering around for days; flagpole sitters perched aloft for weeks—and a time of tabloid sensationalism: front-page sex and crime scandals devoured by the public.

But fueling this revelry was a rebellious outrage over Prohibition. Society was one great frat orgy, spitting in the face of every social and moral convention, cultivating the vulgar and the shocking for effect. Flappers with rolled stockings shimmied the Charleston; free love and uninhibited self-expression captivated the young—smoking, petting, foul language, and swilling hip flasks of bathtub gin in public; "sheiks" and "shebas" caroused in New York's thirty-two thousand speakeasies ("whoopee parlors"); college boys in raccoon coats cruised around in Stutz Bearcats or Model T flivvers. Gangsters and mob violence ruled the bootleg empire. Al Capone pulled in nearly sixty million dollars in 1927, mostly from beer sales, while political listlessness allowed government corruption to go unchecked. New York's "playboy" mayor, Jimmy Walker, addicted to racetracks, nightclubs, and the affections of Broadway showgirls—as his job atrophied—nonetheless won reelection from a hedonistic, free-spending population for whom he was a role model. It was a mad euphoria, a devil-may-care highlife bred from cynicism, boredom, and restlessness. Living for the moment was everything.

Against thoughts of Bolshevik sobriety back home, Theremin walked these streets, past young women with bobbed hair and cloche hats, and boxy black motorcars looking like their carriage forebears, sounding heavy klaxons: "ow-OO-ga!"

At the Hotel Biltmore, the inventor's arrival was attended by a crush of reporters and dignitaries. "This 'prodigieux physicien,' as he was named in Paris," the *New York American* beamed,

> stood beside his invention in his hotel bedroom, surrounded by gentlemen in morning coats with ribbons in their buttonholes, with monocles in their eyes, with enthusiastic words on their lips in French, German and Russian. Professor Theremin is a blushing boy, modest, pink of cheek, blue-eyed and curly-haired.
>
> Polite to everybody. Polite enough to pose precariously on the roof of the Biltmore for the photographers. . . . It couldn't be explained to him in French or Russian either that the visitor to America is expected to do a hula or climb a flagpole to make a snappy picture.
>
> The distinguished-looking gentlemen who besieged the modest young inventor in his suite, testified to the swift recognition by this mechanics-loving country of a machine hailed as greater than radio. The gentlemen were there to date up the professor for demonstrations, concert tours, all varieties of American exhibitions.
>
> Rudolph Wurlitzer, who had hurried up from Cincinnati, bubbling in German about getting Edison right over to meet him. Morris Gest exclaiming that at last a "real miracle has been produced." Violently excited Russian reporters gesticulating. Arrangements being made to demonstrate in Washington before President Coolidge and a group of distinguished scientists. Musicians and composers paying tribute. The union of science and art—the gift of one extremely futuristic country to another.[7]

"First of all," the inventor indicated in Russian to the reporter for *Novoye Russkoye Slovo,* "I am not 'Tair-uh-MEEN.' I wrote my name with French letters for French pronunciation. I am Lev Sergeyevich Tair-MEN." He was being careful. The correspondent could be an operative. "The report in American newspapers that I was offered 35,000 dollars for one performance in Carnegie Hall is not true."[8] The English-speaking press, meanwhile, titillated the public: "Russian Inventor Arrives with Magic Musical Wand."[9] "A musical device which may eliminate radio, phonographs and all other musical instruments, was demonstrated this week by Leo Theremin."[10]

Several days later, the inventor left for Washington, D.C., where his instruments and thirteen boxes of tools had been sent on. At the Hotel Washington he set up a temporary lab and residence to conduct research and prepare for his New York debut in January.

In the capital there was no Soviet embassy, nor was there a consulate in New York. Russia had no formal diplomatic relations with the United States, and the situation was unlikely to improve in the near future. But the Soviets had gained a foothold on American soil anyway by beating the capitalists at their own game. The U.S., though wary of conceding political recognition to the Kremlin, saw every advantage in a business relationship, based on the conviction that a vast untapped market for American goods existed in Russia.

In 1921, the U.S. businessman Armand Hammer set events in motion when he formed the Allied-American Corporation (Almerico), the first American entity to do business with the USSR. By 1924 he was representing Russian commercial interests for thirty-seven major U.S. companies. In May 1924, Almerico merged with two small Soviet firms in New York to form the Amtorg Trading Corporation, the first Soviet-run trading organization in the United States, modeled after Arcos and Wostwag.

While it conducted millions of dollars of legitimate business in the United States, Amtorg—an acronym for "American Trading Organization"—was, in reality, the command center for all Soviet intelligence activities in America. Located in New York, as a check-in point and routing station for Russian agents, it took the place of an embassy or diplomatic legation, but it was better. Its commercial infrastructure disguised its motives; it provided its own funding channels; any exposed acts of espionage would pale in the light of the immense profits generated for American business; and under the pretext of testing potential U.S. exports to the Soviet Union, it could gain unlimited access to American manufacturing plants for industrial espionage. Beyond that, it provided a cover for a vast, always changing pool of employees, many of them agents on temporary missions in the United States.

Amtorg harbored three spheres of activity. The Comintern, in league with the CPUSA (the American Communist Party), masterminded propaganda and revolutionary agitation, channeling funds into local Communist-run unions and organizations such as the *Daily Worker* and the *Daily Freiheit;* the OGPU kept a check on counterintelligence and party loyalty within the network of operatives; and the GRU supervised the siphoning of data on U.S. military technology and American industry. Theremin's "little extra assignment," of course, came under this banner.

≪ ≫

"An invisible plectrum, sounding the music of the 'spheres,' will come true in New York next Tuesday evening with the first American demonstration of the 'ethereal music' of professor Leo Theremin," the syndicated columnist Lemuel F. Parton announced.[11] On January 24, 1928, a parade of illustrious New York gentry, glitterati, and cultural luminaries, streaming out of taxis and limousines, climbed the steps of the Hotel Plaza and headed toward the Grand Ballroom for an 8:30 P.M. demonstration. Rudolph Wurlitzer had mobilized the group, under whose "auspices" Theremin would make his private U.S. debut: Mr. and Mrs. Vincent Astor, Mr. and Mrs. Edsel Ford, Mr. and Mrs. Charles S. Guggenheimer, Mr. and Mrs. Fritz Kreisler, Mr. and Mrs. Herbert N. Straus, Mr. Walter Damrosch, Mr. Felix Warburg, and a host of others. As the five hundred invited guests took their seats in the ballroom, many well-known faces were among them: Arturo Toscanini, Sergei Rachmaninoff, Joseph Szigeti, Cleveland Orchestra conductor Nikolai Sokoloff, and Metropolitan Opera soprano Elisabeth Rethberg.

Up front, on a small stage, the instruments were assembled on tables against a black velvet curtain backdrop. Three green loudspeakers—inverted triangles perched on high poles, like great capital "Y"s—stood guard behind. Following the customary script, the inventor watched in silence while his explanation was read to the audience:

> I consider my work as completely realistic as that of a road builder who must encounter and overcome the difficulties of the rough surfaces to pave a new highway. The technical equipment of music still remains far behind the practical applications of science that have become an accustomed part of our daily life. . . . In music the antiquity of the instrument seems to be regarded as the nearest approach to the ideal. Crude and humble materials serving as the strings of the subtle viola or the noble 'cello, and the long hair from the horse's tail stretched the length of a violin bow, are considered as necessary in music as the electric light, the telephone or the automobile in our everyday life. This address and its accompanying demonstrations may in some degree affect, and even unsettle, such traditional lines of thought.
>
> The triangular apparatus standing before you resembles the loud speakers that are used for the amplification of sound in large halls. . . . By using an alternating current of suitable frequency, tones of varying pitch are secured without difficulty and it has long been possible to produce the entire audible scale by means of these currents.[12]

Schubert's "Ave Maria" opened the program as usual, followed by a Scriabin "Etude," Rimsky-Korsakoff's "Song of India," and works of Offenbach, Saint-Saëns, and Mattheson. "Like an orchestra of humans," the *New York Evening Post* observed,

> this electric instrument several times last night got out of hand, out of Professor Theremin's hands. He began to play Rubinstein's "Night" and there was only a protesting squawk.
>
> He twisted little levers on his left and mixed a more pleasing formula. Docile, his musical wand resumed the melody, lifting notes higher and louder.[13]

"I'd like to know how he does it," a woman in silver lamé whispered to her escort. "I don't know," he replied, "but he's better than Thurston," referring to the contemporary magician.[14] Theremin placed a bowl of colorless liquid before the audience and caused it to pass through the colors of the spectrum by infusing it with varying electric waves. Then he positioned the illumovox to play a spotlight across his face, training over his cheeks the melding rays of "wine red" and "successively blue, yellow and emerald green." "When he switched the electric current and tossed an echo to the back of the room," the *New York Evening Post* reviewer noticed, "people turned their heads incredulously and Rosamond Pinchot, who had been leaning ecstatically on a balcony rail, hastily put on a pair of tortoise-shell glasses." Theremin startled the audience when he played on his "invisible orchestra" music-stand model.[15]

"The novelty wore off to some extent under the long succession of parlor pieces." Someone heard Rachmaninoff caution a woman after her "bravo": "Madame, you exaggerate!" One reviewer thought the instrument's tone suggested "a phonograph's nasal ennui." Another heard "the humming of a giant who could hum exquisitely enough." "About half the audience left before the program was over." Theremin and Goldberg closed with their traditional duet of Glinka's "Elegy."[16]

Musicians collected in an anteroom afterward to greet Theremin. Rachmaninoff put his arm around the inventor. The instrument had a "unique timbre," he admitted. He hoped to experiment with it. Toscanini expressed a desire to try it as well. "A singer is limited by his lung capacity," Szigeti suggested, "and a violinist by the length of his bow, but there is no limitation on this instrument. I have practiced on it and played on it," he told the gathering. "It is not easy to learn. There are no rules or forms. You put your hand in one position. If the sound is wrong, you change its position. It is all empirical. As it stands today, the musician must work out his technique for himself."[17]

Elisabeth Rethberg bubbled with praise: "I believe it has a great future in music. It was surprising to me to find that it had no mechanical tone. It seemed to have a soul. I could sing with it in duet. I was amazed."[18]

Lawrence Gilman registered the first press appraisal in the *New York Herald Tribune:* "It was as close to a miracle as anything we have ever witnessed," he estimated. Gilman christened the instrument the "Theremophone" (in Europe it had mostly been dubbed "the apparatus") and wrote that it showed "actual and potential virtues of a breath-taking sort. . . . There were tones produced last night . . . that were of so mysterious and otherworldly a beauty, a musical quality so alembicated and enchanting, that one's imagination leaped wildly in contemplating their possibilities."[19] "What is before us now," Olin Downes said in the *New York Times,* "is a successful scientific experiment which unfolds new and dazzling horizons for a future that should certainly have much to do with music."[20] Theremin must have breathed a sigh of relief. He had survived the leap through his first American hoop.

Next was to be a concert at the Metropolitan Opera House—his official public debut—scheduled to take place one week later, on January 31. The Rudolph Wurlitzer Company of Cincinnati was the sponsor: "The House of Wurlitzer, with over two hundred years of experience in building musical instruments, has interested itself in the introduction of this marvelous invention, and the occasion also marks the debut of the Wurlitzer Concert Grand."[21]

But one day before the event, Theremin was caught off guard. "The 'musical instrument' by which M. Leon Theremin . . . literally pulls sweet sounds from the air," the *New York Post* explained, "is really an American invention, according to a statement issued today by Dr. Frank E. Miller of 17 West Fifty-fourth Street."[22] "I admire the great skill which has been shown by Professor Theremin," Miller told the *New York Times*, "but he has done nothing which has not been covered by my fundamental patents."[23] Miller, an ear, nose, and throat specialist, claimed he had discovered the principle in 1910 and had patented an apparatus based on the idea in 1921. "Acting under the advice of my patent counsel," he told the *New York American,* "and merely to protect my interests, I have been compelled to notify Mr. Theremin that his instrument is an infringement upon my patent entitled: '*Electrical System for Producing Musical Tones' which was issued to me by the United States Patent Office, under date of April 26, 1921, No. 1,376,228.*"[24] Sniffing a delicious scandal, the *New York American* wasted no time: "Where there should be music in the air there is static on the ether," the paper goaded. "Dr. Frank E. Miller . . . who drags canzoni from the air by pushing a little doofunny on the gadgets that connect up with the thingumys on the radio, and who wrings compelling melodies from the dinguses that are hooked up to the coils, is peeved. Peeved is colloquial for perturbe. . . . M. Theremin is accused by Mr. Miller of . . . producing thereby what might be called bootleg music."[25]

Miller had performed maintenance on the throats of many Metropolitan Opera stars and, as a singer himself, had made a study of the voice, which led to his own voice production method—"Vocal art-science." This research, he said, resulted in the invention of his instrument. One variation of the apparatus was an "audiometer" sounding a range of tones above and below audibility that was sold as a physicians' gauge for testing hearing. In this form, he admitted, it had no musical applications.

But his original model, he insisted, could "supplement an orchestration, because it gave out peculiarly high and low notes impossible of attainment by any other known musical instrument."[26] He was confident it could rival the church organ, but because it "could be used to replace orchestras entirely," his conscience hadn't allowed him to "interfere with the symphony and concert orchestras of the world."[27]

Theremin issued a swift rebuttal: "I have known of Dr. Miller's patent ever since it has been public. It is a step in the series of inventions tending toward electrification of musical acoustics. This tendency we have observed continuously ever since the beginning of the development of electro-technical science—throughout the past half century."[28] The *New York American* put it less delicately: "M. Leon Theremin, the young Russian who last Tuesday night sprang into fame by poking sonatas out of the ether and pulling arias of surpassing sweetness from apparently nothing at all, is perturbe. Perturbe, by the way, is bad French for hot under the collar. . . . M. Theremin . . . declares that Mr. Miller's patents have little to do with art, and nothing at all to do with the manner in which the air is made to sing high C by his method."[29] Conceding nothing to Miller, Theremin nevertheless told the *New York Times*, "I am happy to be able to acknowledge my indebtedness to the long line of work that has been done in the field of technique before me. Without it, the continued progress would be impossible."[30]

But if any American had a legitimate claim to ether music, it was Lee De Forest, and not Miller. Experimenting in his laboratory as early as 1915, De Forest had found that with audion bulbs he could obtain "a succession of musical notes, clear and sweet, of surprising volume, the pitch and timbre of which can be varied almost at will to imitate any musical tone of an orchestra. Here, then, in the laboratory we have for the first time the music of the lamps."[31] That year, De Forest filed for a patent on an *Electrical Means for Producing Musical Notes* and built a rudimentary instrument using audio frequency oscillators to produce up to eight separate pitches from each bulb. Long before Givelet and Mager, De Forest discovered that "the pitch of the notes is very easily regulated by changing the capacity or the inductance in the circuits, which can very readily be effected by a sliding contact or simply by turning the knob of the condenser."[32] In 1915, he also realized that "the pitch of the notes can be changed by merely putting the finger on certain parts of the circuit or even by holding the hand close to parts of the circuit. In this way, weird and beautiful effects can be obtained with ease."[33] Years later, in *Father of Radio,* De Forest even claimed he had experimented with the heterodyne method in 1915 as well, discovering a system that was "the original precursor of the Theremin."[34] De Forest proposed an "audion piano," but in the end, he left the realization of these ideas to others, saying only, "The idea of producing beautiful musical tones by an entirely new method unknown to all our great composers and perhaps offering to future composers new fields for their genius, has truly captivated me."[35]

But Miller, in any case, had little on Theremin. His patent, filed on March 18, 1915, barely a month before De Forest's, described a simple device for generating tones from an audion bulb. It made no reference to the space-control method or the heterodyne system, nor did it offer any possibility for timbre or volume control. The design was set up to produce damped oscillations and utilized an audio, as opposed to radio, frequency scheme.

On the afternoon of January 29, a delegation of reporters gathered on the top floor of Miller's home to assess his apparatus—an instrument with twenty-four keys. The *New York American* found its sound reminiscent of the Thereminvox, but decided that "Professor Miller's device appeared more akin to a descendant of the original typewriter, which had married into the family of the early pioneer washing machines, and risen, so to speak, to the association of the modern radios."[36]

Miller had originally intended to seek an injunction restraining Theremin from appearing at the Metropolitan Opera, but he must have thought better of it. He told reporters, "I do not intend to make any trouble, but I want my fundamental rights recognized."[37]

Ironically for Miller, the sparring in the newspaper drew even larger numbers of curiosity seekers to the Met box office. At prices ranging from $1.10 for single seats in the Family Circle to $55.00 Parterre boxes for eight, the hall quickly sold out, and latecomers were hustled into "an operatically packed horseshoe of standees."[38]

The American music critic and author Sigmund Spaeth served as master of ceremonies and read the inventor's talk:

> No matter how attractive may be the possibility of producing sound with the help of electricity, its application is determined by the direct connection of sounds with the performer and their complete subjugation to his personality. . . . I would not for a moment suggest calling your attention to the idea of utilizing electricity in art, if I were of the opinion that the part it plays must remain limited to the producing of lifeless tones, but I visualize great possibilities in connection with the problem of controlling sound by the simple movement of the hands in the air. This movement . . . makes available not only the expressive power of existing musical instruments but perhaps a greater variety and a greater range of expression than we have thus far even imagined.[39]

"The audience during the preliminary demonstrations was like a child with a new toy," the *New York Sun* reported, "each squeak and rasp, so like they hear on their radios, causing much amusement and some gestures of the well-known pooh-pooh of superiority. When, however, the professor finally tuned his tone to his own satisfaction and produced a clear musical note, amusement was replaced by wonder and spontaneous applause. . . . Whether they agreed that his discovery would eventually junk the Strads and horns and replace them with waving hands, they were pleased, entertained and a bit awed."[40] But the writer for the *New York Post,* was not amused:

In a mechanical age, when the ear for music is being blunted by the raucous and generally dreadful noises on the earth, under the earth and above the earth, and when the taste for beautiful music is being debased by all manner of mechanical substitutes for the reality, it may be that this thing will find public favor just as it is.

On the other hand, the persons whose joy in music is so profound that they regret the radio will merely wait and hope for the best. A few hundreds of years ago Professor Theremin would have been condemned for performing black magic. In the minds of some music lovers today he still has to prove himself innocent.[41]

One audience member, in a letter to the editor of the *New York World*, was ready with a verdict:

With regard to this machine which has been invented by Prof. Leo Theremin . . . I must say it did not interest me much. . . . But with regard to the professor himself I was enormously interested. Such earnestness, such solemn awe, such reverence, almost of a religious quality, in the face of what was in essence a glorified kazoo struck me as pathetic to a fabulous degree. He stood at attention while a gentleman read, in translation, an "address" composed by himself, an address that was compounded of every childish platitude ever uttered on the subject of music; and as he stood there his face bore the rapt expression of a father at the baptism of his first-born. Then he proceeded to demonstrate the possibilities of his invention. . . . And as he pattered about doing these things he displayed all the gravity of an agent for a vacuum cleaner showing how it will pick up dirt, clean rugs, dust books and remove cobwebs from the ceiling. And after all this he played a program, looking more spirituelle than Jascha Heifetz when he plays Brahms. . . .

Through all of it he was so sincere that he made my head ache. The futility of it was simply colossal. Did Anatole France still live he would make this young man immortal.[42]

On the night following the Met demonstration, Theremin was feted at a private reception and dance hosted by Brigadier General and Mrs. Cornelius Vanderbilt at their Fifth Avenue home, toasted by a guest list of prominent scientists. The next evening Goldberg and Theremin performed at the Engineering Club Building on Thirty-ninth Street as part of a Russian cultural exposition sponsored by the American Society for Cultural Relations with Russia. "Dr. Lee De Forest, inventor of the audion tube, was present," the *New York Times* reported, "and congratulated Professor Theremin on the success of his demonstration. He said the inventor had used vacuum tubes for an artistic purpose. The artistic possibilities of the Theremin Vox are tremendous, once its use is taken up by musicians, he said."[43]

In February, Theremin transferred his lab and residence to New York, relocating to the Hotel Plaza Annex, 24 West Fifty-ninth Street. Gradually, the elements for commercial manufacture of his equipment were coming together. RCA invited him to make a private demonstration for its engineers, and on the fourteenth of the month, his radio watchman was officially approved as U.S. patent number 1,658,953—"signalling apparatus." That same evening, he made his Carnegie Hall debut. "The American press has already opened its columns to him," the program booklet declared, "and now the highest tribunal of all, the American public, is to judge his service to science and art."[44] For the occasion, Goldberg added a new work to the repertoire: Stephen Foster's "Old Kentucky Home."

By the end of the month, the inventor was ready to venture out on a sort of American agitprop tour sponsored by Rudolf Wurlitzer. Each metropolitan appearance would follow the tried-and-true formula: a small, private demonstration to whet the appetite of prominent musicians, scientists, and social leaders (and stir up local press coverage), echoed by a major public spectacle at a well-known hall.

In Philadelphia, a Locust Street drawing-room demonstration on the twenty-seventh was the prelude to a large show at the Academy of Music on March 1. "For a few moments . . . last night," the *Philadelphia Record* related, "it seemed as though one of those creatures of fable who summon the thunder and lightning of the skies to earth, and make music while the lightning splits into the hues of the rainbow, were in fact upon the stage. . . . The audience was as enthusiastic as any audience can be that is keyed to that tension which divides the old from the new—which is in the presence of something that may replace all the musical instruments now extant, or may be a mere momentary curiosity soon to be a blight among the inventor's hopes."[45]

Between the two Philadelphia appearances, the application for the space-control instrument, "method of and apparatus for the generation of sounds," was approved as U.S. patent number 1,661,058, on February 28. Apparently the patent examiners found no conflict with Dr. Miller's device.

But lest Theremin become too complacent in his triumph, the *Philadelphia Evening Public Ledger* turned up yet another pretender to the throne—an expatriate Russian inventor named Ivan Eremeeff, living in a "dilapidated old building in an obscure little street between 5th and 6th in Philadelphia."[46] Eremeeff, a pioneer in helicopter research, claimed he had experimented daily, for four years, with "the parent invention of the Theremin device," which he claimed would "be capable not only of producing music but musical tones such as are produced by any of the great artists—and not only music but odors and light beams—and conversely, capable of annihilating sound, absorbing it, transforming it into silence."[47]

The theory was based on the notion that "every sound, every odor, every light beam possesses its own wave length." If each wave length is "known and charted, reproductions of such sounds, odors and lights are possible by the oscillation of a vibrating surface similar to the radio loud speaker."[48]

Eremeeff explained that by using two keyboards, documented wave forms of individual artists could be simulated. In the case of an onion, he postulated, "Having first obtained, by contact with the original, the specific wave length of the onion's odor, the mere setting of the tone keyboard to conform with the odor chart of the onion and 'playing' on the bottom keyboard to regulate the pitch of the vibrating surface, would reproduce the smell of the onion . . . with lifelike faithfulness."[49] Eremeeff imagined an odor instrument adding another dimension to the filmgoer's experience. But the parting shot in the article described Theremin's instrument as "capable of producing the sound of a single instrument or voice at one time, whereas, by referring to charts of known instrumental wave lengths and setting his tone keyboard accordingly, Eremeeff claims to be able to produce the music of any desired combination of instruments."[50]

Back on the road, Theremin passed through Akron, Ohio, where a private showing preceded a public event at the armory. In Cleveland, newspapers ran photos of the inventor coaching the president of the Cleveland Advertising Club through a shot at space-control performance. "They waved their hands . . . announcing that they were playing 'Home Sweet Home,'" the *Plain Dealer* joshed. "It sounded more like a cross between 'The Arkansas Traveler' and the anvil chorus from 'Il Trovatore.'"[51] "Nothing more than the educated squeal of an untuned radio," another caption called it and then added, "The music produced is equal to the finest violin or the cello."[52]

In the ballroom of Chicago's Stevens Hotel on March 12, after a demonstration, Frederick Stock, conductor of the Chicago Symphony, took a "lesson" on the instrument as a stunt for photographers and spectators. "Mr. Stock," the *Chicago Post* reported, "after a vain attempt to play 'That's My Baby' uninstructed, quickly grasped the principles of the instrument after a few pointers by Prof. Theremin and played two or three simple melodies."[53] Before the public demonstration at Orchestra Hall on the eighteenth, the *Chicago Daily Tribune* announced, "One of these days you will be able to pour out your soul in whatever melody happens to appeal to you at the moment, not through the severe, expensive, and laborious drudgery of learning to sing or play the violin or piano but merely by standing in front of a box on your desk and waving your arms gracefully to and fro."[54]

A demonstration in Detroit's Orchestra Hall on March 21 inspired a full-page story on the front page of the *Detroit Free Press*. After lauding the latest wonder of transatlantic telephone conversation and the marvel of a recent television demonstration by Ernst F. W. Alexanderson, the writer declared,

"Now comes Leon Theremin, slim new genius just 31 years old. . . . He has provided two continents with 1928's greatest novelty by extracting music from the ether."[55]

After the demonstration, when the crowd had emptied out, Theremin remained on stage in a darkened Orchestra Hall at midnight, conversing in German with the Detroit Symphony Orchestra conductor, Ossip Gabrilowitsch, and the cellist Hans Kindler. A reporter asked about the cost of the device as a consumer item: "The Russian smiled a bit over the question. 'It depends largely on the general popularity of the instrument,' he responded. 'If it becomes a household thing, it may be one price. If it becomes something for the wealthy, the manufacturer probably will put it in a lovely cabinet with pictures on the panels and charge handsomely. This present arrangement could be duplicated for between $50 and $100.'"[56]

"Music, of course, is but one of the applications of the principle," he continued, describing a divining rod he had invented, capable, he claimed, of accurately detecting certain ores up to a thousand feet underground. It was being used in Russia, he revealed, in connection with rock salt and in archaeological work. Theremin also told the group about his airplane altimeter. "The present barometers of airplanes," one writer that evening learned, "are notoriously unreliable. . . . Below 1,000 feet it is virtually impossible for a flier to tell, except by sight, how close he is to the ground, and the disadvantages of night flying under such conditions are obvious."[57] Theremin told his listeners how his equipment had been installed on various makes of airplanes in Russia and had proved dependable in alerting pilots to their altitude, even if the reading was taken only a foot off the ground.

Getting back to music, Gabrilowitsch ruminated on the Thereminvox. "Its possibilities are limitless. What will happen to orchestra music as now played? What startles me is that it should have been invented in my lifetime. That interests me more than what its application will be 100 years from now."[58]

Working his way back east, Theremin capped off his tour with appearances at Cornell University, the Brooklyn Polytechnical Institute, and a finale on March 29 at the Brooklyn Academy of Music.

By now his three months were up. He had "tested the musical preferences of the American people" and attracted the attention of industrial concerns. But everything he had to show for himself remained on paper. On May 21, in his first letter to the Physico-Technical Institute since November 29, he wrote:

Although I constantly supply information and stay in contact with the local Amtorg, etc., about all my steps in this direction, I would like the Institute to take into consideration the circumstance that in this case the inventor is a citizen of the U.S.S.R. and that is quite new for America. As a result, I have a lot of difficulties in my activity, and it does not move as fast as I would like. On the other hand, I am absolutely sure that my staying here will bring not only use for my future work in the U.S.S.R., because of my acquaintance with American industry and its working conditions, but also it presents a corresponding material interest for the Institute. . . .

I suppose that my staying here for the period of 2 to 3 months will allow me to accomplish what was planned, that is why I ask the Institute, and if it is necessary in further instances, to count the prolonging of my stay abroad as a valid reason.[59]

It was clear he could not wrap up his business and head back to Leningrad—things were only beginning. His six-month temporary visitor's visa had expired, and he would have to apply for an extension. He was comfortably settled in his Hotel Plaza Annex lab, and the prospect of commercial liaisons, in particular, made it difficult to establish a time frame for departure. Katia, who had waited out the spring in Paris, anticipating his return, would sail for America now, over the summer.

《》

In July, writers for two New York Communist organs, A. B. Magil, of the *Daily Worker*, and William Abrams, of the *Daily Freiheit*, dropped in on the inventor for a feature story. "Prof. Leon Theremin led the way into the modestly furnished bedroom of his suite at the Plaza Hotel," Magil wrote.

It sounds a little incongruous to call him professor—he looks so boyish. Tall and slender, with close-cropped brownish-blond hair and a small mustache, he looks several years younger than his almost thirty-two. His face is sensitive—the face of an artist rather than a scientist—and he looks at you out of two soft blue-gray eyes behind which there lies something cool and strong. . . . Theremin is both friendly and reserved, modest yet assured, a person who is evidently intent on his work in a clear, resolute fashion. . . .

He told us of his work, work that never ends. I noticed that every room in his suite is a laboratory. Even in the bedroom where we were sitting odd-looking instruments were installed. And as we talked strange, ethereal sounds came out of the room next door; a familiar melody in unfamiliar tones: a pupil of his was practicing on the new ether-music instrument.[60]

The pupil was Alexandra Stepanoff, Theremin's first student on U.S. soil—a young, recent immigrant to America. Slender and graceful, with delicate features, dark, smartly cropped hair, and an assured smile, she was reminiscent of the very young Garbo. In Russia she had been a concert singer and now, under the professor's spell, she fluently transferred her vocal technique to the ether instrument. Alexandra had come to the inventor's attention through the network of New York's Russian community with which he had surrounded himself, and along with Goldberg she became one of the first disciples of the instrument.

"I have about thirty pupils now whom I am instructing in the art of producing this new music," he told Abrams. "Eventually, when they are fully trained, they will constitute an orchestra that will be able to give concerts such as have never been heard before." Magil reflected on Theremin as "the scientist who has come out of the pain and turmoil of the greatest of revolutions" and concluded, "it is evident that the Soviet Union is close to Prof. Theremin's heart." Then he got to the point:

> At the concerts that Prof. Theremin has thus far given in this country he has appeared before audiences composed largely of scientific and musical experts and the wealthy bourgeoisie. The workers, the great toiling masses who have heard so much of the achievements of this great discoverer, have been unable to hear him because of forbidding prices. But the tables will be turned at the great concert tomorrow evening at Coney Island Stadium where Prof. Theremin will perform. There are not likely to be many members of the wealthy bourgeoisie there. Instead there will be some 25,000 workers listening under the open sky to a new music drawn out of the air by the representative of a new culture at a proletarian music fest arranged jointly by The DAILY WORKER and the Freiheit.

Theremin "expressed gratification that he was able to bring his new music to the American masses in this fashion," and the paper added, "Theremin's appearance tomorrow will be one of his last in this country."[61]

As the interviewers got up to leave, Magil reported, "In the next room the girl was still playing, her hands trembling over the mysterious instrument. Theremin shook hands with us warmly as we left and his soft blue eyes escorted us to the door."

In another article, the *Daily Worker* warned readers that tickets for "the greatest proletarian music event ever held in this country . . . have been selling so fast that it is likely that the demand will surpass the supply. Workers who want to make sure of not missing this event of the century should therefore buy their tickets at once at the office of The DAILY WORKER, 16–28 Union Square." The concert, scheduled for Saturday, July 14—to coincide with Bastille Day—was rained out. "Since the weather on Saturday took such a counter-revolutionary turn," the paper explained, "the great . . . concert . . . has been postponed until next Saturday evening."[62]

On July 21, the event went on. The paper confirmed, "20,000 at Huge Coney Concert; Great Throng Applauds Theremin." Despite a light drizzle through a portion of the concert, "Twenty thousand workers jammed Coney Island Stadium Saturday night . . . for more than three hours."[63] The spectacle centered around a fifty-piece light symphonic orchestra conducted by Arnold Volpe, playing works of Meyerbeer, Wagner, Bizet, and Tchaikovsky, and later lending support to the Roxy Ballet, directed by A. Nelle (former partner of Pavlova), in "Russian and oriental dances." Theremin, the "star of the evening," the "hero of the evening," was "reserved for the climax of the evening's entertainment." He "astounded the vast audience" with Rubinstein's "Night" and Scriabin's "Etude," with piano accompaniment, and Goltermann's *Concerto in A Minor* and the Saint-Saëns "Swan," backed by the orchestra.

But the musical revue was a trimming around the main agenda—a rally by the American Communist Party. Alexander Trachtenberg, a high-ranking CPUSA officer and the manager of International Publishers, the official U.S. Communist book publisher, addressed the crowd, hailing Theremin as "a representative of the new Soviet culture."[64] Then Trachtenberg handed the floor over to Benjamin Gitlow, acting secretary of the CPUSA. Gitlow, a one-time Socialist member of the New York State legislature, was freshly out of jail after serving time for advocating the overthrow of the government. Bellowing to the great assembly, he "riddled the political pretensions of Herbert Hoover and pointed out his role as a faithful servant of Wall St." When Gitlow praised a recent Soviet maritime rescue, "the huge stadium rocked with applause. 'The heroic rescue achieved by these citizens of the first workers' and peasants' republic,' he said, 'is a refutation of the slanders of the capitalist press concerning the Soviet Union. In the future they will be compelled to hesitate before they write their lies about "Bolshevik barbarism."'" An appeal for donations after the concert, from Trachtenberg—himself a major beneficiary of Amtorg funds—"resulted in a generous response."[65]

On July 27, Katia arrived in New York from Cherbourg as a second-class passenger on the *Aquitania*. The months she sat out in Paris had kept her from completing the last semesters of her five-year program at the Medical Institute, and now, short of a diploma and coasting on a temporary visitor's visa, she would have to forage for any menial jobs open in the medical field. Her relationship with Theremin had cooled, and once she arrived, the two lived apart—she in New Jersey, where a job had come up. In a dispassionate arrangement, the couple agreed to rendezvous every few weeks.

A chance to perform outdoors for the great masses of the bourgeoisie came on August 27, when the inventor made his official American orchestral debut. The open-air concert at New York's Lewisohn Stadium, with the New York Philharmonic-Symphony Orchestra, also brought together a full quartet of his instruments for the first time—a miniature prototype of his full electrical orchestra.

Because New York City papers patently boycotted Communist events, the

Coney Island concert was missing from the newsprint paper trail. In any case, hoping to downplay the political ramifications, the inventor took the safe route. "This will be the first time that the novelty music producer will have been heard out of doors here," the *New York Times* announced.[66] Several days before the concert Theremin told reporters, "I consider the performance at the Stadium the most important I have ever undertaken. Although it is not my first orchestral appearance, nor my first concert out of doors, I have never before played in an auditorium as large as the Stadium nor with an organization that is as complete and renowned as the combined orchestra. I believe that the concert will demonstrate that ether music, because of its unlimited volume and variety of shading, is happily suited to the demands of open air concerts."[67] To complete a quartet, Theremin assembled Goldberg, Alexandra Stepanoff, and a "Mr. Olgin." Moissaye Olgin, a Russian emigrant and leading Jewish Communist, was editor of the *Freiheit* and an active member of the CPUSA. Both as an agent for the *Freiheit* and as an individual, he was generously funded by Amtorg.

Theremin and his ensemble manned instruments approximating the ranges of the violin, viola, cello, and double bass. Rehearsals were arranged mostly for the benefit of the orchestra, to acclimate their ears to the new instruments.

Before an audience of twelve thousand, under an open sky, the group performed four selections with the orchestra: Rachmaninoff's "Vocalise" with one instrument, using the timbre of a human voice; Mozart's "Ave Verum" with two instruments; the Saint-Saëns "Swan" with four instruments; and Handel's "Largo" from *Xerxes*, also with the full quartet. The sound, projected out over the musicians' heads through the towering triangular speakers, easily over-whelmed the orchestra in places. "The loud, full tones, with a radio sound similar to a movie theatre vitaphone," noted the *New York Times*, "insisted on acting as the leader for all the musicians, somewhat to the annoyance of the concertmaster and the chagrin of Mr. van Hoogstraten, the usual conductor. But the orchestra always came in strong with the closing bars and generously applauded with the audience. . . . In its first hearing in the open air [the quartet] showed possibilities of practically unlimited volume, tonal color and considerable flexibility." For the public, the honeymoon hadn't ended, and Theremin's performance "was followed by five minutes of persistent applause that brought the rather constrained young Russian back for a half dozen bows."[68]

Theremin closed out his 1928 season with a concert in Boston on October 7. Attendance in Symphony Hall was disappointing. Nicolas Slonimsky, writing in the *Boston Evening Transcript,* observed "a considerable crop of ladies and gentlemen engaged in earnest exploration of the Great Beyond . . . and the mental processes peculiar to believers in cosmic vibrations imparted a beatific look to some of the listeners. Boston is a seat of scientific religions; before he knows it, Professor Theremin may be proclaimed Krishnamurti and sanctified as a new Deity." In the catalog of timbral effects Slonimsky perceived: "Bass tone, huge-massed and monstrously voluminous. High tone, an excursion into the birds' domain. Whistles, tiniest squeaks, insect-like humming, shrill, piercing, almost head-splitting high frequencies swiftly disappearing into the inaudible in the fortieth-thousands of vibrations. The squeaks and the low grumbling of the futuristic triangle aroused applause. Professor Theremin, gentle and condoning, acknowledged it with a civil bow."[69]

At the conclusion, "Professor Theremin and his assistants . . . made for the artists' room where autograph seekers, conjecturers and swarthy gentlemen-believers in cosmic vibrations waited for a chance to talk to the man whose hand makes ether-waves change their course."[70]

At year's end it was time to take stock of the victories and chart a level-headed path. The inventor's two pivotal patents were in place. Between August and December he had registered six more applications with the U.S. Patent Office—refinements of his basic system components: "Improvement in sound producing apparatus," "Method of increasing capacity sensitiveness of conductors," and so forth. American industry was knocking at his door, and the public and press were lined up behind him. The next frontier was the acquisitive consumer.

Nineteen twenty-eight had been a boom year. The stock market soared as more and more people bought into dreams of a materialist Shangri-la. Secretary of Commerce Herbert Hoover—a symbol for the new prosperity—was elected to the presidency in a landslide win in November on the promise of more to come: two chickens in every pot, and two cars in every garage.

Theremin plotted out a commercial strategy, training himself to think like a capitalist. Knowing that he would not, or could not, sell his patents outright to an American concern, he outlined a plan to oversee his own mass-production of the space-control instrument.

In a prospectus for a hypothetical company he called the "Theremin Corporation," he estimated the capital needed for the company would be about $500,000. This would cover "the cost of a well-equipped plant for the manufacture of the musical instrument, the establishment of a sufficient number of studios or schools, the cost of advertising and demonstrations, and leave an ample fund for operating expenses." For the sum of $50,000, he would be willing to transfer all his models and plans to the corporation.[71]

He estimated the production cost of the instrument to be about $100 per unit and the selling price at roughly $150. This would leave a net profit to the company of $50 per instrument. "On the basis of an assumed sale of 10,000 instruments per year," he speculated, "the gross profits to the corporation would amount to $500,000, enough to cover the dividend requirement of $35,000 on the Preferred Stock, and leaving a balance of $465,000 for distribution on the common stock." But this was a conservative estimate. "The assumed figure of 10,000 instruments per year," he wagered, "is exceedingly low."[72] After further calculation, he arrived at a gross annual profit of $1.7 million.

To support his marketing projection, the inventor cited U.S. Department of Commerce figures for 1925 on domestic sales of musical instruments (over $170 million—the majority pianos) and 1927 figures on radios and radio parts sold in the United States ($360 million). Additionally, he proposed the manufacture of a hybrid theremin-radio device. "This combination," he claimed, "ought to incite the interest of not only music lovers but also of the millions of radio fans."[73] A *New York Times* article back in February detailed the idea: "Through the use of a three-position switch and an aerial, Professor Theremin said his 'ether music' box can be converted into an ordinary receiver. With the switch in the first position, the apparatus functions only as an 'ether music' machine, depending on the operator for the music obtained. The second position converts the machine into a combination unit, permitting the operator to receive broadcast music and to accompany it on the machine, while the third position converts it into an ordinary receiver."[74] Assuming that 5 percent of radio buyers would want this dual mechanism, Theremin projected another $9 million in annual income from sales of these devices. It was a bit daring. But these were giddy times.

FOUR

A Theremin in Every Home

With the ethereal piano—and the apparatus will be put on the market quickly—the most musically stupid will be able to practice. What will happen when every office apprentice, at the end of his day, plucks the strings of the ethereal harp and gives expression to his emotions at the open window?

—Andreas Lunus, *Le Courier Musical*, Paris, 1927

The last year of the Roaring Twenties came in like a lion. Stocks had made a gain of more than eleven billion dollars in 1928, the gross national product was ballooning, and the market seemed to be a slot machine with a jackpot for everyone. The lure of easy money seduced the common person into a game that was once the sole province of the wealthy. Buying shares on margin—putting down a small percentage and borrowing the balance from the broker—opened the doors to the multitude. The barber traded tips with his customers; the cab driver kept an ear out for talk of blue chips among his fares. It seemed no one could lose. RCA, one of the glamour stocks, rose from 85 to 420 in 1928 alone.

But the edifice was built on rickety foundations. Less than one-quarter of one percent of all stockholders—the affluent speculators at the top—controlled as much wealth as the rest combined. Small-time investors had extended themselves beyond all reason. With negligible cushions of savings, falling prices could easily wipe them out. And what appeared to these minor prospectors as an honest wager on the American dream was in truth a monopoly held in check by a ruthless pool of men wielding big money. The country had allowed the banker-industrialist-businessman to dictate its destiny, "ousting the statesman, the priest, the philosopher, as creator of standards of ethics and behavior," one economist despaired. And the hubris of the age even appropriated religion itself to the gospel of plenty. The top bestseller for two years running, *The Man Nobody Knows*, recast Jesus as "the founder of modern business," a go-getter who "picked up twelve men from the bottom ranks of business and forged them into an organization that conquered the world." An insurance company pamphlet pictured Moses as "one of the greatest salesmen and real-estate promoters that ever lived." Prosperity was the new deity. In this reckless climate of ballyhoo and lusty optimism, modest investors continued to toss their few nickels and dimes into the shiny machine. Herbert Hoover was inaugurated as president, and the nation settled in for a sequel to the "Coolidge prosperity."[1]

Not to be left out, Leon Theremin rolled out his wares again on March 2, before a "fair-sized Carnegie Hall audience." In a recital of "Dematerialized Music," the lecturer sounded like a pitchman: "Lured by the boundless possibilities of this wide field, Professor Theremin does not wish to wait until time and tradition have placed upon this new departure the seal of their approval. He therefore demands your attention for a short time before the freshness of these innovations becomes stale."[2]

Early in 1929, a company called the Patent and Process Corporation paid Goldberg and Sons five thousand dollars for an exclusive option to negotiate licensing and manufacture of Theremin's U.S. patents. Its first job was to assume negotiations with General Electric, which Theremin had already initiated.

On March 12, Goldberg and Theremin signed an agreement brokered by Patent and Process. The signatory across the table was none other than the Radio Corporation of America, impressed enough to take the leap into electrical music. By the time the inventor put his hand to the contract, RCA had agreed to pay Goldberg and Sons the staggering sum of $100,000 for a two-year option on the exclusive patent rights for the Thereminvox, the radio watchman, and the altimeter.

But the bounty did not stop there. Radio Corporation agreed to pay an additional annual 5 percent royalty on all units sold, with the minimum yearly royalty guaranteed at $25,000—with or without sales. At the expiration of the two-year contract, RCA could take up the option and purchase the entire patent rights for the sum of $500,000 or extend the option period (still guaranteeing $25,000 in annual royalties), with the outright purchase price increasing 20 percent annually to a maximum of $2,000,000 at the end of ten years.

During the '20s, RCA had swallowed up a large share of the commercial broadcast market as a licenser of other companies, and by serving as a distributor of transmitters, receivers, and radio components. The company had no manufacturing plant of its own and acted only as a sales agent for the General Electric Company and the Westinghouse Electric and Manufacturing Company. In 1929, RCA purchased the Victor Talking Machine Company, a leading phonograph manufacturer. Victor had been faltering with competition from the radio industry, and by absorbing the firm and its plant in Camden, New Jersey, RCA hoped to enter the production market. General Electric and

Westinghouse together advanced $32 million to finance the purchase, on the credit of RCA. But since the RCA Victor Company would not be incorporated as a subsidiary of the Radio Corporation until December 1929, Westinghouse and General Electric undertook the manufacture of Theremin's instruments, which would be marketed through RCA.

Under the provisionary banner of the Radio-Victor Corporation of America, a new department in its Radiola division was created for the sale of musical instruments. G. Dunbar Shewell was named RCA musical devices sales manager, with supervision over the merchandising of the new instrument. Shewell had a background in sales—he came to RCA from the Aeolian Company—but he had trained at the Philadelphia Musical Academy, played the piano, and had several published compositions to his name.

The design and manufacture of the instrument would be coordinated through a team of monogram-brandishing engineers from the three cooperating firms: Radiola's president, R. L. Ray, and its vice president, E. A. Nicholas, directed the project; E. F. Kerns of the Production Division and J. W. Rafferty, Production Division manager, supervised the RCA effort; R. H. Emerson of the Radio Commercial Department of Westinghouse and F. E. Eldredge, Radio Commercial Department manager, administered the manufacturing for Westinghouse; Charles J. Young managed production for General Electric.

Planning, distribution, and sales were coordinated at RCA corporate headquarters, 233 Broadway, New York City. All production was carried out at General Electric's Schenectady, New York, plant and the Westinghouse manufacturing headquarters in Springfield, Massachusetts. From his Hotel Plaza Annex quarters, Theremin oversaw and approved every step in the design process. The project was developed under heaviest secrecy, as RCA hoped to enter the musical instrument market with little advance warning to its competitors.

Preliminary planning sessions with the inventor and the three companies began immediately in the spring. "The Sales Department of RCA has indicated its desire that approximately five-hundred Theremin instruments be produced as quickly as possible," an April 4 memorandum explained, "preferably to be available at least during the month of June. It is desired that these instruments be designed for power supply of two sorts—alternating current, 110 volts, 60 cycles, and direct current, 120 volts."[3]

The loudspeaker was to be separate from the rest of the instrument, and the remaining components, including the power device, were to be arranged in one cabinet with legs. Theremin was to prepare two sample instruments using standard RCA parts wherever possible, shipping both to Schenectady to be used as production models. One would be installed in a prototype cabinet furnished by the companies, the other left in a stripped state.

With all this success, Theremin was beginning to line his pockets and enjoy a high profile. He was also learning to work the controls of the free-enterprise engine. By the time he signed the RCA contract, he had secured patents and patent applications for his inventions in Germany, England, France, Italy, Belgium, Spain, Rumania, Denmark, Argentina, Austria, Sweden, and Switzerland. To begin consolidating the world rights, he decided to form a new corporate entity. On April 22 he founded the Migos Corporation and assigned to it the patents and applications from Goldberg/Theremin, covering rights in the United States and its dependencies, Canada, Cuba, and Mexico (the same territories specified in the RCA agreement). Ostensibly, the main function of Migos was to carry out the Radio Corporation contract. In the event RCA took up its purchase option in two years, Migos Corporation would be dissolved after dividends were distributed to its shareholders.

Theremin assembled a board of directors and installed himself as president. He issued the entire capital stock of the corporation—one thousand shares—to seven parties, three of them directors of the company. Among the board were George Goldberg and his brother Maximilian, who, along with Theremin, had the audacious distinction of representing both sides of the negotiations (Goldberg/Theremin as well as Migos), a conceit that actually allowed them to assign patents to themselves.

For the office of Migos treasurer, Theremin appointed Morris Hillquit, national chairman of the American Socialist Party—a distinguished lawyer, politician, and author. Hillquit, who was born Moses Hillkowitz in Riga, Latvia, in 1869, was educated in Russia. At seventeen he emigrated to America, where he started out as a shirt factory worker on New York's Lower East Side. After joining the Socialist Labor Party, he became manager of the weekly *Arbeiter Zeitung* and was admitted to the bar in 1893. As the most prominent of a group of Jewish workers-turned-lawyers, he was active in litigation for labor unions, civil liberty cases, garment trade strikes, and the fight against sweatshop conditions. In 1903, Hillquit wrote the first chronicle of the American Socialist movement, *The History of Socialism in the United States*, and in 1906 and 1908 he made unsuccessful runs for congress. In a 1917 bid for the New York mayoralty he garnered 150,000 votes—more than 20 percent of the total, and the largest number cast for any Socialist candidate in New York up to that time. Hillquit read and spoke a dozen languages and had an international reputation as an eloquent orator and spokesman for Socialism worldwide.

In May, Theremin, Hillquit, and George Goldberg decided to form a second company in Panama, the Theremin Patents Corporation, ostensibly for the disposition of the inventor's patents and applications in all countries of the world *except* the United States and its dependencies, Canada, Cuba, and

Mexico. Both Theremin Patents and the Migos Corporation, of course, came into being with the sanction, and existed at the pleasure, of Amtorg. No American speculators would ever cash in on these firms. Such companies, though they often transacted a modicum of legitimate business, were mainly commercial fronts, engaged in all manner of shady manipulations to divert funds for propaganda and covert activity.

On May 11, two domiciled residents of Panama City, Harmodio Arias and Galileo Solis, "for the purpose of forming a corporation pursuant to the provisions of the Panama Corporation Law," established, formed, and constituted articles of incorporation for Theremin Patents Corporation before a notary public in Panama City. The registered office of the corporation was designated as "15 Central Avenue, in the City of Panama, Republic of Panama."[4]

One important Soviet sphere of operation was in Panama, where a Communist intelligence ring was poised to infiltrate American military installations at the Canal Zone, hoping to seize top-secret U.S. Army documents detailing the plans of Fort Sherman, canal fortifications, and strategic operations. Stolen classified American documents and surveillance photos had to be shipped safely back to New York, and cover mechanisms in Panama were essential, hence the founding of the Panamanian Theremin Patents Corporation. According to the bylaws, all meetings of the stockholders were to be held at that office, "however . . . the directors, by the affirmative vote of a majority of their number, may change . . . to any place within or without the Republic of Panama."[5] Given that all the principal parties lived in New York, this was a convenient clause, one that could lend just enough cover to the job of transferring sensitive documents.

The first meeting of the board of directors convened at Morris Hillquit's law offices in New York on May 31. Hillquit was elected chairman of the meeting. Among the directors of Theremin Patents was a Solomon Fillin, most likely an alias of Simeon Filin, who also went by "Semen Firin," and often simply "Mr. Simeon." Filin was an OGPU officer stationed in New York and an Amtorg employee. After the bylaws were approved, Solomon Fillin tendered his resignation as a director. Fillin's role as an Amtorg liaison may no longer have been needed, or he may have ducked out for reasons that would become apparent in coming months. In the next order of business it was resolved that Theremin Patents Corporation would purchase all of Theremin's patents and applications from Goldberg and Sons/Theremin, for the sum of $25,000 cash and the entire capital stock of the company—1,000 shares, no par value.

On June 12, Theremin Patents borrowed $50,000 from the International Union Bank, of which Hillquit was a trustee. The loan was guaranteed by five individuals—one of them Hillquit—who were liable, in case of default, for up to $10,000 each. The 1,000 shares of stock and $25,000 cash were then transferred to M. J. Goldberg and Sons, the Gesellschaft zür Verwertung der Theremin Patente, m. b. H. (yet another corporate concoction), and Theremin himself, in exchange for full assignment of the inventor's patents to the Theremin Patents Corporation. George Goldberg acted as "attorney-in-fact" for M. J. Goldberg and Sons and the Gesellschaft, and with Theremin, he once again sat on both sides of the table. As buyers *and* beneficiaries, they paid themselves for the rights to the inventions.

The remaining $25,000 was deposited in International Union Bank and sat in a murky region, vulnerable to many forms of channeling and circuitous routing. Amtorg had accounts in a cross section of American, German, Canadian, and British banks, and by bouncing and shifting funds, it effectively maneuvered the resources needed to finance large-scale espionage in the United States.

Meanwhile, RCA was plotting for a large-scale bonanza in the home theremin market. A memo Rafferty wrote to Kerns gave a glimpse of what the Radio Corporation ultimately had in mind: "The manufacturing companies cannot estimate their quotation at this time on quantity of 15,000 to 25,000, but will advise us shortly." For the time being, however, "The manufacturing companies have quoted us a price on 500 Theremin units of $65.00 to $70.00, less tubes, less speaker and less cabinet. . . . The cabinet is estimated at $30.00 and it is believed that Mr. Theremin has a design of cabinet which he requests used for this outfit. . . . It will be necessary to use a complete 106 Loud Speaker for this item to reduce the cost, which is estimated at $30.00."[6]

A patent approval search was conducted, and it resurrected some familiar names from Theremin's recent past. An RCA memo advised: "There is a Miller patent which is apparently involved, and under which we have an option, and also a De Forest patent which may or may not cause difficulty."[7] The suspicions about De Forest, in fact, were sadly underestimated.

To smooth out last-minute details before production, a coordination meeting was held in Schenectady from June 10 to 12 with Theremin and representatives of the three companies. The inventor checked the work to date, and Goldberg submitted a description of the proper playing operation for the instruction booklet, which would be handled at Schenectady. It was decided the instrument would be called "The RCA Theremin."

On June 18, the Radio Corporation issued purchase orders for 500 theremin instruments, 300 to be constructed by General Electric, and 200 by Westinghouse. At $90 each, less loudspeaker and tubes, the GE order would cost $27,000 and the Westinghouse requisition, $18,000. Even with this considerable investment, though, RCA was merely testing the waters with a modest production run to determine if a consumer market existed for the theremin. Referring to the manufacturing quote of $90 per instrument, a General Electric executive wrote to Rafferty, "The above price . . . includes little if any profit for us as we understand that the RCA proposes to dispose of these units at cost or less."[8] Shipment of the 500 instruments was requested for eight to nine weeks from receipt of order at the factories. In an August 14 memorandum to Shewell, Kerns figured the total cost to RCA of a complete theremin instrument with tubes and loudspeaker would be $129.85. Manufacture of the instruments was to begin approximately the first week of September.

That same week stock market prices continued an upward climb from previous weeks in a bull market that elevated the Dow Jones average to its highest point ever. On September 5, when it appeared prices had finally peaked and were trickling down from the summit, Roger Babson, a well-known economist, predicted doom: "Sooner or later a crash is coming, and it may be terrific. . . . factories will shut down . . . men will be thrown out of work . . . and the result will be a serious business depression."[9] When word of Babson's speech reached the trading floor, prices began to tumble. But by the sixth, they turned upward again.

As assembly lines at GE and Westinghouse were cranking up, Theremin tempted the Radio Corporation with another proposition. RCA's tough-minded vice president and general manager, David Sarnoff, knew his company wouldn't rest for long on the laurels of radio. Television was the next frontier, and he was determined to see RCA pioneer the first commercial market for the viewing public. Sarnoff hovered over every minute evolutionary jump in the field, snatching up any ideas or equipment he felt were crucial to success, and ruthlessly buying out or stamping out any serious competition.

For this reason, under a contract of September 13, 1929, RCA bought an option from Theremin on a television prototype for twenty thousand dollars, with the assurance his work would not be sold to anyone other than the Radio Corporation. The inventor promised:

A full-sized picture made up or composed of 86,000 dots. The projection will be simultaneous with the occurrence of the event, including both sight and sound, thus differing from so-called "canned television." The original action or event to be transmitted only requires normal outdoor light or its equivalent in artificial light. The transmitted pictures will be thrown on a standard moving picture screen, 10 by 15 feet, with the usual luminous intensity of a moving picture projection, before an audience of 3,000, or in a theatre of that capacity. The usual distance from the screen for transmission will be accomplished in one short wave of definite length, the distance of transmission being the same as that of sound, and present on the same wavelength.[10]

In the race for a workable system, a handful of U.S. and foreign inventors had raised the art to unheard-of levels over the past two years. While Theremin, newly arrived in America, was caught up with his musical medicine shows, new advances in television were springing up every month.

Starting back in January 1928, when the inventor had been gearing up for his Hotel Plaza debut, Sarnoff was presiding over a General Electric demonstration in Schenectady where Ernst F. W. Alexanderson's mechanical system telecast a moving image of a man talking, gesturing, and smoking, followed by a ukulele performance of "Ain't She Sweet?" The wireless picture transmission came over the experimental station 2XAF, and the sound was sent via radio station WGY. The broadcast was delivered to a darkened room where GE officials and reporters viewed it on a three-inch-square screen. With a resolution of forty-eight lines at sixteen frames per second, it was still a far cry from Theremin's large screen and higher resolution achieved in 1927, but Sarnoff hailed the experiment as an event comparable to Marconi's first wireless telegraphy demonstration.

By May of '28, GE had begun regular telecasts two days a week for half an hour, and radio stations in New York, Chicago, and Boston were airing rudimentary television broadcasts. As people started to take notice, the newly formed Television Society sold 150,000 copies of its first issue of *Television,* an enthusiasts' magazine of technical articles and do-it-yourself tips for building a receiving set. Charles Francis Jenkins, recently granted the first television station license for his W3XK, offered detailed instructions to the public on constructing sets from common materials and made his fully built "Radiovisor" available for purchase. Jenkins hoped to create a wide audience for his thrice-weekly broadcasts, launched on July 2, which he called "the birth of a new industry . . . Pantomime Pictures by Radio for Home Entertainment."[11] The broadcasts were silent dramas of silhouetted figures performing various acts—a girl bouncing a ball, or the interaction of a family over the breakfast table.

In August of that same year, Alexanderson and GE ran an outdoor telecast of New York governor Alfred E. Smith accepting the democratic nomination for U.S. president. Again, sound and picture were transmitted separately. Unlike Theremin's system that accepted images in natural daylight, Alexanderson's apparatus required Governor Smith's face to be bathed in additional illumination from the camera's lighting system in order to be viewed effectively on a receiver. On September 12, GE broadcast the first play ever seen on television: the Victorian melodrama *The Queen's Messenger,* by J. Hartley Manners. Because the two cameras could not move to follow the action, each focused on the head of one of the actors, and a third camera covered the hand motions of "doubles" who handled small items such as wine glasses and revolvers.

In London, meanwhile, John Logie Baird developed a mechanical color system—the first in the world—that used a Nipkow disk equipped with three separate color filters (red, blue, and green), transmitting three individual scans that were reassembled at the receiving end and perceived as approximations of the original scene. Baird demonstrated the device at the annual meeting of the British Association, and while the results were not of high quality, the principles involved pointed the way for color technology in the future. In 1928 Baird also succeeded in transmitting the image of a woman's face across the Atlantic to New York.

By the end of the year, eighteen stations were broadcasting television programs in the United States, and thousands of viewers were building their own sets or purchasing the few commercial models already available. In December, Jenkins formed the Jenkins Television Corporation to manufacture and sell his own sets. A new media boom was underway.

While great progress had been made in 1928, all the major systems were mechanical and involved large, precariously spinning Nipkow disks or, in schemes like Theremin's, rotating mirrors and cumbersome vibrating mechanisms. Jenkins and Alexanderson maintained that the future of television lay in these mechanical designs. But there were others, like Vladimir Zworykin, who gradually nudged the technology in another direction. Zworykin, since his student days in St. Petersburg as a protégé of Boris Rosing, was committed to the idea of an electronic system with no moving parts—one that used electron beams to scan the original image and recreate it at the receiving end. His television research centered around this goal, and in January 1929 he implored the cigar-puffing Sarnoff to weigh the ultimate superiority of electronic schemes. Zworykin wagered that $100,000 and two years of research would see a viable electronic system. Sarnoff was sold, and he agreed to fund the project. Zworykin was set up with his own lab at Westinghouse headquarters in East Pittsburgh, and in February he began a flurry of research with cathode ray tubes. Zworykin's only competition in electronic television systems came from a Utah farm boy, Philo Farnsworth, who, with little financial backing, had already demonstrated a prototype all-electronic system to the press in San Francisco in September of '28.

As 1929 progressed, new advances in mechanical and electronic devices vied for attention. In July, Jenkins expanded his broadcasting to six nights a week, and his silhouette dramas, sent from New Jersey, could now be picked up as far away as Indiana. By August, Zworykin had developed an electronic receiver he dubbed the "kinescope," with a seven-inch cathode ray picture tube, and demonstrated it to RCA and General Electric engineers. In spite of Farnsworth's work, Sarnoff was confident RCA could gain the lead in electronic television. Theremin, with his mechanical system, was now sprinting from behind, but Sarnoff, by offering the inventor a contract, was clearly keeping his options open.

≪ ≫

The first production sample of the RCA Theremin arrived for inspection at Camden, from Schenectady, on September 19. The next day Kerns issued orders to GE and Westinghouse for release and distribution of their theremin instruments to the five regional RCA warehouses. Units were to be shipped to each city in the order in which they occurred on the list:

General Electric:	New York	150
	Chicago	85
	Atlanta	30
	San Francisco	25
	Dallas	10
	TOTAL	300
Westinghouse:	New York	150
	Chicago	50
	TOTAL	200.[12]

On September 23, the *New York Times* announced the arrival of the RCA Theremin. In an official statement, E. A. Nicholas revealed that the first production models had arrived from the factory and were to sell to the public for $175. "It is planned to popularize the Theremin as an instrument available to any unskilled person with a love for music but who is not trained in any instrument requiring years of study," the paper reported. "E. A. Nicholas . . . expresses the belief that the RCA Theremin is ready to take its place as a musical instrument beside the piano, violin and other instruments. 'Any one who is able to hum a tune, sing or whistle is likely to play the RCA Theremin as well as a trained musician,' Mr. Nicholas says. 'Still one may study it and improve continuously.'"[13]

RCA would soon come to regret all the fanfare about ease of playing, particularly because the idea planted false notions about how the instrument operated. A sentence in the flyer for Theremin's Boston recital, "The Player Produces the Desired Music by Definite Hand Movements in the Air,"[14] turned into a press comment on the RCA instrument: "Player Waves Arms and Invention Responds with Piece Asked For."[15] Many columnists, understanding the theremin to be a machine for general use, seemed to confuse it with a home entertainment device, like the radio or phonograph. "All you have to do is wave your hands in front of it in a certain way and it will play 'Ramona,'" one article explained. "Wave them another way and it will 'Snookie-oookie' or 'Wait Till the Cows Come Home' or 'Melody in F.' In fact, it will play anything dictated by the musical taste and knowledge of the operator, and play it good and loud, too, should the performer so fancy."[16]

RCA's theremin promotional brochure was '20s ballyhoo boosted to a deafening level:

> THE RCA THEREMIN
> AN ABSOLUTELY
> NEW
> UNIQUE
> INSTRUMENT
> ANYONE CAN PLAY
> NOT A RADIO
> NOT A PHONOGRAPH
> *Not like anything you have ever heard or seen.*

Inside the pamphlet, the reader was informed:

> Even Aladdin had to rub the lamp . . . and even he could not make music for himself! Now, with an unbelievable, almost magic instrument which you need not even touch, *you* can make, with a gesture of your hands, whatever melody you wish to hear!
> NEW . . . UNIQUE . . . ASTOUNDING!
> RCA has made music, and the enjoyment of music, available to every home, to every person in this land. For Radio, in the development of which RCA has played so vital and so large a part, knows no limitations of space . . . of repertoire; and radio reaches everyone.
> Now: A Further Tremendous Step!
> Having made the *enjoyment* of music universally possible, RCA takes another tremendous step—making possible not merely the *enjoyment* of *other people's* music, but the actual *creation* and *performance* of *one's own music!* Now, for the first time in the history of music, *anyone,* without musical knowledge or training of any sort; anyone, without even the ability to read notes; without tiresome or extended "practice"; without keys, or bow, or reed, or string, or wind,—without material media of any kind—*anyone can make exquisitely beautiful music with nothing but his own two hands!*[17]

Nicholas's press announcement was timed to coincide with the opening of the Radio World's Fair at New York's Madison Square Garden, on September 23. The theremin was exhibited as a new wonder of radio technology, conspicuous in the sea of radio sets. For the consumer, it was the first closeup encounter with the instrument, and periodic demonstrations each day were billed as an "attraction" of the exposition. "It is the instrument of feeling," Theremin told the *Evening World:* "Once we have learned to whistle, we do not need to learn to whistle every new piece. The method of whistling each new melody comes to us naturally, through our feelings. It is so with my Theremin. You play it through your emotions, not by means of a studied rote."[18] The spectacle of the new instrument at the fair drew the usual barrage of press quips: "Finding a use for the pig's 'squeal' has long been the hope of the meat packers, but radio has found a definite use for the radio 'squeal,' which up to this time has only served to harass the radio listener."[19] "Aladdin was a piker compared with Prof. Leon Theremin."[20]

The theremin made its broadcast debut on September 25 from the Crystal Studio at the fair, in a program heard coast-to-coast over the WJZ network. The program featured the inventor playing a Chopin "Etude," op. 10, and Rubinstein's "Romance." It launched a campaign of local and nationally syndicated broadcasts—often in tandem with radio expositions—aimed at making the theremin a commonly recognized sound.

On October 7, a wave of optimism came over Wall Street with a healthy rally, shown especially by a sharp rise in prices of market indicators like RCA and Westinghouse. That evening, the Boston Radio Exposition opened to record-breaking attendance. Back-to-back appearances of dance bands on the exposition stage and broadcasts of the World Series and the "Silver Masked Tenor" mingled with RCA's Pageant of Progress exhibit showcasing displays of television and manmade lightning, along with the theremin. "A young woman waved her hands in the air—and 10,000 men and women who thronged the Boston Garden last night . . . were held motionless and speechless, glued to the spot," the *Boston Post* reported.

> Heads craned. People closed in toward the platform until a thousand or more were jammed together. . . .
> The largest crowd that ever attended a radio show here . . . was thunderstruck. . . .
> The Theremin is the greatest novelty at a radio show filled with novelties and radio sets valued at more than $3,000,000. It is the newest thing and has untold possibilities. In a decade from now the child will be talking about taking Theremin lessons.[21]

Alexandra Stepanoff and Zenaide Hanenfeldt (another recent addition to the inventor's entourage) traded off appearances on the instrument at the demonstration booth and played on the Garden stage four times daily. Hanenfeldt, who had left Russia just after the revolution, when she was ten, had settled in New York with her mother and now taught twenty-five students at the inventor's Hotel Plaza suite. Later she would become George Gershwin's secretary and eventually go to work for Columbia Artists Management. The presentations she and Stepanoff gave at the Garden lasted from ten to forty-five minutes and featured music aimed at the popular taste—Stepanoff played "Mother Machree," "The Pink Lady," and "Because." Every night for a week, during the show, the two performers were also spotlighted in radio recitals over Boston's WEEI.

« »

Changes and adjustments to the RCA Theremin design were still being hammered out as completed units rolled off the assembly line. Some models had been built with the highest playable note set at 1100 cycles (roughly the C-sharp two octaves above middle C)—when the hand was one inch away from the pitch antenna—and other units were constructed to a limit of 1400 cycles (roughly the F-sharp above that). At a coordination meeting on October 10, the 1400-cycle limit was standardized for the instruments that remained to be built.

The first store demonstration took place on October 14 at the Rudolph Wurlitzer Company showrooms in New York before an invited audience. Julius Goldberg performed to the accompaniment of a pipe organ. The tone of the RCA instrument, while similar to that of the inventor's original, could not be changed or made to produce sound effects. But while no method of timbre control was furnished, the characteristics of the individual tubes were designed to allow a pleasing combination of overtones in the sound.

In the store setting, prospective buyers could have a try for themselves. Setting the power switch on the front console to the "on" position lighted a pilot lamp to confirm the instrument was receiving power. After a few minutes the Radiotron tubes heated up, and the left hand was positioned over the volume control loop to avoid a sudden squeal as the "play-off" switch was turned on to connect the speaker.

Before playing, the electromagnetic fields around the antennas were adjusted to suit each person's size and stature. The correct distance from body to instrument was determined by reach. The owner's manual defined proper playing position as the point where the knuckles of the extended right hand touched the pitch antenna. "Tuning" the instrument involved setting the lowest available note to sound when the player stood with the right hand close to the shoulder. Rotating the "pitch" knob clockwise contracted the area where notes would be located in space, so the lowest possible note was closer to the pitch antenna. Counterclockwise motion expanded the scale, pushing the playing area out toward the performer. To set the volume antenna, the left hand was held several inches over the loop while the "volume" knob was rotated clockwise to fix the point in space where the sound was completely silenced.

The owner's manual offered little guidance on playing technique, other than a brief description of proper hand movements and a spread of six photographs showing a model in various postures before the instrument. Right-hand movement toward the pitch antenna "should be made along a straight horizontal line," the copy urged. "The height at which the right hand is moved does not matter; it is chosen arbitrarily to suit the player's stature. The movement of the left hand should be in a vertical direction, above the Volume Control Antenna." The wrists of both hands were to be free and relaxed in all positions of the arm, and vibrato was suggested:

> Vibrato gives the RCA Theremin warmth and expressiveness. The average speed of vibrato which produces a tone of fine quality is about 5 to 6 vibratory movements per second. The hand should move through a distance of about a quarter of an inch, or slightly more, when producing vibrato. While making these movements, the wrist should remain free, otherwise premature fatigue will result. Each distinct vibration is engendered by a double movement of the wrist; first forward toward the Pitch Control Antenna, then back.
>
> Exceedingly deep movements must be guarded against, as the tone then produces an unfavorable impression, while an accelerated vibrato of considerable depth gives the effect of a trill.[22]

With a final word of encouragement, the rest was left to the purchaser's imagination: "After mastering the principles of operation, the player will find himself able to develop variations in technique of his own. The RCA Theremin is admirably adapted to individualism of expression."[23]

By mid-October, instruments were ready to be shown at "a selected number of about fifty outstanding music firms in various parts of the country."[24] Musicians employed by these local dealers were to be invited to New York for a one-week course in playing and demonstrating the theremin. Shewell's office was busy signing new accounts and shooing away office workers poking in to try the instrument, vying for the title of "world's worst." "Facility" was the watchword as the promotional campaign geared up. "As far as technique is concerned," the advertising brochure boasted,

> anyone can begin to play it on the same footing with the finest 'cellist, or pianist, or other instrumentalist in the world! . . . The most familiar instruments are popular because of pleasing tone and relative ease of playing. But the Theremin can rival the tones of any of them. . . . it is easiest of all instruments to play!
>
> A child . . . an elderly lady . . . a skilled musician . . . a blind man . . . all can learn to play this incredible instrument with exactly the same facility! It is destined to be the universal musical instrument; people will play it as easily, and naturally, as they now write or walk.[25]

While Nicholas vouched that the instrument's "place in the home, orchestra, school, club, conservatory and church is obvious,"[26] the target was the home market, and unlike most instruments, a notice in the owner's manual warned that "this device is licensed only for private use in homes as a musical instrument . . . and only where no business features are involved. Not licensed for theatrical or other public or professional performances unless such use is authorized by special, written contract of sale."[27]

On October 17, Kerns submitted a report to Rafferty after personally inspecting twelve instruments at the Bush Terminal Warehouse. He found half to be defective, plagued with everything from reversal of the usual frequency characteristics (high pitches sounding with the right arm at the shoulder) to loosely adjusted parts and noises requiring condenser trimming. Kerns concluded that the customer had a one in two chance of purchasing an operable instrument. Solutions for these troubles were not covered in the instructions, and the layperson, he feared, would be helpless. To avoid "sales resistance," dealers would have to be equipped with instructions for performing minor adjustments.

At General Electric, a concern arose about a possible conflict in the radio frequency band between the theremin and radio receivers. Obviously it would not be good for the theremin to render the family radio set useless. Using a Radiola 66 (an RCA superheterodyne radio) for comparison, engineers ran interference tests. Luckily the trials revealed no problems.[28]

On October 21, as stock prices fell again sharply, GE reported it had only fifty to sixty theremin instruments remaining to be completed. The same day, the eighth annual Chicago Radio Show opened its doors and later in the week played host to the second nationally syndicated broadcast of the theremin, aired over the NBC network on the WEAF chain. Twenty-six major cities from New York to San Francisco heard Alexandra Stepanoff perform on the Studebaker program.

On October 22, the market rallied but was shaky by the end of the day. On Wednesday the twenty-third there was a drop again, and GE and Westinghouse were down. The next day, a precipitous slide touched off a panic—switchboards were overwhelmed with brokers rushing to sell, sell, sell. Thirteen million shares were unloaded, but prices reared slightly on Friday, and hope still remained through the weekend. On Monday, GE fell forty-eight points, and on Tuesday the twenty-ninth, an epidemic of selling by big-time investors as well as small speculators plunged the market into the abyss. Stocks listed on the exchange dropped $14 billion in one day, and with them, the flimsy scaffolding of American affluence came crashing down. Nothing would be the same again. The '20s would go out like a lost sheep.

During the rocky months of September and October 1929, a young Russian composer named Joseph Schillinger had penned the first concerto for RCA Theremin and orchestra, entitled *First Airphonic Suite.* During the previous season, Cleveland Orchestra audiences had been introduced to the music of this composer, recently arrived from the Soviet Union where he had followed and admired Theremin's work. After the Cleveland success of his *March of the Orient,* Schillinger had approached the orchestra's conductor, Nikolai Sokoloff, with a proposal to create a new symphonic work featuring the RCA instrument. Sokoloff, who had witnessed the inventor's Plaza Ballroom debut, remembered being "spurred on by the rumor" that the Philadelphia Orchestra conductor Leopold Stokowski "was thinking of introducing a piece for theremin, and wanting to get in ahead of him with this novelty, I decided to include Schillinger's piece in our annual New York concert, with Leon Theremin as soloist."[29]

Sokoloff recalled the first rehearsal:

> The instrument was wired to a series of outlets on the stage, Mr. Theremin sat in front of it, and we started the rehearsal. . . . suddenly the thing emitted the most unearthly, ear-splitting shriek and, to my horror, I saw our wonderful first horn, Isadore Berv, keel over in a dead faint. It took some time to revive the poor fellow and his instrument was battered by his fall. Theremin was abject in his apologies—his hand had gotten into the wrong position and I was assured that it would never happen again. I wasn't too sure that it wouldn't, but we finished the rehearsal without any more casualties.[30]

Schillinger sugar-coated his piece in a traditional, romantic format, shaped into a sequence of seven uninterrupted movements: Prelude, Song, Interlude, Dance, Postlude, Dithyramb, and Finale.

On November 28, a hardy throng of Clevelanders braved a Thanksgiving Day blizzard to attend the premiere at Masonic Auditorium and see Theremin as soloist. "One may hardly say that even once in a lifetime one hears a new instrument," James Rogers of the Cleveland *Plain Dealer,* noted. "One listens to it both spellbound and baffled."[31]

Two days later Sokoloff repeated the program, then took it to New York on December 3. Dotted among the fashionable Carnegie Hall box holders were Mr. and Mrs. Theodore Steinway, Mr. and Mrs. John D. Rockefeller, and Otis Skinner and his wife. A gaggle of visiting Cleveland dowagers sparkled in gowns and wraps of red taffeta, gold brocade, silver cloth, green velvet, ivory moire, and black georgette. Theremin came on stage, a "grave and slender figure in evening clothes," and "made just the slightest of motions in front of two bars." The hall was filled with "colossal outwellings of sound such as all but baffle description—at times suggesting a balalaika orchestra multiplied by ten" or "a musical saw once heard above the roar of heavy traffic on the streets of London." The sheer decibel power was "at times enveloping the whole orchestra as with a gigantic human voice." "The volume increased until there were oscillations which should have disturbed seismographs in every observatory this side of Tokyo," "a sort of cosmic resonance that fairly takes our breath."[32]

Just how literally it could take the breath, Sokoloff discovered when his earlier fears were confirmed: "We had a huge audience, among them a large lady in the front row whom I could see from the corner of my eye. Mr. Theremin came out, took his place, and we started. Suddenly the thing gave out one of its fiendish shrieks and the large lady toppled over on the floor—out cold. Two ushers who saw her crash landing carried her out as we finished the piece."[33] "At this writing (2 A.M.)," one critic ribbed, "Carnegie Hall still has a roof."[34] But the theremin "seemed to have caught the imagination of the audience, for there was something of a small furore at the close of the composition."[35] "Mr. Schillinger . . . was present to bow many times from a box. Mr. Theremin walked numerous city blocks to and from the wings in responding to the applause."[36]

"From far beyond the doors of Carnegie Hall," Olin Downes lamented in the *New York Times,*

> sounded a strange and vibrant tone. It was the tone of the RCA Theremin, preluding terrifying instrumental days which are just before us. . . .
>
> Joseph Schillinger has composed . . . a simple and rather sentimental ditty. . . . The composition is not important per se, though it is well enough written. It adheres to fairly well-known harmonic formulae, and is evidently constructed with a special eye to simplicity and a background for a sustained melody to be played on the electrical antennae.
>
> For the RCA Theremin may not yet produce a staccato, spiccato, or sforzando tone. These things may lie in its future. Frankly, we hope they do not. We do not like to think of a populace at the mercy of this fearfully magnified and potent tone that Professor Theremin has brought into the world. The radio machines are bad enough, but what will happen to the auditory nerves in a land where super-Theremin machines can hurl a jazz ditty through the atmosphere with such horribly magnified sonorities that they could deaden the sound of an automobile exhaust from twenty miles away?[37]

Schillinger's *Suite* was a milestone that marked the first Western marriage of an orchestra with a solo electronic instrument. David Sarnoff predicted a trend, remarking that since "this new musical instrument will soon be added to the equipment of a number of great symphony orchestras of the country, it will be interesting to note the effect it will have upon music and composition."[38]

Sarnoff's comment wasn't too far off the mark, as there was apparently some truth to the rumor Sokoloff had heard about Stokowski. At a Philadelphia Orchestra concert in Carnegie Hall on December 17, Samuel Chotzinoff of *The World* was "aware at times of noises in fortissimo moments like the heavy respiration of the lowest register of an organ." Olin Downes heard "a fine roar at the thunderous climaxes of Mr. Stokowski's transcription of the organ work of Bach." "The effect was quite overwhelming," Lawrence Gilman reported in the *Herald Tribune.* "A gigantic diapason seemed to underlie the orchestral tone, booming and thundering with an effect which at times was like the menacing roar of some fabulous Bachian Fafner." Chotzinoff that evening was also puzzled by a large "ominous black thing that looked, from its perch between the tympani and the brass, like the canopy over a good sized kitchen range," and Gilman noticed "a shallow black cabinet with open doors." Chotzinoff observed that Stokowski, "always careful to enlighten his customers about his innovations," offered no explanations to the public "regarding the sable apparition, and this department was sent scurrying backstage during an intermission to learn the why and wherefore of the curious intruder."[39]

Chotzinoff discovered it was "only a variation of Mr. Leon Theremin's invention whereby it is possible to draw music from the air."[40] The "canopy," it turned out, was a loudspeaker, broadcasting the "roar" of an electric stringless cello played by Karl Zeise, a regular cellist in the orchestra, disguised among his colleagues in the section. As the critics had suspected, it mingled with the bass forces of the orchestra during Stokowski's transcription of Bach's *Toccata and Fugue in D Minor.*

"No, I'm sorry, but you can't take its picture," the conductor had warned a press photographer after a concert earlier in the year. "We are experimenting so much and are constantly making so many changes that a picture at this stage wouldn't mean anything."[41] Stokowski remained mum about the experiment, referring to the instrument in rehearsals merely as "it."

Stokowski had commissioned the instrument from Theremin, who had built it in November 1928 in consultation with Zeise. At a 1929 New Year's Day concert it was inaugurated with the Philadelphia Orchestra, and Stokowski used it that spring to reinforce the bass line in orchestral works of Bach, "in the way the pedals would be used in a large organ." "This instrument is capable of much greater precision than the previous one," Stokowski said, comparing it to the space-control model. "It is like a 'cello, but without strings. Mr. Theremin and I are working together very closely on the improvements. I tell him we want a little more of this or a little less of that and he makes the changes."[42]

The "fingerboard theremin"—based on the inventor's 1922 original—was designed to mirror string technique. The instrument, positioned on the floor between the knees like a cello, consisted of a black, cylindrical rod about four inches wide, roughly the length of a cello fingerboard, with a lever jutting out at the right. There was no body or box to act as a resonance chamber. When it was plugged in, an electromagnetic charge was created along a celluloid "fingerboard" strip attached to the rod. Notes were produced by moving the fingers of the left hand along the strip. As with the cello, low pitches were closer to the level of the chest, high pitches were closer to the floor. The right hand operated the lever controlling volume and, to a certain extent, articulation. Pressing down on the lever increased the intensity of the sound in the same way pressure exerted on a string player's bow would. One advantage of the instrument, besides unlimited volume, was a considerable range that over-lapped both the cello and double bass registers. The range of the instrument could be set to a high or low region, or could encompass both registers together. A passage that began in the cellos and descended to the basses—or vice ver-sa, moving upward in register—could be performed by a single player on the fingerboard theremin.

The volume control mechanism used a simple lever (an adjustable slide resistance, or rheostat) to produce gradations in volume. When untouched by the player, the lever was held upright by a spring; in this position it produced no sound because an attached arm touched the extreme right-hand side of the resistance. As the lever was pressed down, the arm, in turn, pressed down the sheet metal strip covering the wire-wound resistor, creating a continuously slid-ing contact point, altering the resistance, and increasing the volume of sound as it moved from right to left. Beyond gradual variations of intensity, the sys-tem also allowed articulation of accents and sforzando-piano. Unlike the space-control method, the fingerboard model offered a more natural downward gravitational movement to produce accented notes and increased volume.

The overall timbre of the instrument differed from the tone of the space-control model, sounding more like an organ, or according to Joseph Schillinger, an "idealized cello tone" devoid of the extramusical noises of bow scraping on string. Schillinger also described the tone as "quite close to the double-reeds (nasal)." "Though the manner of playing this instrument more resembles the 'cello than the violin," he claimed, "violinists have found it easy to play. The usual type of 'cello vibrato gives a perfectly satisfactory result."[43]

Stokowski told the New York Times in 1929: "For a long period Professor Theremin and I have been discussing and experimenting with the electrical means of producing tone. The first instrument we have experimented with corresponds to a point midway between the 'cello and the double bass. . . . It is our aim to add to this other instruments which will be higher in tessitura and form a group or choir."[44] But he cautioned, "It is not our intention to re-place the old type of instruments with this new one. The music which was written for the old type of instruments must always be played by those instruments. It is our thought to add these electrical instruments to the present orchestra only for the music of the future."[45]

《》

Far from Stokowski's lofty pronouncements, Shewell's office launched an all-out blitz in the new year to put a theremin in every household. It would be a difficult task to convince the average person of the need to own a strange and little-known luxury item. At $175, the instrument represented a major investment, but in order for it to make a sound, the purchaser was required to lay out an additional $20 for tubes and $35 for an RCA 106 loudspeaker, for a whopping total of $230—a beefy price in lean times. To be welcomed into the home, the instrument would first have to become a household word.

On January 18, the NBC network (a wholly owned subsidiary of RCA), through station WJZ, inaugurated a series of syndicated programs featuring the theremin, to be broadcast every Saturday evening from 7:15 to 7:30 P.M. The first recital spotlighted the inventor himself performing Rachmaninoff, Brahms, and Chopin. On a later show he was interviewed by radio personality Milton Cross. A Pathe Audio Review program offered the inventor playing "Deep Night," followed by a scripted interview:

> "Won't you explain this mysterious musical instrument to me? I'm greatly interested."
> "With pleasure. It is the RCA Theremin, the new electrical musical instrument which produces sound by purely electrical means."[46]

"For weeks radio listeners all over the country have been fascinated by the rich, flowing melody of a strange instrument," the *Hartford Times* wrote.[47] Local recitals began to pop up on the air as RCA instruments were purchased. One regional series was broadcast in Hartford and Boston through Westinghouse stations WBZ and WBZA every Monday evening at 6:30. The featured performer—or in the new coinage, the "thereminist"—was Mischa Tulin, a Russian piano virtuoso and graduate of the St. Petersburg Conservatory, who had studied with Busoni and Glazunov.

RCA mined its corporate ranks to find any possible venue for the theremin, including vaudeville. In June 1928, at the Palace theater in Cleveland, the instrument had first appeared on a vaudeville stage, "surrounded by a fairly lavish presentation, involving a piano accompanist, and a dancer or two."[48] By the following spring, RCA quickened to the idea and was considering the "stage presentation of scientific developments: Television, Televox (electrical man) and Theremin Ether Music." A committee representing Radio-Keith-

Orpheum (in which the Radio Corporation held an interest), General Electric, Westinghouse, and RCA announced that "R-K-O will concentrate on building the mechanical presentations into attractions. . . . General application of science to the stage is regarded as a new form of show business in embryo, bound to progress with the strides of engineering men in the theatre."[49] In January 1930, RKO vaudeville announced new acts in the celebrity roster of Robert L. Ripley's "Believe It or Not": Joe Cook, George Jessel, and "Prof. Theremin and his amazing instrument for picking music out of the atmosphere."[50]

By April, the Ziegfeld Theatre was also involved. "Doree Leslie and Hazel Forbes," the Brooklyn Standard-Union reported, "principals, and five of the famous glorified beauties who appear with Ed Wynn in 'Simple Simon' at the Ziegfeld Theatre, will be given a first course of instruction in the use of Theremin . . . on the stage of the Ziegfeld Theatre."[51] The instrument was on display as a public curiosity in the music room of the New York Paramount, and the Marx Brothers tried one briefly in a stage act in which Harpo gestured at the theremin, pretending it was a blonde. When the instrument responded with the appropriate screams and yelps, the effect failed to go over because the audience couldn't believe the noises were coming from a device no one was touching.

On March 13, 1930, RCA announced that the theremin had been transferred from the Radiola Division to the Victor Division of the new RCA Victor Company. Consequently, the instrument would now officially be known as the "Victor Theremin." G. Dunbar Shewell would relocate his office to the Victor plant in Camden, New Jersey, and would continue as head of the Victor Theremin Division.

Shewell himself toured through the South, the West, and the Midwest, giving lectures and recitals to promote the instrument at theaters, civic clubs and homes of prominent people. His son, Lennington Heppe Shewell, a student at the University of Pennsylvania, traveled the circuit with his father and found himself in demand as a theremin artist. Lennington was living proof that the theremin was the people's instrument. He played the piano by ear but couldn't read a note of music—his father was quick to point out—and with "never a music lesson," he paddled around in the air with an RCA instrument at the Shewell home, playing for his father's business acquaintances after a week. At an electric show in Philadelphia's Convention Hall, when the regular theremin demonstrator failed to appear, Lennington jumped in as a last-minute replacement and his performance career was launched.

Like his father, Lennington had a bit of ballyhoo in him—at sixteen he published his own weekly market letter—and he easily took to the idea of barnstorming around the country with the instrument. Unlike Alexandra Stepanoff and Zenaide Hanenfeldt, Lennington was a homegrown all-American kid and the perfect mascot for amateur music aspirants from the Corn Belt to the West Coast. Shewell swept the country with whistle-stops on RKO stages and in the stores of RCA Victor dealers, tantalizing his prospects with hearty assurances that he too had picked up his technique in only three weeks. Sometimes a whirlwind stump included eight or nine performances a day. "The Victor Theremin," the *Houston Chronicle* reported, "is being demonstrated by Lennington Shewell . . . at Thomas Goggan & Bro. Music Store. The first of these demonstrations occurred at 10:30 A.M. Thursday. There will be three more at Goggan's, in addition to appearances at the four Majestic vaudeville periods today and at 6 P.M. over Station KPRC."[52]

Lennington's tours included spots on local and coast-to-coast radio programs, and soirées in homes of well-known musicians and Hollywood stars. His typical numbers included selections from Romberg's *Student Prince,* Myddleton's "Buck and Wing Dance," "latest popular melodies," Mozart's Overture to the *Magic Flute,* and movements of Rimsky-Korsakoff's *Scheherazade.* In Hollywood, Ramon Novarro hosted Shewell in a reception for film actors in his private home theater and reportedly sang "Pagan Love Song" to the accompaniment of Shewell's theremin. Impressed, both Novarro and Charlie Chaplin stepped forward to purchase their own instruments. In Los Angeles, Shewell performed on the RKO lot, at the Coconut Grove and the Embassy Club, and at the Breakfast Club, where celebrated mezzo-soprano Ernestine Schumann-Heink sang in duet with the theremin.

Shewell brought the instrument to Toronto, cut several 78 rpm recordings of popular favorites on theremin for the newly formed RCA Victor label, and demonstrated the instrument in two motion-picture "talkies." He estimated that his $300-a-week salary, plus expenses—a hefty figure in the Depression— earned him roughly $22,000 the first year.

Beginning in January 1930, Shewell played with Rudy Vallee's orchestra, the Connecticut Yankees, and appeared on radio broadcasts from the Villa Vallee—the first use of a theremin in a popular music setting. When Shewell joined the group as theremin soloist and became a regular fixture on its frequent tours, Vallee developed such a fondness for the instrument that he commissioned RCA to make him a custom-built left-handed model for his own use.

The theremin drew people to stores and public showings with generally favorable reaction, and often a few chuckles. "In a small town in Texas," *RCA News* reported, "after the demonstration had been completed, a teacher of music arose and asked Mr. Shewell if the instrument would play 'Staccato.' A big Texan, who evidently knew what he liked in music, immediately arose and said, 'Hell, no! Who wants to hear that?'"[53] At a New Orleans recital, Alexandra Stepanoff eyed a wasp sitting on the pitch antenna of her instrument. "Distress showed in her eyes," the *Wireless Age* reported. "'Ze bug, ze bug,' she murmured to her accompanist, who happened to be Mr. [G. Dunbar] Shewell. Every man present was sympathetic—and how sympathetic you cannot know unless you have seen Madame Stepanov. Mr. Shewell quickly knocked the wasp to the floor and stepped on it. Applause echoed through the room. The beautiful lady was saved."[54]

The theremin was played at private gatherings, high schools, carnivals, church services and suppers, movie theaters, country clubs, community houses, and benefits. It was demonstrated at a Hadassah membership tea and a $50,000 ball in Philadelphia, and shown at the Cincinnati Music Teachers Association meeting. At the Arkansas School for the Blind "many of the musically inclined students" were given careful instructions and a turn at the instrument.[55]

Occasionally, established musicians performed high jinks with the instrument for publicity photos or made a serious go of it. The Dallas Symphony Orchestra conductor Paul van Katwijk posed with the theremin for photographers, and the Chicago Civic Opera tenor Tito Schipa, pictured in poised concentration over the antennas, said he hoped "to become a good conductor . . . instead of a non-conductor."[56] The instrument's West Coast debut was presided over by NBC's music director, Max Dolin, who coaxed a few operatic numbers out of it at San Francisco's Palace Hotel.

On March 11, 1930, RCA reported to its Victor distributors: "Our first production was limited and was used . . . to lay a broad foundation for merchandising operations on a larger scale. The public response has been very favorable indeed and there is no doubt in our minds that the Theremin faces a very bright future." But the policy of offering a small number of instruments through select retailers across the country would continue, the statement explained, "until we feel that the time is ripe for merchandising the Theremin through our regular wholesaling channels."[57]

George H. Clark, manager of RCA's show division, had occasion to interview over five hundred visitors at radio shows where the theremin was being demonstrated. Clark was afraid RCA faced serious competition from other companies who were on the verge of producing electronic musical instruments for the home. In September 1929 the company had announced publicly that the theremin was but the first of a series of electronic instruments it was developing. Clark realized that major improvements on the theremin principle were in order if the company ever hoped to capture a serious segment of the market.

In March 1930, Clark wrote to RCA executives summarizing his observations at the radio fairs, based on discussions with the public:

> Premised on my firm belief that we could make the Theremin a home musical instrument of great acceptability to the public—in addition to the apparent present plan of having it a high-grade orchestral device—I suggest the following:
>
> 1. That such a home device be made so that the player may operate it while he or she is sitting.
>
> 2. That a control natural to the average person be used, i.e., that the hand be raised high for a high note, or, in the piano analogy, that the hand be moved to the right for a high note, and vice versa.
>
> 3. That some scale be provided for indicating specific notes.
>
> 4. That some form of control be added whereby finger playing may be substituted for hand-waving. . . .
>
> 7. That a form be developed wherein volume control is taken away from manual operation, both hands thus being left free. A second oscillator to be furnished, with hand control, so that two-part music can be obtained.

Clark also recommended an automatic means for creating vibrato, "thus reducing the effort of playing and leaving the mind free to concentrate on note-production." At one radio fair, when he tipped a theremin on its side, allowing the in-out movement of the right hand to be replaced by an up and down motion, he found that "beginners could play it at once."[58]

As Clark systematically dismantled the qualities that made the theremin unique, he essentially wound up with an electronic organ and discovered in the process that the American public leaned toward conventional electronic keyboard instruments. These kinds of devices were growing in popularity anyway, and they began to point the way for commercial success in the field of home electronic musical instruments. Clark, perhaps without fully realizing it, had begun to sound the death knell for the RCA Theremin.

The inventor, however, remained committed to his ideas about an electrical orchestra, and he still hoped to assemble one. From his first months in America, he had found support for this vision from Leopold Stokowski. "I believe we shall have orchestras of these electric instruments," the conductor wrote in June 1928. "Thus will begin a new era in music, just as modern materials and methods of construction have produced a new era in architecture, of which the sky scraper is one phase."[59] Theremin adapted the vision to his own style: "The time is coming when an entire orchestra will play without instruments. Then, before each musician there will stand only a music stand with music, and on it two antennae, and through waves of the air an entire orchestral work will be played—string, winds, drums—all."[60]

After Theremin's vaunted claims at demonstrations, the poetic fancy of critics often took wing. "One dreams of astonishing effects obtained by the assembling of about 20 of these instruments," Emile Vuillermoz wrote. "The titanic chorus of the electro-magnetic voices would have delighted a Beethoven or Berlioz."[61] "Imagine, then," Waldemar Kaempffert suggested in the *New York Times,* "the Theremin electrical symphonic orchestra of the future! A hundred men stand before sheets of music. No horns, no violins, no clarinets— nothing in sight but the players and the music. The conductor raises his baton. The massive chords that open Beethoven's Fifth Symphony are heard— that soul-stirring knocking of Fate at the portal of life. The players simply wave their arms. They seem to grasp the music out of the air."[62] Olin Downes developed the scenario further:

> Wild-eyed musicians will sit at the music racks and flourish their paws in the air. . . . They will stir restlessly in their chairs, describing strange angles and ellipses by their gestures. As the climax gathers to break in a gigantic crashing wave of tone these musicians will leap in the air, reaching for an imaginary mark suspended in the atmosphere above them. The supreme climax can only come for those who are the champion leapers, since the intensity of tone, the amount of the sonority, will be measured by the height that can be reached by the left hand and index finger, held over one of the antennae . . . attached to the music rack! No guest conductor of today will be as athletic as the virtuosi of this odd orchestra.[63]

Back in 1928, Theremin had detailed an actual scheme for a forty-piece orchestra consisting of eight groups of five instruments each. The combined range of the full ensemble would exceed that of the traditional orchestra by one octave above and below. Group 1 would correspond to the string instruments; group 2 would replace the brass; group 3 would replicate the woodwinds; groups 4 and 5 would provide new tone colors; group 6 would act as the "pizzicato" choir, sounding various interrupted tones approximating the timbres of instruments such as the harp, xylophone, guitar, and mandolin; group 7 would consist of instruments for playing chords, including a harmonium; group 8 would contain at least four percussion instruments, approximating the tone colors of the timpani (with variable pitch), large drum (fixed pitch), cymbals and other metallic instruments and would contain a machine for "novelty effects." All instruments would be known by the name "Theremin-Vox" and would be differentiated by numbers.[64]

From his first weeks at the Hotel Plaza residence, Theremin began mobilizing students to fill the ranks of his imagined orchestra. Mostly they came to him voluntarily, drawn by the mystery and romance of the space-control instrument and the lure of belonging to the inner circle of an avant-garde movement. Ildiko Elberth, a professional cellist trained at the Budapest Conservatory, was typical of the ardent pupils in the inventor's orbit. "I loved the cello for its soft tones and because it is so much like a beautiful human barytone," she explained. "But ever since I heard Leon Theremin playing his new instrument . . . I did not receive the same satisfaction from my beloved cello. I often caught myself comparing the music of the cello with the singing of the ether waves and I must admit the comparison turned out for the benefit of the latter." When Elberth finally became Theremin's pupil in October 1929, she recalled, "It was more than I ever expected—too good to be true. Yes, the great man, in spite of his being very occupied—gave me his personal attention. . . . He gave me lessons every day."[65]

In April 1930, Elberth and eight other pupils of the space-control method joined the inventor at his Plaza studio in a semicircle of ten theremins, to rehearse for their first ensemble performance of electric harmony. From left to right, in the horseshoe of hand wavers and antennas, were Eugene Hegy, Anna Freeman, Louis Barlevy, Ildiko Elberth, George Goldberg, Theremin, Lucie Bigelow Rosen, the American composer Wallingford Riegger, Zenaide Hanenfeldt, and Henry Solomonoff. The group was billed as "Ten Victor Theremins" and debuted at Carnegie Hall on April 25 in the first skeletal approximation of an electrical symphony.

John Redfield, professor of musical physics at Columbia University, read the explanatory remarks:

> Mr. Theremin is one of that rapidly increasing number of persons who believe that Music and Science have too long walked in sullen separation, with looks darkly glowering and hostile. Much happier would they both be if they could forget their unreasoning surliness and go arm in arm for the rest of the way. Those acquainted with both of them feel sure that they would find each other surprisingly congenial, and the acquaintanceship gratifyingly profitable. Science now scatters her benefactions to almost every walk of life; she should no longer withhold her gifts from her engaging sister Music.[66]

The layperson's impression of objects on stage was described by the *New York Times* reviewer: "ten tall, triangular, modernistic screens of weird Oriental design, an automobile dial-board, a color disk, radio and phonograph machines and a large and complicated telephone switchboard."[67] Redfield continued, "The keyboard instrument is easily recognized here at my right. The fingerboard instrument is presented on the program by Mr. Wallingford Riegger, the well known composer. The space controlled instrument is the one of which you see several examples here upon the stage. . . . We will now ask Mr. Theremin to demonstrate the control of pitch by playing what is, perhaps, one of the most widely known melodies in the world." The inventor obliged, and Redfield dutifully went on, "I think you will agree with me that the melody you have just heard is one of the most widely known in the world."[68] After further explanations, and a demonstration of sixteenth tones on the keyboard harmonium, Redfield concluded: "Most of the players on tonight's program have played the Theremin for less than six months; and Mr. Riegger first attempted to play the fingerboard instrument on the 15th of this month, just ten days ago. However, it ought to be stated, that Mr. Riegger used to play the cello in the days before he took up composition in a professional way. Mr. Theremin will now present the first number on the program. Ladies and gentlemen, I thank you."[69]

The program featured works arranged by Joseph Schillinger for various ensembles of up to ten RCA Theremins and the fingerboard model. Arie Abileah, on piano, and Stefano di Stefano, on harp, furnished accompaniments. There were solos and duets—the Andante from Beethoven's "Pathétique" Sonata; "Song," from Schillinger's *First Airphonic Suite;* and music of Handel, Ravel, Bach, Boccherini, Hahn, Lieurance, Liszt, Offenbach, Rimsky-Korsakoff, and Bizet. All ten RCA instruments and the fingerboard model joined forces for "Aase's Death" from Grieg's *Peer Gynt Suite,* and Wagner's prelude to *Lohengrin.* Behind each player in the semicircle, a diamond-shaped loudspeaker was elegantly suspended between two poles that rose in a "V" shape. A display of color effects to accompany the music was canceled due to missing equipment, but, as one reviewer sighed, "This was, perhaps, just as well, as it was 11:28 when the end was reached of a rather long, but highly interesting and informative demonstration."[70]

"The thereminic small orchestra produced some imposing effects in the way of sonority and dynamic range," the *New York Herald Tribune* observed, but added, "There is still a speed limit and last night's program was mainly limited to music of a leisurely pace. The finger-board quasi-cello, a promising development in this field, ventured music of a higher speed in Boccherini's minuet. Mr. Riegger . . . played very commendably, except for some wandering from the pitch in the minuet."[71] "Admitting the scientific potentialities of Mr. Theremin's demonstrations last night," the *New York Times* concluded,

the auditor was not impressed with the present musical status of the various instruments. The question of intonation was a vexed one. . . . In the matter of tone-color, the keenest attention failed to find anything more poetic or intriguing than a hollow and literally sepulchral approximation of a 'cello or bassoon in the lower registers and of the oboe, saxophone or perhaps the sarrusophone in the middle and upper. Other characteristic effects which were not heard last night were trills, staccato, and especially no speed above a leisurely andante.[72]

By May, the RCA Theremin campaign was winding down. Attendance records had been broken everywhere—from New Jersey's Trenton Industrial Progress Exposition, where crowds ogled the instrument at the Essex Rubber Company's Malay Hut, to the Hartford state armory, amid "talking motion picture" displays, where a crowd of twelve thousand attended in one night to hear Alexandra Stepanoff perform. At Rhode Island's Providence Home Progress Exposition, the theremin was declared "the most amazing invention of modern times."[73]

Cities where local music dealers hosted promotional events included New Orleans and Cleveland in November; St. Louis in December; Atlanta, Syracuse, and Dallas in January; Little Rock in February; Cincinnati and Houston in March; Decatur, Los Angeles, Colorado Springs, and Buffalo in April; and Denver in May. Cities where concerts and demonstrations were staged in public halls included Boston in November, Baltimore and San Francisco in January, Washington in February, Dallas in March, Topeka and Cleveland in April, and New York in May. A host of regional musicians and trained demonstrators filled in around the scheduled tour dates of Stepanoff, Hanenfeldt, Goldberg, and Lennington Shewell.

The occasional news feature boasted of a local citizen who purchased a theremin and was entertaining folks with the curiosity. A Cleveland paper told of a seventeen-year-old boy who, after hearing Schillinger's *Suite*, bought an instrument at the sacrifice of "a precious collection of 10,000 rare postage stamps." One of only three people in Cleveland who could "play the creation," he was busy with "little else but the melodious classics."[74] Another story profiled a local singer in Texas—"the first artist in San Antonio to master the new instrument"—who played "Pagan Love Song" and "Moonlight and Roses" over the air: "WOAI Family to Hear San Antonio Girl Play Theremin during Tonite's Kelvinator Program."[75]

Despite these successes, G. Dunbar Shewell's merchandising campaign was plagued with defective equipment and a haphazard marketing strategy. Advertising was left to the regional dealers, and after the initial razzmatazz of a store demonstration, there was little follow-up. Many music dealers couldn't tell one end of an oscillator from the other any more than their customers could, and technical support or service ended at the cash register. Salespeople, after a few cursory tips and waves of the hand, sent purchasers home to grope for their own technique on the instrument. With the blithe emphasis on the theremin as a vehicle for the untrained, RCA dropped the principle in the lap of the consumer, expecting instant results with little guidance. Lessons of any seriousness, outside the inventor's circle of protégés in New York, were nonexistent.

Before it was too late, RCA fumbled to address these shortcomings. "As you are well aware," a letter to its Victor dealers began,

> one of the ideal ways to readily learn to play the Theremin is to have someone accompany on the piano. Obviously, Theremin users will not, at all times, have someone available to accompany them, and it has been suggested, therefore, that a Victor record might be used for practice purposes.
>
> We expect to release shortly a Victor record which will be especially adapted for those who are learning to play the Theremin. It will have the fundamental scales and several simple piano accompaniments of familiar melodies.
>
> In the meantime, we have made up a list of standard Victor records which seem best adapted for practice purposes with the Theremin.[76]

Still, the strangest irony of the RCA Theremin was its purported ease of operation. To the average consumer, the freedom of space was really a disorienting weightlessness. Even a fretless fingerboard or a slide trombone had something to hang on to—a point of reference. The theremin called for the acute, inner ear of a singer to sense the location of each note before sounding it, but without any advantage of a physical sensation in the vocal cords or breath. Clark's survey revealed that untrained performers preferred a keyboard orientation, with fixed pitch increments. Adding to the list of hindrances, the theremin was capable of playing only slow music, and it required an accompanying instrument or recording. For a device intended to replace the parlor piano, these were serious defects.

Of course, there would always be a handful of diehard musicians like Ildiko Elberth, bent on mastering the air. "I know that there are millions seeking self-expression," she said, "and I wish I had the chance to tell everyone what I sincerely believe, that the 'Theremin' is the very answer to their yearning."[77] But the housewife, the corner druggist, and the farmer might have little patience for these things. Nevertheless, RCA went ahead with the design of an improved "Victor Theremin" aimed at the broader public. The new mock-up had a built-in speaker and was housed in a boxlike cabinet reminiscent of a large radio set. As a prototype, it represented a cheaper, more self-contained model that the Radio Corporation hoped to mass-produce in the near future.

《》

On July 18, 1930, the *New York Times* ran a front-page story quoting Matthew Woll, vice president of the American Federation of Labor, in a declaration before the congressional committee investigating Communism in the U.S.: "Woll . . . charged yesterday . . . that for the sake of helping American corporations to do business with Soviet Russia the American government was jeopardizing the interests and safety of the United States by being too lenient with Communist agents and representatives of Amtorg." Woll asserted that the "government has winked with one eye and has been asleep with the other, while the agents of Moscow have come among us." He cautioned that visas and permits "enabling Soviet agents to reside and do their subversive work in this country are being extended by the authorities without due consideration of the dangers involved." Woll urged the "wholesale deportation of alien Communists" and warned that American capitalists doing business with the Soviets were "setting up a Frankenstein which may some day come to plague them."[78]

Two weeks later, on July 31, the *Times* carried a front-page headline: "Red Spy Hunted Here as Link of Amtorg to Espionage Groups." Agents of the Department of Justice, the paper reported, working with the radical squad of the New York Police Department, "are seeking a man named Filin, alias Simeon, who, according to information received by the authorities, is the head of two Soviet espionage organizations operating in the United States under cover of the Amtorg Trading Corporation." A raid on a Manhattan drugstore failed to produce Filin, who, according to the *Times*, "had entered the United States on a false passport" and had

> opened a small office for the purchase of medicinal herbs used in the drug industry. This, the authorities say, was done to divert suspicion from his espionage work. Through this office he was connected with the Amtorg, making all his purchases as a subagency of the Soviet commercial agency. This enables him to visit the Amtorg office regularly. There he is said to confer from time to time with representatives of the Soviet Commissariat of War. . . . These representatives are said to bring with them secret messages to Filin from the Moscow chief of the secret military service . . . and Filin in turn gives them information gathered by his organizations in America.

Not long before the raid, in fact, at a hearing of the congressional committee investigating Communism in the United States, a former Soviet chargé d'affaires from Paris, who had broken with the soviet government, reported that information on Filin's U.S. activities had come from a prominent official of the Comintern, and from "Berzin, an officer of the secret military service in Moscow."[79]

≪≫

That same summer, with the RCA Theremin campaign in a temporary lull, the inventor knew he had to act quickly if he wanted to remain in the television race. When David Sarnoff had assumed the presidency of RCA on January 3, 1930, his first order of business was to appoint Vladimir Zworykin head of all television research at RCA, transferring his laboratory to the spacious Victor plant in Camden, New Jersey, and extending him carte blanche to steer investigations in any direction he wished. Sarnoff was betting on Zworykin, but he hedged his options, saving a place for mechanical systems like Theremin's, just in case. "The transmission of sight through radio is now in the laboratory stage," he told the Industrial Club of Chicago on January 23, "and while there is no instrument that I know of either in this country or in any part of the world which is competent today to render it in the form of a service, nevertheless, the faint beginnings are visible."[80] "Meanwhile," an entertainment columnist said of Theremin, "the 33-year-old inventor is supposed to be working on the 'missing link' in television, whatever that is."[81]

To raise capital for a working prototype to impress Sarnoff, Theremin would have to attract investors. The RCA agreement was Theremin's best trump card in this equation—now he could lure backers with a piece of the profits if the Radio Corporation manufactured his system. Since RCA was still planning to put its full support behind the space-control instrument, there was every reason to believe it might also back his television.

Following the lead of Jenkins more than a year and a half earlier, the inventor formed the Theremin Television Corporation on August 18, 1930. The directors were Theremin, George and Maximilian Goldberg, Morris Hillquit, and Frederick F. Umhey, a partner in Hillquit's law firm. The corporation was formed "to purchase and acquire the inventions of Leo S. Theremin or any other person in the field of television . . . to apply for and obtain patents on said inventions in all the countries of the world," and to manufacture devices covered by these inventions. One thousand total shares of a single class, no par value, were issued, mostly to the directors, with the remaining stock distributed to others. Joseph Schillinger ventured a safe five shares, and Theremin Patents Corporation was in for one hundred shares (five thousand dollars, representing 20 percent of its *own* capital).[82]

Television developments had meanwhile taken another leap. On May 22, 1930, Alexanderson had presented his latest mechanical system to reporters and the general public at Schenectady's Proctor Theater. The audience saw and heard life-size musicians and a vaudeville performer whose images were transmitted from the GE laboratory and projected on a six-foot-square screen in the theater. The resolution was forty-eight lines at sixteen frames per second—still not as impressive as Theremin's, but now on a larger screen. In August, Charles Jenkins broadcast a celebrity variety show for CBS, attracting viewers by installing outdoor receivers at numerous sites around Manhattan. By now, Jenkins was also selling television receiver kits for $7.50, including postage.

On August 19, one day after the formation of the Theremin Television Corporation, G. Dunbar Shewell wrote to his Victor distributors:

Most of our wholesalers are familiar with the Victor Theremin and the fact that we have been merchandising the instrument during the past year through about 60 of the leading music houses in the country direct. Our object in doing this was to determine the merchandising possibilities of this product. We feel now that we have received sufficient favorable results to offer the distribution through our regular Victor channels. . . . We will not be in a position to furnish your dealer with merchandise until the latter part of October as our new model with self-contained speaker will not be ready until then. . . . In the meantime, you will find the present model in every way capable of acquainting you with the Theremin possibilities.

Shewell asked that each distributor purchase a current theremin model (plus eight radiotron tubes and an RCA 106 speaker, all at 50 percent discount), "in order that you will have an opportunity to thoroughly acquaint your organization with it." Hoping to smooth out past oversights in the next go-round, Shewell assured his distributors, "We have recently recorded a number of Victor Theremin records especially adapted for accompanying a Theremin performer, as well as an exercise record for the beginner. In addition, we also have Theremin exhibition records which will be especially helpful in showing the proper tone and results to be striven for. . . . but in the meantime, we ask you to do everything possible to have one or more in the organization learn to play the instrument and to have your technicians learn to service it."[83]

≪≫

Suddenly, on October 30, 1930, the Radio Corporation released all claims on Theremin's television. He was free to sell it to another manufacturer, provided he repaid the $20,000 originally advanced to him. This move rendered the Theremin Television Corporation stillborn. No sooner had the certificate of incorporation been drawn up, and the capital raised, than it became clear RCA no longer had any need for Theremin's television work. It now seemed pointless for stockholders to invest considerable amounts to develop a system that the major player in the field had rejected. With RCA out of the picture, it was unlikely GE or Westinghouse would bite, and of the remaining companies involved in serious television research, most had well-ensconced engineers already tackling the problem. To go the route alone, as a manufacturer, would require capital far greater than the $50,000 Theremin's small group of directors had already raised.

The Jenkins Television Corporation, by 1931, was selling the Jenkins Universal Television Receiver for $82.95 (or $47.50 for a kit version), but the company had a capital investment of $10 million in common stock, with its majority stockholder no less than the likes of the De Forest Radio Company. The

Jenkins corporation also owned and operated its own television station that helped furnish a market for its receivers.

As advancements in the field continued, larger and larger funds were required for research, even of the big corporations, and as expectations rose, so did the standards of the major contenders. "While television during the past two years has been repeatedly demonstrated," RCA wrote in its 1930 annual report to stockholders,

> . . . it has remained the conviction of your own Corporation that further research and development must precede the manufacture and sale of television sets on a commercial basis. In order that the American public might not be misled by purely experimental equipment and that a service comparable to sound broadcasting should be available in support of the new art, your Corporation . . . will pursue this development aggressively in the laboratory during 1931, without attempting to market such equipment commercially this year.[84]

Theremin's fascination with television continued, but he cast his research to the sidelines after it became clear that he would not be part of the final rush to the summit of commercial telecasting. Perhaps this was wise, for in 1932, the Jenkins Television Corporation went bust and was liquidated. Eventually Sarnoff bought out its assets and all its television patents for $500,000. He did this not out of any desire to absorb the technology, but only to ensure it would never again challenge Zworykin's work. The documents were filed away and forgotten. Likewise, in April of 1931, Sarnoff visited Farnsworth's lab and made an offer of $100,000 to purchase the whole operation, including Farnsworth's continued research services, but was flatly refused. Seen in this light, RCA's 1929 option on Theremin's television may have been no more than a stalling tactic to hold off a potential competitor just long enough to make sure he could not overtake Zworykin.

With the demise of the Jenkins company, the end had come for mechanical television. Even at a maximum resolution of 240 lines, this technology would be obsolete by 1933, and by November 1931 Zworykin had already tested a successful electronic camera tube—his "iconoscope"—which, with his kinescope, finally made fully electronic television feasible.

《 》

During 1929 and 1930, many small fortunes had passed into Theremin's hands, including RCA's first-year royalty payment of $25,000 in March. But these fortunes slipped through the inventor's fingers, and by October 1930, RCA's planned mass-production of its second-generation "Victor Theremin" had not materialized.

Not surprisingly, the inventor had become weary of the whole corporate tangle, and on November 15, 1930, he registered his lab and residence at the Hotel Plaza Annex as the "Theremin Studio," on a "Certificate of Conducting Business under an Assumed Name," with the State and County of New York. Temporarily free and clear of boards of directors, stockholders, and the like, he would throw himself into his work, presumably with lower financial risk. But at the same time he was broke, and to support his research he would be obliged to take out a series of personal loans from individuals or small companies, guaranteed mainly by worthless shares of stock and the promise of an interest in the sale of future inventions. On October 16, 1930, he had received a personal loan from a Mr. Adolf Klein for $2,000 against which he put up one hundred shares of Theremin Patents Corporation stock as collateral and agreed to repay the loan in twenty-five weekly installments to reach Klein "no later than noon of every Tuesday."[85] On November 26 the inventor signed a promissory note with International Madison Bank and Trust Company for a loan of $3,000, to be repaid within thirty days. A loan of $7,000 from the same bank, which he had taken out in August, was also due in December.

《》

That fall, the *New York Times* reported, "Reverberations fairly rocked the Academy of Music this afternoon as Leopold Stokowski augmented the resources of the Philadelphia orchestra with the electric Theremin in the transcription of Debussy's piano prelude of 'The Engulfed Cathedral.' . . . The modern instrument . . . provided a ground bass for the entire orchestra below the compass of its closest competitors."[86] It was Stokowski's third season with the fingerboard model, but apparently his last. According to Nicolas Slonimsky, "the infrasonic vibrations were so powerful . . . that they hit the stomach physically, causing near-nausea in the double-bass section of the orchestra. Stokowski abandoned the project."[87]

It was perhaps a shock, then, to see Stokowski at Carnegie Hall on December 16, prominently showcasing another inventor's electronic instrument. This was not the product of a reclusive Mager, or a retiring Givelet, or an eccentric Miller, but the invention of a formidable rival with a legitimate claim to the ether wave title. Maurice Martenot had introduced his Ondes Musicales (musical waves), which came to be called the ondes martenot, at the Paris Opera on May 3, 1928, just five months after Theremin's triumph there. The instrument was an immediate success and prompted comparisons with the Russian's achievement. "The public," Max de Vautibault wrote,

hardly over the effects of Leo Therémin's experiments in ether waves, is now brought up with a jolt by Professor Martenot, French inventor of an instrument that goes the Russian's one better in a number of ways. . . . It is an instrument perfect in every detail, an instrument that allows the artist to express his music with a fidelity and finish possible on no other apparatus. It is, at the same time, easy to play and well may come to occupy an important place in solo work, as well as chamber and orchestral music.[88]

Like the theremin, the ondes martenot used the heterodyne system, but with several significant differences. The variable oscillator was controlled manually, rotated with a pulley that was drawn taut or slackened by motions of a ring tugged by the right-hand forefinger. In early models, the pulley was operated over a dummy keyboard that offered the performer an accurate gauge of the distances between notes. The left hand operated a button controlling articulation and could also manipulate a knob to control the sound envelope (the attack and release characteristics of individual notes). Three additional "stops" used in various combinations allowed the choice of eight different timbres. Later models had an actual keyboard of five or seven octaves, the addition of more timbre stops, and the capability of controlling vibrato by shaking the keys with a finger. De Vautibault admired the sound of the ondes martenot, "ranging from warm, vibrant tone to 'white' tone without vibrato . . . sharpest *staccato* to perfect *legato,* with or without *portamento* between intervals . . . tremolo, trills, rapidity . . . permitting the performer to exhibit amazing virtuosity."[89]

Martenot had copied Theremin's itinerary—a European tour followed by a stint in the United States—and made his American debut with Stokowski in Philadelphia just prior to his New York appearance. The Carnegie concert on December 16 spotlighted his instrument in music of Buxtehude and Mozart, and in a symphonic poem by Dimitri Levidis written especially for the ondes martenot. More than half the audience remained after the program for an extra "clinical concert" where the instrument was discussed, and demonstrated in detail.

Martenot, in common with Theremin, was a relentless promoter of his instrument. In many ways the ondes resembled a highly evolved theremin, one that addressed, within six months of the Russian's European debut, many of the defects of his instrument. Theremin's insistence on space-control technique for the performer had caused him to disregard alternative approaches. But Martenot, with his "dummy" keyboard and articulation button, easily overcame many of the deficiencies. The fingerboard theremin and keyboard harmonium, though they solved some difficulties, lacked sophisticated controls for timbre or articulation control. Martenot had found a compromise: a space-control system with a physical mechanism (pulley) attached, to give the player "something to hang on to." This allowed the same expressive hand gestures the thereminist used, but with keener control, and a psychological cushion to bolster confidence. "The tones were not always agreeable," Lawrence Gilman wrote of Martenot's performance, but they lacked the distressing portamento that marred the performances of Professor Theremin and they had far more flexibility of utterance.

It is said that Monsieur Martenot owes nothing to Theremin: that his invention was worked out independently—as to which we cannot speak with assurance.

Monsieur Martenot uses a different kind of apparatus. . . . He has eliminated certain of the earlier crudities and defects. . . . He has not only tamed the "howl," he has taught it politer musical manners.[90]

In April, at the time Theremin was preparing his pupils for their Carnegie Hall debut, one member of the group, the society woman Lucie Bigelow Rosen, and her husband, the trial lawyer and international banker Walter Tower Rosen, poked around Theremin's lab to indulge their curiosity and discovered the extent of his unconventional research. "We visited his first little rooms here," Lucie wrote in a letter to John D. Rockefeller Jr., "and found them overflowing with coils and lamps and mirrors. We saw a vast television machine for a screen twenty times larger than any that is yet deemed practicable, and a microphone without wires. An oscillograph made our voices visible, another instrument measured the beats of sound."[91]

By the time Lucie Rosen joined the Hotel Plaza coterie of students in 1930, Theremin was already on a financial downturn, and the tour of the lab was an eye-opener:

A great many things could not be shown because there was not space, or finished because he had not money, but we did not know that for some time. He had had flattering recognition in Berlin and Paris and London, and received large sums as a new wonder on his arrival in America, which supported his little laboratory and costly independent experiments for a time. But many interesting things are not immediately profitable, and the depression came when no commercial interests felt speculative. We saw him giving up one thing after another without explanation, and felt this was a waste, if ever we saw waste, of creative imagination and tireless energy.[92]

The Rosens owned five townhouses in Manhattan, three on West Fifty-fourth Street and two around the corner on West Fifty-fifth. Lucie's growing devotion to the instrument, and her earnestness in wanting to see the inventor carry out his research, led the couple to offer Theremin the use of their four-story brownstone at 37 West Fifty-fourth Street, next door to their own residence at 35 West. Having the professor in close proximity meant Lucie could pop in and out for regular tips on space-control technique, and she could peer over his shoulder at brash new technologies in their infancy. For Theremin, it meant a residence and laboratory at a modest rent, ample room to carry out unlimited research—in what Lucie called "good old-fashioned spaces"—

and a setting where he could open an informal school to train performers on his instruments.

Given his financial peril, the offer was too good to pass up. In December 1930, more than twelve thousand dollars in debt, and with his corporate dreams in pieces, the inventor transferred his "Theremin Studio" to 37 West Fifty-fourth Street.

Sergei Emilievich Theremin, Lev
Theremin's father. Courtesy of
Lydia Kavina.

Yevgenia Antonova Orzhinskaya,
Lev Theremin's mother. Courtesy
of Lydia Kavina.

Lev Theremin and his sister, Helena, about 1903. Courtesy of Lydia Kavina.

Lev Theremin (right), lieutenant of the Reserve Electrotechnical Battalion, 1917, with his colleagues. From *Sovetskyi Faust*, courtesy of Bulat Galeyev.

Facing page, top: Abram Ioffe in his physics laboratory at the Leningrad Polytechnical Institute, 1924. Courtesy of Vladimir Kossarev.

Facing page, bottom: Lev Theremin (left) performing in duet with Konstantin Kovalsky, about 1924. Kovalsky is using a model of his own design with a foot pedal for volume control and a push-button articulation controller. Courtesy of Ludmila Mikheyeva.

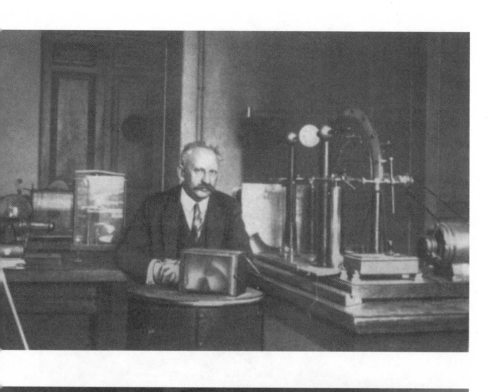

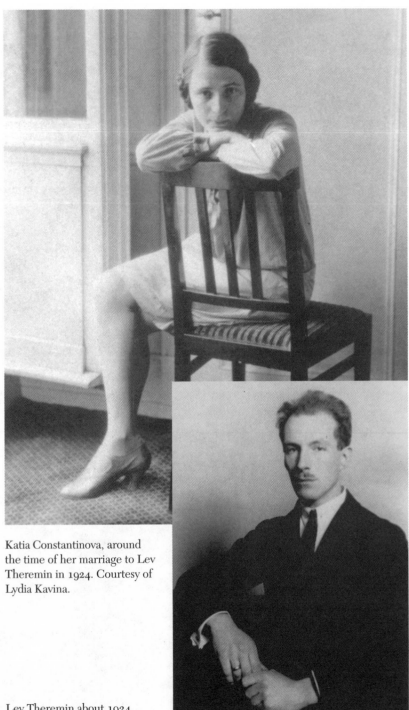

Katia Constantinova, around
the time of her marriage to Lev
Theremin in 1924. Courtesy of
Lydia Kavina.

Lev Theremin about 1924.
Courtesy of Lydia Kavina.

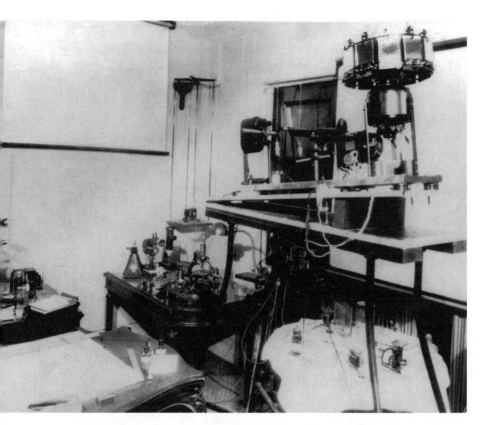

Transmitting apparatus for the third version of Theremin's "electric distance vision" television, 1926. From *Sovetskyi Faust,* courtesy of Bulat Galeyev.

Drawing of Leon Theremin by Fritz Brust. From *Die Umschau*, Frankfurt, 1927.

George Julius Goldberg demonstrating an early theremin model with foot-pedal volume control and push-button articulation controller, Germany, October 29, 1927. Corbis/Bettmann ©.

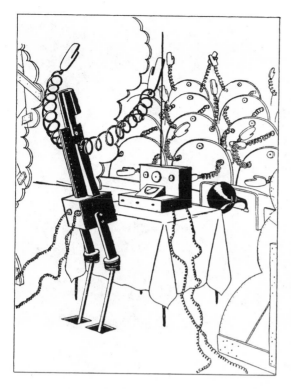

Cartoon by Perrault, France, about 1927: "In 50 Years—Professor Theremin synthesizing himself, plays the finale of *Faust* before applauding machines who will henceforth replace the audience at the Opéra." Schillinger Theremin Collection, Arthur Friedheim Library, Peabody Institute, Baltimore.

Cartoon by Lucien Metivet, France, 1927: "Musiques Radio-electriques— The connoisseur—'I see your trick: you're a ventriloquist.'" Schillinger Theremin Collection, Arthur Friedheim Library, Peabody Institute, Baltimore.

Theremin after his London demonstration at the Savoy Hotel, December 10, 1927, with Sir Henry Wood (middle) and Sir Oliver Lodge (right). *Scientific Monthly*, March 1928.

A cartoon by Percy Arthur Fearon in the *Evening News* (London) on December 12, 1927, places Winston Churchill, then Chancellor of the Exchequer, at Theremin's instrument. Lucie Bigelow Rosen Archive, Caramoor Center for Music and the Arts, Katonah, N.Y.

Cartoon by Arthur Ferrier, *Sunday Pictorial* (London), December 18, 1927. Lucie Bigelow Rosen Archive, Caramoor Center for Music and the Arts, Katonah, N.Y.

MUSIC FROM THE ETHER
FIRST CONCERT DEMONSTRATION IN AMERICA
PROF. LÉON THÉREMIN

Produced by Free Movement of Hands in Air

METROPOLITAN OPERA HOUSE

Tuesday Evening, Jan. 31st, 1928 at 8:30 P. M.

Tickets: $4.40 to $1.10 (Tax Included)

Now on Sale at Box Office

Wurlitzer Piano

RECITAL MANAGEMENT ARTHUR JUDSON

STEINWAY HALL   NEW YORK

Flyer designed by A. Hudiakoff for Leon Theremin's American debut at the Metropolitan Opera House, January 31, 1928. Music Research Collection, New York Public Library for the Performing Arts, Astor, Lenox, and Tilden Foundations.

Theremin demonstrating
his "music stand" model.
Philadelphia Press, February 22, 1928.

Theremin with his keyboard harmonium, 1927. Corbis/Bettmann ©.

Artist's conception of an ether-wave pit orchestra of the future. Illustration by L. U. Reavis, from *New York Herald Tribune*, January 29, 1928. © New York Herald Tribune Inc. All rights reserved. Reproduced by permission.

Creative uses of the space-control technique as envisioned by cartoonist Ving Fuller, about 1928. Lucie Bigelow Rosen Archive, Caramoor Center for Music and the Arts, Katonah, N.Y.

Artist's conception of a theremin-like apparatus used as a divining rod for detecting underground ores. Illustration by Edward McCandlish, *Detroit Free Press*, April 1, 1928. Reprinted by permission of the Detroit Free Press.

The illumovox, about 1928. Archive Photos.

FIVE

The Ether Wave Salon

*Nighttime Broadway dazzles with the light of artificial suns; the auto-
mobile crowds out the pedestrian; the dirigible circles the planet. . . .
And in the meantime . . . sweaty men in tailcoats have raised an inex-
pressible brouhaha. Some rub calf-guts with horsehair. Some, blowing
into cylindrical brass tube. . . . but the powerless voices of their whistles
and shepherd's pipes dissolve in the general clamor of shrieking, moo-
ing, howling, whistling, hissing, scratching and thumping.*

—Joseph Schillinger, 1929

"Lucie Rosen is one of the most original women in New York's social world,"
the *New York Evening Journal* observed. "She has very curly blonde hair which
fuzzes out into a wide halo around her delicate and ethereal face and Mrs.
Rosen's sartorial effects are always extremely picturesque. . . . her *robe de style*
evening gowns are said to be designed by Mr. Rosen."[1] In stark black or her
sweeping white toga mantle, Lucie was a statuesque enchantress at her RCA
instrument.

In the person of Lucie Bigelow Rosen, Theremin could not have positioned
himself more strategically in the echelons of New York society in the 1930s.
Born Lucie Bigelow Dodge in 1890, she was the scion of some of Gotham's
foremost scholars, statesmen, and members of the Social Register. Her ma-
ternal grandfather, John Bigelow, was United States Ambassador to France under Abraham Lincoln, first president of the New York Public Library, and
editor of the *New York Evening Post* with William Cullen Bryant. Her mother, after a brief marriage to Charles Stuart Dodge, married Lionel Guest, the
youngest son of Lord Windburn of the famous Guest family. In 1914, Lucie
married Walter Tower Rosen, a Harvard-educated trial lawyer and international investment banker, the son of a Jewish family in Berlin. The couple had
two children, Walter Bigelow Rosen, born 1915, and Anne Bigelow Rosen,
born 1917.

From 1930 to '39, the Rosens built Caramoor, a sprawling hundred-acre
estate in the hills of northern Westchester, New York. At the heart of the

wooded expanse they erected a vast, Mediterranean-style villa with red-tiled roofs and a central, Spanish courtyard cloister. Inside, over twenty complete rooms from European palaces and villas housed the family's collection of art treasures spanning two thousand years—English and Italian eighteenth-century lacquer furniture, Chinese wallpaper and cloisonné enamels, jades, ceramics, paintings, sculpture, and the gold-burnished bed of Pope Urban VIII.

The entire west wing of the house was designed as a 115-by-40-foot music room. Under its lofty wooden ceiling—carved for a sixteenth-century Italian palace—alcoves, balconies, stained-glass windows, and arched entrances surrounded seventeenth-century needlework upholstered chairs, Turkish rugs, and Flemish tapestries. Walter Rosen's 1912 Steinway piano adorned the music room stage, where he and Lucie often gave recitals for their friends—she on theremin, and he, an accomplished pianist, accompanying her. The Rosens made their home at Caramoor in the summer—from June to October—and commuted to the estate from their New York townhouse on weekends the remainder of the year.

Lucie had kept a keen eye on Theremin during his swing through Europe, and finally, at a New York drawing-room soirée in 1929, she saw him and his instrument in person. Convinced she wanted a career on the instrument, Lucie set aside nine years of violin study to begin active coaching with the inventor. After six months she made her first public appearance as a member of Theremin's Carnegie Hall ensemble, and in February 1931 she joined a quartet of space-control instruments with the inventor, George Goldberg, and Louis Barlevy. Walter Rosen was bent on supporting his wife's dreams, even if it meant putting Theremin under one of his own roofs.

Lucie Rosen saw herself as an adventurer in the arts, and it thrilled her no end to think she could be a catalyst in something really new. In the private world of the Rosens' largess, the inventor now had the luxury of time and physical space to sow the seeds of his theoretical dreams, and Lucie had the makings of a salon. The Theremin Studio was more than a laboratory. It would become a watering hole for intellectuals and cognoscenti drawn to Theremin's ideas—a place for aesthetic discourse—and a hotbed where musicians and artists of New York's avant-garde would labor to breed strange hybrids of art and technology, already in the '30s trafficking in a world of multimedia and arts synthesis.

Thirty-seven West Fifty-fourth Street was a five-story semibasement building of brownstone and frame construction. The facade was narrow—three tall, slender windows placed closely together across the face of each floor—but the building was deep, and spacious enough to assign a separate function to each level. Theremin took the first floor as his lab and as an area to receive visitors.

He set aside the second floor for pupils to practice and take lessons, and for ensemble rehearsals. With so much "old-fashioned" space, he reserved the third floor just for experiments he was making with a dance platform, and the top floor was arranged as his living quarters.

On December 20, 1930, Theremin met with Maurice Martenot, Hans Barth (composer and "virtuoso on the quarter-tone piano"), and Thomas Wilfred, inventor of the "Clavilux" color organ (a silent projector of complex, evolving colors thrown on a screen), in a miniature arts summit to consider a society for "the combined arts of the future." Various proposals were put on the table: an ensemble to present music of the past on viols, rebecs, and harpsichords; current music and music of the future played on quarter-tone piano and on string and wind instruments "tuned fractionally"; ether music, where "a single player at a single keyboard would be able to play a different instrument with each of his ten fingers, in addition to those with pedals . . . and . . . the acoustical equivalents of every sound in nature"; and color projections as "fluid" operatic scenery, "instead of the present-day static scenery which usually must suffice for one scene." Many theoretical and utopian ideas were thrown around, but few practical steps materialized.[2]

Joseph Schillinger arrived at the Theremin Studio early in 1931. Schillinger was an utterly indefatigable, complex Renaissance man. Born in Kharkov, Russia, in 1895, he was originally trained as a conductor and composer at the St. Petersburg Conservatory, but he also studied philosophy, Eastern religions, and Slavic mythology. He learned Hebrew, German, French, English, and Italian, penned thousands of pages of original scientific thought, made hundreds of drawings, designs, and photographs, and wrote a book of mystical poetry. In a single ten-year period he held eighteen separate posts in Russia—deanships, professorships, conducting and lecturing positions, choirmaster and composition appointments, and various consultantships. In 1927 he researched and recorded native folk music of Georgian tribes in the Caucasus and organized the first Russian jazz orchestra. In November 1928 he came to America at the invitation of the philosopher-educator John Dewey and through the sponsorship of the American Society for Cultural Relations with Russia.

Schillinger believed that in an age of technology, art forms should be engineered and executed with the same scientific rigor and formulas as the building of bridges or skyscrapers—taking advantage of the latest scientific tools. His theory of the arts was based on a conviction that natural laws and mathematical formulas operate on the molecular level in every artistic work. By discovering those formulas and reapplying them, talent, he believed, could take a back seat to knowledge. In music, he dissected hundreds of "masterworks" to discover what made them tick and distilled a canon of guiding principles. He applied his theorems ruthlessly, sparing no one. "In melodies composed by a Verdi or a Bellini," he demonstrated, "the mechanical efficiency is so low that it makes us smile if not laugh."[3] Nicolas Slonimsky recalled that Schillinger boiled down Debussy's harmonies to the "first expansion of the melodic minor scale in its third displacement."[4] In his "Excerpts from a Theory of Synchronization," Schillinger even attempted to formulate equations to frame his ideas:

> The integral of rhythm in any art component can be expressed through the following series as a universal law of composition:
> +00
> $5x = -00 -x^n -2 -1 -1/x(-1/x)^n 0$
> -00
> $(1/x)^n 1/x$ 1 x $x^n 00$
> where the negative values indicate the absence of the component or of one of its parameters.[5]

Schillinger put his theory to work in his own paintings, graphic designs, photography, films, and textile designs, and he saw and analyzed "unconscious art" everywhere, even in his own closet. "Joseph was a fastidious dresser," his wife, Frances, recalled, "and possessed about two hundred pairs of socks of different weights and colors. . . . 40 suits, twenty coats, dozens of shirts . . . and countless ties and accessories. He applied his principles of rhythmic design to the colors and fabrics . . . and, using permutations, was able to vary his outfits so that none was ever fully repeated."[6]

Beginning on April 17, 1931, and following every Friday at 8:30 P.M., Schillinger offered a series of lectures at the Theremin Studio based on his theories. The sequence of talks, entitled "Rudimentary Analysis of Musical Phenomena," was advertised with the promise that the "latest electrical instruments devised by Leon Theremin, will be used to illustrate various phenomena." The titles of the twelve weekly sessions were apparently designed to frighten off all but the stouthearted: "The Variety of Musical Experience"; "Prolegomenon to Musical Analysis and Composition"; "Physical and Psychophysiological Nature of Sound"; "Natural and Tempered Systems of Tuning"; "Instrumentology"; "Tone Space and Musical Matter"; "Statics and Kinetics of Musical Matter"; "Processes of Musical Structure"; "Evolution of Styles"; "Theory of Interpretation"; "Methods of Composition"; and "Theory of Musical Perception."[7]

In addition to the lecture series, the Theremin Studio announced the opening of "The Department of Musical Analysis and Composition" under

Schillinger's direction. A prospectus advertised "Group or Individual Courses and Consultations" and described studies in ear training, composition, and "Rudimentary Analysis of Musical Phenomena," including "theory of musical perception based on conditional reflexology."[8]

All high-priced verbiage aside, however, "Schillinger's system seemed to work in practical application," the composer Nicolas Slonimsky remarked. Before long, Schillinger was the cult figure and mentor for a string of composers and arrangers from Broadway and Hollywood—each "in search of practical formulae" and "willing to pay good Broadway money for the initiation into the mysteries of Schillinger lore."[9] Tommy Dorsey, Benny Goodman, and Oscar Levant flocked to study at his apartment; Glenn Miller created his "Moonlight Serenade" as an exercise for a Schillinger lesson. For four and a half years, beginning in the spring of '32, George Gershwin came to Schillinger for three lessons a week. "Gershwin seized upon the Schillinger method with the delight of a precocious child coming upon a complicated network of electric trains," the writer David Ewen remembered.[10] Gershwin loved musical games and delighted in the endless schemes Schillinger came up with, like his claim, in one case, that 46,656 different styles of composition could be extracted from a particular set of chords, or his penchant for showing students how to generate a composition by plotting a cost of living chart or a stock market graph from the newspaper. Schillinger watched over Gershwin's shoulder as the composer worked on *Porgy and Bess,* the *Cuban Overture,* and the variations on *I Got Rhythm* for piano and orchestra; Gershwin's song "Mine" ("Let 'em Eat Cake") was prepared as an exercise for his lessons.

Eventually, Schillinger's method was published posthumously as *The Schillinger System of Musical Composition,* a massive, two-volume tome of 1,640 pages embracing exhaustive studies in music theory, stylistic practice, musical instruments, and orchestration.

Like Theremin, Schillinger worked to extend his theories into all the senses, postulating an amalgam of sound, light, odor, flavor, pigment, and surface in relation to dimensions of space and time. He proposed imaginary devices, or "musmatons," for the synthesis of musical compositions; "graphomatons" for producing linear designs; "luminatons" for projecting light designs. He saw an infinite variety of art forms: television as "pure design combined with solo and choral declamation," or featuring "monodramas with musical accompaniment," or "dance, combined with . . . animated design, cinema"; he saw "dance with light, kinetic setting, puppets as partners, shadow plays, optical projections," and "machinery for composition of design combined with printing, weaving, projecting." He envisioned "instruments for semi-automatic production of design for use in public and private game-rooms, as a means of entertainment. . . . Three-dimensional kinetic Artomatons." Many of these ideas wound up in another posthumous work, *The Mathematical Basis of the Arts*.[11]

In music, Schillinger saw acoustic instruments as relics of a past art, and after the *First Airphonic Suite* the orchestra itself no longer appealed to him. He was a traditional composer by training—in Russia, a state committee had chosen his *Symphonic Rhapsody*, over pieces of Shostakovich and Glière, as the best work composed during the first decade of Soviet rule—but he had come to feel that "the instruments themselves are not scientifically conceived and not scientifically combined with each other. . . . Nobody ever asks the basic question: why should there be such a combination as the stringed-bow, the wood-wind, the percussive instruments?"[12] In an unpublished manuscript he asked why, in a world where "Nighttime Broadway dazzles with the light of artificial suns," "Sweaty men in tailcoats" still "rub calf-guts with horsehair" or blow "into cylindrical brass tube[s]."[13]

Schillinger had met Theremin at the State Institute of Music in Leningrad and remembered the moment in 1922 when he discovered the space-control instrument: "'Here begins the second half of the history of music,' I told my friends then." It was "overwhelming. As if my consciousness had been hurtled through millennia in one instant. For the distance from the bowstring and calfskin to the theremin really must be measured in millennia." The instrument was "a pitiful box," but it was the future of music to him:

> The multifaced Violini, with his unnaturally developed chin . . . greets the box with no particular joy. He tries to smile sardonically, but a vague fear and inexplicable ennui prevent him from doing so.
>
> He poses a question that he considers ironic: "Here I've spent my whole life playing on a little Kinderkoffen and would venture to ask: can your magic box produce several sounds simultaneously, and are staccato, pizzicato and other effects possible on it?"
>
> "Violini. . . . If you can't bear to part with your Kinderkoffen and can't live without swaying like a pendulum while digging your sharp chin (condemned to atrophy) into the chin-rest—at least have the courage to die with dignity. This is all that remains to you, if you don't wish to become a living museum exhibit. I regret to confirm that the little coffin, which was made by diligent Cremoni and which afforded such joy to your ancestors, has become for you a fateful symbol."[14]

In 1931, Schillinger explained his solution:

> I propose to develop, with the aid of the theremin, projects for various machines for the automatic composition of music. L. S. Theremin considers such machines entirely feasible. . . . Under such conditions, musical works can be

broadcast over the radio at the same time that they are being composed by the machine.

The final aim of this work is to construct a synthetic machine capable of composing works of a higher order and with a greater degree of perfection than is accessible to living composers. The machine will be given only a general physico-mathematical idea, and the execution will proceed automatically.[15]

He prophesied: "The men who will be responsible for the music of radio and television of 1950 will be neither composers nor performers, but a new kind of 'music engineer' who will operate the machines that compose and perform music."[16]

While Schillinger waited for "perfected electronic models" of instruments and the "universal use of electronic music,"[17] he played his own space-control instrument, and in 1929 he wrote a "Manual for Playing the Space-Control Theremin," which was never published.

In 1929, Nicolas Slonimsky introduced Theremin to a member of Schillinger's circle—the composer Henry Cowell, who found a kindred artistic spirit in the inventor. Cowell, along with Charles Ives and Edgard Varese, was one of those front-line American composers attempting to pull down the old ramparts between "music" and "noise." His was the very sort of work Arno Huth described as "cramped," because "the instruments are not there." In the '20s Cowell felt he had exhausted the possibilities of the standard piano and reached under the lid to make music with its insides—plucking, sweeping, and brushing the strings themselves. He invented and named the "tone cluster" (a group of adjacent notes on the piano, played by the fist, forearm, or a board) and sifted through Indian and Javanese music for ideas. Cowell explored complex rhythms in his work, and by 1931, as Slonimsky put it, he was "annoyed by the wistful realization that . . . human players will still be human—that is, inaccurate, physiologically limited, rhythmically crippled, and unwilling to reform." He "hit upon the idea of an instrument which would faithfully produce all kinds of rhythms and cross-rhythms. . . . He spoke to Professor Leon Theremin."[18]

Cowell set out the basic ideas for such an instrument in his 1930 book *New Musical Resources,* and on March 7, 1931, he remitted two hundred dollars to Theremin to construct it. "My part in its invention," Cowell said, "was to invent the idea that such a rhythmic instrument was a necessity to further rhythmic development, which has reached a limit, more or less, of performance by hand, . . . what rhythms it should do, and the pitch it should have, and the relation between the pitch and rhythm. . . . With this idea, I went to Theremin, who did the rest."[19] Cowell planned to use the instrument—which he and Theremin called the "rhythmicon"—as a tool for "scientific, physical and psychological experiments with rhythm" and as a practical instrument for new musical compositions. Each of its sixteen keys, when depressed, sounded its own specific rhythm—from one to sixteen equal divisions of a beat—on a pitch that corresponded to the same number in the overtone series. The lowest pitch (or fundamental) sounded one note per beat, the second harmonic (the next adjacent key) sounded two notes per beat, the third harmonic (and next key) sounded three notes per beat, and so on, up to the sixteenth harmonic with sixteen divisions to the beat, the whole instrument spanning a four-octave range. The rhythmicon was polyphonic, meaning it could play any number of rhythms (depressed keys) simultaneously. Essentially it was an early prototype of the drum machine.

Cowell came up with the basic engineering principle—the idea that "broken up light playing on a photo-electric cell, would be the best means of making it practical." Then Theremin "invented the method by which the light could be cut, did the electrical calculations, and built the instrument."[20] When a key was depressed, rotating cog wheels interrupted a beam of light focused on a photoelectric cell, dividing the light into a specific pattern of impulses that triggered the sound of the pitch and rhythm. Theremin worked on the rhythmicon at his studio throughout the spring, hoping for a formal showing when it was finished.

《 》

With the exception of business or artistic contacts like Henry Cowell, or requisite cordialities with the Rosens, the inventor clung to the Russian community for his social recreation. Around the corner on Fifty-fifth Street, he always found a welcoming refuge at the home of the Bolotines, where he often took dinner and could unwind in the comfort of the Russian language. Leonid Bolotine was a former faculty member of Philadelphia's Curtis Institute of Music, and with his wife, Cleopatra, and their children, he frequently dropped into Theremin's studio to chat and test out the inventor's newest handiwork. Nine-year-old Yolanda studied the piano, and with her perfect pitch she found she could easily navigate her way around the space-control instrument. After school she would stop off for lessons with the professor, then practice on the second floor, standing on a box to reach the pitch antenna at eye level.

"My father was the most excellent violinist," she remembered, and when he played Theremin's fingerboard instrument, "he had that vibrato—*professional* vibrato, that only a professional musician can have, and it was *magnificent* sounding."[21] Bolotine's casual trials of the instrument around the studio led the inventor to a new twist on the idea of an electrical ensemble. In June 1931, he assembled a trio to perform light popular music. The space-control

The Ether Wave Salon \ 137

instrument was played by George Goldberg (wearing the temporary new alias of "George Goreff"), Leonid Bolotine played the fingerboard model, and the pianist Vladimir Brenner manned a new keyboard model. The new group, Electrio, debuted on a syndicated broadcast over the WJZ network on June 25, 1931. A male vocal quartet, an orchestra, and soloists provided background accompaniment and played additional selections.[22] The trio was featured in four numbers:

"Lady, Play Your Mandolin" . . . . Electrio, quartet and orchestra
"By the Waters of Minnetonka" . . . . Electrio
"Bye, Bye Blues" . . . . Electrio, quartet and orchestra
"My Hero" from *The Chocolate Soldier* . . Electrio, quartet and orchestra

In early 1932, the group reconvened as the Theremin Electro-Ensemble—with Gleb Yellin replacing Vladimir Brenner on the keyboard instrument—and appeared as a regular syndicated feature each Monday at 3:15 P.M. over the CBS radio network.

≪≫

Temporarily disrupting the peace at 37 West, the stricken RCA Theremin project came to an unexpected, sudden end. Over the past few years as the instrument was manufactured and marketed, RCA had been entrenched in an industrywide tug-of-war over radio tubes. "In March, 1931," Lee De Forest wrote in *Father of Radio,*

> the scene of the far-reaching patent battle between the De Forest Radio Company and the Radio Corporation of America, one which involved millions of dollars and the basic patents of the radio industry, shifted to Baltimore.
> Charging infringement of thirteen patents, the De Forest Company filed suit in United States District Court, seeking a restraining injunction, an accounting, payment of profits earned by use of the patents, and triple damages.
> While the suit was directed primarily at the "Theremin," it involved all instruments employing vacuum tubes in the synthetic reproduction of music. . . . The De Forest Radio Company won and was awarded heavy damages.[23]

In a letter of July 15, 1931, addressed to Samuel E. Darby Jr., lawyer for the De Forest Radio Company, RCA's attorneys spelled out the proposed terms of settlement:

De Forest v. Radio Victor
De Forest v. Pilot Radio

Dear Mr. Darby:
I am advised by RCA Victor Company that the sales of "Theremins" by Radio Corporation of America and its subsidiary companies were in 1929, 178, in

1930, 306, and in 1931, 1. Also, that the sales receipts were $43,332.36, and that the cost of manufacture, not including any selling or advertising expense, or other expenses, was $43,650.

In accordance with our telephone conversations, I am enclosing herewith original and copies of proposed orders of discontinuance and releases in the above suits.[24]

Radio Victor was advised by its attorney to offer payment of $6,000 in damages, in consideration of the orders of discontinuance and the releases in the suit.

In two years, the company had sold 485 of the original production run of 500 instruments, at a loss (when promotion, merchandising, and Theremin's fees were figured in), and had little to show for its efforts in the development of electronic instruments. The difficulties of learning to play the theremin had made it a tough sell with the public, and now, after the De Forest suit, it was clear that the new, prototype "Victor Theremin"—with a built-in speaker— would not be mass-produced. The option on patent rights to Theremin's inventions was not taken up, and the Migos Corporation was left holding worthless shares of stock. Years later, in 1938, Benjamin Miessner, a noted pioneer in radio engineering and electronic musical instruments, wrote to George H. Clark asking if RCA might be interested in his electric pianos. Miessner admitted: "I know and RCA knows that they made a mistake with their Theremin venture. That mistake has caused them to have doubts about all electronic music instruments. . . . But the past few years have proven very decisively that electronic organs and small instruments have a very strong appeal, backed up by fine sales records."[25]

≪≫

In late December of 1931, a young woman with auburn hair and brown eyes— a former debutante from Houston—came to the Theremin Studio. The *New York World Telegram* described Mary Ellen Bute's "flashing smile like the toothpaste ads and a soft Southern voice that reminds one . . . of moonlight and magnolias," but added that she must "bowl over nearly everyone she meets when she says casually: 'We need a new kinetic, visual art form—one that unites sound, color and form. We can take a mathematical formula and develop a whole composition exactly synchronized.' "[26]

Bute was born in Texas in 1906, the daughter of a former debutante queen and a doctor turned cattle rancher. At sixteen, she was a scholarship student at the Pennsylvania Academy of the Fine Arts, and she later studied at the Sorbonne and the Yale School of Drama. She was a painter driven by the work of Kandinsky—at the first sight of it she was "lassoed, bound and branded"—

and she loved the way his abstract forms were "varied, permutated, expanded and contracted . . . building to a stunning *visual* climax. It was like Visual Music." As a painter she was impatient with static canvases and wanted "visual themes" that "could unfold, and permutate and build to a climax before our eyes, as Music does for our ears."[27]

For a time she worked on the Clavilux color organ with Thomas Wilfred—who had also just installed a model at the home of Leopold Stokowski—but she found it couldn't offer the control over design and hue she was looking for. When she came to 37 West, she recalled, "the atmosphere in the Studio was unceasingly creative and free flowing," and with the inventor she began work on a custom-built device. "The work continued at a great clip," she remembered:

> We immersed a tiny mirror in a small tube of oil, connected by a fine wire which was led through an oscillator to a type of joy-stick control. Manipulating this joy-stick was like having a responsive drawing pencil, or paint brush that flowed light and was entirely under the control of the person at the joy-stick.
>
> Mrs. Rosen, who owned the Town House the Studio occupied . . . would come by to practice on the new electronic instruments. The sheer beauty of the sound thrilled her. She would exclaim: "What a lovely sound! I could embrace it!" I felt that way about this little point of living light—it seemed so responsive and intelligent. It seemed to follow what you had in mind rather than the manipulation of the oscillator.
>
> The result on the screen was pristine and pure like a lovely drawing in kinetic light that developed in time-continuity.[28]

Bute and Theremin showed their results to the New York Musicological Society at a lecture demonstration on January 31, 1932. Bute read a paper based on the inventor's ideas, "The Perimeters of Light and Sound and Their Possible Synchronization," and Theremin connected the optical device to one of his electronic instruments, "so that the sound modified and controlled the light." The musicologists were apparently delighted, and Bute credited Theremin with being twenty years ahead of his time. But it was still only an approximation of what she wanted. "At that time," she later reflected, "all of the apparatus was highly erratic and very expensive. . . . it wasn't dependable enough. You could get something you liked one time—but it was hard to repeat. In other words, it was just experimental and not truly usable."[29]

At the studio, Bute met Joseph Schillinger and became enthralled with how "his work correlates sound, time, and shapes." His "Physico-Mathematical Theory of Musical Composition" appealed to her, and she began taking lessons with the theorist, convinced she could find answers in his method. "Schillinger's system helped me over the bump as far as making composition in time continuity and so it freed me to work on visual effects. . . . once I had learned to do the sound composition . . . I was determined to paint in film."[30]

Bute had always been attracted to film, but she had written off Hollywood as commercial fluff. Abstract design was her passion, and as far as she knew there was no cinematic precedent for showing nonobjective forms in motion. But her music composition lessons finally clinched the situation, and what resulted was her first cinematic project—a 1932 collaboration with Schillinger and the filmmaker-historian Lewis Jacobs, called *Synchromy* (derived from a combination of "synchronize," "chiaroscuro," and "symphony"). The five-minute black-and-white short was based on *The Schillinger System of Musical Composition* and on Theremin's ideas in "The Perimeters of Light and Sound and Their Possible Synchronization." Bute and Elias Katz created the Kandinsky-like drawings, and Lewis Jacobs did the camera work and animation. The experiment marked a milestone as the first attempt in the United States to create a film entirely from moving abstract shapes. *Synchromy*, sometimes called *Synchronization*, launched Mary Ellen Bute's fifty-year career as a filmmaker who specialized in dramas composed entirely of animated abstract graphics.

≪≫

Early in 1932, the rhythmicon was ready and made its debut at New York's New School for Social Research at a concert on January 19. Cowell described the instrument's functions to the audience, and he and Joseph Schillinger demonstrated the possibilities. The *Musical Courier* reported the sound to be like "a strong flute in the high register; or a strong bassoon in the low register."[31] The critics were generally unimpressed. Marc Blitzstein quipped that "insofar as one is constrained to represent a single rhythm always upon the same repeated note, and without deviation from the regular beat, the limitations far outweigh the advantages, from the point of view of musical application."[32] "This more or less defeats its own end," *Musical America* concurred, "as the ear, being more accustomed to listen for melody than rhythm, is apt to ignore the latter. The melodic possibilities of the instrument seem small, though its theoretical interest is high."[33]

At the time of the demonstration, Charles Ives decided to commission a second, improved, instrument. This rhythmicon included a sliding rheostat control allowing the performer to adjust the fundamental pitch upward or downward, transposing the whole harmonic series on the sixteen keys with it. Variations in tempo were possible with a second rheostat control. "It relieved my mind," Ives wrote to Slonimsky, "to know especially that the new one would be nearer to an instrument, than a machine. . . . I sent the remitted check to

Mr. Theremin yesterday—and he's started the building. It will be yours and Henry's—I just want to help—and sit under its 'shadow' on a nice day."[34]

Schillinger claimed that with the rhythmicon he could produce drum beats "comparable to the drumming of African natives," and that experts were unable to distinguish between his own records "made in such a way and the genuine recordings made in the Belgian Congo by the Denis-Roosevelt Expedition, which were used in the motion picture, 'Dark Rapture.'"[35] One listener described the tone of the instrument on Schillinger's recordings as "rhythmicized grunts," like the sound produced "by short, heavy strokes of the bow on the string bass."[36] When Cowell brought the rhythmicon to Stanford University in 1932, a writer for the *San Francisco Chronicle* characterized the sound as a "cross between a grunt and a snort in the low 'tones' and like an Indian war whoop in the high tones."[37]

Cowell devised a special system of notation for the instrument, and by December 1931 he had written a four-movement work for rhythmicon and orchestra called *Rhythmicana*. In 1932 he apparently also wrote a second piece for rhythmicon and violin, but the score seems to have been lost. *Rhythmicana* had its first performance after the composer's death, forty years to the month of its composition. At the premiere on December 3, 1971—with the Stanford Symphony Orchestra conducted by Sandor Salgo—the rhythmicon part was realized on a computer-generated tape, with a click-track communicated to the conductor through an earphone to coordinate the solo part with the orchestra.

Of the two original rhythmicons, the first instrument was discarded at Stanford University in 1938, with Cowell's approval, after it fell into disrepair, and the second remained with Slonimsky, who wrote a work for it and used it publicly and privately on several occasions. Later he sold it to Schillinger, whose widow donated it to the Smithsonian Institution in 1966, although it was not in working condition. These were apparently the only two rhythmicons made by the inventor while he was in America.

≪≫

Of all Theremin's pupils—and there were many coming and going at the studio by now—one young woman stood out. From the first moment she stepped up to the instrument, there was a seasoned poise, a knowing intensity to her approach, as though she had always played the instrument. She was a violinist, and that was part of it, but she was no ordinary musician. Clara Reisenberg was born in Vilna (later Vilnius), Lithuania, in 1911. At the age of three, she caused a stir at the St. Petersburg Conservatory when she played the piano and demonstrated perfect pitch. Leopold Auer, the renowned teacher of

Jascha Heifetz and Mischa Elman, accepted her as an "unofficial" violin pupil the following year, and at her entrance examination, perched on a table as a tiny wunderkind, she astounded an august committee headed by the composer Alexander Glazunov, winning a 5+—the highest possible grade. At age five, she was the youngest student ever admitted to the St. Petersburg Conservatory.

In the civil war following the revolution, the Reisenberg family languished under conditions of near famine, and by 1919, with conservatory professors fleeing the ravaged Petrograd, the family retreated to their native Vilna, putting an end to Clara's study. Over the next few years she and her sister, the pianist Nadia Reisenberg—six years her senior—traveled around Poland, Lithuania, Germany, and France, concertizing as youthful virtuosos. "The sisters Reisenberg are children gifted with extraordinary musical talents," a German newspaper wrote. "The older, Nadia, is highly musical, possessing . . . an unusually brilliant technique. Clara, the younger, plays with her little fingers on a three quarter violin, yet she still plays the hardest concert with such earnestness that she enchants the audience."[38]

On December 19, 1921, Clara, her parents, and her sisters, Anna and Nadia, arrived in New York as steerage passengers on a steamer, holding affidavits from American relatives, with plans to settle in the United States. In America, Clara was astonished to come upon Leopold Auer, who had emigrated in 1918, and she again took up lessons with him.

Late in 1928, one of Joseph Schillinger's friends, a chemistry professor named Dr. Vinogradov, took Clara to meet Theremin at his Hotel Plaza suite and see his instrument, simply for the fun of it. "He was being introduced to all various persons," she remembered, "and I was among the various persons that he had to suffer to see." To her surprise, Clara was genuinely intrigued. "I saw this instrument which would fascinate any artist, any musician—the beauty, the esthetic quality of it. And Professor Termen himself was such an interesting and charming person."[39] He offered her a try at the instrument. When she raised her arms before the antennas, it was unlike anything he had witnessed before. Every minute gesture of her finely calibrated violinist's arms and fingers—technique inborn from before she could remember—and a mellowed, old-world musical sophistication beyond her teenage years, as natural as walking or breathing, punctuated the air with a confident music. "I was fascinated," she recalled, "but at the same time, apparently *he* was fascinated, because instinctively, or because of my absolute pitch, or because of violin playing, I could do things immediately that probably people couldn't do."[40]

Clara was charmed, but she was "a busy violinist," with concert engagements to fulfill with Nadia. Suddenly, while preparing a performance of the

Beethoven Violin Concerto, Clara developed a terrible pain and a nagging weakness in her right arm that began to sap energy from her technique. Consultations with doctors brought the problem to light: the malnutrition she suffered as a child during the revolution and the civil war had left her with poorly formed bones. There was little that could be done.

When the inventor presented her with an RCA instrument, Clara kept it at her Sixty-ninth Street apartment, dabbling with it from time to time. But the violin was still paramount in her life. "I made two or three valiant and brave attempts to go back to it," she remembered. Waiting for her arm to improve, she continued to try the space-control instrument. "My interest in the theremin was running parallel with my attempts to go back to the violin . . . and only when I couldn't possibly succeed physically to work my arm, I gave up the violin."[41] By 1932, Clara was committed to transferring her musical sensibilities to the theremin, but she wouldn't attempt a solo debut in public until she had reached the level of artistry she always demanded of herself, even if no precedent existed for it on the space-control instrument.

Theremin, in spite of his de facto marriage to Katia, made no secret of his growing attachment to Clara. As a surprise for her eighteenth birthday, he prepared a magical cake surrounded by an electromagnetic field. When she approached it, the cake rotated and the single candle in the center was illuminated. "Termen and I were very, very friendly quite outside of music," she admitted, "I was constantly there—Russian Easter, Russian this, Russian this— I was always included, and Termen and I had very wonderful memories of dancing together."[42] Often, three or four nights a week, they would hit the New York nightclub scene, he in his tuxedo, she in her polished black concert gowns, following the bands at the major hotels. Clara remembered he was "a marvelous dancer," leading with a suave strength that swept her perfectly into step with him. She remembered they were often taken for professionals, with a spotlight trained on them as other couples stopped and applauded. "He was a handsome man, an agile man. . . . we danced and danced enough that he fell deeply in love with me."[43]

Clara never really studied space-control technique with the inventor beyond about three coaching sessions, which were more demonstrations of basic arm movements than formal music lessons. After that she was able to cut loose with her already acute musicianship guiding her intuitively.

In April, Theremin was to have another Carnegie Hall showing of his newest creations. On the third floor of his studio he was secretly hatching a new species of space-control instrument—something he had seen in his mind's eye for a decade. His "terpsitone," or "ether wave dance stage," was the space-control principle writ large—a dancer could now control pitch with movements of the entire body. An insulated metal plate beneath the dance platform acted as the pitch antenna, registering the stooping and rising of the dancer as relative changes in pitch. Like the space-control theremin, the variable oscillator was heterodyned with a fixed oscillator, and the resulting beat note was sent to an amplifier and reproduced in a loudspeaker. Volume and vibrato were controlled separately by an operator backstage.

Since the performer had no control over volume—and therefore no method of articulating separate pitches by cutting the volume back between notes—the terpsitone used a system of vibrators, tuned to the chromatic scale, which controlled the amplifier and allowed only twelve incremental pitches per octave to be selected for audible reproduction. The electrical circuits, contained backstage in a wall-mounted unit, consisted of four tubes: one fixed oscillator, one variable oscillator (its grid circuit connected to the metal plate beneath the dance platform), one mixer (or modulator), and an audio frequency amplifier. Transformers and tuned coils were housed directly below, in the same cabinet.

In a later model, Theremin added a "visual note indicator" as a guide for the dancer. This system used a panel of colored lights that illuminated, one at a time, as the corresponding pitch for each light sounded. The scheme worked through a set of tuned reeds, one for each light, which vibrated sympathetically as a given note was played, closing the circuit and lighting the lamp. A concealed loudspeaker in the wall projected accompanying phonograph music into the room.

A long search failed to produce a dancer who could manage the terpsitone. Theremin "tried every dancer under the sun," Clara remembered, "but nobody could carry the tune. I could do that, but I certainly wasn't going to jump around and pretend to be a ballerina."[44] Up to this point, Clara had been loathe to appear in public before she was ready. In January she had ventured a cameo appearance with an ensemble in the same New School concert where the rhythmicon debuted. Now, with some hesitation, she agreed to unveil the terpsitone at Carnegie Hall. Despite her reticence, Clara delighted in the variety of choreographic gestures she could use to produce any given pitch:

> I still remember the fascination I had, because here [on the space-control Theremin] you have no choice—you go up the scale, down the scale, and God forbid that you move one pinhead too much, you're in the wrong place—such small intervals. You can't *dance* that way . . . how could you possibly do it? *Here* [on the terpsitone] you had the whole body instead of the whole hand. In other words, you could do *this,* and you didn't have to do *that.* You could move your head, rather than your hand. . . . You could raise your shoulder. Your whole body was in the musical field; you had a *choice.*[45]

The Carnegie Hall concert, Theremin's most elaborate presentation to date of an electrical ensemble, took place on April 1, 1932. Sixteen performers, billed as the "Theremin Electrical Symphony Orchestra," appeared in solos, small ensembles, and as a complete orchestra. The larger groups were directed by the conductor and composer Albert Stoessel, then the music director of the opera and orchestra departments of the Juilliard Graduate School. Among the performers was the pianist Rosalyn Tureck who, as a freshman at Juilliard that year, had undertaken the study of the space-control instrument with the inventor. Her actual Carnegie Hall debut, she later joked, was as a performer on Theremin's keyboard harmonium. Ten-year-old Yolanda Bolotine also performed, standing on her box to play Glinka's "Skylark" on the space-control instrument.

Between 1930 and 1932, the inventor had developed his "keyboard theremin," which would now assume a prominent role in the Carnegie Hall concert. Previously it had been heard in Electrio and its successor, the Theremin Electro-Ensemble, and in the January concert at the New School where a student had played Debussy's prelude "Bruyères" on it. Leopold Stokowski, after he abandoned the fingerboard model, experimented with a keyboard theremin, using one in January 1932 at orchestra concerts in Philadelphia, and on tour in New York and Washington because it was readily portable.

The keyboard theremin, by means of two pedals, a tuning calibration dial, and a series of "stops," could emulate instrumental timbres ranging from the tone of the piano to the sounds of the brass, woodwinds, and timpani. Joseph Schillinger remembered that it offered "well expressed forms of attack, regulated forms of tremulant, fading effects with vibrato automatically performed (as on the Hawaiian guitar), and automatically pre-set varied degrees of staccato etc."[46] The keyboard model had an output of 100 watts and was played through six 12-inch speakers. In addition to its 61 keys (five octaves), it had a "fingerboard channel" offering an alternate interface for string players.

Theremin's Carnegie Hall electronic orchestra, thinner in ranks than his original plan for forty instruments, still operated on the same principle: ten performers played instruments of widely contrasting timbre, approximating the sounds of the orchestral choirs. Fingerboard theremins of assorted timbres and registers covered the strings, and keyboard theremins mimicked the brass, woodwind, and percussion sections. The space-control model was not used within the large ensemble. Among the works performed were arrangements of the *Fantasia in G* and a chorale, by Bach, played by an orchestra of five fingerboard and five keyboard instruments conducted by Stoessel. The rhythmicon was demonstrated, and the "electronic timpani" (from the keyboard theremin) was heard for the first time. According to a preconcert notice in the *New York Herald Tribune,* this function was "operated from an octave of regulation keyboard and said to produce the deep bass notes with sufficient clarity as to make its pitch discernible to the captious ear."[47]

Clara demonstrated the terpsitone by performing the Bach-Gounod "Ave Maria," accompanied by the harpist Carlos Salzedo. Dressed in black, she began the "dance" on her knees in a prayer position, rising slowly.

Demonstrating a new optical apparatus, Theremin showed how pitch accuracy on the space-control theremin could be "read" by the eyes. The "whirling watcher" consisted of a U-shaped glass tube filled with neon gas, wired to the space-control instrument. Electric currents in the instrument excited the tube, causing it to act as a stroboscope and emit regular flashes of light corresponding to the frequency of a particular pitch on the theremin. The alternate ignition and extinction of the flashes were faster than the human eye could perceive and appeared as a constant illumination. Two large disks, one with black-and-white geometric patterns, the other with numerals, rotated at a constant speed. As the theremin changed pitch, the resulting change in the speed of the flashes caused a particular two-digit number and geometric shape to appear due to the phenomenon of "persistence of vision." Alterations in pitch caused the numbers and patterns to appear to jump from one to another, or to rotate slowly, stop, reverse direction, and become lost in the blur of the disk. Inaccuracies of intonation could easily be "noticed" by the audience.

The "Theremin Electrical Symphony Orchestra" was in many ways a last musical hurrah for the inventor in America. Interest in his work was dwindling among critics and audiences, perhaps because by now they were all too familiar with principles drained of their original shock value. Reviewers were turning out in fewer numbers, and what critical reaction there was took on a patronizing, often mocking tone. The *New York Times* commented summarily on the 1932 concert: "An audience of good size was present and followed with close interest and with warmth the various performances. And well it might have, for at times music was played pleasingly. The one thing perhaps that was lacking on the stage was an electrical page turner."[48] A reviewer for *Time* magazine was less kind: "The stage of Manhattan's Carnegie Hall might have been set for Funnyman Joe Cook one evening last week, or it might have been a physicist's laboratory. It was crowded with odd-shaped pieces of apparatus. Wires ran over the floor. Leon Theremin, the Russian who makes music out of radio static, was back again to demonstrate new elaborations of his stunt. . . . Finally the pupils performed altogether, sounded not unlike a group of children, a little uncertain as to pitch, blowing on combs and tissue paper."[49]

For Theremin, a major obstacle in these demonstrations was always the repertoire. As long as his instruments could only borrow familiar music and feebly replicate the original tone colors, their sound would be seen as inferior, and their whole purpose would be called into question. "The prospect, so jauntily suggested . . . of a complete orchestra of Theremophones," Lawrence Gilman had argued in 1928, "(performing, one assumes, the Brahms C minor and the 'Pathetic' Symphony without the use of expensive fiddlers and first horns and woodwind choirs and timpanists) strikes us as highly unlikely of realization; nor would it be desirable. . . . we should lose as much as we could possibly gain."[50] "The electrical musical instrument of the future," Dr. Alfred N. Goldsmith, RCA's vice president, maintained in 1930, "will require great composers just as the piano needed Mozart and Beethoven before its capabilities were realized. Somewhere in the future, probably as yet unborn, are the great composers who will write the master works for these new electrical instruments."[51]

After the Carnegie concert, Irving J. Saxl applauded the idea itself in *Radio News:* "In the line of the various instruments this may mark the first fundamentally new musical development for the last 100 years. It is a beginning of the use of the possibilities which dreamers and scientists attach to music, and with some minor imperfections which show that we are just at the *start* of a new musical development."[52]

The reality of the situation, unfortunately, was expressed more in comments emphasizing the "minor imperfections." Marc Blitzstein's comments following the New School demonstration were typical of those who would put the kibosh on the inventor's demonstrations: "Theremin's electrical instruments have undergone steady perfecting; without much result. Their tone color (it is the same for all—keyboard, space-control and fingerboard instruments) remains lamentably sentimental, without virility. The most perfected one, like a cello, exposes most brutally the cloying sound."[53]

Theremin was never able to realize his plan of an electronic ensemble to mirror the qualities of an acoustic orchestra. The notion, of course, exceeded both the limits of his own instruments and the technology of the time. Only decades later would the complex and subtle sound synthesis required to impersonate the instruments finally allow others to forge his dreams into a workable reality.

While the public moved on, the circle of friends and acquaintances revolving around the Theremin Studio continued to follow the inventor's work with interest. Gerald Warburg, a cellist and a student of Joseph Schillinger, saw further potential in Theremin's musical vision. Warburg was the son of the financier Felix M. Warburg ("dean of American Jewish Philanthropists"—an original sponsor of Theremin's Hotel Plaza debut) and would marry the daughter of Condé Nast in 1933. An alumnus of Harvard, he studied music in Paris and Vienna, and in 1927 he made his solo debut with the New York Philharmonic under Walter Damrosch. With his father, he founded the Stradivarius Quartet, using four Strad instruments from the elder Warburg's collection.

In a letter of January 21, 1932, Theremin, at Warburg's request, agreed to design and build a custom "Electric Theremin-Organ." With Schillinger acting as a consultant and middleman, the inventor was to have the fully functioning instrument completed by March 21, and was to be paid a total of $1,150 for materials but no compensation for his personal work. The elaborate specifications for the instrument included seventy-five keys, seventy-five tuning dials, "vibrato by intensity with speed control," timbre control, a volume control pedal, and a built-in loudspeaker. Schillinger would have the final say on the musical performance and satisfactory functioning of the instrument. Warburg was granted the sole option to finance commercial development of the finished model, on the condition he produce a contract acceptable to the inventor. Theremin would be paid $900 in installments during the construction and was to receive the final $250 upon completion of the project.[54]

On April 4, Theremin wrote to Schillinger,

> The amounts received by me have been already spent for the construction of the instrument and at present I find it extremely difficult to acquire the balance of parts necessary for its completion.
> My efforts to furnish the necessary amount from other sources do not seem to be successful and, being extremely interested in the completion of the instrument, I am compelled to request you to assist me in having the balance of $250, due after completion of the instrument, advanced to me at the present time.
> This would enable me to continue the construction and to complete it within the nearest future.[55]

Schillinger responded by alerting Warburg's attorney, who wrote to Theremin: "we might consider making the advance at this time of the final $250. were we certain that the $900. already paid had been used for the purchase of equipment and construction of the instrument. I point out to you that you are already in default on your obligations under the Agreement inasmuch as the entire instrument was to have been completed by March 21st."[56] Theremin was now to submit the completed phase of his work to Schillinger for examination, to determine if the $900 had indeed been invested in construction costs. "Unless the instrument is promptly completed in accordance with the terms of the Agreement of January 21st," the letter continued, "we shall be compelled to advise Mr. Warburg on his return to hold you responsible for your breach of the Agreement under which you have already received $900."[57]

The Theremin Studio had been a refuge for the inventor—his private sanctuary of art and science. But it could not shelter him against financial realities. Debt was always knocking at the door, and it would be calling again soon.

SIX

Alarms, Magic Mirrors, and the Ethereal Suspension

Walk through a door and a shrieking alarm goes off. Touch a filing cabinet and another alarm goes off. Go to a mirror to set your tie and a light flashes behind the mirror so that you see, not your tie, but an advertisement.

—*Fortune,* April 1935

Yolanda Bolotine recalled an electric doll Theremin made that went toddling across his studio floor. Clara Reisenberg remembered seeing a cradle in his lab with a doll lying in it. The kidnapping and murder of Charles Lindbergh's twenty-month-old son in March 1932 had the nation on tenterhooks, and Theremin's response to the "crime of the century" was a capacitive scheme that threw an electromagnetic ring around a crib, setting off an alarm if an intruder penetrated it. In the July '32 issue of *Radio News,* Irving J. Saxl rated Theremin's system over those that used an electric eye (they could be "fooled" by a flashlight if the beam was not pulsating) or microphone monitors (they could be disabled). In "Radio Guards the Baby," Saxl praised the subtlety of Theremin's method, which could "report the approach of an object by recording and amplifying changes in the inductive and capacitive characteristics of the surrounding medium (air)." He described the apparatus: "If the sensitive metallic rod, which may be hidden in the construction of the cradle, 'feels' the approach of any object within a radius distance of 20 feet from any direction whatsoever, a relay will operate the sounding of a horn, a siren or a loud-speaker in any remote part of the building as a warning signal."[1] "The radio sciences have given us ever watchful eyes, that never wink or sleep," he wrote. "They have given us sensitive invisible fingers that 'feel,' through glass and brick walls over a distance of many feet, the approach of objects which human senses might never notice. May the perfection of devices of this type add to the safety of our beloved ones."

Musical equipment was less and less on the inventor's workbench. Clara recalled trying an ondes martenot that he kept around his studio—a stiff reminder of how competitive the field had become—but new Theremin instruments were not emerging from 37 West. Ironically, the inventor's small blip on the American commercial horizon, though it failed to create a consumer market for the Victor Theremin, managed to make the instrument a generic circuit configuration like the radio. Gradually, people were referring less to *the* Theremin (with a capital "T"), than *a* theremin (with a lower-case "t"), something anyone could build with a few parts from a radio store. No one was manufacturing theremins, so if you wanted one, you had to construct it from scratch, and published schematics were beginning to appear for the hobbyist.

At the Berlin Wireless Exhibition in August 1932, the Heinrich Hertz Institute announced it had come up with a simple electronic musical instrument anyone could build. Based on the theremin, it consisted of a small box with a vertical brass pitch antenna, a volume control pedal, and a left-hand articulation controller button. The construction was designed to be placed near any ordinary radio receiver, using the speaker, amplifier, and one high-frequency oscillator in the set. Nothing else was needed, making it feasible for anyone to "own" the instrument. "As the whole instrument can be built by an amateur in a very short time out of such parts as he has spare," the Hertz Institute explained, concluding with a familiar ring, "it seems not too much to hope that the new device will soon become a very popular 'home music' producer."[2] The same year, Joachim Winckelmann in Berlin published *Das Theremin-Musikgerät*, a twenty-three-page constructor's guide for building a homemade theremin. By 1935, E. L. Deeter was offering the American home tinkerer "An Easily-Built 'Theremin'" in *Radio-Craft* magazine, and *Funk* in Germany ran a similar article, "Selbstbau eines Theremin-Musikgerätes." It was all quite proletarian—music for the people—but not very lucrative in RCA's terms.

Theremin would be driven to more practical work that could woo commerce back to his corner. By now he was on the eighth extension of a sixth-month visitor's visa, and he needed hard evidence to keep the Department of Labor happily signing more postponements of his departure. Likewise, Berzin's office back home had little use for the arcane experiments of a Cowell or a Schillinger, and the inventor could hardly afford to alienate the Kremlin. No military or industrial secrets lay buried in the rhythmicon, but further business contacts could be fertile soil.

When the Rosens transferred Theremin to Fifty-fourth Street they viewed it as a temporary solution. Several months after he arrived at 37 West, Lucie wrote to her neighbor John D. Rockefeller Jr., who was overseeing the construction of Rockefeller Center. "I would like very much to introduce you to our friend Professor Leon Theremin," she began, because I think his work is peculiarly interesting to you.

. . . as a student of the new instruments, I learned that these were by no means the only adventures of the Professor. We learned that his history included early research work in physics and astronomy, radio receiving, and television.

My husband remarked that his quarters were entirely inadequate, and offered temporarily one of the old houses in our street which was waiting to be done over, where at least he had space to work and live. We learned from the little group of men who work with him, that he is no visionary or impractical dreamer, but a physicist and mathematician accustomed to prove to other men his statements, and we have seen plans capable of such useful and energetic expansion that I would like to ask your support for this laboratory and its place in your Radio City. . . .

In this belief, may I ask you to visit this Laboratory which is already your neighbor? or let these men speak for themselves, I will ask them to try. For I found here that science and art are working together for the future, which seems to me the peculiar discovery of our age, and the promise of more beauty in life than people have hoped for, who have not seen how machines could be developed and used.

Believe me, very sincerely yours,

Mrs. Walter T. Rosen.[3]

However well intentioned the letter, nothing materialized, and Theremin hung on at the Rosens' townhouse.

Between October 1930 and July 1931, the inventor had stockpiled six thousand dollars' worth of equipment from the RCA Victor Company, on credit, anticipating a new wave of productivity. But it was no time to be doing business. Although a buoyant Herbert Hoover had assured Americans in March 1931 that prosperity was "just around the corner," in the three short years from September 1929—when the first RCA Theremins came off the assembly line—to July 1932, when prices on the New York Stock Exchange would hit rock bottom, the Dow Jones industrial average slipped from 452 to 58, and stock-and-bond investment slid from $10 million to $1 million. Over those three years, farm income tumbled from $12 billion to $5 billion, the typical weekly wage fell an average of 60 percent, and unemployment was nearing the 12 million mark; 9 million savings accounts were wiped out, and 86,000 businesses failed.

But in September of '31, Theremin found himself entering into a business contract with a Mr. N. I. Stone. In exchange for a loan of $3,000, he agreed to develop a store window display combining the signaling and music patents. Stone would act as business consultant and promotional agent for the device and would realize 10 percent of the gross profits from sale or rental.

Theremin's liabilities had grown so convoluted that he was switching and redirecting paper faster than he could fathom the consequences. As collateral for the loan, he offered Stone nearly a quarter of the shares of the Theremin Patents Corporation (which was now inactive—its resources nearly drained, its credit in default) and an assignment for any monies to be received from Goldberg and Sons' sale of the signaling patent (which was not Goldberg's property at this point, but still under Migos Corporation, and only for limited territories). He also offered to form a corporation to manufacture and sell the invention and promised to install Stone as director and treasurer.

The window display was to involve various turntables, lighting effects, and sound apparatus, and would be activated when an onlooker disturbed a surrounding electrical field. With his two major patents (sound and signal) drawn together in a single machine, Theremin named the common principle "teletouch," literally, "distance touch." It was the perfect label for the capacitive phenomenon and it resonated well with the other recent, and still mysterious, "tele" forms of communication.

As he developed the Teletouch Advertising Display Device, the inventor fashioned other body capacitance equipment, including a door that, when approached with the hand outstretched in a "halt" position, two inches from the surface, opened automatically. If the hand stopped midway, the door stopped as well.

On July 20, 1932, with the display device in progress, Theremin and George Goldberg entered into a new contract, this time with Stone and the Glenbrook Company Limited, for the "exploitation in the United States of mechanical games and amusements using the teletouch system."[4] Theremin was commissioned to create a prototype boxing game to be animated electrically, and Stone would provide the molds for the boxers' figures.

As Theremin fumbled through his miniature corporate mazes, two men, disillusioned with the stock market, sat around a downtown Manhattan office plotting their next venture. M. Boyd Zinman, a successful, self-made man of thirty-six—an accountant by profession—had realized a sizable fortune in the stock market prior to the crash and had purchased a seat on the New York Stock Exchange for $135,000—a record price at the time. By October 1932 he could see no future in the boards and sold the seat for $160,000.

Emanuel S. Morgenstern, thirty-four, was a retired New York realtor. For two years he had tried his hand at the stock market, apprenticing himself at Henry Zuckerman and Company as a telephone clerk to learn his way around. By 1932, he too was fed up.

Zinman and Morgenstern resolved to pool their capital for a new business enterprise. After they tossed about various ideas, Zinman found himself listening to a theremin at a nightclub. When he toured 37 West, Theremin's work struck him as a worthwhile investment.

Zinman's initial interest in capacitive systems centered around burglar alarms. In an October 28, 1932, contract, he and Morgenstern commissioned a prototype device from the inventor for the protection of safes that would "give an alarm when approached by any person within four inches of the safe."[5] Theremin agreed to prepare a model by November 11 and extended an option to order fifty devices by January 1, 1933, at a cost of twenty dollars each.

In two months, Zinman and Morgenstern were satisfied, and on December 22, 1932, they took the plunge with the formation of the Teletouch Corporation in the State of New York. Zinman was installed as president, and Theremin became vice president. Morgenstern juggled the remaining roles of secretary, treasurer, and sales manager. The business was principally set up to manufacture burglar alarms based on Theremin's signaling apparatus, but the space-control instrument would also be produced, and both patents were to become the property of the corporation.

On February 23, 1933, the Migos Corporation (now awaiting dissolution after the RCA option fell through) assigned Theremin's patents and patent applications covering the United States and its dependencies, Canada, Cuba, and Mexico, to Teletouch. Theremin Patents Corporation was still an official entity and retained rights for the remaining world territories. Morgenstern and Zinman agreed to place $10,000 between them in the treasury of the company—a loan to be repaid solely from the profits of the corporation. They would pay themselves, and Theremin, a weekly salary of $150 each.

Morgenstern and Zinman each held a one-third interest in the Corporation, with the last third divided between Theremin (80 shares) and the Gesellschaft zür Verwertung der Theremin Patente (20 shares). A total common capital stock of 300 shares was issued with a par value of $2 each. The "Gesellschaft" (Theremin and the Goldberg brothers) then had the temerity to offer Teletouch a two-year option on its 20 shares (worth $40): $10,000 if purchased in the first year, $15,000 in the second year.

Teletouch moved into the Theremin Studio on Fifty-fourth Street, renovating part of the space as a manufacturing facility and employing ten workers, including George Goldberg. Theremin kept his residence on the fourth floor. "The establishment has a good sized experimental and research laboratory," an auditor wrote in a credit report, "and represents a substantial investment. Premises are kept in a neat and orderly manner and the building in good repair."[6]

Zinman, Morgenstern, and Theremin next created a second company—incorporated on February 10, 1933, as the Teletouch Holding Corporation—to manage all Theremin's work except burglar alarms and the space-control instrument. The inventor agreed to turn over all his other inventions, assets, stock in companies, patent applications pending, future patents, and interest in contracts.

With the holding corporation, it was assumed that Teletouch, in addition to doing a thriving alarm business, could turn a handsome profit on Theremin's other ideas. In a notation under "Inventions—(Not Patented)," a hopeful Zinman specified:

New Burglar Alarm
Electric Fingerboard
Electric Keyboard
Electric Organ
Fire Alarms
Railroad Signalling
Altimeter
Teletouch [Advertising Display Device]
Signals for Vessels
Device for Broadcasting in an extremely narrow band
Photoelectric Recording and Reproducing Device
Wireless Microphone
Polyphonic Keyboard Musical Instrument
Automatic Door Opening and Closing Device
Dance Platform
A Method for Preventing Corrosion
Sound Recording and Reproducing Apparatus
Device for detecting metal or guns when concealed in a person's clothing.[7]

Zinman and Morgenstern appeared to be in control of a potentially lucrative corporate empire, but they were locked into a hard bargain. The holding corporation contract stipulated that if Teletouch had occasion to "fail, neglect, refuse or be unable to pay [Theremin] $150.00 a week, such inventions for which no patents have been applied for, or which have not been exploited or promoted, shall revert back to Theremin." A perplexed Zinman, trying to unravel the inventor's corporate ties, scribbled clues on a lined pad:

Migos Germany owns 337 1/2 out of 1000 shares of Theremin Patents Corp.
Maximilian Goldberg owns 50 shs. of Theremin Television Corp.
M. J. Goldberg and Bros. own 190 shs. of Theremin Television Corp.
Gesellschaft zür Verwertung Theremin Patente had a further interest in 250 shs. of Theremin Tel. Corp. . . .
M. Goldberg owns 25 sh. Migos and M. J. Goldberg and Sons GmbH 325 shares.[8]

Zinman jotted questions to himself: "Why are patents listed 'Theremin Patents Corp. N Y' instead of Theremin Patents Corp. Panama. Is there a N Y Corp. in existence besides the Panama?[9] Does Goldberg owe anything to International Union Bank?"[10] But hoping these knots could eventually be untangled, Zinman and Morgenstern moved ahead.

TELEGRAPH

TELEPHONE

TELEVISION

now

TELETOUCH

OUR PRODUCT SHRIEKS FOR ITSELF

With these words, penciled on note paper in pyramid formation,[11] the company prepared a marketing strategy for its burglar alarms. From the moment the inventor had stepped off the *Majestic* in 1927, the press had already seized on the idea. "Wave of Hand at New Device Brings Police," the *New York American* had announced.

> The man of the future will be only too glad to accede to the demand of a thug who has entered his home or office to lift his hands aloft, for such a gesture will be one of immediate doom to the plans of the intruder. . . . A burglar enters, and at his order the "victim" throws up his hands. THEN THE FUN BEGINS. In going up[,] the hands pass the little rod. Immediately things start happening. Electro-magnetic waves are induced in the rod and these transmit currents over wires to police headquarters, where a loud-speaker suddenly starts letting out unearthly wails. The police arrive, and the episode is ended.[12]

A Teletouch prospectus offered security for "windows, doors, safes, apartments, buildings, stores, banks, warehouses, railroad cars, paintings and sculptures in museums and parks, etc."[13] Any wide-open space where the guarded field had to be invisible could be rigged. Because the alarms were built mainly from parts used in the radio and telephone industries, manufacturing was reduced to assembly work requiring small capital. Teletouch could build a simple device for about $15 or a commercial system to cover large areas for roughly $60. The savings were passed on to the buyer, who also had the option of renting toward purchase for $10 a month. Business was good, but not spectacular.

Teletouch was also considering another application of the patent: a fire alarm system in which the sudden rise of temperature in a room would cause capacitor plates connected to metallic supports to expand, creating a corresponding change in the frequency of the oscillating system, sending out an alarm or signal. The scheme was designed to respond only to sudden increases of temperature—even relatively minute changes—but not to the gradual rise of heat under normal weather conditions. Teletouch was also looking at other system applications for trains approaching a signal block in a railroad signaling system, and warnings for vessels enveloped in fog, to signal the proximity of other ships or objects.

Under the music patent, Teletouch assembled a few space-control instruments, mostly on special order, but it generally avoided the area where the mammoth RCA had already gone belly up. Still, on the outside hope that a market might exist somewhere, Teletouch sponsored a one-time theremin performance on Fred Allen's coast-to-coast radio program, aired on May 17, 1933, over the NBC Red Network. To promote the broadcast, a postcard mailed to music dealers advertised,

30,000,000 PERSONS
WILL LISTEN TO THE NEW, IMPROVED
THEREMIN
ETHER WAVE MUSICAL INSTRUMENT

Here is a new sustaining feature that can be played by one of your staff musicians. Write for particulars.

THEREMIN DIVISION
TELETOUCH CORPORATION.[14]

Apparently few wrote for particulars, and Teletouch had its answer, more than $125,000 cheaper, and two years faster, than RCA.

The theremin, it was evident by now, would not be a household commodity. But there were the few who championed it as a legitimate instrument. Clara Reisenberg was now busy transferring her refined violin virtuosity to the theremin, practicing full time in anticipation of a major New York debut. She drilled herself in space-control technique with the rigor she had applied to the violin, intuiting the most effective gestures as she went. She practiced standard etudes borrowed from violin exercise books to focus her technical precision—scales, and rote melodic sequences such as patterns of two staccato and two legato notes.

Clara devised her own hand positions and gestures. She found that by keeping the tips of her right-hand thumb and forefinger in contact, she could achieve steadiness and control in the vibrato. She also developed "aerial fingering," a system where individual fingers would extend and withdraw from the right hand for subtle, refined control of melody within the electrical field—another technique adapted from violin playing.

Clara's approach stressed complete physical and emotional poise, concentration, and control. "You must not only hit a note," she told a journalist, "but you must hit the center of it. You cannot register any of your internal emotion at all. You cannot shake your head, for instance, or sway back and forth on your feet. That would change your tone."[15]

Theremin was more enamored of Clara than ever and the courtship crescendoed into a marriage proposal. The fact that Katia Constantinova was his de facto wife, though she remained in eclipse in New Jersey, was apparently of little consequence. Her place in his life had become so minor that none of Theremin's associates who were questioned years later had any memory of a Russian wife. Clara, for her part, now entertained marriage prospects with a handful of ardent suitors. Her older sisters wagered bets on the winner. Nadia rooted for Theremin—his Russian lineage, and the common language he shared with Clara, she urged, would complement her temperament well.

But Clara had other ideas. In 1933 she married Robert Rockmore, a distinguished entertainment lawyer she had known since the age of fourteen. Rockmore was well situated in his own practice. He had a long association with the theater as Paul Robeson's attorney, and as a one-time friend and confidant of Eugene O'Neill, whom he had introduced to classical music, the Belmont Racetrack, and the pleasures of chartered weekend yacht cruises around Long Island Sound. Rockmore's latest triumph was his production of the first all-black play in New York, *Run, Little Chillun!*, which opened on Broadway on March 1, 1933. Billed as a "Negro folk drama in two acts," it was a dramatization of Negro spirituals by the Hall Johnson Choir, and it prompted a spellbound Olin Downes to suggeste that it augured "real American Opera."[16] Clara remembered how Toscanini came to *Little Chillun* "five times, and cried five times."[17]

Clara's marriage was a severe blow to Theremin, and he promptly severed all contact with her.

Beyond the emotional sting, a major avenue to his musical work had been cut off. But there was still Lucie Rosen, and there were other occasional chances to see his instrument used. Once in a while composers surfaced to experiment with it. Edgard Varese was drawn to the theremin for the very sounds that would have caused Clara to shudder. He was bent on creating music built of "sound masses" and shifting plains of texture, removed from the traditional sphere of melody and harmony. Percussion instruments had gained ground in his scores recently, and, like Schillinger, he sensed a need for electronics to realize the effects he wanted. In 1929, in the French premiere of his *Amériques,* he replaced a part originally written for a siren with an ondes martenot, and with his *Ecuatorial,* written between 1932 and 1934, electronic instruments moved into the foreground.

Ecuatorial was scored for two fingerboard theremins with an extremely high range (comparable to violins). The instruments were custom built by Theremin to Varese's specifications and were used in a fairly active role with four trumpets, four trombones, piano, organ, percussion (six players), and a vocal bass soloist. The text was drawn from the sacred book of the Maya Quiché, the *Popul Vuh,* part of the incantation of a lost mountain tribe. "The title is merely suggestive of the regions where pre-Colombian art flourished,"

Varese wrote. "I conceived the music as having something of the same elemental rude intensity of those strange, primitive works. The execution should be dramatic and incantory, guided by the imploring fervor of the text."[18] Varese used the theremins in *Ecuatorial* for their timbre and the glissandi and long sustained notes he couldn't find on any other instrument.

Nicolas Slonimsky conducted the premiere of *Ecuatorial* at New York's Town Hall on April 15, 1934. The concert was sponsored by the Pan American Association of Composers—a group founded by Varese, presided over by Henry Cowell, and funded largely by Charles Ives. "Mr. Varese has written music that has power and atmosphere," the *New York Times* began. "It is sometimes unclear; a welter of sound obscures any central meaning in such pages. The Theremins gave the work an unearthly quality at times; in some passages they were mere caterwauling."[19] The *New York Herald Tribune* described the "piercingly shrieking theremin instruments" and commented that "the plan and purpose of the outlines of the music and Mr. Varese's scoring . . . was not always clear, but there were many pungent, massively expressive measures."[20] When Varese later published the score, he reassigned the theremin parts to two ondes martenot.

《》

In 1933, the United States finally granted diplomatic recognition to Moscow. By April 6, 1934, the first visitors toured the new Soviet embassy in Washington. On the twenty-first, the Soviet consulate in New York opened for business at 7–9 East Sixty-first Street, a short seven-block stroll up Fifth Avenue for Theremin from his headquarters at 37 West Fifty-fourth. Now he had more pairs of eyes watching him, and it was around this time that he was assigned the task of investigating life in American prisons.

In 1933, the U.S. government had taken over the military prison on Alcatraz Island off San Francisco and began renovations to convert it into a federal penitentiary by the summer of 1934. Various security arrangements were considered, including surrounding the island with an "electro-static or microwave" field. Because many employees and their families lived on the island, this option was rejected in favor of a more localized detection scheme. Bids were solicited for "a system of detecting electro-magnetically guns, pieces or objects of steel concealed upon any persons . . . and . . . designed as to give an audible and visible signal at a central point whenever any person carrying a pistol, or other object of steel passes through an entrance not more than five feet wide or eight feet high."[21]

On June 29, 1934, the Bureau of Prisons awarded Teletouch a contract to install metal- and gun-detecting devices on Alcatraz. The detectors were to be set up in three locations: on the wharf along the path from boats to the registration office, in the main entrance to the administration building, and at the rear gate used by prisoners passing between the cell block and the workshop.

On July 26, Alcatraz opened as a federal penitentiary, soon to be the home of Al Capone and other notorious inmates. On October 11, Warden Johnston wrote to the Bureau of Prisons, "The gun detectors installed by Teletouch Corporation are in operation and I want to report that they are working to my entire satisfaction."[22] One week later, however, Johnston reported to the bureau, "I wrote to you on October 11th describing the installation and tests in detail. At that time I expressed my satisfaction with the tests. Since that time we have had difficulty in operation on account of the coils getting overheated making it necessary to discontinue use to allow time for cooling."[23] Teletouch was summoned to rectify the problem.

≪≫

One figure conspicuously absent from the Teletouch organization was Morris Hillquit, still a stockholder in Theremin's dormant companies. In the fall of '32 he had again ventured a campaign for New York mayor, capturing a record block of votes for a New York socialist candidate: nearly a quarter-million. But the effort leveled a toll on his already waning health, and on October 7, 1933, within weeks of finishing his autobiography, he died of tuberculosis. Condolences poured in from around the world. International socialist and labor leaders, the British prime minister, President Roosevelt, and New York's Governor Lehman cabled and telegrammed Hillquit's widow. The leader's body lay in state at the Debs Auditorium at the People's House, the Socialist Party headquarters on East Fifteenth Street. Outside, two young socialists posed with red banners. Inside, an honor guard of young party members stood vigil around Hillquit's body, which lay on a catafalque, draped in scarlet velvet and surrounded by wreaths and red and black crepe. Over twenty thousand mourners paid their respects from eight A.M. to midnight. The next day, a cortège escorted by five mounted policemen made brief stops before the headquarters of the Amalgamated Clothing Workers and the International Ladies Garment Workers Union en route to the funeral at Cooper Union. Two thousand attended the service inside, matched by the same number standing outside in the street listening over amplifiers. Nearly twenty speakers eulogized Hillquit as a founder of the Socialist Party, a friend and defender of labor, and a great intellectual and humanitarian. Following the service, the cortège snaked through a maze of streets on the Lower East Side to Clinton Street and passed over the Williamsburg Bridge to Brooklyn, where Hillquit's body would be cremated.

That season, the book also closed on another connection in Theremin's life. After an uneasy ten-year union, the inventor felt it was time to liberate himself, and Katia, from the remnants of their youthful commitment. For the past few years, Katia had been working at Valley View Tuberculosis Hospital in Paterson, New Jersey, as a lab technician and living in the nurses home next door to the facility. In 1934, she and Theremin were officially divorced with an "N 1" certificate filed at the Soviet consulate. Katia immediately wrote to her brother Alexander asking to return to the USSR, but with mass arrests beginning, and the uncertainty of conditions in the country, he advised against it. In a telegram he fiercely reproved his old friend Theremin: "you are responsible for Katia's fate."[24]

On October 30, 1934, Clara made her New York recital debut at Town Hall under her new married name of Rockmore. Though the inventor was still keeping his distance, Clara's involvement with the theremin continued nonetheless. She had surpassed his expectations and developed a consummate technique unmatched by any other player. In her ambitious program she played the "Berceuse" from Stravinsky's *Firebird*, the Andante from Lalo's *Symphony Espagnole*, Ravel's "Kaddisch," and works by Bach, Marcello, Goldmark, Glazunov, Rachmaninoff, and Tchaikovsky. Pierre Luboschutz accompanied on the piano, and Joseph Yasser on the organ. The program closed with a set of spirituals sung by the Hall Johnson Male Sextet supported by theremin and organ. It was the first attempt to sustain the theremin in a full recital of legitimate works from the repertoire.

"From her deft and dainty fingers," Leonard Liebling wrote in the *New York American*, "over the ghostly box, came dulcet and lovely sounds, shaded, diminished and swelled with musical intention and result . . . which was more than Mr. Theremin achieved, and [she] wavered her intonations only now and then when the music took on more rapid movements. She gave evident pleasure to a large audience and received numerous rounds of warm applause."[25] "Miss Rockmore," the *Herald Tribune* reported, "showed that an advance has been made in the technique of theremin performance. The slide from one note to another has been virtually eliminated in the smaller intervals; there is increasing, if not invariable, command of accuracy of pitch."[26] The *World Telegram* concluded that "the Theremin, that machine-age incursion into the sphere of the arts, came closer to proving its rightful place there last evening. . . . The playing . . . has not yet developed to the point of facile execution. Miss Rockmore's success with it as an agency of musical expression, however—limited as its scope is at present—gave a prophetic indication of a future not too distant. No violin or human voice ever was made to give forth such smooth and delicate legati nor was capable of such evenly graduated portamenti."[27]

By 1933, Lucie Rosen was performing actively around the New York area. At the Southampton home of Prince and Princess Kaplanoff she shared the stage in a private musicale with the Metropolitan Opera tenor Rafaelo Diaz. "Mr. Diaz," a local paper reported, "is spending the week-end at Katonah, the guest of Mr. and Mrs. Rosen . . . after which he will motor down to Southampton for a week."[28] Later, Lucie appeared with the singer again at a Diaz "Tuesday Afternoon Costume Recital" in the Grand Ballroom of the Waldorf-Astoria Hotel—a concert sponsored by a substantial segment of the Social Register, including a colonel, a duchess, a countess, and a baroness. Lucie played her theremin every Sunday during the four o'clock vespers at New York's St. George's Church, and once, at the celebration of Harry T. Burleigh's thirty-ninth anniversary as the church's baritone soloist, she performed "Nobody Knows the Trouble I've Seen," in an arrangement the renowned singer/composer had created for her.

Lucie was a tireless advocate for the theremin, often annoyed by attitudes she encountered. "I was asked the other day, 'Isn't it just a few tubes and a couple of antennae you can buy from any radio store?'" she wrote in one of her many unpublished statements. "'Quite easy, a friend of mine said he would build me one—' and one could have answered, 'Yes that is all, and an instrument called a violin is only four pieces of string and a wooden box, but play it if you can.'"[29] She worried that the theremin's reputation had been tarnished by the untrained who played freely in public. "Everywhere I go," she complained, "I meet persons who tell me they are theremin players, but then I find they are vaudeville or specialty artists who have picked up a few simple tunes." "It is really, unfortunately for the theremin, not difficult to pick out one's notes," she despaired.

> Some people have been able to find their way to tunes they knew in four to five weeks. At this point, they were so pleased they stopped inquiring for anything else, and quite a number have astonished the neighbours by simply finding a tune. But the neighbours could not continue to be astonished, and the musical world very properly complained of a deadly lack of interest in an instrument of which all you could say was, notes *could* be found on it. . . . But faith and hope remained in a few devoted souls, and it continues to be studied.[30]

Trailing Clara's appearance by three months, Lucie Rosen made her official New York recital debut in Town Hall on January 20, 1935. With her stylishly posed publicity portraits by De Mirjian, she set the tone for an ephemeral, seraph-like stage manner, aimed to capture the mythical lure of disembodied music. Frank Chatterton was her accompanist in a challenging program of music by Hugo Wolf, Richard Strauss, Wagner, Bach, Debussy, Wieniawski, and others. "Looking like a Burne-Jones come to life," the *New York World-Telegram* mused, "Mrs. Rosen wove with eloquent hands the magical-seeming spell and the theremin responded to her summons with some of the most strictly musical sounds it has yet produced in our concert rooms."[31] "Although at one point," the *New York Times* conceded, "the instrument got out of gear and its inventor, Leon Theremin, was called onto the stage to set it right, Mrs. Rosen was in command of its resources all evening. She plays the theremin, not only with an awareness of its possibilities, but with a knowledge of music."[32] The *New York Herald Tribune* concluded, "She set forth many subtleties of shading and striking contrasts of color in the theremin's tone at various pitches."[33]

《 》

Every week now, Theremin was compelled to rendezvous at a shabby café on Fifth Avenue with two Russian consulate men in gray hats. The routine always began the same way. "Their first words were 'drink!'" he recalled. "So that I wouldn't hide anything I had to drink at least two glasses of vodka. . . . I discovered that by eating butter, alcohol wouldn't affect you. So on the morning of the days I was to meet with them, I ate slightly less than half a kilo of butter. At first it was difficult to swallow, but eventually I got used to it. The people I spoke with drank as well, but not as much as I had to."[34] The inventor's tasks were laid out at these meetings: "I did alot of spying work for the military department in connection with secret information on airplanes. I had my tactics for these things. To find out something new, and foreign, I wouldn't ask about it, I would suggest something new of my own. When you show something of your own it's easier to find out what the other people are working at. So I had some airplane work which the Americans didn't know about—autopilot and remote control devices."[35]

In 1935, Teletouch considered granting an exclusive manufacturing license to the Pioneer Instrument Company for Theremin's "electric capacity altimeter." An elaborate option agreement was drawn up, and detailed specifications of the device were outlined. Theremin guaranteed that his altimeter would indicate correct altitude "within plus or minus 10%" under many complex flight conditions, including changes in "speed, load . . . wing flexure, vibration, barometric pressure, electric field . . . ice formation," and so forth.[36] Pioneer was to install a sample altimeter in an aircraft for test flights. Again, the inventor was instructed to retrieve information for the Soviets. "I could find out whatever was necessary," he remembered, "but I thought all these tasks were too simple, and not very important. For example, I had to find out the diameter of an airplane muffler, and I don't know why this information was needed."[37] Nothing apparently materialized from the Pioneer contract, and Teletouch soon turned to products that, like the alarm systems, could be efficiently produced at the Theremin Studio.

By January 1935, there had been another malfunction of new coils Teletouch had installed in the Alcatraz gun detectors months earlier. Repeated attempts to rectify the defects proved fruitless. When the Bureau of Prisons decided to install a fourth detector in December of '35, the contract was awarded to Federal Laboratories in Pittsburgh, which had lost the original bid to Teletouch. It was bad timing, with Teletouch detectors about to be installed at Sing Sing Correctional Facility in Ossining, New York.

Perhaps for relief, the inventor, recalling his unfulfilled contract with N. I. Stone, returned to the more whimsical mechanisms of a window display device. With a few twists, the idea resurfaced as the Teletouch "Magic Mirror."

Like a gadget from an improbable dream, the Magic Mirror was pure Buck Rogers legerdemain—'30s window dressing of the science fiction variety. The capacitance-sensitive element was the mirror coating itself, which was opaque and reflecting under normal circumstances. When a passer-by activated it by stopping to glance in the mirror, the capacitance relay triggered a light that illuminated the glass from behind, causing it to become semitransparent and reveal a picture or advertising message in the center while the border of the glass remained opaque.

The Magic Mirror startled its first spectators in the windows of Black, Starr, and Frost-Gorham Jewelers at 594 Fifth Avenue. "The mirror faces the sidewalk," a trade magazine reported,

> and when a person comes within two feet of it the lower portion is converted bewitchingly into ordinary glass, illuminated from behind, and a display of jewels is disclosed. The jewelry remains in view while the observer stands near the window, but when he steps back or aside the "magic mirror" reappears.
>
> The sight of someone causing the jewelry to materialize attracted many other Fifth Avenue shoppers so that there was usually a cluster of persons near the mirror, each intent on effecting the change himself.[38]

Lucie Rosen's daughter, Anne Bigelow Stern, recalled seeing animated figures in some mirrors, especially one in a sporting-goods store that revealed sparring boxers—the use Theremin may have found for the prototype figures Stone modeled for Glenbrook's mechanical amusements. Macy's exhibited a modified form of the installation—the Teletouch Magic Crystal—in one of its windows. Designed as a glass sphere mounted atop a small pedestal, the "crystal ball" became transparent as the viewer approached, revealing merchandise on a six-inch diameter platform inside, illuminated by an external spotlight.

By 1936, stores in New York, Boston, Philadelphia, and Lancaster, Pennsylvania, were using the mirror, and exclusive sales rights for the state of Connecticut were granted to a distributor who agreed to purchase forty-eight units from Teletouch at a wholesale cost of $150 each.

On September 14, 1936, the Teletouch Magic Mirror Corporation split off and incorporated as a separate entity. Morgenstern was installed as president.

《 》

After a well-received recital in London on June 18, 1935, Lucie Rosen resolved to take her instrument around Europe in the footsteps of Theremin's triumph nearly a decade earlier. A tour through the major capitals was arranged for April, May, and June 1936. Concerts were scheduled in Naples, Rome, Venice, Zurich, Munich, Budapest, Hamburg, Stockholm, Oslo, Copenhagen, Amsterdam, Brussels, Paris, and London. In the majority of these cities, Lucie was charting new territory with the instrument. "We were forcefully reminded yesterday in Engineers' Hall," Oslo's *Nationen* commented, "that idealists are still to be found in this materialistic and mechanized world."[39] "The Rosens—Mrs. Rosen's husband, son and daughter are with her—are an uncommonly pleasant family," observed Stockholm's *Dagbladet,* "lovable in that amiably hearty manner which is so distinctly American. Mrs. Rosen herself is a striking woman, wholly absorbed in her art; and she has a beautiful and fascinating face which at one moment beams brightly, girlishly, and at the next is deeply soulful and serious. She loves her instrument and enjoys talking about it."[40] Public and critical reaction to the concerts was generally favorable. For Lucie, by now resigned to American apathy over the instrument, it must have been a trip back in time, or a journey to another planet. At a concert in Rome, attended by Marconi, *La Tribuna* reported that Lucie played with the "greatest perfection."[41] Apparently with a degree of journalistic amnesia, the *Münchener Zeitung* commented that "Lucie Bigelow Rosen brought forth a music never before heard . . . a music of the spheres, the resonance and intensity of which no previous instrument has been capable."[42] "Not in three years, we are told, had there been such a demonstration in Munich for any artist," the *New York World-Telegram* reported, "and in Budapest a tidal wave of people broke over the stage eager for encores as long as Mrs. Rosen could play."[43] Budapest's *Nemzeti Ujság* pronounced the theremin's strains "the music of future centuries."[44] "Often," Oslo's *Tdens Tegn* remarked, "this music . . . sounded as if emanating from the most exquisite Amati violin or cello."[45]

The sort of superlatives Theremin had collected in 1927 echoed through Lucie's tour. After an Amsterdam concert attended by the American ambassador, *De Telegraaf* gushed, "this can be the start of an absolutely new instrumental culture. . . . A melody of Debussy became, under her wonderful hands, a fairy-tale of unknown sound. Her method of playing 'Romance' of Wieniawski's Second Concerto became a sensation. . . . She had to play two encores and was loudly applauded."[46] If nothing else, the tour underlined Lucie's convictions with the imprimatur of continental taste.

Ironically, not long after Lucie returned to America, an article on the Teletouch Corporation in *Electronics* magazine began: "Back in 1928, most readers . . . will remember, a new type of electronic musical instrument appeared. It was called the Theremin, after its inventor . . . and for a while it seemed that it might become permanently established in the musical arts. . . . The Teletouch organization, deriving its original impetus from a musical instrument which did not pan out, has applied many of the principles used in that instrument to various forms of electronic control which have met with considerable success."[47]

It was true—most Americans, by the mid-thirties, had to be reminded what a theremin was, but the inventor's technology, in the hands of Teletouch, had achieved a modicum of success. For a brief time, the company found a niche as a wacky, self-styled fun-house factory. A visitor from *Fortune* reported:

> The Teletouch office-factory-laboratory in the brownstone house is a crazy place. Walk through a door and a shrieking alarm goes off. Touch a filing cabinet and another alarm goes off. Go to a mirror to set your tie and a light flashes behind the mirror so that you see, not your tie, but an advertisement. . . . Taciturn treasurer Zinman is used to the din and works right through it. . . . Vice President Theremin spends most of his time at a long laboratory table on the second floor. He is so busy disturbing electromagnetic fields that he scarcely has time to play the Theremin.[48]

Every corner of 37 West, in fact, had some sort of experiment brewing. "All the floors in that house were a mass of wires and tubes and screens," Anne Stern remembered, "—nothing you could possibly have called a home."[49] One of the inventor's pet projects was a closed-circuit television he used to monitor activities on another floor of the brownstone. Stern remembered it as a small black-and-white cathode ray tube receiver modeled after the electronic television Zworykin had pioneered for RCA. Laboratory notes postdating 1931 show that Theremin had studied the television theories of Alexanderson, Rosing, Ekstrom in Sweden, and John H. Hammond Jr. in the United States. Sketches and notes prepared on a Russian typewriter detailed a complete electronic system with three interchangeable camera lenses for variable focusing distances, and a cathode ray receiver screen approximately nine inches in diameter. Theremin's manuscript described the device as a "suggested type of equipment . . . which could be recommended in a case where the receiver must be portable, such as on an airplane."[50] This concept of portability was unique among early sets that were usually housed in unwieldy boxes, and the idea anticipated the smaller, lighter models of later years.

In 1936, Theremin stepped outside his capacitance-driven alarm schemes to explore another design for Teletouch. With security devices like his baby guard, he usually avoided light-activated systems because typical electric-eye mechanisms were unreliable. Because they required two units—a light source and a receiving photocell to be stationed opposite it—the beam of light could be crossed without being broken by shining a substitute light source at the "eye," keeping the alarm cocked. These schemes also required the protected area to lie between two surfaces or objects that could accept mounted units.

In his "Teletouch Ray," Theremin devised a system that housed a light source and phototube side-by-side in a single box. The light source—a small, 200-watt electric bulb—was sent through a condensing lens and could be beamed at any spot, even a surface with low reflective properties. The phototube next to it was focused to "watch" the spot, generating its current from the illumination it "perceived." The circuit was arranged so that the phototube would not operate the relay as long as the intensity of the light spot remained unchanged. When a person or object moved across the path of the beam, the phototube noticed the change in light intensity, causing its current to be altered, triggering the relay and sounding an alarm or setting off any other desired function.

The Teletouch Ray found a novel application in store window lighting. For businesses that balked at the twenty thousand watts typically required to illuminate windows at night, just for a few odd pedestrians, the ray offered a solution. Since stores had no jurisdiction over the sidewalk bordering their windows, it was impossible to install traditional electric-eye mechanisms that would project a light source out the window and require a receiving device in the street. With the Teletouch system, however, a control area could be established anywhere—even beyond a property line—by training a spot of light at it. By shooting the ray at a spot on the street, any passer-by who broke the beam would cause the store window to illuminate temporarily.

On July 6, 1936, Macy's unveiled the Teletouch Ray in seven of its show windows along Thirty-fourth Street, beginning at 9:00 P.M. The system unit, contained in a small black box in a lower corner of the window, beamed a spot two feet from the curb to avoid interruption from passing cars. Each window held its illumination for thirty seconds after a passer-by broke the shaft of light. "I understand the makers of the apparatus claim a saving of many thousands of watts on the electrical meters," a business editorial commented, but this is "small potatoes" compared with the *psychological* results.

Think of the thrill of walking down a deserted street at one o'clock in the morning and having the refulgent glow of brightly-lighted show windows blaze on for *your* special benefit. It's wonderful just to think about it. Next time I'm in New York . . . I'm going down 34th Street all by myself and make the darn things work.[51]

The Teletouch Ray was also installed at the Gimbel's store in Philadelphia, the Brooklyn Edison Company, the Sloate Chevrolet Company of Hartford, and a handful of other establishments.

As the "director of research," according to Teletouch letterhead, Theremin was the goose charged with forging one golden egg after another. Ideas for new inventions streamed from his imagination faster than he could practicably, or financially, realize them. Many, unfortunately for posterity, remain only mysterious and intriguing phrases scrawled incidentally in notebooks. On a loose sheet of lined paper, the words "Ideas to be developed" appear at the top, followed by a list in penciled script.[52] Among the items: "Signal for Automobile Battery; Signal for Automobile Oil Gauge; Radio receiving sets for policemen." And near the bottom, inconspicuously in tiny letters, "Intercity typewriter without wires," suggesting a device allowing the typist of the '30s to clack out a message and transmit it by radio waves to another "intercity typewriter." Facsimile technology for transmitting graphic images over telephone lines—or even through the air—existed at the time, but this idea more closely anticipated the notion of the Internet, and electronic mail, by more than sixty years. But perhaps Theremin's most fantastic unborn brainchild was the one he called the "Ethereal Suspension." He imagined cars driving across an invisible bridge, supported only by fields of electromagnetic waves.

On May 19, 1937, Teletouch was informed in a letter that its contract with Alcatraz was canceled. Federal Laboratories had been contracted to furnish replacements for Theremin's three failed gun detectors, and under government regulations, the Bureau of Prisons was required to "collect from a defaulting contractor excess cost incurred in replacing the supplies or equipment."[53] Teletouch would have to reimburse the government for the amount received under the original contract, plus the difference involved in installing new detectors. The company now owed the government a total of $4,869—an amount that would begin to tip the delicate balance of its solvency.

SEVEN

"I, Leon Theremin . . ."

From Eastport to Sandy Hook—Fresh to strong southeast and south winds shifting to northwest late Thursday afternoon or night and overcast weather with showers Thursday.

—New York marine forecast for Thursday, September 15, 1938

On August 6, 1938, the Russian diesel freighter *Stary Bolshevik* left its home port of Novorossisk on the Black Sea, bound for Istanbul. On the eighth, it sailed across the Sea of Marmara, through the Dardanelles, and continued south, winding a course through the Aegean, the Mediterranean, and the Strait of Gibraltar, to the open Atlantic. From there it set a direct course for the shores of the continental United States. This would be its only voyage to the port of New York that year.

Leon Theremin had been living in America on borrowed time since the day he arrived in December 1927. His original nonimmigrant visa justified his entry into the United States as a "temporary visit—to demonstrate inventions," and the stay was projected at about three months. After nearly a decade, he remained a titular "Professor and Graduate Engineer" at the Leningrad Physico-Technical Institute, though his whole Russian life lay in suspended animation. The Soviet mechanism in New York, however, was never more than one or two steps behind him, in the shadows.

The inventor's tenuous footing with the U.S. Department of Labor was particularly apparent in 1935, when he attempted a brief visit to Cuba to demonstrate his capacitive security equipment in Havana. Stephano Calcavecchia, a Cuban businessman and engineer living in New York, owned an interest in these systems and asked the Cuban embassy in Washington to appeal to the U.S. government on Theremin's behalf. A letter of February 19, 1935, from the embassy to the chief of the State Department's Latin-American affairs division, describes a strong Cuban interest in Theremin's "apparatus for the protection against burglaries, holdups of offices, homes, etc.; for military and police defense and for invisible detectors for the discovery of weapons and bombs in the possession of individuals, or which may be concealed in parts of buildings or in furniture."[1]

Calcavecchia, hoping to assure Theremin's safe return to the United States, asked that the inventor be issued a "re-entry permit, or some sort of guarantee from the Department of Labor . . . in order to return to this country."[2] An assistant to the division chief of Latin-American affairs replied curtly,

> I was frankly surprised that the Russian professor, Theremin, had been able to obtain successive six month extensions of a six month temporary visitor's permit to a total of six years.
>
> "Re-entry permits" are issued only to aliens who have been lawfully admitted in immigrant status. . . .
>
> Should Theremin go to Cuba, he would have to apply to the Consulate General at Habana for a non-immigrant visa, presenting a valid passport. In view of his long residence in the United States and his evident intent to resume such residence, I stated that he would have difficulty in convincing a consular officer of his non-immigrant status.
>
> Should he succeed in obtaining a visa, it would still remain for him to convince the immigration authorities at the port of re-entry from Cuba of his non-immigrant status. He would undoubtedly, in view of his already protracted stay, have difficulty in so doing.[3]

The letter advised Theremin to "regularize his status" by going to a consular office in Canada and applying for an immigration visa to the United States. By doing this, he would be declaring his intention to emigrate to America, a situation that, in light of his "extra assignment" from Berzin, was not a likely option.

In any case, Calcavecchia managed to sell the Cuban government on the security system without Theremin's presence. For more than a year, the political turmoil and instability in Havana had been boiling over with bombings of the customs house, the treasury department, and a Woolworth store and the destruction of a radio station. The April 1935 issue of *Fortune* magazine reported, "In Cuba the offices of government officials, including, of course, Colonel Batista, are being equipped with Teletouch systems to set off alarms if anyone tries to carry a bomb into the room. Big Havana department stores, harassed by terrorist bombers, are also being fitted out with Teletouch friskers."[4]

Teletouch, however, in the aftermath of the Alcatraz failure, was barely holding its own by the spring of '37, and Theremin himself was increasingly tangled in the web of his own fiscal obligations. Facing the emptying hourglass of his visa, he was also living, quite literally, on borrowed money.

By January 1931, the Theremin Patents Corporation had failed to develop or market any products. Its cash assets had shrunk to little more than $8,000 from an original loan capital of $25,000, and by June, a balance of $43,000 was still due the bank. Among the five original guarantors of the loan were an Isaac and Harry M. Marks, who were liable for $10,000 in the event of default. In 1931, when the bank demanded payment, they remitted one-fifth of the balance—$8,788—and sued Theremin Patents for recovery. The company ignored the summons, and a default judgment of $9,400 was entered.

In June 1931, Theremin Patents signed a promissory note to International Madison Bank and Trust Company for a new loan of $40,000, agreeing to pay the principal and interest within four months. By March 1933, Walmor Incorporated—then holding the promissory note for the failed Madison Bank—sued Theremin Patents for the outstanding balance. The company again was mute, and a default judgment of $8,077 was entered in September in favor of Walmor. Both judgments were filed with the New York State Supreme Court.

Theremin himself largely failed to make good on his personal loans, and by 1932 legal action was initiated against him. Walmor, the holder of $3,000 and $7,000 notes for sums he borrowed in 1930, sued in July to recover the balance remaining at maturity. When he neglected to respond, a default judgment for $4,000 was entered against him in New York State Supreme Court in October.

In May 1931, the inventor had signed a promissory note to RCA for $3,000 in exchange for equipment but later defaulted in his monthly payments. RCA sued, and in December 1932 Theremin acknowledged the debt by signing a confession of judgment in New York State Supreme Court for $2,600.

Adolf Klein also litigated to recoup the money he had loaned the inventor in 1930. By May 1934, the parties in the case had arranged to withdraw "an order to show cause to punish the judgment debtor for contempt," when Theremin agreed to supplementary proceedings where he would produce "all written agreements concerning the sale or disposition of his patents and inventions to the Teletouch Corp."[5] In a memorandum of agreement during the formation of the Holding Corporation, Teletouch had stated emphatically that "the Corporation does not assume any of Prof. Theremin's liabilities."[6] Given his credit history, though, this was more an earnest hope than a likely escape hatch.

The issue of how a Soviet alien on a worn-out visitor's visa could pile up this list of delinquencies, in plain view of the U.S. legal system, could only be explained by the temper of American benevolence and naiveté toward Russia in the '30s. The Soviet Union, following the ravages of a world war, a revolution, and a civil upheaval, was viewed as a secondary power—an unlikely threat with its fledgling armed forces and the recent annihilation of huge segments of its population. Even if a handful of spies carried information back to the Kremlin, the effect was thought to be negligible. More important, with the increasing threat of German and Japanese aggression, the United States was loathe to alienate Moscow as a potential ally, merely to slap a few random hands caught in the cookie jar.

Happily anesthetized, the American government held the door open for swarms of Russians moving in on U.S. industry in the '30s. In March 1930, the *New York Times* reported an Amtorg disclosure that "the Soviet Government has about 500 engineers and mechanics stationed in large American manufacturing plants for the purpose of studying methods and operations."[7] Like Theremin, these Russians came to the States through six-month permits issued at the United States consulate in Berlin. Among their known host sites was the General Electric plant in Schenectady where the RCA instrument had been manufactured. Theremin was part of a wave of Soviet engineers sanctioned by the U.S. government to observe American industry in what seemed like a benign spirit of cooperation between the two countries.

Perhaps only the shrewd noted the import of an article on the same page of the *New York Times* that day:

> Flaming front-page editorials inciting the workers and workless of the world to rise in a mighty struggle against capitalism appeared in today's issue of Pravda, Izvestiya and other Russian newspapers in connection with the international demonstrations against unemployment fostered by the Communist International.
>
> Calling the Soviet Republic the "fatherland of all laborers," Izvestiya tells the world's unemployed that socialism and the overthrow of capitalism are their only salvation.[8]

In a third article on the same page, a sympathetic statement was issued by students and professors of Union Theological Seminary: "While professing no allegiance to the political creed of communism, we believe that the social experiment of the Soviet Government should receive the sympathetic and not the hostile criticism of the representatives of the Christian Church."

Despite repeated warnings from the congressional committee investigating Communism in the United States, American business complacently turned a deaf ear on the whistle-blowers. During the '30s, to all appearances, Russia was contributing to the American gross national product with hefty imports of U.S. goods. From 1934 to 1937, Soviet purchases of American products through Amtorg surged from $14,500,000 to $75,000,000. In 1935, RCA alone sold $2,000,000 worth of radio equipment and machinery to the Soviets.

At the same time, Amtorg sniffed out every opportunity to defraud the same companies it did business with. One of the more insidious scams involved a so-called "business directory" in which hundreds of American firms were induced to pay top dollar for full-page display ads, aimed supposedly at prospective clients in the USSR. In the noncompetitive Soviet economy, the catalog was obviously worthless, but the Amtorg publishing department was happy to use the quarter-million-dollar profits to underwrite industrial espionage against the very firms who placed the ads. And through an artful dodging of New York corporate statutes and federal tax laws, Amtorg made sure no crumb was left over for the Internal Revenue Service. Other Amtorg profits—to the tune of $5 million a year, by the mid-thirties—were doled out to Soviet-controlled organizations in the United States.

During the Dies hearings in 1939—the special House committee investigating un-American activities headed by Representative Martin Dies of Texas —many of Amtorg's covert operations finally began to surface. The testimony of Robert Pitcoff, a former Amtorg official, was reported in the *New York Times:* "He pictured Amtorg as a beehive of Soviet spies who used the employees as operatives—'one OGPU agent will ask you to obtain some information, another agent will ask you for something else, and we were continually being asked to obtain information.'"[9] Pitcoff confirmed that Russia had sent many trade missions to the United States for factory tours, and that "much industrial espionage was carried on."

> "In other words," Mr. Dies summed up the testimony, "what the Soviet Union has in the United States is an elaborate spy system, isn't it?"
> "I think it is," Pitcoff responded. "I don't think the Soviet Government denies it. They intend to outstrip all other countries in industry and they will use any means."[10]

《 》

After the April 1, 1932, concert in Carnegie Hall, Leon Theremin largely disappeared from public life. He came forth only sporadically to ally himself with a performance or demonstration of his instruments, but for the most part he was taken up with burglar alarms, electric eyes, and window displays. Little had come of the rhythmicon or the keyboard instruments beyond their initial showings, and Stokowski eventually ended his experiments with Theremin's keyboard models in the Philadelphia Orchestra. Few musicians had actively taken up these instruments.

Clara was a principal exception, of course, but the inventor had maintained his distance and lost touch with her recent playing. When he heard her in a radio performance of Ravel's *Kaddisch*, accompanied by Alfred Wallenstein's *Symphonietta*, he finally broke his long silence. Clara's phone rang. "You played

like an angel," he told her in Russian. He had to see her. By now he was adjusted to the idea of Bob Rockmore and could accept a three-way friendship.
On August 14, 1937, at a Philadelphia Orchestra concert at Robin Hood
Dell, Theremin sat among an audience of 4,500 for Clara's most ambitious
airborne feat to date: a performance of Bloch's *Schelomo* on her RCA theremin, using the full range of the original solo cello part. "I think that put me in
a different, higher level artistically with the theremin,"[11] she recalled. The
Philadelphia Evening Bulletin pronounced her "the greatest virtuoso of the
instrument" and concluded, "One of Mrs. Rockmore's greatest accomplishments has been the nearly total elimination of the glissando."[12]

Clara, with her "aerial fingering," had taken note articulation to the highest precision possible on the RCA instrument, but her technique was capable
of more, and it now demanded a more responsive instrument. "I explained to
him," she recalled,

> that these constant glissandos which people played . . . [were] like molasses.
> The left hand was like molasses—you couldn't shake it off—the sound was
> perpetual. . . . There was no possibility of sharp staccato. . . . Now, what I need-
> ed to begin with was a faster left hand. . . . I was always given the same argu-
> ment from him: "It will be harder." I said, "I don't care how hard it is—just *do*
> it, and I'll learn how to control it. Of course it will be harder, because . . . you
> can hardly *breathe* on that instrument without affecting something."[13]

At Clara's request, the inventor began the design of an instrument custom built
around the real potential of her technique.

《》

If there was any phase of Theremin's American work that suffered from complete neglect, it was his terpsitone. The instrument now sat collecting dust on
the third floor of 37 West after Clara's Carnegie Hall demonstration and one
other showing she had made with it at Columbia University. The inventor determined to fire it up again and find dancers who would exploit its resources.

Even the space-control theremin, as early as 1931, had inspired a dance
collaboration when Sophia Delza used it in her solo dance recital at the Guild
Theatre. "The novelty of the program last night," the *New York Times* wrote,
"was a dance performed to a composition by Gertrude Karlan for the Theremin instrument. In so far as it demonstrated for the instrument a musical legato quite comparable to the legato of physical movement, it can be accounted successful, but . . . Miss Karlan seems to have associated rising movement
with an ascending scale and falling movement with a descending one in a rather
literal manner. . . . The dance has, however, some interesting thematic mate-

rial, and the instrument undeniable possibilities for dancing."[14] In 1933, Harald Kreutzberg choreographed and performed a solo to Friedrich Wilckens's *Dance in the Moon* for theremin and piano at the New Yorker Theatre. The work was written for Kreutzberg and performed by Lucie Rosen, with the composer at the piano. Henry Solomonoff, one of the inventor's students from the 1930 semicircle of "Victor Theremins" at Carnegie Hall, had continued performing under the stage name of Eugene Henry, and in 1931 he accompanied a dance sequence with his theremin for the run of the Roxy Theatre stage show, *Rhapsody of Time*.

Theremin's opportunity to involve himself with a dance company came through Solomonoff, who now managed the American Negro Ballet—a cross-cultural venture founded by the dancer-choreographer Eugene Von Grona— a project that captured Theremin's interest. Baron Von Grona, son of an American vaudeville dancer and a German-born father, came to the United States from his native Germany in 1925 at the age of seventeen and established his own personal style of modern choreography. His 1927 work *Spirit of Labour* was a movement analogue to the "machine music" genre, using sharp, angular, pumping motions and relentless hammering gestures to the accompaniment of steam whistles and pounding mechanistic sounds. When the work was picked up in 1928 by the Roxy Theater, it established Von Grona's name and fostered many stylistic imitators. In 1932 he was invited to perform the piece at the grand opening of Radio City Music Hall.

Following a European tour in 1934, Von Grona returned to the States and the next year presented his *Swastika*, an anti-Nazi dance suite, at Town Hall. The conditions he discovered in Europe were distressing. "It was such a relief to get back here," he told the *New York Herald Tribune*. "I went up to Harlem and I saw the abandon and freedom and spontaneity of spirit of those people. It was so different from the stereotyped Fascist spirit of Europe. I decided to make an experiment."[15]

Late in 1934, Von Grona placed an ad in a Harlem newspaper announcing auditions for "free scholarships" in ballet instruction. Over 150 people showed up—"maids, elevator men, beauticians, porters," according to the *Sunday Worker*—most having a familiarity with dance, but few with any formal training.[16] "They didn't have the opportunity," Von Grona explained. "Such training as they had was mainly jazz—tap dancing and night club work."[17] After the tryouts, about thirty were chosen for the final troupe, divided equally between men and women ranging in age from sixteen to twenty-four. Von Grona christened the company the American Negro Ballet.

Early in 1935, an eighteen-year-old art student named Lavinia Williams became involved with the group. Born in Philadelphia in 1916, Grace Lavinia Poole Williams was of native American, Irish, and African-American descent. After attending Washington Irving High School in Brooklyn, she was offered a scholarship to New York's Art Students League. There, while studying painting and anatomical drawing, she met a member of the American Negro Ballet, who invited her to sketch the company at a rehearsal. Williams had studied ballet since her childhood and had a profound respect for dance. At the rehearsal, Von Grona questioned her about this experience and invited her to audition for the company. When she danced, there was no question. He accepted her immediately, assigning her the role of the thirteenth princess in Stravinsky's *Firebird* for the company's debut concert, promptly ending her career as an aspiring painter.

Rehearsals were held three nights a week for two and a half years as Von Grona shaped and molded his dancers with a dash of ballet and a strong emphasis on relaxation, strength, improvisation, and the development of each individual's inner sense of movement. At Henry Solomonoff's suggestion, Theremin sat in on rehearsals and met Von Grona. When the choreographer heard about the terpsitone, he escorted a group of his dancers to 37 West to try it out. "It was extremely difficult to work with the sound stage to create a sound you could duplicate again and again," Lavinia remembered. "I was never very successful at it."[18] None of Von Grona's dancers, in fact, ever mastered the platform, but Lavinia Williams managed to catch Theremin's eye.

A striking and dynamic woman, Lavinia spoke six languages, painted, danced, and was a voracious reader. She and the inventor—separated in age by twenty years, and in cultural heritage by an even greater divide—were an unlikely couple. In the implicitly racist '30s, theirs was a risky liaison that called attention to itself. But against all odds, they drew increasingly close and fell in love.

On November 21, 1937, the American Negro Ballet presented its debut performance at Harlem's Lafayette Theatre. Von Grona choreographed the entire program and designed it to reflect a balance of movement styles with both classical and jazz scores. Despite the company's name, the technique was decidedly modern dance, not ballet, and the group's collective aura was heavily influenced by Von Grona's own stylistic trademarks. The program included *Children of the Earth*, a Creation allegory that featured two soloists—a man and a woman—against the core ensemble, with music by the English composer Reginald Forsythe; *Air*, a formal, abstract religious piece for eight dancers set to Bach's *Air on the G String; Southern Episode*, a revival-meeting story danced to the holy-roller energy of Ellington's "Sunday Morning" and the blues of W. C. Handy's "Saint Louis Women"; and *Fire Bird Suite*, created to the Stravinsky score, bringing together the entire company. Everything but the

Stravinsky, which was danced to a phonograph record, was accompanied by the New York Negro Symphony Orchestra, conducted by Wen Talbert. The program opened with two movements from James P. Johnson's *Symphonie Harlem*, with the composer conducting. The amplification system was "built and installed by Professor Leon Theremin as a personal contribution to the American Negro Ballet."[19]

In his program notes, Von Grona wrote: "The stirring imagination of the Negro and his innate understanding of the fundamental values have left deep, permanent impressions on the arts. In the dance, however, this talent has been confined chiefly to dance-hall jazz and African rituals." These "limited dance forms," as he called them, seemed unable to express the "deeper and more intellectual resources of the race." Now, through the "Von Grona Free Scholarships," he had made it possible for the members of the group to "enter the serious dance." "Today," he wrote, "enthusiasm and intensive concentration have developed a permanent organization dedicated to the presentation of the modern Negro through the modern dance."[20] Von Grona was no doubt earnest in his purpose, though his tone was often patronizing. He saw his dancers less as individuals than as a "race" whose spiritual heritage he was channeling through the expression of movement. "They are a naive people," he told the *Herald Tribune*, "the stories that are naive and without sophistication they feel and they understand. In the 'Fire Bird' the girls who are the princesses were enchanted with the idea of being princesses playing with golden apples— they took to it naturally. I will always have a fairy story in future programs."[21]

The concert was a fashionable affair that drew both "downtown" and "uptown" segments. The press, which attended in droves, afterward debated the merits of the very idea of a "Negro" ballet. "Park Avenue," *Newsweek* declared, "saw how hoofing and tapping Negroes could also perform the fanciful movements of Stravinsky's 'Fire Bird.'"[22] The *New York Sun* reported that "the downtown element of the audience arrived in a state of divided anticipation, not knowing whether to regard this as the first meeting of a new epochal culture society, or merely as a lark. . . . but all of the performances were animated by the earnestness and zest which the Negro brings with him to the stage."[23] *Vogue* praised the effort as "the first attempt to develop the natural talents of the Negro through the refined technique of the ballet,"[24] and John Martin in the *New York Times* wrote, "No doubt the experience of working with material of this nature, even in the oversimplified choreography provided for them, is of value in their development as a group, however limited its audience appeal may be."[25]

The choreography of the Bach *Air*, described by one writer, was typical of the movement language: "The piece shows eight young women, sheathed in red and gold, shifting and posing in sculpted masses, their arms raised in what looks like either prayer or a Gothic arch. The whole thing is immensely slow and deliberate. One group tilts left, then descends into that deep Grahamesque plié, then rises tilting right, while the other group does the opposite. The entire emphasis is on pattern: the interplay of masses."[26] Ironically, the consensus found the jazz-inspired *Southern Episode* the most successful work, precisely because it was the most indigenous to the interpreters' experience. "That Mr. Von Grona has a valid idea in proposing a Negro ballet was certainly an evidence of the evening's performance," the *New York Sun* concluded, "but its realization requires a vast amount of sober thinking and more technical background than is currently at the performers' disposal."[27] Despite Von Grona's hopes for a "permanent" organization, the American Negro Ballet was short-lived—its last program was presented within five months of its debut.

At some point during the early months of 1938, Theremin and Lavinia decided to be secretly married. "For this I needed the permission of our department," he remembered. "There were no arguments against it, and we were given a marriage certificate."[28] At the Soviet consulate they were issued an N1 certificate for a Russian marriage, but no papers were registered with the New York Marriage License Bureau. At that time, in any case, marriage to an American citizen could not confer U.S. citizenship upon an alien, so Theremin had merely added to the entanglements of his visitor's visa. He and Lavinia took a separate apartment, away from 37 West.

Soon the inventor found himself abandoned by friends who looked askance at the interracial union. In restaurants, he and Lavinia were often seated by the kitchen. The forty-one-year-old Soviet scientist chatting away in Russian with his twenty-one-year-old black American bride, by the clatter of plates and swinging doors, must have drawn a parade of critical glances—annoyingly evident in the couple's peripheral vision. "I loved him dearly," Lavinia reminisced, "he was a very gifted man. . . . he had such lovely blue eyes."[29] Cleopatra Bolotine remembered the naughty pleasure Theremin took at one of Lucie Rosen's concerts when he introduced his new wife to the circles of the Social Register—moving through the audience, sparking jolts of scandal among the jewelry-bedecked.

《》

On April 6, 1938, Zinman, Morgenstern, and Theremin filed a certificate of incorporation for yet another company: Teletouch Industries, Incorporated. With the Teletouch Corporation in financial hot water, this new company offered a legal shelter for the three to continue transacting business, if indeed there was any business to transact. A prospectus hawked the first product:

Aladdin Never Had
A Lamp Like This!
TELETOUCH ELECTRIC EYE[30]

After doggedly campaigning for the advantages of the Teletouch Ray over traditional electric-eye devices using sending and receiving units on either side of a protected area, Teletouch began marketing its own version of the standard system: a light-source unit that directed a beam of up to fifty feet or more toward a photo-cell unit, which, when it sensed an interruption of the beam, sounded an alarm or other warning. The single-unit Teletouch Ray, tested in Macy's windows less than two years earlier, had failed to rout the established technology. Now with a more saleable item, Teletouch hoped to be more competitive. The promotional brochure was aimed at distributors, hoping they would see a market for

> Private Homes . . . As a kidnap alarm it has no equal. . . . Apartments . . . The Teletouch will prevent burglaries. . . . Department Stores . . . As a pilferage detector in stockrooms. . . . Banks . . . To protect openings in cashier's cages. . . . Factories . . . For counting, such as packages, bottles, etc. . . To sound a warning when a person approaches too closely to a dangerous machine. . . . Stores . . . to ring a bell or buzzer when a customer or sneak thief enters. . . . Garages . . . will give a signal in the office each time a person or car goes up or down the ramp. . . . Offices . . . To protect files against pilferage. . . . Gas Stations . . . To ring a bell when a customer pulls up for gas. . . . Hospitals . . . Prevent pilferage of narcotics . . . Prevent escape of dangerous patients from rooms. . . . Museums . . . To protect paintings. . . . Farms . . . To prevent theft from Barns, Chicken Coops, etc. . . . Churches . . . To protect tabernacles against theft of holy relics. . . . Moving Picture Theatres . . . To place by fire exits to prevent "gate crashers."[31]

At a cost of $49.50 for the standard unit, Teletouch hoped to sweep the market. With a sensible, down-to-earth sales pitch, it seemed the company couldn't go wrong: "The TELETOUCH is the first electric eye in the market simple enough for your salesmen to demonstrate in one minute to a dealer, and in turn by him in one minute to his customer. The TELETOUCH is PACKAGE MERCHANDISE."[32]

Along with the electric eye—an eleventh-hour attempt to keep the company afloat—Teletouch had one more product it hoped to exploit. In December 1933, Theremin had filed an application for a patent on a dc-to-ac inverter for use in driving synchronous electric clocks. This device was designed particularly for large metropolitan areas like New York where ac current was generally unavailable. The invention was approved as U.S. patent number 2,047,912 on July 14, 1936, and would be Theremin's only other U.S. patent in addition to the signaling device and the space-control instrument. His six other applications, filed between August and December of 1928, were never approved. The timing-system patent was assigned to Zinman, Morgenstern, and Theremin, but not to any of their companies.

By the spring of 1938, many of Theremin's personal debts, and those of the Theremin Patents Corporation, remained in default. With creditors beginning to close in, the inventor hustled to protect his remaining personal assets from seizure. On May 11, he and Morgenstern assigned their interest in the timing system to Boyd Zinman. With Theremin's personal finances in shambles, his company faltering, his marriage forced into social exile, and his visa extensions fast expiring, the Soviet motherland began to look more and more inviting.

Unlike his compatriot Schillinger, who openly eschewed Communist dogmatism and all it stood for—wearing his newfound U.S. citizenship like an honored uniform—Theremin had a soul that was Russian to the core. His long U.S. residence by no means signaled an embrace of the capitalist free-enterprise system, a weakness for the whimsy and free-spiritedness of American culture, or a desire to break with Soviet life and ideology. After America's open arms stopped short of an embrace and the inventor receded into virtual anonymity, the country simply remained, for a while, a convenient testing ground for his ideas, encouraged especially by the GRU. "Of course, I was there on assignment all the time," he later admitted, "but the assignments dealt with seemingly unimportant issues for military purposes."[33]

As one possibility after another presented itself, the scientist whose ultimate passion was to be constantly inventing saw nothing objectionable in forging deeper relationships with American industry and using its technology to develop his work and his knowledge for the betterment of his homeland. Each six-month visa extension was merely another bookmark to hold a place as he worked his way through the chapters of American commerce. His extended stay was destined to come to an end. Forfeiting his Russian citizenship would have been unthinkable. It was never an option.

Despite his stunts for the paparazzi after his arrival, and his willingness to go along with the public appearances and promotional razzmatazz expected of him, Theremin was never truly assimilated into mainstream American life. His demeanor was colored by an aristocratic distance and decorum left over from his imperial Russian heritage; there was a seriousness in him that precluded any casual American backslapping. He surrounded himself with members of the Russian community—Clara Rockmore, Schillinger, Morris Hillquit, the Bolotines, Zenaide Hanenfeldt, Alexandra Stepanoff, and others —and he spoke Russian whenever he could, even with Lavinia. Anne Stern remembered that he "never learned English properly," and Rosalyn Tureck recalled that in 1932, during her lessons, he used a limited vocabulary repeatedly punctuated with his favorite word, "approximately."[34]

Yolanda Bolotine remembered him with great fondness as a kindly, avuncular figure with a "courtly manner," recalling the time he presented her family with a radio he had made for them. "I think he missed having Russians around him," she remembered, "he missed home. He was homesick." She recalled a playful, spontaneous spirit that emerged when he relaxed in the element of his own language:

> Once the telephone rang in our apartment, and I answered it and I heard a voice—we only spoke in Russian—he asked for my mother, and I said, "Who is speaking?" And he said, "It is I." Like that—but it sounds cuter in Russian: "ah tay AHT." Then another instance: He went to a party, a big Russian party, and the lady there had been a well-known singer whose language was very, very foul. And he rang the doorbell of our apartment, and my mother let him in. He sat, and he was telling her about the party. He said, "I *had* to run away— I couldn't *stand* it any longer. But I didn't go away empty-handed," and he reached inside his coat and brought out a piece of cake wrapped in a napkin, and said, "This is for Yolochka." That's what they called me at that time. Yolanda: Yolochka. He would do things like that. Sweet, nice, cute things.[35]

Theremin was less at home with non-Russian-speaking Americans and their freewheeling comportment. Anne Stern remembered the amusement she and her brother, Walter, once had when they rode out to Forest Hills Stadium with the inventor at the wheel of his roadster. As they crossed the Brooklyn Bridge, Walter kept pushing the stick shift into neutral and feigned innocence as the confused professor tried to figure out why they kept stalling out. She remembered that Theremin liked to play tennis but that he couldn't hit the ball. With his American associates he always maintained an air of formality. To the Rosens he was "Professor Theremin," never "Lev" or "Leon." Stern recalled the long white laboratory coat he constantly wore, "looking like a doctor," and Boyd Zinman's wife, Lucille, described him as an immaculate dresser who changed suits two or three times a day at the sight of the slightest fleck of dirt. Lucie Rosen remembered that he didn't smoke or drink, and that he was a light eater.

Theremin's broad view of American society was tinged with a certain disdain. In 1928, after his Symphony Hall demonstration in Boston, he told a reporter for the *Harvard Crimson*, "Americans do not seem to see any interest in the problems of invention in music. Every people has its own ideas of art, determined by the inherent temperament of the race. The European temperament is enormously different in character from that found in America."[36]

Certainly the U.S. economic climate during the Depression decade did not speak well for the integrity of capitalism. The bank failures and bread lines Theremin witnessed, in contrast to the wealth of the Rosens, the Rockefellers, and others, gave him all the stronger reason to support a Marxist stance. One after another, his companies had fallen victim to the economic famine, and his own debts had left him in financial ruin. In September 1931, he witnessed Morris Hillquit's reaction to a wage reduction by big corporations, and the continued fall in consumer prices. "The capitalistic system has broken down," quoted the *New York Times,*

> and the two major political parties are unable to restore economic stability, Morris Hillquit, national chairman of the Socialist party, declared in a statement today.
> He advised the American voter to turn to the Socialist party as the only hope of working out an "intelligent program of social reconstruction."
> "Private capitalism is breaking down all over the world. It has piled up vast wealth for the few and thrown millions of toilers into the breadlines. . . . Only socialism can cure the devastating ills which capitalism has created.
> "The personnel of our government and law-making bodies, including Congress, must be replaced by faithful and intelligent representatives of the working masses."[37]

As hard evidence of Hillquit's ideas, Theremin saw U.S. citizens flocking by the thousands to the Soviet Union to find work. In August of '31, the Amtorg Trading Corporation announced it had received over 100,000 applications from skilled American workers to fill openings for 6,000 jobs in cities throughout Russia. Stalin's Five-Year Plan had created a new job market due to the shortage of Russian skilled labor, and positions for miners, railroad workers, bricklayers, carpenters, and workers in other trades were available. Although Amtorg announced it had capped the limit at 6,000, applicants continued to storm its offices, and by October, 500 to 600 a day were reportedly being turned away. The majority of those hired paid their own passage to Russia and brought their families with them with the intention of settling permanently in the Soviet Union. "In all cases," the *New York Times* reported, "the American immigrant will receive the same rights and privileges enjoyed by the native worker, such as social insurance, recreation and the education of his children."[38] The 6,000 sent to Russia supplemented 2,500 skilled American workers and more than 1,000 U.S. engineers already employed there.

After 1935, Theremin would even see the American Communist Party begin to insinuate itself into the liberal mainstream. As a result of the Popular Front—an alliance of the CPUSA with liberals and socialists, designed to unite against fascism—Communists could be found in every sector of American life. The newly formed Congress of Industrial Organizations (CIO) had one-quarter of its membership in Communist-run unions by the late '30s; the American Youth Congress, an organization of the largest youth groups in America, was led by Communists; the Minnesota Farmer-Labor Party, the American Labor Party, and dozens of other groups were Communist-dominated. In the early years of the Depression, the CPUSA was the first to lead nationwide demonstrations and violent strikes protesting rising unemployment. The movement crossed racial boundaries as well, adopting an early civil rights platform for blacks. In 1930, the Comintern issued resolutions stating that Communists "openly and unreservedly fight for the right of Negroes for national self-determination in the South" and advocated "confiscation of the landed property of the white landowners and capitalists for the benefit of the Negro farmers."[39] Beginning in 1931, the Communist Party conducted a series of trials in Harlem in a "worker's court" to prosecute members accused of "white chauvinism,"[40] expelling from the Party those found guilty, and in one case, touching off the deportation of a "convicted" comrade to Finland. In 1938, the Party announced that blacks made up 9.2 percent of its national membership, and 6 percent in New York, where major black entertainers regularly performed at Party functions. When nine black youths were arrested in Scottsboro, Alabama, in 1931 and charged with raping two white women, the Party rallied to defend the young men, attracting international attention to the case with the support of such prominent intellectuals as Thomas Mann, Albert Einstein, and Theodore Dreiser. Through causes like this, the Party won many converts among Americans committed to social justice.

One particularly large segment identified with a leftist posture in 1930s America was the community of artists, writers, and intellectuals. As the CPUSA sought new allies in the struggle against the growing threat of fascism, it was forced to mine the ranks of bourgeois culture, once seen as the antithesis to the proletarian movement. Leftist theater groups were particularly active, and by 1934, the League of Workers' Theatre boasted over three hundred affiliated workers' theaters set up to spread the message of the class struggle—organizations like the Workers Laboratory Theatre that presented mobile agitprop plays in New York subways. Writers were attracted to John Reed Clubs emerging around the country and associated themselves with the Communist-dominated League of American Writers and the American League Against War and Fascism. The CPUSA raised substantial funds in Hollywood, and musicians such as Aaron Copland were recruited for the Pierre Degeyter Clubs, named after the composer of the "Internationale."

Because Theremin fraternized within artistic spheres, he invariably found himself in company sympathetic to his Soviet ideology. Leopold Stokowski, in defiance of the Philadelphia board of the American Legion, directed the singing of the "Internationale" at one of his Young People's Concerts in 1934 and, according to the *Daily Worker,* "the conductor declared that the audience itself—at a previous concert—had asked that the 'Internationale' be played so that they could join in the singing."[41] The same year, Stokowski spoke at a Lenin memorial meeting in Philadelphia on his composition *Ode to Lenin,* performed for the occasion by the Pierre Degeyter String Quartette. In 1929, the conductor had presented the world premiere of Alexander Krein's *Ode of Mourning to the Memory of Lenin,* and in 1934 he introduced Harl McDonald's *Festival of the Worker.*

Among the circles of the Theremin Studio, Lewis Jacobs, who provided the camera work and animation for Mary Ellen Bute's *Synchromy,* was an editor of *Experimental Cinema,* a pro-Socialist film magazine. Jacobs himself had made documentaries about the Scottsboro boys, a bloody miner's strike in Harlan County, Kentucky, Depression poverty in a New York working-class neighborhood, and assorted other causes célèbres of the Communist Party. *Experimental Cinema* held an intransigently proletarian view of film as the most potent instrument of social awareness and class consciousness, and it trumpeted the power of socialist realism in Soviet film. "This is particularly desirable," an editorial statement claimed,

> at a time when the current Hollywood movie boasts a banality and a stupidity that seems to wax greater in proportion to the growth in the unsettlement and distress of American life.
>
> It is clear to the editors of *Experimental Cinema* that Hollywood, while it is an almost inexhaustible source of stupefying "entertainment," is also at the same time the tool of American imperialist political policy, which it serves so faithfully and so supinely through the medium of war films, anti-USSR films, news reels, etc.[42]

In an article on Eisenstein, one of many Soviet filmmakers championed in the organ, Jacobs praised the development of cinema in Russia as "organically related to the new social forces and economic implications of the era" and declared that "these forces manifest themselves stirringly in the Soviet film."[43]

《》

By the late spring of 1938, with enthusiasm and support for Theremin's work dried up, the inventor's growing status as a scofflaw seriously threatened to exhaust the patience of the Department of Labor. As far back as December 1934, an FBI memorandum to J. Edgar Hoover had red-flagged Theremin. The report indicated that an inspector from the Baltimore office of the Bureau of Immigration had "called and advised that the Labor Department had been interested for some time in causing the return to Russia of one Professor Leon Theremin, who had over-stayed a temporary residence in the United States." The inspector "stated that recently the Labor Department had attempted to cause Theremin's return to Russia, and was advised by Theremin's attorney, Meyer Bloomfield . . . that Theremin was conducting confidential experiments in the United States in behalf of the Division of Investigation, Department of Justice and in behalf of the War Department. Theremin's experiments were supposed to be in the 'magnetic ray' field."[44]

The memorandum further advised Hoover that the FBI had searched its files but turned up nothing indicating the inventor had been conducting research "by, or in behalf of the Division of Investigation."[45] The statement suggested, however, that agents contact the Bureau of Prisons. Alcatraz, of course, was the work Bloomfield referred to, but the only "confidential" aspect was the observation of the prison on behalf of the Soviet government—certainly not the U.S. War Department or the FBI. In pushing the inventor to prolong his American stay for intelligence reasons, the Soviets outdid themselves with puckish schemes to block his deportation. In an amusingly ironic twist, Teletouch at one point offered the Immigration and Naturalization Service a version of Theremin's signaling device as a snare for illegal immigrants, to be set up at the U.S.–Mexico border.

According to Anne Stern, the inventor was not only a judgment debtor, but he owed substantial tax payments to the federal government. "My father told Theremin," she recalled, "that he really had to do something about paying income taxes and declaring himself as an honorable citizen." Walter Rosen was seriously concerned that Theremin would go to jail. "I think my father put the fear of God in him," Stern continued.

> My father said, "You cannot stay in this country in this absolutely unsuitable way where you don't pay your bills, where you don't have any legal status, where you got an extended visa." . . . My father certainly was a most honorable man, and he was very upset. He was a marvelously educated German Jew. . . . He was not a man to put up with any nonsense, and I think it bothered him terribly that Theremin was dishonorable. And I think one of the things that worried him most was that he knew my mother cared so much about the instrument, and he wanted to make it possible for her to continue to play.[46]

Nearly oblivious to all this, Lucie still occupied herself with refining the space-control instrument design, consulting with the inventor over minute technical details as he tested and repaired instruments at the studio. "We argued about the necessities," she recalled. "It was nearly hopeless to keep in pitch, or play at all in hot weather or wet weather. Was this really because of the difficulties of moving the hands in space—or was it a weakness of the instrument to be overcome by mechanical improvement? It was important to discover."[47] At Lucie's request, Theremin had initially customized her original RCA instrument with an expanded range and the addition of two tone-color choices to supplement the original timbre. Later, she asked for an instrument with still more octaves, and she remembered his reaction: "'Why do you want them?' asked the professor, amused. 'The extra notes will add variety,' I thought. 'The intervals will be closer, fingerwork will be possible.' 'It will be difficult to make,' said the professor, and so it turned out. It took several years to get coils of the necessary extra length that would stay in pitch."[48] In January 1938, Theremin built a custom-designed instrument for Lucie with a five-octave range, a slightly higher frequency, and a smaller resonating coil capacity than the RCA instrument—a model virtually identical to the one he was building for Clara. This version was satisfactory, but Lucie still hoped to fine-tune the circuitry further in one more instrument. Her chance to do this was slipping away, though. Time was running out for the inventor.

By June 9, 1938, Teletouch was sinking so quickly that Boyd Zinman, in a desperate move to raise capital, assigned Theremin's timing-system patent to Westinghouse Electric and Manufacturing Company in Pittsburgh. Gone now was any hope of turning a last-minute profit by exploiting this system that Theremin had signed over to Zinman only two months earlier. But even after the sale to Westinghouse, Teletouch was still unable to pay rent to the Rosens' agent, the 50 West Fifty-fifth Street Realty Corporation, for the continued use of 37 West. It was now apparent to Theremin that the end of the line had come. "Everybody was trying to see if they couldn't make him reform, which was impossible," Anne Stern recalled. "And then he took the leap and said, 'Well, I'll leave.'"[49]

The decision to return to Russia was likely in Theremin's thoughts for some time. He and Lavinia, he later explained, "decided not to have children, because if they were born in America, they would become American citizens, and I was dreaming of returning to the Soviet Union."[50] But lately there were disquieting stories leaking out of Russia. Jan Berzin, who had doubled up in a new role since 1936 as chief Soviet military adviser in Spain during the Spanish civil war, was summoned back to Moscow and had just been executed as a "traitor" in July 1938—a victim of Stalin's bloody purge of the military. The increasing crackdown on the Red Army also weakened the GRU's power abroad—particularly in America—while its archrival, the OGPU, began to gain the upper hand in espionage work as the favored sibling among Stalin's organizations. But Theremin remained confident he could slip comfortably back into his research work at Ioffe's institute as a carrier of American industrial secrets. "There was much talk about the U.S.S.R.," he recalled, "but I wasn't afraid of anything. I thought that if I was a citizen of the U.S.S.R. I would have nothing to fear."[51] U.S. Secretary of Labor statistics, in fact, showed that from 1936 to 1938, Russians were more likely to return home than to seek refuge on American soil: during that time, twice the number of immigrant alien Russians left the U.S. as entered.

In order to make passage home, Theremin needed money. Lucie Rosen wanted one more crack at a hand-built instrument. Walter, who was determined to wash his hands of the inventor as quickly as possible, saw his opportunity and made an appointment for Theremin to meet with him at his 35 West Fifty-fourth street residence. There, he commissioned one final instrument with a down payment of $150 on August 5, with the balance to be paid upon completion of the project. In exchange for a full schematic of the instrument and its amplifier, technical papers describing maintenance procedures, sources for spare parts, and the rights to build similar instruments for private use in the future, Walter agreed to underwrite Theremin's departure. "My father said, 'All right, I will give you ten thousand dollars,'" Anne Stern recalled, "'which will help you pay your travel expenses and whatever else you need, and please depart, but leave me the schematic.'"[52] In a letter of August 12, Theremin granted the Rosens the rights to produce his instrument for their own personal use.

As the inventor carried out work on the instrument, it appeared to Walter Rosen that the job was taking longer than he anticipated, and that Theremin was dragging his feet in orchestrating a smooth departure. On August 25, Rosen's patience finally boiled over into a letter:

> Dear Professor Theremin,
> As I have repeatedly told you and also advised Mr. Zinman, and with all the good will in the world, it is impossible for the 50 West 55th Street Realty Corporation to continue to permit you or the Teletouch Corporation to occupy number 37 West 54th Street. You will recollect that when you originally moved into that house, it was intended to be merely a very temporary occupation. The time has now come where you must make very prompt arrangements to move out. The 50 West 55th Street Realty Corporation must get prompt possession of the house so they can find a tenant who is in a position to pay rent.
> I've been informed that there has been a good deal of difficulty . . . on account of the fact that you have been unable to pay rent. It has been expected for a long time past. I ask of you to be good enough to leave everything in the house that belongs to the 50 West 55th Street Realty Corporation and anything that belongs to Mrs. Rosen or myself, and to see to it that objects that belong to the Teletouch Corporation or yourself, other than theremin instruments which belong to Mrs. Rosen, are removed from the premises. Be good enough to advise me promptly when that has been accomplished.[53]

Rosen's letter finally forced the issue, and Theremin began to do what little he could to put his ramshackle affairs in order before leaving. His manner of handling money matters—ignoring debts, summonses, creditors, and judgments as so many annoying interruptions to the daily progress of his work—was probably encouraged, if not mandated, by his Soviet overseers. And his socialist bent no doubt gave him a disdain for the accumulation of wealth as a capitalist abomination. Even when he arrived on the *Majestic* he had waved off lucrative offers cabled in from American businessmen, preferring to champion his inventions as fruits of a proletarian culture, rather than mere bait for American wealth. His aristocratic demeanor, and his former position as a celebrated scientist at home, perhaps convinced him that support of his research was his due, America being in his debt, and not the other way around. But debt there was, and in the last legal document he put his hand to in America, he attempted to consolidate his obligations, leaving them in the hands of the one person he would trust to handle his affairs after he was gone. On the last day of August, he stepped into a notary's office and signed a statement that would irreversibly alter the course of his life:

POWER OF ATTORNEY
KNOW ALL MEN BY THESE PRESENTS, that I, LEON THEREMIN, of the City, County and State of New York, being about to depart from the State of New York, have made, constituted, and appointed, M. BOYD ZINMAN . . . my true and lawful attorney in fact, for me and in my name to do any and all acts which I could do if personally present, hereby intending to give to said M. BOYD ZINMAN the fullest power . . . to ask, demand, sue for, recover and receive all manner of goods, chattels, deeds, rents, interest, sums of money . . . due and owing or belonging to me on any account and to make, execute, endorse, accept, and deliver in my name . . . all checks, notes, drafts, warrants . . . applications for Letters Patent . . .
With full power and authority to sell, transfer or to do any other act concerning any stocks or bonds, and Letters Patent which I may have or possess, and to transfer the same in any manner required by any corporation . . . and also for me and in my name and stead to appear, answer and defend in all actions and suits whatsoever, which may be commenced against me . . . and perform and finish for me and in my name . . . those things which shall be expedient or necessary . . . in and about, for or concerning the premises . . . as fully as I, the said LEON THEREMIN, could do, if personally present . . .
IN WITNESS WHEREOF, I have hereunto set my hand and seal this 31 day of August, 1938.
[signed] Leon Theremin[54]

The following day, the *Stary Bolshevik* appeared in Raritan Bay, sailed past the southern tip of Staten Island and up the Arthur Kill, and docked at Bayway Terminal in Elizabeth, New Jersey. On the sixth of September it changed berths, moving past Newark Bay, through the Kill Van Kull, and into Upper New York Bay, docking at Claremont Terminal in Jersey City, New Jersey.

By September 8, Theremin had finished Lucie's new instrument, and the day after, Walter asked him in a letter to provide a detailed account of the materials and cost breakdown of the entire project, so as to be able to replicate it in the future. "Please also tell me who can supply the poles for the loudspeaker," he wrote. "Please also give me the name and address of the carpenter who supplied the box for the latest instrument. . . . I would like this for future reference, and would like to know if the carpenter has exact drawings for making this box and stand."[55]

The new instrument represented Theremin's most advanced applications of the space-control principle, and it featured a five-octave range, timbre controls, and an especially sensitive capability for volume antenna regulation. Lucie dubbed it the "September Theremin," to distinguish it from the earlier "January Theremin." The inventor equipped the instrument with six timbral changes, selected by a ten-position switch on the front of the cabinet. Rotation of the switch to the right connected higher constant capacities parallel to plates in the output transformer. The first, or left, position corresponded to zero additional capacity, producing the sound with maximum-high-frequency harmonics. Rotation to the right gradually limited these harmonics. Theremin left the last positions open for Lucie to use other combinations of capacity, or capacity with resistance, in the future. Specific control of left hand responsiveness and incisive attacks could be regulated either by using a greater voltage from the C battery in the volume control system (causing a sharper staccato with the same height of the left hand over the volume antenna) or by decreasing the capacitance in the circuit of one particular tube.

Lucie's technical know-how was generally quite acute when it came to her instruments but, aware that she would no longer have the inventor's guidance, she sat down with him to go over very specific instructions for items like subtle regulation of circuitry, and overall maintenance. In a typescript, under the heading "QUESTIONS answered by Professor Theremin regarding care of his instruments," she noted provisions for future wear and replacement of even the smallest components. Concerning the neon pilot light that indicated the correct adjustment of the pitch circuits, she wrote, "Hardness of the ageing tube will in time cause diminished brilliance but increased sharpness, till the light is entirely lost, and useless for a guide. You can change the tube before this; but if both light and sharpness are defective with a new tube, the trouble is proved not with the tube, but with the circuit."[56]

On September 12, Theremin wrote to the Rosens acknowledging payment of the final installment for his work on the instrument. In another letter, he set Lucie's mind at rest about the future compatibility of the new model with various electrical supply conditions, signing it, ever graciously, "with kindest regards, sincerely yours, Leon Theremin."[57]

Passage out of the country would not be easy. In 1938 there was no direct passenger ship service to the USSR, and travel via Europe would be too risky in light of the inventor's arrears with the IRS, should the U.S. government check his passport. The only hope was through Amtorg, which handled Soviet-owned-and-chartered cargo vessels at United States ports. In the early '30s, the company regularly smuggled its own employees back to Russia aboard its freighters—and there were a few who went against their will when the CPUSA secretly ordered that they be "let go across."

The regular movement of Soviet agents in and out of the United States was engineered through a devilishly precise mechanism. With free access to genealogical records at the New York Public Library, the CPUSA routinely conducted research on birth records, matching them with infant deaths from decades past. With viable names and birth certificates, fictitious life histories were scrupulously assembled for these resurrected babies. Particular care was taken to ensure that nothing was traceable. Schools the person "attended" were chosen from consolidated institutions; childhood home addresses were selected from now-demolished buildings; "former employers" were always defunct businesses. Completed profiles were sent to passport mills in New York and Berlin to be ground out into finished counterfeits.

An agent arriving in New York on a Soviet vessel would carry a forged seaman's book showing him to be a crew member. Once on U.S. soil, the GRU switched the book with a bogus American passport, assigning the agent an identity as a "verifiable" American citizen. Anyone returning to the USSR was filtered through the process in reverse—an arriving "crewman" relaying his seaman's book and identity to the new individual being smuggled out of the United States. In the '30s, the Soviet merchant fleet helped protect its cover by taking advantage of lax regulations. The USSR was not a signatory nation to the international shipping agreements, and its vessels often violated the rules of the sea. And because its ships were self-insured, their technical specifications were not required to be listed with the Lloyds register.

Amtorg happened to have one of its ships, bound for Leningrad, in port at the moment: the *Stary Bolshevik*. "I was assigned as the captain's assistant," Theremin remembered. For a predetermined sum, he was able to arrange a place for himself on the ship and would be allowed to bring his equipment with him. He applied for permission to take Lavinia, but he recalled, "On the last day, my wife was refused papers to leave on the grounds that this was a secret trip."[58] Soviet authorities assured him, however, that she would be sent on after, in about two weeks.

《 》

A light rain fell over New York on the morning of Thursday, September 15, 1938. It was a sticky, muggy day—by 8:00 A.M. the humidity was already at 97 percent and the temperature up to 72 degrees Fahrenheit, in a climb that would reach 82 degrees later in the afternoon. Out on the long pier at Claremont Terminal in Jersey City, next to the tracks of the Lehigh Valley Railroad, the *Stary Bolshevik* waited to be cleared for sailing. Seen from the Battery in Manhattan, Claremont Terminal appeared almost in a direct line behind the Statue of Liberty on the Jersey side of New York Bay. The terminal was used mainly for ore handling, with iron ore or other general cargo unloaded on its piers to be shipped by train. Incoming Russian vessels mainly landed manganese and chrome from the Black Sea at its docks. The *Stary Bolshevik* was a diesel engine, five-hold freighter built by the Severney Shipbuilding Yard in Leningrad in 1933. The ship was 3,974 gross tons, and 2,256 net tons. It was 347.6 feet long, with a breadth of 51 feet 7 inches at the beam. It had a service speed of 9 ³/₄ knots. The *Stary Bolshevik* was a single-deck vessel (no additional decks in the hold), which, in a ship of its size, indicates it was designed primarily for carrying bulk cargoes such as ore, coal, grain, and lumber. If there were any passenger accommodations at all, they would have amounted to no more than a few spare cabins. The ship was operated by the Black Sea branch of the USSR state shipping company, Sovtorgflot, and in New York harbor was consigned to the Moore and McCormack Steamship Company as agents for Amtorg Trading Corporation.

At the appointed hour, in the Fifty-fourth Street townhouse, Theremin met an escort of men—probably from Amtorg—who would see him out to Claremont Terminal. Apparently the inventor had told his wife nothing of what was about to happen. Whether accidentally or by design, Lavinia was present to witness his swift evacuation and she could only assume he was being taken against his will. "I was there at his studio when they came to get him to take him back to Russia," she later recounted. "He said not to try to follow him, nor to try to get in touch with him. I think he was afraid for my safety."[59]

The route out to the *Stary Bolshevik* from Manhattan took Theremin and his escorts through the Holland Tunnel and south to Jersey City, where, at the foot of Linden Street, they crossed Princeton Avenue, traveled along an overpass above the tracks of the Central Railroad of New Jersey near the Greenville Station stop, and out onto a long jetty road bordering a continuous landscape of railroad tracks. Seen from the air, these tracks, and those of the adjacent Pennsylvania Railroad Greenville Yard, appeared like massive networks of dark spaghetti strands, crossing, intertwining, and unraveling down the full length of the piers—more than three-fifths of a mile.

Waiting out alongside this barren, misty terrain was the *Stary Bolshevik,* a dark silhouette with its long, flat cargo deck and huge cranes angled up against the sky. The ship was carrying a crew of thirty-four men and three women, all originating from home ports in Odessa, Leningrad, and Novorossisk. Of the women, one was a doctor, one a barmaid, and the third a charwoman. The men included electricians, firemen, engineers, two cooks, a carpenter, a radio operator, an electrical engineer, a charman, and various classes of sailors, motorists, and ship's officers.

The ship's master was Nicolay Habalov, a thirty-six-year-old native of Leningrad with sixteen years of service at sea. Although he was required by the U.S. Department of Labor to report any additions to his crew prior to departure, he signed a statement indicating that no new seamen were taken aboard. On the clearance records for the ship's departure, the notation "oath," in a column listing numbers of outgoing passengers, indicates he took a sworn oath testifying that no passengers were aboard.[60] "Most immigration services of the day were more concerned with numbers than identities," the Soviet intelligence authorities William R. Corson and Robert T. Crowley have pointed out. "If twenty-four Soviet seamen went ashore, they were pleased to have at least that many rejoin the ship before she sailed."[61] Habalov's crew manifest clearly indicated that thirty-seven seamen had arrived in New York, and thirty-seven were leaving.

As moorings were released and the ship was guided away from the creaking dock by the Moore and McCormack tug, the vessel slowly proceeded around the side of the long pier, past graves of sunken barges and a partly collapsed pile breakwater, and out into upper New York Bay. A trace of precipitation still hung in the air.

Back in midtown Manhattan, a shockwave began to ripple through the community of Theremin's friends and acquaintances. Except for the Rosens, who had had advance warning about his impending flight, he had told no one about his decision to leave. It was a necessity for security reasons, even with Lavinia. "Lev Termen remained, and had to remain, a loyal Soviet citizen in his private life," Bulat Galeyev pointed out.[62] If the inventor had been intending to send for his wife on the next available boat, as he later claimed, she was apparently never privy to this plan. "I was devastated," she revealed years later.[63]

When Theremin absconded, he carried out the operation in such secrecy that no one was aware of the designated time, or the exact circumstances. "I'm not even sure my father knew," Anne Stern recalled, "I don't remember anyone giving me that information. None of us saw him go. He went very quiet-ly."[64] To those who arrived at the Fifty-fourth Street studio in the following days, the sight was jolting. "My father, who knew him very well, after all," Yolanda Bolotine remembered, "came, and found that everything was gone. And a friend of Theremin's told us that Theremin had taken all his plans—the plans of his inventions—with him. He had taken them." She recalled that only "a few theremins were around."[65]

On September 15, as the inventor had prepared to leave, the front page of the *New York Times* ran a series of articles reflecting a sudden and dramat-ic shift in world events. As the struggle in Czechoslovakia between the gov-ernment and Hitler's Sudeten Germans heated up, President Roosevelt cut short his plans and sped back to Washington to be "at the seat of government during the present crisis in Europe." "Chamberlain Off by Plane to See Hit-ler," read the main headline. "Will Make a Personal Plea to Avert War." An-other front-page story reported: "Americans Informally Told to Return Home; Many Ship Bookings to Europe Canceled." Theremin's timing was impecca-ble. "Shipping executives said last night," the article continued, "that Euro-pean developments of the last few days had affected shipping in both passen-ger and freight fields. Tramp ships of foreign registry, which are generally available for service to any part of the world depending upon the nature of the freight, were said yesterday to have been withdrawn from the market. In the passenger field cancellations of bookings have already been reported."[66]

As the *Stary Bolshevik* moved out through the Narrows and into the At-lantic Ocean, the weather began to break. "At Atlantic City, N.J.," it was re-ported, "the barometer reading was 29.62 inches. The wind-shift line which bisects the trough has passed off-shore over most sections of the North and Middle Atlantic States. The winds which were southerly in advance of this line have now shifted in these sections to northerly with a consequent sharp drop in temperature over the interior sections of the Atlantic States."[67]

Perhaps Theremin came up on deck and turned to look back one last time at the receding outline of America from its coastal waters, his hair touseled and whipped by the bracing sea winds. One can imagine him, a solitary figure in a dark coat by the railing, rising and falling with the pitch of the ship, rumi-nating on his American years and pondering his future as he sailed out into a world in turmoil. As he stood among the proletarian population of the Black Sea motorship, among the charwoman and the cooks, the firemen, the elec-trician, and the sailors, he might have flashed back to his triumphant arrival eleven years earlier when reporters shoved their way onto the *Majestic* to catch a glimpse of him, to extract a few words from him for their headlines as he shared first-class amenities with the world's musical elite. But ultimately, he had rejected bourgeois culture in favor of the October Revolution, and now, as he headed back, he knew he had better be ready to defend its principles once again, with all the strength he could muster.

But if he was through with bourgeois culture, it was not yet through with him. Back on shore, every Thursday night, the Mutual Radio network broadcast a popular new sustaining feature, *The Green Hornet,* with the sound of the theremin as the Hornet's buzz:

Announcer: The Green Hornet!

Sound: Hornet buzz up full

Announcer: He hunts the biggest of all game! Public enemies who try to destroy our America. . . . The Green Hornet strikes again!

Sound: Hornet buzz up full.

EIGHT

Yowsah, Yowsah!

Yowsah, yowsah, yowsah. Au revoir. This is Ben Bernie, ladies and gen-
tlemen, and all the lads, wishing you a bit of pleasant dreams. May good
luck, and happiness, success, good health, attend your schemes. And
don't forget—should you ever send in your request-a, why we'll sho' try
to do our best-a. Yowsah. Au revoir, a fond cheerio, a bit of a tweet-
tweet. God bless you, and pleasant dreams!

> —Bandleader Ben Bernie, in his traditional sign-off from *The Ben*
> *Bernie Show*, CBS radio network, 1938

As the dark prow of the *Stary Bolshevik* sliced through the North Atlantic waters on the evening of September 15, 1938, the voices of Sutton Vane's drama *Outward Bound* crackled out over the airwaves along the Eastern seaboard and all across America. Rudy Vallee crooned, and on WEAF, "Good News of 1939" featured songs, comedy sketches, and gags with Frank Morgan, Judy Garland, and Fanny Brice. Americans were in love with radio—not just for the silly banter and idle musical distractions it offered post-Depression listeners, but for the connection it provided with the larger dominion of global affairs. This was, after all, a serious time.

Throughout the month of September 1938—one of the most suspense-charged periods in history—Americans, poised before their radio sets, waited out events that threatened to plunge the world into war again. During eighteen consecutive days at the microphone—from the thirteenth to the thirtieth—the popular commentator H. V. Kaltenborn slept on a cot and held out on sandwiches at his CBS studio in New York. Translating the moment-to-moment dispatches out of Europe from three languages, he droned on with the latest posturings of Hitler, Mussolini, and Daladier. Sales of radios hit a record high that month as anxious listeners witnessed England and France hand Czechoslovakia to Hitler in a wary bargain to avert war. By September 30, the Munich Pact had given Hitler the Sudetenland, and the world managed a guarded sense of peace. Six months later, Germany would take the rest of Czechoslovakia, and the bottom would fall out of the flimsy net of appeasement.

In these moments before the shadow of war moved deliberately over America, a giddy, innocent hopefulness remained in the nation as the Depression clouds dissipated. It was too soon to consider war again—the country needed diversion, and it had to feel its oats once more as an industrial power.

Ironically, Leon Theremin left on the eve of this new strengthening—just as the free enterprise system that stumbled before him began to rise to its feet again. On September 23, 1938, little more than a week after his departure, Westinghouse Electric and Manufacturing Company—his old RCA collaborator, and the assignee of his last U.S. patent—buried a time capsule at Flushing Meadow Park in Queens, New York, containing sundry specimens of late '30s industry and culture. Set to be exhumed in the year 6939, the capsule symbolized the theme of the coming 1939 New York World's Fair: "building the World of Tomorrow."

The most extravagant international exposition ever staged, the fair hosted pavilions from over sixty nations (with Germany noticeably absent) and the majority of the American states. Above all, it was an industrial circus for U.S. companies to parade their handsome new wares. Contained within a twelve-hundred-acre fantasyland of streamlined, art deco structures spilling over with parks, fountains, lakes, and monuments, the fair attracted forty-five million visitors to its food, transportation, amusement, and industrial zones.

In response to the bread lines and bank failures Theremin had witnessed, the fair affirmed the ideal of a strong capitalist economy, fused with industrial progress, as the foundation for world harmony and peace. The architectural focal point and "theme center" of the fair was the seven-hundred-foot tall "Trylon" and its companion "Perisphere"—a massive white globe. Inside the Perisphere, a sprawling diorama of "Democracity" offered an imagined utopian world of 2039. From revolving circular balconies above, fairgoers witnessed a light-and-music spectacle accompanied by the booming voice of H. V. Kaltenborn who, in this role, intoned rhetorically, "this march of men and women, singing their triumph, is the true symbol of the World of Tomorrow."[1]

The fair, with its futuristic agenda of scientific "wonders," would have made an ideal venue for Theremin's work. General Electric staged indoor displays of manmade lightning—ten million volts flashing across a thirty-foot arc; Westinghouse paraded "Elektro" the "Moto-Man," a seven-foot metal robot who could talk, see, smell, and count on his fingers, performing alongside his "Moto-Dog" "Sparko." The RCA pavilion tantalized visitors with reminders of Theremin's own work. Television was a novel attraction at the fair. RCA demonstrated its latest models and offered selected visitors the chance to see themselves on screen. The Radio Corporation initiated public telecasting in New York by carrying the fair's opening day ceremonies to a smattering of local viewers—anyone able to pay several hundred dollars for a set with a seven-inch screen. RCA also displayed an electronic musical instrument—the Story Electronic Piano—and offered a popular interactive display called the "Magic Switch." Like Theremin's baby guard, it featured a doll in a cradle, elevated on a small circular podium ringed by a railing. A sign dared visitors to "try to kidnap the baby." Any fairgoer who reached for the doll set off flashing lights and an alarm. But unlike Theremin's capacitance system, the device was triggered by an electric eye.

The sensation of Theremin's space-control instrument at the Radio World's Fair ten years before was barely a memory by 1939. Visitors to the RCA pavilion would doubtless have been surprised to learn of a Russian inventor who demonstrated several of these phenomena a decade back. Theremin's eleven years in America had come down to very little. But an essence remained, and it continued to have an impact, however slight.

On October 27, Clara Rockmore appeared at Town Hall in her first major New York recital in four years. It was another page from the catalog of ironies in the inventor's life: six weeks to the day he had left, Clara presented the public debut of his improved instrument. The new theremin had a slightly smaller cabinet than the RCA model, and among other changes, it was adapted to incorporate suggestions Clara received from the pianist Josef Hofmann, including a method of preventing the tubes from heating too rapidly, allowing less frequent need for tuning. "Thanks, no doubt, both to the new model and to Miss Rockmore's mastery of its technique," the *New York Herald Tribune* wrote, "the recital marked a significant forward step in the development of the theremin as a concert instrument, especially in the swifter pace which it is now able to attain and the possibility of playing detached notes, as compared with the too much present portamento and the limitations of speed which were still in evidence at its last concert demonstration."[2]

With her sister Nadia at the piano, Clara tackled an ambitious program centering around the complete four-movement violin sonata of César Franck. "That the theremin can respond cleanly and nimbly in speedy passages when the performer has sufficient command of its resources," the *New York Times* declared, "became patent in Miss Rockmore's agile treatment of the second movement of the César Franck violin sonata, which was taken at as high a rate of speed as violinists ever adopt for its allegro sections."[3] For the *Herald Tribune* reviewer, "the program showed that the theremin has accomplished a marked gain as an artistic medium."[4] The critic for the *New York Post* concluded that the instrument "appears to possess no technical limits."[5]

In spite of President Roosevelt's clear call for Americans to return home in September 1938, Lucie Rosen left for a brief tour through several European capitals in the early months of 1939. With the Orchestre Symphonique de Paris on January 24, she performed short works by Wagner, Sibelius, and Debussy, arranged for theremin and orchestra, and the world premiere of a work recently written for her—Mortimer Browning's *Concerto in F.*[6] The budget for the event was considerable: with the hall rental, the orchestra of eighty-five musicians (compensated for two three-hour rehearsals), posters, five thousand circulars and postcards, publicity and management fees, the bill came to $1,630, typical of the resources the Rosens invested to sustain these tours. On February 5, a second concert with the same orchestra featured another work written for her: Jenö Takács's *Mouvements Symphoniques* for theremin and orchestra. On February 23 Lucie played in Venice with the Quartetto Bogo, and on March 9 she wrapped up the tour with an appearance in Budapest.

Though the inventor saw the theremin ultimately as a sophisticated concert instrument—embodied in the meticulous approach of Lucie Rosen, or the elevated musicianship of Clara Rockmore—American culture had made something altogether different out of it. With the exception of Electrio, and its spawn, the Electro-Ensemble, Theremin had never actively pushed his instruments in popular music, but with the appearance of the RCA model, popular culture quickly claimed the instrument for its own.

The tradition began with Lennington Shewell, when he topped off Rudy Vallee's Connecticut Yankees with his lilting theremin sound, early in 1930. Jolly Coburn, a young bandleader directing orchestra dates at Villa Vallee, took notice. Coburn went on to open the Rainbow Room at Rockefeller Center and worked the vaudeville circuit well into the '30s. With a fancy for unique instruments, he was the first to add a harp to the dance band, and by 1934 the theremin had become a trademark item in his NBC ensemble. Coburn demonstrated the instrument in two film shorts for Warner, and in 1936 he carried the idea further, beguiling society columnists with an all-electrical dance orchestra "operated by volts and amperes."[7]

By 1937, Coburn's popular dance orchestra featured the theremin in twice-weekly broadcasts from Manhattan's Riverside Inn, live over the NBC network. "The theremin, you know, is that electrical thing that is played by making passes," the *New York Post* wrote in 1934.[8] The reporter for the *New York Daily Mirror* waited for Coburn to pull a rabbit from the instrument, but added, "actually, it was a greater magic to make the peculiar thing produce music than if it had produced a whole family of rabbits."[9]

Samuel Hoffman, a violinist in Coburn's band, was the next to catch the theremin bug. Hoffman was a chiropodist with an office in Manhattan's Essex House, but his nocturnal soul belonged to music. "Glad to see the maestros coming to the rescue of the doctors," the *New York American* joked in 1934. "A statistician revealed the other day that the average yearly income of doctors, covering the whole United States, is less than $1,500. There's a side line open to the medics. . . . if they can play a fiddle or tickle a piano, there's room for them in the dance bands. Jolly Coburn, court musician to John D. [Rockefeller], has a Dr. Samuel Hoffman on his payroll already. The Doc writes prescriptions for aches and fevers by day and prescribes for the blues with his fiddle by night."[10]

Seeing Jolly Coburn weave the theremin's electronic voice into swing music, Hoffman realized it would make an "interesting novelty instrument as a double" and began studying it seriously. "I used it on a lot of jobs with Coburn, playing solos on ballads and those old standards musicians call 'fake tunes,'" he recalled.[11] "After giving solos nightly I acquired quite a repertoire."[12]

Hoffman formed his own dance band in 1936 under the stage name "Hal Hope," and he found himself "dotted lined" for several seasons with his nightly "revuette" at the Casino-in-the-Air, a swank rooftop restaurant at Lexington Avenue and Forty-ninth Street, atop the Hotel Montclair. The Casino was one of those open-air supper clubs out under the stars—so popular in '30s New York—a romantic setting where elegant couples dined and danced to swing music, silhouetted against a glistening galaxy of city lights. In its ads, the Montclair solicited clientele for lively floor shows "in the beautiful enclosed Fuchsia room, or on cool, breeze-swept terraces," by appealing to "sophisticates like yourself . . . for whom hot-cha and heh-heh are passé." On the dance floor, couples swayed and bobbed—men in white double-breasted dinner coats, dark trousers, and spats, their palms steering women in backless crepe satin or taffeta evening gowns. Hal Hope's swing-rhythm orchestra of nine men in tuxedos—playing violins, accordion, saxophone, guitar, Hammond organ, double bass, and piano, with Hope trading off between violin and theremin—pumped out lush, buoyant harmonies.

The theremin novelty made them the talk of the society pages: "Get a load of HAL HOPE'S Casino-in-the-Airchestra"; "Recommended for diversion seekers looking for something new"; "Walter Winchell enthuses: 'New Yorchids to HAL HOPE and his Swing Rhythms'"; "Hope is an expert on the Theremin, the musical instrument that is played by making strange ritualistic passes in the air"; "By merely waving the hands at it, s'help us . . . that lil' ole theremin goes right to town and 'gives' the grandest tunes that ever shook an eardrum. However, we did neglect to ask whether a Local 802 card or a Master Electrician's license was the proper requisite for participation in this forward movement of the arts."[13]

An added attraction of the Hope Orchestra was an "Electronic Trio" where

Hoffman and his theremin were joined by a Hammond organ and one of the inventor's fingerboard instruments. The composer Charles Paul manned the organ (purportedly capable of "250 million different tone combinations"), and Bill Schuman, the prominent *William* Schuman of later years—American composer, first Pulitzer Prize–winner in music, and president of the Juilliard School and Lincoln Center—played the fingerboard theremin. To heighten the curiosity, Hoffman started offering "how to play the theremin" demonstrations as part of the show. "'Technically speaking,' says the orchestra leader, 'You hypnotize it by waving the hands in front of it, and out comes the music.'"[14]

In 1938, the Hal Hope Orchestra began a run at the Queen Mary Restaurant at 40 East Fifty-eighth Street, and the CBS radio network broadcast the revues live. Off the air, Hoffman provided theremin "lessons" to sporting patrons. "Unless you know how," the *New York Evening Journal* warned, "the funniest grunts, groans and growls come out when you wave your hands at the instrument."[15]

Hoffman's growing notoriety won him a contract directing one of the Meyer Davis orchestras in 1939 at the opulent Park Lane Hotel. In the mirrored, chandeliered Tapestry Room that glowed in hues of the current rage— aquamarine, coral, and brick—he regularly added the theremin to the swing mix. The instrument was billed as a Charlie McCarthy–like musical dummy that "imitates the human voice and any musical instrument."[16] "Guests, too, are at liberty to try their skill at Theremin playing," *Cue* magazine dared, "but the creature isn't easily tamed. Guest produced sounds resemble, as a rule, nothing you've ever encountered in the animal, vegetable, or mineral kingdoms."[17] "The cosmos is not always willing," the *New York Times* cracked.[18]

It was only a matter of time before the theremin's natural proclivity for sliding between notes—the "molasses" Clara Rockmore felt "you couldn't shake off"—became irreversibly identified with the instrument. The audacity Lucie Rosen found in players who performed with a rudimentary technique gradually legitimized the portamento sound with listeners, giving the impression it was idiomatic to the instrument. This caricatured quality—everything Clara Rockmore fought to overcome—combined with the near-sinusoidal electronic sound of the oscillators (and an often heavy, unnatural vibrato), was cultivated as a special effect to evoke dark, spooky, or futuristic realms. The sound relegated the theremin to a specialized musical tool, like an infrequently played percussion instrument, and not the all-purpose expressive medium Theremin hoped it would become. The instrument began to be typed in the popular imagination as a harbinger of the strange and weird—associated with a world outside the boundaries of everyday emotional experience.

The radio mystery-adventure *The Green Hornet* was among the earliest forums to sear this menacing waver of the theremin into the public consciousness. The show was created by the same team that developed *The Lone Ranger*—George W. Trendle and writer Fran Striker—and first aired in Detroit in 1936 on station WXYZ. Beginning in April 1938 it became a syndicated sustaining feature on the Mutual network. The principal character was Britt Reid, a young newspaper publisher who, unbeknownst to his staff, regularly donned mask and cape to become the Green Hornet, stalking his reporters' crime subjects and forging his own personal brand of justice. Britt pursued his criminals—usually swindlers and gangsters—in a huge, powerfully sleek car called the Black Beauty, chasing them down with gas guns and smoke screens, subduing them, and disappearing just in time for the police to arrive and finish the job. Britt was assisted in his work by his ever faithful Japanese valet, Kato, a character modeled somewhat after the Lone Ranger's companion, Tonto. Following the Japanese attack on Pearl Harbor in December 1941, Kato was quickly transformed into a Filipino valet. The Green Hornet's exploits mirrored the turmoil of the real-life mobster world of the '30s so closely that in 1939, when the announcer's opening lines were adapted to read, "he hunts the biggest of all game, public enemies that even the G-men cannot reach," J. Edgar Hoover objected, and the original lines of the script were restored.

The main musical theme for the series was Rimsky-Korsakoff's "Flight of the Bumblebee," but the Hornet's sound effects were rendered on the theremin to suggest the invasion of a giant insect, or an amplified bee. The characteristic Green Hornet theremin buzz was heard nationally by listeners from 1938 through December 1952, when the final episode aired. The thereminist for the entire run of the series was Vera Richardson Simpson, who also played the instrument with the Detroit Civic Orchestra, at the 1938 Michigan State Fair, and in regular concerts on Sunday afternoons and evenings at the Dearborn Inn during the 1930s.

≪≫

On the heels of Theremin's departure in September 1938, Boyd Zinman scrambled to gather up the severed strands of his companies and assess his prospects for continuing. What he found was devastating. When Theremin was present, he had presided personally over the construction of Teletouch equipment. Now it was evident he had never fully disclosed the nature of his inventions, and, in his absence, Zinman's production staff was helpless to recreate its own product line. With documentation missing for unpatented inventions like the Magic Mirror, a large corner of the business was irrevocably stricken. Teletouch Holding Corporation, set up to develop these unpatented devices, was rendered useless, and by December 15, 1938, it was dissolved by proclamation. Occasional sales of burglar alarms based on the signaling device patent, or, here and there, a custom-made space-control theremin, were hardly sufficient to sustain a business.

Zinman was desperate, but he had one last possibility up his sleeve, left for him by the inventor: a "Pilferage Detector" alarm. The system was the most compact, efficient distillation of the electric eye. Contained in a foot-high portable box with a suitcase handle attached to the top, a single receiving lens stared from one of the sides. The device could be set up in any location simply by plugging the box into a wall outlet. "The TELETOUCH must be aimed at a lamp burning in the area where protection is desired," a prospectus explained. "Where complete darkness is preferred, we can supply an infra-red lamp. Should it be desirable to have a photograph of the pilferer, we can provide a moving picture camera which will floodlight the room and run ten seconds each time the intruder passes in front of the Teletouch detector."[19] A variant of the system added an extra feature: "Foolproof against tampering, a hidden alarm inside the unit starts ringing when power line is cut or pulled out of outlet. The alarm, once started in this manner . . . CANNOT BE SILENCED by throwing the switch to 'off' position as the alarm is controlled by a secret combination on the dials which is known only to the owner."[20] On Teletouch Industries stationery still listing "Director of Research, Prof. Leon Theremin," Zinman wrote to J. Edgar Hoover, two weeks after the inventor left, offering the device to the FBI. "May we demonstrate this to you on your next trip to New York?" he inquired.[21]

In another move to shore up his coffers, Zinman entered into a contract with American District Telegraph Company on January 19, 1939. On the basis of Theremin's power of attorney, Teletouch had become the "sole and exclusive owner" of the inventor's U.S. music and signal patents. For the sum of four thousand dollars, Teletouch agreed to license both patents to American District Telegraph for the manufacture of burglar alarms, subject to another license on the signaling patent, granted in December '38, for use in taxicab meters.

These ventures came to little, and in a last-ditch effort to raise capital for his companies, Zinman signed a contract on October 2, 1939, with Radio Wire Television Incorporated, a subsidiary of Wire Broadcasting Corporation of America. In exchange for a loan of five thousand dollars to Teletouch, for the period of one year, Radio Wire obtained an option to purchase the assets of Teletouch Corporation, Teletouch Magic Mirror Corporation, and Teletouch Industries, Inc., for $12,500. The assets Zinman offered for sale included Theremin's music and signal patents in the United States (hardly a bargain since they were both scheduled to expire in three years) and "furniture, fixtures, equipment" and "all models and merchandise on hand in the premises 37 West Fifty-fourth Street or elsewhere."[22] The agreement mandated that the loan from Radio Wire was to be used solely for corporate purposes to operate and maintain Teletouch and guaranteed Zinman a weekly salary of one hundred dollars. Within the year, the option was taken up, and, according to Zinman's son, his father "sold out to Wire Broadcasting for a pittance, because he was broke."[23]

In the fall of 1938, as Zinman reviewed the damage to his corporations, Lucie and Walter Rosen pored over the technical papers they had paid Theremin so dearly to create. Their son, Walter, was home on break from his first year at Yale Law School. As an undergraduate at Harvard he had been a physics and math major and was well versed in reading circuit diagrams. He was curious to see what the inventor had left behind. As he perused the schematic for the September theremin, Anne Stern recalled, "he looked at this stuff and said, 'You know, you've been had—this is absolute nonsense. He's left you something that is utterly *useless.*'"[24]

Cover of sales brochure for the RCA Theremin, 1929. George H. Clark Collection, Archives Center, National Museum of American History, Division of Electricity and Modern Physics, Smithsonian Institution, Washington, D.C.

Alexandra Stepanoff playing the RCA Theremin on a syndicated NBC radio broadcast, 1930. George H. Clark Collection, Archives Center, National Museum of American History, Division of Electricity and Modern Physics, Smithsonian Institution, Washington, D.C.

Rehearsal for the world premiere of Joseph Schillinger's *First Airphonic Suite,* Cleveland, November 1929. Left to right: Leon Theremin, Joseph Schillinger, Nikolai Sokoloff. Photo, Blank and Stoller. American Heritage Center, University of Wyoming.

Rudy Vallee (foreground), with his Connecticut Yankees and Lennington Shewell on the RCA Theremin (center), at an NBC broadcast from Villa Vallee, 1930. George H. Clark Collection, Archives Center, National Museum of American History, Division of Electricity and Modern Physics, Smithsonian Institution, Washington, D.C.

Ether music trio, 1930. Left to right: George Goldberg, Zenaide Hanenfeldt, Leon Theremin, with an unidentified pianist. Lucie Bigelow Rosen Archive, Caramoor Center for Music and the Arts, Katonah, N.Y.

Newspaper ad for the April 25, 1930,
Carnegie Hall presentation of the
"theremin orchestra." Lucie Bigelow
Rosen Archive, Caramoor Center for
Music and the Arts, Katonah, N.Y.

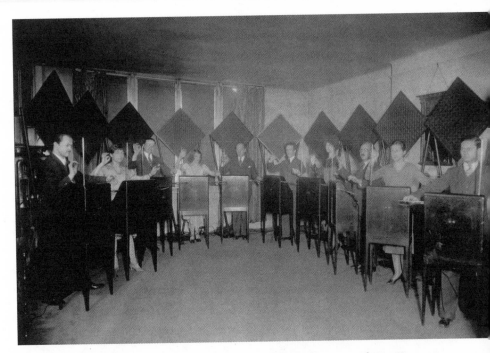

Ensemble rehearsal for the April 25, 1930, Carnegie Hall concert of "Ten Victor Theremins." Left to right: Eugene Hegy, Anna Freeman, Louis Barlevy, Ildiko Elberth, George Goldberg, Leon Theremin, Lucie Bigelow Rosen, Wallingford Riegger, Zenaide Hanenfeldt, and Henry Solomonoff. Lucie Bigelow Rosen Archive, Caramoor Center for Music and the Arts, Katonah, N.Y.

Leon Theremin with a bank of vacuum tubes in his New York laboratory, 37 West Fifty-fourth Street. *Popular Science Monthly,* 1932.

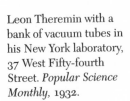

WOAI Family to Hear San Antonio Girl Play Theremin During Tonite's Kelvinator Program

RCA Theremin mania reaches the public: "Miss Virginia Hope is shown at the Theremin. At the piano is Edna June Bump." *San Antonio News,* June 14, 1930. Copyright © San Antonio Express-News.

Joseph Schillinger and the rhythmicon, about 1932. American Heritage Center, University of Wyoming.

Facing page, top: The Theremin Electro-Ensemble at a radio broadcast session, about 1932. Left to right: George Goldberg, Leonid Bolotine, Gleb Yellin. Collection of David McCornack.

Facing page, bottom: Three slender variants of Leon Theremin's electric finger-board instrument. *Electronics* magazine, 1932.

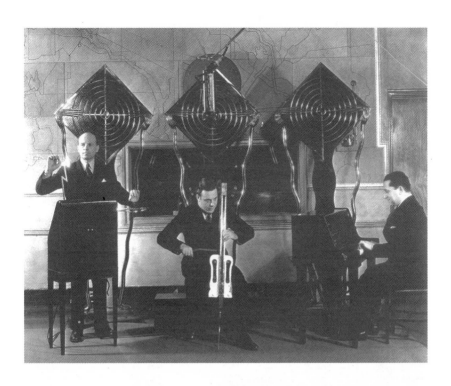

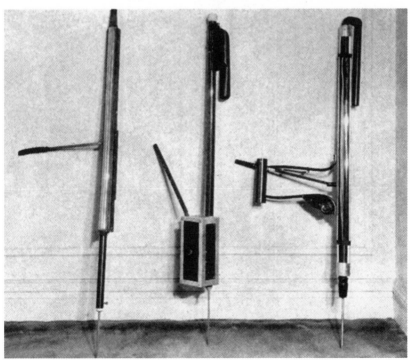

A theremin fingerboard model (right) used by Leopold Stokowski and the Philadelphia Orchestra, with its towering speaker (left). *Electronics* magazine, 1932.

Clara Rockmore performing on the terpsitone, Carnegie Hall, April 1932. *Popular Science Monthly*, 1932.

The keyboard theremin. *Electronics* magazine, 1932.

Theremin demonstrating one of his fingerboard models. *Popular Science Monthly,* 1932.

Theremin with his automatic door opener. *Electronics* magazine, 1932.

The inventor demonstrating his automatic door opener. *Electronics* magazine, 1932.

Flyer for Clara Rockmore's 1934 Town Hall recital debut. Photo, Renato Toppo.
Clara Rockmore Archive, International Piano Archives of Maryland, University of
Maryland, College Park.

Lucie Bigelow Rosen, 1930s. Photo, De Mirjian-Nasib. Lucie Bigelow Rosen Archive, Caramoor Center for Music and the Arts, Katonah, N.Y.

Leon Theremin at a dinner party in the Bolotine home, 1932, among members of New York's Russian community. Cleopatra Bolotine is seated at the head of the table on Theremin's left; ten-year-old Yolanda is peeking out on his right. Maximillian Goldberg is seated on the extreme left; his wife, Sophie, third from left. Courtesy of Yolanda Bolotine Kulik.

Ad for the Teletouch Magic Crystal, about 1936. Michael Zinman Collection, Ardsley, N.Y.

Facing page, bottom: Lavinia Williams, dancing the leading role in Katherine Dunham's "Rites de Passage," 1942. Courtesy of Diana Dunbar.

Macy's Store window at night, with the Teletouch Ray projecting a beam onto the sidewalk. *Electronics* magazine, 1937.

Walter and Lucie Rosen, Hungary, 1930s. Courtesy of Margaret E. Barclay and John B. Scholz.

On the left, 37 West Fifty-fourth Street—the Theremin Studio and headquarters of Teletouch Corporation—with Lucie and Walter Rosen's townhouse residence at 35 West Fifty-fourth,to the right. Photo, Albert Glinsky.

M. Boyd Zinman, 1930s.
Courtesy of Michael
Zinman.

The *Stary Bolshevik* in New York harbor, 1941. Photo, U.S. Coast Guard. Courtesy
of the Steamship Historical Society of America Collection.

On the Yauza: Screws, Politicals, and Radio Street

And are these your wreckers? No, these are engineering geniuses! They were hurled from the twentieth century into the age of the caveman — and, lo, they managed to cope with the situation!

—Aleksandr Solzhenitsyn, *The Gulag Archipelago*

It was a "quivering feeling of coming back to his dear city, to breathe its air" again.[1] From the deck of the *Stary Bolshevik* ("Old Bolshevik"), Lev Sergeyevich began to make out the familiar profile of the august metropolis gradually materializing in the distance. He drew in the old, seasoned atmosphere that so resonated within his soul. He was home.

For shipmaster Habalov and most of the crew, it was just another routine stopover at their home port in the early fall of 1938. Olga Hrennicov, the young doctor, might manage a short respite from the claustrophobic company of her mostly male shipmates; forty-three-year-old motorist Michail Komiz, a seaman since the age of fourteen, could plant himself on solid ground for a short spell; twenty-year-old Ivan Houdoley, second-class sailor, might grab a short visit with his family. But to Lev Sergeyevich it was the romantic embrace of repatriation—a long-anticipated reunion with his mother soil.

He had left in 1927, a celebrated figure, accessory to the security schemes of Lenin and Stalin and a spokesman for Soviet electrification. His odyssey from Berlin and Frankfurt through Europe and the U.S. capitals, to his years with the Rosens and Teletouch, became a gentle downward spiral as he gradually lost popular momentum, retreated into small-scale invention, and bottomed out into a sort of anonymous disgrace in America. Now, with his salvaged instruments and equipment on shipboard, he hoped to start over with a clean record and garner the chance for a new laboratory among old acquaintances. An "electronic Orpheus' lament" was Ioffe's first reaction to the etherphone in 1920, and his words proved strangely prophetic. Lev Sergeyevich, the Orpheus figure who charmed the world with his instrument, was ferried to the underworld now to plead with Hades to deliver his wife and grant him a second chance at life. And there would be a condition: he could not look back.

Leningrad was the youngest of the principal Russian cities, conceived and built as a single project by Peter the Great after New York and Boston were founded. Its cultural milieu resonated more with the famous European capitals it was modeled after than with the older Soviet cities. It was viewed as more progressive, more Western-looking, and so more bourgeois—furthest from the Communist paragon of the great proletarian city. As the late imperial capital, its vestiges of tsarist architecture endowed it with a dignity that even the pettiest bureaucratic occupants couldn't tarnish. And the northern city had an undeniably romantic aura, particularly in the quality of its nocturnal light in the spring. Richard Lourie described the "white nights in Leningrad," when "twilight lasts till dawn. That city of stone, water, and sky becomes even more fluid, as if time itself had dissolved into a gray-white shimmer. But Leningrad also becomes a city of night carnival, with droves of young people out with bottles and guitars, fishermen angling for a bite, lovers disappearing under the shade of trees, the city cut into dozens of islands by the raised bridges, the great flow of ocean traffic always moving by night there."[2]

The city was the incubator of Lev Sergeyevich's character. The nobility and the refined, genteel romance in his demeanor sprang from its spirit—as well as from his continental French ancestry—and this perhaps accounted for his acclimation to European society. Leningrad retained his most cherished associations: the musical, electrical, and astronomical forays of his childhood; his camaraderie with Alexander Constantinov and his wedding to Katia; Ioffe and the Physico-Technical Institute; the birth of the Termenvox, the radio watchman, and distance vision.

While his passage on the *Stary Bolshevik* had been carefully guarded from his American friends and colleagues, and from U.S. immigration authorities, every Russian organization, from Amtorg and Sovtorgflot to the Soviet embassy in Washington and its consulate in New York, would have had advance notification of his arrival in Leningrad. Naturally, he expected a small welcoming delegation of government officials, or a press corps, to be waiting as he disembarked. Instead, he found "empty moorages and dead faces of people afraid of recognizing each other—his motherland plunged into the gloom of Stalin's Middle Ages."[3] The crowds he remembered—pressing forward, craning their necks for him—were gone. The sudden start of reality hit him. This was not the place he had left.

With his cargo of musical instruments and electrical apparatus, Lev Sergeyevich, duly transported, was unloaded on the pier as routinely as a shipment of manganese ore. An unfriendliness, an alien quality, hung in the air.

His contact, Jan Berzin, was dead, and the GRU was apparently out of favor. All the observations and reporting he had carried out in the United States seemed to matter little now. And during his years in America his parents had died—his father, from heart disease, in 1932, and his mother in 1935. Now there was no apartment to return to on Marat Street. Shortly, he boarded tram number nine to Lesnoi, anxious to report to work at the Physico-Technical Institute.

In Ioffe's office he was met with an oddly detached reception. "Settle your business in the big house," his old mentor told him in a flat tone, "and then come out to work."[4] By the "big house" Ioffe meant the NKVD. It was clear he knew the inventor was somehow tainted in the eyes of the government. Lev Sergeyevich noticed Alexander Constantinov was no longer at the institute, and in fact was nowhere to be found. The old acquaintances who remained snubbed him, and others had disappeared altogether. A woman worker at the institute by the name of Butyrskaya was the only person to make overtures of friendship, furnishing him a place to stay while he looked for work.

From America he had known about Stalin's extermination of the top military cadres—Jan Berzin especially—but like most people, he assumed it was a response to subversive activities. What stalwart supporter of the regime wouldn't condemn traitorous acts by "enemies of the people"? But even back among his countrymen—ordinary citizens of the Soviet Union—no one suspected that these publicly censured "crimes" were, in reality, large-scale frame-ups at the tip of a monstrous iceberg of terror—a massive inquisition reaching down into every stratum of government and civilian life. Around the next corner, in the recesses of shadows or the dim corridors of apartment buildings, at the chilling sound of the 4:00 A.M. knock at the door, or with the clasp of the arm from behind on the street and the forced invitation into the back of a waiting car, anyone could slip into oblivion from one moment to the next. Guarded speech, paranoia, fear of betrayal, and perpetual vigilance governed the behavior of every innocent citizen twenty-four hours a day. Lev Sergeyevich was beginning to understand what he had unwittingly stumbled into.

Lenin, the father of the original Soviet terror machine—the Cheka—was the first to legalize violence and mass arrests. His decree "On Red Terror" warned, "it is essential to protect the Soviet Republic from class enemies by isolating them in concentration camps . . . anyone involved in White Guard organizations, conspiracies and rebellions will be shot."[5] He mandated terror as a state institution and made the autonomous Cheka so powerful that tens of thousands were executed in its cellars without a trial. Lenin even took a personal hand in suggesting the most minute details of "custody and surveillance" and initiated the unannounced middle-of-the-night search and arrest of citizens that became standard police procedure under Stalin. In 1921, the terror made its way into the Red Army where, even amidst victory, over four thousand troops and commanders were executed in a Soviet military tribunal, many for simply belonging to the "exploiting class."

But as severe as Lenin's systematic violence was, it proved to be only a foretaste of the devastating carnage Stalin began to level at every sector of the society. Lenin, at least, allowed a measure of dialogue and debate on policy among his highest Party officials. But for Stalin, even discussion was tantamount to treason. He saw threats everywhere—some real, but mostly imagined—and in an ever contracting circle of paranoia, he gradually brought the whole country to the quaking, blind service of his will alone. Between 1930 and 1933, his forced collectivization of farms, and the seizure of every last kilo of grain for export, claimed more than ten million peasant lives from famine and OGPU executions of resistant farmers.

In his drive to subordinate the Party, Stalin quickly silenced the "Old Bolsheviks," and in 1929 Trotsky was arrested and deported to Turkey. By 1930, most of these "oppositionists" were replaced by sycophants who carefully toed the Stalinist line, hoping to rise through the Party ranks by fierce allegiance to his agenda and to the repressions and exterminations he covertly ordered up.

To snuff out the last embers of opposition and assure his unquestioned dominance over Party and country, Stalin plotted in 1934 to institute a widespread purge that would brutalize its survivors into submission forever. When members of the highest Party organs objected, he maneuvered to still their voices as well. To liquidate them within legal boundaries and not arouse suspicion, he masterminded a plot so contrary to logic that his role as the instigator was not divined or believed until many years later.

In what the historian Robert Conquest suggested "has every right to be called the crime of the century,"[6] the popular Leningrad Party leader Sergei M. Kirov was killed on December 1, 1934, by a lone assassin acting on secret orders from Stalin. Kirov presented a mild threat, with rumblings of an alternative leadership, and Stalin now had him conveniently removed. His assassination then became the pretext for setting the purge mechanism into full swing.

Feigning horror and revulsion at Kirov's murder, Stalin—a solemn pallbearer at the funeral—ordered an immediate investigation, implicating every top Party official he perceived as a threat to his leadership. The day after Kirov's murder, Stalin created a "state of emergency" atmosphere and issued a Charter of Terror advancing the already ruthless measures in Lenin's decree "On Red Terror" to staggering levels. The charter exhorted investigative agencies to speed up the processing of cases, demanded that execution was not to be held up for the possibility of pardon—which was no longer an option—and called for executions to be carried out immediately after the passing of death sentences. Hundreds of Party members, including many of the Old Bolsheviks prominent in the revolution, were executed for direct complicity in the assassination. Millions of innocent Soviet citizens were condemned to labor camps, or shot, for some minute part in the alleged conspiracy behind Kirov's murder. His killing was the single justification Stalin had needed to unleash a remorseless whirlwind of imprisonment, torture, and extermination—a relentless four-year bloodbath that decimated the country to the distant reaches of its remote territories.

Prominent members of the Party and the Politburo were fingered in three major show trials from 1936 to 1938. With no real evidence against them, they were subjected to brutal physical and psychological torture to extract absurd public confessions. "These mad dogs of capitalism," Stalin's prosecutor-general, Andrei Vyshinsky, barked at the conclusion of one trial, "killed our Kirov. . . . I demand that these dogs gone mad should be shot—every one of them!"[7] Within months, his demand was summarily carried out. Among the victims of this period was Abel Yenukidze, the Old Bolshevik Kremlin official who had issued Lev Sergeyevich's rail pass on Lenin's orders.

After disposing of his potential adversaries, Stalin went after his supporters. Genrikh Yagoda, the barbaric head of the NKVD who directed much of the genocide during the first two years of the purge, was executed along with twenty thousand of his NKVD officers. The ranks of the army were perilously thinned out, and most of the military intelligence agents and "residents" living abroad were recalled to the Soviet Union and shot. Great numbers of diplomats perished because of their contact with foreigners—guilt by association. In Stalin's relentless search for new purge fodder, industrial accidents, mine explosions, even airplane crashes, were considered acts of sabotage. The plant directors, supervisors, and designers involved answered for these disasters with their lives—accused of being "wreckers," the great catchall term for perpetrators of these "crimes."

To meet the high arrest quotas Stalin routinely set, sentencing by lists and categories rather than individual cases became the norm. Eventually it was a matter of statistics—an anonymous, mass system, often driven by caprice. Robert Conquest cited one instance involving NKVD head Nikolai Yezhov, the successor to Yagoda:

> Orders for further executions came from Moscow. Yezhov telegraphed the NKVD chief in Frunze, capital of Kirgizia: "You are charged with the task of exterminating 10,000 enemies of the people. Report results by signal.". . . . An order to the Sverdlovsk NKVD called for 15,000 executions. Another, to a small town near Novosibirsk, ordered 500, far above normal capacity, so that the

NKVD had to shoot priests and their relatives, all those who had spoken critically of conditions, amnestied former members of White Armies, and so on,
who ordinarily would have got five years or less. In February 1938 . . . Yezhov
himself went down to Kiev to call a special NKVD conference to order 30,000
more executions in the Ukraine.[8]

To stoke the growing purge conflagration, the NKVD recruited "inform-
ers" from among the general population. These *seksots* were omnipresent in
offices and factories, actively hunting their quota of prey against the constant
threat of their own destruction for insufficient vigilance. Arrests were predi-
cated on the smallest remark, the slightest gesture. One man was sentenced
for "'smiling in sympathy' while some drunken dockers at another table in
Odessa were telling one another anti-Soviet anecdotes."[9] A woman received
ten years for "anti-Soviet agitation" for saying that an arrested Red Army
marshal was handsome.[10] The writer Varlan Shalamov spent seventeen years
in labor camps for "the crime of having declared the Nobel Prize laureate, Ivan
Bunin, a classic author of Russian literature."[11]

An accidental slip of the tongue could prove fatal. Failure to report an
indiscreet remark—seen as complicity—played friend against friend, child
against parent. Denunciations became a malevolent channel for sending away
office rivals and irksome neighbors, settling vendettas, or evicting someone
with a coveted apartment. Millions heeded the NKVD call to turn in fellow
citizens by dropping anonymous charges in special mailboxes. Pompous, vocal loyalty to the state—the one strategy for survival—meant coping with an
ever burgeoning individual crisis of conscience and morality. As the waves of
execution and imprisonment moved closer and closer to one's own circles,
betrayal was the only shield against personal destruction.

Less than a month after Kirov's assassination, over thirty thousand citizens
from Leningrad alone were sent to Siberian labor camps. Day after day, Stalin received lists of names to approve for arrest or execution, which he routinely rubber-stamped and sent along to be expedited. "On 12 December 1937
alone," Robert Conquest reported, "Stalin and Molotov sanctioned 3,167 death
sentences, and then went to the cinema."[12]

Lev Sergeyevich hoped to remain in Leningrad, but the atmosphere was
bleak. His only means of support since arriving had been the proceeds from
his final projects for the Rosens, but this resource was short-lived. "The money I had received lasted less than a month," he remembered.[13] He was refused
work everywhere. With few of his old contacts around, there was hardly cause
for optimism. After several months he traveled to Moscow, hoping to appeal
to his old government liaisons for work. "Moscow was unfriendly," he recalled.
"I was up in a tiny room at the Hotel Dnepr near the Kievsky Railway Sta-

tion. There was no job in sight. They wouldn't even take me as a sound operator at the Sound Recording Studio."[14] For a short time he did odd jobs translating from English to Russian, but this was sporadic and impractical work.

Only one route remained: he would have to find a sympathetic ear among the Kremlin circle he once impressed. But who was left? It was early March 1939. Lenin was gone, of course, and Stalin himself would probably be inaccessible. His only hope might be the members of Stalin's high command who presided at the distance vision demonstration in 1927: Ordzhonikidze, Tukhachevsky, Budenny, and Voroshilov.

Ordzhonikidze, Politburo member and close associate of Stalin, had died in 1937—reportedly a suicide in protest over the purge, but according to later evidence, probably a victim of Stalin's design.

Mikhail Tukhachevsky would likely have been Lev Sergeyevich's best choice. Red Marshal, and Deputy People's Commissar of Defense, he was known for his deft military command and a strong interest in advanced technology to modernize the Red Army. Among Stalin's top ranks he was also the most sympathetic to the arts. The composer Dmitri Shostakovich was his close friend, and he would have accepted the inventor's musical work with less suspicion of "bourgeois" pandering than most of the callous bureaucrats in the high cadres. Tukhachevsky was a brilliant intellectual who spoke several languages and had much in common with the inventor: an "ardent belief in Communism. . . . [a] zeal for learning . . . [a] penchant for music—. . . his hobby was to be making violins—and the arts, his leaning towards science and technology."[15]

But Tukhachevsky had been accused of conspiring with the Germans against the Soviet regime—charges based on forged documents ordered up from the Nazis by Stalin—and on June 12, 1937, he was executed by a firing squad. Like most condemned officials, his family was also delivered a bitter fate: on Stalin's instructions, Tukhachevsky's wife, two brothers, and a sister were physically annihilated, along with his mother, who had refused to repudiate him. Three of his other sisters were sent to concentration camps along with his young daughter when she came of age.

Budenny and Voroshilov remained the only choices for Lev Sergeyevich. Both were marshals—the only two survivors of five that Stalin had named to the rank. Budenny, in fact, had condemned Tukhachevsky to death on Stalin's orders. Unlike the marshals who had perished, Voroshilov and Budenny were not professional army men, but each had served with exceptional valor in the civil war as cavalry leaders. Currently, Budenny was head of the Moscow Military District; Voroshilov remained as Commissar of Defense—the same post he held when his office was equipped briefly with distance vision. Lev Sergeyevich decided he would see Voroshilov.

A veteran of many postrevolutionary battles, Kliment Voroshilov was an over-life-sized military legend every schoolboy emulated in play. His deeds were forged into myth in numerous contemporary biographies, and his name was exalted in young soldiers' rallying songs: "when Comrade Stalin sends us to fight, and the first marshal leads us into battle."[16] In 1934 the city of Lugansk was renamed Voroshilovgrad, and several other geographical sites carried his name.

While his pluck and tenacity on the battlefield were celebrated, he recognized his own intellectual limits. He had few original ideas, and his forte was the meticulous dispatch of Stalin's orders to the letter. This dearth of exceptional qualities and independent thought endeared him to Stalin, and through unwavering expedition of every sadistic mandate the leader handed him, he managed to survive the purge and remain in the inner circle among the trusted few whose necks were ultimately spared. Voroshilov became Stalin's intimate friend. The two would "sit together on the platform at meetings, stand side by side on the Mausoleum, go hunting together, take holidays in the south, spend time at Stalin's dacha and at his apartment in the Kremlin."[17]

Voroshilov had been an early member of the Cheka, and he took a central role in the purge, dutifully signing Stalin's lists and rubber-stamping the removal and liquidation of droves of high-ranking army men. After Tukhachevsky's execution in 1937, he set off further cleansing in the armed forces, alleging the existence of huge army and navy spy networks.

Lev Sergeyevich entered Voroshilov's Kremlin office. The supreme Red Marshal of the Soviet Union was an imposing figure: his angry, arched eyebrows met in a knitted brow over a fierce, penetrating stare; his implacable, upper lip was neatly dusted with a close-cropped shadow of a mustache, and a star was prominently emblazoned on either side of his high collar. "He had gotten older and avoided conversation,"[18] Lev Sergeyevich recalled. "Back in the States, I had heard about Tukhachevsky falling out of favour. I also knew about the tragic fates of many talented military leaders. I was surprised to read Voroshilov's nostalgic speeches about the horse published in the press. 'Socialist horse,' 'good horse' turned up again and again in his statements on modern warfare!"[19] Voroshilov and Budenny, the old "Horse Marshals," were tough veterans of cavalry action in the civil war. In 1919 and 1920 Voroshilov had led the First Cavalry Army against the White cavalry, and on the Polish front. Later, during the '30s, he and Budenny had positioned themselves against Tukhachevsky, who warned that Russia's survival in a coming war would depend on greater mechanization and the use of tank and air power.

In contrast to Voroshilov's antiquated cavalry stampedes, Tukhachevsky developed his "deep operation theory," an intricate system of tactical maneuvers brought to the level of artistic or scientific doctrine—something Lev Sergeyevich might have dreamed up. He introduced the notion of "operational shock," involving such strategic theories as "a manoeuvering mass behind the defender's centre of gravity," and "a bolstering, manoeuvering vector."[20]

In 1936, a *Pravda* article, aimed at Tukhachevsky, denounced the use of mechanization to replace the cavalry. The following year, Voroshilov banned publication of Tukhachevsky's essay "The Art of War," and Stalin rejected claims for mechanized warfare as "nonsense," seeing the marshal's independent thinking as dangerous. "Tukhachevsky, who discussed the meaning of Einstein's theory of relativity as it applied to warfare," Shostakovich observed, "stuck in their craw. It was easier for Stalin to talk with the cavalrymen. They looked up to him."[21] Among the accusations at Tukhachevsky's trial, Budenny charged that emphasis on tanks over horses was a military error.

"K. E. Voroshilov received me very coldly," Lev Sergeyevich recalled.

The interview took no more than a couple of minutes. He threw up his hands and said it was beyond his competence to help me find employment. Such a change in the previously well-disposed Commissar must have been due to the fact that he knew I disapproved of his canonization of the horse and the concept of fast war—the concept illustrated by the futurological film, "If the War Breaks Out Tomorrow," featuring our red-starred cavalry bursting into one of [the] West European capitals with bared swords on the third day of the war.[22]

Voroshilov's rejection was a blow, but before there was time to ponder the consequences, the inevitable knock came at the door. On March 10, 1939, a few days after his audience with Voroshilov, Lev Sergeyevich was arrested at the Hotel Kievskaya by NKVD agents. He was taken to Moscow's infamous Butyrka Prison. "All my property," he remembered, "including the electric musical instruments and the equipment I managed to bring back from the States, was confiscated."[23] (The night before, ironically, Lucie Bigelow Rosen had just concluded her European tour in Budapest.)

The inventor wondered what charge could possibly be leveled against him. Complicity with Tukhachevsky to undermine the cavalry? Anything was possible after thousands of common citizens were implicated in the Kirov "plot." Or seeking a job—was unemployment a crime? Evidently Ioffe had been privy to something. On the other hand, at this point in the purge, rounding up souls for arrest quotas was a priority. Justification was usually an afterthought—offenses could be tailored to fit individuals later.

Ironically, Lev Sergeyevich's arrest came as the campaign of terror was winding down. It was clear even to Stalin that the situation couldn't continue at its present pace. By 1938, one in every twenty people had been arrested, affecting virtually every other family. Half the population of every Soviet city had been put on NKVD lists, and files marking most leading officials as spies threatened to topple the political infrastucture. Government agencies were completely overworked, courts were in session around the clock, and with each interrogated prisoner required to name numerous "accomplices," the pyramid effect was close to taking the whole population. Stalin was aware of this, and after the 1937 census uncovered the enormity of the purge, he suppressed the results and had the census board shot as spies. In 1939, he ordered a new census and falsified the results to his satisfaction. But the devastation was still apparent everywhere. On the day Lev Sergeyevich was arrested, Stalin convened the Eighteenth Party Congress—the first in five years. Of the original 1,966 delegates from 1934, 1,108 had been shot, together with over 100 from the Central Committee.

The Butyrka (or Butyrskaya), where Lev Sergeyevich was taken, was the largest of three prisons in Moscow generally reserved for "politicals"—people arrested on "counterrevolutionary" grounds, as opposed to common criminals. Dating from the eighteenth century, the Butyrka contained a series of blocks, each housing large numbers of prisoners. "The arrested man first was taken to a reception point," Robert Conquest noted, "signed in, and submitted to a strict physical search and an examination of his clothes, seam by seam. Bootlaces and metal attachments, including buttons, were removed."[24]

The cells where prisoners waited before interrogation were usually crammed beyond humane limits. A prisoner in the Butyrka described a cell built for 24, filled with 72 men in 1933, and 140 by 1937. "In a woman's cell supposed to hold 25, 110 women were crowded. Planks covered the entire floor and the few beds, apart from a small part of the central gangway, a table and two large latrine buckets. It was impossible for the prisoners to lie on their backs, and when lying on their sides, if one wanted to turn over, it could only be done by negotiating with the prisoners on either side to do it all together."[25] Lev Sergeyevich recalled that he was "put in a cell for 40 crammed with at least a hundred criminals and political offenders."[26]

Like everyone who had remained overseas for an extended time, he was required to write up a detailed report of his activities abroad before he could reenter the work force. Knowing that this account might be his only path back to freedom, he asked to be placed in a separate cell to focus his concentration. But the fact that he was writing the journal in jail did not bode well.

Interrogation was the next step. In preparation, prisoners' resistance was often worn down by sleep deprivation. One man reported being wakened by a guard and made to jump to attention every ten minutes over his allotted six-hour sleep period—a routine that lasted for weeks. Interrogation was usually carried out at night, often when the accused was roused after only a few minutes of sleep.

Lev Sergeyevich was taken for questioning to the interrogator's office, down a Butyrka stairway surrounded by suicide prevention nets. In the office, bright, glaring lights were designed to disorient the prisoner and emphasize his complete helplessness. The typical questioning began: "Do you know where you are? . . . You are in the heart of Soviet Intelligence. . . . Why do you think you are here?"[27] It became the job of the accused to construct a case against himself and fashion an appropriate confession. A sufficient group of others who shared responsibility in the "crime" would also have to be named, and interrogators faced the specter of their own destruction if their victims offered paltry references for additional arrests.

Questioning often began in a polite, almost sympathetic tone, but frequently intensified to violent, abusive hollering and cursing at the prisoner. Interrogators seemed to have infinite strength. One extreme method of torture, the so-called "conveyor," employed shifts of interrogators alternating for days at a time while the prisoner was questioned, without sleep, until the desired confession was extracted. "I was interrogated day and night," Lev Sergeyevich recounted, "made to stand at attention for 90 minutes at a stretch, allowed to relax five minutes, and then made to stand at attention again."[28]

Within the walls of the Butyrka, justice, in the traditional sense, was nonexistent. Prisoners could easily have been sentenced without the lengthy bureaucratic ceremony, but the interrogation routine was another of Stalin's rituals to bully and humiliate the arrested. The whole charade was conducted under the pretext of "legal" process, with each case carefully documented and fed into the vast stream of paper that choked government files.

For Lev Sergeyevich, fashioning a plausible scenario for guilt would not be difficult. Any number of circumstances in his life could have marked him as an "enemy of the people" by Stalin's gauges. Scientists, in particular, fared badly in the purge. In the field of radio technology, especially, many institutes were closed down and researchers arrested. Engineers were generally considered saboteurs, and Lev Sergeyevich, with his previous ties to state security, was a sitting duck in that respect. Another of his interests, astronomy—in which Russia once enjoyed a leading position—was virtually wiped out across the country during the 1930s after twenty-seven leading figures in the field disappeared. Perhaps even more damning was the inventor's work outside the Soviet Union. Ties with foreigners, no matter how insignificant, left citizens wide open for charges of "anti-Soviet activity." Even his early liaisons with the American embassy in Berlin could be grounds for arrest. "All direct contact with foreign consulates was likely to prove fatal," Conquest noted. "Doctors who had treated German Consuls; a veterinarian who had dealt with consular dogs; even more indirect connections, such as the veterinarian's son, were arrested in the Ukraine; and another man . . . explained in prison that he was there as 'the brother of the woman who supplied the German Consul's milk.'"[29] In Lev Sergeyevich's case, he had foreign patents everywhere that revealed the plans of the "signaling apparatus" Lenin had installed in the State Bank and the Hermitage. And these were minor considerations compared with his eleven years in the United States, where he nearly sold RCA the rights to a television more advanced than the top-secret model in Voroshilov's office. It was not a matter of conjuring up an offense but simply knowing which would be used to indict him. Lev Sergeyevich was ordered to "give a complete description" of his life.[30]

On March 19, nine days after his arrest, the interrogators managed to concoct enough evidence against him to draw up a protocol:

I, investigator Yevtikhov of the investigatory department of the NKVD, having examined the evidence of case No. 154, and taking into consideration that citizen Termen, Lev Sergeyevich, born 1896 in Leningrad, non-party member, citizen of the U.S.S.R., has proven beyond a doubt that he was a member of a fascist organization and served as a spy for foreign secret services

RESOLVE:
To name Termen, L. S. as the accused on the basis of Article 58 paragraph 1-a, 58 paragraph 4 of the Criminal Code, and choose a restraining measure to prevent him from avoiding investigation and trial, holding him under arrest in Butyrskaya Prison.
"AGREED"
State Security Junior Lieutenant Yevtikhov,
Investigator of the Investigatory Department of the NKVD of the U.S.S.R.,
State Security Senior Lieutenant M. Barabash,
Senior Investigator of the Investigatory Department of the NKVD of the U.S.S.R.
The present resolution was announced to me on March 20, 1939. The defendant's signature:

[signed] L. Termen[31]

Lev Sergeyevich's signature on the protocol, though compulsory, branded the document a signed confession. Had he harbored any hope of clemency after sketching the report on his American years, it was clear now that his fate was sealed.

The notorious Article 58 of the Criminal Code, under which he was accused, had its roots, ironically, in his hero Lenin's policy of intolerance toward citizens who had collaborated "with organizations supporting that part of the international bourgeoisie that does not recognize the right of the Communist system of ownership to replace capitalism."[32] The fourteen sections of Article 58 covered political offenses ranging from "armed rebellion," "sabotage," "espionage," and "assisting . . . a foreign state at war with the U.S.S.R.," to civil crimes such as the failure to denounce another citizen. Article 58 was a catchall that spread a wide net of entrapment over innocent Soviet people from all social strata.

Section 10—"counterrevolutionary agitation or propaganda"—allowed, in particular, for the widest interpretation of the law. It was *"universally accessible,"* Aleksandr Solzhenitsyn observed, "to aged old women and twelve-year-old schoolboys. To married and single, to pregnant women and virgins, to athletes and cripples, to drunk and sober, to those who can see and to the blind too, to owners of automobiles and beggars of alms."[33] He remembered how "a saleswoman accepting merchandise from a forwarder noted it down on a sheet of newspaper. There was no other paper. The number of pieces of soap happened to fall on the forehead of Comrade Stalin. Article 58, ten years."[34] Even the alleged *thoughts* of the accused were often taken as evidence. A Soviet professor, Falk, captured the helplessness of the interrogated prisoner: "In the NKVD prison, they could tell you with a very serious face that you stole the moon from the sky, with harmful intent. When you relied on the actual fact that the moon is still in the sky, they would answer that it was only because their organs were so alert, and able to prevent the crime, but in your thoughts you had the firm aim to do this. And after that you would be unable to prove you were right."[35] For the prisoner, Solzhenitsyn wrote, "to crush him once and for all and *to cut him off from all others* once and for all—that was the function of interrogation under Article 58."[36]

Two sections (or paragraphs) of Article 58 were used against Lev Sergeyevich: section 1-a, for "treason to the Motherland" (specifically for actions directed against the military might of the USSR), and section 4, covering "aid to the international bourgeoisie." Both were invoked mainly in connection with his work in the United States—abstract charges that could conveniently apply to any number of dealings he had between 1927 and 1938.

Conviction under Article 58 in some cases carried the death penalty, or resulted in sentences of from three to ten years in a forced labor camp (amounting to a protracted death anyway). Section 1 was a sinister pairing: 1-b was punishable by execution, 1-a by ten years' imprisonment. Lev Sergeyevich squeaked by with his head on 1-a. But section 4 could mean ten years, or execution. It would be a tossup.

Following his interrogation and conviction, Lev Sergeyevich was returned to a squalid cell in the bowels of the Butyrka on March 20. Now he would languish while his protocol meandered, with thousands of others, through the vast state bureaucracy for processing and the eventuality of a sentence. In the jammed cell he entered a realm where time was suspended. Nagging fear and uncertainty were the only constants. A life here could turn on a momentary event, or linger, barely tethered to survival, for years. There were more questions than answers, and with what seemed a cruel randomness, individuals were routinely escorted from cells never to be seen again. "Usually, when someone was called from another cell," the inventor remembered, "it was accompanied by horrible screams and cries, as if someone was being killed there."[37] March passed into April, April into May.

Daily life was made bearable only by the ingenuity of the prisoners. Smoking was allowed, and though games were prohibited, chess was sometimes played on the sly using pieces fashioned from bread. Reading was permitted, and the Butyrka library was known for its rich collection of classics and historical and scientific books. "I remember I read some sort of book about a young woman by Lydia Charskaya,"[38] Lev Sergeyevich faintly recalled. May passed into June and July, as he waited out his fate.

The diet was meager, designed to do little more than keep sedentary prisoners alive. A daily soup of cabbage or fish was the standard fare, served with roughly a pound of black bread. The evening meal was a serving of barley, lentils, or groats. This nutritionally empty regimen caused frequent outbreaks of scurvy and dysentery. Scabies, pneumonia, and heart attacks were common as well. "One of [the prisoners] was always picking on me," Lev Sergeyevich remembered. "He was convinced I was an informer. But I never asked anything, and just read all the time. One morning, when they brought tea, he . . . grabbed the mug and tried to pour the boiling water on me, but other prisoners grabbed him by the hand and stopped him."[39]

On the fifteenth of August, Lev Sergeyevich was finally led from his cell to an office in the Butyrka. It was his forty-third birthday by the Old Style, Julian calendar. He could only wonder if he was about to be marched to a courtyard and shot, or whether, by some miracle, a pardon had filtered through the system. Maybe he would merely be routed back in a few minutes to serve additional months or years in the filthy, disease-ridden communal cage. A sentence was read out to him:

Extract from Protocol No. 26
Department of the Special Board of the People's Commissariate
of Internal Affairs of the U.S.S.R.
15 August, 1939

Heard:
47. Case No. 154 on the accusation of Termen, Lev Sergeyevich, born 1895 [sic] in Leningrad. Russian, citizen of the U.S.S.R., nobleman, non-party member.

Resolved:

To imprison Termen, Lev Sergeyevich in a corrective labor camp for participation in a counterrevolutionary organization, for a term of eight years. The
term will be counted from March 10, 1939. The case goes into the archive.

Chief of the Secretariat of the Special Board of the People's Commissariat
of Internal Affairs of the U.S.S.R., Markeyev.[40]

The designation of "nobleman" was a glaring incrimination—one that must
have stung. Despite his unwavering loyalty to the revolution in all his work over
the years, in the end, the legacy of his family emblem was used against him,
to position him outside the proletariat as an "enemy of the people." Sending
the case "into the archive" meant a rubber stamp by the committee and an
incontestable fate tossed into the vaults forever.

According to his original protocol, his long detention in the Butyrka was
designed to "prevent him from avoiding investigation and trial." This was a
sham. There was no trial. Nor was there ever in these cases. The "Special
Board" that sentenced him was an insidious brainchild of Soviet bureaucracy
that let a three-member committee stand in for a full courtroom proceeding
and conduct each "trial" in closed session without the defendant. Solzhenitsyn
speculated that "it would not be a miracle if we should learn someday that there
were never any sessions, and that there was only a staff of experienced typists
composing extracts from nonexistent records of proceedings, and one general administrator who directed the typists. As for typists, there were certainly
typists. That we can guarantee."[41] Lev Sergeyevich's sentence, in fact, was
typewritten.

On the day the verdict was pronounced, halfway around the world, a Mr.
William A. Nickert of Philadelphia took delivery of his new Teletouch theremin. One of a handful of instruments the faltering company labored to crank
out in the inventor's absence, the bill of sale carried a twelve-month guarantee signed by Boyd Zinman on Teletouch stationery—letterhead that still bore
the mark "Director of Research, Prof. Leon Theremin."

In light of the draconian penalties summarily handed out during the purge,
and the norms for sections 1-a and 4 of Article 58, Lev Sergeyevich's eight years
was rather lenient. An old joke among Stalin's prisoners ran:

"What was your sentence?"
"Twenty-five years."
"For what?"
"Nothing."
"Impossible. For nothing they give ten years."

Still, Article 58 prisoners—political "offenders" like Lev Sergeyevich, stigmatized as "58s"—were destined for camps in the most remote regions of Siberia. These penal settlements were known for the severest regimes imposed on forced-labor convicts. Lev Sergeyevich learned that he was about to be transferred to a camp in the vast Kolyma region, the Soviet Union's easternmost outpost of mass imprisonment.

With other starved, disoriented, soon-to-be laborers, he was herded at night into a windowless Black Maria and shuttled to the train platform where each day's wretched lot was customarily disgorged. Ragged, barely human forms, prodded with gunstocks and hollered at by guards, clambered into a cattle car to begin a rail journey often more brutal than the camp life they were about to enter. One hundred or more prisoners were locked into a single car, with little light or ventilation on a trip that usually lasted from four to six weeks. "We were put in the cattle car," Lev Sergeyevich remembered, "and there were three shelves wide enough for nine people to lie side by side."[42] The haul would be from Moscow to the transit camp at Vladivostok on the Soviet Pacific coast, just across the Bering Strait from Alaska. Lev Sergeyevich and his new companions would traverse the entire Russian continent, on more than fifty-two hundred miles of winding track, to reach Vladivostok, the first stop on their migration.

In the August heat, the fetid air inside the cars could quickly climb to a sweltering 86 degrees Fahrenheit, intensified by the reek of a latrine pail that serviced everyone and was emptied only sporadically. The doors were occasionally slid open for short intervals at stops to relieve the gagging stench. Bread was practically the only food. Bits of salty herring were sometimes distributed, but this just heightened the persistent thirst aggravated by water rations that limited a prisoner to eight ounces a day for both drinking and washing. But even this couldn't be counted on. Supervising NKVD convoy troops regularly forgot to pass the water bucket into the cars, and prisoners were known to subsist with no liquid for up to twenty-four hours at a time. Disease was rampant, and doctors assigned to penal trains were more than indifferent. In some cases, bodies of those who died en route remained in the cars for days.

During the '30s, such staggering numbers were condemned to the empire of the Soviet GULAG (the Chief Administration of Corrective Labor Camps) that figures on victims are wildly divergent. The terror had flown so out of control that officials lost count and ceased to take notice. By 1937, some seven thousand camps holding upward of seven million inmates dotted the immense Russian landscape in regional clusters.

Kolyma (kah-lee-MAH), where Lev Sergeyevich was headed, was the largest camp territory—four times the size of France—and registered the coldest temperatures in the Northern Hemisphere, dipping as low as –94 degrees Fahrenheit, inland. For roughly half the year, the coastal waters remained frozen for many miles out. The main camp area was situated around the Kolyma River basin where gold deposits were discovered early in the century. In 1932, Dalstroy, the Far Eastern Construction Trust—an agent of the NKVD—established a network of camps at Kolyma to mine gold using the forced labor population. By 1940, an estimated sixty-six mines were worked by four hundred thousand inmates.

Kolyma's gold—the largest concentration in the country—was accessible by manual labor because it lay fairly close to the surface. But the work of cutting through the permafrost was exhausting. The prison population at Kolyma, consequently, had the largest turnover rate of all the camps: some 30 percent of its miners died each year from overwork and malnutrition and were continuously replaced by incoming convict shipments from Stalin's infinite supply of expendable labor. Gold, actually, was the byproduct of the government's central priority: to kill off prisoners. Kolyma was the deadliest of all the camp complexes. Millions died there. Escape was impossible, given the forbidding terrain outside the walls of the prison barracks and the boundless distances to other pockets of civilization. No free inhabitant, in any case, would have risked life and liberty to harbor a fugitive camp inmate. "Nothing remained for them but to die," Conquest observed, "and they died without thinking of escaping. They died showing once again this national quality . . . patience."[43] Kolyma became a symbol, he noted; "just as Auschwitz has come to stand for the Nazi extermination camps as a whole, so Kolyma remains fixed in the imagination of the Soviet peoples as the great archetype of the sinister system under which Stalin ended, by hunger, cold and exhaustion, the lives of so many of his subjects."[44]

On the interminable train journey, patience was more or less an enforced state of mind. Lev Sergeyevich had plenty of time to ruminate on his approaching destiny. "We travelled a long time," he recalled, "for about a month. The political prisoners again argued and quarreled."[45]

For the second time in a year, he found himself in transit as decisive events in world diplomacy were played out. On August 23, 1939, the Nazi-Soviet Nonaggression Pact—perhaps Stalin's most ill-advised tactical blunder—drew Germany and the Soviet Union into an uneasy alliance. On the surface, it appeared to benefit the interests of both leaders. Hitler won the assurance of Soviet neutrality in his impending invasion of Poland; it would insure him against an attack on two fronts if Britain and France came to Poland's defense. Stalin, in return, was granted the promise of new territory: the eastern part of Poland, and the Baltic States. Along with this, Hitler guaranteed nonaggression toward the Soviets after the fall of Poland. Most important for Stalin, it was a ploy to buy time in what he sensed was an unavoidable European conflagration. But below the surface, his gain of new territory effectively moved his own front further west, offering the Germans easier access when it came time for them to ravage his border.

Stalin's duplicity forced him to backpedal furiously on the Nazi question. The Soviet press followed in step and withdrew all anti-German propaganda. Many people were caught unaware; two teenagers who innocently ordered an anti-Nazi film were sent to a labor camp. Only weeks earlier Lev Sergeyevich had been sentenced for belonging to "a fascist organization," and suddenly the shift of policy forbade the NKVD to use fascist activity as an accusation against anyone. Such was the caprice that steered the destiny of the Soviet people during the purge.

As Lev Sergeyevich rattled along toward eastern Siberia in the steamy cattle car, Hitler attacked Poland on September 1, and on the seventeenth, Stalin penetrated from the east for his share of the spoils.

The tracks of the Trans-Siberian railway finally terminated in Vladivostok. Prisoners were ordered out of the cars. The living heeded the call; any who lay motionless were presumed to be dead. The Kolyma River basin, with its expanse of camps and mines, lay in a remote region of the interior not accessible overland. These territories could be served only by sea.

The transit camp at the port of Vladivostok functioned as a temporary junction where a hundred thousand prisoners at a time poured into barracks, awaiting dispatch to the slave ships of the Kolyma run—the final leg of their journey. In the open air after weeks of confinement, Lev Sergeyevich and the other prisoners were swiftly closed in by guards with dogs and made to squat while papers were checked. Then came the brutal admonition they would hear so often: anyone who stood up would be shot on sight for attempting to escape.

In the transit camp many had their first taste of the malevolent caste system among prisoners. The social order of the Soviet penal world divided along two distinct class lines: "politicals" (58s, or "counterrevolutionaries") like Lev Sergeyevich (or the woman who penciled a number on the newspaper photograph of Stalin, or the man who smiled in sympathy with the dockers' anti-Soviet quips) and common criminals—embezzlers, thieves, rapists, murderers, and the like. Because "political" crimes threatened to erode the authority of the state—which of course was paramount—Stalin took pains to make sure the 58s were dealt the sorriest fate. Politicals were driven into a well-policed underclass, much as the bourgeoisie was trampled under after the revolution. By contrast, hardened criminals and petty thugs—known in the camps as the vicious *urkas*—ruled the roost with relative impunity. They had, after all, merely committed personal crimes against individuals—matters of minor significance to Stalin. But more important, they were regarded as "class allies"—a notion, in Aleksandr Solzhenitsyn's words, "derived from Marxist-Leninist class theory, according to which felons are seen as potential allies in the building of Communism due to their proletarian background."[46] This prejudice naturally was in line with Stalin's own penchant for peopling his top cadres with brutal, sadistic gangster-types of lower intelligence (like the evil Yezhov, who directed much of the purge genocide). Stalin's early activities with Lenin prior to the revolution, in fact, involved authorizing bank robberies in the Caucasus to line the Party's pockets. He clearly resonated with the criminal mentality.

Guards routinely watched dispassionately as urkas assaulted politicals and robbed them of food, warm clothing, and personal belongings. At Vladivostok, urkas thrived in heated barracks with mattresses and blankets, while the politicals, in a segregated zone, were deprived of these amenities and even suffered from a shortage of water. It was in the interest of camp authorities to fortify the fists of the criminals, who served as a de facto, unsalaried terror squad to keep the politicals in check.

The sea route from Vladivostok—a Siberian middle passage—took the prisoners northeast across the Sea of Japan, through La Pérouse Strait, past Sakhalin Island, and northwest through the Sea of Okhotsk to the harbor at Nagayevo. The voyage lasted about a week and was another survival hurdle many never lived to cross. The dreaded "death-ships of the Okhotsk Sea," as Andrei Sakharov called them, were huge tramp steamers ranging in size from two thousand to nine thousand gross tons. Their dark, cavernous holds served as floating dungeons for legions of barely living human remnants en route to the camps. In 1933, the notorious *Dzhurma,* one of the largest vessels, got stuck in the autumn ice and remained lodged there for the winter. When it finally made port the following spring, none of the twelve thousand prisoners in its hold were alive.

Prisoners were battened down under hatches in the freighters' dark recesses by gun-toting guards. The depraved underworld society below was left to its own devices and the whims of heavily armed urkas who dominated in a reign of terror. The writer Eugenia Ginzburg, a former prisoner, recalled her 1939 passage on the Nagayevo run:

> But the worst was yet to come: our first meeting with the real hardened criminals among whom we were to live at Kolyma. When it seemed as though there were no room left for even a kitten, down through the hatchway poured another few hundred human beings. They were the cream of the criminal world: murderers, sadists, adepts at every kind of sexual perversion. . . . Without

wasting any time they set about terrorising and bullying the "ladies"—the politicals—delighted to find that the "enemies of the people" were creatures even more despised and outcast than themselves. Within five minutes we had a thorough introduction to the law of the jungle. They seized our bits of bread, snatched the last of our rags out of our bundles, pushed us out of the places we had managed to find. . . . throughout the whole voyage we never saw a single representative of authority other than the sailor who brought a cartload of bread to the mouth of the hold and threw our "rations" down to us as though we were a cageful of wild beasts.[47]

With the blessing of the guards above, urkas freely raped, maimed, and murdered prisoners in the depths of the convict ships.

The coastline of Nagayevo was a forbidding, stark landscape for the newly arrived. A murky, gray sea washed up on a rocky beach dwarfed by thousand-foot cliffs towering overhead. Convicts disembarked and ambled onto the pebbly shore. The sick were placed in rows of stretchers on the sand; those who had expired were stacked for a head count so death certificates could be issued. All remaining prisoners were ordered into formations of five abreast for the march to the transit camp at Magadan, a few miles inland, beyond the cliffs. "Convicts! This is Kolyma!" The head of Dalstroy shouted his bloodless greeting to the throng of new recruits:

The law is the taiga, and the public prosecutor is the bear! Never expect to eat soup and bread together. What comes first, eat first! What's gone from your hands is lost for ever. You are here to work, and to work hard! You must repay with your sweat and tears the crimes perpetrated against the Soviet State and the Soviet people! No tricks, no monkey business. We are fair with those who co-operate, pitiless with those who don't. We need metal, and you must produce this metal according to The Plan. The fulfillment of The Plan is our sacred duty. Those who do not fulfill The Plan are saboteurs and traitors, and we show them no mercy![48]

Survival to this juncture was already a mark of superior fortitude, but nearly superhuman reserves were needed for what lay beyond these cliffs. "Everyone had moments of perfect despair," Richard Lourie noted. "Even the memory of her child's face was sometimes not enough to make a woman want to live another second. There was a point beyond the reach of love or beauty, an infinite dimness where suicide was the only star."[49] Lev Sergeyevich, the indomitable inventor, fashioned his own unique survival strategy: "Even in my Kolyma exile," he remembered, "I was not afraid, because it was interesting. I felt as though I were watching a new movie."[50]

The earliest convict laborers sent to Nagayevo in 1932 broke ground for the city of Magadan and erected its first structures: a cluster of log dwellings constructed over a desolate swamp near a taiga, a coniferous forest area. In the ensuing years, the area developed into a small city with its own power station, shipbuilding yard, library, post office, and movie theater. As the capital and administrative hub of the entire Kolyma camp network, it served as headquarters for Dalstroy and as a routing station for the constant stream of fresh slave labor headed to the mines just north, in the interior.

Inmates filtering into the camps proper entered a realm of perpetual cold that rapidly broke down the body's resistance. In 1939, the threshold temperature for compulsory outdoor labor was lowered from –58 degrees Fahrenheit to –76. Fur was forbidden, and only canvas shoes, rather than warmer felt footwear, were allowed. Frostbite was common. When Lev Sergeyevich arrived, the brief Arctic summer was just waning, which meant temperatures were somewhat warmer. But under these conditions, workers often toiled in the scorching sun while standing in several feet of slushy, thawing ice. One rhyme among the convict population ran:

Kolyma, Kolyma
Wonderful planet:
Twelve months winter,
The rest summer.

At arrival, each inmate (now called a *zek*—slang from the Russian word *zaklyuchenny*, for "prisoner") was examined by a doctor and assigned to "heavy," "medium," or "light" labor. Politicals were usually charged with the heaviest jobs, though most of them came from nonlabor professions and were not accustomed to strenuous physical work. All lighter tasks, of course, were the inviolate province of the urkas.

A typical work day lasted from twelve to sixteen hours. Prisoners were roused at 4:00 A.M. for a breakfast of gruel or herring, with bread, then marched to the work detail at 5:00 A.M. At noon there was a lunch of cabbage leaf soup, bread, and groats, or gruel and peas. Then work resumed and continued until 8:00 P.M. Any who failed to fulfill their norm were made to labor two additional hours. Back at the camp, various chores were followed by a supper of bread and soup. Then it was over to the board bunks—wooden planks with nothing more. Sleep, especially in summer, was nearly impossible with the all-night battle against an overpopulation of virulent insects. In 1938, a lice infestation caused a typhus epidemic that claimed tens of thousands of lives.

Hunger, the omnipresent obsession of prisoners, was the driving motivation camp authorities used to enforce work quotas. Individual rations were adjusted daily to reflect "fulfillment of norms," but expectations always slightly exceeded a laborer's strength quotient. The result was a calculated, inescapable downward spiral: reduced food allotment for "non-fulfillment of norms" rendered the prisoner less capable of making the following days' work requirement. The pattern repeated itself, and rations continued to diminish by degree, leading to the onset of illness and extreme exhaustion. The sick were expected to work, often with pneumonia and temperatures as high as 105 degrees. The prisoner became so weakened that "only clubbings can force him to drag himself from camp to gold mine. Once he reaches the shaft he is too weak to hold the wheelbarrow, let alone to run the drill; he is too weak to defend himself when a criminal punches him in the face and takes away his day's ration of bread."[51] At this stage the laborer was regarded as fully spent, put on a starvation diet of three hundred grams of bread per day, and allowed to do odd jobs around the camp until death set in. These "goners," as they were called, faced a slow demise.

Others who fell behind in production by the same vicious cycle were condemned to death as saboteurs who refused to work—often by way of Article 58, section 1, for perpetrating an "action directed toward the weakening of state power." Often, at morning and evening roll call, a camp official would read out lists of these doomed—sometimes to the accompaniment of musical fanfares played by urka musicians—after which they would be led through the front gate and shot. Solzhenitsyn recounts the case of a camp chief who, at lineup, liked to "pick out some brigade or other which had been at fault for something or other and order it to be taken aside. And then he used to empty his pistol into the frightened, crowded mass of people, accompanying his shots with happy shouts. The corpses were left unburied. In May they used to decompose—and at that point the 'goners' who had survived until then were summoned to cover them up, in return for a beefed-up ration, even including spirits."[52] The Serpantinka camp at Kolyma was established specifically as an execution barracks for these kinds of liquidations, and in 1938 alone, twenty-six thousand men were executed there. Underground mine accidents also claimed many victims daily, their bodies lifted to the surface and unceremoniously disposed of in the brushwood.

Zeks knew the prospect of survival to the end of their terms ran counter to official policy. Kolyma was set up to destroy its inmates by one method or another and, along the way, produce some gold. "I must tell you that you are not brought here to live but to suffer and die," a camp doctor told one prisoner. "If you live . . . it means that you are guilty of one of two things: either you worked less than was assigned you or you ate more than your proper due."[53] Kolyma gold, it was estimated, cost one human life for each kilogram, or one thousand lives per ton.

Lev Sergeyevich was assigned to a road-building crew. He was lucky to be spared mine work, the time limit for which was, according to Conquest, "at the most, one month, after which either pneumonia or meningitis dispatched the worker into the next world."[54] "I mostly communicated with the criminals," Lev Sergeyevich recalled, "it was simpler. The politicals continued to clarify their positions in heart-to-heart talks."[55] The routine was brutal. "We worked seven days a week," he remembered. "It was ten kilometres on foot to the quarry where gravel was loaded into each convict's wheelbarrow, then 15 minutes for a smoke, and the return journey with the wheelbarrows weighing a hundred kilos each across the cold tundra. One step to the right or left and you could be shot on sight. This went on and on, day after day. Add to it the constant gnawing hunger—our rations were often stolen by the camp authorities. Many died in the tundra."[56] Under the noses of sympathetic guards, urkas also stole the politicals' meager rations and even portions of their days' norms, though their workload was lighter, and their food allotments more generous to begin with. Some stories tell of desperate inmates eating the decaying corpse of a horse crawling with maggots and flies; others devoured half a barrel of wheelbarrow lubricating grease; some picked moss from the ground.

Sometimes, extra rations could be won through a subtle barter system involving the exchange of food and clothing, in delicate strategy and negotiation with guards and urkas. But Lev Sergeyevich found another method. He observed an inefficient use of manpower that cost many lives and, more important for camp authorities, slowed productivity. "Having a good head for inventions," he recounted, "helped me even in those deeper reaches of hell."[57] Under normal conditions, each prisoner could haul one, or at most, two wheelbarrow loads of gravel per day. Lev Sergeyevich suggested laying a wooden track to make a rudimentary monorail system. "I invented special runners for those damned wheelbarrows. . . . it was easier, and now we could do seven or eight wheelbarrows. . . . our productivity soared. So did our rations. . . . All the criminals were very happy with me. They all thanked me."[58]

This kind of ingenuity endeared him to his captors, while droves of his fellow 58s—surgeons, botanists, teachers, engineers, artists, nuns—were being felled by the urkas' unchecked sadism, guards' beatings, mass executions, and random murders for the amusement of the authorities. While the camp administration blithely sanctioned the death penalty for any of them who failed to fulfill a day's norm, the urkas' overt murders went unpunished. Common criminals could volunteer for the Red Army as a possible route out of the camps, but the politicals were so despised and suspect that this path was always closed to them.

Survival of the spirit, even when the body could still drag itself to work in a torpor, required a Herculean effort. "A joke, a sunrise, a line of poetry, the touch of a hand," Lourie observed, "not only helped keep body and soul together but helped keep the soul alive."[59] Momentary glints of culture occasionally flickered through the bleakness of the camps—choirs, glee clubs, theatricals—recruited from the ranks of zeks who were eager to win a day's reprieve from work norms. To Solzhenitsyn, these outlets were a "counterfeit of life, or maybe not a counterfeit, but a reminder, instead, that life despite everything still exists, that it does go on existing."[60] These activities were therapeutic for inmates, but their fundamental purpose was to amuse the bosses, who competed aggressively from camp to camp for claims of the most sophisticated productions.

Inmate orchestras, in particular, were inherently absurd: highly evolved icons of bourgeois gentility amidst a jungle of human predators mangling one another over a scrap of bread. And yet they became a popular custom initiated by camp authorities, much as they did in the German camps. "You hold things dearer in there," one survivor recollected. "Hearing music in there is not like hearing music out here. I would not have missed it for the world."[61] But the juxtaposition was often pointedly bizarre. Solzhenitsyn described a cruel farce perpetrated on a horde of arriving politicals as they marched on foot across the frozen Nagayevo harbor toward Magadan: "[The prisoners] were greeted by the Dalstroi orchestra. The orchestra played marches and waltzes, and the tormented, half-dead people strung along the ice in a gray line, dragging their Moscow belongings with them . . . and carrying on their shoulders other half-dead people—arthritis sufferers or prisoners without legs."[62] Conquest recounted how the orchestra "very often played while the prisoners were at work. To the accompaniment of this music, the guards would fall out prisoners whose work was especially feeble and shoot them, there and then. The shots rang out one after another. The bodies of the murdered men were also buried under the brushwood on the surface of the mines."[63]

Lev Sergeyevich's connection to music initially went undiscovered at Kolyma. Convicts were faceless in camp, their previous identities—aside from basic distinctions such as "Trotskyite" or "counterrevolutionary"—were not always known, and of little consequence to guards and authorities. Lev Sergeyevich was no different. "He was skinny, middle-aged, with an intellectual face," the writer Gyorgy Kiksman explained, "and he did not like to talk about himself. Very little information about him came to the camp . . . and they were saying he was a musician. Why, and what he came here for, nobody asked. It wasn't the custom."[64] By devising wheelbarrow runners, his inventive skills came to the attention of camp administrators. But it was only later that they learned of his musical background. One day he was ordered to "organize music"—to assemble a symphonic ensemble for the camp. Surprisingly, he found at his disposal among the inmates virtually the full membership of the Moscow and Leningrad Philharmonic orchestras. "We performed Ravel's *Bolero*," he recalled. "The chiefs of other camps just died of envy."[65]

Despite these fleeting respites of humanity and civility, the vicious assault of prisoners continued daily. Even if a zek could stay the precarious course between urka violence and underproduction of quotas, traps were everywhere. "Say aloud that the work was harsh, mutter the most innocent remark about Stalin," Conquest explained, "keep silent while the crowd of prisoners yelled 'Long live Stalin,' and you're shot—silence is agitation! . . . No trial, no investigation."[66] Or if an order from Moscow arrived one day mandating the liquidation of a given number of politicals, new interrogations were conducted at the camp. Inmates' original convictions were trumped up to require the death penalty, and the unfortunates were led away to a remote site and shot en masse. Droves of convicts were periodically executed to stem epidemics. In some instances, whole bargeloads of prisoners who could no longer work were sunk in the Arctic seas. Suicide was sometimes accomplished by deliberately stepping out of column during a march, provoking guards who were trained to shoot on sight.

During a trek, those who succumbed to exhaustion, or a guard's pistol, often found their final resting place in the snow where they fell. Prisoners who were buried—just as unceremoniously and anonymously—occupied a brigade of gravediggers full time. Typically, thirty or more corpses were tossed into a single pit dug and dynamited into the rock and permafrost. Sometimes years passed before relatives could verify the fact of these deaths. In all, Conquest estimated, at least 3 million perished at the Kolyma camps from 1932 to 1953; 70,000 in 1938 alone—a common figure for the period.[67]

For zeks who lived to serve out their terms—and there weren't many of them—freedom could never be taken for granted. Their small minority had confounded the system, and the government would still connive to crush them somehow. Often, just as a prisoner was about to complete a term, the Special Board in Moscow would conjure up a fresh sentence to be served out consecutively at the same camp. But release carried no guarantees either. In December 1939, twenty-five hundred freed prisoners sat in the hold of the transit ship *Indigirka* en route from Nagayevo to Vladivostok. When the vessel struck a rock and began to sink, authorities entering lifeboats refused to unlock the hatches and release the prisoners from a dungeon quickly flooding with icy sea water. Only about thirty of the liberated inmates survived the wreck.

Barring legitimate discharge, one route out of the camps, though seldom traveled, involved persuading authorities of some scientific scheme which, if the prisoner were released, could be coaxed into existence for the universal benefit of Soviet power and military advantage. Russian science, thanks to the purge, was in serious eclipse, so proposals were always considered. Lev Sergeyevich might come to mind when Solzhenitsyn wrote: "At line-up before work and after, with hand barrows and picks, these servitors of the muse Urania . . . wrinkle their brows and strive to invent something to astound the government and fire its greed."[68] But although "invention is a form of escape which doesn't involve the risk of a bullet or a beating," he muses, "there are many more inventors—as also poets—among plain ordinary people than we might imagine."[69]

Flirtation with freedom drew many pseudoscientists from the cracks of prison barracks. Solzhenitsyn remembered one who claimed to have "discovered a deviation of the compass needle from the odor of garlic. From this he had envisioned a way to modulate high-frequency waves with an odor and thereby transmit an odor over a great distance. However, government circles did not see any military advantage in this project and were not interested. . . . Either go on bending your back or think up something better!"[70] In a letter addressed to Stalin, one scoundrel proposed to "assist in the secure guarding of the fierce enemies of the people who surround me. If I am summoned from the camp and receive the necessary means, I guarantee to make this system work."[71]

"Meanwhile," Solzhenitsyn added, "really great scientists were done in and perished in camps. But the Leadership of our dear Ministry was in no hurry to seek them out there and to find worthier uses for them."[72] Lev Sergeyevich, who lavished his security apparatus on the government with such flourish the decade before, was now tinkering with wheelbarrows and orchestras— winning a fuller ration, perhaps, but still no closer to freedom than a cunning urka. The ingenuity that safeguarded Al Capone's captivity with gun detectors was powerless to contrive a way past a few extra grams of bread, or a ladle more of hot water and groats at night.

By December, the fleeting Arctic summer had long retreated, and the topsoil of the tundra and the polar taiga were frozen, along with the Kolyma River and its tributaries. The approaching winter would see a two-month period when the sun would not rise at all.

One day a man in an NKVD uniform entered the camp and summoned Lev Sergeyevich to an office at the administrative headquarters. He held out a pile of civilian clothes to the inventor and suggested he change out of his prison rags. Lev Sergeyevich sensed someone in an official capacity must be interested in his work, judging from the man's cordial demeanor—a respect prisoners were unused to. "I was told to get ready to be taken to Moscow," he recalled.[73] And so, just as the *Indigirka* was going down with most of its twenty-five hundred liberated camp inmates, Lev Sergeyevich, in what appeared to be some kind of reprieve, made the long journey back, under escort, leaving this nihilistic "planet" for the "mainland" of Soviet civilization (as the zeks called it), and the sanctuary of the known world again. "One criminal with whom I shared a ration gave me his fur coat," he remembered. "If not for that fur coat I would have frozen to death on that trip."[74] After arrival in Vladivostok, Lev Sergeyevich, under heavy guard, was taken to Moscow on a passenger train, among common travelers.

《》

Stalin's September victory in Poland had strengthened his resolve, but it had cost him a thousand Red Army soldiers. His next move was to bolster Leningrad against invasion by annexing adjacent land in the Finnish region of Karelia. On November 30, the Soviet Army attacked Finland on the Karelian Isthmus in a fierce, relentless assault led by Voroshilov as commander-in-chief. But the divisions of Red Army troops filing across the snow made easy targets. Finnish sharpshooters picked them off in shooting-gallery fashion from tall pines or on skis, flashing out of the blinding whiteness. On March 12, 1940, the Finns' resistance was finally broken and Stalin was ceded his territory, but only after the persistent truculence of endless human waves. The price tag for the new border was enormous. Estimates ranged from fifty thousand to one million Soviet soldiers killed.

The Winter War with Finland exposed glaring weaknesses of the Red Army in morale, leadership, and equipment. Stalin knew better resources had to be summoned. It was then that Lev Sergeyevich was called back from oblivion.

《》

The sight of pedestrians crossing Moscow intersections on a business-as-usual morning must have seemed a strange, surreal transformation. On Saltykov Street, the van pulled up to the imposing iron gates where an NKVD guard checked the driver and waved him through. From the window—this was no Black Maria—Lev Sergeyevich could see they were entering a broad courtyard with monuments to Lenin and Stalin. It was the complex of the Central State Aero-Hydrodynamics Institute (TsAGI). Guards were stationed at every entryway and exit on the premises; some patrolled along the fences and roamed the courtyard. The van halted before a building on the edge of the grounds—the entrance to the KOSOS (the Design Department of the Section for Experimental Aircraft Construction). The KOSOS edifice was an undistinguished eight-story modern structure whose opposite facade overlooked Radio Street by the Yauza River. There, additional guards—in plain-clothes—milled about the sidewalk and along the riverbank.

Security men ushered Lev Sergeyevich into an elevator and escorted him to the eighth floor. Everywhere, he was treated respectfully. He had been brought, he was told, to Central Design Bureau Number 29 (TsKB-29), an NKVD special prison. Standard policy mandated that new inmates read and sign a typed set of procedural regulations. He expected the customary litany of threats: beatings, reduction in rations, added work detail, or, ultimately, the bullet. But among the listed prohibitions was the "consumption of alcoholic beverages." Punishments for errant behavior included denial of exercise or store privileges, and deprivation "of visits." Could this be real? After Kolyma, where convicts had no rights whatsoever—hardly even the right to stay alive—the idea of consent by signature to reasonable, civil conduct seemed like a cruel mockery.

New arrivals were led by guards—or "screws," as the prisoners called them here—along a plush carpeted hallway that abruptly switched directions, right and left, and down a staircase to the "places of residence" on the sixth floor. These were not cells, but three large rooms, and a small one, designated as sleeping areas. Arranged around the periphery of each oak-paneled room were thirty or more army cots with sheets, pillows, and flannel blankets, and a night-stand for each, with packs of Ducat cigarettes placed on them. Leonid L'vovich Kerber, who lived and worked with Lev Sergeyevich at KOSOS, recorded an impression of his first night:

> After a brief interlude, the door opened and yet another guard said something like, "Please, supper's ready." From ingrained habit, I untied my food pack-age, got out my mess bowl, and stood by the door. The screw smiled. "That's not necessary. They'll serve you there."
>
> He led us to the dining area. As the door opened, about a hundred men sit-ting at tables covered with snow-white tablecloths turned their heads at the same time. There were many well-known, friendly faces. . . . At various tables we saw . . . the cream of the Russian aeronautical world. Many friendly eyes looked in our direction, as if to reassure us that everything would be fine now. But I was gripped by fright: seeing all these people meant that it was true, that they, too, had been arrested. What a disaster!
>
> We joined this illustrious group, filling in the empty seats. My mess bowl and spoon now appeared comical and unnecessary. At prison camp you only abandoned them when you were headed for the graveyard. The knives, forks, and plates, which we had grown thoroughly unaccustomed to using, only high-lighted the absurdity of my bowl and spoon. A girl in an apron brought meat with macaroni to our table, asking politely, "Would you like tea or cocoa?" (And this was said to me, who only yesterday was addressed as "you piece of crap"!)
>
> Most of the men had already finished supper and were leaving their tables

when a middle-aged man—it turned out to be the eminent chemist A. S. Fayn-shteyn, who had been a party member since 1915 and once met with Lenin—remarked with irritation, "The cocoa was cold again. What a disgrace!" The newcomers pinched themselves hard: "Good Lord, is this prison or a dream?"[75]

It was, actually, a dream prison—a peculiar oxymoron. Solzhenitsyn, who served half his sentence in one of these places, called them "Islands of Paradise" within the archipelago of the GULAG, because camp inmates who learned of the humane, respectful environments clamored to get into them. Yet for most they were a far-off dream. "No one had seen them," he recalled. "No one had been there. Whoever had, kept silent about them and never let on. On those islands, they said, flowed rivers of milk and honey, and eggs and sour cream were the least of what they fed you; things were neat and clean, they said, and it was always warm, and the only work was mental work—and all of it super-supersecret."[76]

These Paradise Islands were closed research institutes where imprisoned scientists, engineers, and technicians were charged with carrying out secret government projects—slave labor on a higher level than at the camps, but slave labor nonetheless. A group of these institutes was established in the '30s, and a new Soviet word arose to describe them: *sharaga,* or more commonly, its diminutive, *sharashka,* from Russian convicts' slang for "a sinister enterprise based on bluff or deceit." The government, in its customarily enigmatic way, referred to them simply as "special-assignment prisons," or "Special Design Bureaus."

By the late '30s, sharashkas became makeshift patches to cover holes the purge had torn in the country's industrial fabric. With 10 percent of the population imprisoned or executed, the labor force was severely crippled. Especially at the top, scientists and major industrialists were among the disproportionate number of educated citizens seized as "politicals." Many leaders of Soviet heavy industry disappeared, especially in automotive and metallurgical production. By 1940, the paltry number of trained personnel left in the factories were outnumbered by hundreds of unqualified workers assuming the major engineering and technical work. The results were disastrous, and the situation continued to be aggravated by arrests for "espionage" or "wrecking," when factory accidents happened through incompetence.

The design bureau Lev Sergeyevich was brought to was set up to bolster the aeronautics industry. During the '30s the Russian government had promoted stunt flying, record-breaking aviation, and large aircraft, mostly for propaganda, with little attention to modernizing its air force. While the Germans were stockpiling advanced warplanes, the Soviets delighted in bravura displays of socialist technology.

One stunning creation presented to Stalin was a gargantuan civilian airplane—record breaking in dimensions, power, and range—honoring the fortieth anniversary of Maxim Gorky's literary career. Named for the writer, it was a luxuriously appointed, ostentatious, propaganda emblem of Soviet aviation and had cost over six million rubles raised from voluntary donations. The 42-ton behemoth with a 206-foot wingspan boasted a printing press, photographic and film darkrooms, a cinema, press conference salon, telephone station, cabins for seventy people, sleeping berths, a restaurant, kitchen, and buffet—an airborne Titanic.

The *Maxim Gorky* was powered by eight engines, and under its massive red wings, signs and slogans could be electrically illuminated. At completion in 1934, it dazzled Muscovites with dramatic fly-overs above Red Square to flaunt Soviet aeronautical prowess. But on May 18, 1935, an escorting fighter pilot miscalculated his stunt maneuvers within close range of the *Maxim Gorky* and collided with the colossal plane in midair. The huge craft faltered, broke into pieces, and fell into a forest. The passengers and crew all perished. Antoine de Saint-Exupéry, author of *The Little Prince*, who had test-piloted the *Maxim Gorky* the night before the disaster, wrote to *Izvestia:* "Deeply shaken, I feel the mourning into which Moscow has been plunged today. I have also lost my friends. . . . The gigantic airplane was not to be."[77] Pressing forward, Soviet aeronautics celebrated again in the summer of 1937 with the first flights over the North Pole from the USSR to the United States. (Lev Sergeyevich had, in fact, joined the Soviet welcoming delegation for Valery Chkalov and the other pilots on their arrival in the United States.)

But in the shadow of war, all this added up to pure folly. Worse still, the aviation establishment had been cut to shreds by the purge. In the air force, huge portions of the staff and officer corps had been executed along with the best pilots and aviation plant managers in the country. To top it off, Andrei Nikolayevich Tupolev, the Soviet Union's most recognized aviation designer, was in prison. Tupolev, in the '20s, had designed Russia's first all-metal aircraft and built the world's first all-metal twin-engine monoplane bomber. The aircraft made a historic flight from Moscow to New York in 1929 and became the prototype for all future bombers, including the American B-17 and B-29 (Superfortress). Tupolev had designed the *Maxim Gorky* and the record-breaking aircraft that flew over the North Pole. He was admired by Stalin and decorated by the Supreme Soviet with the orders of the Red Star and the Red Banner, and the Order of Lenin—the nation's highest award. He was elected an associate member of the USSR Academy of Sciences and appointed chief engineer of the Main Administration of the Aviation Industry. He was praised publicly by Ordzhonikidze and Voroshilov. But in 1937, like so many others,

Tupolev was arrested by the NKVD and falsely charged with selling plans to the Germans. At a time of national crisis it became a conundrum for the government: his talents were vital to stem a military catastrophe, yet he was an "enemy of the people."

Early in 1939, when it was decided to assemble a special aeronautics sharashka, Tupolev was asked to compile a list of aircraft specialists—an ironic reversal of the denunciation rolls interrogators beat out of prisoners to condemn new victims. He jotted down a list of about two hundred leading names in the field. The majority, as it turned out, were in custody. While searches were conducted in the camps, the TsKB-29 sharashka began to take shape: three separate design bureaus were established, each to orbit around a single prisoner-director. Tupolev was to supervise work on a dive bomber (Project 103); Vladimir Mikhaylovich Myasishchev would handle the design of a long-range, high-altitude bomber (Project 102); and Vladimir Mikhaylovich Petlyakov was assigned to develop a high-altitude fighter (Project 100). As a member of Myasishchev's team, Lev Sergeyevich was delegated work on instrumentation for Project 102.

"We've included you for a long time now on lists of specialists we need for work," Tupolev told a fresh arrival of recruits. "We have pulled many specialists from the Gulag. They have been looking for you in the camps for a very long time now, from Minsk to Kolyma, and from Dzezgazgana to Noril'sk. Praise God, you were still alive. Others, sadly, were not found alive."[78]

Lev Sergeyevich had joined an elite corps of about 150 specialists summoned to TsKB-29. Like some of the others, he had little training in aeronautical engineering, but in a pinch his expertise had to stand in for the vanished aircraft experts. "They were very talented people," J. K. Golovanov wrote, referring to Lev Sergeyevich and his physicist/mathematician colleagues at TsKB-29, "but with all their talents, they could not substitute for the experts."[79] The situation was occasionally frustrating to the directors. "With whom am I working?" Tupolev reportedly snapped. "People from different fields are coming to the designers' office—very often they are not able to distinguish an airplane wing from its tail. And all the aviation engineers are scattered all over the country. . . . What kind of airplanes do you need, made out of crap or metal?"[80] But Lev Sergeyevich's background with altimeters made him more than a simple neophyte in this technology. And the important point was not *who* was putting a mark on each component of an airplane, but that the part functioned within the whole. Each prisoner-specialist had a "facsimile" (a rubber stamp of three digits identifying his design chief) that was affixed on all blueprints and technical papers in lieu of names. Lev Sergeyevich, with his facsimile, would toil as an anonymous cog in Myasishchev's work force.

The evening ritual was taken in with suspicious, guarded pleasure by the new arrivals. Around 11:00 P.M., after dinner, prisoners began gathering in the oak-paneled sleeping rooms, reminiscing, joking, trading stories. No one was ordered to fall in line; screws secured the entranceway, but they were not permitted inside during the sleep period. There were real pillows, sheets, and blankets—no wooden plank beds stacked up like shelves. "The lights were turned off," Kerber recalled,

> which was pleasant, since the ceiling lights burned all night in cells, barracks, and in packed Stolypin railroad cars. . . . The sleeping quarters grew quiet except for the occasional scraping of streetcars which could be heard outside the window as they turned into Volochayevskaya Street and the park.
>
> That night only the newcomers stayed awake: it was too great a shock after the prisons, the camps, and the transit points to lie in a clean bed, anticipating a return to your old work, the access to foreign technical journals, the use of a logarithmic slide rule, the availability of finely pointed pencils and white Whatman paper stretched on the drawing boards. . . .
>
> Just one week before, in my former camp, in the predawn darkness when we marched off to work, a guard with the vacant face of a degenerate shouted, "Sit down! Hands behind your head! I'm warning you: take a step to the left or a step to the right and I'll treat it as an attempt to escape. I'll open fire without warning." But now it was, "Please step into the dining room."[81]

Wake-up call was at 7:00 A.M. "Although they took us for a shower once a week," Kerber explained, "toward morning the air in the sleeping rooms nevertheless reminded you of something between an army barracks and a passenger rail car with unreserved seating."[82] At 8:00, a breakfast of porridge, tea, butter, and kefir (fermented milk) was served. Work began at 9:00.

Filling out the staff were several hundred free workers who labored under the supervision of the prisoner-specialists. These free workers—engineers, designers, and technicians—answered to the prisoners, who could order them to work overtime and grant or deny them leaves or awards. But despite this inverted hierarchy, a sincere camaraderie existed between the two classes. Free workers were expected to address a prisoner as "Citizen Designer," but first names and patronymics were customary. "We were received not as enemies of the people," Kerber reflected, "but as people who had been hurt by life. In the morning we would find signs of touching concern from the free workers in our desk drawers: a flower, piece of candy, pack of cigarettes, or even a newspaper."[83]

Lunch—two dishes and a dessert compote—was served at 1:00 P.M. At 2:00, work resumed.

The Project 102 bomber Lev Sergeyevich was helping to outfit for Myasishchev featured many design innovations including a steerable nose-wheel landing gear, and defensive guns separated from the pressurized cockpit and gunner to be operated by remote control. In fine-tuning the complex calibrations of the system, project engineers evolved their own form of cybernetics—independently from the American Norbert Wiener's ideas. Myasishchev would circle around his workers, inspecting, commenting, advising. "Even in a crowd his appearance was striking," Kerber remembered. "Handsome, with head set at a proud angle, and always dressed in refined fashion, he looked like an actor."[84]

At 7:00, work ended, and a one-hour rest interval was followed by the dinner-leisure period from 8:00 to 11:00. This time brought the most humanizing elements of sharashka life into focus. Prisoners gathered in cliques around the corners of the sleeping rooms according to interest. Poetry clubs took advantage of books from the Butyrka that had been confiscated from purge victims (one collection had bookplates bearing the name of Nikolai Bukharin, former Politburo member shot after a show trial in 1938). Some prisoners drew scenes of life from the design bureau; others fashioned small objects—belt buckles, brooches, cigarette holders, children's toys—from scraps of Plexiglas. Poetry was written; novels were sketched. The music lovers club constructed a rudimentary violin, viola, and cello from scraps of bakelite-finished plywood used for aircraft construction. "They didn't sound like Stradivariuses," Kerber remembered, "but the trio . . . performing Offenbach or Strauss on Sundays invariably attracted enthusiastic listeners."[85]

Once a week, prisoners were permitted to buy small items from an in-house shop using money forwarded to them by relatives via the Butyrka. Cologne, soap, candy, cigarettes, razor blades, and other sundries were stocked. As prisoners gained back weight from an improved diet and sedentary work, exercise could be taken in the "ape house"—a caged-in recreational area on the roof designed for running and strolling.

But all these concessions to normalcy were little more than a child's playhouse analog of life outside the sharashka. Prisoners were perpetually reminded of their reality. Bars were installed on the insides of windows (to mask the true nature of the facility on the exterior); plainclothes screws constantly patrolled corridors and work stations; guards permanently blocked the only staircase connecting the sharashka (which occupied the top three floors of the building) with the lower stories of the KOSOS. Though the screws here were less menacing than in the camps—Tupolev even bullied his own guards—they were still omnipresent. Prisoners could not wear watches, and the strict control of their lives even extended to the practice of putting secret bromine additives in the food as a sexual suppressant.

Infrequent visits with relatives were limited to ten minutes and conducted at the Butyrka under the scrutiny of a guard who censored conversations.

(Once, during a visit, when Kerber's wife introduced him to a young son he had never met, the boy embraced the screw when he was told, "say goodbye to Papa.")[86]

Infringements of rules carried severe penalties. For drinking cologne, two prisoner-specialists were "beaten unconscious and sent into solitary confinement."[87] Attempts to communicate with the outside world through free workers could land a prisoner back in labor camp. And some prisoners feared they would be returned to the camps anyway after their aviation tasks were fulfilled. This very uncertainty worked to the advantage of sharashka officials to control the prisoners through perpetual insecurity. Everyone worried when unexplained disappearances occurred—someone would be summoned away from his desk, never to return again. In one instance, it was discovered later that three prisoner-scientists removed from TsKB-29 (including Karl Szilard, a distant relative of the nuclear physicist Leo Szilard) had been taken away to work on the Russian atomic bomb.

Directors, as well, had their own share of anxieties to contend with, particularly the ignorant intrusions of Stalin's lackeys. Tupolev recalled a typical exchange with Lavrenti Beria, the NKVD chief:

> Beria: "What speed does your 103 [Tu-2] aircraft have?"
> Tupolev: "600"
> Beria: "That's low, it has to be 700! What range?"
> Tupolev: "2,000 kilometers."
> Beria: "That's not good enough, it has to be 3,000! What kind of load?"
> Tupolev: "Three tons."
> Beria: "Too low—it has to be 4. That is all!"[88]

Then, addressing General Davydov, chief of all the prison design bureaus, Beria demanded, "order the military to quickly prepare the technical requirements for the twin-engine dive bomber. Correct the parameters stated by Comrade Tupolev to match my instructions."[89] Failure to carry out these amendments would have spelled doom for Tupolev and his team.

Still, these engineers managed to produce some of their finest work—imaginative, state-of-the-art aircraft—in the shadow of this repression and under the ever-present threat of reprisals for "sabotage" if equipment failed. "Where have I landed?" asked a newcomer in Solzhenitsyn's sharashka.

> "They won't be driving me out into icy water tomorrow! An ounce and a half of butter! Black bread—*out on the table!* They don't forbid books! You can shave yourself! The guards don't beat the zeks. What kind of great day is this? What kind of gleaming summit? Maybe I've died? Maybe this is a dream? Perhaps I'm in heaven."

"No, dear sir," said Rubin, "you are, just as you were previously, in hell. But you have risen to its best and highest circle—the first circle. You ask what a sharashka is? Let's say the concept of a sharashka was thought up by Dante."[90]

≪≫

Saturday, June 21, 1941, was a sunny, balmy day in the western cities of the USSR; people strolled the streets, still buoyed by a TASS announcement on the fourteenth assuring them that Germany would continue to honor the Nazi-Soviet Nonaggression Pact. The massing of 190 German divisions, with thousands of planes, tanks, and artillery, all along the Soviet border over the past months was not to be regarded as a threat. The anxious mood loosened; military vigilance was relaxed.

Stalin, who mistrusted the closest members of his retinue, had trusted Hitler. His ploy to buy time had instead bought a fortified Germany that was harder to defeat now than it would have been in 1939, particularly if the USSR had sided with the Allies in the first place. And Russia's western periphery was now universally vulnerable: by 1941, Nazi resolve had swallowed up every country bordering the USSR from the Baltic to the Black Sea. By sharing Poland, Stalin had also relinquished the buffer zone of an independent country and allowed its conquered resources to be used against him. Worse, in compliance with the 1939 pact, Russia was still furnishing Germany with valuable raw materials such as oil, grain, cotton, manganese, chromium, and foodstuffs, merely fueling Hitler's eastern conquests. The obsolete war equipment Germany delivered in return was hardly an even bargain.

Ultimately, a duped Stalin was happily fattening up Hitler's war machine and nudging his borders up to Germany's to facilitate an all-out Nazi invasion of the Soviet Union. He had been given ample warning of an impending German attack by Soviet intelligence—and the U.S. and British—but he refused to summon his defenses, fearing Hitler would see it as a provocation. To the Germans, the enervated, dilapidated Soviet military that had operated in the Winter War against Finland would appear to offer little resistance, and it emboldened Hitler.

At dawn on June 22, the western Soviet border erupted. A Nazi blitzkrieg of 4.6 million soldiers, 5,000 planes, and 3,700 tanks bombarded along its full length. Within eight hours, most of the regional Soviet air force had been annihilated—1,200 planes were destroyed, 800 on the ground, alone. Those that remained in the air rammed German planes when they ran out of ammunition. A dazed Stalin retreated to his dacha for twelve days, a now famously chronicled period in which he was paralyzed with gloom and indecision and even harbored thoughts of relinquishing power.

Red Army forces led by Voroshilov, Budenny, and Marshal Timoshenko scrambled to repel the enemy. When Stalin emerged from his silence, he ordered the army to stand its ground at all costs, but this proved catastrophic: Soviet forces were encircled and captured in detachments of up to 600,000 troops at a time—3.9 million taken prisoner within the first seven months of the war.

Chaos reigned in the army as commanders lacking battle experience were promoted to replace top tacticians liquidated in the purge. And the "Horse Marshals" severely underestimated the need for tank and antiaircraft units, failing even to organize a successful retreat. On July 1, Voroshilov was relieved of his command and recalled to Moscow.

As the German front clawed its way eastward, the first raid on Moscow came on the night of July 22. Lev Sergeyevich and his prisoner-colleagues at TsKB-29 awoke to the din of wailing sirens and screws hollering as they rushed into the sleeping areas. In the panic "there was a stamping of feet, the cries of guards who had lost their charges, complete darkness, and utter confusion."[91] In the courtyard, trenches had been dug and converted into bomb shelters in response to earlier assaults on Smolensk and Kiev. Now, dark flannel blackout curtains would be cast over the windows. For the past three months the work day had been stepped up to twelve hours, rations were reduced, and gas masks had been distributed. By early August it was clear preparations would have to be made for plant evacuation.

One evening, prisoners were instructed to assemble in groups of sixteen to eighteen men and gather up their personal belongings. Outside in the pitch-darkness, at 10:30 P.M., headcounts were conducted by flashlight and the inmates were hurried onto idling buses. "The gates opened," Kerber recalled, "and the building of the Design Department of the Section for Experimental Aircraft Construction dissolved in the gloom. Would we return here? If so, as what—free men or prisoners? Would this be our city, or would occupiers be lording it over us?"[92]

At the warehouses of Moscow's Kazanskaya railway station, bellowing soldiers with rifles and dogs formed the prisoners into single file; searchlight beams swept arcs across the night sky. "Where were we going?" Kerber wondered. "To Magadan, to Kolyma, to the Eastern Siberia camps, or to another set of camps? And how would we go—as prominent specialists and builders of awesome war machines, or as scum?"[93] The prisoners were herded into three cattle cars with barred windows; there was a final headcount, then the all-too-familiar sound of sliding doors being closed, latched, and locked from the outside. "After shunting here and there, the train departed at about 3 A.M. The wheels clicked at the rail joints; the road to nowhere had begun. As it grew light, the prisoners sat wherever they had found room during the loading. . . . In the half-light of early morning one of the prisoners read a station name through the bars: Kurovskaya."[94]

They were headed east—that they were sure of—but for veterans of this run, like Lev Sergeyevich, it was a disquieting, eerie déjà vu. The next morning saw the routine stop: doors were rolled open, soldiers handed in a pail of water with rations of tea, black bread, and pieces of sugar, and the latrine pail was taken to be emptied out under the cars. "From a small opening accessible from the upper bunks," Kerber recalled,

> a train carrying children could be seen next to us. Their frightened faces stared at the animal-like men behind the bars. It was a train from Murmansk. The city had been bombed, and they took the children directly from the kindergartens to the trains, and then to the east.
>
> It was August, and scorching; there wasn't a cloud in the sky. When the train stopped, the car would heat up. The prisoners would remove clothing and grumble. . . .
>
> The train moved slowly. We crossed the Volga on day 2. The fact that we didn't know where they were taking us and what was happening with our families oppressed us. No one talked. We just lay there silently, with eyes closed. It was easier that way.[95]

One night, near Sverdlovsk, a train carrying the sharashka's free workers wound up on the adjacent track. "The free workers were also in cattle cars," Kerber remembered,

> but with their families, without bars on the windows or an escort. We talked back and forth. They had been ordered to take warm clothing, but they didn't know where we were going either. We learned about the situation at the front only at stations, from the loudspeakers.
>
> After the Urals came the steppes, and the heat became difficult to bear. The prisoner-aerodynamics specialists used materials at hand—paper, cardboard, and rope—to fabricate air intakes, "scavengers," to direct the air flow into the cars.[96]

The following day, a train moving parallel with them on the next track caught the prisoners' eyes. On flatcars, under tarps, they could make out the wingless profiles of the Project 102 and 103 aircraft. This meant the plant was being moved with them—they weren't returning to the camps after all. "Everyone became very happy," Golovanov wrote, "started to talk, and someone even sang."[97]

On the plank bed next to Lev Sergeyevich was Sergei Pavlovich Korolev, future head of the Soviet space program, whom Tupolev had rescued from gold digging at Kolyma. At TsKB-29 he specialized in wing design for Project 103.

Korolev was the cofounder of a Moscow organization that tested liquid-fueled rockets, and he later developed rocket-propelled missiles and gliders at the Reaction Propulsion Scientific Research Institute. His RP-318 was the Soviet Union's first rocket-propelled aircraft, but before it could be scheduled for a test flight, Korolev was imprisoned. "Your pyrotechnics and fireworks are not only not necessary for our country," his interrogator charged, "but also dangerous. You should do real work and build airplanes. But the missiles are probably for an attempt on our leader's life, aren't they?"[98]

At the happy realization that the sharashka was saved, Korolev began to speak excitedly with Lev Sergeyevich and his bunk neighbor on the other side, Gyorgy Korneyev. Now that they looked forward to design work again, the inner rush of creative problem-solving fired them up, and the three resolved to pool their expertise to create a radio-controlled gun-powder rocket to counter Nazi tanks. After so many long months as drones for Myasishchev and Tupolev, a self-initiated project harnessing their deepest personal reserves of invention was life-affirming.

Soon, the rolling design bureau learned its final destination would be the city of Omsk. Its exodus was part of an eastward migration of fifteen hundred factories to the Volga, the Urals, and Siberia, involving millions of workers on miles of snaking freight cars. Dismantled equipment was often reassembled and set back into production as others hustled to get freshly cut timber walls erected around the new sites.

After ten days, the TsKB-29 cattle cars rumbled into the Omsk freight station. This was a provincial city with mostly one-story houses. Lights burned in the windows—there were no blackouts. On the truck ride into town, the roads were rough, "beating up the rear ends of the 'prominent' ones properly."[99] A two-story schoolhouse-like building became the new living quarters for some of the design bureau prisoners. With no local aircraft plant, two motor vehicle factories were hastily converted as temporary production sites. Out in the field, lathes began operating where a more permanent structure would be constructed overhead by urkas and dispossessed kulaks. It was a desperate rush: series production of the aircraft would begin in five months, "and there were no walls, no roofs, no electricity, and no water. Nothing!"[100]

On the opposite bank of the Irtysh River, across from Omsk, Myasishchev's team set up in Kulomzin. There, Lev Sergeyevich resumed adjustments on Project 102 in the aircraft repair shops of the Civil Aviation Fleet. But Sergei Korolev had not forgotten their discussion, and he approached the administrative chiefs of TsKB-29 with a proposal for a rocket laboratory. Eventually, Lev Sergeyevich, Gyorgy Korneyev, and Korolev were allocated a room and twelve civilian employees (mainly young girls) for drafting work. Their rocket project began with a plywood mock-up. But soon the tenuous reality around them shifted again. Early in 1942, Petlyakov—recently freed from custody and sent to Kazan to supervise the series production of his Project 100 (Pe-2) fighter—perished when the plane he was delivering to Moscow caught fire and crashed. Myasishchev, summoned to Kazan to replace him, was forced to abandon Project 102. Without his guidance, and because the necessary engines for it couldn't be found, interest in its completion waned. The 102 design bureau—which Lev Sergeyevich still belonged to—was dispersed, and the inventor was reassigned to a radio sharashka in Sverdlovsk. Gyorgy Korneyev joined a fighter design bureau (Project 110) directed by Dmitry Lyudvigovich Tomashevich in Kulomzin. The rocketry trio fell apart.

In the end, the two years' labor Lev Sergeyevich had given to TsKB-29 bore little fruit. While the design bureaus of Tupolev and Petlyakov bred aircraft that reached series production—5,256 Tu-2s (Project 103) were manufactured—and which saw considerable action in World War II, Myasishchev's Project 102 fizzled to nothing. And the bureaucratic ineptitude and imperious fiats from the Kremlin that led to one blunder and miscalculation after another disgusted Lev Sergeyevich—particularly the neglect of rocket science. "Take the Reactive Institute," he later reflected, "the idea for which was Tukhachevsky's. I met Sergei Korolev and other rocket propulsion experts in prison. I can endlessly cite bitter facts like this. I'm sure that if the Red Army had incorporated the ideas of the versatile Tukhachevsky, rather than those of the technologically-limited Voroshilov, the tragedy of 1941 wouldn't have been so great."[101]

With his approaching assignment in Sverdlovsk, perhaps Lev Sergeyevich would be tapped for his genuine talents in radio engineering. With luck, he would put his peripheral role in aeronautics behind him—a role in which, at the age of forty-four, he was always an apprentice.

But visions of returning to Leningrad and realizing his potential as a free scientist must have gnawed at him. His old mentor, Abram Ioffe—by now the leading physicist in Leningrad, with an international reputation—had set up a special commission at the Academy of Sciences in 1940 to study atomic energy. By 1942 Ioffe was organizing a group with Pyotr Kapitsa (the 1978 Nobel prizewinning physicist) to examine the feasibility of a Russian atomic bomb. In the autumn of '42, Ioffe was welcomed at Stalin's dacha to report on his progress, and his knowledge of American atomic research that was leaked through NKVD operatives. But all this was a far cry from Sverdlovsk, the former Ekaterinburg, where the 1918 execution of Tsar Nicholas II and his family still marked the city as an infamous symbol of Soviet terror. It was a solemn reminder to Lev Sergeyevich of his protracted enslavement and the invisible bars that held him captive from the larger world of scientific research.

Perhaps it was better he did not return to his beloved Leningrad. Under siege since September 8, the city had devolved into a desolate, sprawling urban labor camp where its free population subsisted like prisoners on their own turf, not much better off than their compatriots in the GULAG. Cold and hunger enveloped everything. By December, rationing had shrunk the daily bread allotment to 350 grams for workers and 200 grams for dependents. Household pets—what little was left of them—were killed for their protein value. Furniture was chopped up for firewood. Writing ink froze. In orphanages, lights burned all night to keep ravenous rats from children's cheeks. Signs were posted to advise pedestrians which side of the street was safer from German snipers.

Richard Lourie described the devastation:

> Leningrad had no electricity, heat, or transportation. People had to walk miles through the 30-degree below cold to get to work, then work for twelve hours, and walk back. People were dying everywhere. On the sidewalk, on the assembly line, at their desks, in their chairs at home. People seemed to know when they would die, when there was only a day or two left at most. They would go around and say farewell, a word that in Russian also means, "forgive me."
>
> All the pets were long gone. People were eating carpenters' glue. Women stopped menstruating. Bodies were transported by children's sleds across the frozen city to the cemetery, where the frozen ground had to be dynamited to create mass graves large enough for a population that, at the peak, was dying at the rate of ten thousand a day.[102]

Lourie described schoolchildren who memorialized their fading city in lines of Pushkin, recited to dying teachers:

> *I love you, creation of Peter,*
> *the elegant severity of your regard.*

Lev Sergeyevich, packing his spare belongings for Sverdlovsk in the spring of '42, could not have known that among the numberless casualties that winter was his aunt, Maria Emilievna Termen Nesturkh, who had perished from hunger during the siege of Leningrad.

TEN

Free Music: New Waves on the Home Front

*This is home to me. I feel more kinship to the Russian people under
their new society than I ever felt anywhere else. It is obvious that there
is no terror here, that all the masses of every race are contented and
support their government.*

— Paul Robeson, on his visit to the Soviet Union, 1934.

In late October 1939, Robert Rockmore stood among a welcoming committee on a New York pier, awaiting the arrival of his friend and client Paul Robeson on the SS *Washington*. Robeson was returning with his family after a long
residence in London, wary of the shadow creeping over Europe after Hitler's
September 1 invasion of Poland. His arrival occasioned a strange mixture of
artistic embrace and political controversy.

Robeson, though he enjoyed international renown as a celebrated black
singer and actor, persistently played havoc with his career by freely sounding
off on controversial issues. From his position as a member of an oppressed
race, he seized every opportunity to make political and moral statements.

Between 1934 and 1937, Robeson made four visits to the Soviet Union,
and his experiences were transforming. In contrast to America, which he cas-
tigated for its unstable economy, bitter racism, and lynchings, Robeson saw
the Russian Communist system as one of social equality that supported the
worker. Knowing the famous performer's leanings, Stalin saw in Robeson a
prime Western recruit for the cause. The Russians, inventors of the original
Potemkin Village, were ready with every shining facade to charm their guest
and happily reinforce his impressions. Robeson was fluent in Russian (he also
spoke Chinese, German, and Spanish), and he found himself warmly accepted into the highest artistic and political echelons. On his first visit, in 1934, he
was put up at the National Hotel near Red Square in a lavish suite with a
marble bath and a grand piano. Nights were filled with the theater and the
opera, gala banquets, parties, and receptions. He became an intimate of Ser-

gei Eisenstein, who arranged private screenings of his films and feted the American at a rowdy midnight celebration in Moscow's Dom Kino. The Soviet foreign minister, Maxim Litvinov, hosted Robeson and his wife at a Christmas Eve dinner at his dacha outside Moscow—a large white-columned house surrounded by a sprawling pine forest. At the multicourse feast, topped off with chocolate ice cream, Mikhail Tukhachevsky and Sergei Eisenstein reveled with the Robesons late into the night, dancing, clowning, and listening to Paul perform a set of songs.

On a later trip to the Soviet Union, as Shostakovich described, Robeson was obliged his every wish, to a fault:

> The Jewish poet Itsik Fefer was arrested on Stalin's orders. Paul Robeson was in Moscow and in the midst of all the banquets and balls, he remembered that he had a friend called Itsik. Where's Itsik? "You'll have your Itsik," Stalin decided, and pulled his usual base trick.
>
> Itsik Fefer invited Paul Robeson to dine with him in Moscow's most chic restaurant. Robeson arrived and was led to a private chamber in the restaurant, where the table was set with drinks and lavish *zakuski*. Fefer was really sitting at the table, with several unknown men. Fefer was thin and pale and said little. But Robeson ate and drank well and saw his old friend.
>
> After their friendly dinner, the men Robeson didn't know returned Fefer to prison, where he soon died. Robeson went back to America, where he told everyone that the rumors about Fefer's arrest and death were nonsense and slander. He had been drinking with Fefer personally.[1]

More than anything, Robeson was convinced racial prejudice was nonexistent in the Soviet Union. "Here I am not a Negro," he told Eisenstein, "but a human being. . . . Here, for the first time in my life, I walk in full human dignity."[2] Robeson was so enamored of the Russian "experiment" that for nearly two years, during 1937 and 1938, he enrolled his son Pauli in a Soviet model school along with Stalin's daughter and other children of high-ranking officials. Growing rumors about forced labor, farm collectivization, and the purge terror, if they reached his ears at all, became absurd in the face of "proof" to the contrary that he persistently saw before him. "I was aware that there was no starvation here," Robeson declared, "but I was not prepared for the bounding life; the feeling of safety and abundance and freedom that I find here, wherever I turn."[3]

Robeson's support of Soviet society was not unique among American blacks, and it echoed their increasing numbers among the ranks of the CPUSA—6,900 by 1938, according to the Party. Many intellectuals of the Harlem Renaissance indulged in leftist theater and writing projects—Langston Hughes's blues opera *De Organizer* and his play *Don't You Want to Be Free?* were typical. When he resettled in America, Robeson did not shake off his pro-Soviet stance, but the immensity of his personality covered over, for the time being, any doubts his public may have harbored about his political allegiance.

Bob Rockmore, for one, was happy to see his friend return to the States. Their friendship went back some fifteen years to the time Bob's first wife, Bess, introduced them at the Provincetown Playhouse—the venue where Robeson made his professional debut in Eugene O'Neill's *All God's Chillun Got Wings*. When Rockmore was a foreign drama correspondent in London in 1928, the friendship solidified, and in 1931 Bob produced a London revival of O'Neill's *The Hairy Ape* with Robeson in the lead role. From then on, Rockmore assumed a lifelong role as Paul's attorney, confidant, and artistic adviser. Gradually, he also became manager of Robeson's finances and was even privy to several of Paul's trysts. Rockmore was a meticulous steward of his friend's budget, shrewdly investing his earnings and turning a consistent profit.

In the spring and summer of 1940, Robeson began active concertizing in the United States for the first time in many years. There were political appearances, concerts at Chicago's Grant Park (before an assembly of 150,000) and the Hollywood Bowl (a record crowd of 30,000), and a Los Angeles revival of *Showboat*. In the fall he embarked on a major tour. As a unique adjunct to the concerts, Clara Rockmore came along as associate artist.

Clara and Paul were already good acquaintances, but the tour cemented a deeper friendship. She named him "Pavlik," he called her "Clarochka." They were completely natural together. Often they spoke Russian freely, sometimes to the consternation of onlookers puzzled by the sight of a large black man and a tiny white woman rambling along in a foreign tongue. In concert they performed separately, alternating sets, each with a different pianist. Robeson was backed up by his longtime friend and collaborator Larry Brown; Clara was accompanied by Eugene Helmer. The concert drill was always the same: Paul would perform the first and third sets on the program, with Clara sandwiched in between. After intermission, Clara would open the second half and Paul would conclude the concert.

"Carnegie Hall Thronged as the Negro Baritone Gives First Recital Here in 5 Years," the *New York Times* reported as the tour began.[4] Robeson sang his traditional spirituals, including "Deep River," folk songs from England, Russia, and Mexico, a Jewish prayer in Hebrew, an art song of Mussorgsky, and his most popular request, "Ballad for Americans." Clara played the Brahms scherzo in E-flat (the "Sonatensatz") and works by Bach and Ravel. "Her performances were," Noel Strauss wrote in the *New York Times*, "as always, sensitive and musicianly."[5] Twelve days later the group played for an audience of thirty-five hundred at the County Center in White Plains, New York, and in

November they entertained a sold-out house in Town Hall that was bursting over with fifty standees in the balcony and another fifty seated onstage.

In the course of the tour, Robeson grew increasingly close to Clara, confiding insecurities about his lack of formal musical training—she reassuring him that his natural gifts couldn't have been bought for all the study in the world. She remembered a modest, almost self-effacing man who never felt upstaged—he was genuinely happy for her success. "I warmed them up for you," he would always say as she prepared to go on for her first set.[6]

Clara remembered her frustration as they traveled through the South, when she had to use separate "for whites only" doors and lodgings, and she sometimes forgot herself. "I learned bitter, unforgettable lessons," she recalled. "I wasn't sophisticated enough at that time. I was still young enough and Russian enough to be shocked." She recounted an incident with Robeson's accompanist:

> I kissed Larry Brown on the station, 'cause he took care of our luggage, and he would be on the station first if we traveled by train. And, what do *I* know, it's my *friend*, so I kissed him. The first place we came to he put me on the chair—he said, "Now I have to teach you the facts of life." He said, "Do you know what you did? You kissed me on this station." I said, "I don't care what they think," you know, in other words, I felt I'm not going to treat him differently. He said, "*You* don't *care*, but *I* could be lynched." He said, "I have to teach you the facts of life." So strong these things still were in America in the 40s.[7]

A second tour, in the fall of 1941—this time with William Schatzkamer as Clara's accompanist—took them from the Midwest to Ottawa, across Canada to Winnipeg and Vancouver, and south to Washington State, Oregon, San Francisco, and Los Angeles. In December, Clara returned across the continent by rail on the Santa Fe Chief.

In October 1942, Clara, Paul, Larry Brown, and William Schatzkamer made a third tour—the longest to date—lasting six months and stretching across America from New Hampshire to Idaho, and reaching as far north as Montreal. There were some seventy concerts, averaging one every two or three days, climaxing on April 5, 1943, in Mansfield, Ohio. The final concert drew thirteen hundred people who demanded thirteen encores before Robeson could finally leave the stage. Recalling these tours with Robeson, Clara remembered: "I got beautiful recognition, and big audiences which I would have never gotten on my own."[8]

《》

Following Theremin's sudden flight in 1938, Lucie Rosen's first order of business was to review the maintenance instructions he prepared for her and find a surrogate engineer to keep the instruments in working order. In the basement of their townhouse at 33 West Fifty-fourth Street, the Rosens set up a workshop for the January and September theremins. To oversee maintenance, they eventually hired George Gruendel, an electronics technician and non-commissioned officer employed at the Brooklyn Navy Yard during the war. Gruendel moonlighted for the Rosens on evenings and weekends, often lingering in their basement until the wee hours, poring over tubes and condensers to fine-tune exact adjustments. His first task was to iron out the flaws Lucie's son, Walter, had discovered in the circuit diagram of the September theremin. The inventor's original schematic, labeled "A.C. Instrument (metal chassis)," was clearly missing the feedback circuit altogether, and Gruendel augmented the diagram to match the instrument.

As the technician tinkered with the theremins, always reconciling their temperamental circuitry with the ups and downs of weather or electrical conditions, Lucie stood by, wanting to have a hand in the technical process in the same way she did when the inventor lived next door. In 1940, she began an informal diary, setting down the instruments' chronic maladies and the trial and error cures she and Gruendel cooked up for them. The entries left a poignant glimpse into real afternoons—actual minutes of anxiety and resolution frozen in time—the thought processes of a woman grappling to overcome the technology of her era. "The January Theremin suddenly made scratching crackling noises when warmed to play Saturday," she wrote on July 22, 1940.

> We found three defective tubes. . . .
> The fresh tubes much reduced the offending noises, but they remained potential, to be heard again with every left hand movement increasing the volume. This indicated trouble might be in the battery or its contacts . . . from grit for instance in the contacts, or corrosion. We had recently renewed the battery, so we tried polishing the prongs. . . . Professor Theremin advised keeping strips of emery paper for such polishing of corroded surfaces.[9]

As Lucie was recording these troubles, Boyd Zinman finally moved his company out of 37 West. Teletouch Corporation and Teletouch Magic Mirror Corporation were officially dissolved by proclamation on December 15, 1943, but Zinman retained Teletouch Industries as a banner under which he could carry on entirely new forms of business. In July 1940 he relocated to 74 Trinity Place in Manhattan and was engaged in buying and selling tin plate. A letter dated December 23, 1941—just as the war began to envelope America—showed that Teletouch Industries had received a summons and was involved in litigation. An advertising slogan across the bottom of the stationery left a chilling reminder of former glories: "Keep in touch with TELETOUCH."

It was actually serendipitous for Zinman that he unloaded Theremin's assets with Wire Broadcasting when he did: between 1942 and 1943, the Alien

Property Custodian of the U.S. Attorney General's Office seized the signaling apparatus patent—practically the inventor's only remaining item of property the government could claim against his debt with the Internal Revenue Service.

Unwittingly, however, Theremin had left one gift to the American war effort. Decades later, a former employee at a California aircraft assembly plant revealed that two RCA theremins were exploited in a top-secret testing process at her factory. To gauge the precise mounting of wings, and the degree of flex at the joints, the two space-control models were positioned in a jig test mount, allowing engineers to "hear" the adjustments—a system they found to be more accurate than all other methods. The aviation plant workers were apparently unaware that the theremins were designed for any other purpose, least of all music.

≪≫

On the artistic front, Von Grona was struggling, out of his own pocket, to keep the American Negro Ballet going in 1938. But he found he could remain solvent only by offering its corps for stage shows—precisely the stereotypical casting he had hoped to overcome. Lavinia continued with the group—reconstituted now as the Von Grona Swing Ballet—appearing in Lew Leslie's all-black musical revue, *Blackbirds of 1939*, and in an engagement at Harlem's Apollo Theatre. Despite these compromised efforts, Von Grona found himself bankrupt by late '39, and the group disbanded. Luckily, the solid legacy he left his dancers allowed many of them to find work on Broadway.

Lavinia went on to join the American Ballet Theatre for its inaugural season in 1940, dancing a leading role in Agnes DeMille's *Black Ritual*. The same year she joined Katherine Dunham's company, appearing with the group in the Broadway production of *Cabin in the Sky*, to the choreography of George Ballanchine. The show toured to the West Coast, where Lavinia performed with the Dunham troupe in the films *Stormy Weather* and *Carnival of Rhythm*. After five years with Dunham, Lavinia left in 1945 to join a USO show touring Europe—the Noble Sissle revival of *Shuffle Along*, where she danced the role originated by Josephine Baker. "The 1945–46 show traveled to Italy, Germany, Belgium, Austria, and France," she remembered. "I asked everywhere if anyone had any information about Theremin, but I was unsuccessful in locating him. . . . I thought he was dead for many years. It was very hard for me."[10]

≪≫

As Lucie Rosen set to work planning her next series of concerts, she returned to one of her central concerns: her desire for new compositions. By 1940 she had already commissioned a small body of works: a *Nocturne* of Edward B. Mates in 1933; *Illusion*, written by Sandor Harmati the same year; Ricardo Valente's *Complaint*, of 1934; and Jenö Szanto's *Chant du Soir* in 1939—all for theremin and piano—and larger-scale pieces with orchestra: *Mouvements Symphoniques* by Jenö Takács (1938) and Mortimer Browning's *Concerto in F* (1939). To this repertoire she even added her own unaccompanied *Study of Intervals*. "When composers ask me what general instruction is needed to write for the theremin," she explained, "I would say they should think of a song; a song for an archangel's voice, of five octaves, and incredible power and sweetness, that can dive to the rich low tones of a cello, and include the thin high harmonics of the violin; that can be heard in great spaces without effort, through and above a great orchestra, blending with all other instruments and voices."[11] In the works she commissioned, Lucie had her way—they all reflected the "voice" character of the theremin—and, taken together, they formed the earliest small repertoire of original music designed for the instrument.

While Lucie debated over these concerns, her son, Walter, was serving overseas in the war. Because of poor eyesight, he had been rejected from the U.S. armed forces, but, determined to aid the war effort, he had enlisted in the Royal Canadian Air Force, flying out of England as an American national. On August 18, 1944, in a mission over the Kiel Canal in northern Germany, the landing gear of his plane was shot off by German antiaircraft fire. On an attempted crash landing in Harrogate, in Yorkshire, England, his plane was destroyed. Walter and his crew were all buried at the RCAF cemetery in Harrogate. The family was shattered, and Walter Rosen was never the same.

Lucie continued on, retreating to the private world of her theremins. That fall she reported on a failed concert in Massachusetts in her diary:

> Experience at Paine Hall, Cambridge, and line of inquiry to follow, November 22, 1944.
> Packed instrument in perfect playing condition and travelled the 21st, carrying tubes by hand, others packed in paper and cotton in special drawer of trunk. At once on setting it up when allowed in the Hall, a distorted alteration and weakening of sound was noticeable. We checked again on the light current, it was a true 118 volts A.C. and we were assured we had 60 cycles. . . .
> We went on testing connections and tubes, and changed three of these . . . but it made no difference. . . .
> I was now convinced the instrument was broken, and prepared to talk to the audience that I could not play to.
> When returned to New York the next day, I was taken at once to hear the theremin in my music room. It was playing as loudly and as happily as if it had never heard of Paine Hall. We were mystified. We called in Gruendel. . . .
> He says, we should find out if there is in the building or near it any high-frequency electrical apparatus such as radio or "radar" equipment, or a transmitter, operating around 200–500 kilocycles, and *exactly what* frequency: if

we know this, it may be stopped for the concert, or we may be able to screen it with the help of the technical department.[12]

Lucie was forever wrestling with variable conditions when she traveled. If ac current was unavailable, the theremin wouldn't operate at all. But she was undaunted. In March of '44 she returned to Town Hall with Frank Chatterton—her longtime accompanist—in a recital that included the world premiere of John Haussermann's *Serenade for Theremin and Piano*. In November of the following year, in what was becoming a tradition of annual Town Hall concerts, she premiered Isidor Achron's *Improvisation* and Bohuslav Martinu's *Phantasy for Theremin, Oboe, Piano and String Quartet*, both written for her. In the Martinu, Carlos Salzedo, who helped arrange the commission, played the piano in an ensemble that included the Koutzen Quartet and Robert Bloom on oboe.

Clara Rockmore also welcomed the idea of new works for the theremin— "I want to encourage composers to write for it,"[13] she told a reporter in 1945— but she was much more cautious than Lucie. Occasionally she played pieces in the romantic idiom by living composers like Erich Korngold, Joseph Achron, and Alexandr Grechaninov. But so far her interest in American music extended to the spirituals she had woven accompaniments to under the Hall Johnson Male Sextet at her 1934 debut.

By 1944, Leopold Stokowski thought it was time she had a work tailored to her gifts. The conductor would often drop by her Fifty-seventh Street apartment for a command performance. Pointing to a corner of her living room she recalled, "he would come here and stay on that little couch with his legs sticking out and say 'Play Bach!'" Stokowski had high admiration for Clara—"that girl can make music on a kitchen stove," she remembered him saying.[14]

Thirteen years had passed since the conductor had camouflaged Theremin's instruments within the Philadelphia Orchestra, and the intervening years hadn't seen much progress in the field. In 1939 Stokowski had written to Clara, "The plans for the electric orchestra are going slowly at present because the union have requested me not to make this orchestra, and are not permitting certain instruments to be used as orchestral instruments, which makes it very difficult for me at present."[15] Skirting the union issues, Stokowski decided instead to concentrate on the theremin as a solo instrument. Now he wanted a concerto written for the space-control instrument, designed around its special qualities. In 1944, on Clara's behalf, he commissioned a concerto for theremin and orchestra from the Cypriot-American composer Anis Fuleihan. Composer and soloist conferred closely on technical matters, and Fuleihan produced a full three-movement concerto with fast outer movements.

Clara premiered the concerto with Stokowski and the New York City Symphony on February 26, 1945, at New York's City Center. Wearing a long, sweeping white gown, Clara turned in her usual virtuosic performance. "The best argument for bringing the theremin into the big happy family of music," Louis Biancolli ventured in the *New York World-Telegram*, "was heard at the City Center last night, when Clara Rockmore ran off Anis Fuleihan's specially written concerto. . . . Standing among the high strings, Miss Rockmore coaxed myriad shades of tone from Leon Theremin's wonder-working device. From hushed pianissimi to full fortes, the tone was clear and steady, without any of the stray bleats and wheezes often creeping into the electro-magnetic zone."[16] Harriett Johnson, of the *New York Post,* wrote: "Like most music critics, it has been my fate to hear several concerts by thereminists, but none, in my opinion, has matched the superior quality of Miss Rockmore's performance last night."[17] Louis Biancolli concluded that

> Mr. Fuleihan's Concerto is the solidest score designed so far for theremin solo.
> . . .
> The music makes sound use of the theremin's wide range, which spans four and a half octaves—from low cello C to high F sharp, top note on the oboe. The blending with orchestral colors comes through best in the slow section, drenched in exotic pastoral mood. Mr. Fuleihan's music makes the theremin feel right at home in a busy symphonic huddle.
> Of course, a main factor was Miss Rockmore's playing. The lovely little lady in white always lifted the right note out of the electro-magnetic hideout. Intonation was flawless. . . . Phrasing and line were as expressive as the instrument allowed.[18]

Expressive phrasing and line were always the musical ideal for Lucie Rosen and Clara Rockmore, but thereminists were sometimes reproached for their conservative taste. "Most inventors of electrical instruments," the composer John Cage wrote in his book *Silence,*

> have attempted to imitate eighteenth- and nineteenth-century instruments, just as early automobile designers copied the carriage. . . . When Theremin provided an instrument with genuinely new possibilities, Thereministes did their utmost to make the instrument sound like some old instrument, giving it a sickeningly sweet vibrato, and performing upon it, with difficulty, masterpieces from the past. Although the instrument is capable of a wide variety of sound qualities, obtained by the turning of a dial, Thereministes act as censors, giving the public those sounds they think the public will like. We are shielded from new sound experiences.[19]

For a few composers, the theremin's dreaded portamento was its real freedom. The Australian composer Percy Grainger seized this idea at face value in his *Free Music*. "In this music [Free Music]," he wrote in a letter to Olin Downes in 1942, "a melody is as free to roam thru space as a painter is free to draw & paint free lines, free curves, create free shapes. (Current music is like trying to do a picture of a landscape, a portrait of a person, in small squares—like a mosaic—or in preordained shapes: straight lines or steps.)"[20] In his 1938 article "Free Music," Grainger wrote,

> It seems to me absurd to live in an age of flying and yet not be able to execute tonal glides and curves. . . . If, in the theatre, several actors (on the stage together) had to continually move in a set metrical relation to one another (to be incapable of individualistic, independent movement) we would think it ridiculous; yet this absurd goose-stepping still persists in music. Out in nature we hear all kinds of lovely and touching "free" (non-harmonic) combinations of tones; yet we are unable to take up these beauties and expressiveness into the art of music because of our archaic notions of harmony.[21]

In 1935, Grainger arranged his *Free Music No. 1*, originally written for string quartet, for four theremins. He followed this with *Free Music No. 2*, for six theremins. Using a notation of his own invention in these scores, he indicated the freely moving glissandi of the theremins by continuous lines along the coordinates of a graph, distinguishing each instrument by a different color of ink. What he seemed to be getting at in the end, though, was an automated music of the type Cowell and Schillinger had yearned for. "Too long has music been subject to the limitations of the human hand," he wrote, "and subject to the interfering interpretations of a middle-man: the performer. A composer wants to speak to his public direct. Machines (if properly constructed and properly written for) are capable of niceties of emotional expression impossible to a human performer. That is why I write my Free Music for theremins—the most perfect tonal instrument I know."[22] Ultimately, Grainger envisioned these pieces played on automatic theremins programmed to render the scores in real time, without human operators. In 1937, he and Theremin had postulated the design of such a machine, but the inventor's hasty departure put an end to their plans. Grainger eventually devised, with the help of his wife, Ella, and Burnett Cross, an American physics teacher he met in 1945, a series of mainly electronic machines that gave a fair approximation of his Free Music.[23]

Amusingly, the theremin debate—melodic voice instrument or microtonal sound resource—was easily reconciled among the larger public. Once again it came down to the instrument as simple, quirky entertainment. When average purchasers of RCA instruments threw up their hands after a few months of groping in the ether, they were just as happy to indulge in the common humor. "If your neighbor's radio goes full blast at one A.M.," one writer quipped, "you have only to render a solo on your Theremin, *fortissimo ma espressivo,* and you will put him out of business in short order. Fond mothers will not have to call distractedly up and down the street for little boys that are not where they ought to be. A well chosen note on the Theremin will inform little Johnny, playing ball in the vacant lot four blocks away, that the game has been called."[24]

Parading the theremin as a freak still seemed to be its public fate. The dark role cast for it in *The Green Hornet* radio mystery—the bane of the instrument's existence—would prove to be only a prelude to its lot in subsequent years. In the infancy of sound film, just after its first gurgles and cries in the late '20s, Soviet composers began to discover the instrument. For underscoring scenes of mystery, terror, or the macabre, its tremulous, disembodied electronic howl was irresistible. Dmitri Shostakovich gave it a cameo role in his score for the 1931 film *Alone,* and in 1934 the instrument appeared, appropriately enough, in Gavreil Popov's music for the Russian film *Komsomol—The Patron of Electrification.* With Robert E. Dolan's 1944 score for *Lady in the Dark,* the theremin arrived in Hollywood and began to inch closer to the psychological foreground in motion picture soundtracks.

In 1945, Alfred Hitchcock set out his requirements to the composer Miklos Rozsa for the score of his new thriller, *Spellbound:* a grand, sweeping love theme for Ingrid Bergman and Gregory Peck, and a "new sound" to characterize the haunting waves of paranoia that recur throughout the drama. For the "new sound" Rozsa suggested a theremin. He remembered that Hitchcock and David O. Selznick, the producer, hadn't heard of the instrument and "weren't quite sure whether you ate it or took it for headaches," but they agreed to try it out.[25]

The theremin part Rozsa was conceiving for *Spellbound* was of an order of prominence and difficulty that demanded, for the first time in Hollywood, a professional thereminist to interpret it. The solo line often doubled the violin section, and to render that sort of unison precision, someone with an exacting ear and precise theremin hands was needed. Clara Rockmore was approached first but declined the offer. "*Spellbound* happened to be a very charming melody," she recalled. "I wouldn't hesitate to play it today. But today they would know that I played *Schelomo* and Franck and all this. But at that time, to play in a movie—nobody gave it to me to hear first—I thought it again would be this frightening people, ghosts coming. They were using the theremin for effects of scaring people, of this *woo,* voodoo thing. That wasn't my approach, so I thought, let anybody else do *that.* I won't be a party to it."[26] On principle, Clara refused to be involved with Hollywood. "I have a lifelong . . . different approach from using the instrument to shock people," she said. "I've always been very, very against . . . using it as a sound effect. . . . I approached it as a musical instrument, as a musical possibility, a new voice on which to . . . interpret serious music, not frighten people. In the beginning I probably lost all sorts of possibilities of making money, but I never cared about that."[27] When Clara declined, Rozsa phoned the musicians' union in Hollywood. He found there was only one "thereminist" listed who could also read music: a Dr. Samuel Hoffman.

Hoffman had moved his medical practice from New York to Los Angeles in 1941. Still cloaked in the Hal Hope alias after dark, he played a run on theremin and violin at Leone's Restaurant on Sunset Boulevard, accompanied by a pianist. But away from the thriving New York nightclub scene, he planned to retire from the music business and pack away his instruments. As a matter of course, he had registered with the musicians' local, listing himself as a violinist and thereminist. By 1945 he was completely absorbed in his medical career and was surprised to receive a call from Rozsa: "He came out to see me with a sketch of the part he wanted to write and was delighted when he discovered I could sight-read it. So the theremin part went into the *Spellbound* score."[28]

Hoffman dusted off his instrument and joined the studio orchestra to record a complex soundtrack that placed the theremin in the spotlight: each onset of Gregory Peck's psychotic terror was subliminally announced by the instrument's muffled wail. In one scene, the theremin painted a chilling effect when Peck stood over a sleeping Bergman, brandishing a razor blade in his hand.

The *Spellbound* score won an Oscar, and the theremin gained instant status as an emblem for the unbalanced side of the human psyche. One Hollywood observer noted that after *Spellbound,* "Miss Bergman, the theremin and disordered psyches rose together to new heights of popularity. . . . the theremin became Rozsa's hallmark just as the sarong had become Dorothy Lamour's."[29] Whether Hoffman realized it or not, he had also given the general public its first popular dose of electronic music.

Later in 1945, Rozsa was assigned the score of Billy Wilder's *The Lost Weekend.* The landmark picture was the first to look alcoholism squarely in the eye, and the composer again used the theremin to plumb the shadowy recesses of one man's inner terror. In this case, Rozsa's task was to evoke the pathos of Ray Milland's obsessive cravings for the bottle and the delirium and hallucinations of his prolonged stupor. Rozsa remembered that the film originally previewed with what he called "a disastrously inappropriate temporary score. The opening shots of the New York skyline had some jazzy xylophonic Gershwinesque music . . . and when Ray Milland was fishing in the whisky bottle the audience roared with laughter. As soon as they began to realise the film was actually a stark drama about alcoholism, many started to leave. No applause was forthcoming at the end."[30] The studio considered shelving the picture, but Rozsa prevailed with his own ideas. With Wilder's blessings he put a theremin in the new score. "There was a scene where music had to tell you the utter despair of this man," Rozsa explained, "his craving for alcohol, and the utter degradation that he goes to sell, as a writer, his typewriter. . . . Well, in this scene, it was . . . important that you hear the despair, and the despair is only told to you by the sound of music, and the theremin helped me in this case."[31] Thanks to Rozsa's changes, the film evoked just the right psychological aura. Hoffman was called in again to coax Rozsa's morbid, pathological undertones from the theremin. In the intense score, the instrument became, in Rozsa's words, "the official 'voice' of dipsomania."[32]

Not long after *The Lost Weekend* opened, Rozsa got a call from David O. Selznick's secretary asking whether it was true that he had used a theremin in the score. Hitchcock had seen the film and recognized the characteristic sound. "Apparently Selznick considered he had a monopoly on the instrument," Rozsa remembered. "I flew into a rage and told the lady yes, I had used not only the theremin but also the piccolo, the trumpet, the triangle and the violin, goodbye!"[33] Actually, Rozsa wasn't the only film composer using the theremin in 1945. That year, Roy Webb added it to his score for *The Spiral Staircase,* for the director Robert Siodmak.

≪≫

During the war years, as the second wave of theremin activity—Lucie Rosen, Clara Rockmore, and Hollywood—crested over America, one small part of the first wave was quietly ebbing. In late March 1943, Joseph Schillinger lay dying of cancer. On his deathbed, deep in delirium, he was approached by a strange visitor who spoke in Russian. Frantically he told his wife sitting in the room, "Cherbowsky wants me to return to Russia. I don't want to go. I have been happy here in America. . . . I don't want to go back."[34]

"You are having hallucinations," she told him. "No one is here but you and me." Then she embraced him and he went to sleep.

ELEVEN

Mailboxes and the Invisible Man

It is difficult to make plausible the weirdness of the atmosphere in that room, while this strange scene was in progress. The air of Russia is psychically impregnated, anyway, as ours is not. At this particular moment, one was acutely conscious of the unseen presence in the room of a third person: our attentive monitor. It seemed that one could almost hear his breathing. All were aware that a strange and sinister drama was in progress.

—George F. Kennan, U.S. Ambassador to Moscow, 1952

"Be careful, be careful."

Winston Churchill shook an admonishing finger at his ambassador to Moscow. In front of President Roosevelt and Stalin, Archibald Clark-Kerr had just raised his glass to the Soviet secret police chief Lavrenti Beria, the man "who looks after our bodies."[1] But Churchill was not amused and sat out the toast. He cast a wary glance at the callous, beady-eyed Beria, who had come with Stalin to the 1945 Yalta Conference—the summit where the USSR, Britain, and America would orchestrate the destiny of postwar Europe. Kathleen Harriman, daughter of the U.S. ambassador to Moscow, Averell Harriman, found Beria to be "little and fat with thick lenses, which give him a sinister look."[2]

There was something decidedly unsettling, even demonic, in Beria's face that confirmed the darkest rumors about his reputation. Beria's role at the talks was peripheral, but his noxious, devious presence was a symbol to British and American negotiators of a changed era—he personified the belligerence of the new Russian superpower on the world stage and its calculating duplicity at the bargaining table. The cold war had begun, and he was its frontline general.

In 1948, *Time* magazine ran a cover story on Beria, characterizing him as someone for whom it was as "easy to kill on the party's orders as to drink a glass of water."[3] This was not hyperbole. Like Stalin, Beria was a Georgian and began his climb up the political ladder during the revolution by spying and directing the plunder of personal property in the Caucasus. At the age of twenty-two he was butchering anti-Soviet factions with the Cheka, and even before the purge he had the blood of thousands of Georgian nationalists, Mensheviks, innocent peasants, kulaks, and many intellectuals and former noblemen on his hands.

In 1935 he published a book that distorted the history of the revolution, casting Stalin in a leading role. His strategy worked and won him a court position. He became deputy to the NKVD chief Nikolai Yezhov, the dwarflike, depraved terror lord whose shrieking voice drove the purge machine from 1936 to '38. But Beria soon vanquished Yezhov, who was shot in 1940 as a scapegoat for the heavy casualties of the terror. Beria followed up by sending hundreds of Yezhov's officers to the GULAG, where they joined many of their former victims.

Beria was so inured to murder that killing became a ghoulish pastime. Once he invited a delegation of Cheka officials to a lavish banquet where he announced their arrest and had them shot in the cellar the same night. In 1940 he penned a letter to Stalin that resulted in the massacre of over twenty-five thousand Polish prisoners taken after the Nazi-Soviet pact. The same year he sent agents to infiltrate Trotsky's Mexican villa, perpetrating the brutal ax murder of Stalin's old rival.

As police overlord, Beria was fond of conducting personal interrogations and severe tortures in his office, boasting once that he could take an innocent man for one night and "have him confessing he's the King of England."[4] He savored the desperation of his doomed victims with whom he toyed like a cat before their inevitable executions—dispatches he often carried out himself with relish. Beria was a notoriously heavy drinker, and his unchecked sexual debauchery was well known. Young Moscow women were terrified just at the sight of his picture, aware that he prowled Moscow streets in his bulletproof Z.I.S. limousine, instructing his bodyguards to pluck attractive young females from the street—even teenagers, and sometimes children under ten—and deliver them to his house, where he drugged and raped them. The physicist Andrei Sakharov recalled Beria's handshake as "plump, slightly moist, and deathly cold," from which he concluded that he was "face to face with a terrifying human being."[5]

From the top of the NKVD, Beria looked down on a vast personal empire under his command that included the prison system, the GULAG, the police, firefighters, and troops assigned to the railroads, the interior, and the borders. But it was not enough for him. He joined the Politburo, became a deputy chairman of the USSR Council of People's Commissars, and was made a marshal of the Soviet Union in 1945. He wormed his way into Stalin's personal trust, fawning over the leader with flattery and baiting him like a master rumor monger with constant suspicion over the loyalty of his coterie. Stalin relied increasingly on Beria's counsel, and "in the delicate give-and-take of the Stalin-Beria relationship," Martin Ebon observed, "some people wonder when the master became servant and the servant, master."[6]

Beria favored technology—he held a degree in architectural engineering himself—and he encouraged a retreat from the outmoded strategies of the Horse Marshals, a direction in which the country was already moving. In 1942, the Germans were taking city after city in their eastward sweep across the Soviet Union. Stalingrad, because of its name, was an especially coveted prize. On August 23, a Luftwaffe blitzkrieg of six hundred planes killed forty-thousand of the city's residents in one night, and Stalin resolved to turn the tide. In desperation he was forced to give in to modern warfare. His old nemesis Tukhachevsky's "deep operation" theory was taken out of cold storage and put into practice by the Red Army. Five years too late for its author to enjoy his vindication, the theory began to give Russia the upper hand.

For Beria, science had the potential to amplify the might of the Russian bear, and he led an expansive intelligence ring to seize data on foreign atomic bomb research, passing it to Soviet physicists like Ioffe and Kapitsa. Beria also pushed the USSR into the cold-war offensive by spying on foreign consulates. Winston Churchill's instincts at Yalta were right on the mark: at the 1943 Teheran Conference, unbeknownst to him, his conversations with Roosevelt had been taped with bugging devices planted in residential rooms on Beria's orders. Each day, Beria's son Sergo—fluent in English and German—would transcribe the tapes for a report to Stalin. Kathleen Harriman's uneasiness at Yalta also proved frighteningly prophetic: immediately following the February 1945 conference, Beria started targeting her father's headquarters.

Averell Harriman lived with his daughter at the American ambassador's residence in Moscow. Spaso House, named for its location on Spasopeskovskaya Square, was a two-story yellow stucco-and-masonry mansion built by a sugar baron for his mistress in 1914 and seized after the revolution. In 1933, when diplomatic ties were cemented with America, the building was leased to the United States. Harriman set up his office there in 1943, and Kathleen maintained the day-to-day functions of the complex. "We live in a sort of slum area of cobblestoned streets," she wrote in a letter home, "about five minutes by car from the Red Square, Kremlin & two hotels for foreigners. Our garden consists of some leafless shrubs and a couple of dead trees. . . . Walls are white (dirty and plaster in very bad condition). . . . Up a small flight of stairs . . . the Reception Room . . . has huge Doric columns (white stone) and a chandelier to end all chandeliers. . . . Under your feet is . . . a seasick green & yellow & pink & brown carpet. ('Beautiful,' the chargé d'affaires calls it.)"[7]

The residential nature of Spaso House limited access by Soviet technicians and thwarted attempts to install concealed surveillance devices. The house and garden were surrounded on three sides by high brick walls, and an iron fence guarded by plainclothes Russian officers blocked the fourth side. But Beria was determined. An engineer-magician would be required.

In one of his first dragnets in early '39—just after the ouster of Yezhov—Beria had sanctioned the arrest of an engineer, Lev Sergeyevich Termen. Nine months later, the same Termen had been delivered from Kolyma to the sanctuary of the Radio Street design bureau. Beria knew that—after all, the institution of the sharashka was his creation. After Sverdlovsk, Lev Sergeyevich had been reassigned to a sharashka at Kuchino, near Moscow, a facility for radio electronics and measuring devices. There he had designed a "radio beacon whose signals helped locate missing submarines, aircraft, or secret cargo smuggled into the enemy's rear."[8] In the spring of '45, the Spaso House puzzle would be his next assignment.

Beria's demands were intimidating: there could be no wires, no traditional microphones, and the system had to be encased in something that would not call attention to itself. For Lev Sergeyevich, the stakes were higher than ever. Beria was no one to disappoint. He always had his way, and failure for the inventor could mean a return to Kolyma, or worse. But Lev Sergeyevich forged a working system. The only remaining quandary was how to penetrate the ambassador's residence. With his trademark sleight-of-hand, he soon found his answer in the archetype of the Trojan horse.

July 4, 1945. The annual Independence Day reception at Spaso House was the one event of the year when Averell Harriman threw open the doors to his Russian hosts. A delegation of Soviet boy scouts (Pioneers) presented the ambassador with a large wooden wall plaque—the carved relief of the Great Seal of the United States. It was offered as "a gesture of friendship" and a token of fine Russian woodcarving. Harriman thanked the scouts and hung the eagle emblem on the wall over his desk. Lodged inside was the latest incarnation of Lev Sergeyevich's wizardry—a miniature apparatus bearing the hallmarks of his capacitive work from the space-control instrument to the burglar and fire alarm systems.

Set into a long, trenchlike cavity gouged through an inner surface of the hollow plaque was a small metal cylinder, eleven-sixteenths of an inch deep and roughly the diameter of a quarter. Attached to the cylinder was a nine-inch-long protruding antenna tail. The device was passive—it had no batteries or current, and its lifespan was indefinite. Its presence went undetected by the routine X-ray screening of all objects entering Spaso House. The device became active only when an external microwave beam of 330 MHz was directed at its antenna from a neighboring building, causing a metal plate inside the cylinder to resonate as a miniature tuned circuit. The wood just behind the eagle's beak was thin enough to allow sound waves from human speech in the ambassador's office to filter through to a diaphragm that moved in response to the sounds. The pattern of the diaphragm's vibrations caused fluctuations in the capacitance between the diaphragm itself and the plate of the tuned circuit that faced it, causing it to act as a microphone. This produced corresponding modulations that were registered in the antenna— much like a broadcast transmitter—and reflected out to be picked up as words on a remote receiver. Lev Sergeyevich was careful to select a bandwidth he knew was not under the control of American security. With his experience in tuned circuits from his space-control instrument, and devices like the keyboard harmonium, he was the ideal specialist for the job.

Averell Harriman went about his business, ignorant of the new ear on his wall. In the aftermath of the Hiroshima and Nagasaki bombings, Spaso House was churning with activity and speculation in August, hosting a hero's welcome for General Eisenhower, the visit of a dozen American congressmen, and a White House staff member. In October, Harriman received George Andreychin, a Bulgarian expelled from the Communist Party, who was associated with Trotsky and had spent time in Soviet jails. Andreychin explained that Spaso House had been bugged during the earliest American ambassador's tenure there, and he felt it would be risky to discuss sensitive issues openly. In spite of Harriman's assurances that the building had been exhaustively checked for listening devices, Andreychin insisted on speaking in the washroom, veiling his voice with rushing tap water.

Soviet intelligence was cautious, tuning in the eagle only periodically to avoid detection. Nonetheless, it proved invaluable. Vadim Goncharov, who worked with the team that intercepted the eagle's communications in the monitoring post, later revealed, "for a long time, our country was able to get specific and very important information which gave us certain advantages in the prediction and performance of world politics in the difficult period of the cold war."[9]

With the eagle happily performing its clandestine duties undetected, Beria enlisted Lev Sergeyevich for a second eavesdropping operation in 1947. Again, the charge was to achieve wireless surveillance, but this time there could be no detecting device of any sort planted at the target site. The project would be code-named *Buran* ("snowstorm"). Lev Sergeyevich approached this nearly impossible mandate by studying the natural resonators already in the structural components of buildings. Because sound waves created by the human voice cause window panes in a room to vibrate slightly, he reasoned, a method could be developed to detect and read these vibrations from a distance, reinterpreting them into discernible speech patterns. Considering the complex properties of resonating glass, with many harmonics sounding simultaneously, the trick would be to pinpoint a surface spot of least distortion for maximum clarity of the voice signal. By directing an infrared beam at the window glass and focusing it on a zone of optimum resonance, Lev Sergeyevich was able to reflect the ray back to an interferometer and a photo element, accurately detecting conversations in the room. This technology easily resisted interception (a monitoring unit would have to disrupt the light beam itself) or attempts at jamming (optical overpowering of the signal would be required and was unlikely). The low power radiated by the beam also made it hard to detect. The Buran system was reliable at distances up to sixteen hundred feet from the designated window, but it was not effective in rain, fog, or smog. "In a back parallel street I was given a room where I installed the device," Lev Sergeyevich remembered.[10] At the listening post, part of his job was to reduce the noise element of the received signal.

Using Buran, Beria successfully monitored discussions in the business office of the American embassy (the Chancery), located on the north side of Red Square on Mokhovaya Ulitsa, facing Lenin's tomb. The seven-story building was shallow in depth and easily vulnerable to the infrared system. The new surveillance method was nearly impossible to detect and certainly couldn't be disabled by dismantling anything. Delighted, Beria turned it on the British and French embassies in Moscow as well.

Beria, like other intimates of Stalin, began to observe the leader's growing paranoia over the loyalty of his minions, and his ferocious distaste for the idea of a successor—attitudes that spread an ominous undercurrent of suspicion and fear at sessions of the inner circle. Knowing how seriously to weigh the leader's erratic behavior—his quips, sudden rebukes, or his own Socratic method of diabolical leading questions—became a dangerous survival game. "Stalin was a very distrustful man, sickly suspicious," Nikita Khrushchev recalled. "He could look at a man and say: 'Why are your eyes so shifty today,' or 'Why are you turning so much today and avoiding to look me directly in the eyes?' The sickly suspicion created in him a general distrust even toward eminent party workers whom he had known for years. Everywhere and in everything he saw 'enemies,' 'two-facers' and 'spies.'"[11] Trusted members of his coterie were often forced to tolerate the imprisonment or labor camp exile of their wives or close relatives. Molotov, who remained in the highest plateau of power with Beria and Malenkov, looked the other way as his wife went to jail in 1948 in an anti-Semitic campaign. Late-night dinners at Stalin's dacha turned into vulgar revelries where his subordinates were compelled to drink themselves into a stupor and humiliate themselves, sometimes carried off by body guards at dawn. Often they fell prey to Beria's sophomoric pranks—a tomato placed on a chair, or salt poured into a glass of wine—all to impress Stalin and satiate his sadistic humor. None of them knew exactly where he stood with the leader. Khrushchev later remarked that "it all depended on Stalin's fertile imagination, who was an agent of what imperialistic country from one day to the next."[12] "When we were called to his office, we never knew whether we were going to see our families again."[13] Roy Medvedev described a strange episode after a film screening at a Politburo session, when Voroshilov suddenly appeared to be out of favor:

> Apparently, little tables were laid with cold snacks in the small room where the film was being shown, but nobody would sit with Voroshilov. Yet when the lights went up at the end of the film Stalin turned around and, seeing Voroshilov all by himself, suddenly got up, went over to him and laid a hand on his shoulder. Turning to Beria, he said, "Lavrenty, we really should take care of Voroshilov. It's not as though there are many old Bolsheviks like him around. We must look after him." No-one said a word, as the guests were not sure why Stalin had addressed this remark to Beria in particular.[14]

Fearing for his own security in this charged atmosphere, Beria reportedly recruited Lev Sergeyevich again, this time for the risky operation of eavesdropping on the supreme master himself. The inventor recalled that "most interesting was listening to Stalin's apartment. In his desk and in different parts of his apartment, the MGB [1946 successor to the NKVD] installed special microphones. Very often I had to listen to tapes which were recorded with the help of these microphones and then reduce the noise."[15] Treading this precarious line as servant of two masters—trapped in Beria's web of intrigue and stealth, while, like every citizen, bound in an implicit allegiance to the godhead Stalin—Lev Sergeyevich dug himself in more deeply than ever. He was hostage now to this dirty little secret, and to the tenuous confidence of Beria—something that could hold him indentured for years against the threat of exposure. It was particularly ironic on the eve of his scheduled release.

On June 27, 1947, prisoner Lev Sergeyevich's case again came before the Special Board of the MGB. His original sentence under Article 58 had stipulated a term of eight years, "to be counted from March 10, 1939," the date of his arrest. By now, his promised liberation was already three months overdue.

Extract from Protocol No. 25
Special Board of the Ministry of State Security of the SSR
27 June 1947

Heard:
Case of Termen, Lev Sergeyevich, born 1895 [sic] in Leningrad, Russian,

former nobleman with higher education, non-party member, citizen of the USSR.

Arrested by the NKVD of the USSR on March 10, 1939.

Convicted by the Special Board of the NKVD of the USSR on August 15, 1939 for participation in an anti-Soviet organization, in accordance with Article 58-4 of the Criminal Code of the RSFSR for a term of 8 years in an ITL [corrective labor camp].

Resolved:

To free Termen, Lev Sergeyevich from the previous conviction and everything connected with its restrictions.

Chief of the Secretariat of the Special Board, Ivashin[16]

The fact that freedom came three months late was insignificant. What mattered was that it came at all. For 58s, eight years was a lenient term in the first place, and given the valuable scientific commodity Lev Sergeyevich now signified for the Kremlin, his release was all the more remarkable. But in the erratic machinations of Stalin's oligarchy, a prisoner might be dealt any kind of hand. In certain cases, politicals whose work was highly prized by the government even enjoyed a de facto immunity. Tupolev was freed in 1941, long before he had served out his term, and the nuclear physicist Kapitsa persistently sparred with Beria over atom bomb matters but managed to avoid formal arrest.

In Lev Sergeyevich's case, his release was attended by the crowning Soviet honor in his field, the Stalin Prize—a sort of amalgam of the Nobel and Pulitzer Prizes that recognized work in cultural, scientific, and technical areas. Scores of these awards, totaling millions of rubles, were distributed annually for such achievements as producing new types of tea and cognac, constructing Moscow's fourth subway line, and conducting experimental research on cosmic rays in the upper strata of the atmosphere. Kapitsa and Ioffe were previous winners in physics; Tupolev earned a Stalin Prize in 1943 for his Tu-2 dive bomber (Project 103); Prokofiev and Shostakovich were frequent recipients (Shostakovich in 1942 for his nationalistic Seventh Symphony, penned during the siege of Leningrad). Often, of course, the award was a platform for ideological grandstanding. Stalin's protégé Lysenko, the bully of Soviet biology with his bogus claim that acquired characteristics were inheritable, took the prize more than once; Andrei Vyshinsky, the prosecutor who framed and condemned the scapegoats for Kirov's murder, was honored for his *Theory of Court Evidence in Soviet Law;* writers and cinematographers generally won for propaganda pieces that elevated Stalin or portrayed bourgeois Western capitalists as decadent, insidious plotters.

Lev Sergeyevich, in his last days at the sharashka, was nominated by Beria for a 1947 Class II Prize recognizing his work on Buran. But Stalin himself, who always reviewed and approved the list of nominees, crossed out the "II" and wrote in "I," bestowing the highest decoration. The honor was conferred on Lev Sergeyevich as a "secret" Stalin Prize—a category for achievements of a sensitive nature that were not publicly disclosed. The award came with a bonus of 100,000 rubles ($20,000 in 1947) and a two-room furnished apartment in a Moscow MGB housing complex on Leninsky Prospekt. The premium included the services of a maid—an ironic bow to the notion of capitalist perquisites—something usually reserved for high-ranking officials. But this sort of incongruous pat on the head from the same gangsters that nearly finished the inventor off at Kolyma was a dangerously delicious moment to be savored.

Yet it wasn't freedom in the Western sense. Though Lev Sergeyevich was allowed to take up residence in a large city—a liberty denied most ex-politicals—his new address was stamped in his passport and circumscribed his life: his sphere could not extend beyond Moscow. The sweet Leningrad of his youth would be consigned to his memory, along with his sister and other family who still remained in the dark about his fate after 1938. And an extension of the ban on correspondence, imposed when he was a prisoner, sealed him off completely from his former life.

Cut loose in a restricted, lonely world with an uncertain road before him, Lev Sergeyevich faced a confounding void. Spare radio tubes and a useful application for his work were hard to find. Even in prison, time and purpose had been structured. Life outside the sharashka was vexing. "When I was considered to be imprisoned I had a supervisor who would tell me that I had to do this and that," he recalled. "Then, when I was freed, I had to do it myself. Then I had to fuss, do much more paperwork, keep an office in order; the work became much worse."[17] Remembering the tolerable life of his old free worker colleagues at the design bureaus, Lev Sergeyevich did the improbable: he returned to the MGB and asked to be taken back as a free worker.

The first Russian atomic bomb was in development during the late '40s, driven by Beria's Special State Committee on Problem Number One. It was a pet project he nourished with rich intelligence data harvested from his espionage rings in the United States, Germany, and England. The race was on to catch up with the Americans after Hiroshima and Nagasaki, lest Russia's hard-won superpower status slip through its fingers.

Postwar Soviet defense factories and research centers operated behind a tightly controlled veil of security, much like the U.S. Manhattan Project had. These top-secret facilities were housed in remote, unassuming structures with no visible address—distinguished from abandoned buildings only by a mailbox. Lev Sergeyevich was absorbed into one of these "mailboxes" along with the dark pact of confidence its workers were beholden to. Entry into this sequestered realm drew the curtain on any vestiges of free movement left to him in Moscow. The mailbox was a secret society of initiates sharing a burden of information so volatile, each was like an undetonated bomb. Once in, they knew too much; there was no way back out. Ironically, Lev Sergeyevich had forfeited his freedom again, bartered away voluntarily this time for the comfort of a secure life. But patience and equanimity were still alive in him: "Everything was good: I had work, and all the necessary parts for my work, even from America. I was treated very well, although I did not give any bribes and did not fawn on anyone."[18]

Nine years had elapsed since he had seen Lavinia. No letters could be exchanged, and now he asked the authorities about the possibility of her emigration to Moscow. But everything was governed by the internal laws of the mailbox, and the request was denied. His bosses encouraged him to get married again, but only to someone from within the organization—it had to be "one of ours."[19] All ties with his blood relations had been effectively severed, and he would be compelled to forge a new family from scratch within the alien walls of the secret "box." After so many years of enforced celibacy—though he had no official divorce from Lavinia—Lev Sergeyevich elected to get married again. His pool of eligible candidates could have been captured in an office workers' group photograph.

Maria Feodorovna Guschina, at twenty-six, was the youngest and, to Lev Sergeyevich, the most beautiful of his coworkers. Born in Vladimevskoy County, just outside Moscow, in 1921, she was a secretary and high-level typist in the department he headed. Though she didn't share his Leningrad roots, the two formed a genial union. "What was good about her," he observed laconically, "was that her brother had the same relation to music, he played accordion and mouth organ."[20] The two were married, and on June 24, 1948, twins—Helena and Natalia—were born forty minutes apart. The family remained in the two rooms on Leninsky Prospekt, and Maria, who suffered frequently from the effects of rheumatism and a weak heart, left the mailbox to devote full energy to raising the girls.

Any movement Lev Sergeyevich made outside his workplace was shadowed by MGB officers—"gray sport-coat men." Contact with strangers and acquaintances was heavily monitored at every pace, every glance. George Kennan, the American ambassador stationed at Spaso House in 1952, lived under the same enforced segregation from the populace. "I came gradually to think of myself as a species of disembodied spirit," Kennan later recalled, "capable, like the invisible character of the fairy tales, of seeing others and of moving among them but not of being seen, or at least not of being identified by them. Thus, I thought to myself, might life appear to someone from another age, or another planet, permitted to come to this scene and to observe the comings and goings of a life in which he had no part."[21]

On a summer day in 1950, walking along a Moscow street near the Chancery building of the American embassy, the inventor's cousin, Mikhail Fedorovich Nesturkh, passed a man in a neat dress suit flanked by two gray sportcoat men. There was a sudden glint of recognition—it appeared to be Lev Sergeyevich—and Nesturkh made split-second eye contact with him. For his relatives, Lev Sergeyevich had long since vanished into legend. Most imagined he had died as a nameless casualty of the purge. "I met Levushka today when I was walking on Manezhnaya Square," Nesturkh breathlessly told his wife when he returned from work. "That was him, definitely him. I saw in his eyes that he recognized me as well but he didn't show it and passed me by. . . . He wasn't alone. He was accompanied by two civilians."[22]

Lev Sergeyevich reported the incident to the mailbox, apprehensive that his chaperones might have noticed the exchange. Several days later a black car pulled up in front of the Nesturkh house. Lev Sergeyevich stepped out with his sport-coat men and knocked at the door. He and his cousin embraced, but the warm breeze of familiarity was stifled instantly. It was clear this was official business. Under interrogation from the MGB men, Nesturkh negotiated his family out of dreadful repercussions only by agreeing that he had never seen Lev Sergeyevich and that nothing would be leaked to the relatives.

In the first days of March 1953, as the inventor quietly trod the confines of his guarded life, a twenty-nine-year national stranglehold was relaxing: Stalin lay stricken from a brain hemorrhage at his Kuntsevo dacha, near Moscow. Panicked doctors fretted and rushed about, going through futile motions of resuscitation. Cronies of the inner circle ringed the bedside in solemn vigil. Stalin's daughter, Svetlana Alliluyeva, remembered Beria's "nearly obscene" behavior:

> His face, repulsive enough at the best of times, now was twisted by his passions—by ambition, cruelty, cunning and a lust for power and more power still. . . . He went up to the bed and spent a long time gazing into the dying man's face. From time to time my father opened his eyes but was apparently unconscious or in a state of semiconsciousness. Beria stared fixedly at those clouded eyes, anxious even now to convince my father that he was the most loyal and devoted of them all, as he had always tried with every ounce of his strength to appear to be.[23]

Then the dictator's death throes began:

At what seemed like the very last moment he suddenly opened his eyes and cast a glance over everyone in the room. It was a terrible glance, insane or perhaps angry and full of the fear of death and the unfamiliar faces of doctors bent over him. The glance swept over everyone in a second. Then . . . he suddenly lifted his left hand as though he were pointing to something above and bringing down a curse on us all. The gesture was incomprehensible and full of menace, and no one could say to whom or at what it might be directed. The next moment, after a final effort, the spirit wrenched itself free of the flesh.[24]

Beria, dry-eyed, and certain Stalin had drawn his last breath, could hardly contain his smirk any longer. Exuberantly, he dispatched the dead leader's chief bodyguard to fetch his car.

The next day, waves of mourners, eight abreast—still unaware of Stalin's true role in the terror—shuffled underneath the towering banner portrait of the dictator that draped the facade of the Trade Union House. Inside, they filed into the Hall of Columns, its cream and light-olive-green interior infused with blinding floodlights, to inch past the bier of their leader lying in state in his generalissimo's uniform. Under gilt chandeliers, in the great chamber that once hosted the treacherous show trials of the Old Bolsheviks, sweeping mosaic banks of flowers mingled a sweet perfume with the aroma of steaming borscht from the kitchens below. Guards moved tearful, gaping multitudes along to the constant undertone of Chopin's Funeral March, droned by a two-hundred-member military brass band on a platform to the left of the coffin.

During the funeral, trucks of Beria's security men cordoned off streets and commandeered the main arteries of the city. Several hundred mourners were trampled to death under the throngs of the Soviet faithful massing toward Red Square—Stalin's last victims. As the body was positioned for interment at the mausoleum, Molotov intoned a final panegyric: "Stalin's immortal name will live forever in our hearts, in the hearts of the Soviet people and of all progressive mankind. The glory of his great deeds for the welfare and happiness of our people and the working people of the whole world will live through the ages."[25]

The great edifice of Soviet power hung precariously in the balance now as Stalin's heirs vied to take control of a government with no prescribed system of succession. Malenkov and Beria dominated in the first days. Beria advanced sweeping reforms, many involving amnesty for GULAG inmates and Soviet nationals, suggesting he was maneuvering to seize power as champion of a new anti-Stalinist era. Fearing a Beria takeover, Khrushchev solicited the allegiance of military officers antagonistic to the secret police and rallied the support of his Presidium colleagues Molotov, Malenkov, and Bulganin, in a risky plot of entrapment. (Included among his recruits was a new candidate member, the future Soviet leader Leonid Brezhnev.) At a private Presidium meeting on June 26, Khrushchev, backed by the others, charged a stunned Beria with undermining the unity of the Soviet state. Despite efforts to pass pieces of paper scrawled with the word "alarm" to his officers guarding the Kremlin premises outside, Beria was arrested by Khrushchev's security men on the spot and held until after dark. Beria's guards were then switched with officers of the conspiracy, and he was smuggled out to Lefortovo Prison.

Expelled from the Communist Party and removed from his ministerial post by the USSR Supreme Soviet, Beria was prosecuted under Article 58 (paragraphs 8, 11, 13, and the menacing section 1 leveled against Lev Sergeyevich). Along with six "accomplices" he was indicted for treason, terrorism, conspiracy, and counterrevolutionary activities, and accused of using the secret police network to "seize power and liquidate the Soviet worker-peasant system for the purpose of restoring capitalism and the domination of the bourgeoisie."[26] It was a typically Soviet irony, given Beria's overwhelming record of actual crimes against humanity, that his accusers nailed him solely on fictional transgressions. After a closed trial in December 1953, Beria was found guilty and shot within hours of his sentencing on the twenty-third. Some theories maintained, though, that his role in court was played by a double, and that he had already been killed in June, immediately after his arrest at the Presidium session. His wife, Nino, and son, Sergo, were jailed. After their eventual release, they were prohibited from living in Moscow and exiled to Sverdlovsk.

The new Soviet epoch under Khrushchev was a time of seismic shifts in the power equilibrium. Khrushchev's challenge was to preserve the core of Communist ideology that kept the superstructure of the nation glued together, while loosening the vise of Stalinist despotism that had held the country in the grip of terror for three decades. Beria's deposal precipitated a purge of his police empire (arrests or expulsions from office—not the brutal executions of Stalin's era) and a diminishing of its overall power. After Stalin's death, the organ was briefly reconstituted under the MVD (Ministry of Internal Affairs), and in 1954 it became the KGB (Committee for State Security). Through its various names and identities, though, it remained Lev Sergeyevich's employer.

On the last two days of the Twentieth Party Congress—February 24 and 25, 1956—Khrushchev, in a closed session, delivered his historic "secret speech," denouncing Stalin. "It is impermissible and foreign to the spirit of Marxism-Leninism to elevate one person, to transform him into a superman possessing supernatural characteristics akin to those of a god," he bellowed from the podium. "We are concerned with . . . how the cult of the person of Stalin has been gradually growing, the cult which became . . . the source of a whole series of exceedingly serious and grave perversions of party principles, of party democracy, of revolutionary legality." Khrushchev stripped away layer after layer of the Stalin facade, exposing three decades of intransigent brutality, tortures, forced confessions, mass executions, deportations, the liquidation of military and political ranks, crimes against Soviet nationals, Stalin's World War II military blunders that cost hundreds of thousands of lives, his devastation of peasant agriculture, his alienation of foreign powers, his monopoly on all decision making, and his bloated vanity, which, "using all conceivable methods, supported the glorification of his own person." Khrushchev denounced Beria as an "abject provocateur and vile enemy," who had "murdered thousands of Communists and loyal Soviet people," a "rabid enemy of our party," and a "villain" who had "climbed up the Government ladder over an untold number of corpses."[27]

Of course, the same Khrushchev who addressed his delegates with such indignation had, at the previous Party Congress, in 1952, proclaimed, "Long live the wise leader of the party and the people, the inspirer and organizer of all our victories, Comrade Stalin!"[28] Though Khrushchev's courage was laudable in steering the nation away from its dark legacy, when he cast the first stone he not only distracted attention from his own role in earlier atrocities, but he succumbed to the typically Soviet habit of absolving the whole country's culpability for the terror and genocide by defaming a handful of "culprits." This emphasis on individuals was a Stalinist inheritance that was hard to shake off during the cold-war period. Beria's disgrace, in fact, was manifested by the instant removal of his portrait from all public areas and the extraction of his name from organization titles and thoroughfares—every Beria Street was renamed Malenkov Street. Then, to ensure his complete annihilation—to make him a nonperson—the publisher of a Soviet encyclopedia instructed owners of its volumes to tear out the entry on "Beria" and replace it with a page on the "Bering Strait," which had been sent to them in the mail.

This sort of blatant historical revisionism also had its converse in the practice of "rehabilitation." While individuals in bad odor were written out of history, the mechanism for pardon exhumed the reputations of the buried—both living and dead. Rehabilitation restored honor, dignity, and notoriety, and it permitted a person's name to reappear in publications. But the exorcism of the stigma often meant falsifying history, more to absolve the government than to protect the accused. Frequently, the death dates of purge victims were altered to recast them as casualties of the Second World War.

In his "secret speech," Khrushchev revealed that 7,679 persons had been rehabilitated by the Military Collegium of the Supreme Court between 1954 and 1956. Early in 1957, Tukhachevsky was legally rehabilitated and posthumously restored to Party membership. Later the same year, on October 14,

Lev Sergeyevich was "completely rehabilitated by determination of the Moscow military district Military Tribunal."[29] On paper, this was a heartwarming restoration to good odor, but it hardly altered his personal situation. He would still be enjoined from contacting relatives, and the ban on correspondence would be in effect. As long as he worked for a top-secret mailbox, his whereabouts, even his very existence, would be classified information, and his work would remain anonymous. By contrast, just ten days prior to Lev Sergeyevich's rehabilitation, his old sharashka companion Sergei Korolev presided over the much-publicized launch of Sputnik 1, Russia's inaugural venture into space. Korolev's R-7 ICBM, which launched the spacecraft, served as an experimental prototype for an intercontinental ballistic missile, igniting American concern about the new Soviet capability for deploying nuclear warheads.

Whether he was aware of it or not, though, Lev Sergeyevich had already put his own stamp on the cold-war balance of power with nearly equal magnitude. On May 1, 1960, Francis Gary Powers, a CIA pilot on a high-altitude photographic reconnaissance mission, was downed in his U-2 spy plane over Sverdlovsk. Four days later, Khrushchev announced in the Great Kremlin Hall before 1,300 delegates of the Supreme Soviet: "Comrade Deputies! . . . I must report to you on aggressive actions against the Soviet Union in the past few weeks by the United States of America."[30] A flustered U.S. State Department, in response, vacillated and, dissembling, finally came forward with an announcement explaining that the U-2 had been on a weather research mission for NASA over Turkey. "It is entirely possible," the department ventured, "that, having a failure in the oxygen equipment which could result in the pilot losing consciousness, the plane continued on automatic pilot for a considerable distance and accidentally violated Soviet airspace."[31]

Unfortunately for Washington, this statement crossed by minutes with a cable from the American ambassador in Moscow alerting the State Department to a new suspicion—one that would prove devastatingly true. Two days later, on May 7, again before the Supreme Soviet, Khrushchev unveiled the sly trump card he had been holding in reserve: "Comrades, I must let you in on a secret. When I made my report two days ago, I deliberately refrained from mentioning that we have the remnants of the plane—and we also have the pilot, who is quite alive and *kicking!*"[32] In the dense fallout that followed, U.S. admissions of spying in Russian airspace opened a major rift in Soviet-American diplomacy. On the eve of the Paris Summit, where Russian, American, French, and British heads of state were to huddle over critical issues of détente in the cold-war environment, this was an untimely conundrum for the United States. At the summit, President Eisenhower held out against Khrushchev's demands for a formal apology, and the talks fell apart with the huffy departure of the Russian delegation.

Days later, Khrushchev banged his shoe on the table at a United Nations Security Council debate he instigated, insisting the U-2 affair be condemned as outright aggression. But State Department security agents were standing ready with an unexpected display. Cornered into releasing a long-withheld, if embarrassing, trump card of its own, the department "put on display for a group of reporters samples of the many devices used by Soviet agents of the Soviet bloc to listen in on conversations, official or intimate, of foreigners," the *New York Times* reported. "The disclosures of Moscow's espionage techniques were part of the United States Government's effort to back the argument that Soviet indignation over the fact-finding flight of a U-2 plane over the Soviet Union was exaggerated and unjustified."[33]

At the May 26 Security Council debate, Henry Cabot Lodge held up his prize before the delegates: "Now here is the seal. I would like to just show it to the Council. . . . You can see the antenna and the aerial and it was right under the beak of the eagle."[34] The seal, it was disclosed, had rested on the wall of Spaso House over the tenure of four U.S. ambassadors, from Averell Harriman to George F. Kennan, and during U.S. Secretary of State George C. Marshall's visit to the foreign minister's meeting in 1947, when he used the chamber as his bedroom. In 1952 it was finally unmasked.

For seven years, Lev Sergeyevich's bird of prey had gone undetected until a startled British radio operator in Moscow tuned in the sound of Ambassador Kennan dictating letters in Spaso House. Washington hurried two technicians with electronic sweepers to the residence and asked the ambassador to reenact the scenario, again dictating material to his secretary, Dorothy Hessman. Kennan recalled how on that evening in September 1952, he

> proceeded to dictate to her, in the large upstairs living room–study, a body of prose which was intended to sound like a diplomatic dispatch in the making, and must indeed have sounded that way for all but a historically schooled ear, because it was drawn word for word from just such a dispatch sent from Moscow in earlier years and now included in one of the published volumes of American diplomatic correspondence.
>
> This worked. And what followed was an eerie experience. The family, for some reason, was away that evening—my wife was, in any case. I have the impression that the great building was again substantially empty, except for the technicians, Miss Hessman, and myself. I droned on with the dictation, the technicians circulated around through other parts of the building. Suddenly, one of them appeared in the doorway of the study and implored me, by signs and whispers, to "keep on, keep on." He then disappeared again, but soon returned, accompanied by his colleague, and began to move about the room in which we were working. Centering his attention finally on a corner of the room where there was a radio set on a table, just below a round wooden Great Seal of the United States that hung on the wall, he removed the seal, took up a mason's hammer, and began, to my bewilderment and consternation, to hack

to pieces the brick wall where the seal had been. When this failed to satisfy him, he turned these destructive attentions on the seal itself.

I, continuing to mumble my dispatch, remained a fascinated but passive spectator of this extraordinary procedure. In a few moments, however, all was over. Quivering with excitement, the technician extracted from the shattered depths of the seal a small device, not much larger than a pencil, which, he assured me, housed both a receiving and a sending set, capable of being activated by some sort of electronic ray from outside the building. When activated, as it was on that evening, it picked up any sounds in the room and relayed them to an outside monitor, who presumably had his stance in one of the surrounding buildings.

It is difficult to make plausible the weirdness of the atmosphere in that room, while this strange scene was in progress. The air of Russia is psychically impregnated, anyway, as ours is not. At this particular moment, one was acutely conscious of the unseen presence in the room of a third person: our attentive monitor. It seemed that one could almost hear his breathing. All were aware that a strange and sinister drama was in progress.[35]

Later, Kennan recalled with amusement how he had sat many evenings alone in Spaso House, reading out loud in Russian to keep up his fluency using Voice of America radio scripts:

On several occasions . . . I took the foreign-political commentaries from these scripts, vigorous and eloquent polemics against Soviet policies, and read them aloud to myself precisely in that upstairs study where the listening device was placed. I have often wondered what was the effect on my unseen monitors, and on those who read their tapes, when they heard these perfectly phrased anti-Soviet diatribes issuing in purest Russian from what was unquestionably my mouth, in my own study, in the depths of the night. Who, I wonder, did they think was with me? Or did they conclude I was trying to make fun of them?[36]

The morning after the discovery, Kennan recalled that

the atmosphere of Spaso House was heavy with tension. I had thought it best to close and lock, temporarily, the room where the device had been found. The Soviet servants, their highly trained antennae positively humming with vibrations, sensed serious trouble, and cast terrified glances in the direction of the locked door, as they passed along the corridor, as though they suspected the place to contain a murdered corpse. The faces of the guards at the gate were frozen into a new grimness. So dense was the atmosphere of anger and hostility that one could have cut it with a knife.[37]

The Great Seal bug turned out to be a source of consternation to the CIA, which had never encountered a technology like it before and struggled in vain to figure out how it operated. "The thought of the Soviets eavesdropping on the US Ambassador was serious," H. Keith Melton wrote, but an examination of the device was even more alarming. CIA Technical Services Staff (TSS) experts were studying the first "passive cavity transmitter" to be discovered by Western intelligence services. . . . It . . . elevated the science of audio monitoring to a level previously thought to be impossible. This sophisticated and complex technology overshadowed CIA capabilities in audio monitoring that relied upon commercial law enforcement equipment and antiquated World War II telephone company listening devices.

For the United States to prevail in a "cold war" with the Soviets, improvements in clandestine technology would have to be forthcoming.[38]

Ambassador Kennan also concluded, "It represented, for that day, a fantastically advanced bit of applied electronics. I have the impression that with its discovery the whole art of intergovernmental eavesdropping was raised to a new technological level."[39]

After repeated efforts to bench test the eagle, which quickly became known as "the Thing," American technicians were stumped and turned the device over to MI5, the British internal security service. According to Peter Wright, scientific adviser to MI5 at the time—and a future assistant director of the organization—his hunch about the operating principles of the Thing was borne out in tests he performed on it at Great Badow in Essex. Unbeknownst to the CIA, Wright enlisted the Naval Scientific Service of the British Admiralty to finance a specially built research laboratory to replicate the device. Wright claimed that in eighteen months, six navy scientists assigned to the project at the Marconi Company arrived at a prototype copy they code-named SATYR. Wright first demonstrated the new bug for the deputy director-general of MI5, Roger Hollis:

> It comprised a suitcase filled with radio equipment for operating SATYR, and two aerials disguised as ordinary umbrellas which folded out to make a receiver and transmitter dish. We set SATYR up in an MI5 flat on South Audley Street with the umbrellas in Hollis' office. The test worked perfectly. We heard everything from test speech to the turn of the key in the door.
>
> SATYR did indeed prove to be a great success. . . . Throughout the 1950s, until it was superseded by new equipment, SATYR was used . . . as one of the best methods of obtaining covert coverage. But more important to me, the development of SATYR established my credentials as a scientist with MI5. From then on I was consulted on a regular basis about an increasing number of their technical problems.[40]

Concurrent with the SATYR research, the CIA scrambled to copy the Great Seal bug under the code name EASY CHAIR, a project undertaken in a Netherlands laboratory with the top-secret code names MARK 2 and MARK 3. But as late as 1959, when Peter Karlow organized the CIA's Technical Requirements Board, EASY CHAIR remained on the development docket, and apparently no one at the agency was ever privy to the existence of the British SATYR.

《》

When Henry Cabot Lodge finished displaying the innards of the Great Seal to the UN, Soviet Foreign Minister Andrei Gromyko retorted angrily that the CIA must have fabricated the device. But the Soviet motion to condemn the United States for aggression was defeated by a vote of seven to two, with two abstentions. Only Poland backed the USSR.

As the Western world wondered what had ever become of the dapper, mustachioed conjurer of disembodied song, he had just taken his grandest curtain call ever, at the UN. Only this time the magician had outdone himself. He had dematerialized along with his intangible ether waves.

Arrest photos of Lev Sergeyevich Theremin, Butyrka Prison, Moscow, 1939. From *Sovetskyi Faust,* courtesy of Bulat Galeyev.

Poster for 1945 Town Hall recital of Lucie Bigelow Rosen. Lucie Bigelow Rosen Archive, Caramoor Center for Music and the Arts, Katonah, N.Y.

"Lucie Rosen and Her Friends," oil painting on board by Ernst Fischer, 1930s. Caramoor Center for Music and the Arts, Katonah, N.Y. Photo, Harvey Maisel.

Cary Grant, flanked by
Samuel Hoffman (right)
and the producer Vanda,
takes a turn at the theremin during a break from
the Theatre of Romance
radio production "The
Ghost Goes West." *Radio
Life,* April 14, 1946.
Courtesy of Gary Hoff-
man.

Shirley Temple takes a
lesson with Dr. Samuel
Hoffman, probably in the
late 1940s. Photo,
Vilardell. Courtesy of
Gary Hoffman.

— IN PERSON —
THE THEREMIN
Featured in "Music Out of the Moon" and the motion picture "Spellbound"
with DR. SAMUEL HOFFMAN
Foremost Exponent of the Instrument
and HARRY RAVEL
Composer of the Album

Friday, May 23rd
4:30 P.M.

The album will be on sale
at time of appearance for

$3.15

HOWARD'S
CORNER FOURTH & AMERICAN

Newspaper ad for a live appearance of Dr. Samuel Hoffman and the composer Harry Revel (name misspelled), promoting the Capitol Records album *Music Out of the Moon*, 1947.

Samuel Hoffman (right), with Ralph Edwards, coaching a contestant on the NBC radio show *Truth or Consequences,* 1947. Courtesy of Gary Hoffman.

Facing page, bottom: Operational principle behind the Great Seal bug: from left to right, the path of the monitored sound from point of origin to its interception at a remote listening post. Courtesy of thespymuseum.com, and H. Keith Melton, *CIA Special Weapons and Equipment* (New York: Sterling, 1993).

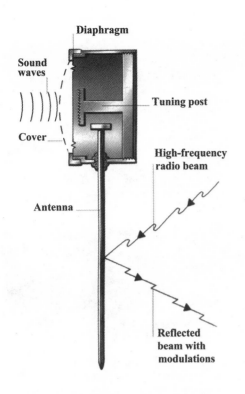

Cutaway view showing the components of the Great Seal's passive cavity transmitter, activated only when an external microwave beam was aimed at its antenna. Courtesy of thespymuseum.com, and H. Keith Melton, *The Ultimate Spy Book* (New York: DK Publishing, 1996).

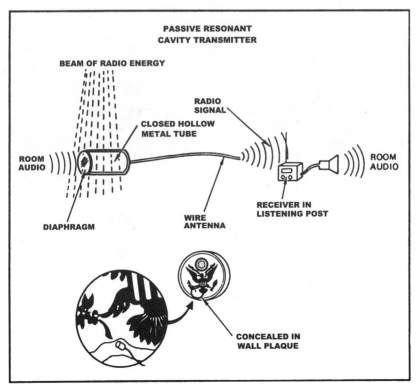

Henry Cabot Lodge, United States Ambassador to the United Nations, unveils Theremin's Great Seal bug before a Security Council meeting at the UN, May 26, 1960. He examines the passive cavity transmitter with its long antenna tail. Corbis/ Bettmann ©.

The Great Seal wall plaque. Left: front view of the carving. Right: cutaway view showing concealed trench containing Theremin's passive resonant cavity transmitter. Courtesy of thespymuseum.com, and H. Keith Melton, *The Ultimate Spy Book* (New York: DK Publishing, 1996).

Cover of a promotional brochure for R. A. Moog Company theremins, 1959. Courtesy of Clare Morgenstern.

Robert Moog playing one of his "Melodia" model transistorized theremins, 1960. Courtesy of Robert Moog.

Paul Tanner with his "electro-theremin," the instrument he used on the Beach Boys' recordings "Good Vibrations" and "I Just Wasn't Made for These Times." Courtesy of Paul Tanner.

Lydia Kavina, age nine, in an early lesson with Lev Theremin, Moscow, 1976. Courtesy of Lydia Kavina.

Lev Theremin playing his own late, handmade model of the "termenvox," Kazan, Russia, 1979. Archive of the "Prometheus" Institute, Kazan. Courtesy of Bulat Galeyev.

Lev Theremin with Bulat Galeyev, Kazan, 1988. Archive of the "Prometheus" Institute, Kazan. Courtesy of Bulat Galeyev.

The "Tonica," a child's theremin, designed by Viacheslav Maximov in St. Petersburg, 1986. Courtesy of Lydia Kavina.

Children at Moscow School no. 1159 in 1997, in a termenvox class taught by Zoya Dugina-Ranevskaya (back row, third from right), a former pupil of Theremin and Kovalsky. The pupil in the foreground plays a "modern termenvox" designed by Lev Korolyov for the Kovalsky school of playing, in which the player is seated and operates the volume with a foot pedal and articulation with left-hand buttons. Courtesy of Ludmila Mikheyeva

The author with Leon Theremin, New York, October 1991. Photo, Linda Kobler.

Youseff Yancy, jazz thereminist, Belgium, 1990s. Photo, N. Huybens. Courtesy of Youseff Yancy.

Facing page, bottom: Lydia Kavina performing at the conference "Electronics, Music, Light"—a commemoration of the hundredth anniversary of Leon Theremin's birth, Kazan, 1996. Archive of the "Prometheus" Institute, Kazan. Courtesy of Bulat Galeyev.

Probably the last photo
ever taken of Lev
Sergeyevich Theremin—
Moscow, September
1993. Courtesy of Lydia
Kavina.

Lev Theremin's grave, Kuncevskoye Cemetery, Moscow. Courtesy of Lydia Kavina.

TWELVE

In the Vanguard: Perfume, Sci-Fi, and Hobbyists

*We literary ones considered ourselves too broad-minded to be bothered
with questions of color. We liked people of any race who smoked inces-
santly, drank liberally, wore complexion and morality as loose garments,
and made fun of anyone who didn't do likewise. We snubbed and high-
hatted any Negro or white luckless enough not to understand Gertrude
Stein, Ulysses, Man Ray, the theremin, Jean Toomer, or George Antheil.*

—Langston Hughes, from *Laughing to Keep from Crying*, 1952

Lavinia had given up all hope of finding Theremin. Back in New York after
her USO tour, she appeared on Broadway in the 1946 revival of *Showboat,*
and in *Finian's Rainbow* and *My Darlin' Aida*. In 1948, she gave in to the affections of Shannon Yarborough, a persistent "stage-door Johnny," as she called
him, and got married, even though her status with the inventor remained in
limbo. By 1950 the couple had two daughters, Sharron and Sara. Lavinia
opened a children's dance studio on Irving Place in Brooklyn and taught nearly
three hundred students at her peak enrollment.

In 1953 she was invited to Haiti to work with members of the National
Folkloric Troupe, and she found the country irresistible. The following year
she packed up and settled there with her daughters, founding the Haitian
Institute of Folklore and Classic Dance. Shannon followed in 1955, after he
had earned a degree in air conditioning and refrigeration, but the already shaky
marriage soon fell apart. After their divorce, he later remarried. Lavinia worked
at the Haitian presidential palace four times a week, giving President Ma-
gloire's children private lessons, and performing for state functions. "We recall . . . the important part which you played in the presentation of those
dances,"[1] U.S. Vice President Richard Nixon wrote to her after a foreign minister's dinner.

It was perhaps better that Lavinia was out of the United States. In cold-
war America, engaged in battling Communists in the Korean War, artists and
intellectuals, academics, liberals, labor union members—anyone with former

ties or sympathies in Communist camps—lived under perpetual threat of "exposure" in Senator Joseph McCarthy's nefarious witch hunts. The furor over former CPUSA members, and fellow travelers, was raging full tilt in a national tempest that had grown out of the Dies hearings a decade earlier. Before it was over, an estimated ten thousand careers were shattered—lives blacklisted and branded with the stigma of "traitor"—locked out of job after job by paranoid employers.

Paul Robeson, who had won a 1952 Stalin Peace Prize—the Soviet counter to the Nobel Peace Prize—was barred from accepting the award in person when the U.S. State Department upheld a ban on his foreign travel and continued to deny him a passport. A Moscow spokesman for the prize hailed Robeson as "the standard-bearer of the oppressed Negro people and all honest Americans struggling against imperialist reactionaries preparing a disastrous war for the Americans."[2] When Robeson finally claimed the 100,000-ruble prize (roughly $25,000)—and its accompanying gold medal bas-relief of Stalin's image—Bob Rockmore was forced into a five-year battle with the Internal Revenue Service to win the money for his client tax-free.

While Theremin, as Beria's lackey, was aiming his ether wave sights on U.S. legations, his musical instrument remained part of the flip side of cold-war life in America—for the segment of American society that could finally enjoy the materialist Shangri-la promised at the 1939 New York World's Fair (dreams held on ice through the war, that now thawed into a warm bath of consumerism and domestic pleasures).

On July 30, 1947, a crowd of forty-five hundred at Manhattan's Lewisohn Stadium heard a theremin there for the first time since the inventor's 1928 appearance, when Clara Rockmore played Fuleihan's *Concerto* with the New York Philharmonic-Symphony, conducted by the film composer Bernard Herrmann. Gerald Warburg played the cello solo in Bloch's *Schelomo* on the same program. Clara was "stunning in a crimson dress" and prompted one critic to remark that "the lady thereminist seemed to be using a deaf-mute signal code as her fingers probed the empty air for the right note."[3] The following January, Clara played the Fuleihan again, with the Philadelphia Orchestra and Alexander Hilsberg, at the Academy of Music.

Lucie Rosen appeared in Town Hall recitals again in 1946 and 1948 and gave new concerts throughout the New York area and the northeast. She played at the Brearley and Horace Mann schools, Philadelphia's Curtis Institute and New York's Mannes School, the New School for Social Research, the National Arts Club and the Eighth Street Theatre, Union College, Harvard, Boston's Jordan Hall, and Washington's National Gallery of Art. She was a soloist with the Starlight Symphony in Scarborough, New York, and with the Buffalo Symphony Orchestra and the Buffalo Philharmonic. She performed benefits for the American Red Cross, the USO, and the National Association for American Composers and Conductors. Often she played in musicales at her New York townhouse and on the music-room stage at Caramoor, accompanied by Walter.

On April 7, 1950, the Rosens left on the *Queen Mary* for what would be Lucie's third and last European tour. The six-week itinerary included London, the Hague, Amsterdam, Zurich, Geneva, Rome, and Vienna. Onboard the ship, the Rosens stowed their Cadillac Minerva limousine, and they had brought along their chauffeur, Joe de Graff, to see them overland from city to city. Joe was a former German pilot who had served in the First World War and had been Lucie's traveling theremin technician and driver since her first road tours in the early '30s. Foreboding signs began to mark the trip when the *Queen Mary* was caught up in a storm, delaying its crossing by twenty-four hours. "Mrs. Rosen is touring Europe on a thereministic crusade," London's *News Chronicle* announced. At a hotel reception, the theremin couldn't be plugged into the mains in time, and Lucie had to speak to the gathering instead: "This model is insured for 2,000 dollars, but if I lost it I should never get another in 100 years."[4]

The performances Lucie turned in on the tour were not up to her old standard, perhaps due to age and waning energy. After the first concert at London's Wigmore Hall, the *Times* likened the theremin sound to "a cow in dyspeptic distress—and that somehow caused laughter in sober Wigmore Hall."[5] "All it offered was an inferior imitation of second-rate strings and a cabaret crooner," the *Musical Opinion* snapped.[6]

Given the progress in electronic music and instruments over the previous twenty years, European critics were less accommodating. While there were respectful bows to Lucie's dedication and skill, reviewers no longer waxed poetic about the untapped potential of the instrument. "Twenty-five years is, perhaps, not a long time to give to the development and perfection of a musical instrument," the once enthusiastic London *Times* estimated. "But it must be confessed that the concert theremin played by Miss Rosen, though claiming improvements in range and tonal variety, is no nearer to music than the model heard at the Savoy Hotel or the instrument which she played at a recital at Aeolian Hall in 1935. Criticism must be bold to say no to it."[7] The *Daily Telegraph* snorted that "Martinu's Phantasy, a well-written piece, showed up the poor theremin's rusticity in the company of such well-bred instruments as string quartet, oboe and piano."[8] One work proved successful. Charles Paul's *Palestinian Song and Hora (Dance)*—written for Lucie—made clever use of rapid, stepwise sixteenth notes that called to mind subtle inflections of Middle Eastern music with small, unavoidable slides between notes. "Microtones are of course not only possible," the London *Times* remarked, "but, alas, all-pervading: they were in place only in this Palestinian Dance."[9]

Critics in other cities were generally as acerbic. "And if the public has already accustomed its ear to the daily threat . . . of an atomic war," Rome's *Il Momento* quipped, "they still have not accustomed themselves to the sound of the Theremin."[10] London's *Musical Opinion* concluded: "we have no hesitation in declaring categorically that unless and until the Theremin is improved and developed out of all recognition it has no future whatever as a concert instrument, though it might conceivably find a haven on the music-hall stage."[11]

The "music-hall stage" in England, in fact, had a proponent of the instrument: J. Forrest Whiteley, who billed himself as "Europe's only Thereminist." Whiteley made the rounds of major theaters—thirty appearances in Albert Hall alone—performing in cabaret and variety shows, and on BBC broadcasts and children's television programs as "television's mystery musician." His solo "act" used the theremin alongside an arsenal of nearly twenty unusual instruments to amuse and educate his audiences about the physics of sound.

Under the heading of "Musaire," Whiteley offered a choice of one-man productions for all occasions: children's parties, resort and hotel shows, school lectures, and functions in private homes. Sometimes he donned costumes to perform "in character" as "McGregor" the Scotsman, or as sundry "authentic dialect characters" of "Irish, Negro, French-Canadian, Jewish, all American and Canadian, many English and Scots" backgrounds.[12] He "modernized" his RCA instrument to seven octaves and concocted a string mechanism for staccato notes and special effects. His instrument was painted a light color and adorned with large musical note decorations and candy cane stripes along the antennas.

On her tour, Lucie carried on a correspondence with Whiteley, trading ideas and experiences. In one letter he related an unusual story: "Yes I could teach it, and have already done so in the case of a young woman who lost her eyesight, her right forearm and most of her left hand, the first day she worked in a Munition Factory. We built a special machine and I trust she still gets some pleasure from it, for of course it is the only thing she could hope to play at all with those handicaps."[13]

Compounding the invective of the press, and other minor annoyances plaguing Lucie's tour, there were anxious moments on the trip from Rome to Vienna. The unwieldy Cadillac was clumsy in negotiating the Brenner Pass through the Alps, especially with Lucie's theremin and its technical paraphernalia lashed to a couple of roof racks, and additional equipment wrapped up and stuffed into the bumpers where Joe stashed it to avoid border duties between countries. On June 1, the trio finally made their way to Cherbourg, where they boarded the *Queen Mary* for New York.

《》

On October 13, 1951, little more than a year after the Rosens' return to the States, Walter was suddenly felled by a serious stroke. For three days he was bedridden at Caramoor, paralyzed on the left side and barely able to communicate with family members standing vigil. On the sixteenth, two weeks shy of his seventy-sixth birthday, he died. Lucie was left to manage affairs at Caramoor and assume the direction of the music series. With less time for playing, public appearances dwindled. Her last concert on the theremin was given for the Music Forum Club of Celina, Ohio, on March 4, 1953, with Alice Sirooni at the piano. Her final selection was the "Swan" of Saint-Saëns.

《》

Samuel Hoffman's star had been rising since 1945. That year he played on Roy Webb's soundtrack for *The Spiral Staircase* and joined a studio recording of the *Spellbound* music for a 78 rpm release. By 1946, *Spellbound* and its soundtrack had reached a virtual cult status, and in April, returning war veterans voted to have Miklos Rozsa appear on "Command Performance" to conduct the score over the Armed Forces Radio Service network. Gloria DeHaven was on hand to emcee the program:

Gloria: Time and again you men have asked to hear the music from the motion picture, "Spellbound." . . . With us here tonight to conduct his own score for "Spellbound," ladies and gentlemen—Dr. Miklos Rozsa . . .
(APPLAUSE)
Rozsa: Thank you very much Miss DeHaven.
Gloria: Dr. Rozsa, there's something I want to ask you about the "Spellbound" music.
Rozsa: What's that?
Gloria: How did you get the eerie effects? The ones that sound like high voices in the ski scene?
Rozsa: That is done by using an unusual instrument called the theremin. I'd like to have you meet the man who plays it, Dr. Samuel Hoffman.
(APPLAUSE)
Gloria: Dr. Hoffman, could you tell us something about the theremin.
Hoffman: Certainly. It is an electrical instrument which has no strings, reeds or percussion. Actually, it's controlled static. I control the static by moving my hands toward or away from the instrument . . . like this. . . .
(DEMONSTRATES)
Gloria: That's very interesting Dr. Hoffman. And now with Dr. Rozsa conducting the orchestra, we shall hear the music from "Spellbound."[14]

This scripted interview-and-performance format was the first of countless celebrity engagements for Hoffman. On this broadcast he shared the stage with stars such as Jim Backus, Sidney Greenstreet, Billie Burke, and Danny Thomas, and several months later he appeared on the same bill with Lana Turner. Now he willingly came out from behind the Hal Hope mask as a single public personality, granting regular interviews to journalists who never tired of hearing about the novelty of his instrument and the strange mix of his two professions. "I am a Dr. Jekyll and Mr. Hyde,"[15] he once quipped to a startled reporter. Virtually overnight he became a Hollywood darling, rubbing shoulders with screen stars and performing at private affairs—Lana Turner's birthday party, Robert Montgomery's anniversary celebration—or coaching such celebrities as Dean Martin on the theremin.

In the wake of *Spellbound,* the recording industry soon seized on the theremin mystique. In 1947, Capitol Records issued *Music Out of the Moon,* a set of three 78 rpm disks (six sides) showcasing Hoffman's theremin in the foreground, in a silky blend with a small orchestra and a vocal choir. The music, by the British-born songwriter and film composer Harry Revel, was arranged and conducted by Leslie Baxter. The six selections on *Music Out of the Moon,* with titles like "Lunar Rhapsody," "Celestial Nocturne," and "Radar Blues," were intended, according to the liner notes, to "play upon the more remote realm of human emotions. . . . It is music that can affect the sensitive mind in a way that is sometimes frightening . . . always fascinating."[16] The racy jacket cover blazoned a scantily clad ingénue sprawled in languorous pose over a spotlighted bed of moon rocks. The recording sold briskly, "breaking all Capitol sales records," according to one society columnist. Reviews were enthusiastic. "Here is an album to be commended," *Variety* wrote,

> a lofty experiment which scores solidly. . . . Revel . . . has really hit here with stunt of using theremin, and could not have made a happier choice than Hoffman, whose memorable work in heightening emotional impact of film "Spellbound" is equaled here. The harmonies are weird and modern and . . . intricate modern rhythms—gamuting rhumba, three-quarters, swing and blues —get excellent interpretation from well-trained choir, which blends beautifully with the theremin's ethereality. The music has character and meaning, and once the public becomes familiar with the unusual mode and structure, it is certain a demand for this fare will sprout. . . . the sex-splashed album cover, probably the lushest art yet adopted by a waxery, will arouse a lot of curiosity as to contents.[17]

Hoffman's career began to accelerate in all directions. "The Theremininduced strains in 'Spellbound' provoked so many goose pimples," a syndicated Hollywood columnist wrote, "that other producers hurried to grab Hoffman and his gadget."[18] *Script* magazine revealed that he was spending "less time on corns and bunions and more time answering calls of movie directors who want him to make with the creeps."[19] "The theremin," *Time* magazine declared, "now is the industry's most fashionable musical device."[20] In 1947 Hoffman played for three film scores, *The Red House, Road to Rio,* and *The Pretender.* He appeared on a spate of radio shows, including *Truth or Consequences, The Charlie McCarthy Show,* and the new *Jack Paar Show,* and made the rounds at B'nai B'rith, Blue Star Mothers of America, and the Marine Corps Reserve. On a project for Columbia Records conducted by Alexander Laszlo, he performed in *The Secret Music of China,* with the theremin again swathed in a celestial veil of orchestra and chorus. For the American postwar palate, the exotic romance of mysterious China, captured in the track titles—"Ghosts of the Great Wall," "Jade Lady," "Lantern Street," "On a Flower Boat," "Cricket Fight," "Rape of Nanking," "Yellow River," and "Pigeon Serenade"[21]—was especially ironic on the eve of Mao Zedong's Communist takeover of the country, and the U.S. refusal to recognize his government.

Hoffman had a knack for capturing the pulse of the nation with his theremin. A decade earlier, when he was fueling the energy on the dance floor of New York's dazzling night spots, his instrument was a swooning melodic balm for Depression times. The theremin voice added a final '30s gloss to the slick dance band arrangements so popular in those innocent moments before the atomic age. In the postwar climate, light, effervescent music with a hint of swing became therapeutic for a population in need of psychological healing, and Hoffman responded by stepping into the new genre of "lounge music" with *Music Out of the Moon.* The following year his second recording venture in this style became the largest commercial exploit with the theremin since RCA mass-produced the instrument twenty years earlier.

The project had its roots back in 1936 when Harry Revel was sitting at the bar of the Hotel George V in Paris, sipping an aperitif. Revel caught a whiff of a captivating scent wafting by on a striking young woman and later remembered, "Her perfume had a dreamy, beautiful fragrance that transposed itself into a melodic theme in my mind." The woman revealed it was Toujours Moi, the famous scent of the French perfumer Corday, and Revel had her pose by the piano for a moment while he extemporized a quick musical sketch. Later that evening he jotted down ideas for a full composition he called *Toujours Moi.* Before he left Paris, Revel spent hours examining essences at the Corday offices and plotting out movements for a suite. When he returned to Hollywood, he found himself "unable to score them in such a way that they would convey the actual ethereal quality of rare perfume," and he put the project on the back burner.[22]

At a party nine years later, Revel again encountered a woman wearing Toujours Moi, and on the same evening he attended a premiere of *Spellbound*. "The sound track used the new Theremin," he recalled, "and the subtle fragrance of Toujours Moi returned. The Theremin was the key."[23] The result was the RCA Victor album *Perfume Set to Music*.

Revel designed the six compositions in the collection as evocative tone poems spun around the Corday fragrances Toujours Moi, Jet, Tzigane, L'Ardente Nuit, Fame, and Possession. Supporting Hoffman's theremin, waltz and beguine beats were scented with an ambrosia of choir, harp, strings, woodwinds, French horn, and the Hammond Novachord—an electronic keyboard instrument. Leslie Baxter again arranged the pieces and conducted the sessions. RCA called the album "the most unusual tie-in promotion in the history of the record industry."[24] Corday sponsored the project and launched a $25,000 national advertising campaign in December 1948 to promote the album with four-color, full-page consumer ads. "Inspired by six of Corday's most famous perfumes," the copy read, "here's an album of unusual, magical music! You hear the strange and hauntingly beautiful tones of the Theremin, with a full orchestra and Chorus."[25]

The three-record 78 rpm set soared to the number one position in *Variety's* chart of best-selling albums for mid-December, topping Bing Crosby's *Merry Christmas Album* and Gene Kelly's *Song and Dance Man*. One week later, *Perfume* had slipped to number seven in the *Billboard* survey but still ran a respectable dead heat with *Christmas Songs by Sinatra*. "The ingredient which makes the difference is the theremin played by Dr. Samuel J. Hoffman," *Variety* wrote. "As a medium to project what Revel seeks to express, the theremin is ideal as well as showmanly; it also is new and exciting enough to captivate quite a few platter purchasers."[26]

In 1948, Hoffman played on the soundtracks of *Corkscrew Alley* and *Let's Live a Little*. By then, he told an interviewer, he had "probably set as many hairs on end on as many heads as just about anybody—outside of Boris Karloff, maybe."[27] On radio he began a regular stint on the *Satan's Waitin'* series.

In 1950, Capitol Records reconvened the Baxter-Revel-Hoffman team for one more excursion into restorative, postwar lounge music. "In everyday life there are times when things seem to go exactly right," the album notes mused. "Our troubled and complex world today offers all too few periods when we can relax in this happy mood. . . . The music in this album is dedicated to such moments. . . . It is written and played . . . with simple relaxed harmonies . . . of a flute in the low register, and themes on the exotic theremin. . . . Turn down the lights, relax in an easy chair and listen. Then, for a few stolen hours, perhaps you will warm to happy memories and blissful hopes: yours, for as long as you may hold it, will be *peace of mind.*"[28] *Music for Peace of Mind* layered the theremin over strings and woodwinds in tunes with titles like "This Room Is My Castle of Quiet" and "My Troubles Fall Away Like Fallen Leaves." In certain passages, Hoffman laid down multiple tracks to create the illusion of a trio of theremins. When the album was released on September 1, 1950, *Variety* named Hoffman "Man of the Week." "This one just can't miss commercially," a reviewer for *Down Beat* wagered.[29]

《》

In postwar life, the theremin popped up occasionally in electronics magazines as a classic circuit formula to be reborn with each hobbyist's variation. In 1949, Ernest J. Schultz described "A Simple Electronic Musical Instrument: The Theremin," in a three-page guide for the builder published in *Radio and Television News.*[30] The article caught the eye of Robert Moog, a fifteen-year-old Flushing, New York, boy. Moog's father was an electrical engineer and an active hobbyist who had shown his son how to read schematic diagrams and solder together circuitry. Since his childhood, Robert regularly constructed simple projects with his father—one- and two-tube radios and a few electronic musical devices. Using Schultz's plan, Moog built the theremin and started experimenting with his own versions of the basic schematic.

In 1951, he displayed his own theremin design (with more "bells and whistles" than Schultz's) before his school assembly at the Bronx High School of Science. Moog's science teacher was duly impressed. Like Theremin, Robert had studied music—piano and theory at the Manhattan School of Music Preparatory Division—a training he coupled with his passion for scientific research. When he entered college in 1952, the theremin remained a preoccupation.

Moog continued to refine his conception of the instrument, and in January 1954, he published his own article in *Radio and Television News* outlining detailed plans for a home-built theremin based on his latest design. "The instrument herein described, in the writer's opinion," he wrote at the end of the article, "is the equal of any in existence, and incorporates added features that make it superior to any that he has seen or heard."[31]

That year, the nineteen-year-old engineering student founded the R. A. Moog Company out of his bedroom and began to sell ready-made theremins based on the schematic in his article. Moog assembled each instrument by hand, one at a time, with the assistance of his father, who also made the cabinets and forged the rose hole design for the built-in speaker using a silkscreen pattern. About ten to fifteen of the units—which he dubbed the model 201—were sold on order.

Moog followed this up with a slick brochure designed by his art teacher at Queens College, promoting a new product line that looked like the work of a serious young company. "All instruments undergo more than forty hours of exhaustive tests and adjustments to achieve uniform and optimum performance," the promotional copy explained. "Because of advanced design, quality control, and thoroughness the musician can own the R. A. Moog Theremin with pride and play it with confidence."[32] For the first time in fifteen years, a preassembled theremin was available for purchase.

Two instruments were advertised in the 1954 brochure: the model 305 and the model 351. Moog called the 305 "the first truly modern adaptation of Leon Theremin's original instrument." Both units were designed as easily portable table-top instruments with a smaller power consumption than a 60 watt light bulb. The 351 had an "overtone selector," and a "synthetic format" that allowed the selection of four different timbres. Both instruments had a range of five octaves. Sales were good, but the company was still really an extension of Moog's hobby—a labor of love—not a business in the strict sense.

«»

In the early '50s, Dr. Ralph Potter, a scientist at Bell Telephone Labs, was adapting another of Theremin's ideas. Potter had been approached by Mary Ellen Bute, who, after two successful decades of making independent non-narrative films, was searching for a new technology. Since the days of her work with Theremin and Schillinger, she had produced thirteen films, collaborated with Leopold Stokowski and Steve Allen, and had enjoyed repeated screenings at Radio City Music Hall. Until 1952, she had relied on traditional animation techniques for her films, hand-coloring thousands of individual frames for a single five-minute short. After twenty years she was discouraged—this method still fell short of her original desire to paint directly with light.

When she met Dr. Potter and described to him the work she had done with Theremin in 1932, he reasoned that the inventor's system was essentially a cathode ray oscilloscope—a device that had since become widely available. With an engineer, Potter designed Bute a modified version of the apparatus to project light patterns in a similar way. Using television principles, any electrical impulse sent through the scope registered on a phosphorescent screen as a beam of light. The advantage was that now, twenty years after her work with Theremin, the newer technology allowed the full, reliable control she wanted. It was possible, using only light, to sketch forms as complex as the animated shapes she had always drawn frame by frame. Bute described the new method—essentially a fulfillment of Theremin's original concept:

The oscilloscope produces a light which you can control by knobs and switches to form lines, shapes, and forms; and it gives you a wonderful sense of three-dimension. This "plain of light," so to speak, can form literally and practically anything on the screen from a waterfall to a dot. . . . When this is completed you take a camera and photograph it as you draw it.

You can also channel music through the oscilloscope and work (draw) right on the oscilloscope with the music on the sound track going through the machine, thus coordinating the two.[33]

Bute also found that the oscilloscope could be set to generate its own patterns in the manner of Schillinger's imaginary "graphomatons" or "luminatons." Her first application of the technology was in the 1952 color short *Abstronic*, described by the *New York Herald Tribune* as "free-wheeling patterns painted on neither canvas nor paper, but on the screen of an oscilloscope. . . . The result—fascinating, complex, rhythmic ribbons of light."[34] The oscilloscope operated only in black and white, so it was still necessary to render color backgrounds for each frame, but the whole system was much more efficient than the hand animation Bute had depended upon before.

≪≫

By 1949, television was a widespread commercial reality, and Sam Hoffman was among the first entertainers to exploit the medium—probably the first to bring a theremin in front of the studio cameras. That year he appeared on Ben Gage's *Rumpus Room* and *Third Dimension Hollywood*. All through the '50s he was a familiar guest on popular syndicated television shows: *Art Linkletter's House Party*, Art Baker's *You Asked for It*, *Truth or Consequences* with Ralph Edwards, *The Colgate Comedy Hour*, *The Steve Allen Show*, Walt Disney's *The Mickey Mouse Club*, *The Loretta Young Show*, and *The Johnny Carson Show*. He recorded background music for *I Love Lucy*, played with Liberace, and, during guest stints on *The Jimmy Durante Show*, clowned in skits with Gloria Swanson and Tallulah Bankhead. On the *Life with Linkletter* show he won a Waste King "Kitchen Pulverator," for "many years of freedom from 'garbage blues.'" Hoffman's singing hands were sought out for commercials—Roma Wine and Alka-Seltzer—and for the theme of *One Step Beyond*.

"I have all the work I can possibly handle and still give proper attention to my patients," he told a *Down Beat* interviewer in 1951. "I get a lot of requests to teach, but just haven't got time."[35] "Dr. Hoffman freely admits he never practices anymore," another reporter divulged, "notwithstanding a number of engagements."[36] Movie work was particularly heavy, and after *The Fountainhead*, *Impact*, and *Devil Weed* in 1949, and *Fancy Pants* and *Let's Dance* in

1950, calls began streaming in for Hoffman's services in a popular new film genre: the science fiction thriller.

By now, the theremin howl was ingrained in the subconscious of the '40s filmgoer as the leitmotif for mental imbalance. In the '50s it emerged as the hallmark of alien space creatures and ghoulish acts. The trend began in 1950 with Ferde Grofé's score for *Rocketship X-M*, where the composer used Hoffman's skills to paint a Martian landscape beheld by a team of space scientists. Bernard Herrmann's classic 1951 score for *The Day the Earth Stood Still* made the theremin's whine and buzz the undertone for the menacing arrival of a flying saucer and its inhabitant droning his strange message: "Klaatu, barada, nikto."

Throughout the '50s, Hoffman was called in to sprinkle his chills in sci-fi pictures: *The Thing, The Five Thousand Fingers of Dr. T, It Came from Outer Space, The Mad Magician, The Day the World Ended*, and *The Spider (Earth vs. the Spider)*. And there was also more-standard fare like *The Ten Commandments*. Movie calls were so regular, Hoffman just "threw his theremin in the back of his Cadillac and went," his son Gary remembered.[37] In *The Delicate Delinquent*, Jerry Lewis's chance encounter and goofy pantomime with an idle theremin in the corner of a laboratory used Hoffman's customized RCA instrument as a prop (with its trademark side handles) and his playing dubbed in on the soundtrack.

By the 1950s, the theremin had settled into the cultural jargon enough to merit its own literary references here and there. Though it was still a curiosity to some, it became an icon of hip esoterica to the initiated. In 1952, in *Laughing to Keep from Crying*, when Langston Hughes spoke disdainfully of the character Caleb Johnson and his ilk for a lack of highbrow savvy—how could Gertrude Stein and the theremin possibly not resonate with them?—the scene was the Harlem Renaissance twenty-five years earlier. "By the end of the 1920's Caleb was just catching up to Dos Passos. He thought H. G. Wells was good."[38] But in 1952, Hughes could be reasonably certain his readers themselves had "caught up" and could appreciate the allusions. No longer the province of Bohemian savants, the names had joined the broader cultural pantheon and Hughes knew his audience could be in on the joke.

Herman Wouk also expected the reader to pick up on the reference when he made the theremin an active prop in his 1955 novel *Marjorie Morningstar*. With no explanation of the phenomenon, the reader's only clue was a passing mention of the poking of hands at the "pole" and the "loop." Even Wouk's characterization of the sound, for full effect, assumed experience with the genuine article: "HEEEEEEE, went the theremin—an unendurable scream, exactly like an ocean liner's whistle, not two feet from Marjorie. She clapped her hands to her ears and ran out of the room, fighting her way through the guests crowding in from the foyer, and stood against the wall near the doorway, panting."[39] For a brief time, the theremin had an invisible cameo role on Broadway in Mary Coyle Chase's 1952 comic fantasy, *Mrs. McThing*, starring Helen Hayes. Mischa Tulin, disguised in a recess behind an orchestra box, played the instrument for the entire run of the show.

≪≫

In 1957, Robert Moog graduated with two bachelor of science degrees: electrical engineering, from Columbia, and physics, from Queens College. In Ithaca, New York, where he began a Ph.D. program in physics at Cornell, he rented a ten-by-eleven-foot furnace room in his landlord's basement to resume construction of theremins. There he developed two new instruments, outlined in a brochure under the rubric of "music's most modern instrument." The "Vanguard" model—a "modern adaptation of Leon Theremin's original design"—included a built-in amplifier and speaker in its wedge-shaped, twenty-inch-high cabinet of hand-rubbed mahogany.[40] Designed to sit on a table, it had a range of three and a half octaves and sold for three hundred dollars. The "Professional" model was completely transistorized and offered a choice of four timbres: principal—"mellow and ethereal, like a flute"; horn—"sharp and nasal"; woodwind—"hollow and woody, like a clarinet"; and string—"rich in overtones."[41] The instrument had a range of four and a half octaves. The Professional sold for six hundred dollars. The catalog also offered custom-made, fully transistorized, battery-operated portables. Moog estimated he sold about fifty instruments in this period, each one constructed completely by hand in his basement workshop, except for the mahogany cases made by a local cabinetmaker.

One of the company's first customers was Arnold Carl Westphal, an itinerant preacher who purchased a Vanguard model. "He and his wife played things like glasses and all these novelty instruments," Moog recalled, "and they went from church to church, putting on services and passing the hat, and the theremin was one thing he played. He played slow melodies, just gliding from one note to the other, without using the volume. That was apparently fine for his audiences, because in addition to using our instruments, he sold a couple dozen Vanguards to other people like him."[42]

In January 1961, Moog published an article in *Electronics World* with a schematic and construction plan for a portable, completely transistorized theremin.[43] At the same time he offered the instrument for sale fully constructed, or in kit form, as the R. A. Moog "Melodia" model. The compact instrument weighed eight pounds and was designed to mount on a microphone stand. The

Melodia was powered by a six-volt battery, had a five-octave range, and was contained in a solid hardwood case with a walnut finish. Kits were fifty dollars, and completely assembled units sold for seventy-five dollars. The instrument was Moog's most popular model, and he eventually sold over one thousand units. The "Troubadour," a high-end version of the Melodia, offered an ac power supply and a continuously adjustable timbre control. Along with the Vanguard and Professional models, which were still being built, these instruments helped sustain Moog's graduate school education.

Soon after he developed the Vanguard, Moog took one of the instruments to Clara Rockmore at her New York apartment on Fifty-seventh Street. To his disappointment, he recalled, the grande dame of the theremin pronounced his instrument "a toy" and encouraged him only by telling him to keep up the good work, and maybe someday he would meet her high standards.

《》

After Walter Rosen's death, Lucie spent the decade of the '50s nurturing what the two of them had started in 1945 as the Westchester Friends of Music, building it into the fully developed Caramoor Festival. In his will, Walter had given Lucie lifetime use of Caramoor and left the entire residuary estate to the Walter and Lucie Rosen Foundation to permanently endow the property for public use as a "cultural, artistic and educational center." Now Lucie was general manager of the festival.

One evening in the late '50s, as Joe chauffeured her home from a visit to Harvard, Lucie was sleeping in the back seat of the Cadillac Minerva. To avoid an erratic driver, Joe swerved, and the limousine plowed into a utility pole. The car sustained minor damage and Joe wasn't seriously hurt, but the impact hurled Lucie out of her slumber and onto the rear floor of the car. At a hospital in Sturbridge, Massachusetts, she was treated for major injuries. After her recovery, the accident left her frail and unable to walk without the assistance of wrist-bracing crutches. In the years that followed, Lucie greeted music festival visitors from a wheelchair at the gates of Caramoor, in her warm and cheerful manner, wrapped in a Venetian doge's cape. On November 27, 1968, the day before Thanksgiving, she died in her sleep from a massive heart attack at her New York residence on Fifty-fourth Street. She was seventy-eight years old.

《》

Samuel Hoffman, in spite of his whirlwind of success with the theremin, would begin to see his musical career overshadowed. During one of his last film jobs, a trombonist in the session orchestra, Paul O. W. Tanner, observed Hoffman's playing. Tanner felt Hoffman was "having a tough time doing his job"[44] and wondered why there was no device such as a "yardstick . . . measured off, like a keyboard," attached to the instrument to gauge the location of given pitches.[45]

As a trombonist, Tanner had performed and recorded with Glenn Miller's second orchestra, and in later years he worked with Les Brown, Tex Beneke, Henry Mancini, Nelson Riddle, Frank Sinatra, Ella Fitzgerald, and Nat King Cole. He came to Los Angeles in 1951, joined the ABC music staff, and worked as a studio regular in the film and television industry. Tanner knew opportunities existed in Hollywood for freelance work on the theremin, but he couldn't imagine himself trying to negotiate the space-control technique.

In 1958 he contracted to create an album in the spirit of Hoffman's collaborations with Revel that would feature a theremin-like instrument of his own construction. With no basic knowledge of engineering, Tanner assembled a rudimentary device in about a week. "I wanted something that would be exact, so that every note would be what you wanted," he recalled, "so I figured out a way to measure a spot, and on that spot I would get such and such a note."[46]

Tanner purchased a variable oscillator, placed it inside a plain wooden box about two feet long, one foot wide, and one foot deep, and attached a length of piano wire to the oscillator as a controller to change the pitch. The wire ran through a hole in the box and out through a small cylindrical tube, where it was attached to a sliding mechanism with a contact switch. The thumb and third finger of the right hand slid the mechanism from left to right, pulling or releasing the wire (much like the ondes martenot), and continuously altering the pitch. The pointer finger in between was left free to touch the contact switch. When the finger touched the contact, a sound resulted. When the finger was released, the sound stopped. Staccato notes were easily performed, and portamentos resulted when the index finger was left on the contact switch as the whole mechanism was slid in one direction. Vibrato was created simply by wiggling the thumb and third finger.

To measure pitch increments, Tanner drew out a keyboard on a strip of cardboard with the "C"s in each octave indicated in red, covered it with celluloid, and placed it beneath the slider mechanism. To tune the instrument, or to transpose a passage to another key, Tanner had only to change the position of the cardboard strip in relation to the slider mechanism. The design provided for three registral ranges, or "sets," as he called them, which could be selected from a switch operated by the left hand. "Set one would go out of hearing range up at the top," he explained—referring to the twenty-thousand-cycle limit—"set three would go out of hearing range down at the bottom, and set two, in the middle, would overlap both of them, so I just stayed in that most of the time."[47] The left hand controlled volume by twisting a simple knob attenuator connected to an external amplifier. Tanner had effectively "solved" the problem of the theremin's inherent pitch glide, but in the process he eliminated the very fascination of the space-control method. Since the instrument was meant only for behind-the-scenes commercial work, though, appearances mattered little to him.

Tanner finished the instrument at 2:00 A.M. one morning and laid down tracks the next day for a complete album of arrangements by Warren Baker—classics such as Glenn Miller's "Moonlight Serenade" and Frankie Carle's "Sunrise Serenade"—accompanied by Andre Montero and his orchestra. The instrument, still nameless, was christened the "electro-theremin" by Cy Schneider, who wrote the liner notes for the album. The recording was issued as an LP in 1958 on the Omega label. The cover art went *Music Out of the Moon* one better, picturing a near-photographic Alberto Vargas illustration of a sensuous nude—with voluptuous curves, red-painted nails, and streaming hair—swimming her way through outer space. *Music for Heavenly Bodies,* according to Schneider's notes, aimed to convey "mood-wise, the awe-inspiring feeling of asteroids and comets. . . . of falling off into the whistling world of infinite space."[48]

Schneider compared the new instrument's sound to "Dr. Hoffman's famous theremin," but he made the point that the electro-theremin produced a pure sine tone with no harmonics, "making it an ideal instrument with which to test your audio equipment." His claim in the liner notes, that the electro-theremin's "advantage over other types of theremins is that it enables musicians to play staccato notes," must have struck a nerve with music business contractors. Word of *Music for Heavenly Bodies* spread quickly, and Tanner began to receive a flood of offers for studio work with the new instrument, cross-fading with the downturn in Hoffman's career. Tanner was so often present for trombone jobs anyway, doubling on the electro-theremin was merely a matter of switching instruments during a session.

Tanner used the electro-theremin for the theme and all the episodes of the popular television sitcom *My Favorite Martian* (1963–66), sounding the trademark accompaniment when the antennas sprouted from Ray Walston's head. Tanner also put the instrument on many soundtracks for *The Lucy Show.* "Anytime she was supposed to be drunk or there was a ghost, or anything like that," he remembered, "they always thought this should be on it."[49] In 1962, Tanner completed a second LP, *Music from Outer Space,* with Frank Comstock and his orchestra, for Warner Brothers records.

《》

After 1960, Sam Hoffman saw his film work, commercial recordings, and major appearances begin to fall off, although he still did occasional studio sessions for the new syndicated television animations *The Flintstones* and *The Jetsons*. By this time, though, his early 78 rpm albums for Capitol and RCA, reissued several times on LP and 45 rpm format in the '50s, continued to sustain his reputation. For over fifteen years he had held the spotlight as the only theremin act on the West Coast, and certainly the only player familiar to the general public. A columnist once predicted that tourists from the east would "feign foot trouble if necessary in order to see Dr. Hoffman and get his autograph."[50] Among other sobriquets, he was once referred to as "Dean of the 'Theremin,' unique radar musical instrument."[51] In a press release for his last major public appearance, he was given the ultimate spurious honor: "Dr. Samuel J. Hoffman, inventor of the Theremin which produces weird outer-space effects used in motion pictures and television, will be spotlighted during the 'Spellbound Concerto' on 'International Hour: Music from Hollywood' *Sunday, May 17* [1964], (9:00 to 10:00 P.M.) on KNXT, Channel 2. Miklos Rozsa . . . conducts the 100-piece Hollywood Bowl Symphony Orchestra."[52] Fittingly, on this broadcast, hosted by Ray Milland, Sam Hoffman's career came full circle, ending with the triumph that launched it.

Despite his successes, and the high profile he brought to the theremin over two decades, the instrument was still a mystery for many. On endless occasions he gave his standard "controlled static" explanation, but there were always some who refused to believe it. In an interview for *Hollywood Citizen News*, he was once asked to refute the theory of a woman—who claimed she was a thereminist—that the instrument was operated "by thought waves to produce melodies which the performer by concentration picks out of the air." His retort: "Tommyrot. Playing the theremin involves no hocus-pocus and no ether waves."[53] Even as late as 1959, after a decade of regular guest spots on television, Hoffman's appearance on a program with George Jessel provoked hundreds of irate callers to light up the network's switchboard, convinced they had witnessed a hoax.

During the last seven years of Sam Hoffman's life, his medical work occupied the better part of his time—some ten to twelve hours a day, five days a week. In December 1967, he died of a heart attack at the age of sixty-three.

≪ ≫

Robert Moog was anticipating his graduation from Cornell in 1963 and examining his future. He was being trained as a physicist and never saw his theremin business as more than an extended hobby to help pay his way through school. Still, there was more he wanted to do in musical electronics, and to get the urge out of his system, he thought, he would take the business one step further. In July 1963, he moved his shop to an abandoned furniture store in an old house in Trumansburg, New York, near Ithaca. His success with the

Melodia Kits prompted him to expand the business to include electronics kits of all kinds.

From Trumansburg he still sold theremins, and for a few years he worked with a sales representative named Walter Sear, who sold the instruments to New York City's music community. In December 1963, Sear rented a booth at the New York State School Music Association meeting to sell tubas he was manufacturing and invited Moog to bring along his theremins. A Hofstra University professor named Herbert Deutsch approached Moog at the booth. Deutsch had recently ordered and built a Melodia kit and was using it for ear-training classes, with good results. He was a composer with a background in jazz and invited Moog to a concert of his music at the studio of the sculptor Jason Seley in January 1964.

Deutsch composed environmental site-specific works to be played in and around Seley's massive constructions made of car bumpers, using live traditional instruments played against a background of pre-recorded electronic music. In one piece, *Contours and Improvisations for Sculptor and Percussionist*, Deutsch asked the percussionist to perform directly on the metal sculpture with an assortment of hammers and sticks, reacting to the taped electronic sounds. "I was very excited about it," Moog recalled. "Herb and I had a correspondence, and I wound up inviting him to come up to Trumansburg. He and I worked together in our little shop for a couple of weeks, and by the end of that we had some of the basic ideas for a synthesizer."[54]

The experiments that spring of 1964 didn't at first strike Moog as anything of great significance. Deutsch simply explained the effects he was after—such as sirenlike continuous pitches—and Moog designed devices to carry them out: voltage-controlled oscillators and amplifiers, a simple voltage-controlled filter, and a rudimentary envelope generator.

The genesis of the envelope generator, in fact, like every other element of the first system, sprang from practical necessity. "The concept of the prototype," Deutsch explained,

> was that there was a keyboard controlling it, and there was no control for articulation as we were working on this prototype. I said, "Somehow we should be able to articulate the attack and decays." And he [Moog] thought about it for awhile, and he literally took out a piece of yellow paper and started scribbling some math on it. And he said, "O.K., do me a favor. Go across the street to the hardware store and pick up a doorbell button." And I went over and I picked up a doorbell button—it cost me 35 cents. I came back and he wired the doorbell button into a little breadboard, and he said, "O.K., now when you play a note, any note that you play on the keyboard, press the button at the same time." And so I would play a note and press the button, and the note would be articulated. He had put two potentiometers there to control the at-

tack time and the decay time. And then within a couple of days he built a second keyboard, and that keyboard had two little switches built in for each note—one switch which was the trigger [for the envelope], and the other switch which was for the regular control voltage for the pitch. And that's where that whole thing came from.[55]

At the Audio Engineering Society convention in the fall of 1964, Moog displayed his prototype model and attracted instant attention. The first order for a system based on this model came from the choreographer Alwin Nikolais. It was, in essence, the first synthesizer Moog sold. In 1965, Moog augmented the original system with new modules. Deutsch now had what he originally set out to find: an instrument that would allow live performance of electronic music on a scale that approached what he could do previously only on pre-recorded tape. Orders for new voltage-controlled modular systems began to come, and with each one, suggestions and demands for specific functions added to the overall number and versatility of the modules. The composer Vladimir Ussachevsky ordered a system of modules that specified a four-stage envelope generator (attack, decay, sustain, and release) that later became standard fare on synthesizers. Bit by bit, specific musicians left their legacy on the evolution of the early Moog modules.

The R. A. Moog Company continued to work from the Trumansburg storefront, but by 1965, the emphasis was on synthesizer manufacture, which showed a growing demand. Interest in the theremin had faded at that point, and the company discontinued production of all its models. The evolution of the modular synthesizer, however, according to Moog, had important precedents in his work with the theremin. The "sound" of the theremin, the knowledge of "what waveforms sounded like what," and the fascination with being able to control something continuously were major influences.[56] The common denominator between the two—at the root of his love for both the theremin and the voltage-controlled synthesizer—was the possibility of stepless distribution of pitch, accomplished on the theremin by continuous motion of the right hand, and on the synthesizer by fluctuations in control voltages. Both systems also represented another of his interests: live performance of electronic music.

By 1965, Moog was completely immersed in synthesizer production, but he still found himself, willy-nilly, involved in occasional projects inspired by the theremin scheme. That year, John Cage approached him about the design of an interactive system for a new collaborative piece with Merce Cunningham. Cage wanted something onstage that could be electronically activated by Cunningham's dancers, causing sounds to be triggered and changed as they moved past it. Cage did not specify a platform, such as the terpsitone, and he wanted something that could be danced around and past, but not *on*. Moog designed twelve individual antennas to be arranged around the periphery of the stage as protruding spears. Unlike the standard theremin, the antennas were not designed to effect pitch changes in circuits per se. Instead, they produced control voltages that were used to change other sounds, via a mixing board they were connected to. In addition to the sounds triggered by the antennas, Cage also used various radios and other noise-making devices of his own creation. In all, the mixer had ninety-six inputs, twelve used for Moog's antennas.

Cage's piece, *Variations V*, was performed at Lincoln Center's Philharmonic Hall in July 1965 as part of the New York Philharmonic's French-American Festival. "If my understanding of John Cage's most recent creation is correct," Allen Hughes wrote in the *New York Times*, "Mr. Cage has discovered a new way for dancers to obtain original music to accompany their works. They can compose it themselves while performing. . . . When Merce Cunningham, or one of the members of his company, danced past a spear, a sound source (or, perhaps, a group of sound sources) began to hum, buzz, beep, scratch, whistle or whir in one of several speakers distributed around Philharmonic Hall."[57] Accompanying this sound environment were various random, distorted film and television clips projected on a huge screen at the back of the stage. At the end of the piece, as Hughes described, Cunningham "put a potted plant in the basket of the bicycle he just happened to have with him and rode merrily through the maze of spears to achieve, I suppose, the kind of bravura closing one usually associates with Rossini scores." Hughes's conclusion about the event bore a striking resemblance to critics' speculations, more than thirty-five years earlier, about the implications of Theremin's work: "Mr. Cage and Mr. Cunningham may have given us a fascinating, if extremely primitive, glimpse into an extraordinary theater of the future. This would be a theater in which dance (possibly drama), music, scenery and, certainly, lighting, could be created simultaneously in the process of performance."[58]

《》

In 1966, Brian Wilson of the Beach Boys contacted Paul Tanner about some projects the group was working on. In a recording studio, Wilson had conceived of an idea for a song based on the notion of "vibrations"—the emotional signals that people and animals communicate to each other telepathically—a phenomenon that had intrigued and frightened him since childhood. Tanner was called in to add tracks on the electro-theremin.

On February 14, Tanner began by adding a track to the song "I Just Wasn't Made for These Times," for the *Pet Sounds* album about to be released. The first session for "Good Vibrations" began at 11:30 P.M. on the seventeenth, at Wilson's Bel Air house. Like most of the follow-up sessions, it ran well into double overtime, through the morning of the next day. Brian Wilson sang Tanner a rough approximation of what he wanted for the theremin part. Tanner, who usually worked from precomposed music, asked if the part could be written out. Wilson explained that the group didn't work that way—they just used their ears—and if he wanted a part he could write it out himself. Tanner scrawled something down and recorded a few takes, but he left with the impression that nothing would come of the session and threw the part out. Later, when Wilson called him, Tanner had to burrow through his garbage to find it.

Tanner found himself caught up in the Beach Boys' prolonged labor of delivering "Good Vibrations." At session after session, musical ideas were changed, thick textures were adjusted and refined using multiple overdubs, and Brian Wilson recorded different parts of the song in four separate studios to capture the distinct trademark sound of each location. After months of polishing the instrumental parts, Mike Love completed the lyrics and Carl Wilson recorded the lead vocal. The final mix was redone four times. Tanner remembered that his part on the completed version of the recording involved not only the familiar high swoops and shakes, but also a low, barely audible section where he played in a register below the other musicians, close to the point where his instrument went "out of hearing range down at the bottom."[59] After seventeen sessions and ninety hours of recording time over a period of six months, the song was completed at a cost of sixteen thousand dollars—a record outlay at the time for a 45 rpm single. The song was released on Capitol in October 1966 and reached number one in Britain by November 17 (remaining for two weeks) and number one on the U.S. charts for the week of December 10. "Good Vibrations" fared well worldwide and became the Beach Boys' only million-selling single.

After the initial success of the song, the Beach Boys asked Tanner to tour with them, but his regular studio commitments and his teaching load at UCLA forced him to decline. "Besides," he told them, "I got the wrong hair, and they said, 'We'll get you a Prince Valiant wig,' but there wasn't any way I could leave town."[60]

Tanner claimed he had no time, or need, to practice the electro-theremin. He remembered one session where he was hired by a studio for a period of two days to master his part—theremins having the reputation of being tricky to play. In fifteen minutes he had learned the music and was free for two days at the studio's expense. In the late '60s, Tanner came to the conclusion that synthesizers could easily create an electro-theremin sound, and he sold his instrument to a Los Angeles hospital as a device to test hearing—a strange echo, forty years later, of the apparatus Dr. Miller had taunted Theremin with before the inventor's Metropolitan Opera debut.

In 1966, when Tanner declined to tour with the Beach Boys, he referred the group to Robert Moog for a theremin. Moog, consumed by synthesizer work, bounced the inquiry to Walter Sear. "The Beach Boys showed up one day," Sear recalled,

> and they wanted to buy a theremin. So I demonstrated it and they tried to play it, and they said, "No, no, this is impossible." I said, "Well a musical instrument does take a few years to learn to play it." They said, "Oh, no, we're guitarists. Can you do anything like a fret board?" And I wrote to Moog . . . and said, "What can we do?" And he came up with what he called the "stringer," which was a resistance strip, you know, just run your finger along the thing. And I remember they came in to buy it, and with a grease pencil I was marking the notes on the stringer.[61]

On the Beach Boys' tours, Mike Love played the device—a ribbon-controlled oscillator—and in the film *The Beach Boys: An American Band* it was seen briefly in a "Good Vibrations" sequence. The stringer became the prototype for what was later a continuous controller on the Moog synthesizer.

In 1967, the R. A. Moog Company incorporated, and in that year the firm first used the word "synthesizer" to describe an "instrument" comprising Moog's modules. Already the name Moog was being associated with the very idea of synthesizers in popular and commercial music applications. Eric Siday, one of Moog's first customers, was pioneering the use of the modular synthesizer in jingles, and Walter Sear was running his own studio where he programmed the instrument for a streak of groundbreaking popular records. By 1969, the Beatles, the Rolling Stones, the Byrds, and the Monkees all owned Moog synthesizers, and the instrument found wide use in studio recordings. One area that remained to be exploited, though—perhaps the most important to Moog himself—was live performance.

In the summer of 1969, the Museum of Modern Art in New York arranged to cap off its Jazz in the Garden series with a program of live music on synthesizers. Moog was asked to furnish an ensemble of real-time modular systems and organize performers who could demonstrate their capabilities in a captivating way. It would be the first time synthesizers were used in public performance on a major scale.

Moog put the finishing touches on the instruments just days before the event, shipping them to a New York hotel the night before, so the musicians could rehearse. The concert, on August 28, marked a historic moment in a summer already distinguished by major events—the first manned moon landing, and the Woodstock Festival only weeks earlier. An audience of thirty-five hundred jammed into the sculpture garden, a space that normally accommodated much leaner crowds. The *New York Times* reported people "sitting, standing, perched on statues and steps, swinging in trees, lying under bushes or doing whatever else they could to obtain a bit of space in the garden."[62] Herb Deutsch remembered that "the concert was relatively under-rehearsed, but the audience didn't really care too much because they were all pretty stoned. There was a good deal of pot wafting around the air that night, and everybody was having a wonderful time."[63]

Two groups performed—one led by Deutsch, the other by the keyboardist Chris Swansen, who had invited the then little-known guitarist John McLaughlin to join him. Deutsch's group opened the evening. Hank Jones played the polyphonic synthesizer, Artie Doolittle supported with the bass synthesizer, and Jim Pirone accompanied on the percussion synthesizer. "Following a few preparatory bleeps, hoots, and grunts," *Audio* magazine commented, "the musicians swung into a pleasantly melodic four-movement suite that seemed strong on treble-bass contrasts. . . . At various times, sounds were reminiscent of trumpet, flute, saxophone, harpsichord, accordion, and several varieties of drum, but, in general, one was content to listen to the music on its own terms, without trying to draw any comparisons with conventional instrumentation."[64]

"After we finished playing," Deutsch remembered,

> Chris's group came on and they had prepared material, and then they realized that without enough rehearsal they would do better just improvising. They went into free-form stuff, which was a good idea, because they got pretty wild, and they were in the middle of a really wild free-form thing, and somebody kicked out the plug which was the main power. So in the middle of this thing—and it was really wild, it had reached a huge climax—suddenly there was dead silence. And of course everybody thought it was the greatest ending that we could have created. So there was this huge screaming applause—it was great. One of the guys who worked for Moog was running around saying, "What shall we do?" And they were all kind of panicked—didn't know what to do. Then somebody finally said, "Forget about it. Just let it go—it's over." And that was the end of the concert.[65]

The great, unplanned final chord, from a pulled plug, that rang out over the neighborhood to signal the end of the concert, reverberated over the sculpture garden wall and onto the adjacent street. Not one hundred yards from the wall stood 37 West Fifty-fourth Street, its dark facade awaiting sale after Lucie Rosen's recent death. Thirty-one years after Theremin had last walked that street, a seminal event of modern electronic music left its audible mark, for a brief moment, in the atmosphere. It was the culmination of the postwar era's response to Leon Theremin.

THIRTEEN

A One-Room Flat and the Microstructure of Time

I heard there was going to be a performance of the theremin instru-
ment. . . . there were only about, probably, forty people in the audi-
ence . . . dark stormy night. . . . a little old man started walking out on
the stage. . . . I assumed that Theremin must have died somewhere in
the '30s or '40s. And as this man began to play, I began to sense that this
must be the inventor, this must be Theremin. . . . he was playing "Mid-
night in Moscow." . . . After the performance there was a reception for
him, but nobody was speaking to him, so I went up and started talking
to him. . . . like a ghost from the past, this man . . . was in fact, the in-
ventor, Lev Termen.

> —Stephen Montague, on his discovery of Theremin at the 1990
> Stockholm Electronic Music Festival

It was May 1962, and Robert and Clara Rockmore were on a Russian vaca-
tion. Bob was determined to acquaint himself, once and for all, with his wife's
roots. In Moscow, they thought about Lev Sergeyevich, but nearly a quarter
century had passed since they or anyone outside the USSR had known for
certain whether he was alive or dead. At a soirée they met a scientist. Quite
offhandedly, almost for the fun of it, Bob queried him: did he know anything
about an inventor by the name of Termen? It was just idle curiosity, for the
Rockmores long assumed Lev Sergeyevich had been swallowed into contemporary mythology like Amelia Earhart—a phantom of history. "I had lunch with
him today," the man retorted casually, and then rushed out. Clara remembered
how she "almost fainted."[1]

She pursued her hostess for details. The woman was circumspect: perhaps
it would be better for Lev Sergeyevich not to meet with foreign visitors. But
this kind of contact, as it turned out, was permissible, provided the inventor
was willing to make application and wait three days for governmental approval.
Clara and Bob, however, were leaving Moscow soon, so their only recourse
was to work through unofficial channels.

The following morning Clara answered her hotel room phone. It was her hostess again. Everything had been arranged, and Lev Sergeyevich would be calling any minute. At the next ring she lifted the receiver: "Clarionic?" It was the same voice, only mellowed now with the craggy overtones of Kolyma frost and years of the well-practiced, hushed inflections of guarded speech. He *had* to see her, he explained, and right away. But the only conceivable way for them to meet, he proposed, was in the rumbling, echoing caverns of the Moscow subway line, where the din and the perpetual tread of anonymous human traffic along the corridors might veil their voices, and paint over any visible sign of emotion. Clara was afraid to go down escalators in New York, she admitted. This was all quite out-of-character for her. She was a "prima donna" who always used taxis and never went near subways, but under the circumstances, she would make an exception.

For Clara it was a strange reunion—sentimental and tender on one level, but necessarily measured and stiff on another. Lev Sergeyevich asked what she would be doing the following evening. She was to attend a theatrical performance she explained nervously, shifty-eyed. It was perfect, he told her. They could meet, but she would have to walk out at the intermission and not go back for the second half of the play. She was being watched as much as he was, he explained. He would be walking back and forth in front of the theater, and she should keep an eye out for him.

The following evening, Lev Sergeyevich spotted Bob and Clara on cue and swept them into a taxi for a surreptitious ride to his place on Leninsky Prospekt. He prompted them to climb the stairs to his apartment. The elevator would be too risky—there were people watching and listening. Helena and Natalia, now almost fourteen, were there to greet the Rockmores in the pair of rooms that also contained two pianos. The girls performed for the guests, and Clara remembered it was a dream come true for Lev Sergeyevich—he hosted her at his apartment. Lost to Clara and Bob, of course, was the irony of the affair: the man who had wired the very air of Moscow had wound up tangled in his own omnipresent net.

The depth of his covert hospitality toward the Rockmores, though, was a sure sign he was still punching a top-secret government time clock—one, in fact, that was right inside KGB headquarters on Dzerzhinsky Square, where he had just been given his own laboratory. "I thought that soon I would start something interesting. Suddenly, for some unknown reason, my task was changed. KGB officials . . . wanted to study some extraordinary phenomena: UFOs, aliens, telepathy, extrasensory perception. They suggested that I work with it. The people in the KGB were for some reason afraid of UFOs. But it was not interesting or serious enough for me."[2] It was the end of the line for him. After seventeen years of mute service to the state, not to mention the forced harnessing of his brain for eight years prior to that, he was ready for assimilation into normal civilian life. By 1964, he had dwelled in the dark regions of government confidence for over forty years, in the long, covert tunnel of the GRU, the OGPU, and the NKVD, and later the MGB, MVD, and the KGB. Now he wanted out.

As the doors of the Committee for State Security closed behind him, he was finally free to seek out his long-lost blood relations. But the reality was sobering. His sister, Helena Sergeyevna Termen Feodorova, who lived her whole life in Leningrad working as a psychologist at a school for deaf-mute children, had died in 1952, still ignorant of his fate. Her husband, Sergei Feodorov, had preceded her in death in 1948, and their children, Boris and Helena, were already grown. Now he could meet openly with Mikhail Nesturkh, the cousin whose dangerous glance pierced his invisible cover in 1950, but the transition into genial society was still awkward and unnatural for him: Nesturkh was startled to see Lev Sergeyevich speaking with the frozen mouth of a ventriloquist—a conditioned defense left over from years of foiling lip readers.

"Retirement" from the KGB meant a pension, but at age sixty-eight Lev Sergeyevich was restless to get back to music, and to his long-dormant independent experiments. The year before, in 1963, he had already begun to peek through the KGB's protective curtain: surfacing briefly under the pseudonym "L. Sergeyev," he had authored his first article in decades—a third-person account of his 1922 meeting with Lenin, "Traits of the Great Man," published in the journal *Radio*.

By 1960 several biographical remnants of his past had begun to appear in articles on the history of electronic music. But these were scattered tributes, not sufficient to reestablish his historical reputation. He emerged from secrecy in 1964 a forgotten man, virtually unknown in his own country. And because he had remained in the service of mailboxes, he had yet to enjoy most of the dispensations granted to revested "enemies of the people." Now he hoped to exploit the benefits of his 1957 pardon—seven years after the fact. But it was not what he was expecting.

His "rehabilitation," it turned out, had been no more than an empty nod to Party process—a mere token of Khrushchev's reforms—not an actual restoration to professional favor. Apparently the covert liaisons of his recent past would prevent him from ever reclaiming the popular ascendancy he achieved in the early '20s. Leaving the KGB was not a simple divorce, or the finality of a gold-watch retirement—it never could be. He had worked on too many top-secret government projects. He would always be a walking file cabinet of

classified state secrets, too sensitive to release into the world under full rehabilitation. "Much of the documentation of his inventions had disappeared or
was being held in secret archives," Nesturkh's daughter Natalia remembered.
"In the 1960s, this man who had been a professor at the Physical-Technical
Institute in Petrograd during the 1920s found himself deprived of all his titles, degrees, certificates and any evidence of his scientific achievements."[3]

Helpless to prove on paper who he was, or even who he had been, Lev
Sergeyevich was compelled to begin all over again, his skills alone forced to
stand for diploma, transcript, and reputation. Added to this was a rigid fact of
Soviet life: without his titles, and retired as a pensioner at his age, he could
no longer hold an appointment as a professor or scientist. The job market was
open to him only as a "proletarian," blue-collar technician.

For a brief period he worked at the USSR Sound Recording Institute, a
studio laboratory that furnished electronically synthesized sound effects for
on-air productions of Radio Moscow. There, he could finally begin to famil-
iarize himself with recent Russian achievements in electronic music—a whole
legacy that had passed him by since 1927. One of his colleagues at the institute, Igor Simonov—whose "noisephone" simulated percussive and everyday
sounds for films and broadcasting—was actually the coauthor of an article in
Radio on the construction of a home-built theremin. But the institute studio
was closed down in 1965, and Lev Sergeyevich moved on to a position in the
acoustics laboratory of Moscow Conservatory.

"It smells of rosin (used for soldering and not for violin bows)," Gleb Anfilov
recalled of the lab. "The technicians are bent over some electrical apparatus
and there is a blackboard covered with formulae."[4] Acoustic research at the
conservatory had nothing to do with the study of electronic music. Experiments
centered around the capture and analysis of sound data provided by students
in order to fine-tune the nuances of their performances. Singers listened to
slowed-down recordings of their voices to dissect their vibrato, or worked with
oscilloscopes to understand the harmonic content of their tone and produce
spectrograms of their voices from a harmonic analyzer.

One of Lev Sergeyevich's workers at the conservatory, Anatoly Kisselev,
remembered how "we students were carried away with his miraculous instruments."[5] But these "instruments," like everything else in the lab, were not for
playing music. They were devices for testing, measuring, and graphing sounds,
tuning musical instruments, and aiding performers in practice techniques. Not
long after the inventor's departure in 1927, Russian electrical music had become a dangerously radical, "bourgeois" notion in official Soviet ideology, and
now his fondest labor of love was something he could carry on only as an av-
ocation. In his years with the KGB he had slapped together a few theremins

to amuse and instruct some guards at the Lubyanka, but beyond that, he found there was no professional outlet for this kind of work.

The low state of electronic and experimental music Lev Sergeyevich found when he reemerged into Soviet life was a symptom of cataclysmic events in the country's recent history. By the '60s, Soviet society was still suffering the aftershocks of Stalin's upheavals, including the subjugation of Russian arts and technology under the same dogmas that had gripped the entire culture with terror.

In Stalin's utopian dream, his empire was an eternal proletarian mecca, beyond the influence of time and changing fashion. To that end, he coopted history, science, and the arts to the service of his own mythology. "In the West," Boris Groys wrote, "the march of progress is 'aimless'—one fashion succeeds another, one technological innovation replaces another, and so on."[6] But for Stalin, "progress" could mean only "an attempt to halt it—as a nationalist reaction to the monotonously unbroken superiority of the West, as an attempt to escape this sphere of domination . . . to flee from time into the apocalyptic realm of timelessness."[7]

In this world that has transcended history, artistic movements would no longer leapfrog for momentary domination, but single idealized styles would reign in a perpetual stasis—perfect archetypes in the highest civilization. "The art of the Stalinist period," Groys observed, "claimed to be building a new and eternal empire beyond human history, an apocalyptic kingdom that would incorporate all the good of the past and reject all the bad."[8] "We Bolsheviks do not reject the cultural heritage," Andrei Zhdanov, Stalin's close political associate, affirmed in a speech. "On the contrary, we are critically assimilating the cultural heritage of all nations and all times in order to choose from it all that can inspire the working people of Soviet society to great exploits in labor, science, and culture."[9]

Just after the revolution, the Russian avant-garde, with its rejection of the past, was a welcome spokesman for the Bolsheviks. But it was Stalin's creation of "socialist realism"—a figurative, representational style of art borrowed from past centuries—which won out as the officially sanctioned mode of expression. Ultimately, the avant-garde in all artistic forms was banished as the stuff of Western bourgeois decadence, stigmatized with the peculiarly Soviet epithet "formalism," a catchall arbitrarily leveled at any work with insufficient "socialist content."

The point of socialist realism was not the representation of reality as an individual artist perceived it, but the projection of an ideal reality—reality as it should be. To be a socialist realist meant "the ability to anticipate the will of Stalin, who is the real creator of reality," Boris Groys wrote, and "to avoid being shot for the political crime of allowing one's personal dream to differ from

Stalin's. . . . socialist realism very quickly succeeded in unifying cultural life by fusing all hearts together with the same love and the same fear of Stalin."[10] Likewise, Stalin exhorted socialist realist authors to "write the truth," which translated as the inner truth of their love for him. Music, as Shostakovich put it, "had to be refined, harmonious, and melodious."[11] Moderate doses of dissonance or experimentation could brand a work as "formalist," threatening its composer with liquidation. Both Prokofiev and Shostakovich were called on the carpet more than once for formalist transgressions.

Stalin and members of his inner circle eventually huddled in a series of conferences, together with a group of writers, to fix the allowable boundaries of the arts. "It is of course irrelevant here to object that Voroshilov or Kaganovich or Stalin himself were not experts on literature or art," Groys argued, "for they were in reality creating the only permitted work of art—socialism. . . . they were as entitled to issue orders on the production of novels and sculptures as they were to direct the smelting of steel or the planting of beets."[12] Ultimately, on April 23, 1932, a Central Committee decree disbanded all artistic groups, replacing them with "creative unions" organized according to discipline—each union head appointed by Stalin. For him, artists were "engineers of human souls," and their works were required to be subconscious reminders to the masses of the socialist vision.

For Lev Sergeyevich, musical experiments with electronics fell outside the sanctioned esthetics of the Soviet doctrine. Music produced by electricity represented needless experimentation in an art that, by decree, had already been officially consummated. Its stylistic ideals had been set and mandated, and no further evolution was called for. Straightforward melodies and harmonies, understandable to the masses and played on traditional instruments, became the lodestar for the official music of the Soviet people. Attempts to expand musical raw materials beyond that implied a rejection of the esthetic ideal and its eternal truth. Worse, it smacked of Western evolutionary "progress," which was anathema in Soviet ideology.

Lev Sergeyevich's musical electronics also ran up against the Party credo from the purely scientific standpoint. The state prescriptions in science and technology, in some ways, were even more daunting than those for the arts. Stalin's mythology had imbued the sciences with supernatural powers. Clearly, in the posthistorical, millennial realm, all things were, and had to be, possible. "Among the characteristic traits of Stalinist literary heroes," Groys wrote,

is their ability to perform obviously superhuman feats, and they derive this capability from their refusal to approach life "formalistically." Thus they can cure tuberculosis by willpower alone, raise tropical plants in the tundra, paralyze their enemies with the power of their gaze, and so on. . . .

The slogan of the age became "Nothing is impossible for a Bolshevik." Any reference to facts, technical realities, or objective limits was treated as "cowardice" and "unbelief" unworthy of a true Stalinist.[13]

Lysenko, by avoiding "formalist genetic methods," claimed that the laws of the plant world could conform to Party directives. His infamous notion that acquired characteristics were inheritable was especially appealing: now the socialist substance of the "new Soviet man" could be passed biologically down through the generations. Everywhere, lone willpower was the directive: among slave laborers competing for overproduction of norms in shock brigades; in Stalin's disastrous order for soldiers to hold out along the Soviet border in 1941; in Beria's impulsive demands to Tupolev for outlandish speed and range on the Project 103 aircraft.

Luckily for Lev Sergeyevich, his Great Seal bugging device and the Buran project seemed like materializations of the miraculous. Remote conversations were intercepted with pure proletarian willpower and, of course, a casual genius for electronic stealth. But his musical instruments were a different story. Traditional instruments were consecrated and symbolized the cream of the past, now frozen in time. Electrical music was of no service to the state. On August 27, 1953, six months after Stalin's death, the government sent out a clear message: the Construction Bureau for Electronic Instruments was suddenly closed down.

Despite this state of affairs, electronic musical instruments occasionally appeared on Soviet stages during the Khrushchev era. In the mid-1950s, Viacheslav Mescherin organized and directed an "Electro-Musical Orchestra" as a resident ensemble of the All-Union Central Soviet Radio and Television. Because the group specialized in folk and popular melodies, Soviet songs, and dance music, it had the government's imprimatur. Clearly it was not an experimental testing ground for new acoustic or esthetic research. The twelve members of the group played electric organs and electronically amplified acoustic instruments: violins, Hawaiian guitars, accordions, and traditional percussion instruments—not "electronic" in the strict sense (with oscillators). The single exception was a space-control theremin played by Konstantin Kovalsky, who had kept the instrument alive in the Soviet Union since the '20s by performing on it as a variety artist.

The Electro-Musical Orchestra had a high profile on radio and television, made records, furnished music for films, and toured widely, even to distant villages. One justification for the ensemble was the notion of introducing listeners to electronic sounds, but this translated as the simple fascination with amplification, and the idea that a small number of these instruments could mimic the power of a much larger group—two violins evoking a whole section of high strings, and so on. The presence of Kovalsky's theremin was a sad irony: thirty years earlier Lev Sergeyevich had charted his hypothetical forty-piece electrical orchestra to replace the symphony, and now, the lone survivor of the scheme, the space-control instrument—in its country of origin—could only sneak in the back door of a folk band.

In 1956, a second all-electrical ensemble similar to Mescherin's was formed in the Soviet army. The repertoire was drawn mainly from popular melodies, and the group included a theremin soloist, Oleg Andreyev, who had constructed the instrument he played on.

With the shift of power in the USSR in 1964, the nation under Leonid Brezhnev saw a degree of backsliding from Khrushchev's reforms, and a reappraisal of Stalin's importance in the latter-day Soviet Union. Needless to say, this was not a positive sign for the arts, and it only reinforced the prevailing paranoia over experimental movements. Electrical music was still tolerated as an occasional curiosity—a 1965 article in *Radio* outlined the schematic for a simple transistorized theremin—but on the whole, research in the field continued underground.

By 1966, Lev Sergeyevich could hold back no more, and he published a thirty-two-page book, *Physics and Musical Art,* as a self-proclaimed musical homecoming. Issued by the Moscow firm Znanie in its series on mathematics, physics, and astronomy, the publication was devoted to "a short analysis of the perspectives, and a prognosis for the future development, of resources for musical art."[14] The slim volume began with a historical review of Russian electronic musical instruments—inventions Lev Sergeyevich had only recently discovered himself since most of them were unveiled while he was in America, or during his years of Soviet hibernation. The survey began with neck rheostat devices like Gurov and Volinkin's "violena" from 1924, N. Ananiev's 1930 variable timbre "sonar," and A. A. Volodin's polyphonic "ekvodin" (winner of a Grand Prix at the 1958 Brussels World's Fair). Electronic keyboard instruments were mentioned: the 1937 "kompanola," the "emiriton" of 1944, and the "krystadine" transistorized electric organ built by Saul Korsunsky at the Sound Recording Institute. Lev Sergeyevich went on to credit Europeans like Mager, Givelet, Martenot, and Friedrich Trautwein—inventor of the Trautonium—and mentioned the American Laurens Hammond. Apparently he was unaware of Moog's work.

After briefing readers on a sampling of his own American achievements, he decried the situation in Russia: "In our country, the use of electromusical instruments is mainly restricted to special effects for movies, and sometimes in variety shows." Mescherin's group, he felt, "did not rise to the scientific or technical level possible in our country, and to the designers' achievements."[15]

He lamented the fact that music schools offered no instruction in electronic instruments, and that few compositions were being written for the medium.

Then, without any details about where and how he had carried out the research, he offered a glimpse of his latest work in musical electronics. In a new space-control theremin, he explained, mere shifts in the performer's glance could trigger changes in its timbre. At a distance of about six to ten feet in front of the performer, lenses arranged across a strip were trained on one of the player's eyes. Behind each lens, a concealed photoelectric cell was attached to its own tone regulator. As the player's eyeball rotated, staring in turn at different lenses, the corresponding photocell behind each one recognized the gaze of the pupil and switched on the associated timbre. Glancing from lens to lens produced a variety of contrasting tone colors, while the hands were free to regulate volume and pitch. The inventor even devised a system to compensate for the swaying of the head: the monitored region of the eyeball was defined by x and y coordinates that met at the corner of the tear duct, following its motions as the head shifted.

Describing another experiment, he wrote: "The sensitivity of modern devices allows for the reception of electrical impulses in the human body, called biopotentials."[16] Using thought processes to generate his body's electrical biopotential, Lev Sergeyevich sought to control volume in a space-control instrument. He worked to focus his thoughts on the idea of increasing loudness. The resulting biological impulses of electricity were to be conducted from a ring on his finger to a power amplifier that would raise the volume of sound in the connected instrument.

He tried every control interface he could think of. "Because the organs which participate in speech and sound making have great mobility in the managing of sound," he observed, "tests were made of different kinds of electric and optical sensors that worked from movements of the lips and tongue, and from whispers and words pronounced by the performer." In the future, he concluded, "those devices will provide very mobile management of important sound parameters."[17]

In 1966, Lev Sergeyevich began to appear at Russian scientific conferences. The year was a turning point in his musical repatriation, and it saw a renewed appreciation for his historical contribution. In an English-language edition of Gleb Anfilov's book *Physics and Music,* ten pages were devoted to the first modern chronicle of the inventor's early achievements to 1929. Under the heading "The Birth of Electric Music," Anfilov's account credited Lev Sergeyevich as the seminal pioneer in the field. A new entry also appeared in the 1966 printing of the *Musical Encylopedic Dictionary* published in Moscow: "theremin," the musical instrument.

Despite this flicker of rekindled interest within the Soviet Union, Lev Sergeyevich still remained dead, quite literally, to the Western world. As late as 1960, Fred K. Prieberg speculated in his book *Musica ex machina* that the inventor's fate was "puzzling. . . . Theremin's relatives in America believe that he had already been shot to death in 1939." Prieberg reasoned that electronic music must have clashed with the ideology of socialist realism. "Theremin, his instrument, and those of the other Soviet inventors," he wagered, "did not fit into the official world view of that time. This appears to be the true reason for their liquidation."[18]

By 1962, Bob and Clara Rockmore, of course, had seen Lev Sergeyevich, but for his protection they had let on nothing. Curiously, Gleb Anfilov, in *Physics and Music,* treated Lev Sergeyevich purely as a figure from the past, but he dropped in one telling clue to the present: a full-page photo of the inventor as a mature man. It was definitely Lev Sergeyevich, but the shot captured the weathered look of a receding hairline and black horn-rimmed glasses. Standing in a dark suit and tie before an unfamiliar model of the space-control instrument, his head was held high, with pursed lips and transfixed gaze, fingers and arms outstretched. The caption below read: "Leon Thérémin is playing Rachmaninov's Vocalise on his Théréminvox, Moscow Conservatoire, 1966."[19] Apparently no one in the West took particular notice.

Harold Schonberg, the chief music critic of the *New York Times,* came to Moscow Conservatory in the spring of 1967. "Mr. Theremin disappeared from sight shortly before the war," he explained in an article, "and nothing more was heard of him. Only a few knew whether he was alive or dead."[20] Lev Sergeyevich remembered that Schonberg approached the conservatory director: "He said, 'We thought Theremin was dead, but it turns out that he's working here; I would like to meet him, to see him, to find out what he's been doing.'"[21] The inventor was summoned to the director's office. "He is very much alive," Schonberg affirmed. "He is a spry, voluble man of 71. . . . He looks and acts like the prototype of the absent-minded professor."[22] Likewise, Lev Sergeyevich was tickled by the reviewer's obvious excitement at having unearthed a long-lost treasure. "Talking a blue streak," he led Schonberg on an impromptu tour of the lab:

> "I have developed an electronic organ tuner," he said, pausing before a knobbed, tubed contraption. "It can tune an organ to any scale, tempered or otherwise."
>
> "Here," he said, turning to another collection of tubes and resistors, "is a machine to photograph sounds. It has 70 channels a half tone apart. And here is my rhythmicon. It can produce any combination of complex rhythms. Let me play you seven against nine. Or would you like to hear 5 against 13? Very

important. A conductor can stand here and learn to beat four with one hand, and five with the other."[23]

The inventor demonstrated other devices: a "piano tester" to measure the evenness of a piano's scale—Steinway was found to be the best among "many fine European pianos"—and an apparatus for comparing and graphing individual pianists' pedaling in the same piece. "He put on a tape of Sviatoslav Richter playing Chopin's C-Sharp Minor Scherzo, and the listener stood transfixed as two colored lines, one for each pedal, arched out, retreated and intersected. 'Richter uses more left pedal than most pianists,' Mr. Theremin said."[24]

Lev Sergeyevich bustled on with device after device like a child in his own toy store. There was a spectrograph for analyzing timbres, and a machine for slowing down sounds without altering their pitch. Then, saving the best for last, he uncovered his dearest, most confidential labors: his musical instruments. Standing before a space-control model, "Mr. Theremin arched his back and faced an imaginary audience. His eyes closed. He looked noble. Suddenly his hands, still strong and beautiful, shot out, and the melodic line of Chopin's E-Flat Nocturne filled the air. Mr. Theremin is still quite an impressive showman." For a grand finale, Lev Sergeyevich led Schonberg into a separate room "in which a small dance floor had been constructed. Mr. Theremin stood on the floor, raised his arms, made motions, and started to play the Massenet Elegy on nothing at all. The room was filled with sound, and it was positively spooky. No wires, no gadgets, nothing visible. Merely electromagnetic sorcery."[25]

Schonberg spun his impressions into an article that ran in the *New York Times* on April 26, 1967: "Music: Leon Theremin." The piece was a journalistic landmark: the formal announcement that resurrected the inventor in the West and opened the floodgates to curiosity and attention. The most astonished readers were probably his old New York associates who, having found him alive, also had a prominent address where they could correspond with him now.

Among the first to dash off a letter was Boyd Zinman. By May 2, Lev Sergeyevich had already responded in handwritten English:

My dearest old friend Boyd Zinman!
It was unexpected pleasure for me to receive your letter with perfect self-design, smiling and sympathetic and a clipping from a newspaper.
Like always you are conducting the business, and I am sure, very successfully. . . .
How do you feel yourself? How is the health of your pleasant wife? Give my regards to her. I hope that she remembers me. What is new about our common friend Morgenstern? If you still have contacts with him, tell him my best regards and my very good reminiscences about our common activity. . . .

Time marches on, but I still hope that again I will be closer to my best friend, assistant and helper. Let me have your photograph for a memory of our past friendship, and to kiss you for advisable restorations of our relations.
Your friend
Leon Theremin[26]

The mostly straightforward letter contained one odd comment. Zinman, who was now an exporter of tractors and construction machinery, had suggested tongue-in-cheek to the inventor that he design a musical tractor. Lev Sergeyevich seems to have taken him at his word: "I am very sorry that it is difficult for me to invent and construct 'musical tractor,' but if you will give me technical requirements how it is supposed to work, I will be glad to switch my work in this direction. Who knows, maybe we will have again such pleasant for me contacts."

Joseph Schillinger's widow, Frances, also wrote after seeing the Schonberg article. Lev Sergeyevich learned for the first time of his old friend's passing almost a quarter century earlier. "I am very sorry that Mr. Schillinger left us," he wrote back, "but I am sure that his work will forever remain in musical art and compositions of the future. . . . *Extremely important* for me to have a copy of music written by my best friend Joseph, 'The First Airphonic Suite.' If we have the score for orchestra we will certainly perform this composition with our orchestra, I am sure with a big success." He inquired after Mary Ellen Bute (whom he recalled in memory as "Helen Beaut") and sent regards to "James" (meaning Gerald) Warburg and Nicolas Slonimsky. "What has happened to the progress in synthesis of painting and music?" he wondered. "Practically I have not a single program of my American concerts and I will be very thankful to you for every even little notice related to my past in the U.S.A."[27]

On August 15 he wrote Frances Schillinger again, reporting that he was practicing the theremin part of the *First Airphonic Suite* and teaching it to some of his pupils. Also, he had shown Schillinger's keyboard works to piano professors at the conservatory, hoping students there would take them up.

Emanuel Morgenstern wrote, proposing a visit to Russia with his wife. "I hope it will be soon," Lev Sergeyevich replied, "and it will be good for me to get a letter from you with the proposed date of your arrival in Moscow, so I will be there to meet you."[28] He invited the Morgensterns to phone him at the conservatory and gave them the number. He felt a new ease in fraternizing with Americans, now that he no longer worked for the KGB.

But it was a false sense of security. Given the low estate of Russian electronic music, the conservatory had merely indulged his back room experiments with terpsitones and theremins so long as they were off-hour tinkerings. When Anfilov wrote in *Physics and Music,* "Thirty years ago, Thérémin could control the tone quality of his Théréminvox with his eyes,"[29] he didn't realize these experiments had been conducted only months earlier at Moscow Conservatory, not decades back, in New York—Lev Sergeyevich had taken such pains in his own book to disguise the location of the research.

Now, Schonberg's article threatened to rehabilitate Lev Sergeyevich as an electronic music pioneer, not only in Russia, but in the world at large. And here he was, carrying on his work under the banner of the venerated Moscow State Conservatory, bastion of official Soviet music. The political complications were enormous. Adding to the discomfort for conservatory administrators was the free traffic of American mail arriving for the inventor. Censors would have grappled with an array of suspicious material in the letters: "musical tractors" designed for an American firm, a planned visit of a former business colleague from the United States, clippings and requests for old concert flyers, inquiries about past acquaintances in New York, curiosity about avant-garde movements (the "synthesis of painting and music"), and the request for the *First Airphonic Suite.*

Lev Sergeyevich was so emboldened, he was even practicing Schillinger's score and training students with it. "I made my last public appearance in 1938," he said at the end of Schonberg's article. "I sometimes think it would be nice to come back once more to the United States and show my latest instruments."[30] It was too much for conservatory officials. They had looked the other way long enough. Not only did the inventor represent an art esthetic contrary to Soviet ideology—and not befitting the conservative stronghold of the conservatory—but he was still a carrier of state secrets (the *Times* article revealed that he contributed "to the war effort, with secret work in electronics"). In his May 2 letter to Frances Schillinger, he made no attempt to mask his bold enthusiasm: "I like to work and to march in the field of new discoveries in science and arts, even if it is sometimes necessary to pass through dangerous conditions."[31] He could not have been more prescient.

One day, the composer Stanislav Kreichi was crossing the courtyard of the conservatory and noticed the inventor's terpsitone sitting by a pile of garbage, chopped up with an ax. Repairs to the acoustics lab were supposedly going on, and Lev Sergeyevich's musical instruments—space-control and fingerboard models, as well as the terpsitone—were thrown out. The "repairs," as it turned out, were actually ideological ones: the conservatory's managing director, N. Nikolayev, rebuked the inventor: "He announced," Lev Sergeyevich remembered, "that 'Electricity is not good for music. Electricity is to be used for electrocution.' So he ordered that all these instruments be removed from the Conservatory . . . and that there be no more such projects at the Conservatory."[32] Lev Sergeyevich was summarily discharged from his post.

The discarded instruments were so meticulously destroyed, nothing could be salvaged. "I made those instruments myself," he remembered sadly, "it took me several months."[33]

The inventor retreated to the two-room apartment on Leninsky Prospekt he shared with his wife and two daughters and set up his lab in a closet. It was a crowded and vexing arrangement, and stifling to his creativity. "My wife and children annoyed me with requests to make a television for the home so they would not have to buy one, but it was of no interest to me anymore. I had new ideas which I wanted to test, to put to life." Working around the family schedule was frustrating. "At the KGB it was better. I could work very late. They would put a guard with a rifle by me and say 'be my guest,' as I worked until morning."[34]

In 1968, he fell in with a group of engineers, inventors, and musicians researching electronic music at the Scriabin Museum—Alexander Scriabin's former residence in Moscow. Every Wednesday, when the building was closed to the public, the group was allowed a room for its experiments. "I went up to the door and pressed the bell," Anfilov recounted.

> The curator of the museum led me through the great composer's modest flat. I walked through the drawing-room, the dining-room, saw the black polish of two grands, and opened one more door when a powerful chord caught me unawares. It was a waterfall of music unlike anything I had ever heard before. . . . It was swelling, filling the air, gaining in strength; then—in an instant— it changed. The chords were now light, sparkling and dying away. Before I knew it, a peal of sound rang out, spreading round in a thousand fragments.
> Silence fell. . . .
> Then I saw several tape recorders and loudspeakers, and two men by what looked like a printing press in a corner. That was where the music had come from.[35]

The "printing press" was the ANS synthesizer, named after Alexander Nikolayevich Scriabin's initials. The ANS was the brainchild of the engineer Evgeny Murzin, who had developed it secretly between 1938 and 1957 (when the first prototype was constructed). It represented the most sophisticated Russian synthesizer of the 1960s. Lev Sergeyevich, working alongside Murzin in the museum lab, scrutinized the instrument's design and operation.

Experiments with the ANS were made at various times by the Russian composers Edison Denisov and Alfred Schnittke and by the American Vladimir Ussachevsky (on a visit to the Soviet Union in 1962). The complexity of programming the instrument, though, made it inferior to the easier, logical manipulation of sound in Robert Moog's voltage-controlled synthesizers. At the time of the landmark Museum of Modern Art concert in 1969, Lev

Sergeyevich apparently had heard nothing of Moog's work or the part he himself had played in influencing it.

《·》

On June 30, 1970, Lev Sergeyevich's wife, Maria, suddenly died from heart disease brought on by the chronic effects of her rheumatism. She was forty-nine. In recent years she had been a shadowy presence in her family's life. Mikhail Nesturkh remembered that Maria was rarely at home when he visited Lev Sergeyevich's apartment, and that she never came with her husband and their daughters on visits to the Nesturkh household. As a widower, Lev Sergeyevich sustained the fatherly devotion he had long had for his daughters—washing their clothes, or bringing them to their lessons at the general music school.

By 1972, the shadow cast by his dismissal from the conservatory had faded, and he was ready to reenter the work force. Rem Khokhlov, a former student at the conservatory, now headed the acoustics lab at Moscow State University's Department of Physics, and he was able to arrange a forty-hour-a-week job there for the inventor. It was not an academic position—Lev Sergeyevich still couldn't hold the title of "professor"—but he was made a "grade 6 mechanic" in radio electronics, specializing in underwater naval acoustics and noise suppression for automobiles. At night, and on weekends, he persisted with musical research in his tiny home laboratory and at the Scriabin Museum. He seemed inured to his brutal treatment at the conservatory. In 1968 he had published an article, "Electronics and Music," in *Radio Amateur Yearbook*, and in 1970 he began teaching theremin students privately at his apartment and in their homes. In 1972 he came forward with the first account of his early life and work, including his triumphs in Europe and America, "The Birth, Childhood, and Youth of the Theremin," in the journal *Radiotechnika*. The same year, an article appeared in *Radio* describing a new transistorized theremin designed and built by a Moscow engineer, Lev Korolyov.

Lev Sergeyevich was buoyed. It seemed like the right moment to address the old complaint that the theremin couldn't utter more than one note at a time. On June 26, 1975, Soviet patent 601742 was registered in Lev Sergeyevich's name for a "polyphonic termenvox." The term "polyphonic" was actually a bit of a misnomer—the instrument really created a "homophonic" texture of melody and accompaniment. It used the traditional space-control interface—right-hand pitch and left-hand volume—but a low-frequency wireless radio transmitter was held in the palm of the left hand, allowing the fingers to select from among six or eight individual frequencies. Each of these frequencies, ranging from 20 to 80 kHz so as not to interfere with the pitch and volume systems, activated, in a separate receiving system, the sound of a corresponding three-note chord that could accompany the right-hand melody being played. To accommodate performance in different keys, the lowest note of each chord automatically doubled the pitch of the melody note sounding in the right hand. In an alternate version of the patent, the palm transmitter was eliminated, and lateral motions of the left hand across beamed infrared light channels triggered the accompanying chords.

The polyphonic instrument was actually created for a demonstration at the university. It was a bold move considering what had happened at the conservatory, but the atmosphere in the acoustics department appeared liberal. For several years the inventor had even coached a regular, devoted circle of students and employees who studied the theremin with him there. This time, while his transgressions didn't cost him his job, department administrators sent him a familiar message: in a reshuffling of room assignments, the polyphonic termenvox was abandoned, and dismantled in stages until it was conveniently beyond repair. When Lev Sergeyevich began work on a new instrument incorporating semiconductors, he was told his work space was needed for nonmusical projects. "The chairman of the physics department considered music not to be a science, that this should not be taking place at the university, and I had to vacate the room."[36]

Ironically, music had become Lev Sergeyevich's secret work. By day, he dutifully played out his role as a technical worker at the university. At a 1975 conference in Kazan he was asked if he should be introduced as "professor," or "winner of the Stalin Prize." "No," he advised, "the Stalin Prize is a secret prize, and the title of professor I had in my past in America. Now I am a six-grade high qualification mechanic."[37]

≪≫

At eighty, Lev Sergeyevich began to entertain thoughts of remarriage. Perhaps he might still have a son to carry on his name. One day in 1976 Natalia Nesturkh and her family were jolted when he showed up at their home with a young woman in her early thirties. Elena, he explained, was to be his new bride. She was an employee of the Scriabin Museum and had lately taken up the theremin. She lived with her adoptive parents, but she suffered from bouts of loneliness because she felt they didn't understand her. Elena admired and respected Lev Sergeyevich and fostered a close emotional bond with him. She had a musical education, and despite the cavernous divide in their ages, she shared the inventor's passion for music.

There was much deliberation on the part of both families, and the question of suitable living quarters for the couple became an issue. Lev Sergeyevich's two rooms on Leninsky Prospekt were crowded as it was—his daughter Natalia and her husband now shared the apartment with him, and under the Soviet system, citizens looking for new living spaces could sit on waiting lists indefinitely, with no guarantees. The prospects for marriage appeared dim. Elena, desperate, jumped from the window of a tall building and died.

After this episode, Lev Sergeyevich drew increasingly close to his cousin, Mikhail Fedorovich Nesturkh, who had just lost his wife and had come to live with his daughter Natalia Nesturkh, her husband, Yevgeny Kavin, and their daughters, Galina and Lydia. Lev Sergeyevich—"Uncle Lova"—was a household regular and one day showed up with a small transistorized theremin he had made for nine-year-old Lydia. His young first cousin twice removed was already musically inclined—she played the piano and wrote her own compositions. Lev Sergeyevich proposed to her parents that he teach her the space-control instrument. "It was his idea to create more students who could keep the instrument alive," Lydia recalled, "so I was just one of his students, but maybe he loved me more than the others because we were related."[38]

Every Friday, at the end of his forty-hour work week at the university, Lev Sergeyevich traversed Moscow from the south side to the north, forty-five minutes by subway and bus—in all types of weather, regardless of fatigue—and climbed the stairs to the Kavinas' fifth-floor apartment rather than take the elevator. "He liked to say, 'I will be there at about 3:16,'" Lydia remembered, and unfailingly his knock came at the precise moment. He was a "very modest, very soft-spoken man, and very humorous at the same time."[39] He always brought cake or candy for tea. Lydia recalled:

> Our lessons were happy moments of light and easy spiritual communication between two people who loved and understood each other. . . .
> His teaching was not strict or formal: I was allowed to play whatever I wanted to play while he sat in an old armchair and listened. Sometimes he sang or whistled to correct my intonation; sometimes he played for me and I would then repeat what he played, gradually learning his style. . . . I am sure that our lessons gave him enjoyment and were balsam for the soul.[40]

The Saint-Saëns "Swan" and Schubert's "Ave Maria"—the standard space-control fare—began to come into focus under Lydia's hands. Lev Sergeyevich coached her through the aerial fingering technique he had learned from Clara Rockmore and imparted the essence of clean vibrato: side to side, for better control, not back to front. But for Lydia, these were "not like lessons to get something, to get to some level. It was just more like making music. . . . I didn't practice between lessons. Sometimes I did, but it wasn't like regular practice and then a lesson. I think it was because he was so soft and he didn't push me at first; and also because it was difficult to understand really what it was, this new instrument, and what level you could reach, and what you could do with it."[41] Lydia's small transistorized instrument was more of a child's toy with only rudimentary possibilities, and it functioned poorly. After a few months Lev Sergeyevich replaced it with one of his more sophisticated hand-built vacuum tube models. "As children often do," Lydia confessed, "I quickly took the miracle for granted."[42]

After two years of Friday afternoon rituals, eleven-year-old Lydia wove the theremin into her own original music for a school play based on Hans Christian Andersen's *Snow Queen*. Since she was acting the part of Herta herself, the score of piano, bells, voices, and theremin had to be pre-recorded on tape, with the space-control instrument used to signal the entrance of the Snow Queen. Lydia's stage flair inspired Uncle Lova to build her a rudimentary terpsitone in the sanctuary of the Kavinas' apartment, housed inside a wooden platform constructed by her father. But the device had no volume control and she never used it for live performance.

Lydia's lessons lasted for five years and climaxed with her public debut in 1981 on the television show *Moscovichka*, where she played her composition "Song of the Bluebird." The following year, Lev Sergeyevich brought her to audition for Mescherin, who accepted her into his Electro-Musical Orchestra as the theremin soloist, replacing Kovalsky, who had recently died.

In 1980, the electronic music studio of the Scriabin Museum—where Lev Sergeyevich had taken refuge for over a decade—suddenly closed under official pressure. All his research was forced back to his apartment and consolidated into his closet lab. But the family situation at home made work there nearly impossible. His daughter Helena had left after she graduated from the aviation institute and was living elsewhere with her husband and two sons. But Natalia and her husband still shared the two rooms with the inventor, and now their daughters, Maria and Olga, added to the crunch. Lev Sergeyevich often had no place to sit down when he came home from the university, and on Saturdays and Sundays the crowding forced him to abandon work entirely and escape to the movie house. In short order he had jotted down in his notebook the titles of hundreds of films he had seen. The space dilemma at home was so severe that two suitcases of his archives—tapes, drawings, notes, and documents—had to be stored at the Kavins'.

In a letter of appeal to the Central Committee of the Communist Party, Lydia's parents deplored the conditions in the Leninsky Prospekt apartment where nine people were now registered (Lev Sergeyevich, his two daughters and their husbands, and four children), though only five were actually staying there. The entreaty pleaded for a decent private living space, the least reward for the inventor's past services to the country, they thought. Lydia's mother persisted with phlegmatic government officials and finally won an audience in March 1981 with the chief of the Department of Higher Educational Institutions of the Moscow Committee of the Communist Party. Eventually a meager compromise was reached: Lev Sergeyevich was offered a temporary living space in a building owned by Moscow University, sparing him the bother of lingering on a long housing list. The single room was essentially a dormitory chamber—about ten by thirteen feet—but a voluminous luxury compared with his share of space in the packed apartment.

As a work environment, though, it was hardly a step up from his old closet. And lately he shrank from electronic music research on Moscow University premises. His work was clearly thwarted. A group of his friends and relatives—the Kavins, Mescherin, Bulat Galeyev, and the engineer Sergei Zorin—petitioned for the formation of an electronic music center with Lev Sergeyevich as director, to focus on research, education, and instrument construction. "It was not possible to organize a private institution in Russia at that time," Lydia's mother, Natalia Nesturkh, explained, "so our activities were limited to writing letters to various government agencies." The group convened at the state recording company, Melodia, courtesy of the Minister of Culture, and by January of '82 they had managed to secure a "Decree of the Soviet Government about the Creation in Moscow of an All-Union Methodological Center of Research in the Field of Electronic and Light-Music." A search began for an appropriate building to renovate, but promise after promise ended in fruitless meetings. It turned out the fiat was a charade. "It was never more than a 'decree,'" Nesturkh realized. "The state bureaucratic system of that period neither wanted nor was able to support new trends in art."[43]

Lev Sergeyevich's dorm room at Moscow University was intended only as a stopgap, and the crusade continued to find him a decent long-term arrangement. Nesturkh and her coterie of the inventor's friends approached a host of organizations. One of Lev Sergeyevich's former classmates, now a well-known academic, refused to help, complaining that the inventor had worked voluntarily for the KGB. Eventually, Valentina Grizodubova—a celebrated woman pilot, official "Hero of the Soviet Union," and deputy of the Supreme Soviet of the USSR, pulled high-level strings and arranged the inventor's transfer to a one-room flat in a communal apartment.

The *kommunalka* was an infamous scourge of the Soviet era—the quintessential proletarian housing solution. An individual, couple, or an entire family lived in one room of an apartment suite shared by many other such families, everyone using the common kitchen and bathroom. The system had all the efficiency of a chicken coop, and just enough mandated square feet per person to still any bourgeois smugness about a place of one's own. In a communal apartment, Shostakovich observed,

> it's easier to make a statement or, to put it bluntly, a denunciation, about your neighbor, since your neighbor's life is on display. Everything is visible—who came, what time he left, who visited whom, who his friends are. What a person cooks for dinner is also visible, since the kitchen, obviously, is communal. You can peek into your neighbor's pot when he steps out. . . .
> There are plenty of diversions in a communal kitchen. Some like to spit into the neighbor's pot. . . . There is the element of risk. The person might come back any second. If he catches you, he'll punch you in the face.[44]

Lev Sergeyevich traded his privacy, and the sterile solitude of a university room, for the din and collective chatter of an apartment crowded with many families. If he gained anything, it was space. His new room measured about ten by sixteen feet, an increase of roughly thirty square feet. The Kavins helped him move in and assisted with his assigned share of the apartment chores (week-long mandatory bathroom cleaning responsibilities cycled regularly through all occupants of a communal apartment). Along with the new room, Lev Sergeyevich was allocated a safe at the Archive of the Academy of Science to secure the historical materials in his two suitcases.

Life went on, but the university job was frustrating. "In the department, people were not interested in science," he despaired. "They mostly worried about money, titles and orders. There were no work results there. At the KGB there had been results."[45] His musical instruments remained his abiding pleasure.

In 1983, the inventor's name was included on the Russian patent of Lev Korolyov's "modern termenvox," an instrument Korolyov had developed with Konstantin Kovalsky between 1971 and 1976. Based on Kovalsky's original design from the '20s with a foot pedal for volume and left-hand buttons for articulation, the modern termenvox was transistorized and incorporated several updated features. A "space neck," or "space fingerboard" visualizer attachment, mounted horizontally along the top surface of the cabinet, allowed the player to see a representation of each pitch played. The visual effect was like a thermometer. Three fluorescent display tubes, collectively covering the full range of the instrument, ran adjacently along the edge of a piano keyboard diagram. As the pitches played became higher (right hand closer to the antenna), their visual analog appeared as a blue-green line moving to the right inside one of the tubes, directly under each corresponding pitch on the keyboard diagram. Pitch indication was accurate to about one-third of a semitone. Since it was possible to move to a new pitch in silence, seeing it precisely on the space neck visualizer before playing it, the old problem of entering on a new note after a rest (which always involved checking intonation quietly in the speaker before playing) was solved. The visualizer also allowed the player to check depth and form of vibrato, and it helped to condition the right hand for relative note distances in space. Korolyov also equipped the modern termenvox with left-hand buttons to preselect timbres approximating the human voice, the oboe, violin, cello, trumpet, and French horn. Kovalsky was a proponent of the instrument, and after his death, Lydia Kavina played one in Mescherin's ensemble.

Lev Sergeyevich's name was added to another Russian patent in 1983: the "'Tonica' Electronic Music Teaching Device," a transistorized children's theremin developed by the engineer Viacheslav Maximov. The small, bright-red plastic box was approved by the minister of culture as a device to improve musical hearing in children. Twenty-five of the instruments were manufactured in 1986, and Maximov devised a textbook method to go along with them. The Tonica made a successful showing at radio exhibitions, and the first production run sold out immediately. But again, the duplicitous government retracted its initial support. "They are easy to play," Lev Sergeyevich contended, "and a wonderful way of developing a child's musicality. But look at the replies I received from culture officials! They say these 50-rouble instruments aren't cost-effective. Then they foist complicated devices on parents, which are expensive and do not help children learn about music."[46] The Ministry of Culture apparently hadn't bargained on popular enchantment over the instruments. Persistent lobbying by the Kavins to manufacture the Tonica as a children's toy came to nothing.

Lev Sergeyevich persevered, passing on his space-control wisdom, one-on-one, to any enthralled pupil with the patience to try. At the Moscow Music Academy "October Revolution," where Lydia was enrolled, he taught a regular studio of theremin students he had assembled there in 1984. Meanwhile, his supporters refused to back down in their drive to amplify his name and better his living conditions. Efim Afanasiev, a writer who published several articles on the inventor, launched a personal campaign, contacting over fifty people and organizations. Predictably, he ran up against official apathy, resistance, and often outright hostility. When he pressed the Physico-Technical Institute for records on Lev Sergeyevich, the administration claimed it had nothing on such an individual in its archives. In March 1987, Afanasiev received a letter from the physics department of Moscow University—where Lev Sergeyevich was currently working—reflecting the inventor's untouchable position:

To Comrade Afanasiev E. F.

In answer to your letter to the Supreme Soviet of the U.S.S.R., we inform you of the following:

L. S. Termen has been working at the Physics Department of Moscow University since 1972. His many years of work activity were recognized with a "Labor Veteran" medal. During this time L. S. Termen took part in research conducted by the department as an ordinary worker and he did not show enough creative activity, nor does he have any achievements on the basis of which he could be recommended for a Government decoration.

We inform you as well that in planning for a celebration commemorating the 70th anniversary of the Great October Socialist Revolution, the question of an award for Termen within the framework of Moscow University has been considered.

The department group knows about L. S. Termen's former achievements, mostly from his oral stories, and some publications in newspapers and magazines, etc. Without official documents supporting Termen's achievements, the Physics Department is not able to evaluate the competence of his former activity in the other institutions.[47]

The letter was signed by the deputy director of the physics department and the acting chair of acoustics.

《 》

On August 21, 1987, in another hemisphere a world apart, an old woman passed away quietly at the Jersey Shore Medical Center in Neptune, New Jersey. The name on the death certificate was Catherine Theremin, eighty-three years old. It was the identity Katia had used all the years she worked patiently as a lab technician in Paterson at the Valley View Tuberculosis Hospital—and later the Preakness Hospital, in its subsequent incarnation. She had lived alone in Paterson through the long decades following her estrangement from Lev Sergeyevich. By night, from the hospital windows, she always glimpsed the distant twinkle of New York lights that had swallowed up her husband in the razzle-dazzle '30s. In 1977 she retired and moved to an apartment complex in Asbury Park on the Jersey shore, overlooking the Atlantic Ocean.

For one month in 1968, Katia had returned to Russia for a warm reunion with six of her siblings and their children and grandchildren. In Moscow she saw Lev Sergeyevich. A relative remembered her saying with satisfaction, "I forgave him." But conspicuously absent from the gathering was her eldest brother, Alexander.

Back when Lev Sergeyevich embarked on his European odyssey in 1927, his brother-in-law, Alexander Constantinov, had stepped in to replace him at the Physico-Technical Institute as head of the laboratory of electroacoustic radio measurements and television. In the early '30s, Alexander had distinguished himself as a television pioneer with a patent on an electronic camera tube similar to the "iconoscope" Zworykin had developed in America. This led to his appointment as a chief scientist at the first television center in Leningrad. But only months later, in the predawn hours of November 1, 1936, he was arrested at his home in a roundup that snared many of the top minds in physics, geology, and astronomy. In America, Katia learned of her brother's arrest and predicted, "they will kill him."[48]

For seven months, Constantinov and his colleagues endured the customary rituals of incessant interrogation and "investigation." On May 25, 1937, the Military Collegium, a three-person high tribunal—in a closed trial with no evidence—accused him of membership in a counterrevolutionary Fascist organization, and of conspiring to construct a bomb using a seismographic device to kill Stalin at a Presidium meeting. He was sentenced to "ten years, without the right of correspondence," which in reality meant immediate execution following the trial. He was shot the next day.[49]

After his liquidation, his wife was sent to Kolyma on an eight-year sentence, still unaware of her husband's fate, and two of their underage daughters together with their grandmother were permanently exiled from Leningrad. Constantinov's family was informed of his death only in 1956, when he was posthumously "rehabilitated" under Khrushchev, but the date was revised to December 1945, and the cause attributed to heart failure. Katia would never know the truth about her brother. In 1988, a year after her death, the family finally learned of his execution, though his burial place remained unknown to them.

According to her wishes, Katia was cremated, and her ashes were strewn over the Atlantic Ocean in the direction of Russia, so she could be closer to home. She never knew that her brother's arrest warrant charged that he had "relatives abroad who did not return, and he is in correspondence with them."[50]

《》

Fresh breezes began to blow over the Soviet Republic in 1986 with Mikhail Gorbachev's call for "restructuring" of the economic and political systems (*perestroika*), and the accompanying "openness," or freedom to speak out (*glasnost'*). His proposal in January 1987 for free, competitive elections coincided with the first of three candid articles *Moscow News* published on Lev Sergeyevich. By March 1988, the paper—which offered an English-language edition—had coaxed out of him a host of frank new revelations about his arrest and imprisonment, his ordeal at Kolyma, and even his secret sharashka work. Glasnost' had put a brazen new wind in his sails: he threw open the curtain on his American years and revealed his marriage to Lavinia; he divulged his liaisons with Jan Berzin, mocked Voroshilov as a blundering cavalryman, unveiled the Buran bugging device by its code name, and even disclosed his "secret" Stalin Prize.

The authors capped off the article with an understated plea for the inventor: "His good manners do not allow him to fight [for] even the elementary comforts like a flat of his own. But he needs it badly, if only to continue his creative work."[51] Five months earlier, Afanasiev was assured by officials that Lev Sergeyevich—who had been in line again since 1986 for another apartment—was slated for a new "living square" (a one-room private apartment) sometime in 1988. Then, in the spring of '88, in the final installment of the *Moscow News* series, Lev Sergeyevich was queried, "Has your living situation improved since the article about you . . . which mentioned your dissatisfaction with your apartment?" "I never wanted to make demands," he assured his interviewers nervously, "and don't want to now. I phoned the housing department three months ago and inquired about my turn to have a new flat. A woman . . . told me that my turn would come in five or six years. Not a very reassuring answer if one is 92 years old."[52]

≪≫

Gorbachev's plan for electoral choice was overwhelmingly endorsed by the Communist Party in the summer of 1988. With it came a sweeping repudiation of Stalinism, a condemnation of the period of "stagnation" under Brezhnev, and a denunciation of the restrictions on freedom of expression and the rights of assembly and organization. The Supreme Soviet was replaced by a Congress of People's Deputies, and free elections were held across the Soviet Union in March of '89.

In Bourges, France, organizers of the annual International Festival of Experimental Music were hoping to capitalize on perestroika and squeeze Lev Sergeyevich through the iron curtain for a cameo bow in the West. But even in the new liberal Soviet climate, the enormity of the invitation raised hackles. Lev Sergeyevich, retired KGB scientist, had not ventured beyond Russian borders since his repatriation in 1938. The diplomatic ramifications were ticklish. "After several months of daily phone calls," Robert Moog recalled, "some of which actually managed to penetrate the Kremlin, Theremin received official permission to leave the Soviet Union little more than a day before he was due to speak."[53]

The symposium—"Synthesis '89"—from June 13 to 16, was sponsored partly by the International Music Council of UNESCO. Under the theme "Rejects from Utopia—Pioneers and Inventors in the History of Electronic Music," the event summoned a hall of fame of trailblazers: Oskar Sala from Germany, developer of the Mixture-Trautonium; J. L. Martenot of France, son of the ondes martenot inventor Maurice Martenot; synthesizer creators Don Buchla and Robert Moog; Jon Appleton and Sydney Alonso, demonstrating the Synclavier; and the composers Hugh Davies from Britain, Eduard Artemiev from the Soviet Union, and others. At the summit of the celebration was Lev Sergeyevich, doyen of electronic music giants—the "Invité d'honneur du Festival"—taking his first tentative steps outside the USSR in fifty-one years.

An exultant press stood ready. Léon Théremin, ancestral compatriot and Albigensian descendant, had returned. "The Western world believed he was dead since 1945," *La Nouvelle République* trumpeted. "Leon Theremin has emerged from Russia."[54] Lev Sergeyevich arrived with two versions of the space-control instrument (one with vacuum tubes, the other with semiconductors), accompanied by his daughter Natalia, and with two Russians in tow—a technician and an accompanist, supposedly. Neither of the chaperons, though, seemed to be competent in his area of expertise, and both were probably KGB men.

For a fleeting moment in flashback, it was December 1927 all over again: the inventor was toasted at a reception of champagne and petits fours, decorated with a medal, and lauded by the deputy mayor of Bourges. Lev Sergeyevich was buoyant: "I am young, I am only 94 years old!" Actually he was ninety-two. But diminished after six decades were the erect, military posture, the proud head, the determined gaze. "Behind a pair of slightly crooked glasses," *La Nouvelle République* observed, "his eyes smile with a great sweetness that lights up his face. Natalia . . . makes gestures of tenderness toward him: her hand caresses the feeble back of the old man." Although "this nonagenarian has a fragile appearance," the paper noted, he "is a rock."[55]

Lev Sergeyevich took the stage on the third morning of the conference. He spoke about his instruments and played Glinka's "Skylark" in a séance of nostalgia recalling his youthful audience with Lenin. Then Natalia offered an ambitious recital on her father's instrument: a Glière concerto, Rachmaninoff's "Vocalise," Debussy's "Clair de Lune," and the requisite "Swan" of Saint-Saëns.

On the final day of the festival, Lev Sergeyevich granted his first full-length interview outside the Soviet Union in sixty years. Speaking through an interpreter who translated his Russian into French, he conversed at length with the American musicologist Olivia Mattis. In the course of their talk, Mattis produced a copy of a letter Edgard Varese had mailed to the inventor from America in 1941. "At that time I was in a special place, so I had no opportunity to receive letters," he confirmed.[56] Then Mattis handed him his mail, forty-eight years late—a strange, exhumed time capsule of thwarted dreams;

expressions of earnest desires that might have been penned the day before; dreams that now would never be, authored by a man already dead twenty-four years:

> Dear Professor Theremin,
>
> On my return from the West in October I tried to get in touch with you. . . . I was sorry—on my account—that you had left New York. I hope that you have been able to go on with your experiments in sound and that new discoveries have rewarded your efforts.
>
> I have just begun a work in which an important part is given to a large chorus and with it I want to use several of your instruments—augmenting their range as in those I used for my Equatorial—especially in the high range. Would you be so kind as to let me know if it is possible to procure these and where. . . . Also if you have conceived or constructed new ones would you let me have a detailed description of their character and use. I don't want to write any more for the old Man-power instruments and am handicapped by the lack of adequate electrical instruments for which I now conceive my music. . . .
>
> With cordial greetings and best wishes in which my wife joins me,
>
> Sincerely,
>
> Edgard Varese[57]

"Can you remember Edgard Varese?" Mattis asked. "How did he look physically? Can you remember?" "No, I couldn't tell you," Lev Sergeyevich apologized. "I met so many people. I did not see Varese much. I cannot remember it. It was so long ago, decades ago." His long-term memory was hazy.

> Mattis: Do you remember Nicolas Slonimsky?
> Theremin: Maybe. I don't remember. It's a familiar name to me—I might even know him—but I don't remember.
> Mattis: How about Henry Cowell?
> Theremin: I recognize all these names. No, I am afraid I don't remember very much about him. Stokowski I remember very well, because I made instruments for him. As for the rest, maybe we talked casually. . . .
> Mattis: Do you remember Joseph Schillinger?
> Theremin: Schillinger, yes, I knew him. I had many conversations with him, but I cannot say anything about his work. I recognize his name; he was famous, after all. . . . he was a composer, but from my point of view he was one of many interesting, good people who were interested in old-fashioned ideas and viewpoints that were not suitable for the development of musical art.[58]

At the end of the interview Mattis prompted him, "Do you have a message now, in 1989, that you would like to convey to the Western world?" His two chaperons were nearby. He would have to weigh his thoughts scrupulously. "What words!" he began.

I knew the Western world pretty well. . . . The only thing I wanted to ask, maybe of some people (if it were allowed by the Soviet government), is that I be allowed to promote my instruments. You must make the impression that I came here, that I was allowed to come here—It seems that there will be no punishment for me if you write in the newspaper about all I have told you. I hope. We'll see what happens. The same with my invention. I want to stress to you that all this needs to be done in a disciplined way, and that when people will be asking about me and writing about me, that all this be done in a responsible way. But if you write that I have said something against the Soviet government and said that it is better to work elsewhere, then I shall have difficulties back home.[59]

His return to Moscow occasioned no more difficulties than usual, and it was easy to slip back into the status quo. But his memory was atrophying in stages. His ephemeral flirtation with the West after half a century had opened windows on people and places of the past that he squinted to make out. In his 1967 correspondence with Frances Schillinger, he had offered a lucid account of his collaboration with her husband and Henry Cowell in designing the rhythmicon. Now these men were little more than shades on the periphery of his recall.

Certain of his American liaisons, on the other hand—Stokowski, Clara Rockmore, Lucie Rosen—were branded into his memory. Lavinia resided in that part of his brain too, indelibly clear. After the death of his third wife, Maria, he had pined for Lavinia especially. In September of '74, after a visit with Clara in New York, Lavinia followed up with a note:

> I enjoyed talking about our wonderful friend Professor Theremin. I have such a deep devotion and love for him that can never be replaced by another.
> I was so happy to know that he is still alive and this news has brought joy into my life. I shall pray always for his safety and happiness. . . .
> When you write to Léon, please tell him of our meeting.[60]

Clara obliged, and Lev Sergeyevich started sending Lavinia letters. "Look, I found her address," he told Bulat Galeyev. "She sent me her picture. Isn't she beautiful? Maybe I should write for my American dancer and marry her again!" "She is rather old now," Galeyev cautioned, "so much time has passed since then."[61] But Lev Sergeyevich was irrepressible. Lavinia confessed to her student and close friend Diana Dunbar in 1988, "We are in correspondence again. He has proposed marriage again."[62]

But aside from a few embers fanned to a warm glow of remembrance, age and cultural taboo were the least of what stood between them now. Time had set them on separate courses quite foreign to the common ground of America where they had met. Lev Sergeyevich had been tied to Bolshevism for fifty years, while Lavinia had knitted her soul profoundly into the fabric of West Indian culture. She had merged with Haitian society and assimilated its folklore into her own teaching and choreography. She had traveled in the summers, founding national schools of dance in Guyana and the Bahamas, teaching and choreographing in Antigua, Jamaica, and Trinidad. Her voracious curiosity absorbed and recast indigenous styles—South Indian Bharatha Natyam and North Indian Kathak. The subtlest cross-cultural inflections were blended in her blood. "A step from Jamaica, Haiti and Africa might be the same," she believed, "but the feelings and meanings are different. You have to understand the meaning of what you are doing."[63] She wrote a book, *Haiti Dance,* as someone who breathed its traditions.

Sporadically she would come back to New York, teaching at the Alvin Ailey American Dance Center School, where her daughter Sara was a member of the company, and at Ballet Arts in Carnegie Hall and other studios. A retrospective tribute to the First American Negro Ballet was staged in December 1981 at the Riverside Dance Festival in Manhattan, and Lavinia danced a reunion with the seventy-three-year-old Eugene Von Grona—who went by "Van" Grona now, to mitigate his Teutonic "baron's" image.

Lavinia remained in the city through 1983, teaching at New York University, Alvin Ailey, and Steps. She was planning an American retirement and even bought a little building in Brooklyn to resurrect her once-thriving dance studio there, but she couldn't find enough students willing to cross the bridge to make the venture float. In February of '84, she returned to Haiti in what would be a fateful trip.

Political ferment and malignant poverty were advancing out of control under the repressive Haitian dictator, Jean Claude "Baby Doc" Duvalier. Lavinia found her adoptive homeland crackling with flames of civil unrest—gunfire, looting, strikes, burning tires, roadblocks, and soldiers showering bullets into crowds of civilians. At the epicenter of the uprising was Jean-Bertrand Aristide, a Salesian Roman Catholic priest who spearheaded the protest movement against Duvalier from his impoverished Port-au-Prince congregation, a Ti Legliz ("Little Church"), or parish of slum dwellers and peasants. Aristide gave sanctuary to many of the ragged, disaffected street youths who stoked the revolutionary bonfires. Lavinia knew and supported Aristide, and like him, she had cast her lot with the poor and exploited.

When Duvalier fled the country in February 1986, a civilian and military junta of his supporters took power. Aristide, the rebel priest, remained a thorn in the side of the government, the army, and even the church hierarchy. He was bombarded with death threats and stalked by assassins brandishing guns, machetes, and stones. After his church was burned down and members of his congregation were slaughtered during a Mass, Father Aristide was expelled by the Salesian order in December 1988. A communiqué from Rome charged him with "incitement to hate and violence" and "exaltation of class struggle."[64] In early 1989 he went into hiding. His supporters—the opposition that agitated for democratic rule and human rights for the indigent and oppressed—were being rounded up by the junta, framed as "Communists" and increasingly detained and tortured.

Lavinia recognized the gravity of the violence all around her—gunfire in the capital close to her apartment once sent her diving under her bed for cover. But she always felt an immunity to the vendettas of Haiti's political factions. She stayed out of the crossfire and avoided politics. She was an artist, a mentor, an ethnographer committed to preserving West Indian and African dance forms for future generations before it was too late. She also traversed social and economic boundaries easily. As a high-profile national icon she mounted great cultural shows and was well-known in the presidential palace—used at one time as a choreographer by the Duvalier regime. Yet she moved intimately among the poor, working within the dance rituals of the voodoo religion—not the spooky elements associated with voodoo by outsiders: black magic, revenge spells, and zombis raised from the dead to do the bidding of their enemies—but the traditional voodoo, with its African roots mingled with Christian symbolism. For her, voodoo was a divine African tradition that ran deeply through the national heritage, an integral part of the legacy she embraced in her mission.

Trading in different social worlds at once, she thought, allowed her to walk safely in a cultural demilitarized zone. The problem now was that Haiti's pluralistic turmoil could no longer guarantee safe passage for such idealism, no matter how neutral or sincere it might appear. Suddenly one day, Lavinia returned to find her apartment broken into and her photo album stolen. Several months later, on July 19, 1989, a month after Lev Sergeyevich emerged in the Western world at Bourges, "Lavinia Williams, a dancer and teacher," the *New York Times* later reported, "died of a heart attack . . . at the Canapé Vert Hospital in Port-au-Prince, Haiti. She was 73 years old."[65] Another obituary attributed her death to "kidney failure, following an attack of food poisoning."[66] The discrepancies only underlined the suspicious circumstances. The operative word, in any event, was "poisoning."

It was hard to imagine why anyone would want Lavinia Williams dead. She was a passionate, life-affirming spirit who mesmerized everyone and was adored by her students—an embodiment of West Indian cultural pride, a national treasure. Admirers vied for her affections: there was Shannon Yarborough (who was still smitten enough with her to follow her to Port-au-Prince with his wife), and there was a boyfriend, and a gentleman in the United States who bought her a condominium apartment beneath his own that she would never live to see. At seventy-three she had the appearance and vitality of a fifty-year-old. She was planning to live to one hundred. But her influence and standing in Haiti invested her with an ideological power, and her closeness to Aristide was perceived as dangerous. More and more, those who worked to educate or raise the estate of the poor were branded as "Communists." She probably had sensed the danger of this for years: in personal interviews she always omitted any reference to Lev Sergeyevich, because, she admitted later, she feared being dubbed a Communist. But despite her vigilance, Aristide's name was emblazoned on her apartment door,[67] and that may have been all it took to undo her.

That the government was not above contaminating the food of anyone inconvenient to its agenda was already documented. Eight months earlier, the swaggering Haitian army colonel Jean-Claude Paul, indicted by a Miami grand jury for cocaine trafficking—whose removal from power was a condition for resumption of U.S. aid to Haiti—died after consuming a bowl of his favorite pumpkin soup. To deflect its culpability, the government ordered an autopsy as a ruse. Poisoning, nevertheless, was confirmed as the cause of death. In Lavinia's case, her burial in the United States was blocked to prevent forensic chemical testing, according to Diana Dunbar; evidence would be harder to uncover in Haiti, where a body could not be exhumed for a year after interment. As it was, the death certificate did not specify a cause.

Lavinia was given a lavish state funeral. It was a magnificent day: a rim of distant mountains under a radiant blue sky; the vivid rainbow colors of Haitian costume everywhere; dancing in the streets to a military band. Just before the burial a girl went into possession. Diana Dunbar flew in from New York for the ceremony. She stood with Shannon Yarborough and later recalled how shaken he was. She remembered him as a big, charismatic and vibrant man, a wonderful storyteller. She could understand why Lavinia had fallen for him. One year later, he too would die of "food poisoning."[68] Ironically, not long after that, Aristide assumed the presidency of Haiti in the first free elections since 1804.

≪≫

There was a loud rapping at the door. Lev Sergeyevich was afraid to answer. It might be the KGB. The knocking came again, and finally he was persuaded to open up. It was October 1990, and organizers of the Stockholm Electronic Music Festival had flown to Moscow to escort him back to Sweden. "Letters never got through," Stephen Montague remembered, "telex was impossible, and the Soviet international telephone exchange was permanently engaged—because there are only 64 international lines for the entire Soviet Union (for surveillance reasons)." The festival representatives "chatted, packed his bags, put the thereminvox in a plastic satchel, and—throwing money at all the Russian officials they encountered—hustled him off to Stockholm just in time for the concert."[69]

Montague, performing at the Stockholm Kulturhuset himself, was astonished to come upon Lev Sergeyevich—the fabled inventor he presumed was long dead—demonstrating his space-control instrument before a scant audience one night at the festival. "I couldn't believe it," Montague recalled. "I was not ready to actually see a man in 1990 that was born ninety-four years earlier walk out on stage and perform. . . . It was the most extraordinary kind of encounter where I thought I was going to go to a concert just to hear somebody *play* the theremin, and then . . . like a ghost from the past, this man walked out on stage who *was* in fact the inventor, Lev Termen."[70] It was an incongruous sequel to the fanfare of Bourges. Here, Lev Sergeyevich shuffled around barely noticed or acknowledged by anyone. Montague rushed in to fill the void of indifference and seized the moment for a private audience at the inventor's hotel. When the thereminvox was reassembled in the room, it "failed to percolate when he first put it together." Montague watched, fascinated, charmed. The elderly legend hunched over his own jerry-built version of the classic instrument, puttering about, coaxing second-rate Moscow-bought electrical components to cooperate, to match his ideal.

> Here's this 94-year-old man . . . [who] gets out a pair of pliers and screw driver. . . . It's still plugged into the mains, and I'm thinking, I don't want to witness a man electrocuted in a hotel room, that I'm the only witness to. And he started sticking it together, and took a little sort of . . . haywire, and sort of twisted this thing, twisted something else, and stuck it back together, and it started working. It looked so simple . . . a kind of homemade look to it. . . . The paint was peeling off from it, and he'd carried it in a kind of a plastic satchel, and part of it stuck out. When we walked down the hall it was bumping into the elevator as we got up there, and it's no wonder it didn't work. But it was just a wonderful kind of image of this mad inventor with his sort of plastic Soviet satchel with this kind of revolutionary instrument in there.[71]

《》

A boyishly ecstatic Lev Sergeyevich waved his new Communist Party card at Bulat Galeyev. It was the spring of 1991. "Congratulate me! I have been accepted into the Communist Party at last!"[72] The card even had his picture on it. It was the fulfillment of a lifelong quest. His first try, on the eve of his trip to Europe and America in 1927, had been denied. In the United States, and later in Kolyma and the sharashkas, it was impossible. "After my liberation I was not trusted for a long time," he recalled. But he was tenacious. He had enrolled at the University of Marxism-Leninism and earned a diploma there in 1981. Then he reapplied to the Party. "Maybe now I could be accepted." But a bureaucrat rejected him on a technicality. "He found some paragraph in the rules of the Communist Party of the Soviet Union that prohibited a person from entering the Party after the age of 80. As it turned out," he explained to Galeyev, "it was possible." The inveterate Bolshevik could finally validate his life's path, even if retroactively. "But why do you need it now?" Galeyev asked. "Now when everyone is trying to flee them?" Lev Sergeyevich scoffed. "What a question! Let them run. I promised Lenin I would do it!"[73] His ironic sense of timing had surfaced again. Within months of posing for his picture on the card, he watched ten republics from the Baltic, Central Asia, Transcaucasia, and the European USSR peel away and declare their independence from the Soviet Union.

In the Western Hemisphere, phone calls were bouncing between coasts. A frantic effort was underway to bring Lev Sergeyevich over for an American reunion while there was still time. People had talked about it for years. Clara hoped for it. But plans always derailed over the same diplomatic obstacles. Now there was a pressing reason to succeed: the New York filmmaker Steven M. Martin was making a Theremin documentary. He had flown to Moscow in 1990 to film Lev Sergeyevich and returned with a sampling of choice vignettes: the inventor in close-up on an old draped chair in his apartment, mumbling his story in a gentle, hoarse voice in halting English; a foreboding escalator descent into the Moscow subway, and an eerie tunneling through its underground passages; an outdoor night shot of the Kremlin in floodlights; Lev Sergeyevich in a red-carpeted, red-walled room of the Glinka Museum, using a pocket knife to calibrate the howling theremin on display there. But it was in America where the inventor had truly had his day, and Martin needed New York footage to bring the story full circle. It would be perfect. Leon Theremin, foster father of American invention, would make a twilight homecoming.

John Chowning, director of the Doreen B. Townsend Center for Computer Research in Music and Acoustics at Stanford University, had been to Moscow the year before and invited Lev Sergeyevich to California for the university's centennial celebration. Now, Chowning rallied his academic machine, secured a visa, and, with Martin's guidance, engineered the inventor's passage to the United States in late September 1991.

Lev Sergeyevich came with an entourage: his daughter Natalia, granddaughter Olga, and the Russian composer Vladimir Komarov with his wife, the poet Margarita Komarova. The four-day centennial celebration kicked off with a campus press conference, and Lev Sergeyevich fielded the inevitable question about the dismantling of the Soviet Union: "I was very involved in revolutionary activity, and I am interested in the changes today," he explained cautiously. With shaky conditions at home, it paid to play both sides, just in case. But Natalia admitted that before Gorbachev, a trip like this would have been "next to impossible."[74]

The following evening—Thursday the twenty-seventh—picnickers started gathering on the grass at 6:00 P.M. in front of the Frost Amphitheater stage, hoping for a close-up view of "Technology and Music: The Beginning and Now." The 7:30 concert would honor Lev Sergeyevich, the father of analog electronic music—in his ninety-fifth year—and Max Mathews—sixty-five—the father of computer music, who pioneered digital music synthesis as early as 1957 with a computer program he developed at Bell Labs. The concert showcased electronic compositions written in 1991 and the world premiere of Komarov's electroacoustic poem *Freedom,* a reaction to the failed Communist coup in August that had finally brought the Party to its knees in Russia.

Max Mathews and Natalia Theremin took the stage for a duet performance of Rachmaninoff's "Vocalise." The vocal part was intoned as usual on the theremin, but replacing the piano was a synthesized orchestral accompaniment, shaped and adapted in live performance by Mathews on his "radio baton." The instrument, which Mathews created in 1986, resulted from his observations of sensing devices for robotics, and he considered it a direct descendant of the theremin. To play it, the performer grasped what appeared to be two timpani mallets, "conducting" them in space over a small white square surface about the size of a tray table. Each mallet housed a radio transmitter that acted upon the five antennas lodged under the surface of the table. Motions of the mallets on or above the table top allowed real-time control of volume, timbre, and rhythm in preprogrammed music played live by a MIDI synthesizer driven by a personal computer. The gestures of the two mallets—which altered the music through a specialized software program Mathews developed—even allowed the "conducting" of a digitized symphony recording in the same way a theremin player could control a monophonic sound. "The difference in 80 years," Mathews explained, "is that computers have digitized the player's motion."[75] It was a page from the book of Theremin's archetypical technology, and it must have stimulated the inventor. Lev Sergeyevich was scheduled only to demonstrate the operating principles of his instrument, but he couldn't resist and broke out in a spontaneous solo rendering of "Midnight in Moscow" that brought the house down. To a standing ovation he was presented with the Centennial Medal.

On Sunday, he took part in a symposium discussion of his work with other panelists—Robert Moog, Leland Smith (who had created the tape realization of the rhythmicon part for the 1971 premiere of Cowell's *Rhythmicana*), Nicolas Slonimsky, and the composer Charles Amirkhanian. Slonimsky was reunited with the inventor at the symposium, but he later told Olivia Mattis that Lev Sergeyevich didn't appear to remember him.

The Stanford visit ended on October 4, and Martin flew the inventor back to New York for location shoots, and a time-crossing to the world of the '30s—a passage to faces and scenes of another epoch.

Clara always felt that the New York decade must have seemed like a dream to Lev Sergeyevich in his later years. But now he was back on the same streets where half a century earlier he had fled in clandestine haste out to the misty pier of Claremont Terminal on that dog day in September of '38. Plunked down again into the noise and bustle of present-day midtown Manhattan, it was a peculiar, sudden reentry.

In a cloud of fading memory, his return was fraught with déjà vu. Martin put him up in a suite at the Mayflower Hotel only blocks from his former studio at the Hotel Plaza Annex and the ballroom where he first titillated the Astors and the Guggenheimers. The Mayflower overlooked Central Park, as the Plaza had. A new generation of students gaped, astonished by his lecture demonstration at New York University. At a glamorous brownstone soirée, surrounded by chandeliers and candelabras, Natalia conjured ether music for a charmed gaggle of New York's cultural elite assembled in her father's honor. From within the party crowd, a handful of elderly former pupils of the Theremin Studio emerged with extended hands. Lev Sergeyevich would return to the scene where he taught them, reminiscing on the sidewalk in front of 37 West for the cameras.

It was hallucinatory time travel—vestiges of the New York he may have remembered, seasoned with a host of adoring new faces standing in for roles others had once played: celebrated musicians, movie stars, photographers, journalists, artists, thereminists. So much was new to him—things he should have recalled, along with much that had escaped him in his decades of insulation from Western culture. In California, Martin had played him the Beach Boys' "Good Vibrations" for the first time. And now he was in a New York without Lavinia, a New York without Lucie and Walter Rosen, or Zinman and Morgenstern, Goldberg, Schillinger, Stokowski, or Mary Ellen Bute—all of them passed on, though most had doubtless evaporated from his memory bank anyway.

Martin took the inventor to Times Square, the American altar of electronic glitz. There he set him loose to amble along the sidewalk at night, the camera panning a few paces in front to record the pivoting of his head at the wonder of it all—his eyes taking in video and pizza store windows, the neon glare, the endless kaleidoscopic light show of electric logos.

Through the dark dream there was one familiar beacon that shined across six decades—Clara. Perhaps Martin's greatest stroke was to reunite her with Lev Sergeyevich. It was the last and most important piece in the puzzle. Clara had trepidations about it, feeling it might be better for them to live with memories of their youthful selves. Twenty-nine years had elapsed since their guarded encounter in Moscow. But it was important now, because this time, on American soil, they could bask in a natural, open warmth. In Clara's Fifty-seventh Street apartment—an Art Deco time capsule largely unchanged since the inventor's last visit there in the '30s—she played for him, and they talked and had tea.

«»

Moscow in the late autumn of 1991 was a surreal awakening for Lev Sergeyevich. In September and October three more Soviet republics had jumped ship. On Christmas Day, a stern Gorbachev came before the nation in a televised address, announcing his resignation as president. The Soviet parliament convened the following day in its final order of business, passing a resolution to acknowledge the formal dissolution of the Soviet Union. On the last day of the year, the functions of the Communist state ceased, and the USSR was no more. Lev Sergeyevich, fellow traveler among his Party comrades for three-quarters of a century—the life span of Bolshevism—had enjoyed club membership for all of eight months.

By early '92, his living situation remained in stasis, despite further efforts by the editors of *Moscow News*, who had appealed to the Lenin District Executive Committee. It was clear now that there would never be a two-room apartment, or any other way out of the living square he still occupied in the communal flat on Lomonosovsky Prospekt. The cluttered room would become the final repository for the remnants of a seven-decade career, distilled to a meager essence. There he struggled to breathe spirit into scattered skeletal remains, objects spewing wires and tubes that lay about the desk and shelves—the detritus of a life worn down.

In one corner, a tall, lean grandfather clock kept sentinel watch against a backdrop of faded, monochrome flowered wallpaper. Next to it, a cello sat propped up against the wall. There was a dusty television with a broken switch, an old, worn brown bookcase stuffed with tilting paperbacks behind sliding glass. Little makeshift shelves supported keepsakes: an abacus with two black-and-white photo portraits of children stashed behind it, drooping dried flowers in clear plastic sheaths next to small clocks, a medal, and a mug. On the desk, an oscilloscope took shelter under shelves crammed with pamphlets in disarray; a smoldering soldering iron lay next to a red intensity lamp; haphazard wires, taped crudely together at junctures, cascaded over the front of the desk.

By the window, near a white radiator, stood a late-model theremin in a U-shaped black wooden cabinet that, like all Lev Sergeyevich's later instruments, he had sawed, painted, and bolted together himself. Behind it, staring back into the room on a pole, was a bright-red diamond-shaped speaker, the only splash of color in an otherwise drab, muted environment—standing in relief like a great, squared-off lollipop.

"We crossed the yard where he has lived for many years," Gyorgy Kiksman wrote after a visit to the flat in 1992,

> and the impression is that not many people know him. We go upstairs to his communal and he sits down on a chair, tired. "I'm sorry, let me rest a bit." He has just returned from his work—the physics department of Moscow University where he has the more than modest position of mechanic. In the tiny laboratory, which is stuffed with devices waiting to be repaired, he spends almost all his time, including his vacation. Summer, Winter, or Fall, his figure in the old sportcoat unfailingly shows up. . . . The exceptions are so rare that his co-workers know unmistakably that Lev Sergeyevich is probably ill if he is absent. The students, who learn about the work of Ioffe and Korolev, know very little about the mechanic who is right next to them. Theremin's communal apartment is the continuation of his laboratory. It's almost half-filled with devices and parts which he made himself, and on which he spends the main part of his pension and salary.[76]

Lev Sergeyevich was always inventing—at his desk, or in his imagination. He ruminated on new ideas with every breath—foraging for gaps he could find anywhere in technical or scientific knowledge that would require his attention. There was an infinite store of problems to solve, if only life were long enough. "I have massive plans," he told *Moscow News*, "but I'm almost a century old."[77]

Work at Moscow University had grown routine and unstimulating, but he could always fire up his brain with schemes for new technologies. "I decided to make useful proposals to the government," he told Galeyev, "—a defense device to search for materials of microwar. I understood a long time ago that two or three bad people could assemble an atomic bomb in a basement somewhere and threaten a whole city. I had an idea for a device which could 'see' any person who carried parts of this bomb in a crowd. But I didn't even get an answer from the university secret department."[78]

Remarkably, the ravages of age that gnawed at his mind seemed to have little effect on his libido. On the way to the airport in Stanford, he had made the composer Paul Lansky promise to set him up with a young woman when he returned for his hundredth birthday. Stephen Montague recalled how the inventor was distracted during a conversation in Stockholm when a "particularly good-looking Swedish woman walked by." He had, in fact, used the distraction to tell Montague about a device he was hoping to develop that would revitalize male potency in old age. "The idea possessed him," Montague felt. "I thought to myself, this was hilarious, talking to a 94-year-old man who's wanting to have enough time to develop a machine to help the aged enjoy their final years in great fulfillment."[79]

As his frame deteriorated, Lev Sergeyevich came closer to a reckoning with his own mortality—something that didn't jibe with the eternal font of invention flowing inside him. More and more his ideas were hypothetical scenarios he could no longer carry out. He was becoming resigned to passing the mantle to others, trusting the evolution of his work to new custodians in a future he would have hoped to remain for. "I think there may be polyphonic dance floors in the 21st century," he prophesied, "operating without orchestras. . . . This is a whole new medium of communication: each dancer . . . cannot only express him or herself, but pick up other partners' moods and make the dance harmonious."[80] His faith in biopotentials led him to believe that "muscular tension and other microelectric phenomena occurring in the body of a performer-composer can be translated into musical signals. This is an opportunity for 'sound tracking' a person's inner world, no less! Excitement, joy and serenity—the entire gamut of emotions can be revealed without words!"[81] Or, as he put it another way, "One variation of the Termenvox is operated with human brain waves. A musician thinks of a tune and the instrument reproduces it."[82] It was a purely speculative idea—there was no prototype—but he told *Moscow News* in 1988 that the Yamaha company of Japan had "announced plans to produce these instruments beginning in the 1990s."[83]

As creature comforts diminished and mental acuity waned, with more and more people disappearing from the screen of his memory, Lev Sergeyevich moved deeper into philosophical realms. He began to push the envelope of the physical world, reaching toward an abstract, idealized conception of reality that, almost in a Stalinist sense, recognized no limits in the conquering of space, matter, or even time. This notion, of course, had been a hallmark of his life's quest, but now he would press it into service, scrambling to crack the last code of material existence itself: mortality.

He mused with Galeyev about KGB intrigue over the idea: "In those times . . . when only the aged were at the top, I was asked to tell them the secret of longevity. I refused, for this secret would be more important than the A-bomb."[84] Searching for a means of life extension had fascinated him since his early speculations over the fate of his coworker, and the eternal frost.

Traditionally, Lev Sergeyevich tackled all problems in the material universe as pragmatic questions, empirically soluble through natural science. Immortality to him was not a transcendental enigma involving the spirit world, but a biological puzzle of the here and now that concerned the preservation of matter. "There is nothing in the world but matter in motion," Lenin had proclaimed, "and matter cannot move save in space and time."[85] Lev Sergeyevich began with this assumption of Marxist dialectical materialism, the official, and only permitted, philosophical movement in the Soviet Union, but added his own motivations, inspired by spiritual elements of Russian cosmic utopia.

Nicolai Fedorovich Fedorov, a Russian philosopher and theologian who lived from 1828 to 1903, was the founder of Russian cosmism, the study of humanity's interrelationship with the universe, and his work had a profound influence on Lev Sergeyevich. Fedorov himself was an ascetic, a devout man who renounced possessions and material comforts, and whose ideas were admired by Dostoevsky, and by Tolstoy, who extolled, "He is very poor, he gives away everything, and is always cheerful and meek."[86] Fedorov's philosophy of the "Common Cause" was erected on the foundations of Christian theology— the idea of resurrection and everlasting life—but adapted to a secular, material view of earthly triumph over natural forces. Under his ideal society—his "psychocracy"—consciousness and action would unite to tame nature's destructive effects. Fedorov advocated the regulation of weather patterns (such as the seeding of clouds), the harnessing of solar energy to replace coal, and the seizure of the earth's electromagnetic energy to allow the steering of the planet outside its orbit on cosmic voyages. The final conquering of the deadly forces of nature would eliminate hunger, diminish the need for obsessive self-preservation, allow a classless society, and obviate hostility between individuals and nations. Most important, dominion over nature would mean the ability to overcome physical death, and with it, an obligation to "resurrect" all ancestors. The resulting overpopulation of the earth would be avoided by colonizing other planets. In the living unity of all humans, past and present, Fedorov saw a kinship with the triune nature of the Holy Trinity—an "indivisibility" so potent it would render the death of any of its members impossible. Fedorov eschewed the idea of the "beyond" and held as his ideal the realization of God's kingdom in this world.

The immortality Lev Sergeyevich sought was part of Fedorov's philosophy: a transformation of earthly matter to a permanently healthy form, freed from entropy. Fedorov's call to resurrect all ancestors was a literal one: "Put together the engine, and consciousness will return to it,"[87] he claimed, and Lev Sergeyevich was willing to take him at his word. The question was how to achieve it. The body would not be transfigured in this "resurrection" and would still require food. But for the mind that materialized the Great Seal bug and Buran, it was not impossible, just a challenge.

Lev Sergeyevich began his investigations at Moscow University with the biologist Lebedinsky, and with the support of Rem Khokhlov—by then the university rector—who, according to the inventor, didn't consider the idea "too abstract." One route of inquiry involved the blood. The inventor speculated: "There are different types of red blood cells, and those types change with a person's age. Several periods of change have been discovered, and during these periods, new 'beings' fight with old ones, and that is what brings on aging. One has to be able to take those 'beings' out of the donor's blood in time—and we would need a lot of the donor's blood! But how to catch them, at what age, I cannot yet tell."[88] He also explored what he called the "microstructure of time," to discover if time could be controlled to decrease entropy. "But to complete my studies of the microstructure of time," he told Galeyev, "—and this is the road to attaining genuine longevity—I need high-speed film-shooting technology. Have you got it?"[89]

The very striving for Fedorov's "transformation"—overcoming material evil (or the forces of nature), and the elevation of souls to a purified state, restored to true goodness—was consonant with Lev Sergeyevich's ancestral heritage from the Albigenses. Both Fedorov and the Albigensian sect adhered to a strong moral and ethical code, both advocated the equality of all people, and both prescribed a life of self-discipline and abstinence, free from material temptations. Each represented an unconventional mutation of Christian doctrine. "Transformation" for the Albigenses, of course, meant liberation of the soul from its prison of flesh, and in Fedorov's common cause it was precisely the opposite: a fortification of material sentience—spiritual liberation on earth. Despite these divergences, Fedorov's theories still echoed many of the Albigensian values at the core of Lev Sergeyevich's ancestral legacy. He had come full circle—like his tuned circuits—to feed back on and amplify the spiritual quest of his progenitors.

《》

On a trip to the Netherlands, Bulat Galeyev was asked by Franz Evers of the Royal Conservatory in the Hague to bring back photos of Lev Sergeyevich for the conservatory archive on his next visit. "I feigned naivete," Galeyev admitted, "and asked if he would prefer that I bring Theremin himself. The reaction was general surprise and excitement."[90] In January 1993 he made good on his word and returned with Lev Sergeyevich. The occasion was the international symposium "Schoenberg and Kandinsky," held jointly by the conservatory and the Municipal Museum of the Hague. The theme was the intersection of music and painting, and the event coincided with the addition of twenty-five new electronic arts studios and workrooms at the conservatory. The symposium also hosted the inaugural ceremonies of the international Academy of Light, where Lev Sergeyevich was the guest of honor, inducted into academy membership in recognition of the kind of work he once carried out with the illumovox and with Mary Ellen Bute.

Symposium participants toured the new studios at the conservatory one evening and viewed the musical instruments collection at the museum, which included a prominently displayed theremin. Natalia played on the instrument, and Lev Sergeyevich surprised everyone, stepping forward to perform a selection. There was still plenty of fortitude in his soul, but his ninety-six-year-old constitution was winding down. Still, on his return from the Netherlands, he planned to resume his work routine—the continual stream of new ideas that sustained him.

As he stepped through his door, the sight of his room in the kommunalka was like an electric jolt through his system. Everything had been vandalized while he was away—his musical instruments smashed, papers ransacked, photo albums stolen. Lately he had received threatening phone calls and letters laced with political overtones—for no apparent reason—but he never took them seriously. The motive for the assault on his property was unclear. The suspect could have been anyone, even a disgruntled occupant in another room of the apartment exasperated with the sound of electrical music seeping through the walls—the rancor of spitting in a neighbor's pot, gone wild. But whatever the intention, his last little corner of creative asylum had been trampled over. Clearly the humanity around him was far from purification.

Natalia took her father back to live at the two-room flat on Leninsky Prospekt for his own protection. It was crowded again—claustrophobic. The threats continued, and Natalia became nervous. Lev Sergeyevich remained isolated there through the spring and summer.

On November 2, Steven M. Martin's finished documentary, *Theremin: An Electronic Odyssey,* premiered across Britain on the BBC's Channel 4 in a special version prepared for television. The inventor had not yet seen it. But in some sense it must have effected a cosmic closure, a purification of his Albigensian soul. On the following day, in a peaceful slumber, Lev Sergeyevich Termen left the material world.

His search for Fedorov's immortal transformation was interrupted by the mundane stroke of mortality, but perhaps his purification came in transcendental form after all, in the company of his ancestors. "I would like to believe," Galeyev ventured, "that if angels exist, they . . . carried away the 'immortal part of the soul' of our Soviet Faust—perhaps even together with his Communist party card and the description of his 'Cathode Electromusical Instrument.'"[91]

Natalia, her two daughters, and her sister Helena delivered the body for burial. Lydia Kavina returned from Hamburg on the tenth, after receiving word. Moscow University officials offered to hold a funeral, but two memorial services were arranged instead—one at Sergei Zorin's Optical Theatre, and a second at the Moscow Composers House on November 14, where Lydia performed a work written in the inventor's memory by Anatoly Kisselev—*Pesnj na ruinach* ("Song on the Ruins"). "In this composition," Lydia wrote, "the theremin part develops out of powerful bass tones that personify a stroke of fate, moving through a sorrowful melody accompanied by sampled chords of a choir's singing to finally reach the lucid moments of the final bars: a very long, slow glissando upwards in the lonely voice of the theremin. This glissando rises to the highest possible tones and loses itself above audible limits."[92]

On the plain, polished brown marble slab that marks Lev Sergeyevich's resting place in Moscow's Kuncevskoye Cemetery, there is a solitary message:

TERMEN

Lev Sergeyevich

28.VIII 1896—1993 3.XI

What possible epitaph could circumscribe the many lifetimes of this single human being?—the nobleman's son in war and revolution; the Kremlin Orpheus sent to bow in prosperity before the cheering of nations, and to stoop in penal destitution under wheelbarrows in Hades; musician, alchemist, spy, court scientist to Voroshilov, magician of Carnegie Hall and Caramoor, slave of Kolyma and Radio Street, Stalin prizewinner and persona non grata; from RCA, magic mirrors, and the terpsitone, to Alcatraz, Buran, and the Great Seal; from Lucie Rosen, Clara, and Lavinia, to Lenin and Beria; a fate coursing through art, science, technology, war, industry, and espionage.

It may just be that he left his own epitaph. Not in words, but, characteristically, in the ether. At his final public performance—as he summoned the waves one last time, with old, knotted, quavering hands at the Hague Museum—he intoned a Russian children's song of the Soviet epoch.[93] It was not a summation, for he never looked back, but only toward the future:

> *Circle of the Sun,*
> *The sky around it —*
> *It is the picture of a little boy.*
> *He has drawn it on a sheet of paper*
> *And in the corner he has written:*
> > *Let the sun shine forever . . .*
> > *Let me be forever!*

Indeed, Lev Sergeyevich . . .

One felt that uncanny feeling as when a door opens on the world of the future and the free winds of unborn centuries stir about the dust of familiar things.

> —Horace Shipp, writing about the theremin in *The Sackbut,* January 1928

I was waiting at the curb on West Fourth Street, in front of the NYU Education Building near the corner of Washington Square Park. Each yellow taxi that veered toward my side of the street and slowed a bit caused my stomach to tighten. But every one accelerated and passed on again. Where *were* they? At last, one cab pulled up precisely in front of me. Steve Martin hopped out, bounded around the side, and unlatched the rear curbside passenger door. Ever so slowly, a hunched figure in a raincoat brought out one leg, then the other, and rose to his feet. Our eyes met. The same eyes that looked into Lenin's eyes, Stalin's eyes. Lev Sergeyevich Theremin was a real person, and he looked just like his recent photos. He smiled gently and we extended our hands for a clasp. Steve took one of the inventor's elbows, and Natalia Theremin—accompanying her father on the trip—supported the other. Lev Sergeyevich shambled his way toward the entrance. I followed behind. It was October 10, 1991.

We stepped out of the elevator on the eighth floor of the Education Building and walked Lev Sergeyevich to the office of the music department director, seating him on a black leather sofa. On Steve's instructions I had bought a quart each of milk and orange juice, which we measured out in cups for Lev Sergeyevich. Natalia was assembling the U-shaped black wooden theremin—the inventor's latest vacuum tube model from his Moscow flat—in a classroom. When Studio E had filled with students and faculty, I began my now standard slide lecture, "Theremin and the Emergence of Electronic Music." Afterward I took questions. Then, I readied the audience for a surprise.

The door opened. A slight figure ambled across the threshold. He wore a light gray suit with the jacket pulled in and buttoned just below the waist, causing the lapels to flair out. His white shirt—with no tie—was open at the neck. Black horn-rimmed glasses were patched near the hinge of the right temple with a winding of white tape. At ninety-five, he made fairly good speed moving across the front of the classroom.

(Flashback to Paris, Salle Gaveau, 1927: *"The door opens at the back of the stage—the buzz of conversation dies down—a little youthful figure crosses the stage to the box . . .*

For a moment he manipulates the interior of his instrument, which emits not unfamiliar crackling and buzzings. Then he stands erect and his fingers grasp the music of the spheres.")

Lev Sergeyevich demonstrated, and Natalia played the Rachmaninoff "Vocalise."

That night there was a soirée musicale Steve had arranged at the brownstone apartment of the writer Michael O'Donoghue and *Saturday Night Live's* music director Cheryl Hardwick. It was a glamorous affair in the style of the '20s drawing-room recitals from the inventor's American heyday. Donald Fagan of Steely Dan was there. *Saturday Night Live's* Hal Willner and the synthesizer pioneer Wendy Carlos came. At the focal moment, Natalia stood before the theremin in the front room, silhouetted against a backdrop of floor-to-ceiling curtained windows separated by a tall mirror that reflected a glistening chandelier. My wife, Linda Kobler, accompanied on the baby grand in the corner, two blazing candelabras framing the music rack. Again, Rachmaninoff's "Vocalise" rose high and howling into the room. Lev Sergeyevich was the toast of the town. I felt as though I had time-traveled to Lucie Rosen's Fifty-fourth Street townhouse in 1930.

I chatted with Theremin and pulled a thick loose-leaf notebook from under my arm. It was my study of his work, in progress. He scanned it with thoughtful eyes, and I flipped through, stopping at key chapters, explaining my chronicle to him as he nodded, smiling. I queried him on certain points. Then he took the book from me and secured it under his arm. Through the rest of our conversation, he gripped it tightly.

《 》

Clara Rockmore died on May 10, 1998. Her CD, *The Art of the Theremin*— a recital of Tchaikovsky, Rachmaninoff, and other Romantics, coproduced and engineered in 1977 by Robert Moog—is venerated by a whole new generation of players. The most prominent of these is Lydia Kavina, who began to appear internationally with the theremin in the 1990s. At the Thalia Theater in Hamburg, Germany, she played in Robert Wilson's production of *Alice*, with music by Tom Waits. She frequently performs her own compositions as well as pieces written for her and is active in both recording and teaching.

Beyond classical recitalists, the theremin has found a home in the most diverse of musical worlds. No other early electronic musical instrument boasts such an eclectic set of uses, from vaudeville to big band, from nightclubs to films, from rock to avant-garde.

After the Beach Boys, other musicians seized on the theremin: Jimmy Page played it in Led Zeppelin's "Whole Lotta Love"; the Jon Spencer Blues Explosion used it; the English pop group Portishead, Bruce Woolley and the Radio Science Orchestra, Père Ubu, Tesla, and a cross section of bands have laced their sounds with the primal scream of electronic music. Lothar and the Hand People began using a Moog theremin in 1965—Lothar was the pet name for the group's theremin—and in their two albums (1968 and 1969) the instrument shared the honors in a psychedelic mix of Moog synthesizers and tape decks. In 1997, the Lothars (four theremins and one guitar) convened as a retro tribute to Lothar and the Hand People.

In jazz, Brussels-based Youseff Yancy began augmenting his trumpet-playing with the theremin in 1968. The multimedia artist Eric Ross has used the instrument frequently in performance, especially as a MIDI controller.

The theremin also continued on in Hollywood. In 1994, Howard Shore scored a theremin part in his soundtrack for the Walt Disney Productions film *Ed Wood,* with Lydia Kavina playing. Danny Elfman mixed a theremin with an ondes martenot and samples of the theremin in his 1996 score for *Mars Attacks.*

In Russia after perestroika, interest in the theremin and its inventor reawakened. In 1992, the Theremin Center, an electronic music studio, was established at the Moscow Conservatory in—of all places—one of the same rooms where Lev Sergeyevich had constructed musical instruments before his rough dismissal in 1967. Andre Smirnov, director of the center, set up a small theremin museum and organized seminars around the history of the instrument. The centenary of the inventor's birth was observed in 1996 with major theremin festivals and conferences held in St. Petersburg, Moscow, and Kazan. In the late 1990s, a new crop of schoolchildren at Moscow's School No. 1159 began regular classroom theremin lessons with Zoya Dugina-Ranevskaya, one of the inventor's former pupils, using models built by Lev Korolyov based on the "Kovalsky School of theremin playing"—with left-hand controllers for articulation, and pedals for volume control.

≪≫

In the nether regions of Theremin lore there lies a body of unfinished or unrealized ideas—strange and intriguing—which we can only hope others might carry forth. Theremin anticipated "virtual reality" by decades when he suggested a "teletouch glove," designed to transfer touch sensations electronically to others at remote distances. It was meant, of course, to be combined with music, light projections, and aromas. In the '60s he spoke of the psychological effects on an audience hearing live music while an ascending and descending image was projected on the back wall of the stage, simulating a rising and sinking floor. He conceived of an experiment to monitor listeners' reactions while strips of rough or smooth fabric moved under their palms, activated from the armrests on their seats.

But beyond his abstract dreams and his musical instruments, Theremin's greatest legacy was to unlock the final sonic door, allowing the free sounds of the imagination to be made real. Without his instrument there could have been no synthesizer, no possibility for infinite combinations of sound with electricity. It is fitting that his tuned circuits, feeding back on themselves in an unbroken cycle with the "music of the spheres," are embodied in the Russian palindrome of his name:

"Termen ne mreT"
"Theremin does not die."

Abbreviations for Manuscript Collections

AFLPI   Schillinger Theremin Collection, Arthur Friedheim Library, Peabody Institute, Baltimore, Maryland

GHCC   George H. Clark Collection, National Museum of American History, Division of Electricity and Modern Physics, Smithsonian Institution, Washington, D.C.

LBRA   Lucie Bigelow Rosen Archive, Caramoor Center for Music and the Arts, Katonah, New York

MZC   Michael Zinman Collection

NYPLLC   New York Public Library at Lincoln Center, Performing Arts Division

Prelude

1. Nathan Milstein and Solomon Volkov, *From Russia to The West: The Musical Memoirs and Reminiscences of Nathan Milstein,* trans. Antonina W. Bouis (New York: Henry Holt, 1990), 223.

2. Dmitri Shostakovich, *Testimony: The Memoirs of Dmitri Shostakovich,* transcribed and ed. Solomon Volkov, trans. Antonina W. Bouis (New York: Harper and Row, 1979), 199–200.

3. Richard Deacon, *A History of the Russian Secret Service* (New York: Taplinger, 1972), 246, 249.

4. Bulat Galeyev, "Face to Face with Mephistopheles, or the Amazing Life of Leon Theremin," *Sputnik Digest* 9 (September 1992): 104.

5. Bulat Galeyev, *Sovetskyi Faust (Lev Termen—pioner elektronnogo iskusstva)* (Kazan: Biblioteka zhurnala "Kazan," 1995), 48. Quotation translated by Tanya Seroka; unless noted otherwise, all translations from the Russian are by Ms. Seroka.

6. Ibid., 68.

7. Nicolas Slonimsky, *Perfect Pitch: A Life Story* (Oxford: Oxford University Press, 1988), 153.

8. Galeyev, *Sovetskyi Faust,* 49.

Chapter 1: Soviet Power Plus Electrification

1. E. Petrushanskaya, "Lev Termen: pod muzikalnoy kryshey," *Muzikalnoy akademia* 2 (1995): 61.

2. Ibid.

3. Ibid.

4. Leon Theremin, "Rozhdenie, detstvo i younost 'termenvoxa,'" *Radioteknika* 27, no. 9 (1972): 109. Quotation translated by Irina Pekelnaya.

5. Petrushanskaya, "Lev Termen," 61.

6. Ibid.

7. L. S. Theremin, "Vospominania," in *Vospominania ob A. F. Ioffe* (Leningrad: Nauka, 1973), 109.

8. Ibid., 110.

9. Ibid., 111.

10. Ibid., 112.

11. L. S. Theremin, "Prodolzhau rabotat," besedy podgotovil L. Magaznik, *Sovetskaya muzyka* 11 (1986): 125.

12. Dmitri Volkogonov, *Lenin: A New Biography,* trans. and ed. Harold Shukman (New York: Free Press, 1994), 236.

13. Ibid., 201–2.

14. "Yudenitch Renews Petrograd Drive," *New York Times,* October 27, 1919.

15. Ibid.

16. "Trotsky Mobilizes All Petrograd Men," *New York Times,* October 25, 1919.

17. Theremin, "Vospominania," 113.

18. Ibid.

19. Ibid., 113–14.

20. Ibid., 114–15.

21. Lee De Forest, *Father of Radio* (Chicago: Wilcox and Follett, 1950), 1.

22. Gleb Anfilov, *Physics and Music* (Moscow: MIR Publishers, 1966), 143.

23. Ibid.

24. Ibid., 145.

25. L. S. Theremin, "The Design of a Musical Instrument Based on Cathode Relays" (abridged text of a public lecture presented at the Second Session of the State Institute for Musical Science, Moscow, November 11, 1921), trans. Oleg Petrishev, *Leonardo Music Journal* 6 (1996): 49–50.

26. L. Kokin, "Unost Akademikov," gl. *Iz Fiztekha in Grand-Opera,* 2-e isd. (Moskva: Sovetskaya Rossiya, 1981), 93.

27. S. Dreiden, "Lenin znakomitsa s termenvoksom," *Muzykalnaya zhizn* 7 (1978): 2.

28. Ibid., 3.

29. Kokin, "Unost Akademikov," 95.

30. Ibid.

31. Ibid.

32. Dreiden, "Lenin znakomitsa s termenvoksom," 3.

33. Petrushanskaya, "Lev Termen," 62.

34. Dreiden, "Lenin znakomitsa s termenvoksom," 3.

35. Petrushanskaya, "Lev Termen," 63.

36. Kokin, "Unost Akademikov," 96.

37. Dreiden, "Lenin znakomitsa s termenvoksom," 3.

38. Petrushanskaya, "Lev Termen," 63.

39. Ibid.

40. Dreiden, "Lenin znakomitsa s termenvoksom," 3.
41. Petrushanskaya, "Lev Termen," 63.
42. Ibid.
43. Dreiden, "Lenin znakomitsa s termenvoksom," 3.
44. Theremin, "Prodolzhau rabotat," 126.
45. L. Kokin, "Istoria o tom, kak iz electroizmeritelnogo pribora rodilas electromuzyka," *Nauka i Zhizn* 12 (1967): 134. Quotation translated by Irina Pekelnaya.
46. Petrushanskaya, "Lev Termen," 63.
47. Lenin to Trotsky, Moscow, April 4, 1922, *The Trotsky Papers, 1920–1922,* ed. and annot. Jan M. Meijer (The Hague: Mouton, 1971), 695.
48. Theremin, "Vospominania," 119.
49. Petrushanskaya, "Lev Termen," 63.
50. Bulat Galeyev, "L. S. Termen: Faustus of the Twentieth Century," *Leonardo* 24 (1991): 575.
51. Natalia Constantinova to the author, St. Petersburg, Russia, January 27, 1997.
52. Petrushanskaya, "Lev Termen," 63.
53. Ibid.
54. Ibid.
55. Ibid., 62.
56. Remark made to Leonid Krasin during a discussion in 1918 on the electrification of Russia, quoted in S. I. Liberman, "Nardodyi komissar Krasin'," *Novyi zhurnal* 7 (1944): 309.
57. Theremin, "Vospominania," 121, 122.
58. Ibid.
59. Ibid.
60. Ioffe to Physico-Technical Institute, Berlin, May 16, 1921, quoted in Kokin, "Unost Akademikov," 119.
61. Theremin, "Vospominania," 116.
62. Ibid., 120.
63. Ibid., 121.
64. Liber vol. B 126, p. 111, Records of the Patent and Trademark Office, RG 241, National Archives.
65. Galeyev, "L. S. Termen," 576.
66. Theremin, "Vospominania," 124.
67. A. Rokhlin, "Chetverty variant," *Radio* 2 (1984): 13.
68. Galeyev, "L. S. Termen," 27.
69. Mikhail Kaplunov and Mikhail Cherenkov, "Lev Termen's War and Peace," *Moscow News,* March 1, 1988.
70. *Saturday Evening Post,* August 14, 1926, quoted in E. E. Bucher, "Radio and David Sarnoff" (TS), part 4, 1943, p. 929, David Sarnoff Library, Sarnoff Corporation, Princeton, N.J.
71. Theremin, "Vospominania," 125.
72. Bulat Galeyev, *Sovetskyi Faust (Lev Termen—pioner elektronnogo iskusstva)* (Kazan: 1995), 40.
73. Henri Barbé memoirs, quoted in David J. Dallin, *Soviet Espionage* (New Haven: Yale University Press, 1964), 46.

Chapter 2: The Greatest Musical Wonder of Our Time

1. L. S. Theremin, U.S. patent no. 1,661,058, "Method of and Apparatus for the Generation of Sounds," filed December 5, 1925, granted February 28, 1928. In his patent, Theremin describes various schemes for interrupting the tone (figures 15–19). Joseph Schillinger described the effect of such a system in an early theremin: "One of the first models of this instrument had a knob contact for producing attacks. By pushing the knob with a finger of the left hand abruptly, one could produce the most abrupt forms of staccato at any desirable speed." Joseph Schillinger, *The Schillinger System of Musical Composition* (New York: Carl Fischer, 1946), 1545. It is unclear why Theremin never developed this system further, especially in response to criticisms of constant portamento in his space-control instrument. In this model, volume was easily regulated with a foot pedal, leaving the left hand free to operate another controller. The patent even specified a method for such an envelope control through hand capacitance in relation to an antenna (patent, fig. 19).

2. "The Latest Marvel in Music," *Literary Digest* 95, (October 1, 1927): 30.

3. Carl F. Pfatteicher, "A Musical Sojourn in Germany," *Musical Observer* (Fall 1927): 26.

4. Ibid.

5. "Electric Instrument Proves the Sensation of the Frankfort Festival," *Musical Courier* 95, no. 13 (September 29, 1927): 7.

6. "The Latest Marvel in Music."

7. "Electric Instrument Proves the Sensation."

8. "Die Grosse Sensation auf der Frankfurter Musikaustellung," *Der Volksfreund* (Frankfurt), August 10, 1927. Quotation translated by Michael Spudic.

9. Arno Huth, "Elektrische Tonerzeugung," *Die Musik* 20, no. 1 (October 1927): 42. Quotation translated by Eric Canel.

10. Quoted in Fred K. Prieberg, *Musica ex machina* (Berlin: Verlag Ullstein, 1960), 213. Quotation translated by Michael Spudic.

11. Quoted in Wolf D. Kuhnelt, "Elektroakustische Musikinstrumente," in *Fur Augen und Ohren*, ed. Rene Block et al. (Berlin: Die Akademie, 1980), 52–53. Quotation translated by Michael Spudic.

12. Ibid., 53.

13. Ibid.

14. Huth, "Elektrische Tonerzeugung," 44.

15. "Electric Instrument Proves the Sensation."

16. Max Eisler, "La Production électrique des sons," *Musique et instruments* 234 (1929): 147. All translations of quotations from the French are mine.

17. Adolph Weissmann, "Prof. Theremins Sphären-Musik," *Hamburger Fremdenblatt*, September 29, 1927. Quotation translated by Eric Canel.

18. "Aetherwellen-Musik," *Düsseldorfer Nachrichten*, September 29, 1927. Quotation translated by Eric Canel.

19. Leon Theremin, "Mein Ziel," *Berliner Tageblatt*, October 1, 1927. Quotation translated by Eric Canel.

20. "Wie wirste das 'Aërophon' auf die Fachleute?" *Berliner Tageblatt*, October 1, 1927. Quotation translated by Eric Canel.

21. Waldemar Kaempffert, "Ether Wave Music Amazes Savants," *New York Times*,

October 2, 1927. When he speaks of "intervals of thirteenths," Theremin is referring to thirteen equal divisions of the octave, not compound intervals consisting of an octave plus a sixth (the interval of a "thirteenth").

22. Ibid.

23. Theremin, "Mein Ziel."

24. Margot Epstein, "Professor Theremin erzählt," *Berliner Tageblatt*, November 17, 1927. Quotation translated by Richard and Edith Kobler.

25. Gerhart Herrmann Mostar, "Theremin," *Der Deutsche Rundfunk*, October 21, 1927. Quotation translated by Elisa Fahnert.

26. Epstein, "Professor Theremin erzählt."

27. *Daily Telegraph* (London), December 10, 1927.

28. Kaempffert, "Ether Wave Music."

29. Epstein, "Professor Theremin erzählt."

30. Ibid.

31. Leon Theremin, nonimmigration visa, November 25, 1927, General Records of the Department of State, Visa Division, RG 59, National Archives.

32. "Dernière Heure," advertisement in *Le Guide du Concert* 14 (1927–28): 267.

33. "M. Léon Théremin nous parle de sa prodigieuse découverte," *Petit Journal* (Paris), December 8, 1927.

34. "Music from the Air," *Belfast Telegraph*, December 9, 1927.

35. "Music from the Air; Scientist Who Plays on Nothing," *Daily Mail* (London), December 9, 1927.

36. "Music from the Air," *Belfast Telegraph*.

37. "Le Professeur Theremin fait un début triomphal en présentant la 'musique éthérée,'" *Petit Journal* (Paris), December 7, 1927.

38. Charles Fraval, "La Musique des ondes," *La Lanterne* (Paris), December 10, 1927.

39. Caby, "Une Admirable découverte," *L'Humanité* (Paris), December 8, 1927.

40. "Une découverte sensationnelle: la musique des ondes éthérées," *L'Humanité* (Paris), December 8, 1927.

41. "Paris Musicians Won by New Instrument," *New York Times*, December 9, 1927.

42. Andreas Lunas, "Une Révolution acoustique," *Le Courier Musical* (Paris), December 1, 1927.

43. Henry de Varigny, "La Musique des ondes éthérées," *Journal des Debats* (Paris), December 10, 1927.

44. Henry Prunieres, "Ether Wave Used," *New York Times*, December 25, 1927.

45. "Une Démonstration de la musique des ondes," *Le Journal* (Paris), December 9, 1927.

46. May Birkhead, "All Paris Thrilled by Radio Invention," *New York Times*, December 18, 1927.

47. A. Givelet, "Les Instruments de musique à oscillations électriques," *Le Genie Civil* 93 (September 22, 1928): 273.

48. Prunieres, "Ether Wave Used."

49. "Paris Hears Concert of Musician Who Does Not Touch His Instrument," *Paris Times*, December 7, 1927.

50. Artigny, "Billet du matin," *Le Figaro* (Paris), December 10, 1927.

51. "New Wonders in Air Music," *Daily Herald* (London), December 10, 1927.

52. "Electricity Turned into Music," *Daily Chronicle* (London), December 10, 1927.

53. Peterborough, "Theremin Again," *Daily Telegraph* (London), April 15, 1950.

54. "Music Out of Space; Sir O. Lodge, Shaw and Bennett Get a Shock," *Sunday News* (London), December 11, 1927 ("ordinary wireless," "young Russian"); "Music from the Air; Plucking It Out by the Hands," *Sunday Chronicle* (London), December 11, 1927 ("grave-looking); Julia Chatterton, "Music from the Air," *Musical Standard* (London), December 17, 1927 ("slightly built," "conveyed to audience").

55. Ernest Newman, "Melody from the Air," *Sunday Times* (London), December 11, 1927.

56. "Music from the Ether," *Daily Telegraph* (London), December 12, 1927.

57. Newman, "Melody from the Air."

58. "Music Out of Space."

59. Newman, "Melody from the Air."

60. "Music from the Ether," *Daily Telegraph.*

61. "Music Out of Space."

62. "Music from the Ether," *Daily Telegraph.*

63. Newman, "Melody from the Air."

64. "Music from the Ether; 'Howls' Transformed," *Irish Independent* (Dublin), December 13, 1927.

65. "Music from the Ether," *Daily Telegraph.*

66. "Music from the Air," *Sunday Chronicle;* Peterborough, "Theremin Again"; "Music Drawn from the Air," *Daily Express* (London), December 13, 1927.

67. Chatterton, "Music from the Air."

68. Newman, "Melody from the Air."

69. Candidus, "The Sense of Things; Playing on Air," *Newcastle Chronicle* (England), December 13, 1927.

70. "Mr. Theremin's Magic Muse," *Daily Mail* (London), December 12, 1927.

71. Ibid.

72. Candidus, "The Sense of Things."

73. "Drawing Music from the Ether; Demonstration of Russian Professor's Invention," *Birmingham Post* (England), December 12, 1927.

74. Ibid.

75. "Music from the Air," *Newcastle Journal* (England), December 14, 1927.

76. "The Electrical Ventriloquist," *Daily Mirror* (London), December 15, 1927.

77. Ernst Toch, "Theremin und Komponist," *Neue Badische Landes-Zeitung* (Germany), December 6, 1927. Quotation translated by Richard and Edith Kobler.

78. Ibid.

79. Kaempffert, "Ether Wave Music."

80. "Russian Invents Electric Apparatus Which Mysteriously Reproduces Music," *Chicago Tribune,* December 7, 1927.

81. L. S. Theremin, "Method of and Apparatus for the Generation of Sounds," U.S. patent no. 1,661,058, filed December 5, 1925, granted February 28, 1928.

82. "Melody from the Air," *Eastern Daily Press* (London), December 12, 1927.

83. Theremin, "Mein Ziel."

84. "Drawing Music from the Ether," *Birmingham Post.*

85. "The Electrical Ventriloquist."

86. "A Marvel; Magic Music; Holds Thousands Enthralled," *Daily Dispatch* (London), December 13, 1927.

87. "Recognisable Tunes," *Daily Sketch* (London), December 14, 1927.

88. "Magic Music Fills the Albert Hall," *Daily Chronicle* (London), December 13, 1927.

89. Arthur Eaglefield Hull, "Music from the Ether," *Monthly Musical Record* (January 2, 1928): 8.

90. Ernest Newman, "The World of Music," *Sunday Times* (London), December 19, 1927.

91. "Ether Music Inventor Sails Today," *New York Times,* December 14, 1927.

92. "Bad News for Burglars," *Daily News* (London), December 15, 1927.

93. Joseph Szigeti, *With Strings Attached* (London: Cassell, 1949), 214.

94. Arthur Ferrier, "When the Ether Becomes Our Fairy Godmother," cartoon, *Sunday Pictorial* (London), December 18, 1927.

95. "The Music of the Spheres," *Daily Chronicle* (London), December 10, 1927.

96. Emile Vuillermoz, "Music and the Ether Waves," *Christian Science Monitor,* January 21, 1928.

97. Birkhead, "All Paris Thrilled."

98. Candidus, "The Sense of Things."

99. "Music Drawn from the Air."

100. Alfred Einstein, "Aetherwellen-Musik," *Dur und Moll* 6 (October 25, 1927): 5. Quotation translated by Richard and Edith Kobler.

101. "Paris Musicians Won by New Instrument," *New York Times,* December 9, 1927.

102. "The New Musical Instrument," *Truth* (London), December 14, 1927.

103. "Paris Musicians Won by New Instrument."

Chapter 3: Capitalism Plus Electrification

1. "Sensacionny uspekh izobretenia L. C. Teremina," *Russkaya Gazeta* (New York), December 10, 1927. Quotation translated by Irina Pekelnaya.

2. "Inventor to Exhibit 'Ether Music' Here," *New York Times,* December 22, 1927.

3. "Gets Music from Ether," *New York Sun,* December 21, 1927.

4. "Inventor to Exhibit 'Ether Music' Here."

5. "Gets Music from Ether."

6. "Inventor to Exhibit 'Ether Music' Here."

7. Don Ryan, "Russ Inventor Turns Air Waves to Music," *New York American,* December 23, 1927.

8. "Prof. L. S. Termen v New Yorke," *Novoye Russkoye Slovo,* December 23, 1927.

9. "Russian Inventor Arrives with Magic Musical Wand," *New York Evening Post,* December 21, 1927.

10. "Air Wave Device Produces Music," *New York Zits Weekly,* December 31, 1927.

11. Lemuel F. Parton, "Music to Be Created by Wave of Hand," *Oakland Tribune* (California), January 20, 1928.

12. Leon Theremin, "New Trails in Musical Creation," *Musical Leader* 58, no. 10 (March 6, 1930): 19.

13. Norman Klein, "A Toy? No, a Soul Is This Music Wand," *New York Evening Post,* January 25, 1928.

14. Ibid.

15. Ibid.

16. Klein, "A Toy?" ("phonograph's nasal"); "Ether Concert Stirs Musical Stars Here," *New York Times,* January 25, 1928 ("novelty," "humming"; "'Strays' from the Laboratory," *Radio Broadcast* 12, no. 6 (April 1928): 428.

17. "Ether Concert Stirs Musical Stars Here," *New York Times,* January 25, 1928.

18. Klein, "A Toy?"

19. Lawrence Gilman, "Wave of Hand Draws Music from the Air," *New York Herald Tribune,* January 25, 1928.

20. Olin Downes, "Theremin Opens a Musical Vista," *New York Times,* January 29, 1928.

21. "American Debut of Theremin Invention Also Marks Concert Premier of Wurlitzer Nine Foot Concert Grand," *Music Trade Indicator* (Chicago), January 28, 1928.

22. "N.Y. Man Says He Made Music Wand," *New York Post,* January 30, 1928.

23. "Disputes Invention of 'Ether Music,'" *New York Times,* January 31, 1928.

24. "Both Rivals Claim to Own First Patent," *New York American,* January 30, 1928.

25. Ibid.

26. "Music from Air Is Old, He Says," *New York Sun,* January 30, 1928.

27. "N.Y. Man Says He Made Music Wand."

28. "Disputes Invention of 'Ether Music.'"

29. "Both Rivals Claim to Own First Patent."

30. "Disputes Invention of 'Ether Music.'"

31. Lee De Forest, "Audion Bulbs as Producers of Pure Musical Tones," *Electrical Experimenter* (December 3, 1915): 394.

32. Ibid.

33. Ibid.

34. Lee De Forest, *Father of Radio* (Chicago: Wilcox and Follett, 1950), 331.

35. De Forest, "Audion Bulbs," 395.

36. "Both Rivals Claim to Own First Patent."

37. "Disputes Invention of 'Ether Music.'"

38. Samuel Chotzinoff, "Music," *New York World,* February 1, 1928.

39. Theremin, "New Trails in Musical Creation."

40. "Prof. Theremin Demonstrates Music from Ether," *New York Sun,* February 1, 1928.

41. "Mechanical Music at the Metropolitan," *New York Post,* February 1, 1928.

42. C.M.J., "Ethereal Music," letter to the editor, *New York World,* February 4, 1928.

43. "Theremin in New Concert," *New York Times,* February 3, 1928.

44. "Music from the Ether; Concert Demonstration," concert program, February 14, 1928, Carnegie Hall, New York, courtesy of Olivia Mattis.

45. Henry G. Hart, "Notes Produce Colored Hues as Physicist Calls Music from Air by Waving Hands," *Philadelphia Record,* March 2, 1928.

46. "Asserts Device Produces Odors," *Philadelphia Public Ledger,* March 2, 1928.

47. Ibid.

48. Ibid.

49. Ibid.

50. Ibid.

51. "Step Right Up! No Strings to Pull in Playing Thereminvox," *Cleveland Plain Dealer,* March 10, 1928.

52. "Pulls Music out of Air," *Marietta Times* (Ohio), March 13, 1928.

53. "Stock Takes a Music Lesson," *Chicago Post,* March 15, 1928.

54. Edward Moore, "Static Turned into Music by Wave of Hand," *Chicago Daily Tribune*, March 13, 1928.

55. W. C. Richards, "Ethereal Orchestra Plays for Detroiters," *Detroit Free Press*, April 1, 1928.

56. Ibid.

57. Ibid.

58. Ibid.

59. Theremin to the Leningrad Physico-Technical Institute, May 21, 1928, Archive of the Physico-Technical Institute RAN, RG 3, Inventory 3, vd.hr. 2179, s. 20.

60. A. B. Magil, "Drawing Music from the Air," *Daily Worker* (New York), July 13, 1928.

61. Ibid.

62. "Thousands to Hear Theremin Play Tomorrow," *Daily Worker* (New York), July 13, 1928.

63. "20,000 at Huge Coney Concert," *Daily Worker* (New York), July 23, 1928.

64. Ibid.

65. Ibid.

66. "Outdoor 'Ether' Music to be Heard Monday," *New York Times*, August 24, 1928.

67. Pitts Sanborn, "Theremin's 'Ether Music' for Final Stadium Week," *New York Times*, August 25, 1928.

68. "'Theremin-Voxes' Heard in Open Air," *New York Times*, August 28, 1928.

69. "From the Ether a 'New' Music in New Manner," *Boston Evening Transcript*, October 8, 1928.

70. Ibid.

71. Leon Theremin, Prospectus for Theremin Corporation, 1928, Theremin Corporate Papers, MZC.

72. Ibid.

73. Ibid.

74. "Makes Radio Set of Ether Music Box," *New York Times*, February 14, 1928.

Chapter 4: A Theremin in Every Home

1. The economist Stuart Chase, quoted in Allen Churchill, *Remember When* (New York: Golden Press, 1967), 231 ("ousting statesman"); Bruce Barton, *The Man Nobody Knows: A Discovery of the Real Jesus* (Indianapolis: Bobbs-Merrill, 1925, fourth and fifth unnumbered pages ("founder of modern business"); Metropolitan Casualty Insurance Company pamphlet, quoted in *The American Heritage History of the Twenties and Thirties*, ed. Ralph K. Andrist (New York: McGraw-Hill, 1970), 82 ("greatest salesmen").

2. Leon Theremin, "The Thereminvox and Its Tonal Resources," paper read at Leon Theremin's demonstration of his newly invented musical instruments, Carnegie Hall, New York, March 2, 1929, reprinted, *Pro Musica Quarterly* 7, no. 3–4 (March–June 1929): 41.

3. Radio Corporation of America, memorandum of meeting with Professor Theremin, Hotel Plaza Annex, New York, April 4, 1929, GHCC.

4. Theremin Patents Corporation, Articles of Incorporation, Panama City, May 11, 1929, MZC.

5. Ibid.

6. Rafferty to Kerns, Radio Corporation of America memorandum, May 9, 1929, GHCC.

7. James G. Norton to D. J. Bennett, Radio Corporation of America, June 20, 1929, GHCC.

8. G. W. Henyan to J. W. Rafferty, General Electric Co., June 3, 1929, GHCC.

9. Babson, quoted in *American Heritage History of the Twenties and Thirties,* 153.

10. Migos Corporation, amendments to Articles of Incorporation, Schedule B, New York, 1930, LBRA.

11. David E. Fisher and Marshall Jon Fisher, *Tube: The Invention of Television* (Washington, D.C.: Counterpoint, 1996), 89.

12. E. F. Kerns to C. J. Harrigan, General Electric Co., September 20, 1929; E. F. Kerns to R. H. Emerson, Westinghouse Electric and Manufacturing Company, September 20, 1929, both in GHCC.

13. "Radio Corporation to Sell 'Ether Music' Device; Plans to Popularize Theremin Instrument," *New York Times,* September 23, 1929.

14. "Leon Theremin; Russian Scientist Playing His Ether-Wave Music Instrument," flyer for concert in Symphony Hall, Boston, on October 7, 1928, courtesy of Olivia Mattis.

15. Sam Love, "New Instrument with Extensive Repertory to Be Put on Market," *Louisville Courier Journal* (Kentucky), September 23, 1929.

16. Ibid.

17. RCA Theremin promotional brochure, Radiola Division, Radio-Victor Corporation of America, 1929.

18. "Instrument of 'Feeling' Demonstrated by Russian," *Evening World* (New York), September 28, 1929.

19. Robert Mack, "Radio Squeal Transformed into Fine Music by Science," *Worcester Gazette* (Massachusetts), September 25, 1929.

20. "Aladdin a Piker," *Elizabeth City Independent* (North Carolina), October 4, 1929.

21. Howard Fitzpatrick, "10,000 See Radio Show's Marvels," *Boston Post,* October 9, 1929.

22. *RCA Theremin Musical Instrument,* instruction booklet, (New York: Radio-Victor Corporation of America, 1929), 9.

23. Ibid.

24. "Radio-Victor Corporation Begins Production of 'RCA Theremin'; G. D. Shewell in Charge of Sales," *Talking Machine and Radio Weekly,* September 25, 1929.

25. RCA Theremin promotional brochure.

26. "Radio-Victor Corporation Begins Production."

27. *RCA Theremin Musical Instrument,* 10.

28. B. R. Cummings to T. R. Bunting, Schenectady, October 18, 1929, GHCC. The fixed and variable pitch oscillators of the RCA Theremin, at zero beat, resonated at approximately 172 kilohertz, and the volume control oscillator operated at about 420 kilohertz—sufficiently separated in frequency from the pitch oscillators to avoid interaction. The tests proved successful, revealing slight interference only in relation to the volume control oscillators. Cummings wrote: "The tests showed prominent beat interference only at 840 KC, which is the second harmonic of the volume oscillator. Direct comparison of this interference with that caused by a Radiola 66 indicated that the two were of approximantely equal intensity. The super heterodyne people considered the interference level to be well under the limit which they set for their super-

heterodynes." Interestingly, Marc Ellis, in the process of powering up an antique RCA Theremin in 1991, reported: "I knew that the 420-kHz volume-control oscillator was operating . . . because I could hear its second harmonic at about 840 kHz on a transistor radio." Marc Ellis, "The Theremin: A First Look Inside," *Popular Electronics* (September 1991): 94.

29. Nikolai Sokoloff, "Reminiscences," TS, 1965, Cleveland Orchestra Archives.

30. Ibid.

31. James H. Rogers, "Finds Theremin Has Warmth and Power," *Cleveland Plain Dealer*, November 29, 1929.

32. Oscar Thompson, "Novelties and Sonorities, with an Exhibition of Scientific Magic, in Clevelanders' Concert," *New York Evening Post*, December 4, 1929 ("grave and slender," "made just," "colossal outwellings," "musical saw," "volume increased"); D. K. Bradley, "Airphonic Music," *The Sackbut* 10, no. 7 (February 1930): 187 ("cosmic resonance"); Pitts Sanborn, "Sokoloff Leads the Cleveland Orchestra through New Works," *New York Telegram*, December 4, 1929 ("gigantic human voice").

33. Sokoloff, "Reminiscences."

34. Thompson, "Novelties and Sonorities."

35. Bradley, "Airphonic Music."

36. Thompson, "Novelties and Sonorities."

37. Olin Downes, "Glazounoff Draws a Rising Tribute," *New York Times*, December 4, 1929.

38. David Sarnoff, "Where Opportunity Beckons," *New York Times*, September 22, 1929.

39. Samuel Chotzinoff, "Music," *The World* (New York), December 18, 1929; Olin Downes, "Music," *New York Times*, December 18, 1929; Lawrence Gilman, "Mr. Stokowski Takes Leave of His New York Public until the Spring," *New York Herald Tribune*, December 18, 1929.

40. Chotzinoff, "Music."

41. Laura Lee, "Stokowski Adds 'It' to Orchestra Tone," *Evening Bulletin* (Philadelphia), April 30, 1929.

42. Ibid.

43. Joseph Schillinger, *The Schillinger System of Musical Compostion* (New York: Carl Fischer, 1946), 1546.

44. "'Ether Wave' in Orchestra," *New York Times*, April 30, 1929.

45. "'Electric' Concerts Now Possible," *Musical Advance* (June 1929): 4.

46. Pathe Audio Review, script for audio recording, November 11, 1929, Film Division, Library of Congress, Washington, D.C.

47. "Theremin Played at Armory To-Day," *Hartford Times* (Connecticut), March 19, 1930.

48. *New York Telegraph*, June 10, 1928.

49. "Mechanical Acts for Keith's Vaude; Television-Televox-Theremin," *Variety*, April 17, 1929.

50. "Ripley Will Make a Vaudeville Tour," *Milwaukee Sentinel* (Wisconsin), January 5, 1930.

51. "Learn Use of 'Theremin,'" *Brooklyn Standard-Union*, April 1930.

52. "Victor Theremin Is Demonstrated in Houston Store," *Houston Chronicle*, March 27, 1930.

53. "The Theremin Wins Famous Musicians and Stars for Stars on Tour," *RCA News* 11 (September 1930): 25.

54. "Everyone Craves to 'Make Din' on the New Theremin," *Wireless Age* (January 1930): 14.

55. "Theremin Draws Large Audience," *Little Rock Gazette* (Arkansas), February 28, 1930.

56. "Schipa Trying a New One," *Detroit Free Press*, February 20, 1930.

57. Victor Division, RCA Victor Company, Inc., to all Victor distributors, March 11, 1930, courtesy of Floyd Engels.

58. G. H. Clark, memorandum to Vice President and Director of Patent Development, Radio Corporation of America, March 26, 1930, GHCC.

59. Leopold Stokowski, "Wonderful Music Promised by Electrical Production," *Santa Barbara News* (California), June 9, 1928.

60. Elinor Elgin, "How Eerie 'Wave-of-Hand' Music Box Works, Explained by Inventor," *Boston Sunday Post*, February 4, 1928.

61. Emile Vuillermoz, "Music and the Ether Waves," *Christian Science Monitor*, January 21, 1928.

62. Waldemar Kaempffert, "Music from the Air with a Wave of the Hand," *New York Times*, January 29, 1928.

63. Olin Downes, "Theremin Opens a Musical Vista," *New York Times*, January 29, 1928.

64. Robert Marks, "Theremin Plans Electrical Orchestra," *Musical Association* (September 15, 1928).

65. "Ildiko Elberth Chats about Playing Theremin," *Newark News* (New Jersey), April 24, 1930.

66. Leon Theremin, paper read for Theremin by John Redfield at Theremin's demonstration of his newly invented musical instruments (TS), Carnegie Hall, April 25, 1930, p. 2, Clara Rockmore Archive, International Piano Archives of Maryland, University of Maryland, College Park.

67. "Theremin Presents 'Ether-Wave' Recital," *New York Times*, April 26, 1930.

68. Theremin, paper.

69. Ibid.

70. "Prof. Theremin Offers Recital of Ethers Waves," *New York Herald Tribune*, April 26, 1930.

71. Ibid.

72. "Theremin Presents 'Ether-Wave' Recital."

73. "Unusual Home Exposition at Armory," *Providence News-Tribune* (Rhode Island), May 19, 1930.

74. "Boy Plays Theremin," *Cleveland Press*, January 20, 1930.

75. "WOAI Family to Hear San Antonio Girl Play Theremin during Tonite's Kelvinator Program," *San Antonio News*, June 14, 1930.

76. Victor Division, RCA Victor Company, Inc., to Victor Theremin dealers, March 14, 1930, courtesy of Floyd Engels.

77. "Ildiko Elberth Chats about Playing Theremin."

78. "Woll Says Amtorg, in Federal Favor, Plots Revolution," *New York Times*, July 18, 1930.

79. "Red Spy Hunted Here as Link of Amtorg to Espionage Groups," *New York Times*, July 31, 1930.

80. E. E. Bucher, "Radio and David Sarnoff" (TS), part 4, 1943, p. 937, David Sarnoff Library, Sarnoff Corporation, Princeton, N.J.

81. Richard Massock, "About New York," *Austin American* (Texas), October 24, 1929.

82. Theremin Television Corporation, Certificate of Incorporation, New York, August 18, 1930, New York County Clerk's Office, Circuit Court House, New York.

83. Shewell to Victor Distributors, August 19, 1930, courtesy of Floyd Engels.

84. Radio Corporation of America, Annual Report 1930, New York, 1931, 26.

85. Theremin to Klein, New York, October 16, 1930, MZC.

86. "Low Tones for Stokowski," *New York Times*, October 18, 1930. From the description, it would appear that this instrument represented a further development over earlier models used by Stokowski, as the range evidently extended below that of the double basses. Additionally, timbre control may have been possible with this instrument, or another similar model used by Stokowski at the time, indicated by a remark in a 1930 flyer for one of Theremin's Carnegie Hall demonstrations: "This type instrument with amplification and a mechanical arrangement for the control of tone color by means of a foot pedal is being used by the Philadelphia Symphony Orchestra." Leon Theremin, promotional flyer for April 30, 1930, concert at Carnegie Hall.

87. Nicolas Slonimsky, *Perfect Pitch: A Life Story* (Oxford: Oxford University Press, 1988), 150.

88. Max de Vautibault, "Will Robots Make the Music of the Future?" *Musical Digest* 8, no. 7 (July 1928): 28.

89. Ibid.

90. Lawrence Gilman, "'Music from the Ether' Heard at the Philadelphia Orchestra Concert," *New York Herald Tribune*, December 17, 1930.

91. Lucie Bigelow Rosen to John D. Rockefeller, New York, April 9, 1931, LBRA.

92. Ibid.

Chapter 5: The Ether Wave Salon

1. "Mrs. Rosen to Play Theremin in Concert at Town Hall," *New York Evening Journal*, February 3, 1936.

2. "Move for Recitals of Unique Music," *New York Times*, December 21, 1930.

3. Joseph Schillinger, *The Schillinger System of Musical Composition* (New York: Carl Fischer, 1946), 283.

4. Nicolas Slonimsky, "The Schillinger System" (TS), n.d., courtesy of Olivia Mattis.

5. Joseph Schillinger, "Excerpts from a Theory of Synchronization," *Experimental Cinema* 5 (1934): 29.

6. Frances Schillinger, *Joseph Schillinger: A Memoir* (New York: Greenberg, 1949), 35–36.

7. Theremin Studio, flyer for lecture series by Joseph Schillinger, 1931, collection of Mrs. Joseph Schillinger.

8. Ibid.

9. Nicolas Slonimsky, "Schillinger of Russia and of the World," *Music News* (March 1947): 3.

10. David Ewen, *George Gershwin: His Journey to Greatness* (Englewood Cliffs, N.J.: Prentice-Hall, 1970), 213.

11. Joseph Schillinger, *The Mathematical Basis for the Arts* (New York: Philosophical Library, 1948).

12. Schillinger, *Schillinger System,* 1485.

13. Schillinger, "On the Theremin (In Place of an Interview)" (TS), New York, November 1929, trans. D. G. Nakeeb, AFLPI.

14. Ibid.

15. Joseph Schillinger, "Outline of the Work" (TS), December 1931, trans. D. G. Nakeeb, AFLPI.

16. "Music Makers to Be Engineers," *New York Sun,* May 11, 1940.

17. Schillinger, *Schillinger System,* 1486, 1547.

18. Slonimsky, "The Schillinger System."

19. Henry Cowell, "The Rhythmicon, a New Musical Instrument Invented by Henry Cowell and Executed by Leon Theremin, 1931" (TS), Henry Cowell clipping file, NYPLLC.

20. Henry Cowell to Olive Cowell, 1932, quoted in Leland Smith, "Henry Cowell's Rhythmicana," *Anuario Interamericano de Investigacion Musical* 9 (1973): 135.

21. Yolanda Bolotine Kulik, interview by the author, August 13, 1996.

22. "Electrio in First Concert Features Novel Instruments," *New York Times,* June 21, 1931.

23. Lee De Forest, *Father of Radio* (Chicago: Wilcox and Follett, 1950), 385–86.

24. Fish, Richardson, and Neave to Samuel E. Darby Jr., July 15, 1931, GHCC.

25. Benjamin F. Miessner to George H. Clark, March 10, 1938, GHCC.

26. "Color, Sound, Light Dance with Harmonious Steps in 'Synchromy,' Art Form Created by Texas Girl," *New York World-Telegram,* July 20, 1936.

27. Mary Ellen Bute, speech presented before the Pittsburgh Filmmakers, Pittsburgh, June 30, 1982, (MS), courtesy of Kit Basquin.

28. Ibid.

29. Mary Ellen Bute, "Abstract Films" (TS), c. 1954, courtesy of Kit Basquin.

30. Ibid.

31. "More Horrors," *Musical Courier,* January 23, 1932.

32. Marc Blitzstein, "Premieres and Experiments—1932," *Modern Music* 9, no. 3 (March 1932): 127.

33. "Demonstrate New Theremin Instruments," *Musical America,* January 25, 1932.

34. Ives to Slonimsky, New York, January 1932, in Nicolas Slonimsky, *Music since 1900,* 5th ed. (New York: Schirmer, 1994), 1039.

35. "Music Makers to Be Engineers."

36. Smith, "Henry Cowell's Rhythmicana," 139. Two acetate disks revealing the rhythmicon's possibilities exist in the Schillinger Collection, NYPLLC, probably made by Schillinger around 1940.

37. Quoted in Smith, "Henry Cowell's Rhythmicana," 141.

38. Quoted in "Gardner Theatre," *Gardner News* (Massachusetts), January 1922.

39. Clara Rockmore, interview by the author, New York, July 31, 1991.

40. Ibid.

41. Ibid.

42. Ibid.

43. "Look! No Hands—The Story of the Theremin," feature documentary, British Broadcasting Corporation, Radio 2, June 11, 1996; "In Clara's Words" (TS), November 1, 1997, courtesy of Clara Rockmore.

44. Clara Rockmore, interview by the author.

45. Ibid.
46. Schillinger, *Schillinger System*, 1547.
47. "Theremin Shows Four New Devices Friday Evening," *New York Herald Tribune*, March 27, 1932.
48. "Theremin Concert Given," *New York Times*, April 2, 1932.
49. "More Theremin," *Time*, April 11, 1932.
50. Lawrence Gilman, "Wave of Hand Draws Music from the Air," *New York Herald Tribune*, January 25, 1928.
51. "Music Lurks in a Glass Bulb," *New York Times*, September 7, 1930.
52. Irving J. Saxl, "Music from Electrons," *Radio News* 14, no. 2 (August 1932): 74.
53. Blitzstein, "Premieres and Experiments" 127.
54. Theremin to Warburg, New York, January 21, 1932, Schillinger Collection, NYPLLC.
55. Theremin to Schillinger, New York, April 4, 1932, Schillinger Collection, NYPLLC.
56. Ralph F. Colin to Theremin, New York, April 8, 1932, Schillinger Collection, NYPLLC.
57. Ibid.

Chapter 6: Alarms, Magic Mirrors, and the Ethereal Suspension

1. Irving J. Saxl, "Radio Guards the Baby," *Radio News* 14, no. 1 (July 1932): 44.
2. "Electrical Instruments for the Home," *New York Times*, October 9, 1932.
3. Rosen to Rockefeller, New York, April 9, 1931, LBRA.
4. George Goldberg and Leon Theremin, memorandum of agreement with N. I. Stone and Glenbrook Company Limited (TS), New York, July 20, 1932, MZC.
5. Leon Theremin, agreement with Emanuel B. Morgenstern and M. Boyd Zinman (TS), New York, October 28, 1932, MZC.
6. R. G. Dun and Company, credit report for Teletouch Corporation (TS), New York, March 2, 1933, MZC.
7. Teletouch Holding Corporation, memorandum of agreement between Prof. Leon Theremin, Emanuel B. Morgenstern, and M. Boyd Zinman (TS), New York, January 28, 1933, MZC.
8. M. Boyd Zinman, notes on Theremin Television Corporation, handwritten on lined paper, New York, 1933, MZC.
9. M. Boyd Zinman, notes on Theremin Patents Corporation, handwritten on lined paper, New York, 1933, MZC.
10. Zinman, notes on Theremin Television Corporation.
11. Teletouch Corporation, draft of advertising slogan (MS), about 1933, MZC.
12. "Wave of Hand at New Device Brings Police," *New York American*, January 27, 1928.
13. Teletouch Corporation, prospectus for burglar alarm (TS), New York, about 1933, MZC.
14. Teletouch Corporation, promotional postcard, New York, 1933, MZC.
15. "An Afternoon with a Theremin Player," *P.M.*, April 8, 1945.
16. Olin Downes, "American Idiom for Opera," *New York Times*, April 2, 1933.
17. Clara Rockmore, interview by the author, New York, July 31, 1991.

18. Edgard Varese, *Ecuatorial*, 1934, conductor's score (New York: Ricordi).

19. "New Music Given by Pan-Americans," *New York Times*, April 16, 1934.

20. "Pan-American Composers Give Spring Program," *New York Herald Tribune*, April 16, 1934.

21. Specification of Gun Dectector System, June 26, 1934, Records of the Bureau of Prisons, RG 129, National Archives.

22. J. A. Johnston to Director, Bureau of Prisons, Alcatraz Island, October 11, 1934, Records of the Bureau of Prisons, RG 129, National Archives.

23. J. A. Johnston to Director, Bureau of Prisons, Alcatraz Island, October 18, 1934, Records of the Bureau of Prisons, RG 129, National Archives.

24. Natalia Constantinova to the author, St. Petersburg, Russia, January 27, 1997.

25. Leonard Liebling, "Theremin Concert by Clara Rockmore Has Novel Effect," *New York American*, October 31, 1934.

26. "Miss Rockmore Gives Recital on Theremin," *New York Herald Tribune*, October 31, 1934.

27. "Theremin Takes Forward Step," *New York World-Telegram*, October 31, 1934.

28. "Southampton," unidentified newspaper clipping, July 20, 1933, LBRA.

29. Lucie Bigelow Rosen, "Three Articles on the Return of the Theremin" (TS), LBRA.

30. Ibid.

31. "Theremin Music at the Town Hall," *New York World-Telegram*, January 21, 1935.

32. "Lucie Bigelow Rosen in Theremin Recital," *New York Times*, January 21, 1935.

33. "Lucie Rosen Appears in Concert on Theremin," *New York Herald Tribune*, January 21, 1935.

34. E. Petrushanskaya, "Lev Termen: pod muzikalnoy kryshey," *Muzikalnoy akademia* 2 (1995): 65.

35. Ibid.

36. Teletouch Corporation, specifications for electric capacity altimeter (TS), New York, September 1935, MZC.

37. Petrushanskaya, "Lev Termen," 65.

38. "Black, Starr & Frost-Gorham Has 'Magic Mirror' Gem Display," *Jewelers' Circular-Keystone*, 1936.

39. "Yesterday's Concert Halls," *Nationen* (Oslo), May 15, 1936.

40. "Amerikansk thereminspelerska i Stockholm," *Dagbladet* (Stockholm), May 10, 1936.

41. "Concerto di Lucie Rosen," *La Tribuna* (Rome), April 18, 1936.

42. "Aetherwellen-Musik," *Münchener Zeitung*, April 29, 1936.

43. "Mrs. Rosen Success in Europe," *New York World-Telegram*, June 16, 1936.

44. "Étherhullámhangverseny," *Nemzeti Ujság* (Budapest), May 3, 1936.

45. "Sfaerenes musikk," *Tidens Tegn* (Oslo), May 15, 1936.

46. *De Telegraaf* (Amsterdam), May 26, 1936.

47. "Teletouch Corporation," *Electronics*, February 1937.

48. "Theremin," *Fortune*, April 1935.

49. Anne Bigelow Stern, interview by the author, September 18, 1991.

50. Leon Theremin, opisanie skhemy elektricheskogo dalnovideniya, priblizitelno 30-h godov (pechatnaya rukopis), MZC.

51. Paul Talbot, "The Back Yard," Boston, United Business Service, 1936, reprinted on Teletouch Corporation stationery, MZC.

52. Teletouch Corporation, "Ideas to be developed," penciled list on lined paper, MZC.

53. W. T. Hammack, Assistant Director, Bureau of Prisons, to Teletouch Corporation, May 19, 1937, Records of the Bureau of Prisons, RG 129, National Archives.

Chapter 7: "I, Leon Theremin . . ."

1. Cuban Embassy, Washington, D.C., memorandum to Edwin C. Wilson, Chief, Division of Latin-American Affairs, Department of State, February 19, 1935, General Records of the Department of State, RG 59, National Archives.

2. Ibid.

3. U.S. Department of State, Division of Latin-American Affairs, memorandum to Edwin C. Wilson, Division Chief, Washington, D.C., February 25, 1935, General Records of the Department of State, RG 59, National Archives.

4. "Theremin," *Fortune*, April 1935.

5. City Court of the City of New York, County of New York, withdrawal of order to show cause to punish the judgment debtor for contempt, New York, May 25, 1934, Civil Court, New York City.

6. Teletouch Holding Corporation, memorandum of agreement between Prof. Leon Theremin, Emanuel B. Morgenstern, and M. Boyd Zinman (TS), January 28, 1933, MZC.

7. "Soviet's Engineers Study Our Plants," *New York Times*, March 7, 1930.

8. "Soviet Papers Urge World-Wide Revolt," *New York Times*, March 7, 1930.

9. "Says Americans Act as OGPU Spies," *New York Times*, October 15, 1939.

10. Ibid.

11. Clara Rockmore, interview by the author, New York, July 31, 1991.

12. "At the Dell," *Evening Bulletin* (Philadelphia), August 16, 1937.

13. Rockmore, interview by the author.

14. John Martin, "Sophia Delza Pleases in Dance Concert," *New York Times*, November 16, 1931.

15. "First All-Negro Ballet Makes Debut in Harlem November 21," *New York Herald Tribune*, October 27, 1937.

16. Quoted in Joan Ross Acocella, "Van Grona and His First American Negro Ballet," *Dance Magazine* (March 1982): 24.

17. "First All-Negro Ballet Makes Debut."

18. Lavinia Williams, interview by Diana Dunbar, New York, December 1988, courtesy of Diana Dunbar.

19. American Negro Ballet, program booklet, New York, November 1937, NYPLLC.

20. Eugene Von Grona, "The Story of the Ballet," notes in The American Negro Ballet program booklet, New York, November 1937, NYPLLC.

21. "First All-Negro Ballet Makes Debut."

22. Acocella, "Van Grona," 30.

23. "Negro Ballet Has Performance," *New York Sun*, November 22, 1937.

24. "American Negro Ballet," *Vogue*, December 15, 1937.

25. John Martin, "Negro Ballet Has Debut in Harlem," *New York Times*, November 22, 1937.

26. Acocella, "Van Grona," 31.

27. "Negro Ballet Has Performance."

28. E. Petrushanskaya, "Lev Termen: pod muzikalnoy kryshey," *Muzikalnoy akademia* 2 (1995): 66.

29. Williams, interview by Diana Dunbar.

30. Teletouch Corporation, "The Teletouch Electric Eye," prospectus for distributors, New York, 1938, MZC.

31. Ibid.

32. Ibid.

33. Leon Theremin, interview by Olivia Mattis, Bourges, France, June 16, 1989, trans. Nina Boguslawsky and Alejandro Tkaczevski, courtesy of Olivia Mattis.

34. Anne Bigelow Stern, interview by the author, September 18, 1991; Rosalyn Tureck, interview by the author, December 1990.

35. Yolanda Bolotine Kulik, interview by the author, August 13, 1996.

36. "Jazz Characteristic of America—Theremin," *Harvard Crimson*, October 8, 1928.

37. "Advises Socialism as Only Slump Cure," *New York Times*, September 28, 1931.

38. "6,000 Americans to Work in Russia," *New York Times*, August 24, 1931.

39. Harvey Klehr, *The Heyday of American Communism: The Depression Decade* (New York: Basic Books, 1984), 326.

40. Ibid., 327.

41. "Legion or No Legion, Stokowski to Play the 'Internationale,'" *Daily Worker*, January 27, 1934.

42. Edward Weston, "Statement," *Experimental Cinema* 3 (1931), first unnumbered page.

43. Lewis Jacobs, "Eisenstein," *Experimental Cinema* 3 (1931): 4

44. E. A. Tamm to J. Edgar Hoover, Division of Investigation, U.S. Department of Justice, Washington, D.C., December 11, 1934, Files of the Federal Bureau of Investigation.

45. Ibid.

46. Anne Bigelow Stern, interview by the author, August 27, 1996.

47. Lucie Bigelow Rosen, "A New Sound in the World," *Music News* 39, no. 6 (June 1947): 3.

48. Ibid.

49. Anne Bigelow Stern, interview by the author, August 27, 1996.

50. Petrushanskaya, "Lev Termen," 66.

51. Ibid.

52. Anne Bigelow Stern, interview by the author, August 27, 1996.

53. Walter Rosen to Leon Theremin, New York, August 25, 1938, LBRA.

54. Leon Theremin, Power of Attorney, New York, August 31, 1938, MZC.

55. Walter Rosen to Leon Theremin, New York, September 9, 1938, LBRA.

56. Lucie Bigelow Rosen, "Questions Answered by Professor Theremin on his Space-Control Istrument" (TS), New York, September 1938, LBRA.

57. Leon Theremin to Walter Tower Rosen, on Teletouch Corporation letterhead, September 1938, LBRA.

58. Petrushanskaya, "Lev Termen," 66.

59. Williams, interview by Diana Dunbar.

60. Record of Vessels in Foreign Trade, 1938, Records of the U.S. Customs Service, RG 36, National Archives.

61. William R. Corson and Robert T. Crowley, *The New KGB: Engine of Soviet Power* (New York: William Morrow, 1985), 293.

62. Bulat Galeyev, *Sovetskyi Faust (Lev Termen—pioner elektronnogo iskusstva)* (Kazan: 1995), 49.

63. Williams, interview by Diana Dunbar.

64. Anne Bigelow Stern, interview by the author, August 27, 1996.

65. Yolanda Bolotine Kulik, interview by the author, August 13, 1996.

66. "Americans Informally Told to Return Home; Many Ship Bookings to Europe Canceled," *New York Times*, September 15, 1938.

67. "The Weather over the Nation and Abroad," *New York Times*, September 16, 1938.

Chapter 8: Yowsah, Yowsah!

1. Larry Zim, Mel Lerner, and Herbert Rolfes, *The World of Tomorrow: The 1939 New York World's Fair* (New York: Harper and Row, 1988), 54.

2. "Miss Rockmore Gives Recital on New Theremin," *New York Herald Tribune*, October 28, 1938.

3. "Miss Rockmore Gives Recital on Theremin," *New York Times*, October 28, 1938.

4. "Miss Rockmore Gives Recital on New Theremin."

5. "Clara Rockmore Theremin Recital," *New York Post*, October 28, 1938.

6. At this performance, Rosen premiered only the first movement of the Browning Concerto.

7. "Electrified Orchestra," *New York Sun*, September 5, 1936.

8. *New York Post*, October 31, 1934.

9. Candide, "Only Human," *New York Daily Mirror*, about 1936.

10. Louis Reid, "The Loudspeaker," *New York American*, October 31, 1934.

11. Charles Emge, "Dr. Hoffman Tells Whys, Wherefores of Theremin," *Down Beat* 18, no. 8 (February 9, 1951): 9.

12. Ian Ledgerwood, "Portrait of a Doctor as . . . Theremin Player," *Los Angeles Herald Examiner*, December 30, 1962.

13. W. S. (Bill) Farnsworth, "Sidewalks of New York," *New York Evening Journal*, June 8, 1936 ("Get a load"); Farnsworth, "Sidewalks of New York," *New York Evening Journal*, June 16, 1936 ("Recommended"); Hotel Montclair, newspaper display ad for "Casino Montclair," New York, about 1936, collection of Gary Hoffman ("Walter Winchell enthuses"); "Around the Tables with Chester King," *Brooklyn Daily Eagle*, June 5, 1936 ("Hope is an expert"); "Where to Dine and Dance," *Long Island Daily Star*, August 1936 ("By merely waving").

14. "For Your Information," unidentified newspaper clipping, 1936, courtesy of Gary Hoffman.

15. W. S. (Bill) Farnsworth, "Sidewalks of New York," *New York Evening Journal*, 1936.

16. "Dining and Dancing," *New York Herald Tribune*, March 27, 1940.

17. "Table Talk," *Cue*, December 4, 1939.

18. Theodore Strauss, "Certain News and Notes of Night Club Life," *New York Times*, December 24, 1939.

19. Teletouch Industries, Inc., "Pilferage Detector" prospectus, 1938, Files of the Federal Bureau of Investigation, Washington, D.C.

20. Teletouch Industries Inc., "Electric Eye Burglar Alarm" prospectus, 1938, Files of the Federal Bureau of Investigation, Washington, D.C.

21. Zinman to J. Edgar Hoover, New York, September 30, 1938, Files of the Federal Bureau of Investigation, Washington, D.C.

22. Teletouch Corporation, agreement between Teletouch Corporation, Teletouch Magic Mirror Corporation, and Teletouch Industries, Inc., and Radio Wire Television, Inc., New York, October 2, 1939, MZC.

23. Michael Zinman, interview by the author, December 13, 1996.

24. Anne Bigelow Stern, interview by the author, August 27, 1996.

Chapter 9: On the Yauza

1. Related to the author by Sergei Zorin, through Lydia Kavina, March 27, 1997.

2. Richard Lourie, *Russia Speaks: An Oral History from the Revolution to the Present* (New York: HarperCollins, 1991), 213.

3. Bulat Galeyev, *Sovetskyi Faust (Lev Termen—pioner elektronnogo iskusstva)* (Kazan: 1995), 51.

4. Vladimir Kossarev, "Stranizi istorii," materiali konferezii Lev Termen pioner elektronnogo iskstva, neopublikovanaya rukopis, St. Petersburg, 24–29 Noyabr 1996.

5. Dmitri Volkogonov, *Lenin: A New Biography,* trans. and ed. Harold Shukman (New York: Free Press, 1994), 234.

6. Robert Conquest, *The Great Terror: A Reassessment* (New York: Oxford University Press, 1990), 37.

7. Ibid., 102.

8. V. Petrov and E. Petrov, *Empire of Fear* (London: 1956); *Pravda Ukrainy,* May 4, 1989, quoted in Conquest, *The Great Terror,* 287.

9. Simon Wolin and Robert M. Slusser, *The Soviet Secret Police* (New York, 1957), 188, quoted in Conquest, *The Great Terror,* 284.

10. Eleanor Lipper, *Eleven Years in Soviet Prison Camps* (London, 1951), 48, quoted in Conquest, *The Great Terror,* 284.

11. John Glad, foreword to Varlam Shalamov, *Kolyma Tales,* trans. John Glad (New York: Norton, 1980), 12.

12. *Moskovskaya pravda,* February 10, 1989, quoted in Conquest, *The Great Terror,* 235.

13. Mikhail Kaplunov and Mikhail Cherenkov, "Lev Termen's War and Peace," *Moscow News,* March 1, 1988.

14. Ibid.

15. Shimon Naveh, "Mikhail Nikolayevich Tukhachevsky," in *Stalin's Generals,* ed. Harold Shukman (New York: Grove, 1993), 258.

16. Roy Medvedev, *All Stalin's Men,* trans. Harold Shukman (Garden City, New York: Doubleday, Anchor Press, 1984), 1.

17. Ibid., 11.

18. Galeyev, *Sovetskyi Faust,* 56.

19. Kaplunov and Cherenkov, "Lev Termen's War and Peace."

20. Naveh, "Mikhail Nikolayevich Tukhachevsky," 256–57.

21. Dmitri Shostakovich, *Testimony: The Memoirs of Dmitri Shostakovich*, transcribed and ed. Solomon Volkov, trans. Antonina W. Bouis (New York: Harper and Row, 1979), 100.

22. Kaplunov and Cherenkov, "Lev Termen's War and Peace."

23. Ibid.

24. Conquest, *The Great Terror,* 264.

25. Ibid.

26. Kaplunov and Cherenkov, "Lev Termen's War and Peace."

27. Conquest, *The Great Terror,* 278.

28. Kaplunov and Cherenkov, "Lev Termen's War and Peace."

29. Beck and Godin, *Russian Purge and the Extraction of Confession,* 119, quoted in Conquest, *The Great Terror,* 271.

30. E. Petrushanskaya, "Lev Termen: pod muzikalnoy kryshey," *Muzikalnoy akademia* 2 (1995): 66.

31. Narodnyi Kommissariat Vnutrennikh Del, nachalnik razvedivatelnogo otdela, postanovlenie, dela no. 154, Lev Sergeyevich Termen, Moskva, 19 Mart 1939, Arkhiv Komitet Gosudarstvennoy Bezopasnosti.

32. V. I. Lenin, *Polnoe sobranie sochinenii,* ezdanie 5-e, (Moskva: 1970–85), quoted in Volkogonov, *Lenin,* xxxviii.

33. Aleksandr I. Solzhenitsyn, *The Gulag Archipelago: 1918–1956; An Experiment in Literary Investigation III-IV,* trans. Thomas P. Whitney (New York: Harper and Row, 1975), 298.

34. Ibid., 293.

35. Vladimir Kossarev, "Stranizi istorii."

36. Aleksandr I. Solzhenitsyn, *The Gulag Archipelago 1918–1956: An Experiment in Literary Investigation, I-II,* trans. Thomas Whitney (New York: Harper and Row, 1973), 504.

37. Petrushanskaya, "Lev Termen," 66.

38. Ibid.

39. Ibid.

40. Iz Otdela Osobogo Soveschaneya pri Narodnom Kommissariate Vnutrennikh Del, Vipiska iz protokola nomer 26, Lev Sergeyevich Termen, Moskva, 15 Avgust 1939, Arkhiv Komiteta Gosudarstvennoy Bezopasnosti.

41. Solzhenitsyn, *The Gulag Archipelago, I-II,* 283.

42. Petrushanskaya, "Lev Termen," 66.

43. Varlam Shalamov, "Kolymskii Napiski," unpublished Russian manuscript by a Soviet ex-prisoner, published in French as *Récits de Kolyma* (Paris, 1969), quoted in Robert Conquest, *Kolyma: The Arctic Death Camps* (New York: Viking Press, 1978), 153.

44. Conquest, *Kolyma,* 13.

45. Galeyev, *Sovetskyi Faust,* 58.

46. Aleksandr Solzhenitsyn, *The Gulag Archipelago 1918–1956: An Experiment in Literary Investigation V-VII,* trans. Harry Willetts (New York: Harper and Row, 1978), 534.

47. Eugenia Semyonovna Ginzburg, *Krutoy Marshrut* (Milan, 1967), first-hand account by a Soviet woman writer, published in English as *Journey into the Whirlwind* (London and New York, 1967), quoted in Conquest, *Kolyma,* 30–31.

48. Michael Solomon, *Magadan* (Toronto, 1971), first-hand account by a Rumanian ex-prisoner in the postwar period, quoted in Conquest, *Kolyma,* 66.

49. Lourie, *Russia Speaks,* 197.

50. Galeyev, *Sovetskyi Faust,* 6.

51. Elinor Lipper, *Elf Jahre in sowjetischen Gefängnissen und Lagern* (Zürich, 1950), first-hand account by a Swiss former Communist prisoner, published in English as *Eleven Years in Soviet Prison Camps* (London and Chicago, 1951), quoted in Conquest, *Kolyma,* 128.

52. Solzhenitsyn, *The Gulag Archipelago, III-IV,* 129.

53. Solomon, *Magadan,* quoted in Conquest, *Kolyma,* 64.

54. Vladimir Petrov, a former Soviet prisoner now in the West, published a memoir in English as *Soviet Gold* (New York, 1949), quoted in Conquest, *Kolyma,* 50.

55. Galeyev, *Sovetskyi Faust,* 58.

56. Kaplunov and Cherenkov, "Lev Termen's War and Peace."

57. Ibid.

58. Kaplunov and Cherenkov, "Lev Termen's War and Peace"; Petrushanskaya, "Lev Termen," 66.

59. Lourie, *Russia Speaks,* 196.

60. Solzhenitsyn, *The Gulag Archipelago, III-IV,* 494.

61. Lourie, *Russia Speaks,* 189.

62. Solzhenitsyn, *The Gulag Archipelago, I-II,* 582.

63. *Dark Side of the Moon,* with an introduction by T. S. Eliot (London, 1946), contains two first-hand accounts by Polish women, pp. 118–21 and 155–64, respectively, quoted in Conquest, *Kolyma,* 62.

64. G. Kiksman, "Chelovek iz kommynalki," *Svet, priroda i chelovek* 12 (1992): 46.

65. Bulat Galeyev, "Face to Face with Mephistopheles, or the Amazing Life of Leon Theremin," *Sputnik Digest* 9 (September 1992): 105.

66. Conquest, *Kolyma,* 53.

67. Ibid., 218, 227.

68. Solzhenitsyn, *The Gulag Archipelago, III-IV,* 478.

69. Ibid.

70. Ibid.

71. Ibid., 481.

72. Ibid., 482.

73. Kaplunov and Cherenkov, "Lev Termen's War and Peace."

74. Galeyev, *Sovetskyi Faust,* 58.

75. L. L. Kerber, *Stalin's Aviation Gulag: A Memoir of Andrei Tupolev and the Purge Era,* ed. Von Hardesty (Washington: Smithsonian Institution Press, 1996), 151–52.

76. Solzhenitsyn, *The Gulag Archipelago, I-II,* 590.

77. Quoted in Kerber, *Stalin's Aviation Gulag,* 105.

78. Ibid., 155.

79. Jaroslav Golovanov, *Korolev: fakti i myfi* (Moscow: Nauka, 1994), 295.

80. Ibid.

81. Kerber, *Stalin's Aviation Gulag,* 156.

82. Ibid., 176.

83. Ibid., 160.

84. Ibid., 179.

85. Ibid., 199.
86. Ibid., 207.
87. Ibid., 175.
88. Ibid., 190.
89. Ibid.
90. Alexander I. Solzhenitsyn, *The First Circle*, trans. Thomas P. Whitney (New York: Harper and Row, 1968), 9–10.
91. Kerber, *Stalin's Aviation Gulag*, 231.
92. Ibid., 233.
93. Ibid., 234.
94. Ibid.
95. Ibid., 234–35.
96. Ibid., 235.
97. Golovanov, *Korolev: fakti I myfi*, 305.
98. Kerber, *Stalin's Aviation Gulag*, 167.
99. Ibid., 236.
100. Ibid., 239.
101. Mikhail Kaplunov and Mikhail Cherenkov, "Another Look at Lev Termen's Long and Eventful Life," *Moscow News* 17 (1988): 2.
102. Lourie, *Russia Speaks*, 233.

Chapter 10: Free Music

1. Dmitri Shostakovich, *Testimony: The Memoirs of Dmitri Shostakovich*, transcribed and ed. Solomon Volkov, trans. Antonina W. Bouis (New York: Harper and Row, 1979), 198–99.
2. Comment to Sergei Eisenstein in Moscow, 1934, quoted in Susan Robeson, *The Whole World in His Hands: A Pictorial Biography of Paul Robeson* (Secaucus, N.J.: Citadel Press, 1981).
3. Vern Smith, "'I Am at Home,' Says Robeson at Reception in Soviet Union," *Daily Worker*, January 15, 1935, quoted in *Paul Robeson Speaks: Writings, Speeches, Interviews, 1918–1974*, edited, with an introduction and notes by Philip S. Foner (New York: Brunner Mazel, 1978), 95.
4. Noel Strauss, "Several Ovations Welcome Robeson," *New York Times*, October 7, 1940.
5. Ibid.
6. Clara Rockmore, interview by the author, New York, July 31, 1991.
7. Ibid.
8. Ibid.
9. Lucie Bigelow Rosen, diary entry from "Theremin Notebook" (TS), New York, July 22, 1940, LBRA.
10. Lavinia Williams, interview by Diana Dunbar, New York, December 1988, courtesy of Diana Dunbar.
11. Lucie Bigelow Rosen, "A New Sound in the World," *Music News* 39, no. 6 (June 1947): 3.
12. Lucie Bigelow Rosen, diary entry, November 22, 1944.
13. "An Afternoon with a Theremin Player," *P.M.*, April 8, 1945.

14. Rockmore, interview by the author.

15. Stokowski to Rockmore, Philadelphia, April 22, 1939, Clara Rockmore Archive, International Piano Archives of Maryland, University of Maryland, College Park.

16. Louis Biancolli, "Theremin Heard Again in Concerto of Its Own," *New York World-Telegram*, February 27, 1945.

17. Harriet Johnson, "Stokowski and Theremin," *New York Post*, 27 Febraury 1945.

18. Biancolli, "Theremin Heard Again."

19. John Cage, *Silence* (Middletown: Wesleyan University Press, 1939), 3–4.

20. Percy Grainger to Olin Downes, 1942, quoted in Teresa Balough, comp., *A Musical Genius from Australia: Selected Writings by and about Percy Grainger* (Nedlands, Western Australia: University of Western Australia, Department of Music, 1982), 141.

21. Percy Aldridge Grainger, "'Free Music'; December 6, 1938," in Balough, *Musical Genius from Australia*, 143.

22. Ibid., 144.

23. These devices, collectively known as the "Cross-Grainger free music machine," were developed from 1945 until Grainger's death in 1961. Both *Free Music No. 1* and *Free Music No. 2* were later realized in electronic music studios at the BBC about 1970, at the Swedish Radio EMS about 1972, and at the University of Melbourne in 1976 and 1978.

24. Philip Gordon, "The Theremin," *New Jersey Journal of Education* (February 1930): 13.

25. Miklos Rozsa, *Double Life* (New York: Hippocrene Books, Winwood Press, 1989), 126.

26. Rockmore, interview by the author.

27. Ibid.

28. Charles Emge, "Dr. Hoffman Tells Whys, Wherefores of Theremin," *Down Beat* 18, no. 8 (February 9, 1951): 9.

29. Lawrence Morton, quoted in Christopher Palmer, *Rozsa: A Sketch of His Life and Work* (London: Breitkopf and Härtel, 1975), 33.

30. Rozsa, *Double Life*, 128.

31. Miklos Rozsa, "Lecture in London (October 1972)," *Pro Musica Sana* 4, no. 1 (Spring 1975): 22.

32. Rozsa, *Double Life*, 129.

33. Ibid., 128.

34. Frances Schillinger, *Joseph Schillinger: A Memoir* (New York: Greenberg, 1949), 222.

Chapter 11: Mailboxes and the Invisible Man

1. Amy Knight, *Beria: Stalin's First Lieutenant* (Princeton: Princeton University Press, 1993), 131.

2. W. Averell Harriman and Elie Abel, *Special Envoy to Churchill and Stalin: 1941–1946* (New York: Random House, 1975), 416.

3. "Communism's Beria; The Cop at the Keyhole Is King," *Time*, March 22, 1948.

4. Michael R. Beschloss, *Mayday: Eisenhower, Khrushchev and the U-2 Affair* (New York: Harper and Row, 1986), 168.

5. Andrei Sakharov, *Memoirs*, trans. Richard Lourie (New York: Knopf, 1990), 146.

6. Martin Ebon, *Svetlana: The Story of Stalin's Daughter* (New York: New American Library, 1967), 59.

7. Harriman and Abel, *Special Envoy*, 235.

8. Mikhail Kaplunov and Mikhail Cherenkov, "Lev Termen's War and Peace," *Moscow News*, March 1, 1988.

9. E. Pozdnykovi V. Goncharov, "Orel vse slushal i peredaval Russkim," *Sekurity* (Yanu, 1996), 45.

10. E. Petrushanskaya, "Lev Termen: pod muzikalnoy kryshey," *Muzikalnoy akademia 2* (1995): 67.

11. Translated text of speech delivered by Nikita S. Khrushchev, First Secretary of the Communist Party, at a secret session of the party's Twentieth Congress in Moscow, February 24 and 25, 1956, reprinted in "Text of Speech on Stalin by Khrushchev as Released by the State Department," *New York Times*, June 5, 1956.

12. Nikita Khrushchev, *Khrushchev Remembers*, vol. 1, trans. and ed. Strobe Talbot (Boston: Little, Brown, 1970), 281.

13. Harriman and Abel, *Special Envoy*, 522, fn.

14. Roy Medvedev, *All Stalin's Men*, trans. Harold Shukman (Garden City, N.Y.: Doubleday, Anchor Press, 1984), 20.

15. "Mehanik Lev Termen: 'Ya podslushival Kreml,'" besedy podgotovil Dmitriy Lihanov, *Sovershenno sekretno 4* (1991): 30.

16. Osoboe Soveschaniye pri Ministerstve Gosudarstvennoy Bezopasnosti Soiuza SSR, Vipeska iz protokola nomera 25, Lev Sergeyevich Termen, Moskva, 27 Iun 1947, Arkhiv Komiteta Gosudarstvennoy Bezopasnosti.

17. Leon Theremin, interview by Olivia Mattis, Bourges, France, June 16, 1989, trans. Nina Boguslawsky and Alejandro Tkaczevski, courtesy of Olivia Mattis.

18. Bulat Galeyev, *Sovetskyi Faust (Lev Termen—pioner elektronnogo iskusstva)* (Kazan: 1995), 68.

19. Ibid.

20. Ibid.

21. George F. Kennan, *Memoirs 1950–1963: Volume 2,* (Boston: Little, Brown, 1972), 117.

22. "Informazia o L. S. Termen" (TS), Informazia sostavlena Nataliey Mikhailovnoy Nesturkh, Moskva, 1992, Arkhiv Lydii Kavinoy.

23. Svetlana Alliluyeva, *Twenty Letters to a Friend*, trans. Priscilla Johnson McMillan (New York: Harper and Row, 1967), 7–8.

24. Ibid., 10.

25. H. Montgomery Hyde, *Stalin: The History of a Dictator* (New York: Da Capo, 1971), 599.

26. *Pravda,* December 17, 1953, quoted in Knight, *Beria,* 218.

27. "Text of Speech on Stalin by Khrushchev as Released by the State Department."

28. "A Revised Biography: Joseph Stalin," *New York Times,* June 5, 1956.

29. Komitet Gosudarstvennoi Bezopasnosti—Afanasievu, Moskva, 14 Iun 1991, Arkhiv Lydii Kavinoy.

30. Session of the Supreme Soviet, May 5, 1960, quoted in Beschloss, *Mayday,* 43.

31. Statement read by Lincoln White, State Department spokesman, at a press conference, May 5, 1960, quoted in Beschloss, *Mayday,* 51.

32. Session of the Supreme Soviet, May 7, 1960, quoted in Beschloss, *Mayday*, 58–59.

33. William J. Jorden, "Spy Devices Used by Soviet Shown," *New York Times*, May 28, 1960.

34. Beschloss, *Mayday*, 313.

35. Kennan, *Memoirs*, 154–56.

36. Ibid., 156, fn.

37. Ibid., 156.

38. H. Keith Melton, *CIA Special Weapons and Equipment: Spy Devices of the Cold War* (New York: Sterling, 1993), 6.

39. Kennan, *Memoirs*, 156.

40. Peter Wright, with Paul Greengrass, *Spy Catcher: The Candid Autobiography of a Senior Intelligence Officer* (New York: Viking, 1987), 22–23.

Chapter 12: In the Vanguard

1. Nixon to Williams, Washington, April 19, 1955, Dance Research Collection, NYPLLC.

2. "Stalin Is 70 Plus 3 But Has No Party; Paul Robeson Praised," *New York Times*, December 22, 1952.

3. "Novelty Feature at the Stadium," *New York Times*, July 31, 1947 ("stunning"); Louis Biancolli, "Theremin in Concert Spotlight," *New York World-Telegram*, July 31, 1947 ("lady thereminist").

4. "But the Theremin Wouldn't Play," *News Chronicle* (London), April 15, 1950.

5. "Electrophonic Music," *The Times* (London), April 21, 1950.

6. "Lucie Bigelow Rosen and the Theremin," *Musical Opinion* 73, no. 872 (May 1950): 483.

7. "Electrophonic Music."

8. "The Limitations of the Theremin," *Daily Telegraph* (London), April 19, 1950.

9. "Electrophonic Music."

10. "Una Thereminista al Teatro delle Arti," *Il Momento* (Rome), May 17, 1950.

11. "Lucie Bigelow Rosen and the Theremin," *Musical Opinion* (May 1950): 483.

12. J. Forrest Whiteley, "Versatility Plus Originality," promotional flyer, London, early 1960s, collection of Hugh Davies.

13. Whiteley to Rosen, London, May 8, 1950, LBRA.

14. Radio script for "Command Performance #225," U.S. Armed Forces Radio Service, April 18, 1946, collection of Gary Hoffman.

15. *Parklabrea News* (Los Angeles), clipping from 1950, courtesy of Gary Hoffman.

16. Liner notes from Harry Revel, *Music Out of the Moon*, cond. and arr. Leslie Baxter, Capitol CC-47.

17. Al Scharper, "Music Out of the Moon," *Variety*, 1947.

18. Harold Heffernan, "Mood Music," *Detroit News*, July 18, 1950.

19. "Creeps!" *Script*, January 1948.

20. "Music," *Time*, clipping from 1947, collection of Gary Hoffman.

21. *The Secret Music of China*, orchestra, chorus, and cast conducted by Alexander Laszlo, Columbia C-172.

22. Liner notes from Harry Revel, *Perfume Set to Music*, cond. and arr. Leslie Baxter, RCA Victor P-231.

23. "Rhythm and the 'Scent-ses,'" *Cue*, November 1948.

24. "$25,000.00 National Advertising Campaign Scheduled for 'Perfume Set to Music' Album," *Your RCA Victor Distributor's Record Bulletin* 1, no. 16 (November 8, 1948): 1.

25. RCA Victor Records, display ad, *Los Angeles Times*, December 9, 1948.

26. Al Scharper, "Record Reviews," *Variety*, December 21, 1948.

27. Jim Joseph, "Foot Doctor Coaxes Music from Nowhere," unidentified newspaper clipping, 1948, collection of Gary Hoffman.

28. Liner notes from Harry Revel, *Music for Peace of Mind*, cond. and arr. Billy May, Capitol CC-221.

29. "Concert," *Down Beat*, clipping from 1950, collection of Gary Hoffman.

30. Ernest J. Schultz, "A Simple Electronic Musical Instrument: The Theremin," *Radio and Television News* 42, no. 4 (October 1949): 66–67.

31. Robert Moog, "The Theremin," *Radio and Television News* 51 (January 1954): 39.

32. R. A. Moog Company, "The R. A. Moog Theremin," promotional brochure, Flushing, N.Y., 1954, collection of Robert Moog.

33. Mary Ellen Bute, "Abstract Films," unpublished essay (TS), ca. 1954, collection of Kit Basquin.

34. *New York Herald Tribune*, undated, quoted in a promotional brochure on the films of Mary Ellen Bute, after 1965, collection of Kit Basquin.

35. Charles Emge, "Dr. Hoffman Tells Whys, Wherefores of Theremin," *Down Beat* 18, no. 8 (February 9, 1951): 9.

36. Polly Pope, "Dr. Samuel Hoffman Makes Music with Static Control, Invisible Waves," unidentified Los Angeles newspaper clipping, 1950, courtesy of Gary Hoffman.

37. Gary Hoffman, interview by the author, August 21, 1997.

38. Langston Hughes, *Laughing to Keep from Crying* (New York: Henry Holt, 1952), 2.

39. Herman Wouk, *Marjorie Morningstar* (Garden City, N.Y.: Doubleday, 1955), 404.

40. R. A. Moog Company, *The R. A. Moog Theremins*, promotional brochure, Ithaca, N.Y., 1959, courtesy of Clare Morgenstern.

41. Ibid.

42. Robert Moog, interview by the author, August 17, 1997.

43. Robert A. Moog, "A Transistorized Theremin," *Electronics World* 65 (January 1961): 29–32, 125.

44. Dr. Paul Tanner, interview by David Miller, 1997, courtesy of David Miller.

45. Dr. Paul Tanner, interview by the author, August 13, 1997.

46. Tanner, interview by David Miller.

47. Tanner, interview by the author.

48. Cy Schneider, liner notes from *Music for Heavenly Bodies*, arr. Warren Baker, Omega OSL-4.

49. Tanner, interview by the author.

50. Harold Heffernan, memo to Samuel Hoffman, Detroit, July 21, 1950, collection of Gary Hoffman.

51. Southern California Council of National Federation of Temple Brotherhoods, "Men's Club Dinner," flyer, Los Angeles, May 1952, collection of Gary Hoffman.

52. "Inventor of Theremin Is Soloist during 'Spellbound,'" press release, May 13, 1964, for "International Hour: Music from Hollywood," collection of Gary Hoffman.

53. Margaret Harford, "Playing by 'Thought Waves' Discounted," *Hollywood Citizen News,* March 22, 1948.

54. Moog, interview by the author.

55. Herbert Deutsch, interview by the author, August 25, 1997.

56. Robert Moog, interview by the author, October 5, 1991.

57. Allen Hughes, "Leaps and Cadenzas," *New York Times,* August 1, 1965.

58. Ibid.

59. Tanner, interview by the author.

60. Ibid.

61. Walter Sear, interview by the author, August 29, 1997.

62. Allen Hughes, "Moog Approves of Moog-Made Jazz," *New York Times,* August 29, 1969.

63. Deutsch, interview by the author.

64. Bertram Stanleigh, "Moog Jazz in the Garden," *Audio* (November 1969): 96.

65. Deutsch, interview by the author.

Chapter 13: A One-Room Flat and the Microstructure of Time

1. "Look! No Hands—The Story of the Theremin," feature documentary, British Broadcasting Corporation, Radio 2, June 11, 1996.

2. Bulat Galeyev, *Sovetskyi Faust (Lev Termen—pioner elektronnogo iskusstva)* (Kazan: 1995), 68.

3. Natalia Nesturkh, "The Theremin and Its Inventor in Twentieth-Century Russia," *Leonardo Music Journal* 6 (1996): 58.

4. Gleb Anfilov, *Physics and Music* (Moscow: MIR Publishers, 1966), 99.

5. Anatoly Kisselev, "Theremin and the First Synthesizer in the World" (TS) 1991, courtesy of Anatoly Kisselev.

6. Boris Groys, *The Total Art of Stalinism: Avant-Garde, Aesthetic Dictatorship, and Beyond,* trans. Charles Rougle (Princeton: Princeton University Press, 1992), 80.

7. Ibid.

8. Ibid., 73.

9. Andrei A. Zhdanov, *Essays on Literature, Philosophy, and Music* (New York, 1950), quoted in Groys, *The Total Art of Stalinism,* 40.

10. Groys, *The Total Art of Stalinism,* 52, 53, 71.

11. Dmitri Shostakovich, *Testimony: The Memoirs of Dmitri Shostakovich,* transcribed and ed. Solomon Volkov, trans. Antonina W. Bouis (New York: Harper and Row, 1979), 146.

12. Groys, *The Total Art of Stalinism,* 35–36.

13. Ibid., 59–60.

14. L. S. Termen, *Fizika i muzykalynoye izkusstvo* (Moskva: Znanie, 1966), 4.

15. Ibid., 7.

16. Ibid., 18.

17. Ibid., 17.

18. Fred K. Prieberg, *Musica ex machina* (Berlin: Ullstein, 1960), 209–10.

19. Anfilov, *Physics and Music,* 193, facing page.

20. Harold C. Schonberg, "Music: Leon Theremin," *New York Times,* April 26, 1967.

21. Leon Theremin, interview by Olivia Mattis, Bourges, France, June 16, 1989, trans. Nina Boguslawsky and Alejandro Tkaczevski, courtesy of Olivia Mattis.

22. Schonberg, "Music: Leon Theremin."

23. Ibid.

24. Ibid.

25. Ibid.

26. Theremin to Zinman, Moscow, May 2, 1967, MZC.

27. Theremin to Frances Schillinger, Moscow, May 2, 1967, AFLPI.

28. Theremin to Morgenstern, Moscow, 1967, collection of Clare Morgenstern.

29. Anfilov, *Physics and Music,* 246.

30. Schonberg, "Music: Leon Theremin."

31. Theremin to Frances Schillinger, May 2, 1967.

32. Theremin, interview by Olivia Mattis.

33. Mikhail Kaplunov and Mikhail Cherenkov, "Another Look At Lev Termen's Long and Eventful Life," *Moscow News* 17 (1988): 2.

34. Galeyev, *Sovetskyi Faust,* 69.

35. Anfilov, *Physics and Music,* 206.

36. Olivia Mattis and Robert Moog, "Pulling Music Out of Thin Air," *Keyboard* (February 1992): 54.

37. Galeyev, *Sovetskyi Faust,* 71.

38. Lydia Kavina, interview by the author, July 13, 1996.

39. Ibid.

40. Lydia Kavina, "My Experience with the Theremin," *Leonardo Music Journal* 6 (1996): 51.

41. Kavina, interview by the author.

42. Kavina, "My Experience with the Theremin," 51.

43. Nesturkh, "The Theremin and Its Inventor," 59–60.

44. Shostakovich, *Testimony,* 91.

45. Galeyev, *Sovetskyi Faust,* 72.

46. Kaplunov and Cherenkov, "Another Look."

47. Zamestitel dekana Fizicheskogo Fakulteta, MGU, i Ispolnyaushchiy obiazannosty Zaveduiushchego Kafedroy akustiki, MGU—E. F. Afanasievu, Moskva, 16 Mart 1987, Arkhiv Lydii Kavinoy.

48. Natalia Constantinova to the author, St. Petersburg, Russia, January 27, 1997.

49. Vladimir Kossarev, "Stranizi istorii," materiali konferenzii Lev Termen pioner electronnogo iskusstva, neopublikovanaya rukopis, St. Petersburg, 24–29 Noyabr 1996.

50. Natalia Constantinova to the author.

51. Mikhail Kaplunov and Mikhail Cherenkov, "Lev Termen's War and Peace," *Moscow News,* March 1, 1988.

52. Kaplunov and Cherenkov, "Another Look."

53. Bob Moog, "Bourges Electronic Music Festival; A Gathering of Giants," *Keyboard* (October 1989): 22–23.

54. Catherine Buchet, "Le viel homme et la musique," *La Nouvelle République,* June 17–18, 1989.

55. Ibid.

56. Theremin, interview by Olivia Mattis.

57. Varese to Theremin, New York, May 5, 1941, courtesy of Olivia Mattis.

58. Theremin, interview by Olivia Mattis.

59. Ibid.

60. Williams to Rockmore, Georgetown, Guyana, September 2, 1974, courtesy of Reid Welch.

61. Galeyev, *Sovetskyi Faust*, 81.

62. Lavinia Williams, interview by Diana Dunbar, December 1988.

63. "Lavinia Williams: History in Motion," *In Step*, April 1980, 16.

64. Amy Wilentz, *The Rainy Season: Haiti since Duvalier* (New York: Simon and Schuster, 1989), 401.

65. Jennifer Dunning, "Lavinia Williams, 73, a Dancer," *New York Times*, August 10, 1989.

66. Joe Nash, "Obituaries," *Dance Magazine* (February 1990): 114.

67. Diana Dunbar, interview by the author, December 1, 1996.

68. Information about Lavinia Williams's last months in Haiti, the suspicious circumstances surrounding her death, and her funeral ceremony was provided by Diana Dunbar. Speculation about Williams's death by "food poisoning" arose, in Ms. Dunbar's words, from "many sources in Haiti that I interviewed." Personal communication to the author, August 28, 1999.

69. Stephen Montague, "Rediscovering Leon Theremin," *Tempo* 177 (June 1991): 22–23.

70. "Look! No Hands."

71. Ibid.

72. Galeyev, *Sovetskyi Faust*, 79.

73. Ibid.

74. Paul Hertelendy, "The Soviet Who Sired an Electronic Revolution," *San Jose Mercury News*, September 26, 1991.

75. Olivia Mattis, "Tuning In on Electronic Music Pioneers," *Stanford University Campus Report*, October 9, 1991.

76. G. Kiksman, "Chelovek iz kommynalki," *Svet, priroda I chelovek* 12 (1992): 46.

77. Kaplunov and Cherenkov, "Lev Termen's War and Peace."

78. Galeyev, *Sovetskyi Faust*, 72.

79. "Look! No Hands."

80. Ilya Vais, "Lev Termen's New Music," *Moscow News*, December 28, 1986–January 4, 1987.

81. Ibid.

82. Kaplunov and Cherenkov, "Another Look."

83. Ibid.

84. Bulat Galeyev, "Face to Face with Mephistopheles, or the Amazing Life of Leon Theremin," *Sputnik Digest* 9 (September 1992): 105.

85. Vladimir Ilyich Lenin, *Materialism and Empiro-Criticism*, trans. I. Kvitko (Marks and Lawrence, 1927), quoted in N. O. Lossky, *History of Russian Philosophy* (New York: International Universities Press, 1951), 348.

86. Lossky, *History of Russian Philosophy*, 76.

87. Ibid., 78.

88. Galeyev, *Sovetskyi Faust*, 72.

89. Galeyev, "Face to Face with Mephistopheles," 105.

90. Bulat Galeyev, "Special Section Introduction" for "Light and Shadows of a Great Life: In Commemoration of the One-Hundredth Anniversary of the Birth of Leon Theremin, Pioneer of Electronic Art," *Leonardo Music Journal* 6 (1996): 45.

91. Ibid., 47.

92. Kavina, "My Experience with the Theremin."

93. Lev Oshanin, "Pust vsegda budet solnse," *Lev Oshanin: Lirica, Balladi, Pesni* (Moskva: "Hudozhestvennaya Literatura," 1983), 348–49.

ALBERT GLINSKY is a composer whose music has been heard across America, in such venues as Lincoln Center, Kennedy Center, and the Aspen Music Festival, and throughout Europe and the Far East. He has received awards from the National Endowment for the Arts and the American Academy of Arts and Letters. His music has been published by C. F. Peters and recorded on the BMG/Catalyst label. Glinsky holds degrees from the Juilliard School and New York University. He is an associate professor of music at Mercyhurst College in Pennsylvania. Glinsky writes and lectures extensively on the life and work of Leon Theremin and conducts an interdisciplinary presentation, TERMEN-ology.

Music in American Life

Songprints: The Musical Experience of Five Shoshone Women   *Judith Vander*
"Happy in the Service of the Lord": Afro-American Gospel Quartets
   in Memphis   *Kip Lornell*
Paul Hindemith in the United States   *Luther Noss*
"My Song Is My Weapon": People's Songs, American Communism, and the Politics
   of Culture, 1930–50   *Robbie Lieberman*
Chosen Voices: The Story of the American Cantorate   *Mark Slobin*
Theodore Thomas: America's Conductor and Builder of Orchestras,
   1835–1905   *Ezra Schabas*
"The Whorehouse Bells Were Ringing" and Other Songs Cowboys Sing
   Guy Logsdon
Crazeology: The Autobiography of a Chicago Jazzman   *Bud Freeman, as Told to
   Robert Wolf*
Discoursing Sweet Music: Brass Bands and Community Life in Turn-of-the-
   Century Pennsylvania   *Kenneth Kreitner*
Mormonism and Music: A History   *Michael Hicks*
Voices of the Jazz Age: Profiles of Eight Vintage Jazzmen   *Chip Deffaa*
Pickin' on Peachtree: A History of Country Music in Atlanta, Georgia
   Wayne W. Daniel
Bitter Music: Collected Journals, Essays, Introductions, and Librettos
   Harry Partch; edited by Thomas McGeary
Ethnic Music on Records: A Discography of Ethnic Recordings Produced in the
   United States, 1893 to 1942   *Richard K. Spottswood*
Downhome Blues Lyrics: An Anthology from the Post-World War II Era
   Jeff Todd Titon
Ellington: The Early Years   *Mark Tucker*
Chicago Soul   *Robert Pruter*
That Half-Barbaric Twang: The Banjo in American Popular Culture   *Karen Linn*
Hot Man: The Life of Art Hodes   *Art Hodes and Chadwick Hansen*
The Erotic Muse: American Bawdy Songs (2d ed.)   *Ed Cray*
Barrio Rhythm: Mexican American Music in Los Angeles   *Steven Loza*
The Creation of Jazz: Music, Race, and Culture in Urban America
   Burton W. Peretti
Charles Martin Loeffler: A Life Apart in Music   *Ellen Knight*
Club Date Musicians: Playing the New York Party Circuit   *Bruce A. MacLeod*
Opera on the Road: Traveling Opera Troupes in the United States,
   1825–60   *Katherine K. Preston*
The Stonemans: An Appalachian Family and the Music That Shaped
   Their Lives   *Ivan M. Tribe*
Transforming Tradition: Folk Music Revivals Examined   *Edited by
   Neil V. Rosenberg*
The Crooked Stovepipe: Athapaskan Fiddle Music and Square Dancing in North-
   east Alaska and Northwest Canada   *Craig Mishler*
Traveling the High Way Home: Ralph Stanley and the World of Traditional Blue-
   grass Music   *John Wright*
Carl Ruggles: Composer, Painter, and Storyteller   *Marilyn Ziffrin*
Never without a Song: The Years and Songs of Jennie Devlin, 1865–1952
   Katharine D. Newman

The Hank Snow Story   *Hank Snow, with Jack Ownbey and Bob Burris*
Milton Brown and the Founding of Western Swing   *Cary Ginell, with special assistance from Roy Lee Brown*
Santiago de Murcia's "Códice Saldívar No. 4": A Treasury of Secular Guitar Music from Baroque Mexico   *Craig H. Russell*
The Sound of the Dove: Singing in Appalachian Primitive Baptist Churches   *Beverly Bush Patterson*
Heartland Excursions: Ethnomusicological Reflections on Schools of Music   *Bruno Nettl*
Doowop: The Chicago Scene   *Robert Pruter*
Blue Rhythms: Six Lives in Rhythm and Blues   *Chip Deffaa*
Shoshone Ghost Dance Religion: Poetry Songs and Great Basin Context   *Judith Vander*
Go Cat Go! Rockabilly Music and Its Makers   *Craig Morrison*
'Twas Only an Irishman's Dream: The Image of Ireland and the Irish in American Popular Song Lyrics, 1800–1920   *William H. A. Williams*
Democracy at the Opera: Music, Theater, and Culture in New York City, 1815–60   *Karen Ahlquist*
Fred Waring and the Pennsylvanians   *Virginia Waring*
Woody, Cisco, and Me: Seamen Three in the Merchant Marine   *Jim Longhi*
Behind the Burnt Cork Mask: Early Blackface Minstrelsy and Antebellum American Popular Culture   *William J. Mahar*
Going to Cincinnati: A History of the Blues in the Queen City   *Steven C. Tracy*
Pistol Packin' Mama: Aunt Molly Jackson and the Politics of Folksong   *Shelly Romalis*
Sixties Rock: Garage, Psychedelic, and Other Satisfactions   *Michael Hicks*
The Late Great Johnny Ace and the Transition from R&B to Rock 'n' Roll   *James M. Salem*
Tito Puente and the Making of Latin Music   *Steven Loza*
Juilliard: A History   *Andrea Olmstead*
Understanding Charles Seeger, Pioneer in American Musicology   *Edited by Bell Yung and Helen Rees*
Mountains of Music: West Virginia Traditional Music from Goldenseal   *Edited by John Lilly*
Alice Tully: An Intimate Portrait   *Albert Fuller*
Long Steel Rail: The Railroad in American Folksong (2d ed.)   *Norm Cohen*
The Golden Age of Gospel   *Text by Horace Clarence Boyer; photography by Lloyd Yearwood*
Aaron Copland: The Life and Work of an Uncommon Man   *Howard Pollack*
Louis Moreau Gottschalk   *S. Frederick Starr*
Race, Rock, and Elvis   *Michael T. Bertrand*
Theremin: Ether Music and Espionage   *Albert Glinsky*

Typeset in 10/13 New Caledonia
with Orbital display
Designed by Paula Newcomb
Composed by Jim Proefrock
at the University of Illinois Press
Manufactured by Thomson-Shore, Inc.

University of Illinois Press
1325 South Oak Street
Champaign, IL 61820-6903
www.press.uillinois.edu